THE
ENCYCLOPEDIA OF
TAROT

A figure of the tarot: "He is the Hermit. Friend to solitude. Poet and wanderer. With his lantern he searches for truth in the darkness and finds it everywhere.... The Hermit is an elusive figure. He travels mostly alone, yet he can appear in our lives at any time.... He doesn't sermonize. He offers us only the simple poetry of his experience...."

(9 The Hermit, Cosmic Tribe Tarot,
art by Stevee Postman, text by Eric Ganther)

THE ENCYCLOPEDIA OF TAROT

Stuart R. Kaplan

Jean Huets

VOLUME IV

Published by
U.S. GAMES SYSTEMS, INC.
Stamford, CT 06902 USA
www.usgamesinc.com

First published in 2005 by
U.S. Games Systems, Inc.
179 Ludlow Street
Stamford, CT 06902 U.S.A.
www.usgamesinc.com

PRINTED IN CANADA

Library of Congress Cataloguing-in-Publication Data available upon request.

ISBN 1-57281-506-X   Item # BK7

10   9   8   7   6   5   4   3   2   1

Editor and Graphic Designer: Jean Huets
Dedication page art from Celestial Tarot, by Kay Steventon

Works by Stuart R. Kaplan

BOOKS ON TAROT

Encyclopedia of Tarot, Volume I
Encyclopedia of Tarot, Volume II
Encyclopedia of Tarot, Volume III
Encyclopedia of Tarot, Volume IV (with Jean Huets)

James Bond 007 Tarot Book
Tarot Cards for Fun and Fortunetelling
Tarot Classic
Tarot of the Witches

TAROT INSTRUCTION BOOKLETS

Angel Tarot
Cagliostro Tarot
Cary-Yale Visconti Tarocchi
Devil's Tarot
Egipcios Kier Tarot
Egyptian Tarot
Enoil Gavat Tarot
Hanson-Roberts Tarot
Hermetic Tarot
    (with Godfrey Dowson)
Minchiate of Florence
Oracle of the Sibyl
    (with Giorgio Tavaglione)
Oswald Wirth Tarot
Papus Tarot
Pierpont Morgan-Bergamo
    Visconti-Sforza Tarocchi

Prager Tarot
Ravenswood Eastern Tarot
    (with Dirk Dykstra)
Royal Fez Moroccan Tarot
Sicilian Tarot
Solleone Tarot
Spanish Tarot
Starter Tarot (22-card deck)
Starter Tarot (78-card deck)
Swiss 1JJ Tarot
Tarocchi of Mantegna
Tarot Classic
Tarot of the Witches
Tarot of Valentina Visconti
Ukiyoe Tarot

HISTORY AND CURRENT EVENTS

The American Historical Playing Card Deck:
    Portraits in American History
Political Satire Playing Card Deck Instructions

MINING

Mining, Minerals and Geosciences:
    A Guide to Information Sources

DEDICATION

To the people
who make the
world of tarot:
artists, scholars,
dreamers, booksellers,
writers, collectors,
magicians
…to all believers

CONTENTS

PREFACE

THE ENCYCLOPEDIA OF TAROT was first published over twenty-five years ago as a single volume work describing some 250 tarot decks. The aim was to bring together obscure information on the early origins of tarot and to document the different types of tarot decks in existence.

At the time, tarot decks were packaged in simple tuck boxes with a small booklet of instructions, available primarily in "head shops" and esoteric bookstores. During the 1980s, tarot entered the mainstream, becoming available in many types of stores. The growing interest in tarot led to the subsequent publication of volumes II and III of the *Encyclopedia,* in 1986 and 1990 respectively. These two volumes featured 700 additional tarot and tarock decks, both published and unpublished.

During the last fifteen years, an explosion of new tarot packs has reached the marketplace, aided greatly by the same technology that has so profoundly changed other areas of our culture. Graphic design software has facilitated private publication of packs, many in limited editions available solely through the Internet. Artwork that has not achieved publication in print can be viewed on-line. Besides opening new avenues of distribution, the Internet has contributed to the exchange of ideas about tarot with chat rooms, reviews, web sites, e-zines, and the like. In addition, beautifully designed and packaged tarot decks are being mass-produced in print form by more publishers than ever before.

Increased interest in tarot has spread all over the globe. Spanish-language books on tarot were once relatively rare, but on a recent trip to Buenos Aires, I found more than fifty books dealing with tarot. Numerous books and decks have been published in other European languages, including Polish and Czech. Previous volumes of the *Encyclopedia* featured a handful of Japanese tarots; volume IV includes a section dedicated to some 100 tarot decks created and published in Japan.

The expansion of interest in tarot has come with developments in its iconography. Until the late twentieth century, most decks were variations of the Tarot of Marseilles, with arrangements of the suit signs on the pip cards. Since 1909, when the Rider-Waite deck first appeared, many decks have followed suit with full illustrations on all the cards of both the Minor and Major Arcana. Steadily, other influences have been assimilated. A burst of creative design and innovative interpretation came when artists discovered how aptly the tarot expresses themes and reflects cultural currents. The 1990s Celtic revival inspired decks such as Greenwood Tarot, Arthurian Tarot, Sacred Circle Tarot, Celtic Dragon Tarot, and Glastonbury Tarot. (Interestingly, the images of the Rider-Waite Tarot reflect the Celtic revival of the early twentieth century.) Motherpeace Tarot and Tarot of the Goddess are inspired, in different ways, by feminist values. Multicultural perspectives are reflected in decks as diverse as Native American Tarot, Buckland Romani Tarot, Roots of Asia Tarot, African Tarot, and Royal Thai Tarot. Great artists of the past come to life in Dante Tarot, Giotto Tarot, and Golden Tarot.

Uses for the cards have evolved since the Milanese nobility in the mid-fifteenth century gamed with them. Many people use the tarot for guided meditation and self-realization, gravitating to decks like One World Tarot and Jungian Tarot. The occultist can find decks that enhance the study of numerology, Kabbalism, witchcraft, Golden Dawn, alchemy, and other areas of spiritual investigation. The most famous of the esoteric decks is the Rider-Waite Tarot, with Book of Thoth Tarot coming in second. The tarot also amuses us with light-hearted decks such as Halloween Tarot, Medieval Cat Tarot, and PoMo Tarot.

From the earliest extant decks, created in Renaissance Italy, to the packs of today, tarot artwork in itself is fascinating. Complex and richly colored decks such as Spiral Tarot and Cosmic Tribe Tarot reveal more details, more intriguing interpretations and stories, every time they are viewed.

Tarot holds tremendous interest for scholars, too, as tarotologists delve into the history and artistic development of tarot cards. Curiosity drove me on the quest to unravel the secrets of tarot and especially to separate fact from fiction. Collectively, the four volumes of *The Encyclopedia of Tarot* aim to reveal the rich imagery of tarot, from the fifteenth century to the present, and to provide reliable information about its history—the theories and the known facts—as well as traditional and nontraditional interpretations of its symbolism. The information is presented in an unbiased way, so that people can explore for themselves the different theories on how and why tarot was conceived, making their own discoveries and gaining deeper appreciation in the process.

Unfortunately for tarotologists, it is not always easy to view the impressive tarot collections housed in libraries and museums. Antique tarot decks are often put away in cabinets and are not readily available for examination. Even when access to collections is arranged, the opportunity for viewing is usually limited to one deck at a time. *The Encyclopedia of Tarot* allows people to compare the works of many tarot artists and to study each artist's unique interpretation of the tarot's meaning.

Among the most passionate of tarot lovers are collectors, many of whom own dozens, even hundreds of decks. Whenever possible, the *Encyclopedia* provides publication facts and other information, such as tax stamp descriptions found in volume II, to help identify and date each deck featured. Thus, it functions as an archive and as a reference tool for collectors.

The majority of the published decks featured in the *Encyclopedia* are from The Stuart and Marilyn R. Kaplan Collection of Tarot Cards and Playing Cards. Many people have suggested that the collection be donated to a museum. After considerable reflection it was decided that the tarot community would be better served by making individual decks available to other collectors. Some tarot decks from the collection have been sold through Sotheby's and others on eBay. In this way, collectors have the opportunity to acquire out-of-print and rare decks and to enjoy the cards at their leisure. As a fellow collector, it is very rewarding to hear from new owners of their joy in finally having the opportunity to possess a deck that was previously unavailable.

Tarotists are as diverse in style, personality, background, and appearance as the characters on the cards themselves. At the same time, we are drawn together by a common interest. We gravitate to each other, in person and on-line: collectors, scholars, art historians, occultists, business people, artists and fortunetellers who read the cards. The pages of the *Encyclopedia* are a gallery of the people of tarot, living and long-dead, as much as they are a gallery of tarot cards. I'm proud that this group of artists and patrons has allowed U.S. Games Systems to help open the world of tarot to a rainbow of cultures, images, and ideas, growing far beyond the earliest extant decks in Italy and France.

Volume IV is the largest volume of the *Encyclopedia* to date, with artwork from 850 tarot decks. Even so, not every new tarot pack created since publication of volume III will be found in it. Each week brings news of yet another tarot deck. The authors extend their sincere apologies to tarot artists whose works could not be included in this volume due to the publication deadline. To the artists who furnished material for volume IV, we are deeply grateful for your contributions. To those artists not included, perhaps there will be a fifth volume of *The Encyclopedia of Tarot*. Tarot artists are welcome to contact the authors at U.S. Games Systems, using the address shown on the copyright page.

The authors would be remiss in not making mention of a very special contributor, Laurie Amato. Laurie furnished an extensive amount of material from her personal collection. Of particular value was the information, both textual and visual, concerning tarot cards published in Japan, which we might otherwise have overlooked. We are also grateful for the photographs of Laurie's own tarot artwork. The book is richer for her gracious assistance and numerous contributions.

A wonderful source for tarot packs that deserves special mention is tarotgarden.com located in West Des Moines, Iowa. The assistance and support of Jeanette Roth and Lorraine Sharkey-Dolan enabled the authors to acquire many unusual tarot packs especially from Japan, Poland, Germany, Italy, France, and Brazil.

I thank Allen Stairs for permission to include his thought-provoking essay on reading tarot cards.

I wish also to express my profound appreciation to Jean Huets, co-author of volume IV of *The Encyclopedia of Tarot*. Jean's keen eye and deep understanding of tarot enabled her to piece together the threads of information gathered from many tarot artists and sources. Without her tireless effort, expertise, and dedication over the past several years, volume IV would not have seen publication. The caliber and integrity of this volume attest to her talents.

In the tarot deck, the card numbered zero is The Fool. The tarot Fool, as contrasted to a foolish person who is generally considered deficient in judgment, is a bold optimist willing to step out into new adventures. The Fool card attracted my attention to the tarot, because I was born on April Fools' Day. Like the Fool, I have always been drawn to new challenges. The purchase of my first pack of tarot cards, at the Nuremberg Toy Fair in 1968, changed the focus of my personal interests and led to the founding of U.S. Games Systems, Inc.

Fortune dealt me the ability and resources to pull together this archive of tarot, to publish and disseminate it. Towards that end I've devoted thirty-six years to researching, finding, acquiring, and documenting as many tarot decks as possible, and to featuring them in *The Encyclopedia of Tarot*.

However passionate the artist or the occultist, however dedicated the scholar or the collector, the tarot remains a boundless mystery. Perhaps that is the true allure of the cards; their secrets are never completely revealed. The tarot is like an unbound book whose pages rearrange themselves with every shuffle of the cards. The cards reveal a never-ending story, an eternal cycle.

The primary joy and responsibility of my occupation has been to serve as a conduit for tarot. The *Encyclopedia* is the culmination of this endeavor. In future years, I hope that someone will look at the *Encyclopedia* the way I look on each tarot deck that comes my way — as a world of knowledge and wonder.

Stuart R. Kaplan
Stamford, Connecticut
March 2005

The Fool   A handful of published and unpublished designs shows a variety of topics and sensibilities.
TOP ROW: Inner Garden Tarot, by Laurie Amato; PoMo Tarot, by Brian Williams; Andrey Bezukladnikov Tarot.
SECOND ROW: Unity Tarot, Linda J. Franks; Lover's Path Tarot, by Kris Waldherr; Childhood Arcana, by Sarah Scott Parry.
BOTTOM ROW: Gaian Tarot, by Joanna Powell Colbert; Rambles into Arkanas Tarot, by Alexander Egorov; Tarot of the Saints, by Robert M. Place.
The illustrations of decks throughout the Encyclopedia include 0 The Fool wherever possible, so that interpretations of the same card by hundreds of different artists can be compared.

I

UNPUBLISHED TAROT DESIGNS

The meaning of the word "published" became ambiguous during the last decades of the twentieth century. Tarot decks that are sparks of light on a computer screen can be considered published when they are posted on the internet and seen by many people.

Traditionally, a published tarot deck is printed as cards on paper in quantities that allow access to more than a handful of people. This chapter comprises artwork that exists only in the original, as well as designs appearing not as decks but as t-shirts, decks posted on the Internet, very limited editions, sculptures, art in magazines, and so on. (Note that some decks included as "unpublished" may have been published after production of this book.)

Acquiescent Tarot Saskia Deneuve aimed to "represent the original meaning and representation" of the tarot cards. Her designs date from 2003.

Adflatus Tarot Adflatus is Latin for "breath" or "inspiration." "Adflatus came to birth in early 2000," says Australian artist Zach Wong. "It was a new millennium, and I wanted to achieve an understanding of my past, my present, and the endless possibilities of my future." The double-ended designs can be seen upright or reversed. "The cards are drawn in the style similar to stained glass. Iconic images represent a lesson to be learned, a being to be studied, or a situation."

Collection of the artist

Adflatus Tarot Zach Wong, 2000 Descriptions are by the artist.

Each character in the **Major Arcana** wears a "mask," depicted by lines that break each face down to sections. The mask is a representation of a "human" relation, similar to that of the mythical gods who stand in human form amongst us to ease our comprehension of the messages they deliver.

KNIGHT of SWORDS

FIVE of SWORDS

TWO of SWORDS

KING of WANDS

SEVEN of WANDS

FOUR of WANDS

QUEEN of CUPS

EIGHT of CUPS

THREE of CUPS

PAGE of PENTACLES

TEN of PENTACLES

NINE of PENTACLES

Adflatus Tarot (continued)

The **Minor Arcana** represent the lesser lessons. The suits are broken up into four different themes. Each is reflective of the element with which the suit is aligned.

The **suit of swords** is associated with the element of air, thought, intelligence, mentality, and matters of the mind. The characters of the suit are warriors, highly ornate and decorated, firm and serious. They embody the logic and sensibility that can be found only in those who remove themselves from the burdens of emotion. With their swords they cut through life as well as protect themselves.

The **suit of wands** is associated with the element of fire, intuition, magic, the powers of creation, and matters of the soul. The characters in the suit are magicians, warriors, sages, and opulent individuals. They embody the use of magic in daily life. With their staves or wands, they move to create or fight.

The **suit of cups** is associated with the element of water, emotions, and matters of the heart. The characters of the suit are mer-people of the oceans and seas. They embody movement freed from restraint of the land and the fantastical luxury of living life for the pleasures it presents. With their cups, they swim through the oceans of life searching for contents to fill their vessels.

The **suit of pentacles** is associated with the element of earth; the sensations of touch, sight, sound, and taste; physical pleasures; and the matters of the body. The characters of the suit are metallic humanoids that are one with their element. They embody the fruits of the earth: metals, the built environment, material possessions, and the ingenuity of creation. With their pentacles, they go through life enjoying what the earth has to offer them.

Acquiescent Tarot   Saskia Deneuve, 2003

Collection of the artist

Tarocco di Afrodite Amerigo Folchi, 1992
X The Wheel of Fortune. XI Strength. XIV Temperance. XVII The Star. XXI The World.

Tarocco di Afrodite (Tarot of Aphrodite) Amerigo Folchi describes the Tarot of Aphrodite as "an aphrodisiac of the feminine body." The art was created circa 1992.

Aleph-Beth Tarot Michele Jackson created the Aleph-Beth Tarot as a way to learn the Hebrew alphabet. Each card of the Major Arcana deck shows somewhere the literal meaning of the letter to which the card corresponds. For example, a pair of oxen in the corner of the Fool card indicates the letter aleph. The deck was created in 1999, using collage technique.

Alien Tarot April Pedersen's tarot designs feature big-eyed aliens of the so-called Gray Type. The clever and humorous renditions tap into alien lore. For example, Death shows the "alien autopsy" from an alien spacecraft that supposedly crashed near Roswell, Texas. XV The Devil shows Devil's Tower, Wyoming, a bluff that was the site of the alien saucer games in the film *Close Encounters of the Third Kind*. XX Judgement shows an imminent alien abduction. The artist's sentiments are ambiguous; her self-portrait as the Empress shows her holding a book with a question mark on it. The artist's Nevada roots are apparent in the Six of Eyes, in which an alien plays the slots. The Alien Tarot was created in 1999.

Aleph-Beth Tarot Michele Jackson, 1999
The caption gives the corresponding Hebrew letter and location of the image showing the meaning of the letter.
TOP ROW: **Fool,** aleph; oxen in the lower right corner. **Magician,** Beth; house in the lower right quadrant of the card. The portrait is from the 1919 work *Picture with Light Center*, by Kurt Schwitters. It portrays Paschal Beverly Randolph, a nineteenth-century Spiritualist, Rosicrucian, and sex magician. **High Priestess,** gimel; camels in lower left corner. The woman shown is a Masai of Kenya. **Empress,** daleth; door in the lower left corner. The figure is from *Hope*, by Gustav Klimt (1903). **Emperor,** heh; the window frames Emperor Hirohito of Japan.
SECOND ROW: **Hierophant,** vau; nails are at the bottom border. The figure is Ann Duckworth, High Priestess of the Three Witches Church of Philadelphia and the artist's spiritual teacher. The gods and goddesses are (from upper left, top) Cernunnos, Baba Yaga, Venus of Willendorf, and Oshun. **Chariot,** cheth; a fence is at the bottom. **Strength,** teth; the snake is at the bottom right. The card shows *The Moorish Chief*, by Eduard Charlemont (1878). **Hermit,** yod; the hand. The wall hanging shows the eight auspicious symbols of Buddhism. The spire is part of a stupa, or holy structure, and the candles read "Love" (left) and "Peace" in Japanese.

Wheel of Fortune, kaph; fist is at bottom left. The wheel is from an alchemical text, and a part of a photo of Jupiter is in the lower right corner.
THIRD ROW: **Justice,** lamed; the ox goad is in the lower left corner. The figure is St. Michael from the triptych *Judgment*, by Hans Memling (1472). **Hanged One,** mem; water is in the lower half, in the background. The figure is *Hope*, by George Frederick Watts (1885), and the line drawing of the hanged figure is a sketch by Russian poet Aleksandr Pushkin (1825). **Death,** nun; fish is at lower right. The woman is *The Madonna*, by Edvard Munch (1894). **Temperance,** samech; a staff (prop) is on the right. The woman is from the *Doni Tondo*, by Michelangelo (1503). **Devil,** ayin; eye is in the lower right corner. The devil card in the woman's hand is from a Mexican lotteria deck.
BOTTOM ROW: **Tower,** peh; mouth is at the center bottom. The nude is from a pre-Raphaelite nude study (1920). **Star,** tzaddi; fish hook is at the bottom right. The figure is from *Air Castles*, by Maxfield Parrish (1904). **Sun,** resh; a head is at the bottom right. **Judgment,** shin; a tooth is at the bottom left. The figure is from *Jeune Homme Nu Assis au Bord de la Mer*, by Hippolyte Jean-Flandrin (1836). **World,** tau; the tau cross is at the lower right. The statue in the hand is *Sheer Lust*, by Gabriele Johannmann (1991).

Alien Tarot April Pedersen, 1999   TOP ROW: 0 The Fool. I The Magician. III The Empress. VI The Lovers. VII The Chariot.
SECOND ROW: VIII Justice. IX The Hermit. X Wheel of Fortune. XII The Hanged Man. XIII Death.
THIRD ROW: XV The Devil. XVI The Tower. XVIII The Moon. XX Judgement. XXI Emergence.
BOTTOM ROW: King of Eyes. Eight of Eyes. Six of Eyes. Four of Eyes. Five of Saucers.

Collection of the artist

Tarot of the Ancient East   Greg Harold Fiorini, 1990

TOP ROW: 0 The Fool. 1 The Magus. 2 The High Priestess. 3 The Empress. 4 The Emperor.

SECOND ROW: 5 The Hierophant. 6 The Lovers. 7 The Chariot. 8 Strength. 9 The Hermit.

THIRD ROW: 10 The Wheel of Fortune. 11 Justice. 13 Death. 14 Temperance. 15 The Devil.

BOTTOM ROW: 16 The Tower. 17 The Star. 18 The Moon. 19 The Sun. 21 The World.

Tarot of the Ancient East   The Tarot of the Ancient East is based on artist Greg Harold Fiorini's investigation of Zoroastrianism and its offshoots. Fiorini wished to "devise a fresh deck with unused symbolism.... Zoroastrianism, above all, is a dualistic religion, and this lends itself well to the tarot system, good–evil, dark–light, etc., figuring highly in its doctrine." The Ancient East in the deck is the region extending from the eastern shores of the Mediterranean east into India and from Arabia north to Armenia. The time period is from pre-history to Mohammed's migration in 622 CE. The images on the deck are mostly drawn from the faces of ancient coins. The deck was made in 1990.

Ancient Millennium Tarot The tarot illustrations by Al Duffy are based on astrological, elemental, numerological, and Hermetic symbolism. The illustrations combine ancient imagery with modern icons such as the skyscrapers of New York City. They were rendered in pen and ink in 1993.

Tarot of Angels Australian artist Cree Marshall used classic artwork to form collages as tarot images. In a letter to Stuart Kaplan, she states, "My reason for using a variety of angelic images from a wide range of artists [is] so that those consulting these cards have a better chance of finding the depiction which comes closest to their own angelic vision, rather than the too-personal one of a single artist." The manuscript by Marshall describes the images as well as the "bright face" and "shadow face" of each image. The cards also each have a "Journey's Song" and "Journey's Psalm" written by Marshall. The Fool, for example, has the following verses:

Journey's Song
Angel child, innocent,
pagan yet reverent,
dancing life's harmonies
endlessly.

Journey's Psalm
Angels know: my answers
lie
in harmony
simplicity
and trust.

The deck follows the Jungian archetypal "hero's journey," the symbolic passage that each of us must make in order to realize the authentic self and one's full potential. It dates from circa 1995.

Collection of the artist

Tarot of Angels Cree Marshall, circa 1995

TOP ROW: **0 The Fool** is ruled by Metatron and Messiah, the two angels of the Garden of Eden. **I The Magician** is Amazarak, an angel who taught magicians, and Armers, a fallen angel who also taught sorcery. **XV The Devil** is a collage of William Blake prints showing Satan, Adversary, and Lucifer, Light Giver. The Fallen Angels are at their feet. **XIX The Sun** is ruled by Galgaliel, chief of the angelic order of galgallim, equal in rank to the seraphim, and Uriel, Fire of the Sun, regent of the sun. **Amazon of Blades** depicts Giorgione's depiction of Judith, a Jewish heroine who defeated the Babylonian enemy by luring their leader Holofernes into a drunken stupor and then beheading him.

BOTTOM ROW: **2 of Blades** shows David's rendition of the Sabine woman Hersilia separating her Roman husband Romulus from her vengeful father Tatius. **6 of Staves** depicts Marie de' Medici as Victor of Jülich. **Child of Vessels** is Caravaggio's *Bacchus*. **Ace of Vessels** depicts a Byzantine chalice that is said to have been owned by Lorenzo de' Medici. The angel of the cup looks to a white dove of peace and purity, and a raven of solitude and sin. **5 of Pomegranates** shows Pablo Picasso's couple facing a Renaissance angel who holds a pomegranate, symbol of the riches of the earth.

Ancient Millennium Tarot   Al Duffy, 1993   The descriptions are based on the artist's statements.   TOP ROW: **VIII Strength** shows an elephant breaking down the walls of fear, old concepts, habits, and thoughts. The angel riding the elephant signifies the balance of forces and shows that our strength is led by spirit. **XV Ignorance** is a ghostly figure leading his ill, perverse, and wicked pageantry of human disgrace throughout the universe. The people are twisted and in bondage to the impure material life of experience. **XVI The Temple** illustrates the destruction of the ancient civilization of Atlantis. Sunshine breaks through the storm, offering the hope that the disruption will bring enlightenment. **XVII The Star** has at its center the symbol of the astrological sign Aquarius. **Knight of Wands.**   BOTTOM ROW: **Seven of Wands** shows an angel standing before a schematized skyline of New York City, when the World Trade Center still stood. **Knight of Cups. Ten of Pentacles** is a scene of wealth and plenty. In the background is a coat of arms featuring a bull's head, a dollar sign, and a key. **Five of Pentacles** shows a man imprisoned physically, mentally, and spiritually. He crouches, trying to escape the energy of the sun. **Four of Pentacles** shows a bull with a briefcase full of money looking out at the same view shown on the Seven of Wands.

Tarot of the Angry Moon   Chris Bivins brought twenty years of experience as a graphic designer and illustrator to the tarot, completing a set of designs in 2001. "As a designer I am constantly challenged to combine words and images to convey a particular message or feeling," Bivins writes. "The artistic tradition of the tarot along with its oral interpretation makes it an excellent candidate for this creative process.

"Each card exists as several different layers, adding depth and texture while also hinting at the layers of meaning that can be found in each turn of the card. Some elements are brought sharply into focus, while others remain obscure, or blurred. The text that floats on the surface of each card moves in and out of focus, hinting at the sometime elusive interpretations of each card.

"Some cards, such as The Tower and Strength, were fairly simple manipulations of strong, single photographic images. Others, like The Magician, Death, and the Hierophant, were layered combinations of several different elements brought together to creatively express an idea. Still others, such as The Wheel of Fortune, The Fool, and the Chariot, required extensive work in creating objects and shapes in a drawing program, and then adding texture and color in Photoshop [graphics software] to create recognizable symbols.

"I wanted the deck, as a whole, to have a somewhat

dark and edgy feel to it, retaining some of the traditional symbolism within a more contemporary framework. The strong use of black as an underlying color helped achieve this look while creating an overall dark tone."

Antoni Tarot   New Zealand artist Chris Fincham created tarot designs in 1997 using the graphics software CorelDraw. The artist writes to Stuart Kaplan: "I have tried to stick with the traditional symbolism of the tarot, but I have updated the images. The whole pack has many quirks and I have incorporated a few new ideas more relevant to today's lifestyle."

Antoni Tarot   Chris Fincham, 1997

9

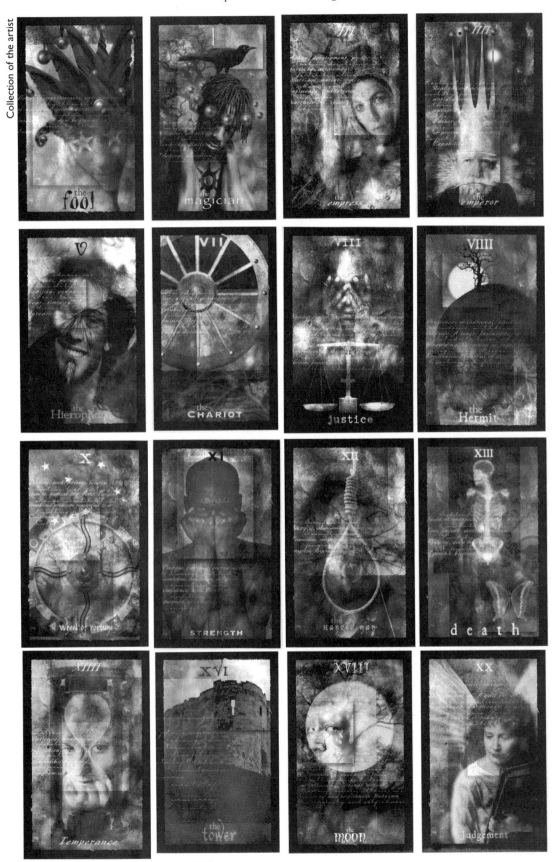

Tarot of the Angry Moon   Chris Bivins, 2001

Tarot des Artiste Cassandra Saulter created the Tarot des Artiste [sic] in pen and ink, colored with gouache and gold illumination. She then produced a limited edition of ten decks, using color laser photocopies, cut and laminated, and accompanied by a hand-lettered book, also photocopied and hand-assembled. An unusual feature of the Major Arcana deck is the horizontal orientation of several of the cards. The deck was created in 1990. The artist says, in the book accompanying the deck, "Tarot figures are little archetypes reflecting the atmosphere surrounding you."

Artist's Tarot Curator Amy Lipton assembled a show "The Wheel of Fortune" that represented seventy-eight artists, one for each card of the tarot. The show took place at Lombard-Freid Fine Arts gallery, New York City, in December 1995. Lipton compares the Fool to today's artist: "Card number 0 in the tarot deck pictures a youthful figure dressed in colorful garments wandering aimlessly. He/She pauses at the brink of a precipice among the great heights of the world with no fear. He/She is full of intelligence, but at the same time naïve, as if in a dream. He/She is in search of experience and self-expression. The world is full of opportunities, and unlimited possibilities are waiting. This archetype for the Fool card can easily be attributed to the artist as well. Culture relies on this type of perpetual seeker, one who is unrestrained by the normal confines of society and is able to move freely back and forth from dream state to reality. Living in a condition of suspense with one foot on the ground and the other ready to step off a cliff at any moment enables the artist to transcend time. Though much of our society is not prepared to listen, artists often predict the future, inadvertently if not intentionally."

Ascension Tarot Lisa Elizabeth Berg describes her tarot as "a tool for awakening the sleeping soul." Each image of the Major Arcana deck has an English title and a Hebrew name. Berg made the pen-and-ink deck in 1999.

Astrologic Tarot Brazilian artist and astrologer Pedro Eugênio Gomes Pazelli created the Astrologic Tarot, a deck comprising Major Arcana only. The deck was completed in the late 1980s, with titles in Portuguese. The titles are traditional, with XIII left untitled.

Tarot Aurore Michele Richards and Jeff Hill worked together to create the Tarot Aurore. Hill made the drawings, and Richards colored them. The title Aurore, French for Aurora, reflects the colors that Richards applied, using Prismacolor pencil, to Hill's pen-and-ink drawings. Says Richards, "I colored the deck to suggest the emotional qualities each card summons up, so that simply by looking at the cards one could get a sense of their meanings." The images of the deck are based on the Tarot of Marseilles, with the Rider-Waite Tarot hinted at, for example, in the pomegranates at the feet of the figure on III L'Imperatrice (The Empress), and in the pentacles, rather than coins, for the Minor Arcana suit. Richards hand-produced the deck by laminating color photocopies of the card faces onto blue cover stock, on which she drew the back design. Each back design is slightly different from the rest, since they are hand-colored. The deck was created in 1991.

Tarot of Awakening Tom Mann of Portland, Oregon, painted the images of the Tarot of Awakening: A Guide for the Modern Mystic in 1998. "The Tarot of Awakening can be thought of as a mystical map for those who have embarked upon the journey of awakening to their soul's purpose," says Janet de Coriolis, author of the manuscript accompanying the deck. "The Tarot of Awakening was inspired and guided by beings or intelligences whose only desire is to support the mystical journey of our awakening souls."

Tarot de Michel Bassot et René Chassagny Michel Bassot designed his twenty-two-card tarot in gouache, pencil, and gold leaf in 1995. The accompanying text is by René Chassagny. The color scheme is symbolic of the three planes of divine, astral, and physical. Gold represents the divine plane; silver is for the astral plane; the material plane is represented in different colors, neither gold nor silver. The images on the cards allude to classical and biblical themes.

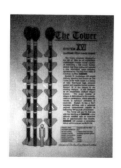   

Artist's Tarot 1995
16 The Tower, by Gregory Green. Laser print.
Page of Swords, by Vik Muniz. Gouache, acrylic, and pen.
Ten of Swords, by James Elaine. Ink on paper.
Ten of Cups, by Joanne Howard. Charcoal and chalk on sandpaper.

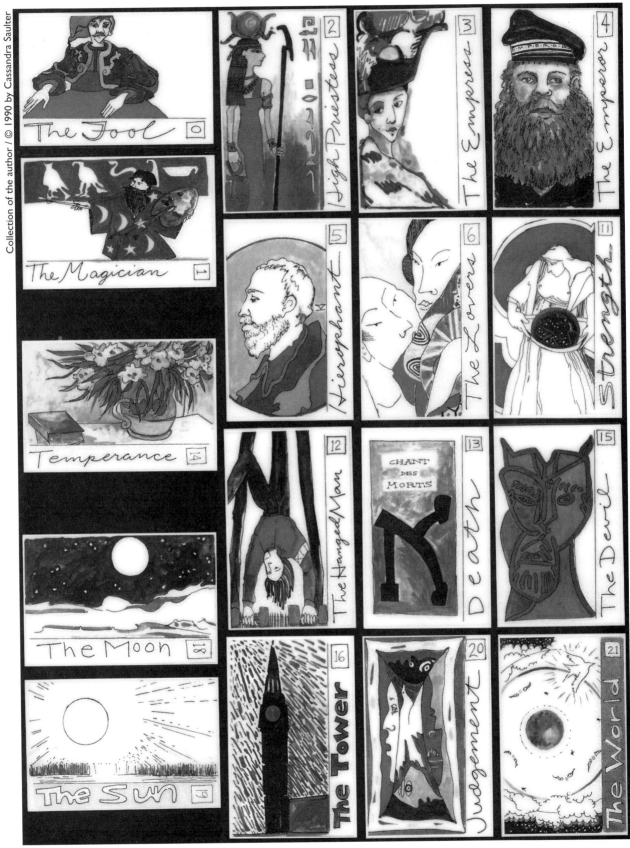

Tarot des Artiste   Cassandra Saulter, 1990

Ascension Tarot Lisa Elizabeth Berg, 1999 The caption is based on the artist's descriptions of the cards.

TOP ROW: **0 faith** shows a child following a dove, symbol of the omnipresence of the divine. The tiny cup on the child's belt signifies receptivity. **I the principles** shows a figure who is buoyant in spirit from her faith. The radiant fire is her heart, full of the brilliance of God. The crown suspended over her head represents the ruling nature of the principles of harmony in life. **2 the way** represents the path we choose to take in life. The seeker portrayed is in a dense forest. The dove of divinity is a constant inspiration. **3 great mother** carries a basket representing the bounty of her nature. She and her child walk into the dark, representing the unmanifest potential, and fruition, the house of earth itself. **4 great father** makes an offering of smoke, representing the spirit. The eagle is his all-seeing spirit helper.

SECOND ROW: **5 the guide** is represented as a woman receiving others in council. She offers guidance in the development of the ascending body of light. **6 inner voice** shows a young man seeking counsel of his own inner voice, the higher self. The light of illuminated knowledge floods the scene, as time and space stand still. **7 self discipline** portrays the seeker sitting on a throne carried by the serpent of wisdom. About her head is an aura that reveals the radiance that comes from a disciplined life. The star tetrahedron represents Father-Mother-God, primary sacred geometry, as above so below, and the merkaba (body of light). **8 spiritual**

strength depicts a spiritual practitioner. She makes a canopy over her head, signifying what must be kept within the heart and mind. The incense smoke represents the spirit, and also human DNA, which will be fully utilized on realization of godhood. The fire in the incense burner represents the first spark of otherness sent from the totality of all. The griffin signifies the taming of the lower nature, including desire, fear, control. **9 sovereignty** shows a person who wears a prayer shawl over one shoulder, and carries a candle, which signifies the light of god. The dove of the spirit sits on his shoulder. The elemental, in the form of a bright, winged creature, keeps spirits light and joyful.

BOTTOM ROW: **10 cycles** has at its center the seed of life and the ourobouros, the snake biting its own tail, a symbol of eternity. Anubus, at the bottom of the card, is the guardian escort for transition through the cycles. **11 accountability** holds scales that bring light to what was once hidden. She wears a yin-yang symbol over the third eye, offering balance of vision. In the palm of her left hand is the eye of Horus, symbolic of the ancient Hermetic schools and the development of innate wisdom. **12 divine order** shows a Melchizedek teacher offering knowledge of the divine order of the universe. **15 discernment** shows a boy who gently opens the door of perception for discernment and careful consideration. **16 inevitable change** shows the feeling of being dashed by giant waves, which can come with change.

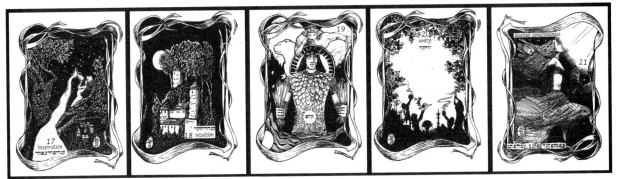

Ascension Tarot *(continued)*   **17 inspiration** shows a figure pouring god-light from a vessel. The mundane world surrounds her. Within the challenge of a seemingly separated world is the continual upliftment that a spirit-inspired soul may provide for himself and others. **18 intuition** shows a full moon over a still, small mountain hamlet. The moon is partially obscured, as can be the spiritual life within.

19 (sun) is portrayed as a young man holding rays of light. The angel over his head represents higher authority, a hierarchy of divine order. **20 unity** represents a great celebration of unity, in which all life is honored and flourishes. There is enough for everyone. **21 exalted consciousness** leaps forward with the dove of peace into the light of the absolute, perfectly willing to be transformed into the new race.

Astrologic Tarot   Pedro Eugênio Gomes Pazelli, 1980s

Collection of the author

Tarot Aurore   Michele Richards and Jeff Hill, 1991

0	II	III	IV
Fool	High Priestess	Divine Mother	Divine Father
XII	XIV	Princess of Swords	Ace of Swords
The Hanged Man	Art	Inner Music	Clarity
Princess of Wands	Ace of Wands	Princess of Cups	10 of Disks
Freedom	Transformation	Self-Awareness	Wealth

Tarot of Awakening Tom Mann and Janet de Coriolis, 1998 Descriptions are based on the manuscript by Janet de Coriolis.

TOP ROW: **0 Fool** has a crystal ball to remind him of purity, perfection, and knowledge of Spirit, and a double wand to ground him to the Earth and bring him courage, wisdom, and compassion. **II High Priestess** meditates atop the lotus of enlightenment. **III Divine Mother** rules the cycles and rhythms of creation. **IV Divine Father** is the sacred masculine principle of creation, which rests on a solid foundation of truth, integrity, and the ethical use of power.

SECOND ROW: **XII The Hanged Man** indicates values turned upside down and the need to question beliefs and habits that no longer support psychological or spiritual growth. **XIV Art** shows the goddesses of light and dark as alchemists balancing the transmutation of the physical body as it becomes a vessel for a soul on fire with divine love. **Princess of Swords** wears a red turban, indicating a quick mind and passionate nature. The wolf is a fierce and gentle creature that devours fear, awakens intuition, and reunites the soul with its spiritual family. **Ace of Swords** bursts through dark clouds on a beam of life. Her wings propel her above illusions; her many eyes see new possibilities.

BOTTOM ROW: **Princess of Wands** has awakened to the power of Spirit within her. **Ace of Wands** is illumined by the glory and power of the Lady Isis. **Princess of Cups** is in transition from childlike innocence to a mature expression of the feminine nature. **10 of Disks** shows a high priestess who extends her hands in blessing. Her aura is alive with symbols of freedom, love, and clarity.

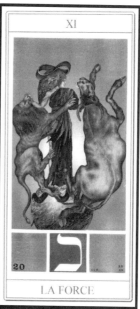

Tarot de Michel Bassot et René Chassagny 1995
The cards are in order of the planes, as described by the artists.

TOP ROW: (The Divine world) **IIII L'Empereur** (The Emperor) is the god Jupiter, master of fire. **XVI La Maison Dieu** (The House of God) depicts the myth of Prometheus, who stole fire from heaven and was punished by being chained to a rock, an eagle repeatedly pecking out his liver. (The Astral world) **II La Papesse** (The Popess) rests her feet on the world. She holds open the book of nature and life. The pillars Joachim and Boas symbolize that life is created and maintained in the tension of opposites. **XI La Force** (Strength) shows a woman, coifed with infinity, subduing with a gentle gesture the animate world, symbolized by the lion, and the physical world, symbolized by the bull. At her feet is a serpent, symbolizing the world spirit.

BOTTOM ROW: (The Physical world) **XII Le Pendu** (The Hanged Man) is suspended from two trees, one whose roots are in the sky, while the other's roots penetrate the earth. The Hanged Man is passive to superior energy, an instrument of the union of sky and earth. **XVIII La Lune** (The Moon) shows a scorpion who travels in the past and in the subconscious. The column symbolizes yang, or masculine, energy. The canvas reminds us that this card governs the imagination and thus artistic creation.

Hilary Baumann Tarot Graphic artist Hillary Baumann describes the goal of her tarot designs, "to create a beginner tarot deck that had interesting artwork and a description simple enough for a beginner but accurate enough to not insult more advanced users." The cards were composed of illustrations and computer-generated type and borders in 2001.

Hilary Baumann Tarot 2001

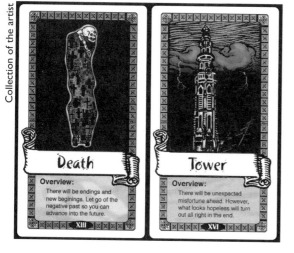

Beginner's Tarot Samantha Lynn of Woodhull & Desmoulins Press calls the Beginner's Tarot a "color-coded deck targeted towards the beginning student of tarot who wishes to drill on the basic associations of the cards." Major Arcana are printed in yellow, swords in gray, wands in red, cups in blue, and coins in green. The deck was made circa 1996.

Andrey Bezukladnikov Tarot Andrey Bezukladnikov has been a photographer since he was fourteen. As a child, he had aspirations of being a botanist, and he collected cacti. His dream took a different turn when he bought his first camera to photograph the flowering of the cacti.

Bezukladnikov's tarot designs have a central photograph framed by smaller photos. The artist describes the way in which the deck was inspired: "When I turned thirty-three, I decided to sum up my life and to create a series of images of the phenomena of the material world which had influenced my destiny. At that time I was under a strong influence of books on magic. I decided that tarot symbols would serve best for this purpose." The collages are composed of pictures chosen from those the artist had taken during the previous twelve years. The deck is also known as the Perestroika Tarot. The titles are in Russian. The designs were made circa 1995.

Beginner's Tarot Samantha Lynn and Woodhull & Desmoulins Press, circa 1996

Andrey Bezukladnikov Tarot Circa 1995 0 Fool. 1 Magician. 3 Empress. 4 Emperor.

Andrey Bezukladnikov Tarot *(continued)*
TOP ROW: 6 Lovers. 7 Chariot. 8 Justice. 9 Hermit.
SECOND ROW: 10 Wheel. 11 Strength. 12 Hanged Man. 14 Temperance.
BOTTOM ROW: 15 Devil. 16 Tower. 17 Star. 18 Moon.

Biblical Tarot English artist Robin Rudolph says of the Biblical Tarot, "As the stories of the Bible and biblical imagery are deeply imbedded in Western consciousness, I felt that a tarot deck based on the Old and New Testaments would be easily accessible in terms of understanding and grasping the archetypal truths of the tarot." The deck was completed in 1995. The four suits are crosses (swords), staffs, roses (cups), and coins. The court cards are sage (king), seer (queen), messenger (knight), and acolyte (page).

Biblical Tarot Robin Rudolph, 1995 The descriptions are based on correspondence with the artist.

TOP ROW: **0 The Simpleton** reflects the saying of Jesus, "Be as a child to enter the kingdom of heaven." **1 The Archmage** is Jesus walking on the water, the four suits around him. **2 The High Priestess** is Mary Magdalene. According to legend, she was a prostitute who became a disciple of Jesus. **5 The Pharisee** studies a scroll. The Pharisees were a sect of Judaism that relied on law and learning. **9 The Hermit** is John the Baptist in the desert.

SECOND ROW: **14 Faith** recalls the saying of Jesus, "Consider the lilies of the field. They toil not, neither do they spin. Yet Solomon in all his glory is not arrayed as one of these." (Matthew 6:28–29) **15 Temptation** shows Adam and Eve caught in the serpent twined on the Tree of Knowledge. **17 The Star** shows a Magus and a shepherd boy looking at the star that will guide them to the place where Jesus has been born. **18 The Moon** depicts Joseph, in his many-colored dream coat, in prison. **19 The Sun** recalls the end of the cataclysmic flood that drowned the world, except for those aboard Noah's ark. A dove holding an olive branch heralds the end of the flood.

BOTTOM ROW: **21 Creation** depicts the Garden of Eden, where predator and prey rest peacefully together. **Eight of Crosses. Four of Staffs. Ten of Roses. Seer of Coins.**

Collection of the artist

Black and White Tarot Linda Kazyak, 1993

Black and White Tarot Linda Kazyak created cards with black backgrounds and figures in white. Her deck was made in 1993.

Louise Janitsch Blake Tarot Louise Janitsch Blake originally designed her round tarot images as astrological art. "My idea is to tie in the zodiac and tarot, using the feminine aspects of the systems, but keeping the symbolism fairly traditional," the artist says in correspondence with Stuart Kaplan. The illustrations have appeared in the magazine *Aquarian Voices* and as t-shirt designs.

Louise Janitsch Blake Tarot 1989 Gemini (The Lovers). Virgo (The Hermit). Libra (Justice). Scorpio (Death).

Collection of the artist / © 1989 by Louise Janitsch Blake

Axel Bohnenkamp-Seiler and Inge Peitzsch Tarot
Circa 1985
The Magician. Three of Cups.
Two of Cups.

Collection of the artist

Axel Bohnenkamp-Seiler and Inge Peitzsch Tarot
Author Axel Bohnenkamp-Seiler and artist Inge Peitzsch collaborated to create tarot images. The style of the art could be called naive, although the composition and color schemes are complex. The original art is in gouache. Of the tarot, Bohnenkamp-Seiler says, "Man at the closing of the twentieth century suffers imperceptibly from the fact that the bridge between subconscious and conscious thinking has collapsed. He relies on words, sentences, theses, and has lost sight of imagery, the language of the heart. The ancient wisdom of man is first repressed and then forgotten. Tarot cards are the key to this ancient wisdom…. They help to reconstruct the bridge—they are the bridge…." The cards were created circa 1985.

John M. Bradley Tarot   John M. Bradley painted Minor and Major Arcana cards primarily for use in divination. In a 1996 letter to Stuart Kaplan, he explains, "I have been a student of tarot for about 15 years. During that time I have become familiar with various decks. I have found that the illustrations of many of them are too structured and rigid for fluid divination, and I thereby set about designing one that retains traditional symbols while breaking down the concrete structure that can inhibit many readers. The images on the cards are often surreal and at times Picassoesque." The designs were completed in 1995.

Bush Tarot   W.N. Bush created a tarot deck based on Renaissance cards. Most of the cards were modeled after the extant cards of the Visconti-Sforza tarot. For missing cards, Bush used other works. For example, he modeled his Devil card after an illumination in a French psalter. The deck was made in 1997 with drawings in pen and ink.

Collection of the artist

Bush Tarot   W.N. Bush, 1997   TOP ROW: I The Magician. VII The Chariot. XVIII The Star. XXI The World.
BOTTOM ROW: Queen of Swords. Page of Swords. King of Staves. Knight of Cups.

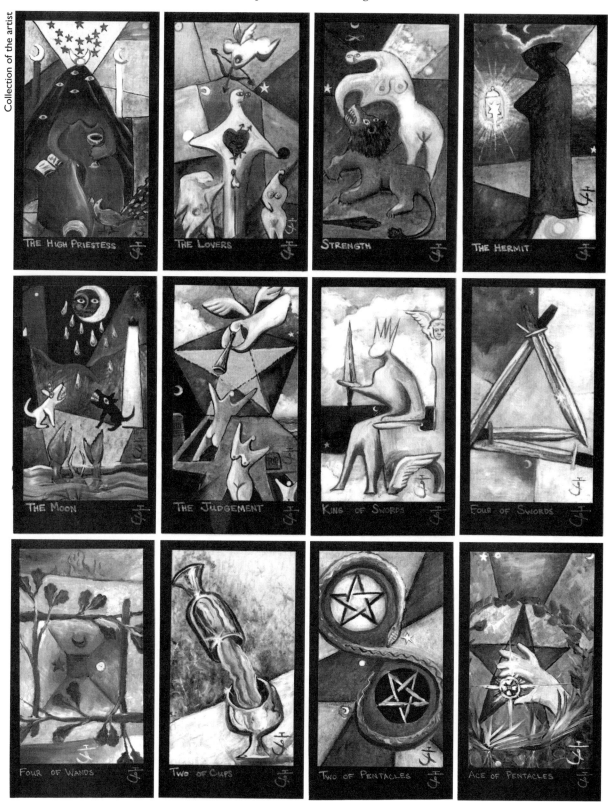

John M. Bradley Tarot 1995

Carbonic Tarot "The Carbonic Tarot is so-called because it has been totally designed with graphite, a pure form of carbon," says artist Adriano Monteiro. "Carbon is the element that exists in the most quantity in the universe; it's present in everything, in all forms of life, vegetable, animal, or mineral. Carbon is responsible for the formation of the largest and most complex chains.... The Carbonic Tarot is composed of twenty-two cards, the Major Arcana; they correspond to the Tree of Life Paths, the universe and its energies manifested. At the same time, they're stages of the Initiation Path that ascends level by level, as well as the aspects of the human being." The black and white drawings were made in 2001.

Gli Arcani di Casanova The engravings by Italian artist Carla Tolomeo show the life of Casanova (1725–1798) in the framework of the tarot. Ninety sets of the engravings were issued numbered with Arabic numerals, and twenty were issued numbered in Roman numerals. A book, *Gli Arcani di Casanova,* published in 1988 by Raffaele Bandini Editore, is illustrated with the deck and describes the cards.

Giacomo Girolamo Casanova was a Venetian adventurer. His memoirs, which describe in detail his sexual exploits and mirror the politics and culture of his time, brought him lasting fame.

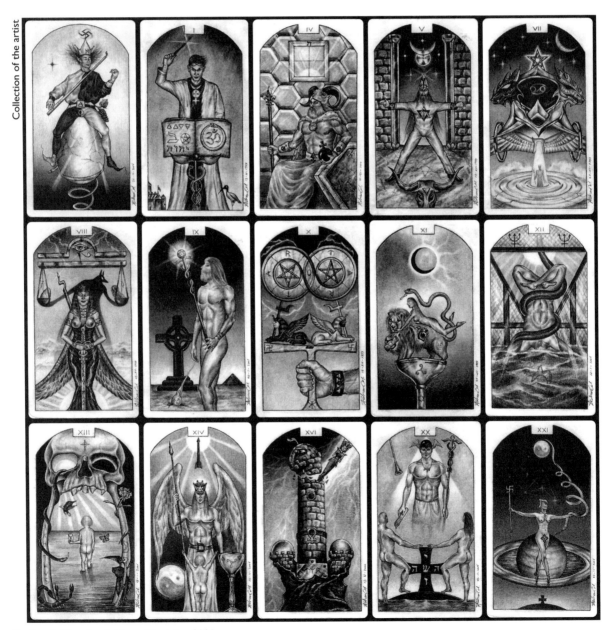

Collection of the artist

Carbonic Tarot　Adriano Monteiro, 2001

Collection of the author

Gli Arcani di Casanova Carla Tolomeo, 1988

TOP ROW: **1 Il Mago** (The Magician) is Casanova, who swindled Marquise d'Urfe by convincing her that he could give her birth as a man. **3 L'Imperatrice** (The Empress) is "M.M.", a nun with whom he had an affair. **4. L'Imperatore** (The Emperor) is Abbé de Bernis, the French ambassador to Venice, who also had an affair with M.M. **8 La Giustizia** (Justice) portrays Manon Balletti, a young woman from a theatrical family. She fell in love with Casanova.

BOTTOM ROW: **9 L'Eremita** (The Hermit) reflects a period of relative solitude in Casanova's life, as librarian at Count Josef Karl Emmanuel von Waldstein's castle in Dux, in what is now the Czech Republic. **11 La Forza** (Strength) depicts the count Edoardo Tiretta, called *"six fois ou six coups"* (six times or six blows). **12 L'Appiccato** (The Hanged Man) shows dueling pistols. In 1766, Casanova quarreled over an actress with Count Xavier Branicki. They fought a duel, and the count was seriously wounded. Casanova had to flee but was proud that a nobleman condescended to fight with him. **15 Il Demonio** (The Demon) portrays Marianne Corticelli. She agreed to help Casanova in "regenerating" the Marquise d'Urfe as a man. However, when she demanded too big a cut, Casanova told the Marquise that Corticelli was possessed by an evil demon.

Cathar Tarot The twenty-two-card Cathar Tarot was named after the gnostics who lived in Languedoc, in the south of France during the Middle Ages. Artist Rossetta Woolf, who worked in partnership with Aleph Kamal and Peter Lamia, writes to Stuart Kaplan: "In our culture so many threads lead back to [the Gnostics of Languedoc]. At this time it seems to us crucial that they be looked at anew, for therein lie the seeds both of what is great and what is wicked in Western culture and spirituality. The tarot itself was…quite possibly developed by them into its present form." The illustrations are in watercolor.

The Cathars believed that the universe was engaged in a fight between two equal powers: good and evil, good being the kingdom of God and evil being the material world. In 1209, Pope Innocent the Third launched a crusade against them.

Celestial Tarot Artist and tarot aficionada Laurie Amato created the Celestial Tarot by montaging images of outer space with silhouettes of figures from medieval, Renaissance, and neoclassical paintings. The compositions are simple, but the effect is complex and colorful. The Celestial Tarot was created in 2000.

Other decks by Laurie Amato are the Inner Garden Tarot, Inner Landscape Tarot, Stained Glass Tarot, Starlight Tarot, and Victorian Tarot. Amato also designed the "Egyptian Temple of Tarot," a three-dimensional rendering illustrated with cards from the Ibis Tarot, by Josef Machynka.

Cathar Tarot   Rossetta Woolf, Aleph Kamal, and Peter Lamia, circa 1990

Collection of the author

Celestial Tarot   Laurie Amato, 2000   TOP ROW: 0 The Fool. I The Magician. II The High Priestess. III The Empress.
SECOND ROW: IV The Emperor. VI The Lovers. VIII Strength. IX The Hermit.   THIRD ROW: XII The Hanged Man. XIV Temperance.
XV The Devil. XVII The Star.   BOTTOM ROW: XVIII The Moon. XIX Tarot Sun. XX Judgment. XXI The World.

Tarot of Celtic Legends Gerry Ryan and Kate Hepworth, circa 1995 **The Fool** depicts Gawain, the Arthurian knight who underwent trials to his strength and his virtue. **The Empress** is the goddess Danu. Legend has it that, with the Cosmic Snake Ophion, she gave rise to the people who later populated Ireland, known as the Tuatha De Danaan. **Death** is Macha, a great woman of the Danaans, who collected the heads of men killed in battle and ruled as queen of Ireland. **The King of Wands** is the Norwegian Viking king Cormac, the main character of an Icelandic saga of love, battle, and Celtic magic. **The Four of Cups** depicts part of the story of the female magician Etain and the Irish king Midir. Their story of love takes bizarre, magical twists (such as Etain turning into a beautiful purple fly).

Tarot of Celtic Legends Irish writer Gerry Ryan and California artist Kate Hepworth worked together to create the Tarot of Celtic Legends. Says Ryan, "We seek to reinforce the elementary clarity and availability of the tarot by shaping the deck with the images of the Celtic characters and legends. They contain fundamental ethical truths, which precede and are intertwined with our modern religious symbols. They are totems of bold nature, our own bold human nature, with its mixed feelings of soul and body, and its opposite pushes towards progress and apathy." The deck was made circa 1995. Hepworth used painting and computer graphics to create the images.

Changing Woman Tarot The "Changing Woman–Every Woman's Journey" paintings, completed in 1996, were not originally intended to be tarot cards. Artist Ezshwan Winding developed with Cay Randall-May the tarot correspondences after the series was complete. The deck has twenty-two Major Arcana. Cards 22 through 34 are not Minor Arcana but rather images that "give insights into modern life," as described by Ezshwan. Says Ezshwan about the series, "The Changing Woman series is my way of honoring the goddess in every woman as she moves from the Disempowered Feminine Energy to her personal revelation and transformation. I call on the Goddess to come through me with love, fervor, and directness." The cards have numbers, but no titles.

Chaos Tarot The awesome beauty of fractals illustrates John Berger's Chaos Tarot. "The Chaos Tarot is a road map to surreality," Berger writes. "Derived from the Mandelbrot Set, the deck's images evoke power on both emotional and magical levels. The basic deck contains twenty-three Major Arcana, One Fool, and four element-based suits of ten numbered cards each." The two extra Major Arcana are XXII Anamnesis and XXIII Eschaton. The suits are fire (swords), earth (wands), water (cups), and skies (pentacles).

The Mandelbrot Set is a "fractal," a computer-generated graph of a mathematical equation. Benoit Mandelbrot was the mathematician who first plotted fractals on computer by assigning colors to numbers. Before Mandelbrot's work, the equation was too complex to plot.

"The Chaos Tarot uses 'pure' fractals," Berger writes, "that is to say, fractals that have not been altered from their original shape and color relationships in any way.... Because these are 'pure' fractals, they immediately offer the user an intense and direct connection to the fundamental and elemental qualities of reality."

Changing Woman Tarot Ezshwan Winding, 1996 Titles of the cards are by the artist. TOP ROW: **0** Fool: Spring. **1** Magician: Everywoman. **2** High Priestess: The Oracle. **3** Empress: Baubo is a primordial goddess who personifies the mother of divine races. **5** Hierophant: Diviana is a motherly, protective Roman goddess.

SECOND ROW: **6** Lovers: Aphrodite is the Roman goddess of love. **10** Wheel: Ushas is the Indian goddess of dawn, adorned each day by her mother, the sky, to bring anew the gifts of day. **11** Justice: Brigit is a Celtic goddess with many attributes, including the power to mediate between people at war. **12** Hanged Man: Vestal Virgin is a priestess of the goddess Vesta and is committed to celibacy for life. **13** Death: Kali is the Indian goddess of destruction and war.

THIRD ROW: **14** Temperance: Waiting by the Well portrays the Samaritan woman who gave Jesus water to drink at

a well. She was surprised and honored, as normally she would be considered too low in status to serve someone of Jesus's social class. **15** Devil: Without love there is no life. **16** Tower: Giving birth to self. **17** Star: Juno is the queen of the Roman pantheon. **18** Moon: Moon goddess.

BOTTOM ROW: **19** Sun: Gaia is the Earth Mother of Roman myth. **20** Judgment: The Mature Inanna was a Sumerian goddess of war and passion. She is also known as Ishtar. **23** Examine the Heart: Inanna. **25** Mother Love: Demeter was the Greek goddess of agricultural fertility. She stopped the return of spring when her daughter Persephone was abducted by the king of the underworld. The cold lifted only when her daughter was permitted to return to earth for half the year. **32** Inform Yourself: Lady of the Lake guards the sword Excalibur, by which the ruler of Britain was known.

Collection of the artist

Chaos Tarot John Berger, 2002 The descriptions are by the artist.

TOP ROW: **I. The Magician** is a visual roadmap to magic and arcane knowledge. The Mandala is here, the Qabala, the Star of David ringed with sacred scarabs. Energy disperses in these patterns, emanating from the divine spark—the Mandelbrot—within a soul. **II. The Priestess** represents consecration, sensuality, fertility. The complex crest rises over tendrils of color, the flows of kundalini energy climbing into rolling pearls of energy, transforming as they make the transit. In the Priestess card, there lies a model for bringing cycles into harmony, as all things flow into a single point. **VI. The Lovers** are born in the division of a single cell. What was one becomes two, then ever seeks to become one again. The path to reunion remains, a thread between the sundered, showing the way. **XII. The Hanged Man** is suspended, a fly snarled in a spider's web. Lines of force constrict movement. The way to escape is not obvious. Fighting the flow will not succeed. Escape is taking the web into one's self, absorbing the lines of force as a black hole absorbs matter, until a new gate opens onto the next level of reality.

SECOND ROW: **XIII. Death.** Do not be afraid to go into the light. Death is transition. It marks the mutability of the world. Time passes and all things end. In each ending, there is a beginning. **XV. The Devil.** The name Lucifer means "Morning Star." The Devil was born into the light, and from

Chocolate Tarot Lynn Atkinson, circa 2000 TOP ROW: **VIII Strength: Chocolate for Perseverance** shows an advertisement for Cadbury's Cocoa that includes the slogan, "Makes strong men stronger." **XIV Temperance: Creating Frothy Chocolate** was illustrated in the early Aztec Codex Tuleda. The froth provided a bitter spicy taste prized in that culture. **Princess of Swords: Chocolate Victory!** A little girl carries a chocolate sponge cake, as a policeman stops all traffic for her. **6 of Swords: Chocolate goes to Europe.** Hernan Cortez brought the first chocolate to Spain in 1528. BOTTOM ROW: **Queen of Cups: The Pretty Chocolate Maker** is a painting by Jean-Etienne Liotard. The portrait inspired a wealthy aristocrat to marry its subject, a chambermaid. **Six of Cups: Hot Chocolate—a childhood Treat.** Chocolate was considered medicinal; children remind a laughing servant that they need their daily dose. **Ace of Cups: A Chocolate Break in Eight-Deer's Journey.** Eight-Deer was the ruler of the Tilantango Aztecs. He drank up to fifty cups of chocolate daily. **Eight of Coins: Grinding Cacao Beans.**

Childhood Arcana Sarah Scott Parry drew images from fairy tales and nursery rhymes for the Childhood Arcana.

Child's Play Tarot The Major Arcana of Ratna Pappert's tarot show children dressing up in larger-than-life archetypal roles. Says the artist, "A mismatched jumble of patterns and images on the clothing and toys of the children and in their surroundings allows the symbolism of the tarot to hide in plain sight." The characters of the Minor Arcana are dolls, in the suits of pencils (swords), candles (wands), fishbowls (cups), and buttons (coins). Ratna Pappert created the art in 2002.

Chocolate Tarot Lynn Atkinson's tarot "reflects the cultures and themes that are found in the life and history of chocolate and remains true to that theme as every card is a part of that world—no fudgin' (pardon the pun)." The deck was composed circa 2000.

Christmas Arcana Sarah Scott Parry blends religious imagery with traditional English Yuletide festivity.

Clavicle Tarot "The core of the Clavicle deck is the skeleton, the core of humanity," says artist Atanielle Annyn Rowland Noel. "The skeleton evokes the universality and eternity of humankind. Except to the trained eye, all human skeletons look alike. King and commoner, Stone Age hunter and modern scholar, man and woman, young and old, ebony, ivory, saffron, and bronze—we all have remarkably similar bones.... All but a few figures have their skeletons clad in an ectoplasmic human form. This signifies the potentiality of tarot symbols. The figures wear suggestions of clothing and carry emblems of the roles they play in the Universal Dance. Traditional tarot symbology and Rider-Waite modifications are retained for ease in reading." The Clavicle Tarot deck was completed in 1994.

light he takes his essence. The Devil is still an angel, fallen or not, and the card depicts a bright being displaying its wings with childlike pride. **XVI. The Tower.** "Ashes, ashes, all fall down...." The Tower is the card of explosions, of chaos manifesting itself swiftly and violently, falling in a rain of ashes and sparks. Fireworks and lightning strikes. This card represents creation from destruction, or simply destruction itself, in all its stark and beautiful glory. **XVIII. The Moon** reaches out to us with chunky convoluted arms of gravity and magic, influencing our nights and coaxing forth the ocean's menstru-

al-tidal flow. The Moon is complex, involving, layered. Its secrets are difficult to decipher, its meanings and truths are often hidden. Look beneath the surface for answers.

BOTTOM ROW: **XXIII. Eschaton.** The object at the end of time grows nearer with every moment. Gaze into the abyss. You will see it grow larger before your eyes. This is a dangerous card, a working card. But do not be afraid of what lies at the end of the tunnel. Put your will into this card, and the Eschaton WILL come sooner. **Ten of Fire (Swords). Ace of Skies (Wands). Five of Water (Cups).**

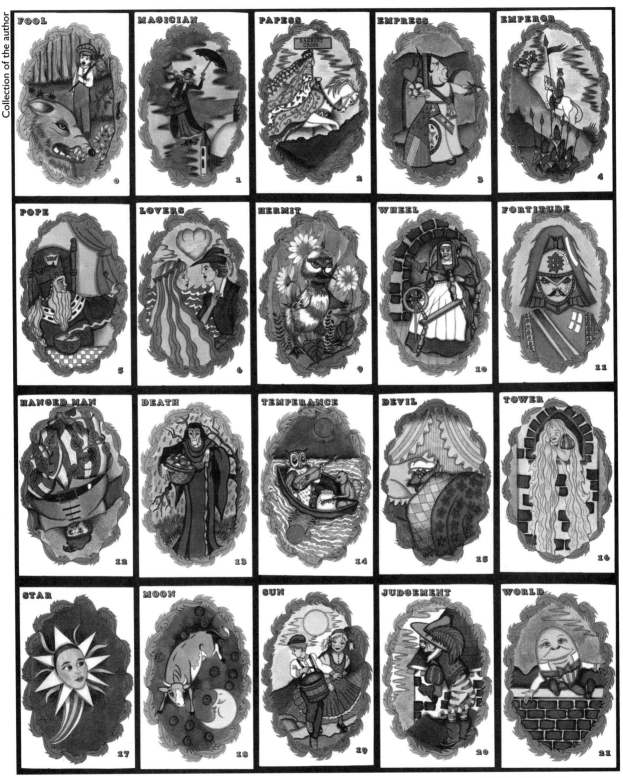

Childhood Arcana   Sarah Scott Parry, circa 1990   TOP ROW: **0 Fool.** "The Boy Who Cried Wolf." **1 Magician.** Mary Poppins, the magical nanny. **2 Papess.** "Ride a cockhorse to Banbury Cross to see a fine lady upon a white horse." **3 Empress.** Queen of Hearts from *Alice in Wonderland.* **4 Emperor.** "The Brave Old Duke of York."   SECOND ROW: **5 Pope.** "Old King Cole." **6 Lovers.** "The Little Mermaid." **9 Hermit.** "The Ugly Duckling." **10 Wheel.** Spinning wheel from "Sleeping Beauty." **11 Fortitude.** "The Little Tin Soldier."   THIRD ROW: **12 Hanged Man.** The giant from "Jack and the Beanstalk." **13 Death.** The wicked queen from "Snow White." **14 Temperance.** "The Owl and the Pussycat." **15 Devil.** The big, bad wolf from "Little Red Riding Hood." **16 Tower.** "Rapunzel." BOTTOM ROW: **17 Star.** "Twinkle, twinkle, little star, how I wonder what you are…" **18 Moon.** "Hey diddle diddle, the cat and the fiddle, the cow jumped over the moon…" **19 Sun.** "Jack and Jill." **20 Judgement.** "Puss in Boots." **21 World.** "Humpty Dumpty."

Child's Play Tarot   Ratna Pappert, 2002

Christmas Arcana Sarah Scott Parry, circa 1990   3 is Mary, 4 is Joseph and 21 is the baby Jesus. 13 is King Herod, who ordered the slaughter of children under two, in jealousy of rumors that Jesus would someday supplant him.

34

Collection of the artist

Clavicle Tarot   Atanielle Annyn Rowland Noel, 1994

Cooperstown Tarot Jim Markowitz and Paul Kuhrman, 1988 20 The Umpire. Ace of Gloves. Veteran of Bats. 10 of Balls.

Contemporary Tarot Lois Polansky blended old and new symbols and methods to create the Contemporary Tarot. She says in her artist's statement, "I developed my personal interpretations of the cards through intensive research of traditional tarot iconography, hundreds of sketches and by immersing myself completely in contemporary 'pulp print.' For each card I selected media-derived imagery to correlate with the archetypal symbols that appear in the historical tarot decks.... The finished collage drawings were scanned and digitized on a computer … and then transferred onto five-inch by four-inch zinc etching plates through a photo etch process. The plates were bitten in acid, inked, and hand-printed. Prior to processing the images on the plates, I overlapped two positive Kodaliths for each of the figures, thus transforming them into double mirror-image fantasy people with all the ambiguities of a Rorschach test." The Polansky deck adapts the correspondences of Hebrew letters to Major Arcana from the Eliphas Levi, Papus, and Oswald Wirth decks. The suits are represented by circles (swords), triangles (wands), crescents (cups), and squares (coins). The Contemporary Tarot was completed in 1994.

Cooperstown Tarot Jim Markowitz and Paul Kuhrman named their tarot deck Cooperstown in honor of the New York home of baseball. The designs derive from the Tarot of Marseilles, with a baseball theme. The originals are acrylic paintings. Three of the paintings from the deck were included in the Smithsonian Institute's traveling exhibition called "Diamonds Are Forever: Artists and Writers on Baseball." The deck was completed circa 1988.

Costume Arcana The costumes in Sarah Scott Parry's tarot carry the symbolism of the cards. Parry says, "All the costumes are actual costumes of Great Britain, from the Druids to the Tutors."

Cross-Cultural Tarot Welsh artist Linda Cattrall created the Cross-Cultural Tarot with imagery and symbols from existing and ancient cultures worldwide, including European tradition, Hindu mythology, and Buddhist folklore. The artist says in correspondence to Stuart Kaplan, "This approach avoids narrow categorization and leads toward a global consciousness. In creating the ideal of an integrated planet, where tolerance, understanding, and celebration of cultural differences occur, peace on earth will naturally ensue." Several of the Major Arcana designs were published as greeting cards in 1997 by Tarot as Greeting Cards.

Crystal Fusion Tarot The Crystal Fusion Tarot was created by Jeanne Auger and Jeff Fisher of Canada. The images are collages of photographs, paintings, and pencil drawings. Each card shows various correspondences, including Hebrew letters, astrological signs, I Ching hexagrams, chemical formulas, and atomic elements. A primary influence on the artists was the shamanistic teachings of Native Americans, known to many from the books by Carlos Castaneda, who described his experiences with his teacher Don Juan. The deck was completed in 1991.

Contemporary Tarot Lois Polansky, 1994 The caption is based on descriptions by the artist.

TOP ROW: **0 The Fool** is a composite dancer, a Nureyev/Baryshnikov figure that can leap beyond the temporal world and into the air. **1 The Magician** was inspired by the film actor and sleight-of-hand artist Ricky Jay, whose mercurial energy mesmerizes audiences. **2 The High Priestess** plays with the role of women in religion and submits to chance by overlapping the positive and negative images of a gorgeous super-model in flowing loungewear and elaborately coiffed hair. **3 The Empress** is the archetypal

feminine mother, queen, and earth-goddess, combining Psyche with a ceramic Marilyn Monroe doll. **4 The Emperor** is a winged television psychiatrist, a gentle father figure wearing a sheepish grin and holding a scepter pointing upward.

SECOND ROW: **6 The Lovers** lean toward one another, bisected by the tree of life in which the "Angel-America" appears. **8 Justice** weighs the value of our legal system and tries to maintain the delicate balance between all the opposing forces at work in the world today. **9 The Hermit** comprises double monk figures locked together, rocking and

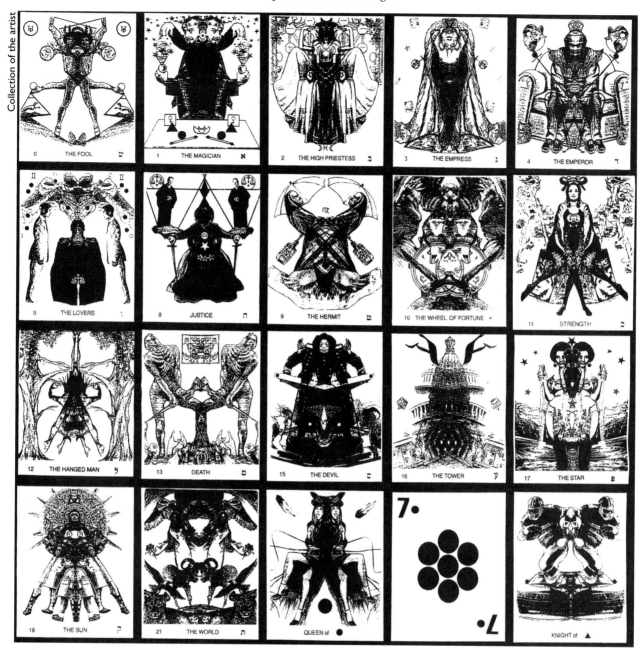

rolling to an ethereal gospel rhythm under their clear plastic umbrella-walking sticks. **10 The Wheel of Fortune** represents the artist's belief in the irony of destiny. The traditional wheel is replaced with a double Rolex watch inscribed with TARO and the Tetragrammaton. The archetypal creatures are the "Lion King" of the Walt Disney movie, a cow skull by Georgia O'Keefe, the sphinx of Hollywood, and Jonathan Livingston Seagull of the book by Richard Bach. **11 Strength** alludes to the link between industry, investment, and the marketing of beauty. The "Beauty/Beast" theme is explored as the twin icons of sex and power.

THIRD ROW: **12 The Hanged Man** is based on an inverted image from a poster from Joyce Theater, a dance theater in New York City. **13 Death** is based on a photograph of a Mardi Gras figure dressed in a body stocking that displayed the human skeleton. **15 The Devil** expands the duality of good and evil by representing the devil as a fallen angel, a famous superstar idolized and then hurled from star-

dom in disgrace through a tragic character flaw. **16 The Tower** shows the U.S. Capitol struck by lightning that resembles the Hebrew letter ayin. A sense of resilience comes through. **17 The Star** is the "star's star," actress Elizabeth Taylor, shown in the film *Cat on a Hot Tin Roof*. She holds a cocktail glass in each hand and pours a never-ending stream of false hope.

BOTTOM ROW: **19 The Sun** depicts the two children of President John F. Kennedy following their father's assassination. The "Billy Bud Aztec Sun God" behind them is renewed hope/sunlight, overcoming one of America's darkest nights. **21 The World** weaves together air/east, fire/south, water/west, and earth/north, symbolized respectively by the Angel in America, lioness, bird, and ram. **Queen of Circles** is Barbra Streisand, the popular American singer. **Seven of Circles. Knight of Triangles** is the football star Joe Montana, clutching his football/light bulb and charging off the masthead of his sports car.

Collection of the author

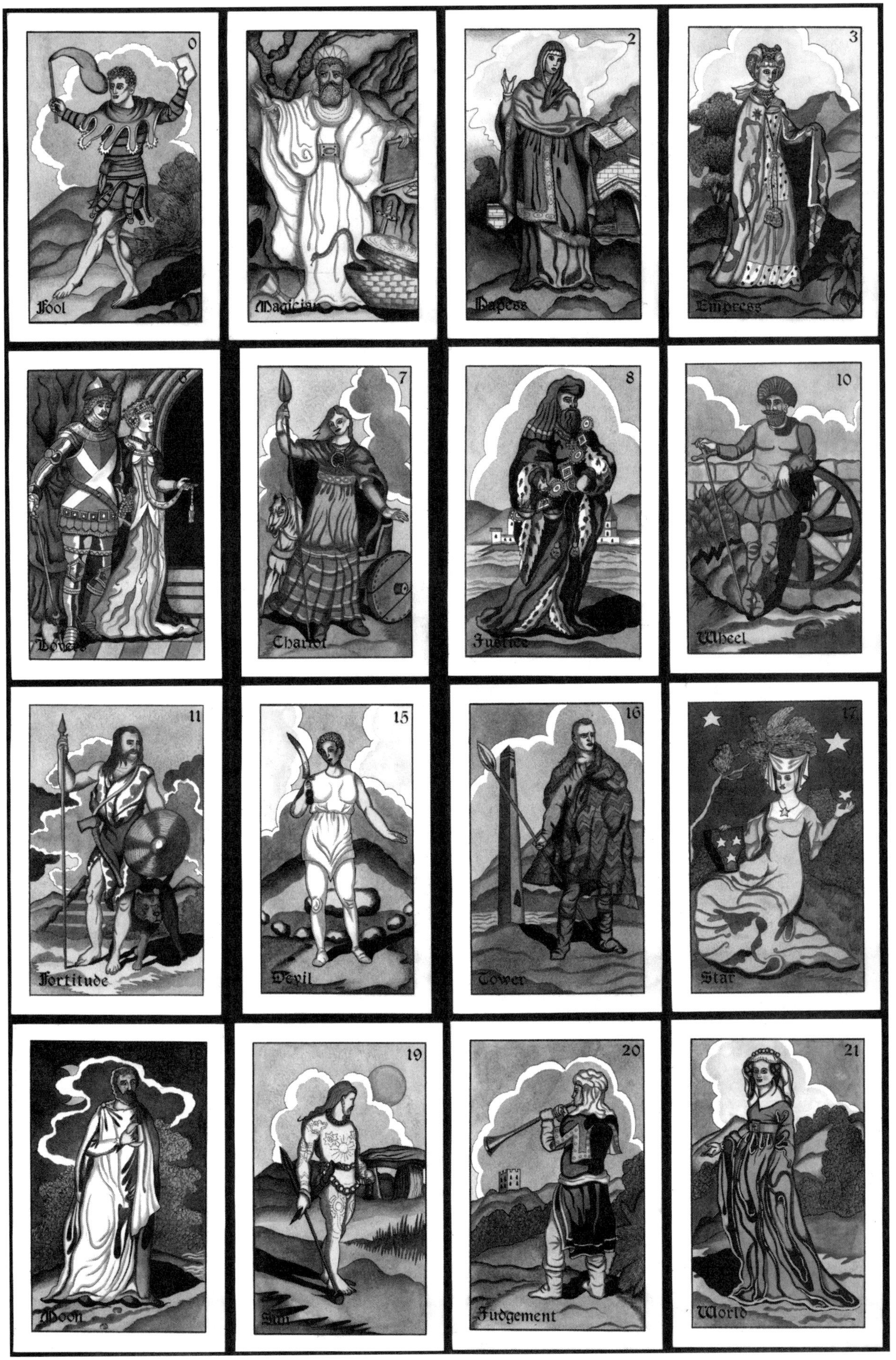

Costume Arcana   Sarah Scott Parry, circa 1995   The following descriptions are by Sarah Parry.

TOP ROW: **0 Fool.** His costume dates from 1272. The introduction of the jester, or fool, was by the East. Idiots were believed to be favored of heaven. Here we see an early jester. The bag is an inflated bladder. The parchment in the left hand is probably a grant of intended benefit. **1 Magician** is an arch-Druid in his judicial habit. Around his neck is the Jodhain Morain, or breastplate of judgment. It is said in the Irish fables that if one utters false judgment, the collar has the power of "squeezing the neck." **2 Papess** is an Anglo-Saxon woman of rank, from 850 CE. The Anglo-Saxon women were celebrated for their embroidery; accordingly, we find her gown embellished with needlework and beads. **3 Empress,** 1446, wears a reticulated headdress and coronet richly studded with jewels. She wears a surcoat and a mantle trimmed with ermine. Over her shoulders is a mantel with her paternal coat of arms.

SECOND ROW: **6 Lovers,** 1425. He wears the armor worn by the "great" from the middle of the reign of Edward III to the end of the reign of Henry IV. **7 Chariot** depicts a costume from the time when the Romans entered Britain. The figure is almost Boadicea-like. Her cloak is fastened by a fibula, and from her neck depends a golden torque. **8 Justice,** 1392. A man wears a stately habit. The robe is deep purple, lined with ermine and hooded in crimson. On his chest he wears a cross pattee of gold, and over the left shoulder hangs a superb belt of gold and precious stones. **10 Wheel** shows a man who wears a corset or *wambas* of leather, a kind of half armor. In his hand is a "hammer."

THIRD ROW: **11 Fortitude** shows a Briton of the interior. He wears the skin of a brindled cow, called in his native tongue *brych.* Attached by a thong is a *bwyell-arv, arv-vwyell,* or *bwyell-ennilleg,* the battle ax. At his side is a dog, not only the trusty guardian of his hut, but a fierce and steady companion of war. **15 Devil** shows a woman known as a priestess, or

fola, a descendent of the Druids. The large stone behind her was used for human sacrifices. It was said that the *fola* could foretell the future by the flowing blood and the intestines of her victims. **16 Tower** shows how an Irishman would have been dressed in the time of James I. His *coccula,* or cloak, is "shagged" and woven like braided hair. His temples and face are shaved, while the hair on the top of the head was gathered at the back into a single lock or glib. **17 Star,** 1420. The woman's costume was designed to display the neck and shoulders, and it shows off the symmetry of the body. The headdress is of the crescent or horned kind.

BOTTOM ROW: **18 Moon** shows a Druid holding a *cornan* or crescent, termed by the Irish *cead-rai-re.* The first quarter of the moon was a symbol of the sacred ship known as the Ark of Noah. The Druids wore white, the emblem of holiness and truth, as well as being the color of sunlight. **19 Sun** portrays a Caledonian around 45 CE. The men preferred to adorn their bodies with tattoos rather than clothes. The process of tattooing was extremely painful, and the men who were able to endure it were highly esteemed as brave men. His spear, or *aseth,* is made of ash. Around his waist and neck are ornaments made of twisted iron wire, which his people prized as others prized gold or silver. The background represents the Lan-y-Chomlech in Cornwall. The stone arch was so high that a man on horseback could ride underneath it. Lan-y-On signifies the "enclosure of On," the Arkite divinity, and therefore implies that all Cromlechs were representations of the "Noachic Ark." **20 Judgement,** 1375. This man is a trumpeter. The Saxon kings thought of their minstrels as an essential part of the household. The costume, though prettily embroidered, was in fact fairly comical. The love of the grotesque was obvious as early as the reign of King Edward III. **21 World** shows a pregnant woman from around the time of Henry VI. On top of her veiled headdress is a wreath of embroidery and pearls.

Cross-Cultural Tarot   Linda Cattrall, 1997   Captions are based on descriptions by the artist.

The Fool is a youth on the point of making his own way in life. He steps into an abyss, carrying the tools that he will later use as the Magician. His white clothes symbolize purity. **The Magician** is in ritual garb, red for dynamic action and white for purity of intention. He points skyward with his wand and earthward to indicate his awareness of celestial and terrestrial forces. The puppy of the Fool is now a wolf. **The Pope** shows Buddha (center), Krishna (left), and Jesus (right) surrounded by rainbow light. **The Lovers** show

two people surrounded by red roses, ripe grapes, and laurels. The woman holds a golden apple. In the sky, a manifestation of a parent or an ex-lover tries to prevent Cupid from shooting his arrow, but the couple is protected by the fruits and flowers of Earth herself. **The Chariot** shows a man in crown and regal costume, reflecting the gravity of the news he brings. The steeds are lying down, their tails forming a caduceus shape. The animals gossip, reflecting the role of the charioteer as messenger of both good and bad news, often a voice from the subconscious.

Cross Cultural Tarot (continued)

TOP ROW: **Justice** has scales for weighing up and balancing events, moralities, and ideas as disparate as a sphere and a pyramid. The word is passive but displays its potential for cutting down, slicing through, and getting straight to the point. The costume is Egyptian, reminding us of how ancient our need is for law, justice, and truth. **Death** (Rebirth) has a red pig head of brutishly destructive, instinctual animal aspect, while the emerging fetus represents new life, hope, and new beginnings. She holds a crescent knife for action, and her consort is symbolized by her staff. **Temperance** is an androgynous angel turning water into wine. One foot is on a golden sphere and the other on a triangle of lead, showing the angel as the alchemist, artist, and poet, creating beauty and wonder from inspiration, apparently performing miracles. **The Tower** is struck by lightning. A baby amidst the flames at the top is Dionysus reborn from catastrophe. **The Star of Hope** shows a young pregnant woman between two pools, remembrance and forgetfulness. She is associated with the goddess Astarte, mother and consort of Dionysus.

BOTTOM ROW: **The Moon** is three of the Moon's phases: new, full, and old. At the center, a woman in her prime emerges from a deep pool, reminding us of the Egyptian goddess Isis. On her right, a prepubescent girl sits before a silver pillar. On her left, a postmenopausal woman sits before a golden pillar. She holds the Egyptian rattle, indicating her immense wisdom and revered status. **The Sun** depicts the three stages of a man's growth and development: initiation, adulthood, and maturity. Initiation is shown by a young boy leaping through a ring of fire. The adult acknowledges the youth, who looks forward to maturity and becoming the sage. **The Earth** is viewed from outer space, the ozone layer like a fragile, precious bubble. We are watching the Earth rise while simultaneously sitting on a beautiful hill surrounded by her flora and fauna. **Ace of Wands** portrays the essence of fire, with a reference to the William Blake poem "The Tyger" ("Tyger, Tyger, burning bright..."). **Ace of Pentacles** shows a pentacle rooted in the ground by a point on either side of the valley, a rainbow arching over it. At the base of the card, the Green Man, spirit of nature, awakens and stirs, causing plants to sprout and grow.

Crystal Fusion Tarot   Jeanne Auger and Jeff Fisher, 1991   The caption is based on text by Jeanne Auger and Jeff Fisher.

TOP ROW: **I The Magus. II The High Priestess** stands facing us, her hands and head upholding the "horns of the Moon." She is semi-clothed, revealing her mysteries. Although she traditionally "carries" nine moons, only six are shown—another fully manifest one encompasses her body, while two more are absorbed into the infinite point above her head. These six manifest in two triangles, which interrelate in many ways, one being the apparent distance between her pineal gland, or "third eye," and the lunar receptive crown of her head. Her simple element is water, the cradle of all life on this planet, in both ocean and womb. **VIII The Balance. XII The Hanged Man.**

SECOND ROW: **XXI Universe. Queen of Swords: Air Stalker,** her head bowed, contemplates a luxurious plant with sword-shaped leaves, while behind her a train rushes by. A whippoorwill flies up from the plant, spreading its wings over the solar plexus, while another of the queen's allies, the thrush, covers her feet protectively. Both are songbirds, one of day and one of night. A bell hangs from her belt, ringing in sympathetic harmony to the feelings of others. **7 of Wands: Vindication. Ace of Wands** shows a rough hand, its wrist surrounded by flames, reaching into the card, holding delicately a sectionally marked candle. This is the sky-ladder of will, marked with thirteen degrees, rising from the center to the Seventh Heaven and going down from the center to Death. The flame has four sheaths, for the four Kabbalistic worlds.

BOTTOM ROW: **Queen of Cups: Water Stalker. 6 of Cups: Absorption. King of Disks: Earth Warrior,** a bass drummer, plays while his drum burns. A freshly sacrificed bull's head looks up at him in amazement; the drummer himself wears a bull-horned helmet. In the background, the minarets of Istanbul rise from the four-columned temple ruins of the Hellenic city of Constantinople. Two Chinese coins float on either side of the drum. An enormous sun, almost hidden, sits on a horizon punctuated by smokestacks. **Queen of Disks: Earth Stalker.**

Crystal Visions Tarot Hollywood psychic Dana Weiss created the Crystal Visions Tarot using photographs, many of celebrities. She completed the deck in 1995, but considers it a "work in progress." In a letter to Stuart Kaplan, she writes, "I am always finding new photos and replacing others. This explains why I have two cards for some."

Crystal Wolf Tarot Ylva Faith Trollsveden, the Swedish artist of Crystal Wolf Tarot, explains in correspondence with Stuart Kaplan the name of her deck: "To show animals and crystals, because many people in Sweden know that I work with crystals, and my name, Ylva, is Latin for wolf." The suits of the deck are represented by crystals and animals: rock crystal and polar bears for swords, citrine and lions for wands, rose quartz and swans for cups, and amethyst and wolves for pentacles. The artist is one of the founders of the Swedish Tarot Association. The Crystal Wolf Tarot was created in 1995.

Tarot Cuní & Masats The Tarot Cuní & Masats was painted by Catalan artist José Cuní Alfonso using a technique of Japanese Ukiyoe artists of the fifteenth century. Josep Masats Safops, who collaborated with him on the deck, describes in a letter to Stuart Kaplan the medium: "It is a method of painting that is between watercolor and gouache. The binding agent of vegetable gum is so transparent that it provides the colors with their maximum intensity as well as a unique, captivating brightness…. Cuní's colors embody the spontaneity and gracefulness of a child at play and that of a learned man submerged deep in thought." The figures on the cards, he says, are "spiritual and immortal characters according to the symbolism each one of them has…. The borders represent abstract elements, made of squares and perforated with holes through which to search for heaven, earth, spirit. They are like eyes open to the Infinite, to the Whole, or to Nothingness." The deck was completed in 1996, with titles in French.

Collection of the artist

Crystal Visions Dana Weiss, 1995 TOP ROW: **The Dreamer** (Fool) shows rock singer Elton John. **The Emperor** shows William Shatner as Captain James Kirk, of the television science fiction show *Star Trek*. **Silence** (The Hermit) is silent film star Charlie Chaplin. **Wheel of Fortune. The Hanging Spirit** is the pop star John Lennon in the film *Help!*

SECOND ROW: **The Star** is singer and actress Cher. **Queen of Swords** is jazz/folk singer Joni Mitchell. **The Wish** (9 of Cups) shows the artist with Lindsey Buckingham. "My wish was to meet Lindsey B.," she says, "and 'when you wish upon a star, your dreams come true.'" **8 of Cups** shows the 1960s fashion model Jean Shrimpton. **6 of Coins** shows the San Francisco intersection of Haight Ashbury, a counterculture gathering place in the 1960s.

Collection of the artist

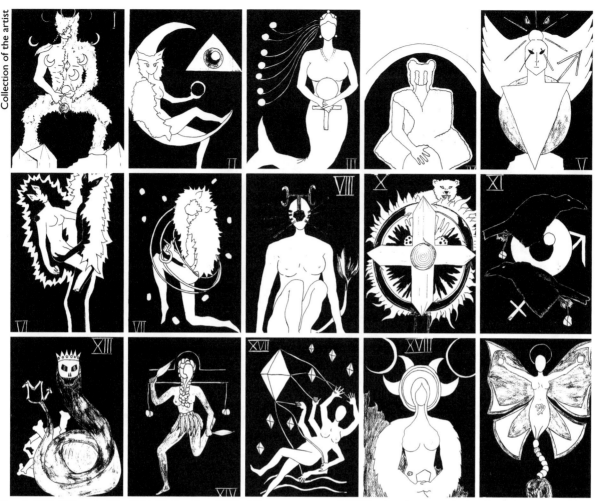

Crystal Wolf Tarot   Ylva Faith Trollsveden, 1995   The descriptions and titles are based on the artist's text.

TOP ROW: **I The Magician** stands on the four rocks of the earth, ready to take new steps. He holds the star symbol Mercury and a full moon. He has thrown eight moons to balance the forces. He is half wolf, and his coat is old to show wisdom. The nine colored balls in his hair show chakra wisdom, and the feather is for freedom. **II The High Priestess** has insight into dark forces but can control them, as symbolized by her sitting on the waxing moon. She is half lynx, an animal that is mystic and solitary. Near her is the triangle, symbolizing the mystical eye. She holds a ball of obsidian, which stands for magic insight. **III The Empress** is half bottle-nosed dolphin to show her connection with water, the living energy of creation. She holds the symbol of Venus in front of her stomach, as a sign that she is pregnant. In her hair are pearls of wisdom. **IV The Emperor** sits inside the world. He is half bear, to show his strength and wisdom, and he holds a globe of jade, an earthbound stone. **V The Master** has eagle eyes and wings, and a meteorite.

SECOND ROW: **VI The Lovers** are connected in the sigil of Jupiter. He is part dog, and she is part cat, to portray polarity. The ruby she holds is a symbol of their love and

trust. **VII The Leader** is symbolized by a fox person, who stands for cleverness. The Leader moves in freedom with the three rings of Saturn around its body. Stones of fire opals circle around. **VIII Strength** shows a garnet shining right and left for balance, power, and structure. The symbol of Uranus is on top of it. **X The Wheel of Karma** holds the flood of life in its rotation. The stones point toward the four elements. **XI Justice** shows two ravens of myth, symbolizing knowledge of all things. The hematite they hold in their claws shows balance of energy.

BOTTOM ROW: **XIII Death** is shown as a snake, the power to transform, to grow out of our skin and learn from experience. He has eaten experience and thrown out the bones that are no longer needed. Malachite is in the form of an egg. **XIV The Balance** shows the turkey, the earth eagle, dancing to show freedom and harmony. The topaz hanging from the symbol of Libra indicate cleverness, warmth, and experience. **XVII The Star** refers to the spider, an animal that weaves together experience. The stone is fluorite, for mental power. **XVIII The Moon** is shown in five phases, waning to waxing. The swan-woman wears aquamarine, a stone that shows spiritual depth. **Knight of Cups.**

Tarot Cuní & Masats   José Cuní Alfonso and Josep Masats Safops, 1996

Collection of the artist

Temperance   Tosca Cunningham, 1998

Tosca Cunningham Temperance   Tosca Cunningham describes her 1998 image of Temperance as "my conception of my Spirit Guide and your Spirit Guide inspired by the Royal Fez Moroccan Tarot card. It's my favorite card in the deck because it exemplifies the story and purpose of life."

Cyber Tarot 2101   Magnus Johnstone's tarot exists in a world of robots. "The year is 2101. The Revolt of the Robots was 69 years ago. It wasn't as glorious a victory as the history files indicate. By then, the earth's ecosystem had collapsed and most life forms had already become extinct. The humans offered little resistance, yet it was a little sad to see the passing of what was, after all, our prototype." The artist offers a unique "cyber" explanation of how the tarot works. "An ingenious conjunction of chaos theory and telekinesis, the tarot deck…is used to laterally access unconnected databases. The cards are a frequency analyzer of the magnetic patterns of the moment, both the sidereal time in the universe at that moment and the questioner's own personal field. By concentrating on a question while shuffling a deck, the inquirer's psychokinesis reveals the wave patterns of the present moment, previous moment, and subsequent moment." The deck comprises Major and Minor Arcana, with the court cards personifying the robots. Cyber Tarot 2101 was made in 2000 with computer-generated images.

Cygnet Tarot   "I initially approached the Cygnet Tarot through the back door, as it were," says Kevin Grey Harris, the artist of the deck, "with an increasing fascination with the medium of collage and an abiding love for the paintings of the Pre-Raphaelites…. It quickly took on a life of its own, however, which continues to astonish me. Because of this method of discovery, it took some time for it to reveal itself for what it was, namely a tarot of the Western mystery tradition, as defined by John and Caitlin Matthews [see Arthurian Tarot].… It is my sincere belief that, if approached with the proper reverence and humility, the tarot is, not unlike the works of

Shakespeare, a map of the world in which every aspect of the human condition can be found." The Pre-Raphaelite movement flourished during the Victorian era. Its proponents were particularly fascinated with medieval lore; their artworks combined heightened realism with a dreamlike magic. The Cygnet deck, which was six years in the making, was completed in 1997.

Dark Shadows Tarot   Lynn Atkinson based the 2001 Dark Shadows Tarot on the *Dark Shadows* television series that ran from June 1966 to April 1971. The show was a gothic soap opera featuring the Collinwood mansion, and populated with ghosts, werewolves, vampires, and even Satan himself. The deck, handmade from color printouts, includes an "Introduction Card" and a "Dedication Card." The Introduction Card states, "*Dark Shadows* is the first show to regularly feature the tarot for divination & magic. The tarot was always successful in its magic and divination uses in meeting the needs of the residents of Collinwood, whether living or dead."

Tarot of the Dead   Artist Monica Knighton writes to Stuart Kaplan, "The Tarot of the Dead [is] inspired by the Mexican Day of the Dead, Dias de los Muertos…. All human figures on the cards are represented by skeletons. In the spirit of artwork created for the Day of the Dead, the images are not dark. They colorfully, sometimes humorously, portray figures engaged in various activities." The artwork, in pen and ink and watercolors on Bristol board, was completed in 1998. The Minor Arcana are double-ended, with suits of pens (wands), guns (swords), coffins (cups), and film reels (coins). The deck generally adheres to the imagery of the Rider-Waite Tarot and the Tarot of Marseilles, despite the macabre protagonists and a few twists. The deck has only one non-skeletal figure.

Death Tarot   Luigi Scapini made tarot designs based on the Death card of the Medieval Scapini Tarot. "It is a deck full of joy," the artist writes to Stuart Kaplan, "much more than you can think at first sight." The concept of the deck was inspired by Santa Muerta (Holy Death) of Latin America, where the Day of the Dead is an important holy day. The designs were made in 2001.

Collection of the author

Medieval Scapini Death card
Luigi Scapini continued the theme from this card in his designs for the Death Tarot.

Collection of the artist

Cygnet Tarot   Kevin Grey Harris, 1997   Titles were furnished by the artist.   TOP ROW: The Magician. The Lovers. The Hanged Man. Art (Temperance). SECOND ROW: The Star. Queen of Swords. Princess of Swords. Ten of Swords. BOTTOM ROW: Eight of Swords. Three of Wands. Seven of Cups. Ten of Disks.

Cyber Tarot 2101   Magnus Johnstone, 2000
Descriptions of the cards are by the artist.

TOP ROW: **0 Fool** corresponds to the electron—there and not there, quantifiable as a wave, negligible yet essential, electricity. **1 Magician** is the operator. **3 Empress** represents the system's ability to regenerate. **6 Lovers** represent system interface compatibility. **9 Hermit** is mountains of firewalls, impervious to virus, worm, or hacker.

SECOND ROW: **12 Hanged Man** is the sublimation of module to an intranet. **18 Moon** is temporarily inaccessible files. **19 Sun** is light, energy, and heat, and controlled fission. **20 Judgement** is the end of time, the new millennium. **21 World** is the user.

THIRD ROW: **8 Swords** indicates that all access is denied, and previous authorization has been revoked. **3 Swords** means that an intruder has gained access and damaged files. **Queen of Wands** is a feline model professional robot. **Knight of Wands** is a business adventurer robot. **10 Wands** means that a hard drive overload is slowing down the system.

BOTTOM ROW: **5 Wands** indicates that systems operation is unstable, and an adjustment may prove beneficial. **King of Cups** is a research and development robot. **7 Cups** shows multitask overload, with imminent system crash. **Page of Pentacles** is a new model business robot. **Ace of Pentacles.**

Dark Shadows Tarot   Lynn Atkinson, 2001

Tarot of the Dead   Monica Knighton, 1998

TOP ROW: 0 The Fool. I The Magician. II High Priestess. III The Empress. V The Hierophant.

SECOND ROW: VI The Lovers. VII The Chariot. VIII Justice. IX The Hermit. X Wheel of Fortune.

THIRD ROW: XI Strength. XIII. XV The Devil. XVIII The Moon. XIX The Sun.

BOTTOM ROW: XXI The World. Page of Guns. Queen of Pens. King of Coffins. Title card.

Collection of the artist

Death Tarot   Luigi Scapini, 2001   XIII La Santisima Muerte (Holy Death). Two of Swords. Prince of Coins.

Definitive Tarot   Guy Palm describes his deck as "an ambitious attempt to connect the symbolism of current tarot decks to logically deduced patterns in nature, while steering completely clear of the ambiguous mystical rhetoric that has surrounded tarot over the years.... By structuring the tarot around scientific, logical, observable patterns in nature, a never-before-seen symmetry takes over in the design of the deck that allows for comparative analysis to be made between each card of the deck, both Majors and Minors. In other words, in The Definitive Tarot, no card stands alone. Each card has a place on a matrix of cross-referencing ideas." Ten years in the making, the deck was completed in 1999.

Definitive Tarot   Guy Palm, 1999   Descriptions are by the artist, who also chose the order in which to present the cards.

TOP ROW: The **Beautiful Goddess** typifies all that is good about a "three" with her beauty and grace. By rearranging the Major Arcana into two different progressions of 1 thru 9, the card formerly known as The Hanged Man becomes The **Vicious Beast** to our "beauty," typifying all that is bad about a "three" with his animalian ways. Likewise, the following **Three of Pentacles** correlates with traditional interpretations by showing a craftsman's handiwork, while the **Three of Roses** conveys the idea of love and affection. In opposing fashion, the **Three of Wands** reveals the savage hand of The Vicious Beast at work. While...

SECOND ROW: The **Three of Swords** conveys the opposing idea of hate. As each card is reversed, bad becomes good and good becomes bad. The craftsman becomes a persnickety perfectionist, and hate becomes tough love. The **Cognizant Genius,** formerly The Magician, shows how some symbols remain more or less intact. The **Hopeless Sickling** shows how some symbols are re-interpreted, as The Star is viewed as a symbol of faint, failing energy. The **Mighty Hero** replaces The Emperor as a more universal symbol of strength. And the **Blessed Guru** rides a magic carpet instead of The Chariot.

THIRD ROW: The **Wretched Heathen** replaces The Tower as a symbol of disaster as well as opposing The Blessed Guru with the idea of spiritual bankruptcy. The **Consummate Sage** replaces The Hermit and symbolizes a culminating good ending at the number nine. The **Terminated Corpse** replaces The Moon (and Death) as the real symbol of death and all culminating bad endings. The **Nine of Pentacles** restates the idea of a culminating end with a mountain peak. The **Nine of Wands** restates the idea of death with a tombstone.

FOURTH ROW: The **Eight of Roses** conveys the idea of a climactic release and wide open spaces, while the **Eight of Swords** conveys the idea of limited space or bondage. The **Seven of Roses** correlates with the spirituality of The Blessed Guru as shafts of heavenly light filter through the branches of a tree. The **Seven of Swords** opposes that with a spiritual connection to the dark side in the form of a frightening hallucination. The **One of Pentacles** restates the idea of a new start, found in The Magician card, or Cognizant Genius.

Collection of the artist

FIFTH ROW: The **Morbid Zombie** replaces the Page of Swords, as each court card is given a unique name that reflects the two numbers of numerology that influence each card. The **Witty Entertainer** is the Page of Pentacles. The **Frightening Assassin** is the Knight of Wands. The **Forthright Philanthropist** is the Knight of Pentacles. The **Barbaric Blowhard** is the Queen of Swords.

BOTTOM ROW: The **Sympathetic Medium** is the Queen of Roses. The **Sovereign Patriarch** is the King of Pentacles. The **Insidious Totalitarian** is the King of Swords. The **Noble Saint** is the King of Roses. And finally, the **Nine of Swords** restates the idea of insanity and the dark abyss found in The Terminated Corpse.

Hélène Delvaux Tarot 1990 TOP ROW: **I The Magician** wears a rainbow scarf. His baton is blue at the top end and red at the other end. **II The High Priestess** holds sun and moon keys. **III The Empress** sits at the bank of a stream in the desert. A pelican is beside her, the bird that mythically feeds its children with its own blood. She treads a snake. **IV The Emperor** also sits beside the stream, in a grassy land. In the sky behind him is Jacob's ladder, after the Hebrew patriarch's vision of a ladder that extended from earth to heaven and was attended by angels. SECOND ROW: **V The Pope** has a throne like a castle. **VI The Lovers** includes a man who resembles the Magician. **VII The Chariot** depicts a warrior in red and green armor, a crescent and star decking his hair. The two horses seem to merge with the chariot itself. **VIII Justice.** An owl, a snake, and a sprig of grass are at the woman's feet. BOTTOM ROW: **IX The Hermit** walks in the night by the light of stars and a partially cloaked small lamp. An hourglass is tied to his waist, and a snake twines his staff. **XI Strength. XII The Hanged Man** dangles between two trees. A cloth is at the roots of the left tree. A flower, the same as that of the Magician, is at the roots of the right tree, along with a tiny man driving an ox. A nest is in a crook halfway up the right tree. **XVII The Star** shows a maiden pouring water from a gold pitcher into a stream and from a silver pitcher onto the ground. The planets are above her.

Maria Dillen Tarot   1988
The Wheel. The Star. The Sun.

Hélène Delvaux Tarot   Belgian artist Hélène Delvaux painted twenty-two Major Arcana. The images are traditional with artistic variations. The motif of red (left) and white (right) pillars recurs repeatedly throughout the deck, and the figures are clad in strong colors, such as black, dark blue, and red. The deck was completed in 1990.

Maria Dillen Tarot   As part of a class given by Guido Gillabel, tarotist of Belgium, Maria Dillen designed a set of Major Arcana. She made six copies of the deck by hand. The decks were made circa 1988.

Divine Mother Tarot   Claire Blanche Dougal created the Divine Mother Tarot together with a series of prayers. The artist says the deck is "designed to be used as a tool for spiritual growth and transformation." The deck comprises twenty-two Major Arcana and sixteen Minor Arcana, which are king, queen, jack, and ace in the playing card suits of spades, hearts, clubs, and diamonds. The deck was completed in 1994.

Tarot of the Doorways   Chicago artist David C. Rogers was inspired by the Major Arcana of the Rider-Waite and Builders of the Adytum (BOTA) Tarots. The artist's intention, as described in correspondence with Stuart Kaplan, was to create "portals for meditation." The artist continues, "One method [of meditation] consists of staring at a card until one has memorized its symbols and content, and then building it piece by piece in the mind until the total image is complete. At that point, one may actually enter the scene (in one's own mind or by astral projection of the body…) and therein communicate with the archetype of the card or even become the archetype itself. Thus the cards represent a kind of doorway into the archetypes of the mind. They symbolize the many energies, attitudes, and forms that make up our complex psyches." The Tarot of the Doorways was painted in 1996.

Divine Mother Tarot   Claire Blanche Dougal, 1994   14 Guardian Angel. 18 Moon Goddess. King of Clubs. Jack of Diamonds.

Tarot of the Doorways   David C. Rogers, 1996   The caption is based on correspondence from the artist and reflects mainly the artist's variations on the Rider-Waite or BOTA decks.

TOP ROW: **0 The Fool** has the sigil of Uranus on his clothes. **I The Magician** is painted as a mirror image, as (the wand is usually shown in his right hand), so that the meditator can see the image as a reflection of the self as an aspiring magician. **II High Priestess** has a rose at her heart, symbolizing the sacrificed god of the Kabbalistic Sephirah Tiphareth. **III The Empress** has dove and swan attributes of Venus. **IV The Emperor** includes a symbol for sulphur on his breastplate, and solar epaulets, reflecting the fire element that rules this card.

SECOND ROW: **V The Hierophant** holds a scroll on which is a pentagram, the symbol of spirit residing over the four elements and the number five. **VI The Lovers** stand below an angel, who represents the Super-consciousness, the Higher Self. **VII The Chariot** shows a charioteer with geomantic symbols on his tunic. According to Israel Regardie, geomancy is "an archaic method of divination by means of the element of Earth." **VIII Strength** depicts a woman who tames a red lion. She has in her hair the rose of desire. Above is a heart with six rays, representing the sun or Tiphareth, the sixth Sephirah of the Kabbalistic Tree of Life. **X Wheel of Fortune** represents Jupiter, god of expansion and wealth.

THIRD ROW: **XI Justice** has the allegorical figure holding a scale with a weight in one pan and in the other pan the

54

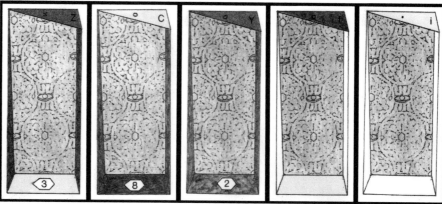

Double-Sided Tarot Alex Kiy, 1993 Titles are by the artist. VI Lovers. VII Chariot. IX Hermit. Princess of Wands. 6 Swords (Science).

Collection of the artist / © 1993 by Alex Kiy

Double-Sided Tarot Rather than make images to be printed on the faces of the cards, Alex Kiy created back designs. Says Kiy, "This unique approach to using the Tarot designates individual standard cards with back markings/colors that are intended to represent Archetype matrices, or patterns that some people consider astrologically significant." The system involves matching the card associations with a chart created by Kiy. The designs were completed in 1993.

Dreamer's Tarot Samvado Gunnar Kossatz created the Dreamer's Tarot in 1995 as collages of photography and watercolor painting, composed by computer using Adobe Photoshop and CorelDraw. The German artist is the creator of the Experimental Tarot (U.S. Games Systems, 1997) and the Colman-Smith Tarot, a recolored Rider-Waite Tarot (unpublished).

Deck of the Dreamers Ethan Petty created his tarot using Photoshop software. The twenty-two Major Arcana were finished in 1997.

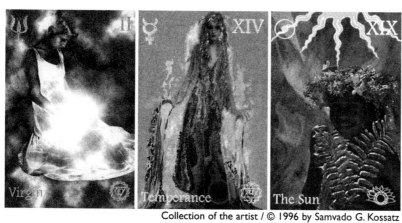

Dreamer's Tarot
Samvado Gunnar Kossatz, 1995
II Virgin. XIV Temperance. XIX The Sun.

Collection of the artist / © 1996 by Samvado G. Kossatz

feather of Ma'at, judge in the ancient Egyptian underworld. On her shoulder is an owl, totem of Greek Athena, goddess of wisdom. **XII Hanged Man** is before an ocean, in correspondence to Neptune, the sigil on the gallows. **XIII Death** has fish on the bridle of its horse, denoting the Hebrew letter nun, which means fish. The fish swim in the Great Sea of Binah who, in turn, represents Kali, the Hindu destroyer goddess. **XIV Temperance** is a card of alchemy and the balancing and refining of adverse elements such as water and fire. Thus, fiery yods fall on the eagle of Scorpio, a water sign, and alchemical water falls on Leo the lion, a fire sign. **XV The Devil** depicts bondage to the material world, sexual lust, drunkenness, and violence.

BOTTOM ROW: **XVI The Tower** shows lightning purging a tower of hubris and pride. **XVII The Star** shows a maiden pouring water in a pond and on land. The seven smaller stars in the sky are painted the colors of the celestial bodies they represent: indigo for Saturn, violet for Jupiter, red for Mars, orange for the Sun, green for Venus, yellow for Mercury, and blue for the Moon. **XVIII The Moon** has violet grass, to represent the color of Yesod, Sephirah of the Moon. **XX Judgement** shows man, woman, and child rising from tombs at the blast of an angel's trumpet. **XXI The Universe** represents a seal to the completion of the great work, the attainment of integration, when all elements and archetypes of the self are in balance.

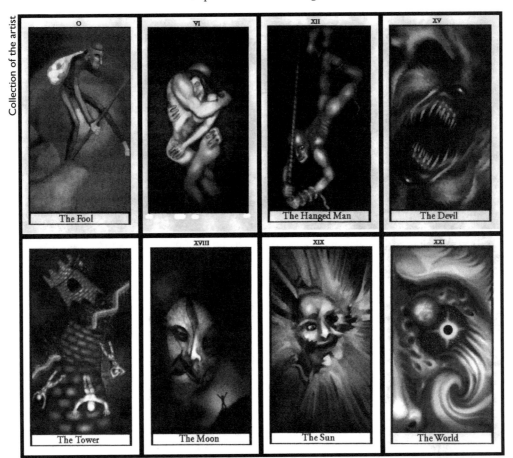

Deck of the Dreamers Ethan Petty, 1997 The caption is based on the artist's descriptions of the cards.

TOP ROW: **0 The Fool. VI The Lovers** is dark to make the atmosphere more personal for the couple. The plant life in the back brings out the pure nature of the lovers. **XII The Hanged Man** represents a sacrifice of one thing for another without making any progress, and in the end keeping oneself hung. I chose to have the character holding himself up to show this process. The blue skin, I felt, made the situation seem a bit more moody. **XV The Devil.**

BOTTOM ROW: **XVI The Tower. XVIII The Moon. XIX The Sun. XXI The World.**

The Economist **magazine** Four renditions of tarot cards were shown on the cover of the May 14, 1994, issue of the English magazine *The Economist*. The artist was not credited. The threat implicit in the cards was based on fears of a financial debacle caused by failure of derivatives, financial instruments whose value is derived from bonds, equities, and other assets.

The Economist **tarot cards** Anonymous, 1994

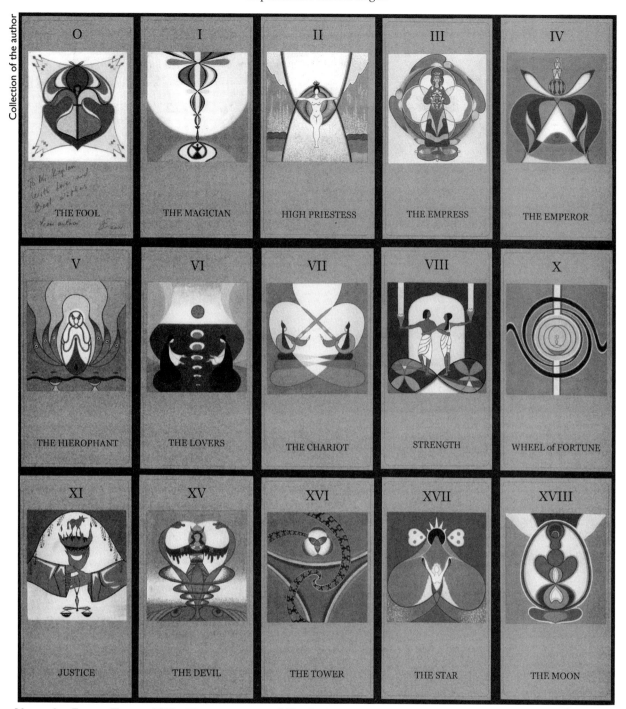

Alexander Egorov Tarot   2001   The inscription on 0 The Fool reads, "To Mr. Kaplan / With Love and / Best wishes / from author / [artist's sigil] 2001."

Alexander Egorov Tarot   Russian artist Alexander Egorov created a Major Arcana in watercolor. The designs were mounted on paper printed with titles. The Major Arcana were made in 2001, but some of the designs are based on earlier work by the artist. Egorov also created a deck called the Egorov Tarot, with different artwork, which was published by Piatnik of Vienna.

Eleda-Arome Tarot   Crystal N. Chase (Eleda) and Wm. Wooton (Arome), 1991

Eleda-Arome Tarot   "Imagine a world filled with magical creatures. Imagine a golden city with mighty powers, and now imagine those magical creatures aiding you to discover your own mighty powers…just gaze into the Elede-Arome Tarot deck." So writes one of the co-creators of the Eleda-Arome Tarot. Crystal N. Chase (Eleda) designed and Wm. Wooton (Arome) illustrated the deck in 1991.

Elementals Comic Book   The cover of number 5 in the comic book series *Elementals* shows the characters of the series as tarot card illustrations. The artist is Bill Willingham. The story itself does not connect with tarot, and no interpretations are given in the comic book, which was published in 1989 in Canada by Comico: The Comic Company.

Tarot of the Elements   Beverly Lee Gray painted the Tarot of the Elements in oil on canvas. About the deck, the Australian artist writes to Stuart R. Kaplan, "As a self-evolving artist, these works grew out of my philosophies and meditations, and were channeled through me. I appreciate that the artwork is primitive and the images varied…. I have been using the pack for readings/counseling and for teaching, and I have found that the images and symbols integrate when used as a pack. In fact, the naivete and free-flowing essence of the designs trigger responses within people…. Every card has been painted to show the positive aspects behind every experience or situation." The deck was created circa 1989.

Elusive Realities Tarot   Judith Green Golden describes her deck: "The Elusive Realities Tarot uses butterflies to symbolize metamorphosis, transformation, and the soul." Golden considers the Major Arcana to represent the archetypes of the collective unconscious. "The journey through the twenty-two trump cards suggests the path to individuation, self-realization, and enlightenment. The Minor Arcana suits reflect the four elements: fire = spirit, passion, intuition; water = emotions, feeling; air = mental, mind, thinking; earth = the physical, tangible reality, the senses." The images are drawn from original photographs by Golden. She made four of the Major Arcana in the early 1990s, then resumed the project in 2002. "My transparencies are printed as Polaroid transfers," she says. "This print is scanned into Photoshop and sometimes new backgrounds or other elements are added. The size was determined by the size of the Polaroid 669 film I use."

Elementals comic book cover
Bill Willingham, 1989

Tarot of the Elements
Beverly Lee Gray, 1989

0   THE FOOL

I   THE MAGICIAN

II   THE HIGH PRIESTESS

V   THE SHAMAN

VII   THE VOYAGER

IX   THE HERMIT

XIII   DEATH

XIV   TEMPERANCE

XV   THE DEVIL

XVI   THE TOWER

XVIII   THE MOON

XIX   THE SUN

CONTEMPLATION

ILLUMINATION

CHANGE

II OF AIR

ACE OF FIRE

KNIGHT OF WATER

II   EARTH

Elusive Realities   Judith Green Golden, 2002
Descriptions are based on those by the artist.

TOP ROW: **0 THE FOOL.** Fearless, the Fool laughs at Death. A youthful, androgynous adventurer, instinctive and curious, the Fool journeys into the unknown accompanied by a small dog. He is in the costume of a court jester from the Middle Ages. His tunic and hat are half green and half red, suggesting the yin/yang of the balance of feminine and masculine. A large butterfly with human eyes leads the Fool into the darkness. Ruled by Uranus. **I THE MAGICIAN.** A messenger between heaven and earth, the Magician has everything she needs to create magic on the tangible plane: fire (snakes and lizards), water (fish and shells), air (birds), and earth (plants). An infinity sign of tiny butterflies flutters over her head. She represents purity, passion, and conscious intellect. Ruled by Mercury. **II THE HIGH PRIESTESS.** A dark, mysterious woman, the High Priestess reflects the inner wisdom of the unconscious. She wears a black lace mantilla and holds a full moon. Behind her, the constellations float in the night sky. She is the powerful feminine blessed with psychic ability. Ruled by the Moon. **V THE SHAMAN** is the masculine aspect of inner knowledge. He wears a dark cape and holds a replica of the sun. A small butterfly rests on his staff. Trained from childhood in the secrets of his tradition, he is a spiritual leader, a teacher, and a healer. Ruled by Taurus.

SECOND ROW: **VII THE VOYAGER** is an adventurer who explores uncharted spaces. He is focused, determined to reach his goal, and he trusts he will return triumphant. A map of the constellations guides him, with Leonardo's figure of man's relationship to the cosmos as inspiration. Stars from a distant galaxy float behind him. Ruled by Cancer. **IX THE HERMIT** withdraws from the outer world in order to delve deeply within to seek the truths of the universe. Her dark red cloak and hood hide her true self until her inner vision ignites, burning brightly and illuminating her path. The owl, symbol of wisdom, sees in the darkness and protects her. Ruled by Virgo. **XIII DEATH.** A laughing skeleton in a dark jacket offers a bouquet of dried flowers, reminding us that Death is always with us. Death is not meant to suggest a physical death but the periodic need to allow a radical transformation to occur in life. Fluttering butterflies with eyes remind us that they have transformed from caterpillars into their current mystical state of being. Rebirth. Ruled by Scorpio. **XIV TEMPERANCE.** A beautiful red-haired angel with butterfly wings pours liquid from one chalice into another, signifying the alchemical union of opposites, the harmonizing of the psychic and the physical world. The many butterflies around her symbolize the metamorphosis taking place. Ruled by Sagittarius.

THIRD ROW: **XV THE DEVIL** is a woman in a Devil mask and black robe. A heavy chain circles her throat. The Devil symbolizes carnal desire, lust, decadence, and addiction to all things pleasurable.

Temptation and indulgence. A creation of the church to represent evil, the Devil is similar to the gods Bacchus and Dionysus from Greco-Roman cultures. Ruled by Capricorn. **XVI THE TOWER.** A symbol of power, the Tower topples in flame when struck by lightning. The Eye of God, found on U.S. dollar bills, is rocked off its pyramid. A male and a female figure fall from the heights. Disaster from without suggests the need to rethink our attitudes regarding power and to consider power with others rather than power over others. Ruled by Mars. **XVIII THE MOON.** Moonlight is silvery, a reflection of light without its own light source. La Luna is the ultimate seductive female, beautiful, desirable, tantalizing, yet cold and distant. A nude woman with a butterfly on her head holds the full moon in her hands. Ruled by Pisces. **XIX THE SUN.** An Aztec god prepares to fling the Sun into the heavens for its daily march across the sky. A small butterfly sits on the cactus beside him. Streaked with yellow, the sky is warm and illuminating. The Sun represents conscious masculine energy. Ruled by the Sun.

BOTTOM ROW: **II OF AIR: Contemplation.** In her right hand, the rational, logical side, a woman with long brown hair holds a bird, representing air, the intellect. In her left hand, she holds a heart representing water, the emotions. She considers both her heart and her mind before making her decision. **ACE OF FIRE: Illumination.** The Aces represent the pure beginnings of the energy of each suit. The Ace of Fire is playful, sparkling, quick, and creative. She illuminates everything near her. **KNIGHT OF WATER.** Romantic and charismatic, the Knight of Water is pale blue, the color of clear water. He plays a flower flute as he continues his quest to find the Holy Grail. He is dreamy, passionate, and charming. Others gravitate to him and join him on his journey. **II OF EARTH: Change.** The boy dressed like Peter Pan squats down; the girl, like Wendy in a long white dress, jumps up. Then they immediately reverse their positions. Change is called for; it can be playful rather than difficult.

The Lens of Tarot
With the Mountain Dream Tarot, Bea Nettles created one of the first tarot decks using original photography. (See The Encyclopedia of Tarot, volume I.)
More tarot photographs by Nettles are featured in her book Knights of Assisi.
Some tarot artists use photographs with little alteration beyond cropping; others alter and recompose images substantially, by using computer software. Tarots in volume IV that use original photographs (taken by the artist of the deck) are:

Bezukladnikov Tarot
Cosmic Tribe Tarot
Dreamers Tarot
Elusive Realities Tarot
Energy Cards
Gateway to the Gods
Knights of Assisi

Tarot de Paris
Photographic Tarot
Photographique Tarot
Settanni Tarot
Seventh Ray Tarot
Share Tarot

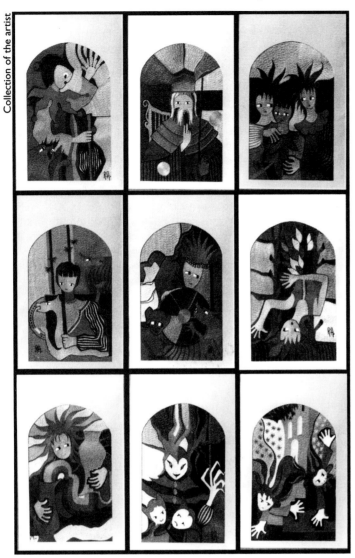

Embroidery Tarot   Caroline Roussel-Abiker;
individual cards, 1987; large design, 1990

Embroidery Tarot Parisian textile artist Caroline Roussel-Abiker put needle and thread to creating tarot designs in embroidery, both as a large montage and as separate "cards." (Previous embroidery designs by the artist were included in *The Encyclopedia of Tarot,* volume 3.) The artist wrote to Stuart R. Kaplan of the large design: "I worked a big embroidery, showing the figures mixed as a kind of kaleidoscope of tarot's magic world." The large design measures approximately 24 by 71 inches (60 × 180 cm) and was completed in 1990. The individual designs measure about 6 by 8 inches (15 × 20 cm) and were completed in 1987.

Enchanted Path Tarot Robbin Kornrumph Platt, 1989

Enchanted Path Tarot The Enchanted Path Tarot "lends itself to readers of all ages and levels of awareness," says the artist, Robbin Kornrumph Platt. The colors of the deck are bright and the forms are mostly abstract. The suits are awareness (swords), spirituality (wands), emotions (cups), and abundance (coins). The deck was created in 1989.

Energy Cards Utah native Janice Rae Petersen, together with Jim Burris, created the Energy Tarot with photographs of the American Southwest. Petersen says in correspondence with Stuart Kaplan, "Energy cards are reflective of the energies of nature and of your inner energy. Connecting to these energies enables one to get in touch with self and with others." The deck includes seventy-eight tarot cards, as well as sixty-six "spirit" cards by which the reader, says Petersen, "can explore in greater depth his inner spirit." The Energy Tarot was completed in 1993.

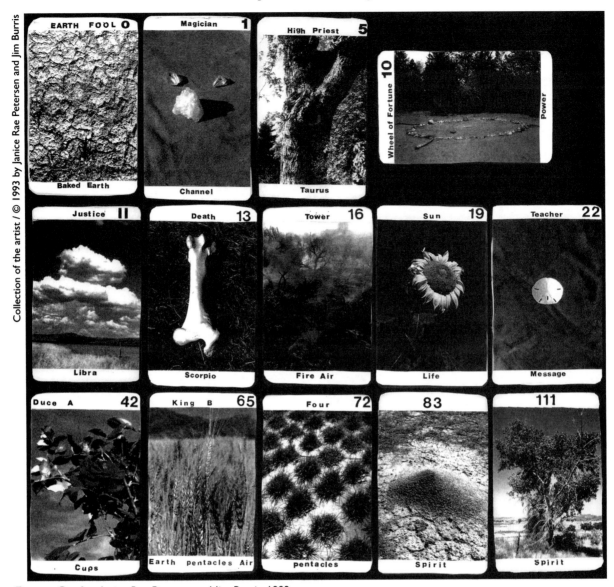

Collection of the artist / © 1993 by Janice Rae Petersen and Jim Burris

Energy Cards Janice Rae Petersen and Jim Burris, 1993

Essential Tarot Gail Fairfield describes the Essential Tarot as "just that. It's a tarot deck that is stripped of frills so that the essence of each card can shine through." Sheila Mohn illustrated the deck with simple lines and colors, and Gail Fairfield wrote interpretations of the cards. The art was completed in 1990.

Esther's Australian Tarot Artist Esther Abizdris painted tarot card images, circa 1994, that reflect the flora, fauna, and landmarks of Australia. As the artist says in a letter to Stuart Kaplan, "Some of the animals depicted were introduced by the immigrants to Australia in the last century and the turn of this century. All of these animals are now considered just as much a part of Australia as the native dingo. Some of the traditional names for the

tarot cards within this pack have been changed to suit the Australian culture and geographical area. Different nationalities in their various ethnic style of dress are on the cards, as Australia is a multi-cultural country. As there is no one royal family that can truly represent Australia, there are no kings, queens, knights or pages. Instead, the courts are man, lady, messenger, and child."

Ethyrial Tarot Gigi Miner, also known as Ladyfogg, says of the Ethyrial Tarot, "The deck was birthed from a strong urge to create. I wanted to find a way to communicate without words and hope this deck is able to do just that." She composed digital photographs for each card. The deck was created in 2003.

Essential Tarot Sheila Mohn, 1990 The caption and subtitles are based on the descriptions by Gail Fairfield.

TOP ROW: **0 Fool: Faith,** as it almost dances off the card, expresses total innocence and appreciation for the adventure of life. **I Magician: Discernment** has stars in his eyes to show that he sees clearly with sparkling vision. **II High Priestess: Transcendence** has a gaze slightly unfocused as she tunes in to a non-usual reality. **IV Emperor: Power** wears the crown of others' tribute as he comfortably holds his power. **V Hierophant: Morality** wears the symbols of his beliefs right out front where everyone can see them.

SECOND ROW: **VI Lovers: Cooperation** may face opposite directions but they are joined in their commitment to a common cause or desire. **VIII Strength: Survival** shows the strength of the lion that protects itself and its young with fierce tenderness. **X Wheel of Fortune: Release** indicates that as the Wheel spins around, it's impossible to calculate where it will stop; all results are possible. **XI Justice: Equilibrium** only occurs if the needs of the body (bread) and the needs of the spirit (roses) are truly balanced. **XIII Death/Rebirth: Transition** says, the door into Death/Rebirth is inviting, but it will close behind you.

BOTTOM ROW: **XIV Temperance: Artistry** shows two different substances tempered or adapted as they're combined into a new substance; water and light are mystically blended to make magic on earth. **XVII Star: Resourcefulness** pours its abundant light and gifts down on the earth. **XVIII Moon: Guidance** is never far away; in fact, it surrounds the left (logical) part of the mind with intuitive insight. **Page of Wands. Queen of Cups.**

Collection of the artist

Esther's Australian Tarot   Esther Abizdris, circa 1994   TOP ROW: **Mastery** (Magician) depicts the Sydney Harbor, with the Opera House on Bennelong Point. **Hidden Knowledge** (High Priestess) shows the Book of Knowledge under the "all-seeing Eye of God," the eye in the triangle. **Spirit Guide** (Hierophant) is a cross-cultural person, an Aborigine wearing Torres Island headgear. **Storm of Life** (Tower) is the Cape Byron Lighthouse, the most easterly point in Australia.

BOTTOM ROW: **Eight of Spears** shows limestone formations in the Pinnacles Desert, Nambung National Park, Western Australia. **Two of Spears** shows two fish in the Great Barrier Reef. **Two of Cups** shows a pair of Major Mitchell cockatoos kissing. **Seven of Pentacles** depicts Jedda, the artist's Blue Heeler dog. Blue Heelers were bred in Australia from collies and kelpies as cattle dogs.

Ethyrial Tarot   Gigi Miner (Ladyfogg), 2003   TOP ROW: Hierophant. Temperance. Devil. Moon. BOTTOM ROW: Three of Swords. Six of Batons. Ace of Batons. Ace of Coins.

Collection of the artist

Evolving Tarot   Michele Jackson, 1999

Evolving Tarot   Michele Jackson created the Evolving Tarot to teach herself collaging techniques. "Consequently, you see a myriad of styles and moods," she says in correspondence with Stuart Kaplan. Each of the cards includes an astrological sigil at the lower left corner and a path or Sephirah on the Kabbalistic Tree of Life in the lower right corner. The Evolving Tarot was created in 1999.

Fairy Lore and Mythology Tarot   Texas artist Lee Seed sketched designs for the queens of a tarot deck that would "embrace the elegance of the fae as well as have an elemental theme, for, in lore, fairy magic was based on the elements," as she says in a letter to Stuart Kaplan. The designs were made in 2002.

Fairytale Tarot   "The tarot is like a faith," says James Stewart, creator of the Fairytale Tarot, "which has grown, changed, and adapted from one generation to the next for a long time…. Each age and each individual has their own personal viewpoint regarding the tarot. No viewpoint is necessarily the last word, but rather merely a contribution to an extraordinary tradition of spirit and a remarkable deck of cards."

About his deck, which he commissioned Billie Wolf to illustrate in 1989, he says, "Fundamentally, the Fairytale Tarot teaches you how to build a 'spiritual fire' for a happy heart. The method used to accomplish this fairytale feat is defined as Coue's Law, which states: 'If there is ever a contest between the imagination and the will, the imagination will win.' In other words, the Fairytale Tarot offers effective images that instruct your heart 'to live happily ever after.'"

Fairy Lore and Mythology Tarot   Lee Seed, 2002   Queens of Swords, Wands, Cups, and Pentacles

Collection of the artist / © 1989 by James Stewart, Ph.D.

Fairytale Tarot Illustrated by Billie Wolf under direction of James Stewart, 1989   16 The Tower. Queen of Cups. Queen of Pentacles.

Collection of the artist / © Melisa Fauceglia

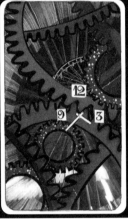

Fauceglia Tarot Melisa Fauceglia, 1998   Magician. Wheel. Ace of Swords. The artist is pictured at left.

Fauceglia Tarot Canadian artist Melisa Fauceglia created tarot designs using a combination of collage and drawing. Her designs were completed circa 1998.

Floral Ellipse Tarot Beth Crawford describes the Floral Ellipse Tarot as "the combined idea of my husband and me. I enjoy painting, and he thought of the perfect ellipse." The suits have been translated to flowers, which also represent the seasons: poinsettia for swords and winter, dogwoods for wands and spring, roses for cups and summer, and daisies for pentacles and fall. The artist used color to convey the moods of the cards. "For instance, in the Two of Dogwoods, the color is subdued and quiet, meaning a calm coming together of talents." The deck was completed in 1994.

Tarocco le Fontane Divinatore (Prophetic Sources Tarot) The Prophetic Sources Tarot, by Amerigo Folchi, was founded on historical and mythical water elements, such as springs and fountains, associated with prophetic powers. The designs truly show Folchi's diversity in style, with a collagelike combination of black and white statuary figures against colorful abstract backgrounds.

Fortune Teller Greeting Cards The Fortune Teller Greeting cards published in 1998 by New Legend have scratch-off gold seals that reveal randomly placed symbols numbered to correspond to Major Arcana cards. To use the card, the reader scratches off ten gold seals, then writes the revealed numbers in blocks that correspond to positions of a tarot spread. For example, if the first seal that is scratched off reveals the number 0, the reader writes "0" in the first block of the spread. Brief interpretations of the Major Arcana are given. The artwork on the faces of the cards is by Kessia Beverley-Smith of Interactive Illustration, with creative ideas by Phil Irwin. The Major Arcana were published in 2004 as part of a full tarot deck by U.S. Games Systems.

Free Hand Tarots Artist Ernesto Fazioli writes, "The tarots are eternal oneiromantic [divinatory with dreams as the medium] images that live their own life within each heart, within each mind. They are poems that stimulate new stanzas and new rhymes. They are always the same, and yet always different. Neither beautiful nor ugly." He created the twenty-two Arcana of the Free Hand Tarots circa 1999.

Collection of the artist

Floral Ellipse Tarot Beth Crawford, 1994 The caption is based on correspondence from the artist. She gives names and personalities to the court cards "enabling either you or someone around you to identify with them."

TOP ROW: **Fool.** A young innocent man dances and plays with his dog among baby's breath. He puts his hands in the air in a gesture, saying, "What? Me worry?" and goes on his merry way. **II Priestess.** Wildflowers and azaleas keep an ageless woman company. She and the cat know things that shallow beings do not. **VIII Justice.** A wise woman stands among the prickly poppy and, like it, holds the softness of beauty and mercy in one hand and the sharpness of the sword or thorn in the other. **X Fortune.** Lady Luck holds a wreath of the four seasons and the four suits. As she strolls through creeping phlox, she slowly turns the wheel, thus changing the way of life, love, and happiness. **XI Strength.** A bold young woman walks barefoot with her friend, the lion. She has become strong by facing the beast we call fear, thus making him her ally and strength.

SECOND ROW: **XII Hanging.** The man hanging, like the bell flowers, in a yoga position has accepted what life has given him, knowing that calmness and patience will make life serene. **XIII Death.** A ghostly figure floats among evening primrose. It is an illusion from another dimension that we cannot quite grasp, but above flies the phoenix risen from

the ashes, symbolizing the hope that there is something more. **XIV Temperance.** The angel amidst tulips patiently measures the waters of life. She is aware, as the butterfly is, of her purpose in life. **XV Devil.** A deviate creature, overgrown with bergamot, with a gleam in his eye, rests his claw foot on a skull. Is he laughing at us for taking material objects and life too seriously? **XVII Star.** A proud, radiant woman sits nude, basking in the glow of the star above and the star flowers beside her. Like the swan and the water lilies, she commands admiration.

BOTTOM ROW: **XIX Sun.** The happy couple and the sunflowers dance the dance of perfect harmony. They whirl in the rays of the sun, delighting in their congenial relationship. **XXI Universe.** The woman floating in a ring of forget-me-nots reaches full cycle. She is ready to emerge, as if from a womb, to start the dance again. **Prince of Poinsettias.** Kevin, the logical, technical, and mathematical prince, pursues life head-on, armed with his abilities. He is sometimes touched by the unknown, but prefers to seek the scientific rather than the spiritual, because the eeriness of it all will unbalance him. **Ace of Poinsettias. Queen of Dogwood.** Amanda, the creative queen, is secure in her talents, mature, and proud of her accomplishments. She feels it is her destiny to teach and guide, resulting in a perpetuation of her creativity throughout the ages.

Tarocco le Fontane Divinatore (Prophetic Sources Tarot) Amerigo Folchi, circa 1990 TOP ROW: III The Empress. IV The Emperor. V The Pope. IX The Hermit. XV The Devil. BOTTOM ROW: XVII The Star. XXI The World. Ace of Wands. King of Cups. Six of Cups.

Fortune Teller Greeting Cards
Kessia Beverley-Smith and Phil Irwin, 1998

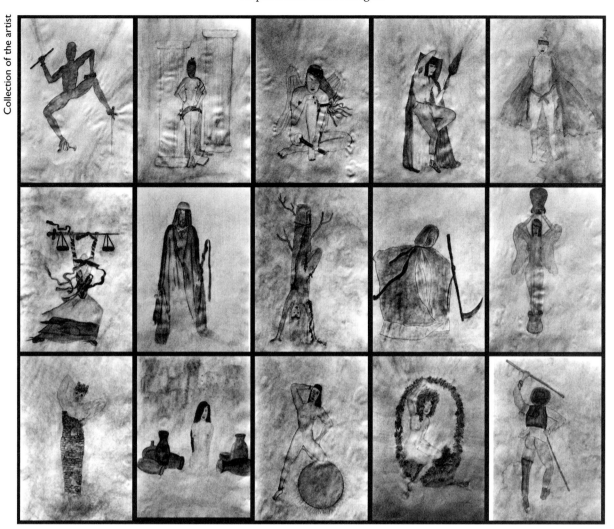

Free Hand Tarots   Ernesto Fazioli, 1999   The text and titles are drawn from a manuscript by the artist.

TOP ROW: **I The Androgen.** Without a face or sex, the androgen jumps around with its four elemental instruments. It jokes with life, which in him is in the embryonic stage. **II The Lady in Waiting** is the lady who waits, expecting a child, the mother with the veiled face who doesn't want to know who he will be, where he will come from, and where he will go. **III The Fairy** is the good fairy godmother who will follow the flight of the child from the earthly womb that protected him to the most beautiful flower upon which she will go to rest. **IV The Naked Prince** is the child finally grown up. He protects his shoulders with his shield: Nothing can wound him; he is ready to command. **VI The Tied Up Man.** Tied hands, a strong wind. It is a moment of crisis, time to remove the string that keeps his mantle closed and covers his sex, in order to discover who and what he will be. In order to live, one needs love and an identity.

SECOND ROW: **VIII The Dance of the Blind.** A hurricane sways the purple dress of the goddess of justice. The bandage of the eyes of the goddess will not indicate the way. Real justice can be found only within ourselves. **IX The Desert Man.** The pale color of burnt sand accompanies the solemn movements of the man in the desert. He is the only person able to live alone, in silence. **XII The Executed.** The athlete hangs from the pole like a man who has been execut-

ed. He shows no pain or regret. He continues to speak under his breath; he laughs and looks deeply into the spectators' eyes. **XIII The Empty Mantle.** Divine shivers tickle my skin. The shadow of death has passed by. An empty black mantle sways beside the man, who puts on the mantle and becomes the subject of his own macabre death, his transformation. **XIV The Purification Ritual.** The water from above flows below; the water from below flows above. The purification of dross brings to life a new skin.

BOTTOM ROW: **XVI The Man of Stone** knows that, to destroy the tower in which he is imprisoned, strong hands are necessary. Other peoples' hands are always too weak, and instead of destroying they always create new patterns. **XVII The Mermaid.** In the same way the mermaid attracts navigators, the stars seduce the man on earth. **XIX The Sun Man** is all of gold. He is all splendor, brightness, and heat. **XXI The Wing.** The light has brought man within the womb, which is no longer a mother but flowers, petals, and leaves that are celebrating. Now the androgen is itself. The laurel of victory transports it to Olympus. Lead has been transformed into gold. **XXII The Boogie-Man.** In all fairy tales, there is always a boogie-man that causes great fear. But he is half-naked and dirty, running away. Let's follow him for once and see where he brings us. I am certain that beyond the abyss another child waits for us.

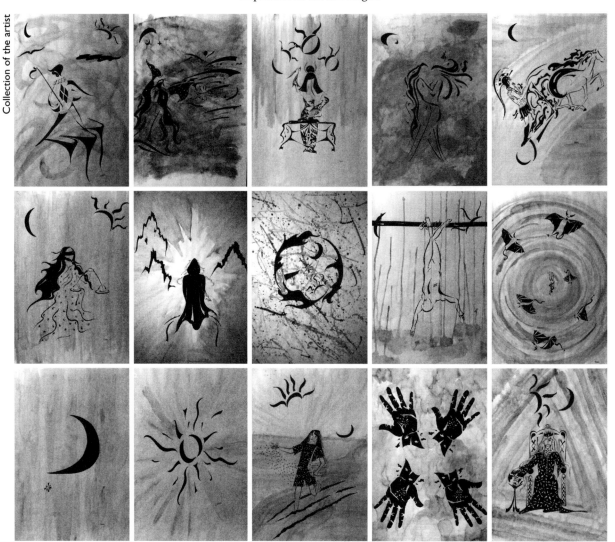

Friends Tarot   Deborah Ennis, circa 1991   Titles given are based on traditional titles.
TOP ROW: 0 Fool. 1 Magician. 2 High Priestess. 6 Lovers. 7 Chariot.   SECOND ROW: 8 Justice. 9 Hermit. 10 Wheel of Fortune. 12 Hanged Man. 15 Devil.   BOTTOM ROW: 18 Moon. 19 Sun. Page of Hands. Four of Hands. King of Worlds.

Friends Tarot   Deborah Ennis called her deck the Friends Tarot because she asked friends to participate in writing descriptions of the cards. In a letter to her friends, she says, "One of the things that drew me to the tarot was the fact that friends could learn a lot about each other and how they are perceived through reading cards....Wanting to recreate some of the intrinsic symbols of the tarot that I found so beautiful, combined with the challenge of creating my own symbols, led me to design my own version of the modern deck. I hope that having my friends describe the artwork and symbolism of the deck will bring in other viewpoints and add some dimension to the work." Each card has a watercolor wash background, stamped with linoleum block prints. The colors of the background correspond to the symbolism as well as to the suits of the cards. Swords are reddish, pertaining to opposites, decisions, and dialectics. Hands (wands) are in earth tones, indicating work, labor, or craft. Cups are blue and purple for spiritual issues.

Worlds (Coins) are green for material and worldly concerns. Most the cards have a sun symbol for comfort, awareness, and happiness, or a moon symbol for confusion, change, and turmoil. The deck was created circa 1991.

Full Moon Dreams Tarot   Lunaea Weatherstone made a collage tarot deck, using computer software. She issued the deck as numbered printouts. The presentation card dates the deck October 1998. The suits are air, fire, water, and earth, and the courts are king, queen, guardian, and child.

Amy Funderburk Tarot   Amy Funderburk painted tarot designs in oil on canvas. The images have a Nordic theme. They were completed in the mid-1990s.

Full Moon Dreams Tarot Lunaea Weatherstone, 1998

Amy Funderburk Tarot Circa 1995 XII Suffer to Learn
(Odin) corresponds to The Hanged Man. XIV Sacred Water,
Sacred Flame (Brighid) corresponds to Temperance.

Collection of the artist / © 1993, 1995 by Amy Funderburk

Gaian Tarot
Joanna Powell Colbert, 2002

Gaian Tarot Joanna Powell Colbert describes the Gaian Tarot as "centered in earth spirituality, with imagery and symbolism drawn from the natural world and the people who live in harmony with it." She continues, "The deck's message reflects the world view of contemporary Pagans and nature lovers: an awareness of planetary consciousness, a concern for the local and global community, and the desire to celebrate and protect Gaia, Mother Earth." The deck was made in 2002 using colored pencil and paint.

0 • The Fool

2 • High Priestess

8 • Strength

17 • The Star

18 • The Moon

19 • The Sun

Gateway to the Gods

Michiyo Fujihara created the images of the Gateway to the Gods Tarot with original photographs manipulated by computer. The images were released in 1997 on a CD-ROM, with poetry by Meir Raibalow. The publisher was Nippon Columbia of Tokyo in partnership with Blue Apple Fine Art Photography of New York.

Generation X Tarot The artist of the Generation X Tarot, Jonathan Schlackman, writes to Stuart Kaplan of his deck: "It utilizes the traditional card names and symbolism, but in a nineties teenager through early thirties kind of way." The images were created circa 1995 using photographs altered by computer. The term "Generation X" is the title of a 1991 novel by Douglas Coupland. The book described a generation of people born in the 1960s, "purposefully hiding itself," and in relative obscurity to their parents, the post-World War II "Baby Boomers."

Generation X Tarot Jonathan Schlackman, circa 1995

Gateway to the Gods   Michiyo Fujihara, 1997

Genesis of Enoch Tarot   D.P. Douglas, 1991   Collection of the artist / © 1991 by D.P. Douglas

Genesis of Enoch Tarot   The Major Arcana of the 1991 tarot by Dean P. Douglas depict interpretive scenes from the Bible. Five "Missing Keys" cards correspond to the final five letters of the Hebrew alphabet and are drawn from the Book of Revelation. The suits represent four ancient civilizations: swords for Rome, wands for Egypt, cups for the Philistines, and disks for Babylon. Court cards interpret the visions of Zachariah, and the numbered cards are based on the Kabbalah as described by the Order of the Golden Dawn. The back design shows the Tree of Life with the four living creatures of the Bible.

Sandra Gerö Tarot   Austrian artist Sandra Gerö completed a full deck with oil pastels on paper. The artist says, "Life is a dance, and talking and thinking about life should be fun, like a child's game. This tarot is designed to encourage your playfulness and help you open your mind to get in contact with the child inside you, so the wisdom of the cosmos can come to you." The designs were made circa 1995.

Collection of the artist

Sandra Gerö Tarot   Circa 1995   The description is by the artist. TOP ROW: **3 The Empress** rests her feet on the moon, indicating her connection with the High Priestess (virginal aspect of woman) and the Moon (crone aspect). Twelve stars above her head represent the twelve solar months of the year, and she is the thirteenth, signifying the matriarchal order of thirteen lunar months. **8 Justice** holds a pair of scales and the sword of analysis. Her physical power is represented by her wild red hair. **9 The Hermit** walks from the dark triangle into the light. His orange walking stick represents the power of knowledge and information as well as communication. **10 The Wheel of Fortune** carries the sphinx, the brown earthly serpent and the green fertile Anubis. These forces alternate to maintain a cycle of perfection, destruction, and new construction. **12 The Hanged Man** has light and multicolored energies surrounding his head. The trees are the gate to the inner world, for the Hanged Man is an apprentice shaman.

BOTTOM ROW: **14 Temperance** is a blue angel pouring water from one cup into another. Behind, a path leads to a highly energetic place, a place of worship. **17 The Star** shows a naked green figure pouring water to the earth and sea. She is the bright star surrounded by her seven sister, seven priestesses. **19 The Sun** shines on boy-and-girl twins, dancing and playing in a blooming garden. **Queen of Swords** is dressed in blue and violet and wears a radiant crystal on her head. Her throne is made of smaller crystals. She represents the black moon. **Eight of Wands** shows a hypnotic sun burning over the desert while the last of the eight wands is thrown over a dune.

Sandra Gerö Tarot *(continued)* **Prince of Cups** is dressed in green and red and sits on a multicolored snail shell. He represents the cardinal point west and the evening. **Nine of Cups** portrays a woman in a violet dress sitting with her twin babies. Green cups of fertility surround them. **Three of Cups** shows three women, dressed in white, red, and black, dancing together in front of three orange cups of communication. **Six of Pentacles** shows blue and yellow pentacles shared between the positive and the negative, two sides of the same person. **Ace of Pentacles** is shown as a plant with good roots, surrounded by new sprouts.

Collection of the artists

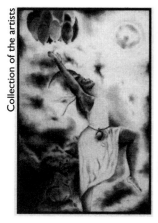 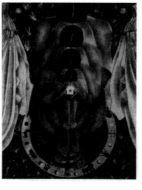 

God the Mother Tarot Lorena Johnson, illustrator, and Kathya Alexander, 2001 The description is based on that by Kathya Alexander. **0 The Fool** is a young woman about to step off the edge of a precipice, as though the earth has little power to restrain her. The vast void symbolizes the unknown. The feather in the headband is associated with virility and strength. The pale gray cat sitting separate from the woman indicates that she is free from animal forms of desire, and also shows that nature and humans can exist together in harmony. **II The High Priestess** shows a woman emerging from herself. She is the spiritual Bride and Mother, the daughter of the stars. This is perhaps a purification ceremony, for the woman is bowed and unclothed, signifying purity of spirit, mind, and body. She sits on a disk of the zodiac, her feet resting on the phases of the moon, representing mastery of nature and the universe. The two hooded women indicate things mysterious and unrevealed, initiating the novice into the Secret Church, the house which is of God and humanity. **IX The Hermit** is completely shrouded in a black cape, holding her staff in her hands. The darkness of her cloak symbolizes her inward quest for truth. The cloak is wrapped loosely around her, indicating that it does not restrict her, but is worn of necessity in the surroundings. Around her head she wears the white band of pure thought, this time surrounded by the black hood of isolation. Behind her is a star that represents the light that will lead her through the darkness, and the sign of Saturn, which represents her karmic destiny. The staff represents the Magician's wand and the rod of Moses.

Gnostic Tarot The Gnostic Tarot was drawn on computer (with Aldus Freehand) and hand-colored in pencil. The deck is based on creation myths described in *The Secret Book of John, The Nature (Hypostatis) of the Archons,* and *The Origin of the World,* which are manuscripts of Gnosticism, a religious movement that arose during the first century CE. The Gnostic Tarot was created by Richard A. Dengel in 1993. Dengel first created a Gnostic Tarot in partnership with Maureen Proietta in 1984 (see *The Encyclopedia of Tarot,* volume III); the one included in this volume is redesigned from that deck by Dengel alone.

God the Mother Tarot "The illustrations in God the Mother Tarot include all the women of the world, but women of African descent are the primary focus.... We created the images of God the Mother Tarot to illuminate the beauty of the Black woman and to illustrate that, in her, there is no cause for fear." The creators of the deck, Kathya Alexander and Lorena Johnson, based the deck on "Christic principles, the principles that accept Jesus as the Son of God and the Bible as their most sacred book." The designs, illustrated by Johnson and described by Alexander, were made in 2001.

Gnostic Tarot   Richard A. Dengel, 1993

Tarot of the Goddess   Elisabet Lund, 2002
TOP ROW: 0 The Fool. 3 The Great Mother. 4 Consort. 5 Mystery Keeper. 7 Chariot.
BOTTOM ROW: 9 The Wise One. 11 Strength. 13 Death. 17 Star. 18 Moon.

Tarot of the Goddess   Elisabet Lund created the Tarot of the Goddess "to evoke the mythologies and Goddesses that I feel lie beneath the traditional tarot images," she says in correspondence with Stuart Kaplan. "The main source is Sumerian mythology, but the whole Middle East and also India have contributed with various Goddesses. Often, this has lead me to an interpretation of the cards that is slightly different from the traditional, and therefore, also quite different images. This is a very female deck; the only male appearing is the Consort (Emperor)." The artwork is watercolor and was made in 2002.

Goddess of the Lake Tarot   Gregory DeLaCastro claims the Goddess of the Lake Tarot to be "an authentic 47,000-year-old shamanic tarot." The deck, he says, was "drawn by 10 Ocelotl, a divine incarnation of the sun god, who is shown in cave paintings from the Olmec period near Oxotitlán, Mexico. Yet one of the earliest references to the 10 Ocelotl occurs in the text on a fossilized elephant bone that was found in Valsequillo, Mexico. This clearly makes [the Goddess of the Lake Tarot] older than the Egyptian tarot decks of Seti I and Ramses the Great." The artist describes the designs of the deck as being made on rawhide colored in mottled sky-blue. "The ground on the backs of the cards was stained multi-color to look like stone or marble." DeLaCastro writes that the images came into possession of the Ute, in the present United States Southwest, and surfaced again in the 1980s. The Goddess of the Lake Tarot comprises twenty-five trumps. The backs of the cards have astrological formulas "translated into contemporary astrological notation, together with the addition of the more familiar European names for each card." The deck was made in 1994.

Tarot of the Golden Ribbons   Dragana Kovacevic of Yugoslavia added two cards to the traditional seventy-eight-card tarot. "Reading through the literature, two things struck me. First, tarot has even today an aura of black magic, even among quite a lot of people who are engaged with it. Second, in the book *Transcendental Magic*, by Eliphas Levi, I found that the tarot set originally had eighty cards, but that they had been lost somewhere far in the past. That persuaded me to try to pair the Major Arcana by opposites. It was apparent that every system that incorporates death and devil, and does not incorporate life and God, is by definition proclaimed black magic. After this discovery I added the cards Life and God to this tarot." The deck was colored in pencil on paper and finished in 1996.

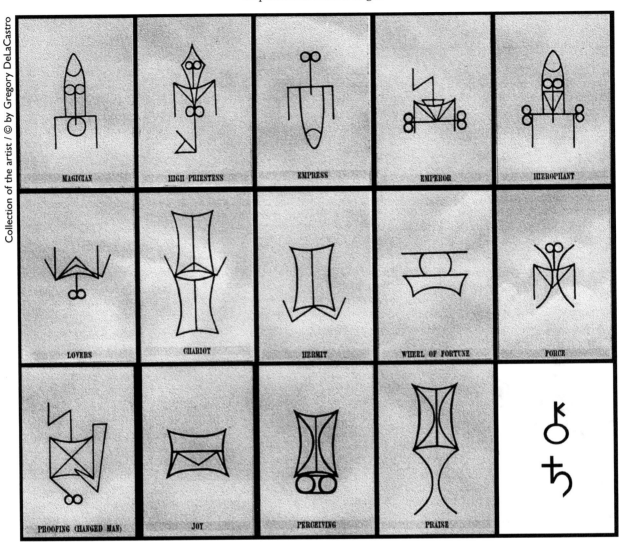

Goddess of the Lake Tarot Gregory DeLaCastro, 1994 The bottom right card is the back design.

Tarot of the Golden Ribbons Dragana Kovacevic, 1996 The caption is based on descriptions by the artist.

TOP ROW: **0 The Fool** is an androgynous figure, symbol of spiritual innocence, dancing Shiva's dance above the sun surrounded by a universe simultaneously in chaos and perfect order. **I The Magician** wears a robe red with life. **II The High Priestess** stands between the pillars that lead to the secret. **III The Empress** is green for fertility. She holds a horned ball for the astrological sign Taurus. Stylized plants symbolize earth. **IV The Emperor** is red. He sits on a globe, meditating over a bird-cross, symbol of compassion and responsibility, with crystals for order.

SECOND ROW: **V The High Priest** is triple-crowned for earth, life, and unity. He holds a ball-cross, a juncture of material and spiritual, surrounded with eternal flames. **VI The Lovers** are orange, symbolizing the sun, and rise from the violet sea of unity, surrounded by the blue eternal sky. **VIII Strength** shows a woman caressing a man-lion of fierce instincts, chained by a double-headed snake of wisdom. **IX The Hermit,** wrapped in a gray, hooded cloak, follows the light of spiritual guidance into the cave of inner truth.

XIII Death shows a white portal leading into a labyrinth of final truth.

THIRD ROW: **XIX The Sun** shows a boy dancing, surrounded by green leaves of nature's motion and fertility and the blue sky of spiritual renewal. **King of Swords** is blue for intensely strong intellect that creates and destroys. He flies in disturbed skies in search of a target. **Eight of Swords** shows a bird symbolizing both mobility and repose in an orange and blue background with swords, symbolizing concentration and distraction. **Seven of Wands** shows seven wands for seven degrees of matter, consciousness, and evolution surrounded and protected by fire and unity. **Three of Wands** shows a lotus of divine purity surrounded by colors of change and enlightenment.

BOTTOM ROW: **King of Cups** levitates over the ocean in meditative lotus posture, surrounded by a rainbow. **Princess of Cups** dives into the sea for a cup of secret treasure and knowledge. **King of Coins** is horned, as he stands for Prima Materia. He sits on a crystal throne. **Nine of Coins** is a helix of orbs, signifying endless variety and possibilities of life. **Back design.**

Gothic Elemental Tarot Kelly Vossos, 1996

TOP ROW: 0 The Fool. V The Hierophant. IX The Hermit. X Wheel of Fortune.

SECOND ROW: King of Swords. Six of Swords. Knight of Wands. Three of Wands.

BOTTOM ROW: Queen of Cups. Seven of Cups. Princess of Disks. Nine of Disks.

Gothic Elemental Tarot Kelly Vossos created the Gothic Elemental Tarot using watercolor, acrylic, and pencil. "My major intent on creating this deck was to provide a visually easy-to-understand approach that was unique in presentation and filled with primordial symbolism," Vossos writes to Stuart Kaplan. Many of the figures on the deck are composites of human and animal. The deck designs were completed in 1996.

The Fool

The Fool

You are unafraid of the unexpected.
You open new doors and set new trends.
You are a natural entertainer, whose shrewdness
is hidden behind a mask of innocence.

The Empress

The Empress

The Empress brings to your life abundance and
magical elements. She shows you the great potential that
lies within you and supports you in your
good fortune and continued success.

The Lovers

The Lovers

The Lovers signify a loving relationship with
oneself. A respectful union with another.
Two spirit mates unified in a single embrace.
They now dream the dream of love together.

Strength

Strength

Strength tells you to follow your passions and dreams
at all costs. Never give up, never surrender.
Use your strong heart and yet remain gracious as you
approach your object of desire. Know that
all will be delivered.

The Wheel of Fortune

The Wheel of Fortune

This card signifies happiness, success
and unexpected gains. The great
universal wheel showers you with gifts and well being
emerging from a time of hardship.
Remain still within giving thanks and acceptance.

The Moon

The Moon

This is not a time for commitment or concern. Watch
and listen for your own messages. The tides change
now in your favour, bringing you rewards.
Know that once again you will stand in the
full embrace of the sun.

Prototype collection of the author / Artwork collection of the artist

Grace Tarot Hannah
Alvarez Blanco, 2002

Grace Tarot Hannah Alvarez Blanco of Canada designed the Grace Tarot using collage technique. She wished her cards to "appeal to a society seeking positive reaffirmation." She created a prototype that packaged three cards in a folder, so that the cards could be collected gradually, rather than bought as a complete deck. The designs were created in 2002.

Tarot des Grands Initiés du Moyen Age (Tarot of the Great Initiates of the Middle Ages) French cartoonist Willy Vassaux is well-known for his comic book histories of the battles of World War II. However, his wide-ranging interests also capture alchemy, tarot, and other esoteric topics. His designs for Tarot des Grands Initiés du Moyen Age, rendered in pen and ink, have Kabbalistic references and other symbols worked into the figures and background. The Tarot des Grands Initiés du Moyen Age was made circa 1995.

Tarot of the Hands "In the hand is represented one's entire life, the flow of existence," writes Morena Poltronieri, artist of the Tarot of the Hands. "It expresses strength and dominion.... With our hands we create and work, and here is present the symbolism of alchemy that permits man to rise above materialism to reach the higher spheres of knowledge. According to Buddhism, the closed hand is a symbol of esotericism, of mystery, as opposed to the open hand, the emblem of revelation. From this is born the idea of the hands as a symbol of the tarot, which represents the journey of man on earth. This man is neither devil nor angel, but only man, the man who holds in his hands the secret of his destiny and the knowledge of being able to realize it." The black and white ink drawings of the Tarot of the Hands were made in 1999.

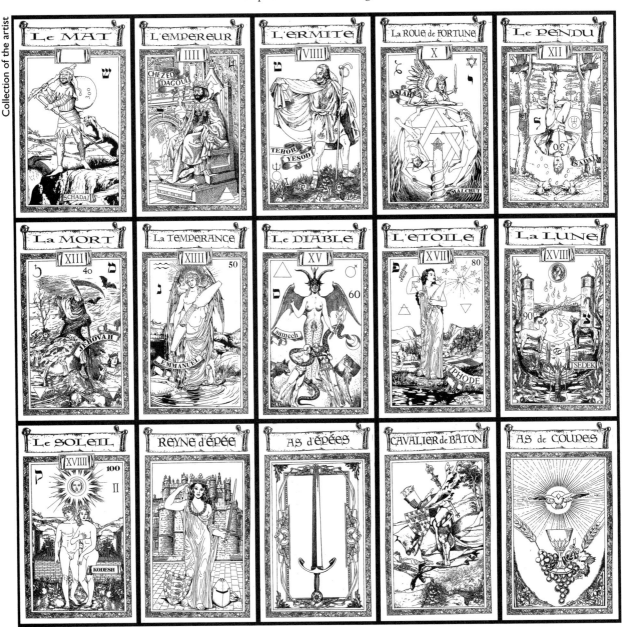

Tarot des Grands Initiés du Moyen Age (Tarot of the Great Initiates of the Middle Ages)   Willy Vassaux, 1995
TOP ROW: Le Mat (The Fool). IIII L'Empereur (The Emperor). VIIII L'Ermite (The Hermit). X La Roue de Fortune (The Wheel of Fortune). XII Le Pendu (The Hanged Man).   SECOND ROW: XIII La Mort (Death). XIIII La Temperance (Temperance). XV Le Diable (The Devil). XVII L'Etoile (The Star). XVIII La Lune (The Moon).   BOTTOM ROW: XVIIII Le Soleil (The Sun). Reyne d'Epée (Queen of Swords). As d'Epées (Ace of Swords). Cavalier de Bâton (Knight of Batons). As de Coupes (Ace of Cups).

Tarot of the Hands   Morena Poltronieri, 1999   The descriptions are based on those by the artist; the titles in the caption are given in a manuscript and are not translations of the titles on the artwork.

TOP ROW: **I The Instruments** are the four elements, always active, ready to react. From the cup of knowledge and the hat of ideas extend the hands that exert their power through actions. **II The Guardian** is the eye that guards the entrance to the mysterious world of dreams and imagination. The hands are about to lift the veils and reach wisdom. **III The Flight** shows the hands holding the scepter, symbol of power, ready to fly off with light and spiritual wings. **IIII The Sceptre** is held in the hand that emerges from the cube of the world. The scepter reminds us that nothing can separate man from concrete action and his responsibilities. **V The Fusion** shows two hands joined together, emerging from the sacred hat, symbol of wisdom and spirituality.

SECOND ROW: **VI The Arrow** comes from high in the sky as a symbol of unforeseen action and of the trials inflicted by destiny. The hand is wounded by it and unable to react. The card represents the *coup de theatre,* but also love at first sight, which blocks every action and pierces the soul. **X The**

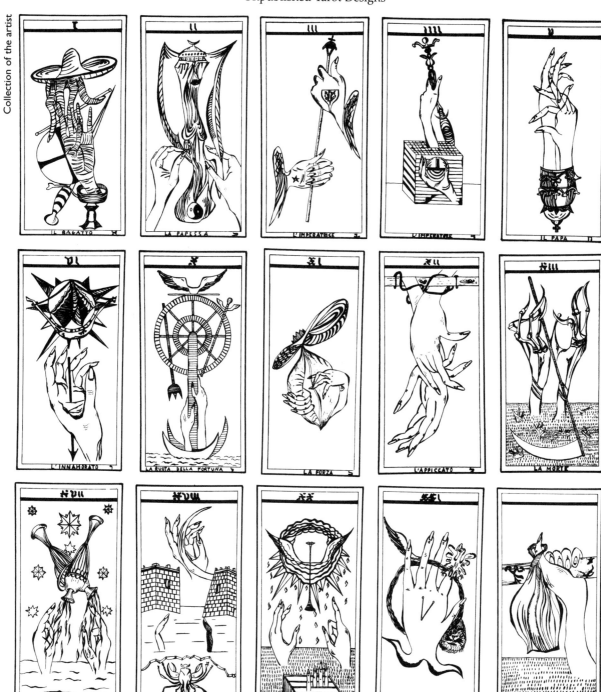

Wheel completes its cycle in the same way that life continues its course. The crescent moons on the waters symbolize an idea navigating the unconscious, trying to ascend the wheel. **XI The Mouth** is the source of vital breath and words, the place where the creative process takes place. The hands put all this into practice. **XII The Rope** ties two hands that dangle down loosely, without vital energy. The rope represents the bonds that block action and enterprise. **XIII The Sickle** is guided by two skeleton hands. **XIII** represents the passage from one life cycle to the next life cycle.

BOTTOM ROW: **XVII The Source** gives birth to new hands and new projects. **XVIII The Crab** purifies the pond from harmful dross, beneath the moon that transmits its

vibrations and under the towers of silence. Two fingers point to the sky, indicating that one must be inspired, even if one's course seems difficult and full of shadows. **XX The Prison** shows two hands lifted by the message of new objectives and destinies, given by the trumpet. Another hand is trying to rise, but is trapped in the prison of old memories. **XXI The Union of the Instruments** symbolizes that a conclusion has been reached, a final stage has been attained, for better or worse. **Zero** shows a hand picking up a sack of rags and some souvenirs, ready to begin a new journey. This is the moment of risk, the possibility of starting a new life, time to start anew.

Hannah's Deck Ana Noriega, 1990
TOP ROW: 0 The Fool Child. 1 The Magical Gypsy. 2 The High Priestess. 6 The Lovers. 7 The Chariot.
SECOND ROW: 8 Justice. 9 The Seeker. 11 Strength. 14 Temperance. 15 The Horned Shadow.
THIRD ROW: 16 The Tower. 17 The Star. 18 The Moon. 19 The Sun. The Lord.
BOTTOM ROW: The Lady. Air & Air. Air & Water. Fire & Spirit. Earth & Earth.

Hannah's Deck Hannah's Deck has twenty-two Major Arcana aligned with traditional tarot and twenty-two Minor Arcana comprising two cards titled The Lord and The Lady and twenty cards based on combinations of fire, water, air, earth, and spirit. The deck, by Ana Noriega of Puerto Rico, was created circa 1990 as photomontages. Noriega told *The Winged Chariot* (cycle 7, issue 8): "Although I've always been attracted to the tarot, because of lack of understanding, I also sort of feared it…. It was only about two years ago that the book *Tarot for Yourself* [by Mary K. Greer] crossed my path…and something inside seemed to click…. It so inspired me that I challenged my own ingenuity and spent days mentally conceiving images for the cards. Although the symbolic correspondences for each card are determined by tradition, there was space enough for the individual expression of those ideas. It implies, however, a trip across the corridors of the self with only one's

Mother

WIND

penetration

KNIGHT OF SWORDS

©1996USGAMES

XXI THE WORLD

hohe

Hohepriesterin
High Priestess

Galadriel's mirror shows many things, but wisdom lies in understanding what is shown.

Kelche
Cups
4

The High Priest
V

XI FORTITUDE

SIX OF WANDS

VI   The Lovers

ACE OF WANDS

DRAGON TAROT

FERRARA TAROT: The Chariot (90% actual size)

II

THE HIGH PRIESTESS

The Lovers

VENUS

VULCAN

ORIENS

OCCIDENS

LOVER'S PATH TAROT (before publication)

XVII

The Star

OLD ENGLISH TAROT

©1996 US GAMES

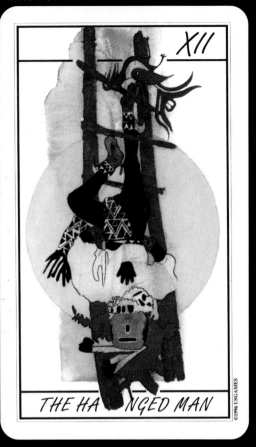

XII

THE HANGED MAN

8

FORCE
KYLLIKKI

Four of Buffalo

SANTA FE TAROT

Sangue / Blood
Sang / Blut
Sangre / Bloed

9

TAROT OF THE ORIGINS

VI DIE LIEBENDEN

Lights
Luci 10

Lumières
Luces

Lichter
Lichten

XXI

IL MONDO

TAROCCHI ROMANTICI (80% actual size)

Love

2

RÖHRIG TAROT (75% actual size)

Five of Rods

THE SYLPH
LA SYLPHIDE

XIV

DER LUFTGEIST
LA SÍLFIDE

LA SILFIDE

II

O

THE FOOL.

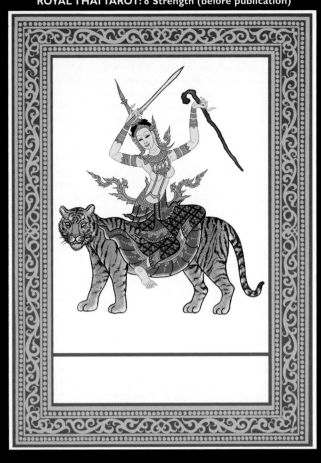

ROYAL THAI TAROT: 8 Strength (before publication)

CONNOLLY TAROT

XIV TEMPERANCE

TWO
of CUPS

TAROT OF A MOON GARDEN

XIII Death

HALLOWEEN TAROT

3 THE EMPRESS

10 WHEEL OF FORTUNE

The Fool

GREENWOOD TAROT

2 OF KOSHES (STAVES)

BUCKLAND ROMANI TAROT

Six of Air

Dawn Chorus

SEVEN OF CUPS

ANCESTRAL PATH TAROT

The Fool

TAROT OF THE TRANCE (95% actual size)

5.

Der Prophet   A Proféta
The Prophet   Le Prophète

The Chariot

III   The Empress

0   The Fool

UNIVERSAL TAROT (Miller)

Five of Disks

GODDESS TAROT

VIII ◦ JUSTICE

ATHENA

Q

Reason

GILL TAROT

THE MAGICIAN

1

CRYSTAL TAROTS

The House of God

PERFECTION

The Universe

Prince of Wands

5 Swords

THE HIGH PRIESTESS

◄ XXI ►

THE WORLD

7
of Wands
Persevere, Endure

CROW'S MAGICK TAROT

QUEEN

WANDS

VERTIGO TAROT
(first edition, shown at 85% of actual size)

own consciousness as guide. At the least, I've become aware of aspects of myself which went unrecognized before." She explains the name of the deck: "Hannah is part of the name I adopted for myself toward the end of the deck's creation. The complete name is Hannahisis. Hanna or Anu is the dark female ruler of the underworld and Isis is the Good Mother goddess archetype."

Hanslian Tarot The artist of the Engel Tarot also created designs for a seventy-eight-card deck. Alois Hanslian painted scenes of lifelike figures in dreamlike settings. The artwork was completed circa 1998.

Collection of the artist

Hanslian Tarot Alois Hanslian, circa 1998 TOP ROW: Fool. Magician. Emperor. Wheel of Fortune. SECOND ROW: The Devil. The Tower. The Star. Judgment. BOTTOM ROW: Ace of Swords. Four of Wands. Princess of Cups. Four of Disks.

Iolsta Hatt Tarot   1995

Iolsta Hatt Tarot   Dragons are the motif in Iolsta Hatt's tarot deck. The Major Arcana include runes and astrological signs, and the titles are nontraditional. The Minor Arcana courts are titled matron (king), mistress (queen), maiden (knight), and messenger (page). Aces are called auroras. The deck was created in 1995.

Haunted Tarot   The Haunted Tarot is based on sites in the United Kingdom. Lynn Atkinson created the deck as collages of photographs and artwork circa 2002.

Haunted Tarot   Lynn Atkinson, circa 2002   **XVIII The Moon.** In 1888, prostitute Mary Ann Nicholls of Durward Street, Whitechapel, was the victim of the serial killer called "Jack the Ripper." The true identity of Jack the Ripper has never been discovered, and until it is Mary Ann Nicholls will haunt Durward Street. **XXI The World.** Lucy Lightfoot, a farmer's daughter, fell in love with the effigy of a crusader at Gatcombe, Isle of Wight. The crusader was Edward Estur. In 1831, while Lucy was visiting her medieval "lover," a storm hit the island and was followed by a total eclipse of the sun. Lucy's horse was found tethered by the church, but Lucy herself was never again seen. The jewel and lodestone in the hilt of the crusader's sword were missing. More than thirty years later, a record was discovered. It told that Estur had been accompanied in his crusades by Lucy Lightfoot of the Isle of Wight. The little dog at the foot of the effigy dances on its hind legs every 100 years on Midsummer's Eve. **King of Cups.** David Rizzio was Mary Stewart's personal secretary. Their devotion to each other aroused the jealousy of the queen's second husband, Henry, Lord Darnley. He commissioned the murder of Rizzio at Holyrood Palace. The bloodstain in the hall of the palace has never been effaced. **9 of Coins.** Amy Dudley was the wife of Robert Dudley. Her husband was close to Queen Elizabeth I, and when Amy died after a fall down the stairs at Oxford, gossip held that she was murdered by Robert. The room where she was examined after her fall is known as the haunted room of Worchester College.

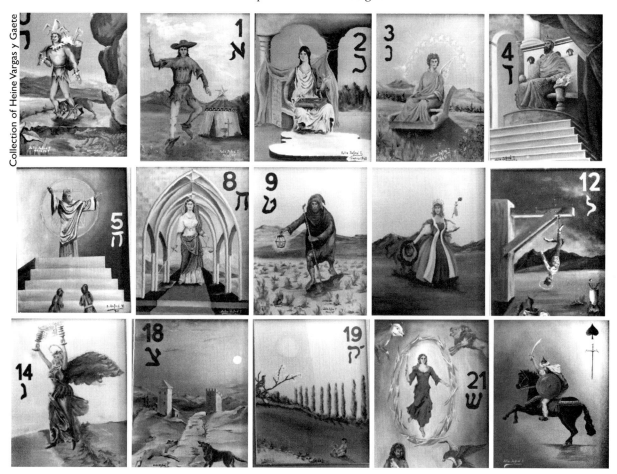

Collection of Heine Vargas y Gaete

Heliopolis Tarot   Julio Jofré Tijou, 1970s

Heliopolis Tarot   Collector and tarot scholar Heine Vargas y Gaete of Chile relates a strange story about how the Heliopolis Tarot came into being. He tells of how a Chilean lawyer, Julio Jofré Tijou, lost his license and became a wandering circus clown. A friend, Carlos Gómez, suggested that he paint the tarot. Julio Jofré Tijou had no background and so began studying at the National Library in Santiago. "It was then that strange things began to happen. Julio Jofré went to bed dead tired at midnight having studied all day long. Surprisingly, he would wake up at dawn sleeping over his books, not knowing how he got there. He began to paint the pictures, hanging them up in his improvised studio, but many times he found them the next morning all over the floor. Many strange things happened, but the strangest of all is that he got back his license as a lawyer. A well-to-do friend of his set him up in a comfortable studio…. It so happens that an old tradition says that whoever paints the tarot dies, and in this case Julio died suddenly of a heart attack, leaving Strength and The Wheel of Fortune unfinished." Vargas Y Gaete acquired the paintings in the 1970s. Each is painted in oils. The collection comprises the Major Arcana and four Knights, of the suits Spades, Clubs, Hearts, and Diamonds.

Hexagraphic Tarot   The Hexagraphic Tarot is described by its artists Marc Mesmer and Charles Harvin as a "Retro-Modern conception, giving a new look and feel to traditional tarot symbolism." They go on to explain, "The extraordinary shape of the cards was inspired by the recurring appearance of this form in Nature. The hexagonal shape has also been chosen to allow for a wider 'window' for the image, for facility in projection exercises. It also allows for the creation of interlocking layouts of kaleidoscopic complexity and more degrees of distinction between upright and reversed interpretations." The deck was created as acrylic paintings on card stock in 1993.

Hexagraphic Tarot
Marc Mesmer and Charles Harvin, 1993

TOP ROW: 0 Fool. V Shaman. VII Chariot.

SECOND ROW: VIII Strength. XIII Death. XIV Temperance.

BOTTOM ROW: Two of Cups: Love. Four of Pentacles: Earthly Power. Back design.

Melanie Hibbert Tarot Melanie Hibbert created tarot designs when she was fifteen years old; she had been collecting tarot cards since age thirteen. "They have surrealistic and futuristic styles," she said in a letter to Stuart Kaplan. "Many famous people or pop icons are in them." The hand-collaged designs were made in 1997.

Jeff Hill Rosenwald Tarot In correspondence with Stuart Kaplan, Jeff Hill writes, "I have spent many agreeable hours poring over the unique tarots, especially the more primitive ones [in *The Encyclopedia of Tarot*]. The one tarot of them all that I've found the most interesting is the tattered images in the two sheets in the Rosenwald Collection." (For Rosenwald cards, see volume I, pages 130–131). Hill followed his interest to redraw the Rosenwald tarot, adding Minor Arcana pips of his own design. "I have invented my own pip system, continuing in the antique style. My glyphs, just above the suit symbols, are 'shorthand' for P.C. Smith's picture-book illustrations in the Rider-Waite deck." The designs were completed in 1995.

Melanie Hibbert Tarot 1997 XV The Devil. XVIII The Moon. XIX The Sun. XX Judgement.

Collection of the artist

Jeff Hill Rosenwald Tarot Jeff Hill, 1995

Hindu Astronomy Theological Tarot P.B. Dhuri, artist, and Kishor N. Gordhandas, 1989

Hindu Astronomy Theological Tarot A very unusual deck was commissioned by Kishor N. Gordhandas, a playing card collector in India. The deck was hand-painted by P.B. Dhuri on heavy, stiff paper, with gold borders. The backs are orange-red, and the cards are gold-edged and lacquered. The cards are hard and have a distinct scent due to the lacquer treatment. The illustrations are in the style of Sawantwadi, a town in Sindhudurgh, in the south of India, that is known for its lacquerware on wood as well as the round Ganifa playing cards.

The deck is contained in a wooden box hand-painted with images from the deck. The Major Arcana of the deck depict planetary and astrological signs with Hindu deities. The Minor Arcana suits are pothi (Book of Knowledge), corresponding to the god Brahma; lotus for Vishnu; trident for Shiva; and vajra (thunderbolt) for Indra. Court cards are king, queen, vehicle, and abode. The deck includes a presentation card that reads [sic]: HINDUASTROMY THOLOGICAL / 78 CARDS TAROT / INDIA - 1989 / KISHOR N. GORDHANDAS / BOMBAY / ARTIST - P.B. DHURI / SAWANTWADI LACQUER-WARES.

Hindu Mahabharata Tarot Sunit Kumar Gupta created a tarot deck based on the great Indian epic *Mahabharata*. The round designs were completed in 1996. Extra cards, such as Injustice and Birth, are added to the basic seventy-eight. The designs on the pips of the Minor Arcana recall those of the Rider-Waite Tarot.

Hindu Mahabharata Tarot   Sunit Kumar Gupta, 1996

Barry Robert Hoffman Tarot   New York artist Barry Robert Hoffman created tarot designs in intricate ink drawings. The drawings were made circa 1990.

Hollywood Tarot   Artist Ed Stone created a collage painting of the Major Arcana. Many of the cards have a Hollywood theme. The acrylic painting measures 24 by 48 inches, and it was completed in 1990.

Barry Robert Hoffman Tarot circa 1990

Hollywood Tarot   Ed Stone, 1990

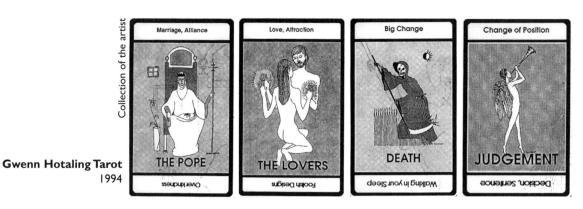

Marriage, Alliance	Love, Attraction	Big Change	Change of Position
THE POPE	THE LOVERS	DEATH	JUDGEMENT
Over kindness	Rookh Designs	Walking in your Sleep	Decision Sentence

Gwenn Hotaling Tarot
1994

Holy Grail Tarot "Round about Halloween, in 1995, I began to have incredible visions of a procession of the Hallows of the Holy Grail. I began to draw and, in the course of three months, ended up with eighty magical drawings comprising a tarot deck based on the Holy Grail legends. Material continued to be channeled through as I painted, down to the minute details of the costume." So Arlene Whiteswan introduces her tarot paintings. The richly colored scenes illustrate the Arthurian legend, centering around the Quest for the Grail. The artist worked on the paintings for two years.

Gwenn Hotaling Tarot Gwenn Hotaling created tarot designs that give upright and reversed meanings at the top and bottom of each card. The designs were completed circa 1994.

Helen Houlston Tarot The playful tarot by Helen Houlston features a cast of the artist's relations and friends. The English village of Blanchland, where the artist lives, is pictured on several cards. The artist says of the deck, "This is a personal set of Tarot Trumps whose cards combine the symbolism of a conventional pack with characterization based on real people known to me.... I was very much influenced by the Visconti-Sforza Tarocchi Deck (I used its Popess as my own Female Pope), and I used metallic gold paint a great deal to try to create something of the richness of the beautiful cards which were my inspiration." Many of the cards feature a quote from a literary or popular source. The paintings were completed circa 1985.

Hugobian Tarot Peter Wood of England used watercolor to portray teddy bears in 1998. The word Hugobia, coined by the artist, means "Land of Bears."

Hugobian Tarot Peter Wood, 1998

Holy Grail Tarot   Arlene Whiteswan, 1995   TOP ROW: **0 The Fool** is Parsifal. **1 The Magician** is King Solomon on his ship. **2 The High Priestess** is the Lady of the Lake. **3 The Empress** is a composite of the Irish goddess Brighid and the Virgin Mary. **9 Grail Hermit.**   SECOND ROW: **13 Death** shows the Raven Morrigan on the battlefield of the Crusades. **15 The Devil** is the Green Knight. **18 The Moon** shows the Three Marys of the Sea. **Queen of Swords** is Gwenevere. **Knight of Swords** is Sir Lancelot.   THIRD ROW: **Seven of Swords. Two of Swords** is Tristan and Iseult. **Knight of Lances** is Merlin. **Queen of Grails** is Dindraine. **Knight of Grails** is Sir Galahad.   BOTTOM ROW: **King of Pentacles** is Sir Bercilak, Lord of the Hunt. **Knight of Pentacles** is Sir Gawain. **Nine of Pentacles** is the Faery Queen of Avalon. **Two of Pentacles. Ace of Pentacles.**

Helen Houlston Tarot Circa 1985 The descriptions are by the artist. Her story demonstrates the tarot as an illustration of "Every Woman's" life.

TOP ROW: **0 The Fool.** Everybody wanted to be The Fool, but I'm the one setting off to find a new life. The journey is mine. Carefree, careless, and innocent, I sit precariously on a hill overlooking the tiny village that was to become my home. Money is already slipping away. Perhaps if I'd known what lay ahead of me I may not have worn such a broad smile. **2 The Female Pope.** The innocent and holy Popess is just a cardboard cut-out. That's me, behind her, wheeling her about. She holds the Book of Wisdom and the keys to inner knowledge, mystery, and intrigue. Her eyes are fixed towards Heaven, but I'm the one lurking behind, and I am watching you. **3 The Empress** is a school teacher and one-time colleague. Successful and indulgent, she is a great lover of life and works hard to enjoy its luxuries. She likes expensive holidays and good food, and her only fear is of growing fat. Perhaps a fault might be that being so successful herself she has some difficulty in understanding deficiency in others. **4 The Emperor** is my son. In this card he luxuriates in his executive office with imperial-crested coffee cup and personalized chocolate biscuit. All the gadgets that surround him work smoothly. The pencils in the crown are well sharpened. Happy in his success, he sports a boutonniere and his granddad's opal tie-pin. **5 The Pope** is my father, a grammar school teacher, science graduate, hard worker, able craftsman, and above all, quiet humorist. He had a joke or quotation (more often a deliberate misquotation) to suit most occasions. Gentle and amenable, he was a wonderful family man. As a committed agnostic he knew the Bible well, and we envied the way he could quote from it to illustrate what in those days were unusual views. For a short time at the end of his life he developed, as many very old people do, a strange extra wisdom, and we would sit by his bed fascinated with his profound-sounding but often meaningless talk. Because of this we called him Guru, Wise Man, and Pope.

SECOND ROW: **6 The Lovers** are my daughter and son-in-law. They made the right decision when they chose each other and, with puppy Daisy, make the strongest bonding unit of all, a triangle of love. These lovers are warm and happy on a cold high mountain. Summer roses bloom from their pockets and kisses fall instead of snowflakes. **8 Justice** is my mother. Caring, loving, and endowed with exceptional common sense, my mother worked hard to make a good home for us. Practical and creative, she would tackle any job and do it well. Although a perfectionist herself, she was not over-critical of others. "A bit of help is worth a lot of criticism," was one of her mottoes. She had a passion for flowers, cakes, and expensive hats. Often she would threaten to snickersneeze a naughty grandchild with her hat-pin, and in this card a hat-pin is her sword. **9 The Hermit.** This friend stands on the empty terrace watching the dogs race past. He says the most difficult thing in life is "Timing," and sometimes he wonders if he's ever been able to get it quite right. The zodiac at the bottom left came out the day before the artist began the painting: "At the beginning of the week you will find it difficult to face the thought of work." **10 The Wheel of Fortune.** The Fool is king, and I'm at the bottom sleeping. I wish I could stay asleep forever. "Always be kind to the people you meet when you're on your way up. You may meet them again when you're on your way down." **11 Strength.** The Lovers are having a fun-fight on a slippery pole over a river. He wears the mask of a fierce lion, but she is not afraid. The lion's foot has slipped. It is he who will get his feet wet.

THIRD ROW: **12 The Hanged Man.** A Fool traveling alone toward a new life encounters many people determined to rob him, cheat him, and kill all his dreams. I met many such people on my journey, and this hanging man represents all of them. The money falling from the pouch he holds was mine. **13 Death** plays a board game with lives. As he moves round he marks his future victims with a cross, just as men mark trees that stand in the way of a new motorway. Behind him are the people he has already visited, some of whom I have known and loved. He moves on. Who will be next? **14 Temperance.** To characterize this card I had to go back nearly half a century to a fellow Girl Guide [English Girl Scout] in the Primrose Patrol. Truthful, pretty, and really nice, she was everybody's favorite. I wonder if anyone else disliked her as much as I did! **15 The Devil** sweeps in and out of Hell holding between finger and thumb of each hand a person I believe to be evil. The flames of Hell are stoked by anti-nuclear badges thrown in by nuclear devils. So Hell gets hotter and nearer to the Earth. **16 The Tower.** Two school boys, and I was one of their teachers. (Was that spray-can pinched from my art room cupboard?)

BOTTOM ROW: **17 The Star.** After going through a rough time, this friend pinned her hopes on her own lucky star. She got her wish. It works! **18 The Moon.** At the time of painting this card the Moon Dogs had been howling in this dear friend's life for many years. Nobody knows how she survived, but she did. Known for her compassion, loving nature, and good sense, she is simply, "The Best." Everybody feels better for knowing my wonderful friend. **19 The Sun** shows the Thryft House Fields of my art school years. The sun was always shining. The corn was as high as an elephant's eye. Joyful, romantic, and incurably hopeful, we painted, dreamed, sang, and laughed in our own special "Golden Cornfields of Home." **20 Judgement.** This is the exception. I know nobody in this card. However, St Michael's vest is made of the same material as a "New Look" dress I bought when war-time rationing was over. The skirt was so long that people stared at me. I loved it, saved it, and some years later used the material again to make holiday beach clothes for my children. **21 The World.** My Husband. He was our world. Highly educated and cultured, a historian, teacher, and family- and home-loving man. Strong and gentle and very good-natured, he had an enormous sense of justice and fairness. He was loving, sensitive, and kind, and well known for his sense of humor. He died very young, greatly loved and enormously missed as father, son-in-law, husband and friend.

Collection of the artist

Harrie Huisman Tarot Circa 1998 XVII The Star. XVIIII The Sun. XX Judgment.

Harrie Huisman Tarot Harrie Huisman of the Netherlands painted twenty-two Major Arcana circa 1998. The oil paintings measure 75 by 100 centimeters.

Jack Hurley / John Horler tarot kings William Jack Hurley and John Horler were two of the artists who created the New Tarot deck, which was published in 1974 (see *Encyclopedia of Tarot,* volume I). The two kings here are "the kings that did not make it into the New Tarot deck," says Hurley. "The final court cards were based on a more elaborate system. These are mostly astrological. I provided John Horler a list of about twenty people per sign that he knew around Big Sur." Horler drew composites of real people to represent the kings. The original drawings, by Horler, and the linoleum blocks for the prints, by Hurley, were made in 1969. These prints were pulled by Jack Hurley in 1994.

Hutchinson Publishing A single Star card mounted on folded stock is hand-drawn in black ink and hand-painted in red, blue, yellow, and green. The back is blank. The card is labeled "from Hutchinson Pub. / Mr. Robinson." The card is modeled after the Rider-Waite Tarot and was probably made in the 1970s. No other information is known about the card.

Infinity Tarot The intricate artwork of the Infinity Tarot, by Catherine Buck and Jonathan Martin, includes symbolism of color, the Kabbalah, astrology, and numerology. At the side borders are lemniscates, the mathematical symbol of infinity. The Major Arcana include astrological or elemental symbols at the top, and at the bottom a Hebrew letter and two Sephiroth from the Tree of Life, indicating the path to which the trump is assigned. The system is that of the Golden Dawn. The artwork was completed in 1998.

Hutchinson Publishing
1970s

Collection of the artist

Collection of the author

Jack Hurley / John Horler tarot kings 1969/1994 King of Wands (Aries). King of Circles (Gemini).

Infinity Tarot   Catherine Buck and Jonathan Martin, 1998

TOP ROW: **Fool** plays a flute, an instrument by which the breath of life is formed. A phoenix feather, symbol of sacrifice and regeneration, floats over him. His knapsack carries karmic responsibilities. A dog warns the Fool to step careful-ly. **Magi.** The yellow background is for the creation of thought, and for light and manifestation. The black and white floor shows positive and negative energies. **High Priestess** wears a gray crown that holds the columns of Justice (white) and Severity (black). She is the embodiment of the middle pillar. Her throne is the heart of mysteries. She is veiled, for knowledge must be sought. **Empress.** At her feet, the lion and the lamb sit together peacefully. The red of her clothes, the heart she holds, and the roses near her symbolize pas-sion and love. **Lovers** represents two halves of the whole: male and female. They sit in a green landscape of fertility, with a pool of the waters of life below them. The lotuses are for life everlasting, and the evergreens are the renewal of life.

SECOND ROW: **Chariot.** A blanket of stars shows endless possibilities; the golden road indicates the path of experi-ence. The charioteer is humankind in search of answers. He wears his heart on his sleeve. **Justice** sits on the foundation of the law. The blindfold demonstrates judgment through inner sight. The sword is the mind that penetrates through a situation. **Death** is Azrael, the angel of death. The black and white body represents the transition from one reality to

another. He is in a womblike cave. Six candles around him represent the heart; the flames are the human life force. A snuffed candle indicates an individual's transition into death. The sun and the vegetation outside promise new life. **Temperance** is Raphael, angel of fire. He has a golden pot of alchemy, to blend the essence of creation. The separation of black and white on his body indicates the hidden and the illuminated, male and female, peace and aggression. **Devil** holds a man and a woman prisoner. The grapes on the woman's tail indicate passion; the flames on the man's tail indicate sexual desire. The chains that hold them also hold the keys of release. The inverted pentagram indicates spirit forced to earth, or energy used to a negative end.

BOTTOM ROW: **Star** shows Fortuna holding a golden ves-sel of the sun, the silver vessel of the moon at her feet. The stars are beliefs and wishes. The standing stones form a win-dow to the universe. **Moon.** A man symbolizes the scattered seeds planted in the womb of life; and he is also a man con-fronting his feminine side. The broken bridge is the inability to confront or control the hidden or unknown. **Sun.** A child, the soul of man, rides a white horse, the connection of the spirit to the earth. The Lovers are in the background. **World** shows a woman on one foot, the human spirit upright and balanced. The wands she holds are the fire of creation. The wheel behind her has on it the Hebrew alphabet, the record of creation. **Page of Cups.**

Inner Garden Tarot   Laurie Amato, 2001   TOP ROW: 0 The Fool. 2 The High Priestess. 5 The Pope. 6 The Lovers.
SECOND ROW: 8 Strength. 9 The Hermit. 10 The Wheel of Fortune. 12 The Hanged Man. THIRD ROW: 15 The Devil. 16 The Tower.
18 The Moon. 21 The World. BOTTOM ROW: Four of Swords. Knight of Wands. Two of Cups. Seven of Coins.

Inner Garden Tarot Laurie Amato made the Inner Garden Tarot by collaging photographs of lush, formal gardens and antique sculpture. The deck was completed in 2001.

Inner Landscape Tarot The Inner Landscape Tarot is a montage of images of sculpture, paintings, and nature photographs. Laurie Amato created the deck in 2000.

Inner Order Tarot Raphaela Pulera painted the designs of the Inner Order Tarot under the direction of Robert Zink, in 1996. The imagery is drawn from the symbolism used by the Order of the Golden Dawn.

Inner Order Tarot Raphaela Pulera, artist, and Robert Zink, 1996 FIRST ROW: 1 Magician. 4 Emperor. 8 Strength. 9 Hermit. 10 Wheel of Fortune. SECOND ROW: 11 Justice. 13 Death. 14 Temperance. 15 Devil. 20 Judgment. BOTTOM ROW: 21 World. Princess of Swords. Knight of Batons. Queen of Cups. Ace of Pentacles.

Insight Tarot Elaine Seymour, the artist of Insight Tarot, created the deck circa 1990 as a therapeutic tool for women. "Insight Tarot is a mirror," she says. "Totally honest, challenging, and sympathetic, it provides never-ending private and intimate revelation. It is a pathway that brings the unconscious to light and sends the shadows packing without the reader even knowing that this process is taking place within her. Insight is very special; it offers women the opportunity to heal themselves and keep their dignity intact at the same time."

International Icon Tarot Robin Ator describes the International Icon Tarot as based on Pamela Colman Smith's designs for the Rider-Waite Tarot. "One could argue that tarot is like a set of signposts for life," says Ator. "Hence, it might not be inappropriate to recast the cards as a set of flattened graphic icons. The approach is one of graphic simplification, in an attempt to make the best-known tarot cheerful and modern, yet retain its usefulness, historical gravity, and clarity." The artwork was made in 2001.

Inner Landscape Tarot Laurie Amato, 2000 TOP ROW: 0 The Fool. I The Magician. II The High Priestess. IV The Emperor. SECOND ROW: V The Hierophant. VI The Lovers. VII The Chariot. VIII Strength. THIRD ROW: IX The Hermit. X The Wheel of Fortune. XI Justice. XIII Death. FOURTH ROW: XIV Temperance. XV The Devil. XVII The Star. XXI The World.

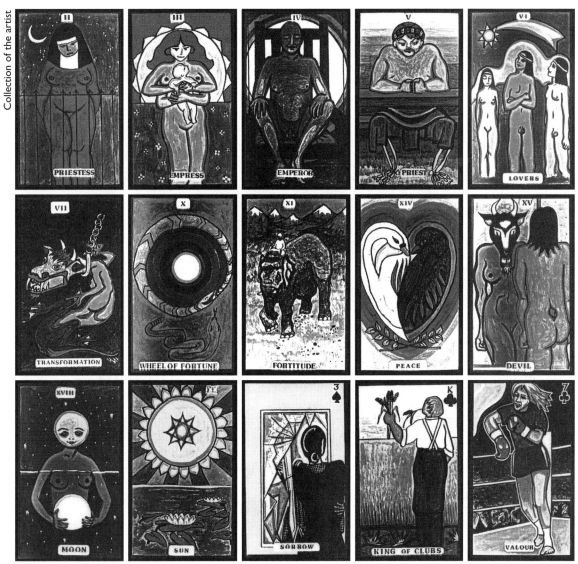

Insight Tarot   Elaine Seymour, circa 1990

International Icon Tarot   Robin Ator, 2001

Intuitive Tarot Patricia Sands describes her tarot deck: "The images on the cards are graphic and contemporary with the feel of a Matisse cut-out. The cards are color-coded. One can look at the tale of the color and 'read' whether it is a positive card or a darker toned, more somber card….The language of the cards has been softened. In the Intuitive Tarot deck, the traditional Death card is now the Completion card, etc. It makes it more user-friendly, so people will be more willing to pick up the cards and develop their own intuition." The suits are intellect (swords), spirit (wands), emotions (cups), and physical (coins). The courts are masculine (king), feminine (queen), movement (knight), and message (page). Sands issued the cards using computer printouts cut and collated by hand. The first edition of the deck featured a back design showing the title of the deck. The second edition was redesigned, using the same illustrations with a different layout treatment. The back design is a spiral of lavender. Both editions were issued in 2000.

Iona Tarot The Iona Tarot, by Italian artist Giona Fiocchi, comprises zinc-plate etchings in sepia or blue. The etchings were executed in the 1990s by Roberto Giudici in Varese. The etchings were intended to be a signed, limited edition of forty-nine sets of Major Arcana. However, according to the prospective art dealer, the plates were seized in a legal action and the edition was never issued. Only photocopies were available for reproduction here.

Iona Tarot
Giona Fiocchi and Roberto
Giudici, 1990s
3 The Empress. 11 Strength.
13 Death. 16 The Tower.
19 The Sun. 20 Judgment.

Collection of the artist

Intuitive Tarot   Patricia Sands, 2000

Jacobowitz Esoteric Tarot "This is an attempt to create a 'spontaneous' Major Arcana deck," says Leon Jacobowitz Efron. "The whole set was created in less than a week in my spare evening time. I did not make any preparations, that is, make symbolism lists, nor did I sketch beforehand. The only time spent thinking about the cards was during the painting process. My attempt was to create a series of Majors based on my associations of the various cards while drawing them. I began by drawing all the cards in ink and finished the coloring (in watercolor) at the end. The coloring was also done without planning beforehand. Many of the cards were naturally affected by the designs of my Jewish deck [see Jewish Tarot], but I think mostly they have a new touch. They are definitely not Kabbalistic nor do they have a reference to the Hebrew alphabet. I used whatever symbolism came to my mind at the moment I sat to draw, be it alchemy, Christian iconography, mythologies (Greek, Celtic, whatever) or the Bible. Some cards present an understanding of the card I had and not necessarily the actual scene usually depicted. For example, The Lovers are self-knowledge, wisdom, id versus ego, etc.; Judgment is the Phoenix." The deck, which the artist also called the Watercolor Tarot, was created circa 2000.

Ernie James Tarot The tarot designs by Ernie James are montages of electronic clip art put together on computer. They were made circa 1990 to accompany James' manuscript on reading tarot cards.

Ernie James Tarot Circa 1990

Collection of the artist

Jacobowitz Esoteric Tarot Leon Jacobowitz Efron, circa 2000 TOP ROW: 0 Fool. 5 Hierophant. 7 Chariot. 13 Death. 15 Devil. BOTTOM ROW: 17 Star. 18 Moon. 19 Sun. 20 Judgment. 21 World.

Collection of the artist

106

Collection of the artist

Jewel in the Lotus William A. Freiday, circa 1990 TOP ROW: 0 The Wise Fool: Eris. 1 The High Priestess: The Peace of the Mothers. 2 The Soothsayer Medium: Breezes' Gentleness. 7 The Chariot: Element: Mountain. 8 Strength: Element: Wind. SECOND ROW: 9 The Seeker: Inner Truth. 11 Balance: Abundance. 14 Temperance: Balance. 15 Fixation: Standoff. 17 The Star of Hope: Element: Lake. BOTTOM ROW: 18 The Moon: Element: Water & Moon. 19 The Sun: Element: Sun & Fire. Deuce of Swords: Meditation. Queen of Cups: Unity. King of Pentacles: Flow.

Jewel in the Lotus The artwork for Jewel in the Lotus is paper cutouts mounted on Bristol board. The artist, William A. Freiday, describes his work as "inspired by Matisse's paper cut-out phase, as well as by Zen sumi-e drawings in the formal arrangement and use of empty space." The designs were completed circa 1990.

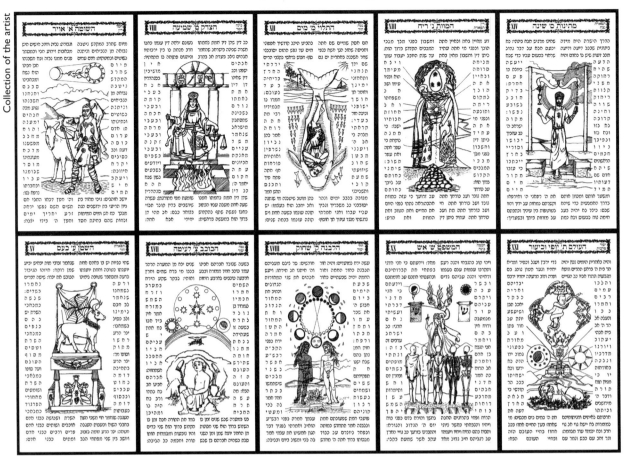

Jewish Tarot   Leon Jacobowitz Efron, 2002   Leon Efron describes the form of the cards: "Each card is designed as a Talmud page, the middle of which contains an illustration of the subject instead of the main text appearing in a regular Talmudic page. This image is framed in text that explains the image…. This text is composed of quotations from a list of Jewish sources that are relevant in one way or another to the subject of the card, its Jewish astrological correlation, or its assigned Hebrew letter's meanings. On the right top of the card, the title of the card is given in Hebrew square letters (all in accordance to the Talmudic design). In the middle is the Hebrew letter assigned to the card. To the left is the title of that letter (for example: the letter gimel is assigned the title 'Wealth and Poverty'); this title is written in Hebrew as well. On the far left corner of the card, where in a regular Talmudic page the number of the page appears in Hebrew letters, I have put the number of the card in Roman Numerals so that any person familiar with the tarot will have no problem recognizing it by its number and image (even if the image is slightly different)."

TOP ROW: 0 Fool. 8 Justice. 12 Hanged Man. 13 Death. 14 Temperance.

BOTTOM ROW: 15 Devil. 17 Star. 18 Moon. 20 Judgment. 21 World.

Jewish Tarot   As a final project for his degree in Design and Illustration from Tel Aviv University, Leon Jacobowitz Efron created a tarot deck that draws from Jewish traditions and Kabbalah. The artist says, "It is important to note that this deck is not standard in its design; it is not meant for beginners. It is based on Jewish ideas and on the Hebrew language. However, any tarot reader with experience will have no problem using it right away…." The Jewish Tarot was completed in 2002.

Kabbalah Tarot   David Sheen used strong black and white, rounded images to create the Kabbalah Tarot in 2002. Sheen says, "In the course of my research of the tarot, I discovered that [regular playing cards evolved from tarot cards, and that] tarot cards draw heavily on knowledge of Kabbalah, ancient Jewish mysticism. In the last several centuries, however, the tarot has transmuted, and it now contains only vestigial references to its Kabbalistic origins. I made it my goal to reverse-engineer a Kabbalah Tarot, and I believe that I have achieved this goal." The process: "I reverted the order of the Major Arcana of the tarot to their original order and channeled Hebrew words that begin with the corresponding alphanumeric letter of each card and that encapsulate the theme the card has historically represented. I have also unearthed a historical narrative that runs through the entire Major Arcana, a narrative of the history of humanity, which I have documented in my correspondences." The Minor Arcana comprise pip cards in four suits, plus ten "unsuited" cards.

Kabbalah Tarot   David Sheen, 2002   Descriptions are excerpted from the artist's explanations.

TOP ROW: **0** (untitled). According to the Kabbalah, a mysterious twenty-third letter is in the Hebrew alphabet. This letter is supposed to be the key that has the power to unlock all of the secrets encoded in Hebrew texts. **1 Magician** presents the information within tarot cards. **2 High Priestess** is the primary female, the mother of all humanity. **3 Empress.** The child no longer depends on its creator for survival. It takes its first steps out into the world on its own.   SECOND ROW: **5 Pope** ideally represents guidance in learning right from wrong. **6 Lovers.** The two figures loosely hold hands, but also point in opposite directions, indicating their respective path of choice, choice of path. **7 Chariot.** The chariot and rider symbolize control. To plant seeds in the ground is to control it, to wield power over it. **8 Justice.** Law has three components: legislative (symbolized by the figure on the left), executive (right), and judicial (center). Justice is about achieving balance.   THIRD ROW: **9 Hermit** is withdrawn from human contact and the comforts of the physical world in order to live a truly spiritual life, at one with nature. **10 Wheel of Fortune.** An object is cast on the Wheel, and eventually the forces of nature decide where it lands. We have worked hard, and now we wait for our efforts to bear fruit. **12 Hanged Man.** When newcomers establish a foothold in territory, they attempt to conquer it by military means, represented here by the closed fist, hidden behind the back. The Hanged Man has historically signified being suspended in time, waiting for the other shoe to drop, so to speak. **13 Death.** Critical mass has been achieved, and the military forces wreak death and destruction on the people.   BOTTOM ROW: **15 Devil.** Colonization has been institutionalized, and the people are enslaved. Tilt your head to the left, and the people are on their hands and knees, crawling as slaves once did. Tilt your head to the right, and the figures are sitting at desks mindlessly typing away on computers or holding onto a steering wheel, driving like drones through rush hour, as slaves do today. **17 Star.** The people shrug off their shackles, break through the lines of their oppressors, and storm the ramparts. **20 Judgment.** With this new revelation, you are able to see the world for what it really is. **Two of Spirit.**

Collection of the artist / © 1999 by Arnsten-Russell

Kabbalist's Tarot   Susan Arnsten-Russell, 1999

Kabbalist's Tarot   Susan Arnsten-Russell describes her tarot: "The Kabbalist's Tarot combines tarot, Kabbalah, and personal experience in an effort to provide a tarot that recognizes that the cosmos is a coherent and meaningful whole and that each aspect of creation is vitally connected to everything else." Each Major Arcana card has on its left border a Hebrew letter, a diagram of the Tree of Life, and an astrological symbol. The Minor Arcana have an extended Tree of Life diagram with the archetypal "world" highlighted. The court cards feature elemental and astrological symbols; the pips feature astrological symbols. The deck was completed in 1999.

Knezek Tarot   Teresa Knezek created tarot designs in 1998 using Adobe Photoshop software. Her intention,

she explains in a letter to Stuart Kaplan, was to create a deck "to fill the gap between pictorially traditional tarots, like the Hanson-Roberts and Rider-Waite, and the more symbolically original ones, like the Motherpeace and Voyager decks."

Knights of Assisi Tarot   Bea Nettles went to the beautiful region of Assisi, Italy, to create tarot photographs. "From a distance I read about the hill town of Assisi with its pink stone fortresses and St. Francis's Basilica…. There one finds ancient manifestations of the military, agricultural, mercantile, and spiritual activities upon which the respective suits of swords, wands, pentacles, and cups were based." The photographs were published as a book, *Knights of Assisi: a journey through the tarot.* The book was published in 1990 by Inky Press Productions, Urbana, Illinois.

Teresa Knezek Tarot   1998

X The Hermit

XVII The Tower

XIX The Moon

XX The Sun

Ace of Swords

Ace of Wands

Ace of Cups

Ace of Disks

Knights of Assisi Tarot

Bea Nettles, 1990
Descriptions are based on Nettles' book. **Knight of Swords. Four of Swords.** This is masculinity at its most aggressive and phallic—brave, cool, and keenly intelligent. In the extreme, the sword can lead to death, and the four of swords alludes to this final sleep.

Knight of Wands. Two of Wands. Also masculine in the traditional sense of the word is the Knight of Wands. Images in this suit show mock battles, parades, and other displays of strength and pride. **Four of Cups.** The cups are reminiscent of the holy Grail, the spiritual, the romantic, and the emotional. **Two of Pentacles.** These coin-shaped discs represent the emerging merchant class, and it is in this suit that one finds students, men and women going about their daily work in shops, cultivated fields, and studios. This is the suit of the everyday, where it is safe to dance.

Kundalini Tarot The Kundalini Tarot has a traditional Major Arcana. However, the Minor Arcana have seven suits, corresponding to the seven *chakras*, or energy centers, described in Hindu spiritual physiognomy as located along the spine, up to the crown of the head, in the human body-mind-spirit. Rachel Parti, artist of the Kundalini Tarot, describes kundalini as "a female serpent lying coiled around the base of the spine." When the serpent, a metaphor for spiritual energy, moves up the chakras, "it is transformative and mind-altering." Each chakra suit has a *yantra*, or visual meditation, a *mantra* called a *bija*, an animal called the vehicle, a lord, and a *shakti;* some of the suits have additional elements as well. Parti painted the designs for the Kundalini Tarot in 2000, using watercolor, and gold and silver inks, drawing from traditional tantric images as well as elements of the Rider-Waite Tarot.

Collection of the artist

Kundalini Tarot Rachel Parti, 2000 Descriptions are by the artist. TOP ROW: **0 Fool: Ganesha** dances on the edge of a precipice. A mouse is at his feet. In one hand is a *damaru* (hand drum) and in another is a lotus. Ganesha is carefree because he has no attachment to his ego or his illusions. He knows that his destination is wherever he ends up, not where he thinks he is going. **2 High Priestess: Sarasvati,** the Flowing One, goddess of learning and talent, sits on the throne of the High Priestess. She strums a *vina* and holds a sacred text and a *mala* (prayer beads). She is a river goddess. She sits between the pillars of dualistic delusion; we may choose to look at the world as black and white, but the reality is far more diverse and colorful. The sacred texts are the wisdom she will impart to any sincere seeker of the truth. The *mala* aids the tantric practitioner in concentration and discipline of the mind. She strums songs of beauty and sacred sounds. Behind her is a pomegranate bush heavy with the fruit of knowledge. **One of Aum: Yantra.** Aum is the "third eye" chakra, and it precedes the crown chakra. The Ajna yantra is a simple white circle with two petals. The complexity and multiplicity of the lower five chakras has become focused and simplified in the sixth chakra. **Two of Aum: Bija.** The Aum is the most sacred of mantras, the sound of the transcendent, infinite, absolute supreme, and nameless Godhead. It is pure consciousness, the Supreme Self, the Void, the One. **Three of Aum: Hamsa.** Hamsa is the sacred swan. It represents the individual soul at the moment of its merging with the divine. **Four of Aum: Lord Ardhanarishvara** is the merging of the illusion of duality. One half is Shiva, the other half is Shakti.

BOTTOM ROW: **Five of Aum: Hakini** has six heads with which she can see all that is. She holds a *damaru*, which guides the steps of the tantric on the path, a skull to help the tantric remain detached from delusion, and a *mala* to help the tantric keep the mind centered. She gives the *mudra* (gesture) of granting fearlessness. **Four of Crown: Sahasrara Chakra.** The crown is the highest chakra and represents ultimate enlightenment, when the tantric becomes one with the Supreme Self.

Collection of the artist

2. WITCH	9. ALANE	14. SOBER	19. SUN	Faither
Yin o' Spades	Mither	nine	five	Lassie
fower	three	Laddie	six	fower

Kyle Tarot   Mary Anne Gordon, 1995

Kyle Tarot   Mary Anne Gordon of Scotland designed a tarot deck using Scottish motifs. The cards are titled in Scottish, and the portraits on the court cards feature plaids in a tartan that identifies the suit. The name Kyle derives from the ancient kingdom of Kyle, now called Ayrshire, in southwest Scotland. The images of the Major Arcana float on a black background, while the Minor Arcana have backgrounds of the Scottish landscape and wildlife. The suits are spades (swords), sticks (wands), cups, and coins. Gordon painted the originals in acrylics in 1995.

Latex Tarot The tarot designs by cartoonist Keith O'Brien and others were made as rubber stamps by The Artery of Boise, Idaho. The designs were made circa 1994.

THE WORLD

Latex Tarot Keith O'Brien, circa 1994
TOP ROW: The Hanged Man. The World.
SECOND ROW: The Fool. The High Priestess. The Emperor. Temperance.
BOTTOM ROW: The Star. The Magician. The Emperor.

Stamped material collection of the author / © by the artists

The Magician

The Emperor

J.K. Lawson Tarot J.K. Lawson created intricate pen-and-ink tarot designs. He explains in a letter to Stuart Kaplan, "I share the same birthday as Salvador Dali and, in memory to him, use the same titling and numbering system [as the Dali Tarot]." The artist plans to execute the final designs as stained glass or reliefs carved in Indonesian wood. The designs are dated 1996.

Tarot Light Mark Valenza and Barbara Hess describe their 1992 deck as "drawn in a very positive manner, with a sense of humor that does not take away from the depth found in traditional tarot." The deck has five parts: Major Life Event cards and the suits of love, creativity, self, and fortune.

Collection of the artist

Tarot Light Mark Valenza and Barbara Hess, 1992

J.K. Lawson Tarot 1996

Maat Tarot Julia Cuccia-Watts painted the illustrations for the Maat Tarot in 2002.

Maat Tarot
Julia Cuccia-Watts, 2002
TOP ROW: Fool. High Priestess. Empress.
BOTTOM ROW: Strength. World. Ace of Cups.

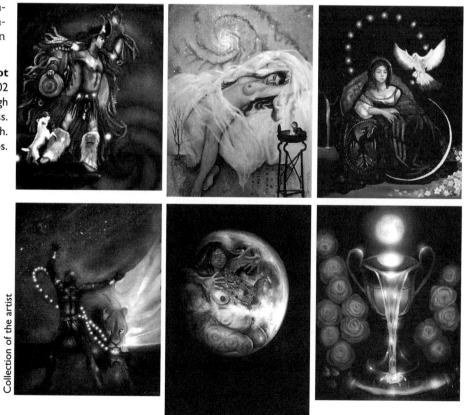

Magic Mirror Tarot   David Bergen, 1998

Magic Mirror Tarot   David Bergen created the Magic Mirror Tarot in 1998. He "drafted" the cards by using photocopies of extant artworks in order to "press on with pumping out the basic ideas." Each card has at its top the "seal for the deck"—two winged heads forming the artist's personal logo, pattern bars adapted from "the sides of an inlaid box in which my wife keeps her own deck," oracle heads, which the artist sculpted "to resemble a fragment of antique statuary" and incorporated into the deck "as a way of showing the unknowable." An icon for the Major Arcana or each suit is at the bottom of each card. Each Major Arcana card has a hand-lettered quotation.

Bergen explains the title of the deck by referring to the mirrors used by mystics and shamans to reveal "certain secrets from worlds invisible.... Mirrors which serve a symbolic function are therefore to ordinary mirrors what the tarot is to a deck of playing cards, and those who gaze into the depths of these magic mirrors perhaps see unexpected or deeper aspects of themselves reflected back to themselves—a familiar experience for those who work with the tarot, which can at times be like holding a conversation with one's own subconscious.... I had been working on the creation of my own deck for some fifteen months when I came across a reproduction, from a sixteenth-century work (*Splendor Solis,* by S. Trismosin), which portrays an alchemical androgyne holding a circular object whose appearance echoed the circular device in which a landscape is invariably shown in The World cards of fifteenth-century tarot decks. The caption described the object as being a kind of mirror in which the whole world could be seen reflected.... The name Magic Mirror Tarot came to mind, and it does indeed strongly express what I feel about the tarot in general and my own deck in particular."

The World David Bergen, in his manuscript "Magic Mirror Tarot," points to the similarity between the title page from *Splendor Solis*, a sixteenth-century work by S. Trismosin, and The World card from the fifteenth-century Gringonneur Tarot (see *The Encyclopedia of Tarot*, volume I for more information on the Gringonneur deck). The double-headed figure in the book illustration holds a mirror that reflects the whole world.

Magical Tarot of the Golden Dawn Jonathan A. Pierce, a student of the Ra Horakhty Temple, California, created drawings for the Magical Golden Dawn Tarot under direction of Patrick Zalewski. The Major Arcana and Minor Arcana numbered cards, the artist explains, "are based on the original drawings from the Whare Ra Temple [of New Zealand], with some differences in artistic interpretation, and input from Mr. Zalewski. The court cards are unique, derived from the descriptions provided by Mr. Zalewski, documents written by [MacGregor] Mathers, and the sketches of Wynn Westcott." Mathers and Westcott were founders of the Hermetic Order of the Golden Dawn in England. Arthur Edward Waite, who commissioned the Rider-Waite Tarot, was also a member of the Golden Dawn. The Whare Ra temple was founded by Dr. Felkin, a member of the original Golden Dawn under Mathers.

Magical Tarot of the Golden Dawn Jonathan A. Pierce, artist, and Patrick Zalewski, 1995

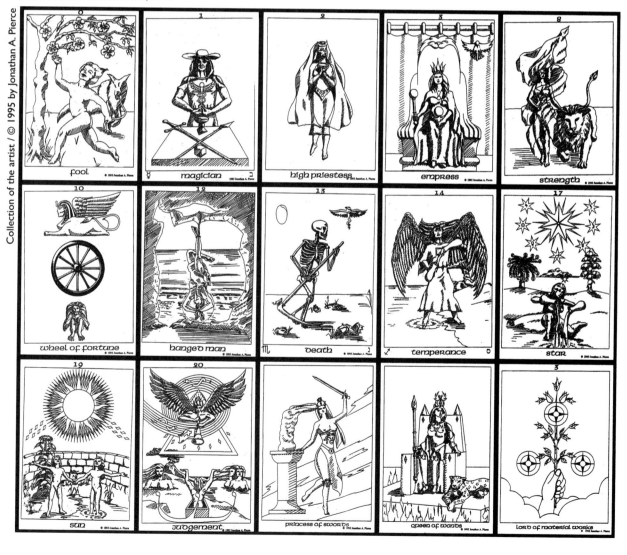

Malone Tarot The Moon was published in 1995 as a greeting card by Giftworks/Chronicle Books. The artist, Peter Malone, has illustrated several books as well.

Ewa Mann Tarot Welsh artist Ewa Mann created her tarot, she says, "loosely based on the Marseilles Tarot deck…using images that relate easily to life at the close of the twentieth century." For example, VIII Justice shows a woman who "touches her flat stomach like somebody who lost quite a bit of weight recently." The original art was rendered in gouache and finished in 1999.

Ewa Mann Tarot 1999 TOP ROW: 0 Fool. I Magician. II High Priestess. VIII Justice. SECOND ROW: IX Hermit. XI Strength. XV Devil. XVII Star. BOTTOM ROW: XVIII Moon. XXI World. Knave of Wands. Ace of Cups.

Card, collection of the author / © 1995 by Peter Malone

XVIII The Moon
Peter Malone, 1995

Collection of the artist

Mary-el Tarot Marie White, 2002

Marciniak Typology Tarot Jane Marciniak "painted the Major Arcana abstractly," she says in a letter to Stuart Kaplan, "going beyond the symbols to which we are accustomed in most tarot decks to the actual archetypal pattern." Her work is based on the archetypes described by Carl Jung. It was created over a period of years during the 1990s.

Marine Tarot In choosing what kind of fish to represent each Major Arcana card, Sarah Scott Parry considered the name of the fish and its physical appearance. For example, of the Magician, she says, "A fish that can fly is surely verging on magical!" The Marine Tarot was completed in 1998.

Mary-el Tarot "The main concept behind the Mary-el Tarot," writes artist Marie White, "is about achieving a balance and symmetry between the dualities of masculine and feminine, light and dark, inside and outside, etc. Rather than a focus on any one point in the swing of a pendulum, the focus has been on a holistic universe and self. Inspiration for the images was drawn from the iconography, symbols, and mythology of the people and nature from all over the world." Marie White created the images in oil paint in 2002.

Tarot of Maud Joyce Maud Daley created the Tarot of Maud using computer graphics software. The designs were made in 2002.

Marciniak Typology Tarot Jane Marciniak, 1990s **The Magician** represents the Great Work of the alchemist, the process by which the Divine is freed from nature where it is imprisoned. He represents the catalyst, the quick active mental force that unites ego and shadow and causes a collapse of the existing ego structure. The Magician was known to the alchemist as Mercury, the Prima Materia, or the First Matter. He was also the substance that acted upon the First Matter to produce the Philosopher's Stone. When the Magician moves through your psyche, a fire is being lit. (From Jane Marciniak's manuscript, "A Tarot of Personality: Correlations to C.G. Jung's Analytic Psychology.")

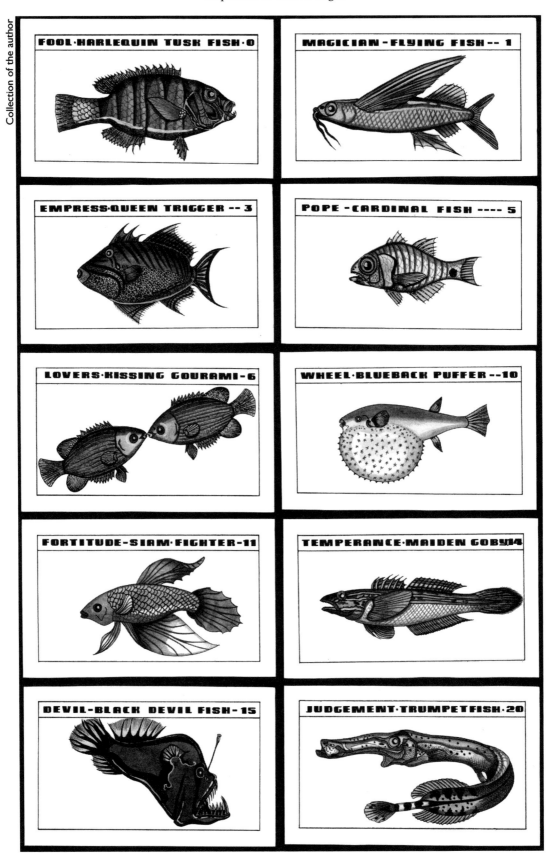

Marine Tarot Sarah Scott Parry, 1998

Tarot of Maud
Joyce Maud Daley,
2002

Mayan-Olmec Tarot Lia Machel illustrated the Mayan-Olmec Tarot circa 1999 in watercolor and ink. She tells of the Mayan-Olmec people in a manuscript: "The magnificent cities and pyramids built by these peoples of the Black and the Red races testify to an unbroken history in the Americas that dates from before the Pre-Classic period of 1500 BCE to CE 200, to Post-Classic CE 1541. There is much evidence of a world-wide trade route between them and Egypt, Africa, Syria, the Polynesian Islands, and possibly Northern Europe, in that long-ago past.... The Mayan-Olmec Tarot Deck records the costumes and lives of these peoples in the Minor Arcana suits. The Major Arcana cards are designed to feature more of the significant roles of their leadership and religious practice. All connected to the heavens and the major constellations.... The Mayans adopted much of the Olmec imagery and their social institutions, and were located from the Yucatan down into today's western Honduras, Guatemala, and El Salvador."

Mayan/Pre-Columbian Tarot Carol Miller commissioned Mexican artist Pedro Friedberg to render designs for the Major Arcana Mayan/Pre-Columbian Tarot. The designs were made in 1992. The titles of the cards, except for card 22, are days of the Aztec calendar.

Kerri Shawn McIntire Tarot The 1995 design of the Empress, says Kerri Shawn McIntire in a letter to Stuart Kaplan, "owed much to Cicely Mary Barker." Barker's illustrations of fairies, originally published in the 1920s, have been reprinted many times in books, calendars, and greeting cards. "The popularity of such fairy and angel images in today's culture is very welcome," McIntire continues. "Their charming, powerful presence brings us inspiration and hope." The Empress was painted in watercolor.

Medicator Tarot The Medicator Tarot was made by a Belgian artist and tarotist whose pseudonym is Medicator. The Major Arcana deck was published in 1987 in a limited edition of eighteen numbered copies. Included are two cards printed with a poem in Flemish and a page giving English and French translations of the poem. The back design shows a diamond and the words "Medicator Tarot."

The cards of the Medicator Tarot represent "the genesis of man," according to the artist. Card 0 shows "Man as a Being of Light in the Absolute." Cards 1 through 9 represent "involution, or the descent in substance in the Universe." Cards 10 through 18 show "evolution, or the ascent." The last three cards, 19 through 21, show "three aspects [of Man who has reached his completion]."

Mayan-Olmec Tarot Lia Machel, circa 1999

Medicator Tarot 1987 Descriptions are based on those by Medicator.

TOP ROW: **0 Pleroma.** Man as Being of Light in the Absolute. **1 Pneuma.** Entry in the Universe of man as divine spirit-particle with all potencies in himself. **2 Nyx.** First experience with substance; the primeval waters envelop the Light particles. **4 De Vier Zuilen** (The Four Elements). The spirit orders the primeval waters, by which the basic elements are made. **5 Fiat.** Creation of the universe and the human soul-body according to the Image, with the elements as building materials.

BOTTOM ROW: **9 De Pelgrim.** The complete expression of man in the physical world. Becoming conscious of his divine essence and that he must go back. **10 De Spiraal.** Acting in accordance with and the use of the laws and cycles. **11 Het Vuur in de Aarde.** Controlling and efficient use of lower and higher selves. **13 De Mystieke Dood.** Transmutation of forms in energy. **14 Anima Mundi et Spiritus Mundi.** Efficient use of life energy for development of latent capacities.

Kerri Shawn McIntire Tarot 1995 **"The Empress** combines the magic of the new age with the mystery of the old. The choice of green Luna moth wings reflects the fertile, elusive nature of femininity." (Kerri Shawn McIntire to Stuart Kaplan)

Collection of the artist

Collection of the author

Mayan/Pre-Columbian Tarot Pedro Friedberg, artist, and Carol Miller, 1992 TOP ROW: **1 Cipactli** is a period of days ruled by the crocodile god of creation and fertility, Tonacatecuhtli. **7 Mazatl** is the day on the Aztec calendar for hunting. Tepeyolotl is called the heart of the mountain, and Tlazolteotl is the earth goddess. **8 Tochtli** is "rabbit," and is associated with a calendar year. Xihuetecutli is the senior god of the Aztecs, a god of fire and warmth. Xipe Totec is the Aztec god of agriculture, spring, and the seasons, the symbol of the death and rebirth of nature. BOTTOM ROW: **14 Ocelotl** is a good day for doing battle. Tlazolteotl, the protector of the day, is Aztec earth and mother-goddess, and goddess of sex and purification. **XVI Cozcocuahtli,** "vulture," is a thirteen-day period protected by Xolotl, the evening star and a shape-shifter. This is a good period of time to confront discontinuities, disruptions, and failures. **22 Tezcatlipoca/Quetzalcoatl.** Tezcatlipoca means "smoking mirror." He symbolizes youth and is the brother of Quetzalcoatl, the god of intelligence and reflection. They represent dark and light, respectively.

Tarot Meditations: A Christian Reflection   Richard E. Kuykendall, circa 2000   The caption is based on descriptions by the artist.

TOP ROW: **0 The Fool** symbolizes the quality of being able to be childlike—to skip out into the world, whistling a tune—without a care and without fear. **1 The Magician** symbolizes one who is able to bring to pass one's will in one's life. He lives in balance with the four areas of life represented by the suit signs. **4 The Emperor** is the card of the archetypal masculine. Ideally, he is one who would rule his realm with a sense of responsibility as to the needs of his subjects. **5 The Hierophant** symbolizes organized and institutionalized religion. The two monks bowing before him suggest his authority from an external perspective, spirituality that is dogmatic rather than intuitive. **7 The Chariot** sym-

bolizes one who is in control of the various forces of one's life, able to bring together different and even opposite elements in pursuit of a goal.

BOTTOM ROW: **8 Strength** depicts Samson of the Old Testament wrestling a lion. Though outwardly it denotes physical power, this card is more symbolic of the inner strength that enables people to overcome the various obstacles that confront them in life. **9 The Hermit** shows a medieval monk who has set out alone on his quest for truth. Thus the card represents someone who needs to work alone for a time. **11 Justice. 13 Death. 18 The Moon** shows the way that we are moved by our subconscious influences, just as the moon depicted seems to influence the two howling dogs in some mysterious way.

Tarot Meditations: A Christian Reflection   Richard E. Kuykendall created the Tarot Meditations "to show that one can be a Christian and still claim these cards as one's own." The art was drawn in pencil circa 2000.

Metaphysic Tarot   Chilean artist Cecilia Mayer-Rechnitz hand-constructed the Metaphysic Tarot. The Major Arcana feature photographs of her original paintings glued on heavy stock, then hand-lettered with titles. The Minor Arcana have elemental sigils as images. The backs are blank. The deck was packaged in a hand-made round silk pouch, with a silk-covered book describing the meanings of the deck in Spanish. The deck was completed circa 1992. The artist says in a letter to Stuart Kaplan, "The Major Arcana images were born of certain archetypes from my personal history. In 1984, when this idea was conceived, I didn't know that I could express myself by painting. At that time I was getting deep in my studies of tarot, and I felt the need to materialize these special faces, full of color symbols and memories of past lives that were inside of me."

Michael's Tarot   The tarot by German artist Michael Kutzer shows skill in several media, as it was made, the artist describes, "as a mixture of engraving, relief etching, etching, and aquatints." The cards were hand-colored. Rather than a title, each card bears a motto in Latin or Greek, except for the Devil card, which has an Italian motto. It took nearly two years to complete a limited edition of twelve copies of the Major Arcana deck, which was published in 1989 and packaged in a tooled, suede box. Each card is signed and numbered by the artist.

Millenia Tarot   Catherine Inslee describes the tarot she created with artist Joe Diorio "a reductionist form that expresses the esoteric function encoded in each card." She continues, "Through gesture, posture, and inclusion of arcane symbols and objects, I hope to use this chiefly androgynous form to bridge a gap between sex, race, and age." The drawings were made circa 1994.

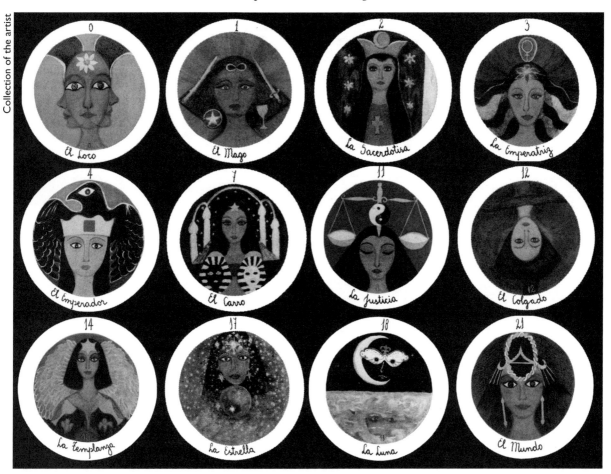

Collection of the artist

Metaphysic Tarot   Cecilia Mayer-Rechnitz, circa 1992

Michael's Tarot   Michael Kutzer, 1989   LEFT GROUP, TOP ROW: Magician. Wheel of Fortune. Justice.   BOTTOM ROW: The Moon. The Devil. The Star.   AT RIGHT: The Hermit as Chronos/Saturn is an extra proof that was not included in the published decks.

Images courtesy of Tarot Garden (tarotgarden.com)

Collection of the author

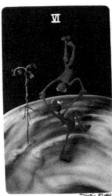

Collection of the artist / © 1994 by Inslee and Diorio

Millenia Tarot Joe Diorio, artist, and Catherine Inslee, 1994

Millennium Tarot Julia and David Line, 1995
Temperance. The Sun.

Collection of the artist

Millenium Tarot The Millenium Tarot applies medieval imagery to the Book of Revelations in the New Testament. The circular design is intended to allow interpretation depending on the way that cards fall against compass points. Julia and David Line created the designs circa 1995.

Millsennium Tarot Denis Mills describes his Major Arcana as "unashamedly romantic in its concept. It employs bright colors with flowers, astrological signs, and mystic symbols. All designs have a basic architectural format with the figures woven into the picture, often as part of the background pattern." Mills is an architect, graphic designer, and painter living in Wales. The originals were painted in gouache in 1995.

Mimotarot Mexican artist Alfredo Valero R. created a deck that merges tarot symbolism with the art of pantomime. In a letter to Stuart Kaplan, he writes, "This deck follows a minimalist principle in which the performers stand by themselves with no scenery, no colors—even their bodies are painted flat. However, the brain 'reads' them accurately, thanks to the principle of continuity. The mime's only interaction is with the typography, and she/he is supposed to represent each Major Arcana only with his/her performance. Just the art and body communicate the concept of every Arcana." The Mimotarot was created in 1993 in black and white. The artwork includes a title card and back design.

Minimalist Tarot The Minimalist Tarot was created "for those who might have given thought to taking up tarot, but have been put off by a perception that more traditional pictorial decks are too 'occult' and incomprehensible," according to Samantha Lynn, editor at Woodhull & Desmoulins Press, England. The deck was created circa 1996; no credit for the artist was given with the samples of the cards.

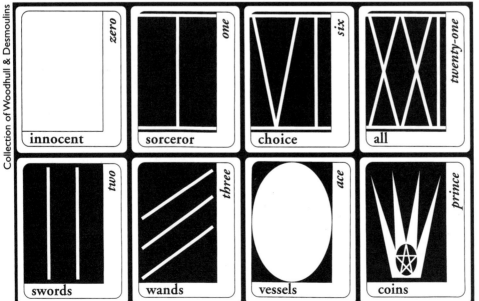

Collection of Woodhull & Desmoulins

Minimalist Tarot Artist unknown (from Woodhull & Desmoulins Press), circa 1996

Collection of the artist

Millsennium Tarot Denis Mills, 1995 The titles of the cards are from the artist's correspondence with Stuart Kaplan.
TOP ROW: 0 The Fool. 1 The Magician. 2 The Female Pope. 3 The Empress. 4. The Emperor.
SECOND ROW: 5 The Pope. 6 The Lovers. 7 The Chariot. 8 Strength. 9 The Hermit.
THIRD ROW: 10 The Wheel of Fortune. 11 Justice. 12 The Hanging Man. 13 (untitled). 14 Temperance.
BOTTOM ROW: 16 The Tower. 17 The Star. 18 The Moon. 19 The Sun. 21 The World.

Mimotarot back design The skillful fingers of the Mime hold a card that is like a dark and empty stage. With lights or without them, the Mime will be able to enliven this stage as he performs an exercise of style in twenty-two acts.

Mimotarot Alfredo Valero R., 1993 The descriptions are by the artist.

TOP ROW: **El Loco** (The Fool). Most observers will call him "mad"; that's the price he must pay for being original and "different" from the rest. **1 El Mago** (The Magician). The Mime's hands are the base and focal point of his corporal expression. With them, he manipulates objects made of pure imagination. He creates a bird whose flapping stirs up our senses. **6 Los Amantes** (The Lovers). The Mime finds inspiration in any phenomenon of nature, but the most sublime inspiration comes from his lover. He gets on his knees and kisses her hand to show a deep respect. When she is not there, he feels lonely and empty. **11 La Fuerza** (Strength). Tense muscles, frowning, and fists are minimal demonstrations compared to the internal strength that floods her body. She wants to demonstrate that her weakness isn't and has never been real.

BOTTOM ROW: **13 La Muerte** (Death) The She-Mime's body imitates the form of a scythe, while her head follows the horizon and lets her last breath escape. To her, death is another transformation of matter, so whatever she did with her living energy doesn't matter anymore. **15 El Diablo** (The Devil). His evil and threatening expression is a logical result of the certainty that floods his mind. He justifies his attitude by calling himself an essential part of balance and demanding fifty percent of all merit. After all, good would never exist without evil and vice versa. **17 La Estrella** (The Star). Watching the sunset, the extremities of the She-Mime represent the five points of a star. Balancing on the invisible threads of the celestial vault, the stars present a pantomime with bears, scorpions, twins, and a whole variety of mythological characters. **18 La Luna** (The Moon). Who has ever wished to touch the moon? The She-Mime surrendered to the temptation and now balances on her arms the only natural satellite of our planet. Her torso and legs form a moon in first quarter. Her inspiration increases when she perceives the mystical light of the nocturnal body. **19 El Sol** (The Sun). The Mime discovers that his hands are like two suns. One tries to eclipse the other. Both of them have their own brilliance and can dazzle the most skeptical of spectators. His flaming fingers caress high temperatures in the scale of expressiveness. When on stage he radiates warmth and joy.

Tarot Mobile The Tarot Mobile by Emilio C. Ramirez of Mexico is meant to inspire meditation on relations between cards. The mobile comprises eleven small Tarot of Marseilles cards, with a face on both sides of each card so that all the Major Arcana are represented. The mobile came with a leaflet giving thoughts on the relations between some of the cards, with the final thought: "There is a long list of relations about this Tarot Mobile and the Wisdom of the Ages, but the important thing is that you meditate and see within yourself."

Modern Folk Tarot Eric E. Roberts made the Modern Folk Tarot in 2003, using a primitive style in the tradition of folk art.

Tarot Mobile Emilio C. Ramirez, 1989

Modern Folk Tarot Eric E. Roberts, 2003

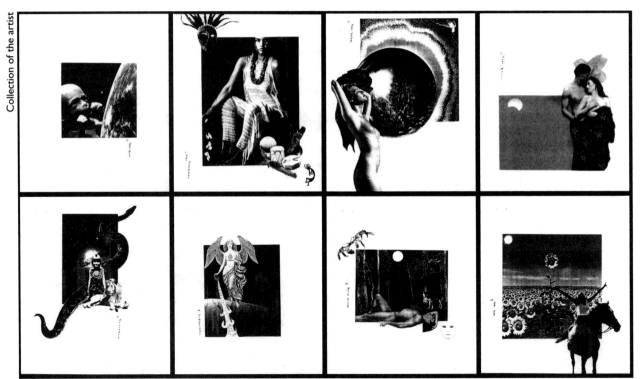

Moon Dreamer's Web Tarot Anna Noriega used montage technique to create the Moon Dreamer's Web Tarot. About the tarot, the artist says, "Within the context of the here and the now, the perceived physical surroundings are interpreted by all of us in a purely individual manner. Similarly, the tarot cards' traditional interpretations are like mirrors pointing to the heart's path." Moon Dreamer's Web Tarot was made circa 1991.

Motherwell Tarot Dickie Motherwell of Canada describes the Motherwell Tarot: "These cards speak of the New Age, where humanity finds peace through simplicity and positive thinking. We are moving into a time when a universal currency will stabilize our economic system. A universal language will enable us to communicate and consequently enhance acceptance and understanding. Mankind is evolving and, through this, is forming an alliance which promotes respect for the human spirit as well as any and all beliefs that connect us to our higher selves. The Motherwell Tarot deck attempts to relate these ideas and promote healing and higher consciousness." The artwork was created in different places in the United States and Canada in 1991 and 1992.

Moon Dreamer's Web Tarot Anna Noriega, circa 1991
TOP ROW: 0 The Fool. 1 The Shaman. 3 The Lady.
6 Soul Mates.
BOTTOM ROW: 11 Strength. 14 Temperance.
18 Moon Dreamer. 19 The Sun.

Mundane Tarot Mary Beth Cantwell's goal in creating the Mundane Tarot was "to make the ideas of the tarot more accessible for the 1990s and to create a household oracle that would be simpler for everyday readings. The basic meanings behind the cards remain the same, but modern imagery replaces the arcane, demystifying (undressing) the tarot, leaving it in its natural form. Supernatural beings have been replaced by ordinary ones, making this the Mundane Tarot."

Mundane Tarot Mary Beth Cantwell, 1990s

Motherwell Tarot   Dickie Motherwell, 1992
Descriptions are based on those by the artist.

TOP ROW: **I The Magician** conjures up the love vibration to heal the planet. Diplomatic Maggie, the cat, watches his creative visualization. **III The Empress** is a loving Hawaiian queen who cuddles a small child, displaying her natural affinity for motherhood and creativity. **V The Hierophant** depicts the judicial authority found in religious institutions. He is a Holy Man, and the ceremonies he performs are symbols of our solidarity with the church. **IX The Hermitess** has withdrawn from companionship, as she finds her path more productive when traveling alone. She lights the way for the world with her knowledge and fulfills her sense of purpose while being a recluse. **X The Wheel of Fortune.** A soft breeze moves through this wind harp, creating sound vibrations seemingly at random. The symbols floating around the harp represent the variables of chance.

BOTTOM ROW: **XV The Devil.** Associated with a ball and chain are the addictions of pain, alcohol, cocaine, marijuana, and sex. All of these compulsive behaviors will produce a state of bondage if not kept under control. **Two of Swords.** Maggie is expertly balancing two swords tip to tip. She cannot afford to look at anything other than the swords, and her concentration must remain focused. One can find an element of peace while being so absorbed because one becomes detached from outside influences. **Eight of Wands.** Maggie and Jiggs love each other very much and always stay in touch. The telephone poles represent speedy communication and news. **Nine of Cups.** A smiling Hatoi holds two black pearls while being encircled by nine cups. This is a picture of happiness, material wealth, and physical well-being. This monk has transcended negativity and found freedom through inner peace. **King of Disks** holds a globe disk in his hand and envisions the future with purpose. He is a mastermind in the circulation of money and uses his natural resources in creating sound finance.

Mwezi Tarot   The Mwezi Tarot is described by artist Judith Elaine as an African form of divination. "The African Sangoma believe that the ancestral spirits play a vital role in life and that lessons can be learned from their age-old wisdom." The deck, which was completed in 2000, comprises five elements: the Minor Arcana, which correspond to air, fire, water, and earth, and the Major Arcana, or spiritual element. Symbols on each card give clues as to the interpretation. For example, a running stick figure indicates joy and happiness. The court cards are messenger, warrior, queen-chieftain, and king-chief. The Major Arcana has an extra card, which is called the "blank" card, even though it has artwork. "The large eye on the blank card represents seeing too much, or not being able to see." In a divination, the blank card indicates that the question or situation should not be addressed at the time.

Mythological Tarot   Sarah Scott Parry peopled the Mythological Tarot with the deities of ancient Greece and Rome.

New Millennium Tarot   "My inspiration for this deck was to create strong, colorful designs that boldly express the core energy of each card," says Amy Ericksen, creator of the New Millennium Tarot. "The characters are not of any particular race or religion, but are representatives of the spirits I see embodying the energies that create our universe…. The characters in the Major Arcana are timeless mythological beings who share their limitless love and zest for creation and wisdom with whoever requests it. The Minor Arcana are four elemental families. The pip cards illustrate how the numbers one through ten manifest in each family's elemental realm, and they are based on the book *A Beginner's Guide to Constructing the Universe,* by Michael S. Schneider." The New Millennium Tarot was completed in August 1999 in gouache and watercolor on watercolor paper.

Mwezi Tarot   Judith Elaine, 2000   Titles are by the artist.

TOP ROW: 0 The Fool: Purity. 1 The Magician: Four Elements. 7 The Chariot: Determination. 9 The Hermit: Learner. 10 Wheel of Fortune: Cycles.

SECOND ROW: 14 Temperance: Balance. 16 Tower: New Beginnings. 17 The Star: Inspiration. 18 The Moon. 19 The Sun: Success.

BOTTOM ROW: 21 The World: Completion. Messenger Bird of Clear Quartz (Messenger of Thoughts and Conflict). Warrior of Jasper. Three of Rose Quartz: Celebrations. Four of Tiger Eyes: Greed.

Mythological Arcana   Sarah Scott Parry, circa 1990   Descriptions are by the artist.

TOP ROW: **0 Fool: Icarus.** Daedalus made for himself and his son wings, to escape from an island prison. Icarus flew too near the sun, and the heat melted the wax by which the feathers were fastened. He fell into the sea and drowned. **1 Magician: Circe** was the goddess of prophecy. **2 Papess: Athena** sprang fully grown and armed from the head of Zeus. She was goddess of Athens and personified wisdom. **3 Empress: Aphrodite** was goddess of love and fertility.

SECOND ROW: **4 Emperor: Zeus** was looked on as the highest civic god, the father of gods and men, and most powerful of the immortals. **6 Lovers: Eros** was the Greek god of love. In Hellenistic times he was portrayed as Cupid, a mischievous child. **9 Hermit: Hypnos** was the Greek god of sleep. He lived in the underworld and never saw the light of day. **10 Wheel: Cyclops** was a gigantic being with a single eye in the center of the forehead.

BOTTOM ROW: **11 Fortitude: Heracles** was a son of Zeus by a mortal woman. His strength and prowess were incomparable. Even as a newborn infant, he strangled two serpents that attacked him in his cradle. **13 Death: Charon** ferried the souls of the dead across the River Styx. His fee was a coin placed in the mouth of each corpse. **15 Devil: Siren** was a nymph whose enchanting song lured sailors to their deaths on the rocks. **19 Sun: Helios** was the Greek god of the sun.

133

New Millennium Tarot   Amy Ericksen, 1999   The descriptions are by the artist.   TOP ROW: **0 Fool.** A unisex spirit steps with the limitless flow of the universe through space and time. A golden beam of divine energy guides and protects her. Her decorations and antlers express mystery and play. **1 Magician.** An artist combines and balances male and female energies. He allows himself to become a channel for divine creation. **3 Empress.** A giant goddess gives birth to the universe. She expresses the abundance and variety of all that is. **4 Emperor.** A god seeds the growth and form of creation. His clear vision uplifts, liberates, and expands reality. **5 Priest.** A man in communion with nature sees the connection of all within heaven and earth.

SECOND ROW: **6 Lovers.** Two spirits express the limitless joy and love of the universe. They are amused by what is known without words. **9 Hermit. 11 Justice. 13 Death. 15 Devil.** An angry being expresses the frustration and confusion of outward separations.

BOTTOM ROW: **17 Star. Knight of Air. 5 of Fire. 7 of Water. Queen of Earth.** A tree woman reigns in the beauty and bounty of nature. Her gifts are freely given.

New Millenium Tarot   Lee Varis created Major Arcana designs by combining digital photography, illustration, and 3D rendering on computer. About his cards, he says, "The New Millenium Tarot is conceived as a bridge between the esoteric knowledge of past ages and the new Aquarian Age of enlightenment we are now entering. The advent of the computer has provided new tools for the expansion of human awareness, and these tools provide a way to re-imagine the tarot for the modern, quantum-conscious, multimedia-inspired cyberculture. This tarot uses computer imaging techniques to create a repository of knowledge about the human condition encoded in multilevel symbolic imagery." Some of the designs were printed in the April 2001 issue of *PEI: Photo>Electronic Imaging* magazine.

New Millenium Tarot   Lee Varis, 2001

Nimue Tarot "The Nimue Tarot deck is a random collection of sketches inspired by poems, fragments of literature, and songs both classical and contemporary, dreams and visions," writes Vivien Stewart-Jones. "The name Nimue Tarot reflects my name Vivien and the legend of Nimue, though this theme was not used in the deck." Nimue, or Vivienne, is the Lady of the Lake, of Arthurian legend. The designs were first sketched, then composed with graphics software in 2001.

Tarot Noir "From whatever vantage point, we gaze through life's smoke and mirrors at the stuff we're all afraid to see," Sandy Sussman writes, introducing her tarot designs. "From whatever level of comfort, we ride currents of night, shadow, and romance and its intrigue in order to figure what's real. In an authentic language of painted imagery and channeled messages, Tarot Noir builds a bridge across the hot, asphalt streets of the human condition to reach the other side, where the sultry, poetic voice of an angel whispers to us that 'knowledge is love.'" The designs were painted in black and white, with colored borders, and completed in 2002. The deck has twenty-two Major Arcana numbered in Roman numerals. The Minor Arcana are replaced by Arabic numbered cards 22 through 72.

Nimue Tarot   Vivien Stewart-Jones, 2001

Tarot Noir Sandy Sussman, 2002 Descriptions are excerpted from text by the artist.

TOP ROW: **0 TRICKS.** Fleet-footed Messenger, bearer of Dreams, the Fool heralds an Experience of Journey and Destination. Camouflaging Grace with the swift pace of ordinary events, the inner Trickster teaches that there is Nothing to lose, Everywhere to go, and that the only way around a problem is Through it. **I MAGIC.** Like the snake, the Magician is a master of charm and Power. When goals are clearly connected to the great work of Evolution, the resulting Alchemy produces golden Understanding. **III LADY IN RED.** Giver of Life, mother of Self-invention, Intelligence behind the great Wheel of karmic connections, the Empress authors an Earthsong to which all souls resonate. **IV HE.** The Male Soul personifies responsible Leadership, yet the Man is always surprised to gaze within Life's Mirror at a young Boy who wears the Emperor's new clothes. If he is wise, he balances the cherished Image of Youth with the Authority of his sacred Command; only through Compassion will he discover the treasured goal of a place in History. **V RITUAL.** The Hierophant overcomes obstacles through the art of Confrontation.

SECOND ROW: **XII EGO.** The Hanged Man projects his own image onto Reality's silver screen. Until karmic Truth is accepted, outside Activity will threaten his ambivalent position; he will hang, in mute suspension, until a message arrives, bearing the possibility of Rebirth. **XIII REBIRTH.** When the veil of Ignorance lifts, an untranslatable Beauty is revealed, whose Light shines on in the Before and Hereafter. **XIV**

PURITY. Consciously stalking the purifying baptism of Temperance helps one master the skill of Balance; Eagles and Lions merge to reveal a true picture of Wholeness. **XX MEMORY.** Accompanied by a trumpet-like Sound, a Moment arrives when bands of Remembrance loosen and the Ark opens to reveal mirrorlike jewels of true Memory. Illusions of Individuality vanish in the regenerating Sight of one eternal Self. **25 AWAKENING.** The Past is gone, and a new Archetype emerges from its cocoon, wanting only to dance, like a butterfly, on platforms of Vision.

BOTTOM ROW: **27 TURNING POINT.** When one Path ends and another begins, there is a Moment wherein only one Action is possible; the Initiate understands how to consciously surrender Will as this state of Suspended Animation appears. **28 REUNION.** Seeing the longed-for face of Love lights up the Soul and completes a Cycle. **45 EXPERIENCE.** The Fool falls into a World of Experience just as the Art of Detachment is mastered. Acknowledging ones' personal History is valuable, for it is then no longer doomed to karmic Repetition, and the Future can be entered with a lighter Heart. **48 CLOUD DOG.** The variegated Colors of Nature sharpen and reveal a pantheon of friendly, half-remembered Shapes in the Sky: castles in clouds, cats in boots, scary monsters with long tails. Sometimes, one has to lose Focus in order to truly See. **65 DON'T LOOK BACK.** Like Orpheus pausing for a fatal glimpse of his lover, Doubt can drown Hope in the Underworld's depths. Crawling through Yesterday's dark tunnel toward the Light of an everpresent, ever changing Now is a necessary Ascent.

Omaggio a Galileo Chini (Homage to Galileo Chini)
Amerigo Folchi, 1992

Omaggio a Galileo Chini (Homage to Galileo Chini) Amerigo Folchi created this deck in homage to his fellow artist Galileo Chini (1873–1956). Born in Tuscany, Chini was known for working in the flowing, decorative Liberty style of the 1920s and 1930s. Chini worked in a wide variety of media, including painting, glass, fresco, ceramics, and costume. According to K. Frank Jensen, writing in *Manteia* (no. 7, July 1992), Folchi was inspired to make the deck after seeing Chini's decorations in the central pavilion of the Venice Biennàle. The Homage was made in 1992.

Paul O'Meara Tarot   Paul O'Meara conceived his tarot deck "whilst walking my dog under rolling summer clouds. The images that I had programmed into my subconscious over many years began taking form in the ever changing sky. This is why clouds form the basis of the images in this deck. I have tried to portray the exact images that I saw coming alive far beyond the usual painted two-dimensional card." O'Meara made his designs using computer software and completed them circa 1998.

Paul O'Meara Tarot   Circa 1998

The Magician

The World

King of Wands

Queen of Wands

One in Ten Tarot   Shandra MacNeill, 2001

One in Ten Tarot   Shandra MacNeill created a limited edition of ten Major Arcana decks, each one drawn in ink and hand-painted in watercolor. The deck in the author's collection has gold borders applied in thick gold paint. The backs are heavily textured maroon paper. The decks were issued in 2001. The deck came in a blue silk pouch on which is hand-written, "One in Ten Tarot / #9/10 / Shandra MacNeill / 2001."

The deck was also issued in reproduction editions, in 2004, with faces printed, not hand-painted. The Gold Edition was 100 decks with gold edging, and the Silver Edition was also of 100 decks, with no decorative edging. Both Gold and Silver editions were signed and numbered by the artist.

Ouroboros Mail Artists' Tarot The Ourobouros Mail Artists' Tarot was coordinated by tarotist K. Frank Jensen of Denmark. Thirty-three artists from all over the world were requested by mail to design two Major Arcana cards each. Jensen provided each artist with templates labeled with the titles of the cards requested. In the booklet accompanying the deck, Jensen describes his production process. "The cards were color-copied on 160-grammes paper, four on a sheet, and the copier was adjusted so they received an extra silicone oil covering during the copying process. When finished, the sheets were mounted on black Chromolux cardboard, trimmed, and corners rounded, one by one." Jensen adds, for anyone considering a similar project, "Beware, however, the method is extraordinarily time consuming!"

The deck was issued by Ouroboros of Roskilde, Denmark, in 1998 in a numbered, limited edition of twenty-five. Additionally, each contributor received a deck of twenty-three cards: a full Major Arcana including one of the cards designed by the artist, plus the other card designed by the artist. The book accompanying the deck includes all sixty-six cards represented in color, so that each artist can see the contributions by the other artists, and to give credit to all the artists.

Jensen also produced mail art tarots, which were documented as photocopies in booklets, in 1993, 1994, and 1995.

Mail art emerged in the 1970s; the American artist David Zack is credited for coining the term. The process begins when the coordinator invites contributions to a mail art project. Usually the project will have a theme, for example, tarot in general, or one tarot card. The solicitation for art and the art itself is sent by post or by e-mail. The project may be documented in the form of a photocopied book, with copies sent to the contributors, or as a web page. Sometimes the art is also exhibited in a gallery. Mail art is not so much about the actual artwork as about the process: coordinating a project, and creating, mailing, receiving, and documenting the art. Other media associated with mail art are collage and montage, postage-type stamps, rubber stamps, and zines.

Ovum Tarot The Ovum Tarot was first made by Klaus Müsebeck in 1986 as a series of primitive drawings (see *The Encyclopedia of Tarot,* volume I). The graphic designer Katharina von Saalfeld redrew the deck to be published in Müsebeck's book *Jeder ist ein Tarot-Mensch* (Everyone Is a Tarot Person). The book was published by Aurum Westermann Verlag Braunschweig in 1990. The author describes the deck: "The name of Ovum Tarot evolved from the idea that the visual images of the archetypes arise *ex ovo,* which means from the DNA code.... If all tarot systems are compared, it is possible to imagine the existence of a *kollektives Unbewusstes* (collective unconscious). The categories and the numbers of the Major Arcana are exactly the same. Ovum Tarot has been adapted to the triune brain model [developed by neurobiologist Paul McLean]. The figures of 0 to V are a metaphor of the functions of the neocortex. VI to VII represent the limbic system, and XVIII to XXI correspond to the basic arousal system which refers to biorhythms. [This system is also called the reptilian brain as it is considered to have evolved earliest.] The white figures arise in the consciousness out of the dark background of the unconscious."

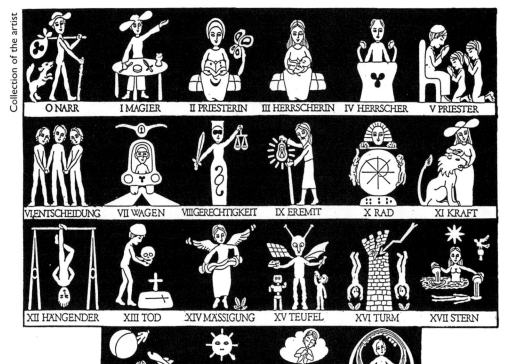

Collection of the artist

Ovum Tarot
Katharina von Saalfeld, artist, and
Klaus Müsebeck   1990

Ouroboros Mail Artists' Tarot   K. Frank Jensen, coordinator, 1998   TOP ROW: **0 The Fool** by Monica Talamas, Uruguay. **0 The Fool** by Henk van Setten, The Netherlands. **0 The Fool** by G.M.W.K.S.J., Denmark. **I The Magician** by Louise Heroux, Canada. **IV The Emperor** by Michael Kutzer, Germany.   SECOND ROW: **V The Hierophant** by Ivan A. Antonazzo, Italy. **V The Hierophant** by Georg Lipinsky, Germany. **V The Hierophant** by Georg Lipinsky, The Netherlands. **VI The Lovers** by Claudio Parentela, Italy. **VIII Strength** by Marilyn Dammann, USA.   THIRD ROW: **IX The Hermit** by Ralf Schröer, Germany. **IX The Hermit** by Klaus Rupp (Merlin), Germany. **XI Justice** by Guido Vermeulen, Belgium. **XII The Hanged Man** by Judith Nems, France. **XII The Hanged Man** by Barbara Hilmer Schröer, Germany. BOTTOM ROW: **XIV Temperance** by Anne Nomrowsky, Germany. **XV The Devil** by Dietmar Vollmer, Germany. **XVI The Tower** by David Dellafiora, Australia. **XVII The Star** by Arnell Ando, USA. **20 Judgement** by Willi Melnikow, Russia.

141

Magazine collection of the author

Oz Magazine Tarot   Martin Sharp, 1967

Oz **Magazine Tarot**   The May 1967 issue of the London magazine *Oz* included a poster with Major Arcana by Martin Sharp, a renowned pop artist. Most of the cards were made as montages of printed and original illustrations. The style captures the psychedelic wave of the 1960s. The London *Oz* magazine was published from 1967 to November 1973. (Its predecessor, the Australian *Oz*, started publication on April Fool's Day of 1963 and lasted only a few years.)

Tarot of Paper   The Tarot of Paper is made of paper cutouts painted in watercolor. Each "card" is actually a mini-theater, with the cutout figures posed against painted backdrops, and props and paper clothes glued to

Anna Gioia Del Fauro at work on the **Tarot of Paper**

them. The artist, Anna Gioia Del Fauro, photographed the dioramas to form the card illustrations. The Major Arcana scenes were created circa 1994.

Collection of the artist

Tarot of Paper Anna Gioia Del Fauro, circa 1994 TOP ROW: 0 Il Matto (The Fool). I Il Mago (The Magician). II La Papessa (The Popess). III L'Imperatrice (The Empress). SECOND ROW: VII Il Carro (The Chariot). VIII La Giustizia (Justice). VIIII L'Eremita (The Hermit). X La Ruota Della Fortuna (The Wheel of Fortune). THIRD ROW: XI La Fortezza (Strength). XII L'Appiccato (The Hanged Man). XIII La Morte (Death). XIIII La Temperanza (Temperance). BOTTOM ROW: XV Il Diavolo (The Devil). XVII La Stella (The Star). XVIII La Luna (The Moon). Gli Attori (The Actors) is an assembly of the entire "cast" of the Tarot of Paper.

Parry Tarot   Sarah Scott Parry, circa 1995

Sarah Scott Parry is a prolific artist of the tarot. From the 1980s on, she has created many one-of-a-kind decks focused on themes, such as toys or holidays. Her medium is usually pen and ink and watercolor, with titles and numbering applied by stick-on letters. A sense of childlike fantasy runs through her works. • Sarah Scott Parry's decks included in this volume are: Childhood, Christmas, Costume, Marine, Mythology, Parry, and Shell. • Tarot designs by Parry (then listed as Sarah Scott) were also featured in volume 3 of *The Encyclopedia of Tarot:* Acuna Arcana, Bird Tarot, Butterfly Tarot, Dibujar Arcana, Fantasy Arcana, Geometrize Tarot, Insect Tarot, Jungle Arcana, Natalie Arcana, Old Fashioned 1940s Tarot, Oriental Arcana, Picture Arcana.

Natalie Parry Tarot   The daughter of Sarah Scott Parry has followed in her mother's footsteps to create a tarot design. Her rendering of the Moon was made in 1992, when she was nine years old.

Parry Tarot   The Major Arcana set to which Sarah Scott Parry gave her own name combines elements that thread through her works: nature, fantasy, and myth, and childlike characters who may find themselves in dark situations.

Tarot de Parthenay   Different artists designed postcards featuring Major Arcana. The edition was limited to 650 sets, issued in December 1986. Club de Tarot de Parthenay is a French club dedicated to the game of tarot.

Pete's Brewing Company Tarot   In 1997, Pete's Brewing Company of Palo Alto, California, issued a limited edition of glasses and coasters with four tarot images. The company calls its beer "Pete's Wicked Brews." The name of the artist was not indicated.

The Moon
Natalie Parry, 1992

Tarot de Parthenay 1986 The names of the artists follow the titles of the cards. TOP ROW: **0 Le Fou** (Yvon Kervinio). **2 La Papesse** (Charles Berg). **3 L'Impératrice** (Camille Gougnard). **4 L'Empereur** (Jacques Lardie). SECOND ROW: **6 L'Amoureux** (Tinou). **9 L'Hermite** (J.B. Garon). **12 Le Pendu** (E. Quentin). **14 La Tempérance** (Michel Bordas). BOTTOM ROW: **16 La Maison Dieu** (Pierre Jeudy). **17 L'Etoile** (Marc Ledogar). **19 Le Soleil** (Danny). **21 Le Monde** (Flo).

Pete's Brewing Company Tarot 1997 The caption is "the tarot's wicked symbolism," from the back of the coasters. **The Fool** and his dog symbolize fun, folly and the all-around enjoyment of life—the things drinkers of Pete's Wicked Brews cherish. The spilled beer signifies a major party foul. **VIII Strength.** The strong man carrying the keg symbolizes the struggle to choose between each of the finely crafted Pete's Wicked Brews. And the exalted, all-powerful King of the Jungle represents…well…a big lion. **XX Judgement.** Weirdness aside, the flying woman symbolizes the unselfish nature of anyone serving Pete's Wicked Brews. The patrons with raised glasses represent anyone who wants her to just hurry up and pour something Wicked.

Photographic Tarot Photographer, author, and artist Martin Timm describes the Major Arcana he created: "The deck consists of twenty-two metaphorical still lifes showing preponderantly religious motifs in a polarity between artificial and realistic imagery: A photo of a doll is an 'image in an image'—the image of a baby in a photographic image. The medium is photography, a technique that is said to cause a higher illusion of reality than painting or sculptural art. The images are abstract. The message does not necessarily deal with the objects themselves. Those objects mostly represent nothing but symbols; they may produce associated pictures in our minds.

"The extreme horizontal format represents the wish to stay comfortable, which carries the danger of stagnation. The illumination of the objects plays a certain role. Referring to the words spoken by Jesus, 'I am the light of the world,' the evangelist John develops his metaphysics of light and illumination. According to Plato, light is truth, purity, and beauty. Black means night, sleep, dream, the unconsciousness, the shadow of C.G. Jung's theory—the attributes that we fear as extremely immoral. But in the darkness, it is easier to produce free imagination." The deck was first shown at the gallery "in focus" in Cologne, Germany, in 1993.

Photographic Tarot Martin Timm, 1993 Descriptions are by the artist.

TOP ROW: **Narr** (Fool) is Shakespeare's fool giving advice to King Lear. He is also our own childhood in its unspoiled wisdom and its wish to become adult. He marks both the first step in the Major Arcana sequence and its climax. The toys symbolize: In the beginning there was and is always the game. The feather stands for the ease and lightness that we lose when growing up and wish back or find again in the relaxation of old age. Sometimes this *animus simplex* helps us to dare jump from one step of development to the next. **Hierophantin** (High Priestess) represents the *femina saga,* that wise old woman turning the Magician's "fire into a flame." From the old Greeks and Egyptians we know her as the female hierophant in the mysteries of initiation. The middle ages taught us about the midwives, women of herbal lore and natural medicine and fortune-tellers accused as witches tied to Satan, so that many of them had to die on the pyres of the Inquisition.

SECOND ROW: **Regentin** (Empress). The composition of an orchid, the queen of flowers, and two apples combines the superiority of majesty and a Biblical symbol of worldly womanliness and fertility, and erotic, clerical sin. We can find these two apples in the "Song of Solomon." The Empress expresses the mystery of womanliness, beginning with the antique goddesses of love and fertility, the Madonnas, and the matriarchs reflecting C.G. Jung's *anima.* **Regent** (Emperor) shows us C.G. Jung's *animus* in his "male honor," respectable, sovereign, and capable and, on the other side, a non-spiritual patriarch, violent and addicted to big objects. He is the archetypal father fighting between real, true, and conscious authority and worldly, primitive strength. He represents the antique image of manliness by the simplicity of typical male accessories.

THIRD ROW: **Siegeswagen** (Chariot). Triumphing over the parental family life of his home, the aspirant goes out to find his individual place and how wide his personal area is. The children's bikes symbolize that leaving home at the right time is a positive step forward. The Chariot is also a show of success. With the Chariot you follow your desire to show off and gain prestige. **Gerechtigkeit** (Justice). Weighing is aimed

at producing symmetry, balance, and compensation. Justitia's scales are determined to compare guilt and expiation, deserving and reward, symbolized by the fir cones. She is trying to find all bountiful beauty and harmony. She asks for morality and the essential guilt of man.

FOURTH ROW: **Hangene** (Hanged One) can represent punishment, humiliation, unwilling martyrdom, or the initiation of a contemplative. The doll boy hangs in isolation from the doll family. **Mond** (Moon). Noctiluca, the Goddess Who Shines in the Night, reminds us that the image of the moon is full of legends and myths of darkness and night, sleep, dream, and unconsciousness, symbolized here by the totem pole. The connection between the female image and the moon is found in the female cycle and in the phases of the moon, as well as the traditional correlation of Empedocles' element water because the moon causes the movement of the tides. According to tradition, the moon reflects the energy of the mythological male sun.

BOTTOM ROW: **Sonne** (Sun). The sun has been, for most cultures, a male character. So this card brings together brightness, symbolized by the flash bulbs, and manliness, symbolized by a man's hairy thighs. These "objects" are set into a formal analogy by their visual resemblance to each other. The sun gives life and mental brightness, and according to the evangelist John, light is beauty, purity, and truth. But where there is light, there is shadow, too. The sun can blind us and destroy life by dryness, as in a desert. So, the sun confronts us with the polarity of brightness and darkness as well as life in nature and its destruction. **Welten-Ei** (World Egg). In the end, there is as a king over the Heavenly Jerusalem the great resurrected sacrifice of the New Testament: an innocent, pure, and white lamb, symbol of the resurrection and of Christ himself. The lamb on this card is the only full, living object in the Major Arcana sequence, so the last card stands for transcendence, an end and at the same time a new beginning on a higher level. This last card symbolizes the analogy between the lost paradise of the Old Testament and the newly gained paradise of the New Testament in the image of the Heavenly Jerusalem. After having got back the original union of man, soul, nature, and God, life can start again—nowhere else but on the littlest step, the Fool.

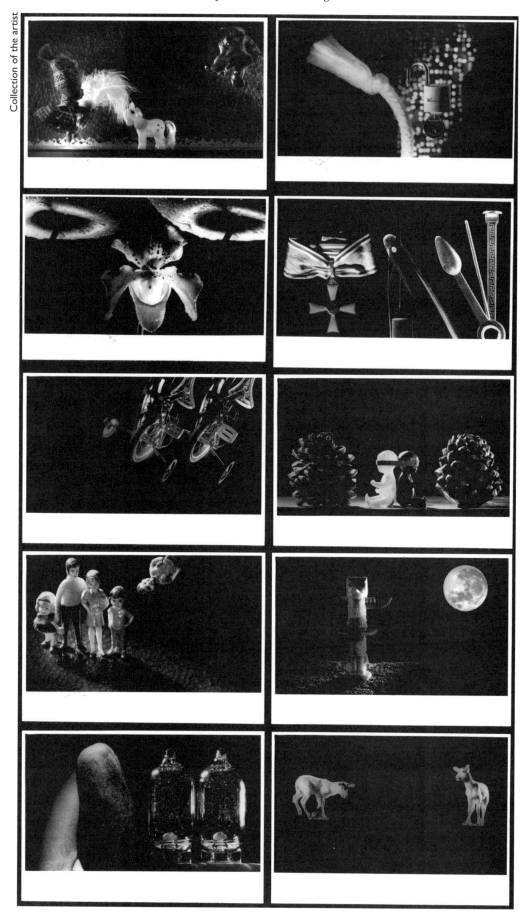

Photographique Tarot   J.J. Salavador, circa 1993
TOP ROW: 0 The Fool. I The Magician. II The Popess. III The Empress. IV The Emperor.
BOTTOM ROW: V The Pope. King of Batons. Page of Cups. Ace of Cups. Three of Coins.

Photographique Tarot   Fashion photographer J.J. Salavador describes his tarot deck as based on the esthetic of the Visconti Tarot and the symbolism of the Tarot of Marseilles. "This game of tarot has the ambition to confront its user with an updated spirit of tarot." The photographs were made circa 1993.

Planet Earth Tarot   The cover of the Aries 1989 issue of *Welcome to the Planet Earth* magazine featured three tarot cards. The cards illustrated an article by Mark Lerner, "The Tarot Comes to Life: Death of the Patriarchy." The article says, "It's not often that the tarot cards literally spring to life through the names and personages gracing the world stage. However, the inspiration for portraying these three cards came to me on Feb. 23 and 24. Just as President Bush was attending the funeral of 'Emperor' Hirohito in Japan, the Senate Armed Services Committee suddenly 'decked' former Senator John Tower, a man striking to become Defense Secretary, as allegations about his use of alcohol and womanizing began surfac-ing.... Then I realized that the Salman Rushdie/Ayatollah Khomeini affair—which reached white-hot proportions as Pluto went stationary in mid-February—had been a version of the Death card." (The Ayatollah Khomeini of Iran considered Rushdie's book *The Satanic Verses* blasphemous and offered a reward to anyone who would kill the author.) *Welcome to the Planet Earth* was published by The Great Bear Press, Eugene, Oregon.

Tarot of the Porta della Luna   The Tarot of the Porta della Luna comprises forty-four cards: the traditional Major Arcana and the "other face" of the Major Arcana, showing the images turned around in some way. "Each card presents its double, and like magic they become forty-four mysterious secrets." The deck was created circa 1998 by La Porta Della Luna, a center for research on magic, located in Bologna. The drawings are by Laura Verzellesi. Each card corresponds to an allegorical tale by Morena Poltronieri and Ernesto Fazioli.

Planet Earth Tarot
Mark Lerner, from the cover of *Welcome to the Planet Earth* magazine, 1989

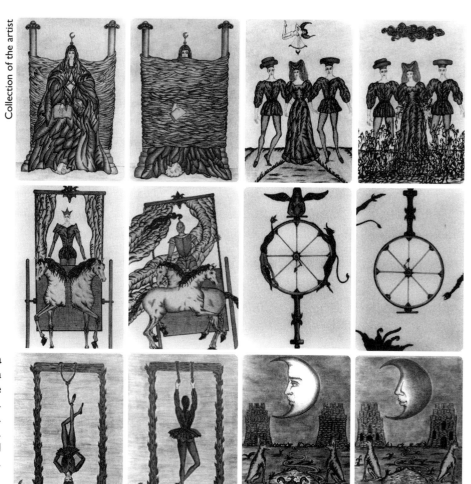

Collection of the artist

Tarot of the Porta della Luna Laura Verzellesi, circa 1998 TOP ROW: The Priestess. The Lovers. SECOND ROW: The Chariot. The Wheel of Fortune. BOTTOM ROW: The Hanged Man. The Moon.

Practical Tarot Ariell Huff thought up the Practical Tarot after a series of encounters with psychics "suggested almost every thinkable earthshaking possibility that could befall a human." However, those dramatic events did not come to pass. "I guess the problem is that like many fortunate people, my life is not earthshaking.... The above methods of prophecy are too drastic and dramatic to define my life." Tongue in cheek, she described in an article the two parts of the Practical Tarot as the Mini Arcana and the Somewhat Bigger Arcana. The article by Huff on the Practical Tarot was printed in the November/December 1990 issue of *Body Mind Spirit* magazine. The illustrations are by Sarah Johnson.

Practical Tarot Sarah Johnson, artist, and Ariell Huff, 1990

Magazine collection of the author

Collection of the artist / © 1996 by Melinda Frank

Practitioner's Tarot
Melinda Frank, 1996

Practitioner's Tarot Melinda Frank created the Practitioner's Tarot as illustrations for a reference diary. Each card would be tabbed and spaces on the pages would allow the tarotist to fill in personal interpretations and notes on the card. The tabs would allow quick access during a tarot reading. The original artwork was painted in acrylics on 2-ply board, then scanned, with lines and titles added on computer. The project dates from 1996.

Pragmatickal Tarot Paul Greener's 1989 Pragmatickal Tarot is based on the Kabbalah "with overtones of the Golden Dawn system," as the artist says in correspondence with Stuart Kaplan. He adds, "I have not hesitated

to use symbols from various other cultures and systems when I felt they did the best job in revealing the essence of a particular card." The artwork was painted in acrylics.

P$ynner Tarot "My inspiration for the P$ynner Tarot deck came from my interests in the occult, namely shamanism, witchcraft, voodoo, Buddhism, or any occult belief having the visual information of fetishes/designs found on ceramics, metalwork, textile, and architecture," says Cindy C. Arriola, artist. "I view each card as a self-portrait and symbolic of my own life, using my own personal imagination, but keeping in the guidelines of the original meanings of the tarot.... The characters look like me—they have big eyes and teeth like me, and the same sarcastic, but happy grin." Arriola made the art in pen and ink and colored pencil in 1993. She used every color of the rainbow in each card, outlined in black. Cindy the P$ynner is the artist's pseudonym. In an interview published at psynner.com, she says, "P$YNNER is a parody of the word 'sinner.' PSY - originates from every word in the dictionary starting with those 3 letters, such as psyche, psychedelic, psycho, etc. The "$" signifies money, which is the root of all evil."

Pragmatickal Tarot Paul Greener, 1989 2 The High Priestess. 12 The Drowned Man. 19 The Sun. Knight of Swords. Ace of Swords.

Collection of the artist

P$ynner Tarot   Cindy C. Arriola, 1993

Peter Ra Tarot 1989 3 The Empress. 4 The Emperor. 5 The Pope. 14 Temperance. Knight of Swords.

Peter Ra Tarot Scottish artist Peter Ra cites as his influences Franco Gentilini, David Palladino, Sergio Minero, and Schikowski, whose work he saw in volume I of *The Encyclopedia of Tarot*. In a letter to Stuart Kaplan, he says, "Most of my work is based on a Rider [Rider-Waite Tarot] foundation. However, I was waiting for the correct feelings to emerge when I was manifesting my Major Arcana, and the deck almost drew itself in a short period of time." The artist left no space for titles on the proto-type cards he created. "It is my belief that anyone who seriously wants to study a beautiful deck would rather have pure pictures impress their unconscious when they go in search of answers within their meditations." Ra created his designs in 1989.

THE MAGICIAN
Art

THE HIGH PRIESTESS
Intuition

THE CHARIOT
Will

THE HANGED MAN
Enlightenment

DEATH
Rebirth

THE STAR
Grace

Rainbow Bridge Tarot Lauren Raine and Duncan Eagleson named their tarot designs Rainbow Bridge Tarot "because it bridges an eclectic mix of contemporary experience and traditional wisdom that constitutes not only the authors' personal inner journey, but the 'rainbow' mix that is evolving into the new spiritual paradigm," the authors say in a letter to Stuart Kaplan. "The 'Rainbow Bridge' is being built by all of those who have been seekers in postmodern urban Western society. It spans the gap between the worlds for those of us who have lost faith in institutionalized religions, but do not come from native cultures with tribal spiritual traditions, and seek new spiritual perspectives." The paintings were made circa 1990. Psychic, author, and poet Lori Lothian also had input on the design of the cards. Several Major Arcana were made available as signed prints.

Rainbow Bridge Tarot Lauren Raine, Duncan Eagleson, and Lori Lothian, circa 1990

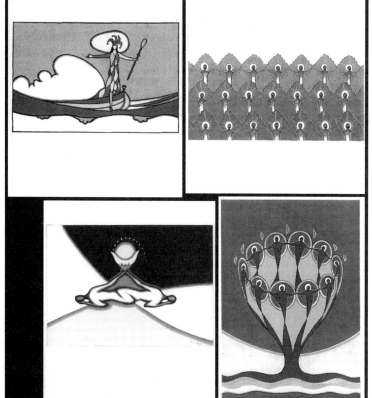

Rambles into Arkanas Tarot   Alexander Egorov, circa 1993   The captions are by the artist   The Fool: The mirror of Master in the desert of freedom. The Empress: The Song. The Lovers: The meeting with myself. The World: The Dance.

Rambles into Arkanas Tarot   Russian artist Alexander Egorov drew a series of pictures based on tarot symbolism, calling them Rambles into Arkanas. The images recall Bauhaus design, with repetition and soft geometrical patterns. The drawings were made circa 1993.

Hovav Rashelbach Tarot   Hovav Rashelbach describes his tarot work in a letter to Stuart Kaplan: "My designs, although modern, use a classical medieval atmosphere, expressed in rich colorful pictures, giving the cards a new style, yet preserving a mystical appeal.... The symbols are based on those described in *The Pictorial Key to the Tarot,* by A.E. Waite, and *Tarot Packs,* by Pierre Louis Ductbartre." The set was made in 1990 as a final project for graduation from the Israel Academy of Art and Design, Bezalel. It was issued as signed prints.

Susan Rashkis Tarot   Montage tarot designs by Susan Rashkis were published in issue 23 (1989) of *Magical Blend* magazine. In the accompanying article by Eileen Katz, she describes the process of putting them together. "I start out with boxes and boxes of images that aren't organized in any way at all. Once I've decided what card I'm working on, I'll take out a big pile of images and, keeping the card in mind, just go through them. I pull

out anything that vaguely relates to the card I've chosen. Then I just keep narrowing it down so that the pile gets smaller and smaller. That's when the really creative, organizational work begins. The whole process is a microcosm of drawing from the creative unconscious." About the tarot itself, Rashkis says, "There are a lot of jokes in my tarot. I think that happens with anything you study for years and years. Eventually all you can do is laugh at it. I think that helps in letting go, and absorbing it."

Razor's Edge Tarot   Jefferson Powers explains the thought behind his tarot designs: "What I have attempted to do here is create new imagery to fit within the traditional tarot framework, imagery that will be easier for a resident of the modern age to interpret. I strongly encourage readers to decide for themselves what each card is supposed to mean, using the provided descriptions as loose guidelines. The only major deviation I have made from tradition has been the creation of a new suit to replace the coins, which seem too limited to financial concerns, and the subsequent pentacles, which are tied too closely to cheesy mysticism. This new suit includes all the day-to-day aspects of existence, and has been renamed clocks to signify time and the way it is used." About the name of the deck, he says, "Here at the end of the 1990s, as we dovetail into a new millennium, many of us feel as though we're dancing on the edge of a razor—one bad step and we're sliced in half before we know what's happened.... What we need, then, is something that will help us to better know our own minds.... For this, I suggest we turn to a tool of self-discovery that has been around for over 500 years: the tarot."

The black and white artwork of the Razor's Edge Tarot was created by manipulating photos with computer software and was completed in 1997.

Hovav Rashelbach Tarot   1991

Susan Rashkis Tarot 1989
TOP ROW: The Magician. The High Priestess. The Chariot. The Hermit.
SECOND ROW: The Moon.

Razor's Edge Tarot Jefferson Powers, 1997

Red Rose Tarot Graeme Davison's circa 1995 tarot designs recall the work of Frank Lloyd Wright (1867–1959) and the Glasgow School movement, which influenced graphic design in the early twentieth century. Davison made two versions: one in black and white, highlighted in red, and the other in full color.

Redneck Tarot Karen Marie Sweikhardt used oil pastel for the Redneck Tarot. She was inspired by the cowboy culture of the American Southwest. The artwork was made circa 1998.

Collection of the artist

Redneck Tarot Karen Marie Sweikhardt, circa 1998 18 The Moon. Ace of Smokes. Two of Pickups.

Red Rose Tarot Graeme Davison, circa 1995

Collection of the artist

THE FOOL · THE MAGICIAN · THE INCARNATION · THE VEHICLE · THE HERMIT

WHEEL OF FORTUNE · BALANCE · THE GARDEN · THE DEVIL · THE TOWER

THE MOON · JUDGEMENT · THE WORLD · MOTHER of WANDS · of COINS

Reincarnation of Adam and Eve Tarot   Mark Timchak, 1996

Reincarnation of Adam and Eve Tarot   Mark Timchak made tarot designs in 1996 using computer graphics. Although inspired by the Rider-Waite deck, the artist made several changes to the traditional tarot. Seven Major Arcana cards are renamed, and Power (Strength) is card 12 while The Hanged Man is card 8. The court cards are named father, mother, son, and daughter.

Diana Reynolds Tarot   Tarot cards are matched with astrological signs in Diana Reynolds' artwork. The Australian artist made the designs circa 1988.

Tarot of the Rishis   The Tarot of the Rishis combines the Hindu pantheon with tarot symbolism. The deck was conceived and designed by Mary Devlin and Thomas K. Dye, and illustrated by Steven Johnson Leyba. Mary Devlin explains, "The rishis are the seers, or diviners, of India…. Ancient Hindu scripture…contains certain goddesses, gods, and other characters whose correspondence with the traditional tarot images and their esoteric, divinatory meaning is too eerily exact to be coincidental." The designs were made between 1994 and 1996.

Diana Reynolds Tarot Circa 1988

Tarot of the Rishis Designed by Mary Devlin and Thomas K. Dye, and illustrated by Steven Johnson Leyba, 1996 Descriptions are by Mary Devlin.

TOP ROW: **O Svetaketu** (The Fool). Svetaketu, the young Brahmin, is just starting his journey toward Self-realization. He stands at the beginning of the Path, looking out at its twists and turns as it advances toward the Light and disappears into the distance. He is leaving behind the trappings of his earthly life. Svetaketu, son of the great seer Uddalaka, is represented in Hindu tradition as a personification of the Brahmin, born to the priestly function, who is still shackled to earthly prejudices and conceits. Yet, in spite of his shortcomings, Svetaketu is a sincere Seeker, committed to his journey. **III Draupadi** (The Empress). Draupadi, a princess in her own right, the wife of five kings including the Samraj of all India, sits enthroned. Her marriage to the five Pandavas certainly proved beneficial for all concerned. Not only did the marriage cement a powerful political alliance that lasted

for many years, Draupadi proved a strong, loyal, and powerful companion. On several occasions Draupadi is credited with actually physically saving lives, and her wisdom proved a constant source of valuable guidance for the Pandavas. Draupadi was also the best of wives in that she bore many children, including five fine sons, one to each of the Pandava brothers. **VI Krishna and Radha** (The Lovers). Lord Krishna sits under a tree and plays his flute, while his lover Radha looks on. Krishna was a young man of unsurpassed beauty, and the village maidens pursued him relentlessly. His favorite was Radha, whom he loved from the moment he first set eyes on her. She was a lovely maiden with black hair, sloe eyes, and honey-golden skin, and she loved Krishna devotedly. Radha is viewed as the ideal wife—faithful, loyal, never wavering in her love. Radha is also perceived as the personification of the soul, and her union with Krishna symbolic of the ultimate reunion of the soul with God.

157

SECOND ROW: **XII Mandavya of the Stake** (The Hanged Man). Arrested by soldiers who suspected him of thievery, Mandavya, the rishi who had taken a vow of silence, refused to defend himself, and so he was condemned to death. The executioners strung him up on a stake, where he remained hanging for days. When his vow of silence expired, he called for his devotees. Aghast, they told the king who he was. The king was mortified, and he lowered the sage to the ground. Mandavya, in spite of the great wrong done him, had faith in the innate justice of the Universe, and therefore accepted his fate and was quick to forgive those responsible for his pain. **XIII Shiva** (Death). Shiva is the God of Death, and thus is a frightening figure, capable of striking terror in the hearts of all who have visions of him. But he is also the God of Rebirth, which has caused some to claim that he is actually more of a lord of sleep than death. Thus Shiva is linked with transformation and regeneration, which can be an inner transformation or regeneration of the human psyche. He is also the god associated with Self-realization, or the dissolution of the individual personality which gives way to Divine Consciousness. Ultimately, Shiva is the death of death—or the God of Eternal Life. **XV Kali** (The Devil). Kali is a war-goddess, slaying all her foes, symbolizing Time which eventually dissolves all creation into the ultimate energy where all distinctions disappear. In our world, where joy and pleasure are associated with bondage to worldly pleasures and possessions, Kali symbolizes a stage where all attachments dissolve. Thus to most humans she appears hideous and fearsome. Kali also personifies the lie that death and leaving behind all we cherish is something to be feared. Yet on the highest level of all Kali signifies no more than the gateway to Supreme Bliss, which all of us, when we reach that gate, will welcome with all our hearts.

THIRD ROW: **XIX Surya** (The Sun) Surya, resplendent god of the sun, oversees the world which he rules. The ancient Hindu masters saw the sun as the giver of light, warmth, knowledge, energy, and life itself. Surya, the sun god, and his sphere are believed to be the gateway to the path of the gods. The sun stands at the center of all creation and symbolizes the ultimate in bliss, manifested as both earthly pleasure and divine ecstasy. Surya is seen as the ultimate source of all earthly pleasure and joy, and he is worshiped with song and dance. **XXI Lakshmi** (The World). Lakshmi, Goddess of Abundance, sits on her lotus in the sky, showering her largess upon all beings. Lakshmi is perhaps the most attractive of goddesses in the Hindu pantheon. She is the goddess of fortune, luck, prosperity, wealth and abundance, and fortunate transitions. Lakshmi, who actually does the work of creating and destroying worlds, is also the ultimate hope of renewed life. Even after the ultimate dissolution of Universes, whether they be personal or cosmic, the hope of future rebirth and new cycles is Lakshmi. Lakshmi is she who ultimately awaits all Seekers. **King of Wands** (Vidura). The sage Vidura is honored with the title of King of Wands. Half-brother to King Pandu and King Dhritarashtra, royal blood runs through his veins, yet since his mother was a member of the Sudra, or peasant class, he was banned from being a king himself. His Sudra blood, however, makes him the perfect King of Wands, the suit traditionally associated with the peasant class. Stories in Hindu literature show that he personifies everything the King of Wands stands for: wisdom, fairness, cleverness, confidence, and idealism.

Collection of the artist / © 1994 by Vladislav Zadrobílek

Rota Tarot   Vladislav Kužel, 1994

Rota Tarot   Vladislav Kužel designed black and white Major Arcana illustrations for Pierre Lasenic's book *Tarot: Klíč Iniciaci,* in 1938. The designs were also published as a color deck some time before World War II. (See *The Encyclopedia of Tarot,* volume III.) Another edition of the book was published in 1994 by Trigon of Prague. In this edition, the illustrations are more filled in with black.

Royal Britain Tarot   Lynn Atkinson created the Royal Britain Tarot from portraits of English royalty, with subjects from the period of the Norman Conquest in 1066 to the end of the Edwardian era in 1910. The roles they take as tarot characters interpret their historical roles. The deck was created in 2001.

Tarot of the Royal Court   Artist Annie Rioux writes, "The forty-two cards of the Tarot of the Royal Court were hand-painted…in acrylic and ink on canvas frames. Great attention is paid to the layering of color, intricately coded by light, luminescent shades, and hues. Overlaid and slightly skewered rectangular frames fan out around the figures. The representations themselves, simplified, stereotypical, and light-hearted in their historicity, are nearly always figural characterizations and are shorn of all but the most essential accouterments of symbolic imagery.… This divestment and the framing color schemes have the effect of emphasizing the portraiture of the individual figure.

"Inspired by the historical context of the Italian Tarocchi, the Tarot of the Royal Court is given a social, historical, and economic context.… The figures carry their historical baggage with the most unconcerned naivete and sport the few symbolic accessories with frank matter-of-factness.…" The paintings were made circa 1996.

Jacob Ruijling Tarot   Dutch tarotist Jacob Ruijling constructed a deck for personal study of Kabbalistic correspondences in the tarot, using a diagram of the Tree of Life, Rider-Waite images, Hebrew letters, and astrological symbols. He notes, "Don't look at the design, for I am not an artist, and don't look at the way it has been made, for I am not a craftsman. If I may bid you politely, only look at the deck as one being made by an amateur, a lover of meditating on and working with the tarot." He made the deck in 1991.

Samantha's Tarot   Samantha Kocsis describes her tarot as "a simple and down-to-earth depiction of tarot's essentials. This deck uses bright and romantic jewel-tone colors as well as a mix of new and traditional images to express a vision of what tarot means to me, in a personal but still accessible way, retaining the intended meanings of the cards." The artwork was done in acrylics and watercolor in 2002.

Collection of the artist

Royal Britain Tarot   Lynn Atkinson, 2001

TOP ROW: **0 The Fool: King George III** is noted for his bouts of insanity and for having "lost" the American colonies. **III The Empress: Queen Victoria** saw the greatest growth of Britain as a major world power. **V The Hierophant: King James I** commissioned translation of the Bible into English, and also authored a major work on the persecution of witches. **XII The Hanged Man: King Charles I** was overthrown and executed by Oliver Cromwell. **XIII Death: Queen Mary I/Bloody Mary** earned her sobriquet with relentless persecution of non-Roman Catholic subjects.

BOTTOM ROW: **XIV Temperance: William & Mary** took the throne with no violence. **XV The Devil: King Richard III** earned the throne by murdering contenders, including children. **10 of Swords: Lady Jane Grey** was queen for 10 days; then she was imprisoned and executed. **8 of Swords: King Henry VI** was the last ruler of the House of Lancaster. **King of Coins: King Henry VII** succeeded Richard III and was first ruler of the House of Tudor.

Collection of the artist

Tarot of the Royal Court
Annie Rioux, circa 1996
TOP ROW: I The Magician. III The Empress. V The Pope. VI The Lovers. VII The Chariot.
SECOND ROW: XIII Death. XIV Temperance. XV The Devil. Knight of Batons. Queen of Coins.

Collection of the artist

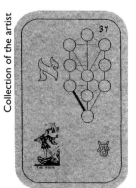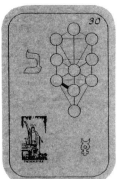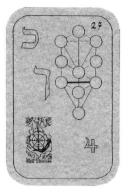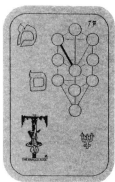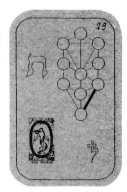

Jacob Ruijling Tarot 1991

Collection of the artist

Samantha's Tarot Samantha Kocsis, 2002

Luigi Scapini Tarot Luigi Scapini created a Major Arcana series that blends myth and tradition from the ancient, medieval, and Renaissance worlds. Most of the cards are untitled, although some have titles hand-written in pencil on the margins of the art. The hand-colored etchings were issued in a signed and numbered edition of twenty, dated 1976. Like the Medieval Scapini Tarot (published by U.S. Games Systems) by the same artist, the images have many details that enrich the symbolism while adding touches of light-hearted humor.

Tarot der Schatten (Tarot of the Shadows) Marcel Kastaun created the Tarot of the Shadows to depict the dark side of the human psyche. The Major Arcana deck was issued in a signed, numbered edition of thirty copies. The deck was made in Cologne, Germany, in 1995. The backs are solid black.

Scriptorium Tarot Canadian artist Roland Hui began the Scriptorium Tarot in 1991 and worked on it into the year 2000. The deck expresses his interest in children's book illustrations, Pre-Raphaelite art, and the images by Pamela Colman Smith in the Rider-Waite Tarot. The images are watercolor and ink on illustration board.

Luigi Scapini Tarot Luigi Scapini, 1976
TOP ROW: The Fool. The Magician. The High Priestess. The Empress.
SECOND ROW: The Emperor. The Lovers. The Chariot. Strength.
THIRD ROW: The Hanged Man. Temperance. The Devil. The Tower.
BOTTOM ROW: The Moon. The Sun. Judgment. The World.

Seasons of the Tarot The Seasons of the Tarot was created by Tori Hartman and Kim Dalton, and illustrated by Rasputon Mims. The suits of the Minor Arcana are named after the seasons: swords are winter; cups are spring; pentacles are summer; and wands are autumn. The seasonal motif is shown in the Major Arcana with settings that emphasize the seasons. The designs were made circa 1998.

Tarot der Schatten (Tarot of the Shadows) Marcel Kastaun, 1995

Collection of the artist

0. NARR. II. HOHEPRIESTERIN. V. HOHEPRIESTER. VII. WAGEN. VIII. GERECHTIGKEIT. X. SCHICKSALSRAD. XI. KRAFT. XII. GEHÄNGTER. XIII. TOD. XIV. ALCHEMIE. XV. TEUFEL. XVI. TURM. XVII. STERN. XIX. SONNE. XXI. UNIVERSUM

Collection of the author

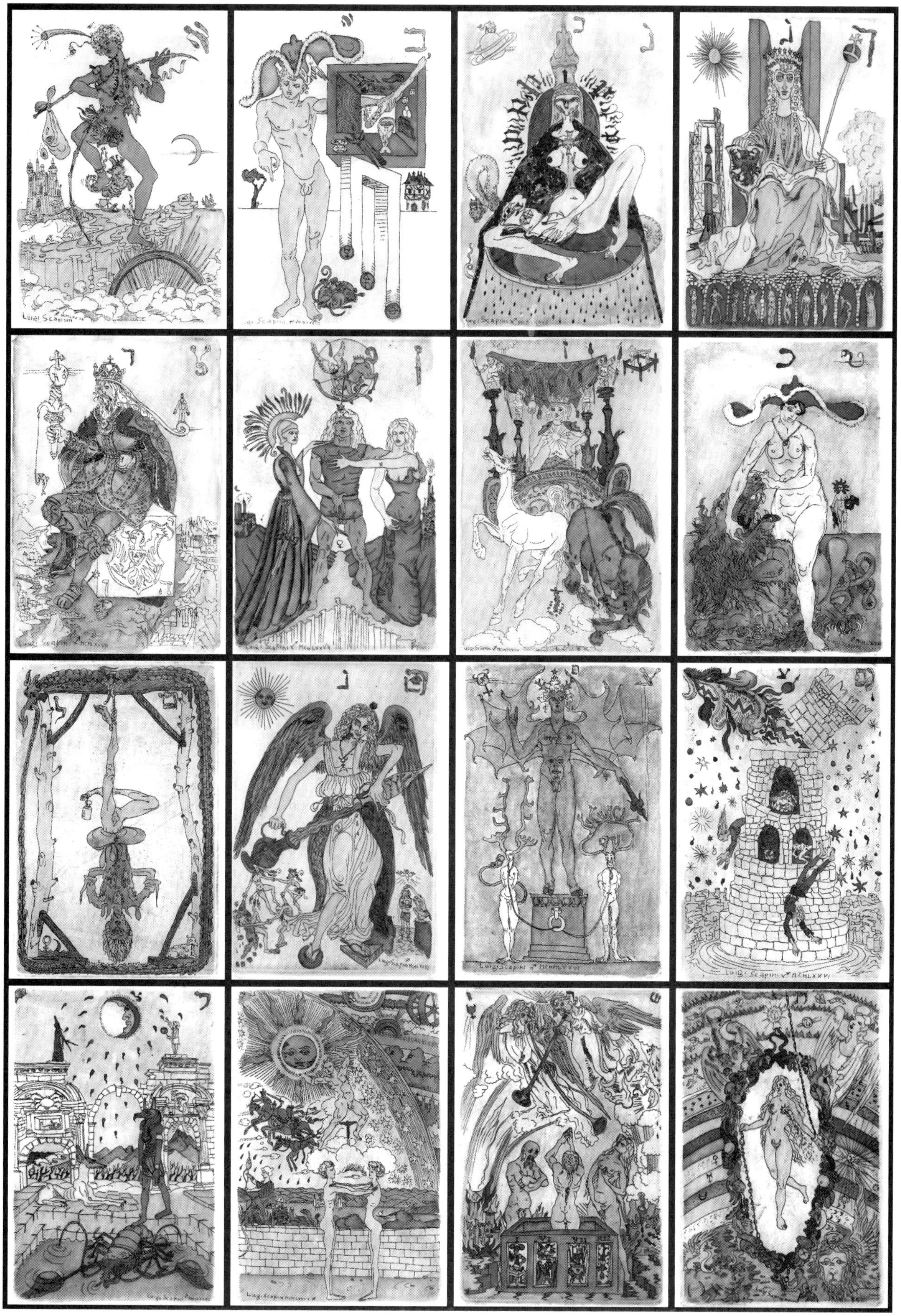

Collection of the artist

Scriptorium Tarot   Roland Hui, 2000   The description is by the artist.

TOP ROW: **II The High Priestess** sits between two pillars. One hand clutches an amulet on her breast, while the other guards a book of sacred text cradled by the moon. **VI The Lovers.** Under a statue of Eros, a pair of young lovers kiss. **X The Wheel of Fortune.** The medieval symbolism of the capricious nature of Fortune is invoked here. A figure climbs toward a crowned individual whom he wishes to replace. Once set high, the former king (on the right) has been cast down and falls from the spinning wheel. **XI Justice.** Amidst the cosmos, Themis, personifying Justice, grasps a pair of scales which harmoniously balances Alpha and Omega, the beginning and end. **XVII The Star.** A monk studies the heavens from the window of a monastery with an astrolabe. In the distance a great star is in sight, bringing hopes of new discoveries at hand.

BOTTOM ROW: **Ten of Swords.** Amidst a background of drawn swords, imminent violence is at hand. **Three of Swords.** A winged heart lays trapped helplessly in a bed of thorns, pierced by three swords. **Queen of Cups.** A hooded queen clutches a cup from which sweet incense arises, inducing her trancelike state. **Knight of Cups.** Completing the Grail quest, a kneeling Sir Galahad is miraculously offered communion by the sacred vessel. **Ten of Pentacles.** The dynastic line of descent of a great noble family is depicted.

Seasons of the Tarot   Rasputon Mims, under direction of Tori Hartman and Kim Dalton, 1998

Collection of the artists

IV OF WINTER   KNIGHT OF AUTUMN   II OF SPRING   QUEEN OF SUMMER

Share Tarot   Dante, 1993 (Peyto Books)

Seron Deck   Jennifer Seron hand-made four signed and numbered tarot decks with photocopies and collages of original art, in 1996. The cards are gold-edged, with a back design of a blue and orange pattern. A handmade booklet accompanies the deck. The expressionistic Major Arcana are called Archetypes, with Kabbalistic concepts and Hebrew letters; the courts are environments, with I Ching and Taoist concepts, and show landscapes; and the pips are characters, people drawn from New York City subways. The suits are spades, clubs, hearts, and diamonds. In addition to seventy-eight cards, the deck includes a Joker, a presentation card, and an introductory card. The introductory card reads, "The best tarot deck is no better than the honesty and creativity of the person who uses it. The Seron deck is meant to tell stories—illustrated stories without words about any well-thought out question you ask in an open-ended manner. The 'answer' depends upon you to interpret, so be honest with yourself & open to new viewpoints!"

Tarot of the Seventh Ray   Mark P. Smith describes his tarot deck as "devoted to exploring the connection between self and spirit.... By visually interacting with the world around me, I have found imagery to support my theory that we are surrounded by the varying influences of the tarot all of the time. Tarot is everywhere; it is a 'mirror of the soul.'" The artwork was made in 1994 from black and white photographs by the artist, mostly of his native North Carolina. The numbering of The Moon and The Sun are switched.

Lefebure Severine Tarot   French artist Lefebure Severine created several tarot designs in 1999.

Share Tarot   Dante used computer software to compose art for the Share Tarot. The images were published as a book, *Share: Tarot Meditations*. Dante says, "*Share* is a book based on my direct experiences with The Light. I used certain archetypes from the tarot card deck to communicate what I have learned. Nothing in *Share* is based on any particular belief systems because they cannot teach you what a part of you always knows." The book was published by Peyto Books in 1993.

Seron Deck Jennifer Seron, 1996 The descriptions were written and the cards arranged by the artist.

TOP ROW: **Fool** is composed of darkness above giving birth to light below, and vice versa. To each side of this birthing is the passage through which change / life passes. The shape is that of the aleph, a kind of / X, which in the context of the Fool connotes hyperbola or hyperbole. The edge upon which the traditional Fool walks is nothing but this birth and rebirth between flesh of space and flesh of matter: the birth of Energy from Time. **Magician** contains all the Hebrew letters within the petals of expanding cosmos / consciousness. The new thought contains all possibilities for

expression, yet all expression is limited within the symbols we choose to envision. Beth, the Magician, is the house within which we choose to live today. The door on one side is entirely open, as we must be in order to express what we conceive. **Empress** is utterly feminine. Daleth, the Hebrew letter, means door. The Empress is the verdant vegetable door through which we all pass. Birth and the stork embrace and reflect. At the edges of the door, there are embers so hot they are blue / white and look to be cubes of ice. Bright chartreuse leaves of flesh form the lips which open to speak in language wordless, earthy yet ethereal. Through the door one might expect to see solid red flesh, or darkness, but there is light, a clear ivory glow ever gyring nearer that yet unmoving moves. The image of our world-womb embedded in feminine flesh. **Lovers** are opposites that mirror one another exactly. Tension created by exact opposites is energy / time / space / matter. They are twin zain, or Hebrew swords / weapons / pricks. One faces another like the Yin /Yang of Tao. One dark, one light, both encased in orange. To one side the sun, darkness, sky, matter, and male. To the other side, the moon, paleness, water, time, and female. Reversals of old matched pairs predominate. Two masculine zain surround the dual feminine inner hearts. The Lovers are an endless turmoil of energy, a frictionless machine with no beginning or end, only opposed parts in fluid, dynamic relationships.

SECOND ROW: **Death** connotes the fish which is the meaning of the Hebrew letter nun. This fish has a gaping abyss of an open mouth about to close (or not) on a nun-shaped hook. The abyss of the fish's mouth is the same abyss seen in the Fool card. White and black spines surround the fish's body, barbs of Boaz and Joachim, which like the nun-shaped hook can entrap prey. The fish is in solid brown / russet water. One golden eye is shaped like an egg, the other like a baby fish. What we see of Death contains all time and rebirths in itself. The fish is the symbol for a shining soul swimming in the sea of space. Unmoored, this fish is Death. Either about to be hooked, or the predator of smaller fish, this fish is life. **Nature** used to be the Devil in a traditional deck. Platonism and Christianity did much to malign Nature and the primacy of the "physical" world. Today people acknowledge and celebrate sexuality. People are no longer afraid of "mother earth" now that our science and industry have bound her to our service. Nature is defined by the Hebrew letter ayin, or eye. Three blood-red tears fall from Nature's eye. The Devil we loathed is nothing more than a humbled embarrassment to us now—a constant reminder of our own irresponsibility and unchecked greed. Polluted air, tainted ground water, species extinctions, increasing ocean and air temperature now characterize "Nature." Soon enough we will realize that our nature is Nature. **Moon** is a crescent climbed by a cooked-but-living lobster, which trails a scarab / dung beetle, which in turn pushes the black sun into / under a bloody menstrual sea of sky. At the upper end of the crescent moon, cycles of full moons' spiral widening. The Hebrew letter is qoph, which means ear, or monkey, according to a modern translator. Upon the back of the lobster, qophs exist within the gyres of DNA. The crescent moon connotes an ear and the spirals, and dung / sun connote the passage of the inner ear within a sea of blood. Instinctual precognition, life in death, darkness in light, and menstrual cycles are visually represented in the Moon. **Universe** is a Tree of Life set in an ultramarine sea of apparent space filled with stars / souls. Above are the branches, whorls, flames—expressions of the fulfillment of a Fool's promise. Below is the earth, two houses on either side of the roots. Each house is a tau, or the Hebrew letter which means "sign." The tau is similar to a beth, but the tau is open to the bottom. The trunk of the tree is composed of interwoven black, white, and gray pillars: judgment, mercy, and loving-kindness, respectively. In truth, the Universe is a tree

whose source is contracted earth, whose trunk blends all possible action, and whose end is whorling expansion, which itself ends, eventually, in contracted earth. The Universe is the inverse of the Fool card. Hyperbola / Hyperbole—as above, so below.

THIRD ROW: **King of Diamonds** means "Shining within Deeps." Air and Earth. Father below Mother. The image of the pale moon in a black sky: a bright soul illuminating all around. **Queen of Clubs** means "Tree on a Mountain." Earth and Wind. Youngest Son below Eldest Daughter. The image of a stubborn twisted tree (representing wind) against a gray sky, upon a barren harsh purple mountain: personal tenaciousness in a hard spot, and / or providing solid sustenance for fragile but important purposes. **Princess of Spades** means "Fire and Water." Middle Daughter above Middle son. The image of golden fire above royal water: love and hate, action and passivity, energy and time, masculine and feminine, day and night, static and dynamic. Opposites attracted to one another are resolved not by losing individuality; rather, each increases power of other via their closeness. Intensity. **Jack of Hearts** means "Thunder in Swamp." Thunder and Water. Youngest Daughter above Eldest Son. The image of growth of green rice seedlings in a paddy field of navy water. To the seed, growth is tumultuous and bizarre, shocking, and wrenching; to the outsider, this same growth is utterly seamless, smooth, slow, and natural. To be at rest is to be at ease with change.

BOTTOM ROW: **Ace of Spades** shows a Cheshire cat whose fur is striped magenta and purple, and whose eyes are yellow. Aces are the root element of their suit. Spades are fire, sword, the shape and color of flame with the same point. This root of fire is the root of cutting wit, humor. The Cheshire cat, like fire, passion, and humor, is present only under the right conditions. As soon as there is a wet blanket, no more cat, flame, desire. The spades choose conditions for confrontation. **Three of Diamonds** is represented by two animatedly gossiping women. These two women are close, sharing whispered confidences. Taurus and Neptune together bring earthy turbulence, the Old Man of the Sea and the Stubborn Bull of the Earth together peaceably. Each is the complement of the other, each respectful of the other's strengths and weaknesses. Equals. Friends. Two such together generate a third soul of lovingkind actions which follows in their wake. **Two of Hearts** is a sad older family man returning home from a long day at work. He is as strong as circumstances demand, always. Pisces in Pluto and Mercury together implies a balancing, tenuous and strained with work. Ethereal, instinctual, wandering Pisces is either bound to deep Pluto or tethered to fickle Mercury. The only hope for positive is if Pluto is so deep as to be shallow, and Mercury is so fast as to be immobile such that the dreams of Pisces become reality. **Nine of Clubs** is represented by a foreigner or a person alienated. S/he is hopeful, but is able to see only the bounds of his/her own reality. Aquarius in Neptune balances hope with the reality of a changeable world. Also, the worst aspects of xenophobia may be implied by this white-on-white aryan. Only when airy hopes for a better world are tied to the degraded emotionality of fanaticism is a person capable of the worst this card implies.

The High Priestess · II

The Hermit · IX

The Hanged Man · XII

The Devil · XV

The Tower · XVI

The Sun · XVIII

The Moon · XIX

Page of Swords

Five of Swords

Ace of Cups

Two of Disks

Ace of Disks

Tarot of the Seventh Ray Mark P. Smith, 1994   The descriptions are by the artist.

TOP ROW: **The High Priestess II** (Winston-Salem, NC). The High Priestess connects the purity of Kether with the perfect beauty of Tiphareth; she is the ideal representation of the moon. In this card we find the principle behind all manifestation, the source of inspiration in all things creative. **The Hermit IX** (Pisgah National Forest, NC). It is this place to which we are guided when overwhelmed by the world around us. It is here that we can find our comfort. The glistening heights beckon to us, inviting quiet contemplation and deeper understanding. **The Hanged Man XII**

(Winston-Salem, NC). The Hanged Man shows us the principle of an "enforced sacrifice." This is a path of ultimate giving that cannot be avoided. Again, as in so many other places, we are asked to remember that with every death comes a rebirth, that all is not lost, that redemption follows suffering. **The Devil XV** (Hwy. 74, between Asheville and Bat Cave, NC). The devil shows us our chains. Much like Jacob Marley, we are reminded that the shackles which bind us in our existence are fully self-created. Here we must remember that the dreadful apparition we see in the mirror is but a passing moment in our lives, and can be overcome through the direct confrontation of our fears.

Collection of the artist

Lefebure Severine Tarot 1999 The Hanged Man. Death. Temperance. The Tower.

Shell Arcana Sarah Scott Parry chose shells to represent the Major Arcana based on name, appearance, and qualities. The images are framed with symbols matching the cards' symbolism.

Silvano Silva Tarot Italian artist Silvano Silva created a seventy-eight-card tarot deck with colorful, often macabre images in a primitive visionary style. The artworks were created in 1994.

Simple Tarot "The Simple Tarot reshapes traditional tarot symbols in simple, geometric shapes," says graphic artist Willie Hewes. "I believe the simplest image, freed of unnecessary detail, can give you the clearest meaning, while still being open to varied interpretation, precisely because there are no details to pin down the meaning." The artwork was computer-generated in 2003.

Skeleton Tarot David Stoddard describes his Skeleton Tarot as "inspired by the Rider-Waite Tarot deck, but with a humorous feel to it." The tarot was made in 2002.

Sobel Tarot Sculptures Metal sculptor and blacksmith Ray Sobel created sculptures that incorporate tarot cards. The three works, collectively titled "Wheels of Fate and Fortune," were finished in 1993. Of the works, the artist says, "I consider it my *Meisterstuck,* as it is masterful in both technique and artistry and the best work I have ever done in over twenty years of blacksmithing." Sobel used iron, gold leaf, wood, paint, and tarot cards in his work.

Solayá Tarot The Solayá Tarot was made by three different artists under direction of Solayá Mircault. The art was made circa 1993.

SECOND ROW: **The Tower XVI** (a model). Here the angel falls from the mountain; the current state of affairs is utterly destroyed. The material makes way for the spiritual, and we can no longer avoid the Tao. We are swept away by the current, and our illusions are shattered on the rocks. **The Sun XVIII** (Asheville, NC). The darkness is cast aside, and our joy illumined. The sun bursts radiantly forth from a world of shadow, and we can rejoice once again. We are safe, and we are in love! **The Moon XIX** (Winston-Salem, NC). She is finding her power now. After a long time in the dark vacuum of space, her face begins to rotate and reflect the rays of the sun. Receptivity reigns; illusion and deceit are cast out of the garden. **Page of Swords** (Pisgah National Forest, NC). Quietly intelligent, the Page contemplates the nature of being. Both whimsical and stoic, this youth represents the perfection of intelligence and the art of discernment.
BOTTOM ROW: **Five of Swords** (Max Patch, western NC). Here we feel the pain of defeat; after trying hard, we have failed. The mind is still young. There is promise, however: We are reminded that every death brings a rebirth, that in horror we can always find profound beauty. **Ace of Cups** (Hwy. 74 between Asheville and Bat Cave, NC). The essence of our emotion; the wellspring of our joy. This place is sacred and fine, fueling our greatest pleasures and our darkest rages. Be respectful of this elemental treasure, or drown in the raging flood. **Two of Disks** (Linville Falls, NC). The earth's energy divides. On the one hand, it empowers and supports us, and on the other, it reminds us of our responsibility to return this nurture in kind. The polarity here is the essence of the number two; one gives, the other receives; one rushes forth, the other retreats; one laughs, the other cries. **Ace of Disks** (Bat Cave, NC) This card embodies the primordial power of the earth, that from which we are created and from which we create. Here we see a birthing of this energy, with the radiance of the sun receiving it from above. The solidity and stability of the stone reminds us of the earth's majestic strength.

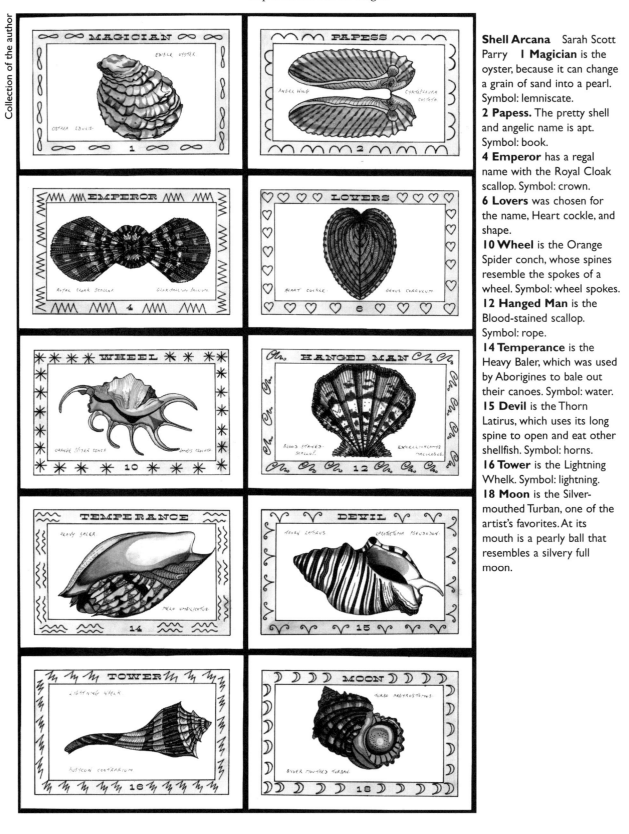

Shell Arcana Sarah Scott Parry **I Magician** is the oyster, because it can change a grain of sand into a pearl. Symbol: lemniscate.

2 Papess. The pretty shell and angelic name is apt. Symbol: book.

4 Emperor has a regal name with the Royal Cloak scallop. Symbol: crown.

6 Lovers was chosen for the name, Heart cockle, and shape.

10 Wheel is the Orange Spider conch, whose spines resemble the spokes of a wheel. Symbol: wheel spokes.

12 Hanged Man is the Blood-stained scallop. Symbol: rope.

14 Temperance is the Heavy Baler, which was used by Aborigines to bale out their canoes. Symbol: water.

15 Devil is the Thorn Latirus, which uses its long spine to open and eat other shellfish. Symbol: horns.

16 Tower is the Lightning Whelk. Symbol: lightning.

18 Moon is the Silver-mouthed Turban, one of the artist's favorites. At its mouth is a pearly ball that resembles a silvery full moon.

Silvano Silva Tarot   1994

Skeleton Tarot David Stoddard, 2002 TOP ROW: I The Magician. III The Empress. IV The Emperor. IX The Hermit. XII The Hanged Man. BOTTOM ROW: XV The Devil. Four of Swords. Queen of Wands. Two of Cups. Four of Pentacles.

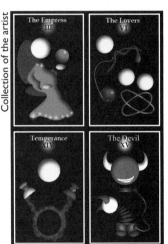

Simple Tarot
Willie Hewes, 2003

Sobel Tarot Sculptures
Ray Sobel, 1993 The square piece (TOP RIGHT) and the wheel mounted on blue painted wood (BOTTOM) incorporate the Tarot of Marseilles. The wheel mounted on butternut wood (LEFT) uses the Tarocchino Bolognese, published by Edizioni del Solleone.

Solayá Tarot
Solayá Mircault, circa 1993 Magician. Queen of Swords. Queen of Arrows.

magician

chariot

Strength

Death

Princess of Wands

8 of Wands

7 of cups

3 of Pentacles

Solstice Tarot Bev Patterson, circa 1995

Solstice Tarot Bev Patterson became interested in painting a tarot deck when her husband Paul had a reading done for his birthday. She began by painting her interpretations of each card in his spread. Paul Patterson, himself a student of the tarot, in turn wrote interpretations for the images she painted. The symbols and figures reflect different streams of spirituality and thought, including Native American and Celtic lore, astrology, and transpersonal psychology.

Southwestern Tarot Sacred symbols of the Southwestern Native American people illustrate Lora Anderson's Southwestern Tarot designs. The artwork was made in 1994 using CorelDraw software.

Southwestern Tarot
Lora Anderson, 1994

EMPRESS

EMPEROR

STRENGTH

SUN

Spirit of the Animals Tarot   Denise Satter, 1998
Descriptions are based on those by the artist.

TOP ROW: **0 The Fool.** A happy and unaware dog chases a ball to the edge of a cliff. The Fool is a card of enthusiasm about the moment, without thought of the future. **I The Magician.** A solemn kangaroo stands in the universal "as above, so below" posture. **II The High Priestess.** A watch-ful, wise Siamese cat holds the scroll of knowledge in her chamber of secret and hidden knowledge. **III The Empress.** A proud, strong lioness sits in her springtime garden, a true empress to her lion emperor. **IV The Emperor.** A fiercely powerful lion takes command of his world.

SECOND ROW: **V The Hierophant** is a careful mountain sheep, a leader to his group in the high peaks. **VI The**

174

Spirit of the Animals Denise Satter, of Studio Le Chat in California, used watercolors to depict in brilliant color animals as symbols of the tarot cards. In a letter to Stuart Kaplan, she describes the source of her inspiration. "I have been painting animals for many years and feel closely connected to them. My household has always been a zoo of sorts, and in the past years has been a home for many wonderful creatures…. The animals [of the tarot designs] are from all over the world and encompass all walks of life. I chose each one according to their unique characteristics as the perfect spiritual archetype of the particular card represented." Satter created the Animal Tarot in 1998.

Star Tarot Artist Cathryn McClelland explains the name of her deck in a letter to Stuart Kaplan, "I believe that symbolically, spiritually, and consciously people look to the stars for guidance and hope. The stars, like us, are part of the spiraling universe—all part of one, in a state of constant multi-level transition." The artwork was done in 1993. McClelland made another set of images called the Star Tarot, circa 1998.

Collection of the artist

Star Tarot Cathryn McClelland
TOP ROW: (cards from 1993) III The Empress. King of Swords. (cards from circa 1998) 0 The Fool.
SECOND ROW: I The Magician. II The High Priestess. III The Empress. Page of Cups.

Lovers. Two entwined swans glide blissfully down the river of life as they mate for all time. **VII The Chariot. VIII Strength.** An immensely strong elephant succeeds in supporting the entire world. **IX The Hermit** is a bear retiring to its cave to rest, meditate, and build strength for the upcoming year. He glances back one final time at the vagaries of life.

THIRD ROW: **XI Justice.** The unblinking, all-seeing owl holds the scale of Justice. **XII The Hanged Man.** A slow-moving and timid three-toed sloth is unable or unwilling at this time to change his fortune and therefore accepts all that comes to him in a somewhat victimized fashion. **XIII Death.** Butterflies are so ephemeral: They are a caterpillar, they become a pupa, they emerge and become a butterfly for a short life, and then the whole process is repeated. **XIV Temperance.** The patient, enduring camel carries water to the other side of the desert. **XV The Devil** is a subtle, ven-omous spider. It warns not to get enmeshed in another's web without being entirely aware of the situation.

BOTTOM ROW: **XVII The Star** portrays two cosmic dolphins, psychically linked. They are guided by the brightest star and seven lesser stars in their search for serenity and knowledge. **XVIII The Moon.** A wolf bays longingly at the moon, with a dog looking on and a crayfish in the water. **XIX The Sun.** Two zebras celebrate summer in Africa, the place of the sun. **XX Judgement.** A family of wolves in a desolate landscape at the height of winter hears the horn of Gabriel. This is one of the oldest images: the magic of family. Although the card is about judgment and choices, it is also about family—biological and family of friends or choice—and staying together through the lean times. **XXI The World.** A seal rests on a planet in space, holding up the earth in perfect balance.

Starlight Tarot Laurie Amato, 2002

Starlight Tarot Rich detail and inviting textures are part of the textile art of the Starlight Tarot. Artist Laurie Amato composed the deck by gluing fabric, faux gems, and pieces of jewelry over the Rider-Waite Tarot Major Arcana. The work dates from 2002.

Darin Stelting Tarot Darin Stelting's tarot designs recall the exuberant paper cut-out art of Matisse. She completed the art in 1991.

Bonnie Stern Tarot Bonnie Stern's tarot paintings are based on the letters of the Hebrew alphabet. She began the work in the mid-1980s and continued through the early 1990s.

Alison Stone Tarot Poet and painter Alison Stone painted tarot designs in oil, in 2000.

Darin Stelting Tarot 1991
TOP ROW: Magician. Justice. Death.
BOTTOM ROW: Sun. World.

Alison Stone Tarot 2000

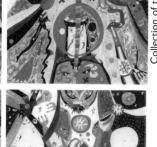

Bonnie Stern Tarot Circa 1990

Montage/Collage

An art technique that burst into the tarot world in the 1990s is montage, compositions made by assembling other pictures, such as printed photographs (for example, from magazines) or reproductions of art. The montage decks in volume IV were made by hand as well as by use of computer software. Montage decks (not including decks that feature original photographs taken by the artist) in volume IV are:

Aleph-Beth Tarot	Melanie Hibbert Tarot
Tarot of Angels	Inner Garden Tarot
Blue Rose Tarot	Inner Landscape Tarot
Celestial Tarot	Moon Dreamer's Web Tarot
Crystal Fusion Tarot	Ourobouros Mail Artists
Crystal Visions Tarot	Tarot
Curious Tarot	Oz Magazine Tarot
Cygnet Tarot	Susan Rashkis Tarot
Ethyrial Tarot	Royal Britain Tarot
Evolving Tarot	Rock and Roll Tarot
Fauceglia Tarot	Stained Glass Tarot
Full Moon Dreamers Tarot	Tarot of Transformation
Golden Tarot	Victoria Regina Tarot
Grace Tarot	Victorian Tarot
Hanna's Deck	Janet Wheeler Tarot

Tarot of the Storm Philippe Rouchier used paint and pencil as well as the computer graphics program Adobe Photoshop to create the Tarot of the Storm in 1999. Of the deck, he says, "The particularity of Tarot of the Storm is such that it stimulates the user's subconscious with strong and unusual images that correspond to the symbols of the traditional tarot and thus allow the user to instinctively grasp the meaning." The suits correspond to elements of nature: swords with lightning, wands with fire, cups with water, and circles with earth.

Straight and Narrow Tarot The Straight and Narrow Tarot is illustrated with figures of Christian tradition, including saints and a few villains. It was created in 2002 by Dutch artists Claudia Dominguez-Vargas and Sicko van Dijk from illustrations manipulated with the software program Adobe Photoshop. The artists say, "We think tarot is primarily a card game. A game of reflection and inspiration, in which people are invited to compare concepts and situations portrayed on cards with their own position and direction in life."

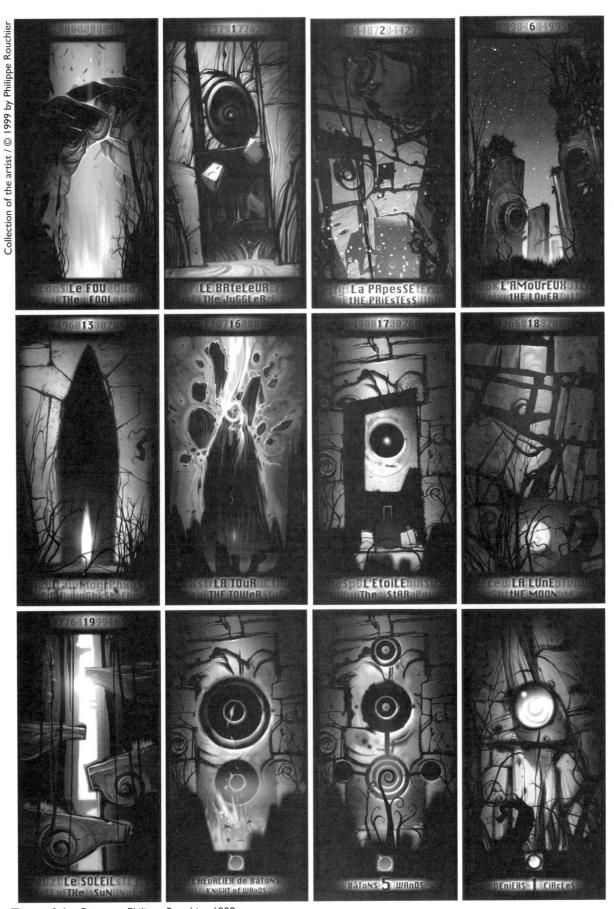

Tarot of the Storm   Philippe Rouchier, 1999

Collection of the artist

FRANCIS OF ASSISI — JOHN THE BAPTIST — TERESA OF AVILA — ANTHONY THE HERMIT — SIMEON STYLITES

LAZARUS — TITUS BRANDSMA — CHRISTOPHER — GEN 41: 18 — MATTHEW 2: 13-15

GEN 11:27 — MAT 20: 1-16 — EC 1:7-8 — KINGS 7: 13-14 — LUC 19:1

Straight and Narrow Tarot   Claudia Dominguez-Vargas and Sicko van Dijk, 2002

TOP ROW: **0 Francis of Assisi** renounced wealth, prestige, and even his family to become a mendicant. His purity of heart allowed him to preach love to all, even the animals. **I John the Baptist** was among the first to recognize the importance of Jesus. **II Teresa of Avila** became a nun in 1531. In her late thirties, she experienced ecstatic spiritual visions. She eventually founded a new order, the Discalced Carmelites. **IX Anthony the Hermit** lived circa 251, in Egypt. He is called one of the "Desert Fathers." He underwent violent temptations, which he overcame. **XII Simeon Stylites** subjected himself to bodily austerities, culminating in his taking residence, circa 423, on a twelve-foot-square platform at the top of a pillar.

SECOND ROW: **XIII Lazarus** was raised from the dead by Jesus. **XV Titus Brandsma** spoke out against Nazism and was sent to the Dachau concentration camp. Despite the inhumanity around him, he asked his fellow prisoners to pray for the salvation of the guards. He was executed in 1942. He is shown standing at the gate of Dachau. **XVIII Christopher** is known in legend for seeking a great king to serve. He was disappointed in worldly kings. One night, as he

carried a child across a ford, the child grew so heavy he could barely carry him. The child told him, "You have been carrying the world. I am Jesus Christ, the king you seek." **IX of Swords: Gen 41:18** concerns the dream of the Pharaoh, which Joseph interpreted as warning of famine. **VI of Swords: Matthew 2:13–15** illustrates the flight to Egypt of Mary and Joseph with the infant Jesus.

BOTTOM ROW: **III of Clubs: Gen 11:27** concerns the lineage of Tera. One of his descendants was the patriarch Abraham. **VIII of Cups: Mat 20:1–16** shows the vintner paying his laborers according to their agreement: one denarius regardless of how late or early they arrived for work. "Thus the last will be first, and the first, last." **VII of Cups: Ec 1:7–8** "Into the sea all rivers go, and yet the sea is never filled, and still to their goal the rivers go. All things are wearisome. No man can say that eyes have not had enough of seeing, ears their fill of hearing." **VIII of Pentacles: Kings 7:13–14** shows King Solomon. The verses describe the king's Hall of Justice. **IV of Pentacles: Luke 19:1** illustrates the story of Zacchaeus, a tax collector who climbed into a tree in order to see Jesus amidst the crowd and was later host to Jesus.

Sumerian Tarot Michael Gerbrandt of Canada created the Sumerian Tarot in 1996.

Sumerian Tarot Michael Gerbrandt, 1996

Jillian Suzanne Tarot San Francisco artist Jillian Suzanne made prints of tarot designs in 1995.

Sydna Tarot Canadian artist Sydna painted her tarot designs in watercolor in 1989.

Josie Taglienti Tarot Josie Taglienti made tarot designs on love and relationships, with clearly defined, intense colors. The designs were made in 1993.

Sydna Tarot 1989

Josie Taglienti Tarot 1993

Jillian Suzanne Tarot 1995

Tahuel Thoth Tarot
Carsten Wockel, 1989
I The Magician

Tau Tarot Illustrator Thomas Manigart and occult student Dennis Kennedy worked together to make the Tau Tarot, based on mythology, philosophy, symbology, and Jungian color psychology. The designs date from 1993.

Grand Tarot Taurin Golo (Guy Nadaud, also spelled Nadeau) is an acclaimed artist of *bandes dessinées,* translated as "comic strips." He designed his tarot deck, circa 1999, in tribute to the sport of bullfighting. He calls his tarot *traité d'art tauromagique,* "treatise on the art of bull-magic," playing on the French word for bullfighting, *tauromachie.*

Tahuel Thoth Tarot Carsten Wockel's 1989 paintings are connected with the Kabbalistic Tree of Life. "I tried to form the pictures in such a manner that the tarot can be used as an ordinary deck for divination as well as mediation, to get in contact with one's own spiritual processes to reach the subconscious experience of one's mind," the artist writes Stuart Kaplan.

Taromino de Jean-Didier Jean-Didier created Major Arcana printed in red, green, and black on plain wooden domino-shaped pieces. The designs are symbols adapted from the Tarot of Marseilles. Taromino was issued by Jean-Didier Diffusions in 1990, boxed with a folded gameboard giving a spread diagram.

TarotPro After studying the concept of tarot, software designer Elisabeth Fürhauser Chironne hand-painted a rough draft of each card. The drafts were scanned and corrected pixel by pixel to be low-resolution screen images. Heavy colors were used as appropriate for sixteen-color monitors. The deck was created for use with TarotPro: Tarot Professional for Windows. The software includes three different decks, many layouts, instructions for designing one's own layouts, music, and more. The publisher is PAW-Software, and the program was published in 1994.

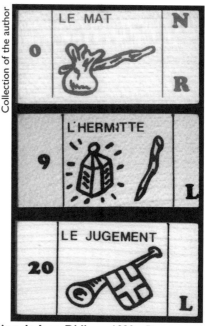

Taromino de Jean-Didier 1990 Pieces are shown at actual size

Tau Tarot Thomas Manigart, artist, and Dennis Kennedy, 1993

Grand Tarot Taurin
Golo, circa 1999

Grand Tarot Taurin The artist Golo portrays himself, in the lower left corner, studying *tauromagique*.

0 The Fool — I The Magician — II The High Priestess — III The Empress — IV The Emperor — V The Hierophant
VI The Lovers — VII The Chariot — VIII Strength — IX The Hermit — X Wheel of Fortune — XI Justice
XII The Hanged Man — XIII Death — XIV Temperance — XV The Devil — XVI The Tower — XVII The Star
XVIII The Moon — XIX The Sun — XX Judgment — XXI The World — Knight of Cups — Queen of Pentacles

TarotPro   Elisabeth Fürhauser Chironne, 1994

Teddy Tarot Jo Covalt, 1991

Teddy Tarot Jo Covalt drew teddy bears in tarot scenes in 1991. "I created this Teddy Tarot for personal use…. It's amusing (I hope), but the serious meanings are still there (I hope)."

Temporal Tarot The twelve-sided designs of the Temporal Tarot are to enable the reader to make predictions as to when the events seen in the cards will take place, according to the signs of the zodiac. Lani Faust created the deck and accompanying manuscript in 1989.

Terra Tarot "The Terra deck is about the community of the world, to celebrate both our cultural similarities as well as individual uniqueness," writes artist Toni Truesdale of her designs. "The four races, four elements, four directions, and four colors set the patterns of the four suits." The African race is represented by the Yoruba Orisha, the element fire, the color black, and the direction east. The European race is represented by the Arthurian cycle, the element of water, the color white, and the direction north. Indigenous peoples are represented by the Iroquois, the element of earth, the color red, and the direction south. Asians are represented by Tibet, air, yellow, and west. "The Major Arcana show archetypes that are common symbols to our world experience and reflect our multi-cultural world. The world has housed many kinds of people and traditions. Although civilizations have been extinguished, seeds exist in material fragments left behind. Tangled webs of information confuse modern investigators as people change and became absorbed into the next generation of civilizations…. It is the purpose of this deck to help in those steps towards a better understanding of each other individually and socially into a multi-cultural world future. And to aid in the process of putting aside the feelings of superiority, alienation, and mistrust and to build a co-operative continuation of ideas as well as values." The artwork was made to be studied either end up; it was completed in 1995.

Terra Nova Tarot Jan H.N. De Jong of the Netherlands made Major Arcana designs by copying the Multicopy Tarot (see *The Encyclopedia of Tarot,* volume III) and re-drawing and re-coloring by stencil the illustrations. The deck was printed circa 1991 on cards intended for use by CB radio hobbyists.

Temporal Tarot Lani Faust, 1989 XIX The Sun.

Terra Tarot Toni Truesdale, 1995 Descriptions are by the artist.

TOP ROW: **0 Utopia/Palmares.** *Utopia* was a sixteenth-century novel of a more perfect society. Palmares was a sev-enteenth-century Brazilian settlement made up of escaped slaves, white servants, and Indians fleeing colonization. Both came to mean human paradise. **I Alchemist/ Shaman.** Alchemist symbolizes the western search for knowledge,

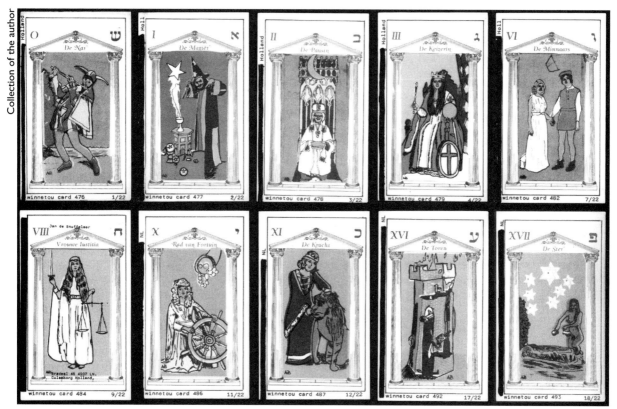

Terra Nova Tarot Jan H.N. De Jong, 1991

often for the material gain of wealth in creating gold. The Shaman is the tribal healer, spiritual guide, and counselor. **II Fates/Sisters** are associated with the fabric of life, spinning, measuring, and cutting human existence. **III Crone/Maiden.** The Crone is a woman coming into midlife. She will now be able to fulfill goals and offer wisdom. Maiden is the promise of life to be. She is the threshold of the future and the living bridge between the ancestors and descendants.

SECOND ROW: **IV Gate to Heaven/Sun, Moon, Stars.** Gate to Heaven is the passage from this world to the next. Sun, Moon, Stars is a reminder of one's small place in the cycle of the universe. **VII Passage** represents reflection, change, travel, challenge, and the search for inner truth. **VIII Feathers/Civilization.** Feathers is a message of the indigenous people to consider the fate of the earth. The prophecies of many cultures warn that the time of crisis approaches, with wildlife and plantlife endangered. Civilization is the plunder of the earth's resources without regard to the natural world and the effect on all Earth's life. **X Labrinth/Maze** is a symbol of life's journey with false leads, surprises, and turns. It can mean trials, travel to the source, mystery, and possible mastery.

THIRD ROW: **XII Solitude/Community.** Solitude shows the need to return to the solace of nature and heal. Community is the joy of family, friends, and neighborhood. To be included and appreciated is a necessity of all human life. **XIII Tree of Life/Rebirth.** The Tree of Life is a symbol of the continuity of life. She is usually regarded as a female sym-

bol, representing life, family, love, and nurturing. Rebirth is the tree of the initiated, the pole the shaman travels both to the heavens and underworld to seek instruction and aid of the spirit world. Only through the death of the old self can the new emerge. **XIV Twins/Balance.** The Twins represent the duality of negative and positive, dark and light, night and day. The brothers in many creation stories struggle with their opposite natures to create the world. Balance is the nature of the grandmother/mother of the twins. She keeps their struggle from getting out of hand. She is the balancing influence. **XVI Stairs/House.** The dreams of all of us are filled with houses of the past and stairs leading us somewhere.

BOTTOM ROW: **XVII Ritual/Festival.** Humans celebrate the major events in the individual life, holidays, and holy days. We invoke the spiritual with dance, song, and theater. Each culture has different rituals, each religion different rites, yet the meaning is similar; we are a human family. **XIX Crossroads/4 Directions.** Choices are always difficult. But that great challenge links us to the human symbol of the cross. It is also the four directions, four winds, four races, and four elements. **XX Lost Generations.** Generations remain unborn due to premature death through accident or violence. When someone is killed, so, too, are their possibilities and descendants. Many are also lost to abuse, neglect, and abandonment. Without direction, they continue the cycle of violence. **XXII Trickster.** Tricksters instruct with humor and make us laugh at ourselves. Some of their names are Coyote, Raven, Br'er Rabbit, and Spider.

Tesselating Tarot (Tarots a la Escher) GianCarlo Ghirardi was interested in trying to express "the totally pervading character of the psychological moments represented by the images of the cards by a graphic technique that exhibits the same feature." The technique Ghirardi employed is "tesselating," covering a plane by repetition of the same figure. Ghirardi cites the artist M.C. Escher as a master of tesselating. "The world in which the cards 'live' is a two-dimensional world of plane figures. It became then a logical necessity and a stimulating challenge to try to fill up the plane with figures which, by infinite repetition, are always identical to themselves and leave no space for anything but the symbol itself." The artist is head of the Department of Theoretical Physics of the University of Trieste. His tarot work dates from circa 1988.

Texas Tarot Dana DeYoung was inspired to make the Texas Tarot by the concepts in Sallie Nichols' book *Jung and the Tarot*. The Major Arcana prints hinge on using the tarot cards as metaphors for stages in life. The prints were prepared for a thesis exhibition that took place in January 1988.

Theofana Abba Tarot The Theofana Abba Tarot was created by Martin Stejskal under direction of Theofanus Abba, pseudonym of Josef Louda. The images were published as an unbound book of Major Arcana prints by Auroboros, Prague, in 1973. The images are based on the Oswald Wirth Tarot, but the numbering and titles of some of the cards is different. For example, card 11 Strength shows a nine-headed dragon instead of a lion;

19 The Sun shows four people instead of two. In a letter to Stuart Kaplan, Stejskal described the person for whom the deck is named: "Theofana Abba was one of the last pre-war [WWII] Czech hermetics, a great specialist in alchemy.... I got acquainted with him in the last period of his life, and the thin book I am sending to you is the result of our collaboration." The prints seem to have been made by printing the color with a rough screen, then overprinting the black line art.

3CDCG Tarot Japanese graphic artist Tetsuya Kagami designed a tarot deck using a three-dimensional modeling computer program. The deck, completed in 2001, shows the images of each card from several different angles.

3D Tarot Patrice Warner used computer illustration graphics to create tarot designs in 1999. The artist explains the concept of the deck: "With the tarot the visual aspect is the centerpiece; for the first time tarot users can go beyond a two-dimensional reality and experience the tarot in 3D. 3D Tarot will allow users to feel as if they could reach out and touch the rich textures and color of each image. Each card will pull you into a 3D photo-realistic environment as if you were there."

3-Dimensional Tarot Toni Truesdale made tarot designs with the intention of applying them to cubes, for a three-dimensional deck. "The placement and turning of the cubes would constantly change in numerous probable combinations." The artwork was made in 1995.

Texas Tarot Dana DeYoung, 1988

Collection of the artist

Tesselating Tarot (Tarots a la Escher)   GianCarlo Ghirardi, circa 1988

Theofana Abba Tarot Martin Stejskal under direction of Theofanus Abba (Josef Louda), 1973

Collection of the artist

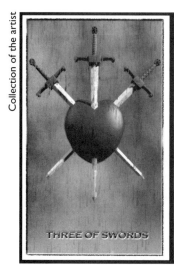   

THREE OF SWORDS   ACE OF SWORDS   FOUR OF RODS   TEN OF CUPS

3D Tarot   Patrice Warner, 1999

Collection of the artist

3CDCG Tarot   Tetsuya Kagami, 2001
Two views each of 16 The Tower (top) and
the Page of Wands.

Collection of the artist

3-Dimensional Tarot   Toni Truesdale, 1995   1 The Magician. 2 The High Priestess. 3 The
Empress.

Tiffany Tarot Eugene Tiffany used the computer graphics program Freehand to create a set of Major Arcana. Of the art, Tiffany says, "The imagery of the Tiffany Tarot harkens back to some of the earliest decks known. These include, for example, various woodcut versions. The Tiffany Tarot is without the many relatively recently tacked-on embellishments. However, the stylization of the Tiffany Tarot does incorporate contemporary graphic design principles both old and new." The art was created in 1995.

Tarot of Timeless Truth Leila Vey completed the Tarot of Timeless Truth, using computer software, in 2003. Of her designs, she writes, "Tarot of Timeless Truth honors nature-based spirituality.... I have consciously stayed away from depicting man-made structures, except in three cards where it was absolutely necessary in order to convey the meaning of the card."

Davide Tonato Tarot Davide Tonato's cards draw from fantasy illustration and the esoteric tradition of the tarot. The Major Arcana were done in oils, and the Minor Arcana was done in tempera and watercolors. The artwork was completed in 1989.

Davide Tonato Tarot 1989

Collection of the artist

Tiffany Tarot Eugene Tiffany, 1995

Tarot of Timeless Truth   Leila Vey, 2003   Descriptions are by the artist.

TOP ROW: **III Empress.** I provide sustenance for all children of the earth, and love them equally. I am the giver and preserver of life. I offer beauty, passion, sensuality, and pleasure to all who connect with me. I am the nurturing mother, ever pregnant with new life and new possibilities. Take what you need. There is plenty for all. **VII The Chariot.** High above the world below, I meet the dragon. I summon the strength of the dragon chariot to fight my battles, some of which are physical and some of which are struggles within my own mind. I gird myself with strength to fight off the monsters that haunt or torture me, and when I face challenges head-on, I am always the victor. **XIII Death.** Whenever something is lost, there is opportunity to gain something precious and new. This is my lesson. To be transformed, we must first shed away everything that is unnecessary and keeps us chained to the meaningless, until we are stripped to our most basic skeleton. This can be a painful process, for we are not comfortable with loss. At this time, the future may be unclear, but have faith that you are in God's hands now and always. You are a work in progress, on your chosen path to greatness. **XIX The Sun.** I am the welcome burst of good fortune and clarity that floods your senses like the midsummer sun. I bring understanding and glory, happiness and freedom. I bestow vitality and radiance and usher in times of success and confidence. Bask in this moment and enjoy, for this time is fleeting. Just as the sun sets and makes way for darkness, so my brilliance must, in time, give way to rain.

SECOND ROW: **XXI The Universe.** We are the successful completion of a great cycle. Our world is in a state of perfection. We are now whole, and in balance with creation. Our conversations with God have brought great blessings to us and have given us supreme satisfaction. Our sense of peace and harmony contributes great healing energy to the universe, with which we are inextricably connected. Let us savor this wholeness and allow its healing to renew us so that we may embark on a new cycle of life. **King of Swords.** I am the master problem solver. I can process large amounts of information and find the solution, and with equal ease convey the answer to others. I am the just and impartial judge. I cut through chaos with truth as my sword. I see through confusion and can quickly arrive at the source of any issue. I live to the highest standards of ethics and morality, and challenge all who have contact with me to do the same. **6 of Swords.** I feel whipped. I can muster only enough energy to function at the most basic level. If I suffer yet another setback, I am not sure I can survive. I have fought hard to avoid sinking into a deep pit, and I need rest. I need change and renewal. I seek guidance out of the murky turmoil of my life into calmer waters. I hope and trust that a new day is on its way. **2 of Swords.** I am a rock. My emotions are well-guarded, and I hold everyone at arm's length. I believe that as long as I stand firm and resist unpleasant choices, I can be at peace. I work very hard to drive doubt and worry from my mind so that I will not have to face decisions that will rock my world. Life may have become stale and meaningless, but at least I survive and do not feel pain.

THIRD ROW: **Prince of Wands.** I am a great hunter, warrior, and hero. I face danger when others do not dare. I succeed at everything I try. I have had many adventures, and tomorrow I shall embark on yet another. My blood runs hot. I work hard. I play hard. I love deeply, and I hate deeply. My joy can turn to anger in a flash. Some people may say that all I do is blow smoke and make empty promises, and yet they continue to flock to me. I tire of routine quickly, and when I become bored, I must move on. I am tied to no one and I treasure my independence and freedom. **6 of Wands.** I am the spirit of triumph, the euphoric feeling of being recognized for a job well done. After much hard work, preparation, and practice, I have earned this victory, and I am deeply proud of my accomplishment. This is the success that spurs me on to even greater heights. **Princess of Cups.** I am the expectant mother in all of us, dreaming of romance and fulfillment. I surround myself in beauty, peace, and love. My voice is quiet and musical. My gentle nature attracts creatures more timid than I am, and I celebrate the intimacy I share with them. **6 of Cups.** I am the innocent happiness of childhood, the spirit of simple trust and unconditional love. I care for others as others care for me. I relish the joys of life: rolling in the tall meadow grasses, collecting seashells on the seashore, playing in the sun all day long, and sharing secrets with a best friend. I represent the simple pleasures that will be remembered in your fondest memories.

BOTTOM ROW: **2 of Cups.** I am the energy created when two people, groups, ideas, or abilities come together and connect in a meaningful way. I am the fun, harmony, and joy that results from the bond that can be felt only in love and acceptance. My energy heals all. It is playful and exciting, yet at the same time peaceful. Enjoy this happiness now, for these feelings subside as the union matures and becomes even greater. **Queen of Pentacles.** I am the supreme mother. I offer warmth, security, and comfort to all. Everything I have is also yours, for we are in this together. I will stand by you, come what may; I will never forsake you. I will help you find what you need, for my ability to provide knows no bounds. I will teach you to make do with what you have, to take care of matters that need attention in the most efficient way. Life should not be a complicated chore; it should be filled with laughter, children, furry creatures, and lush greens. Together, let us celebrate this amazing gift of life, and all the beauty and abundance mother earth provides. **7 of Pentacles.** I pause a moment to enjoy the fruits of my labors. I think about how things have gone and how I might make better choices in the future. I have learned some valuable lessons from my work thus far. I shall consider trying new approaches where the ones I have used did not serve me as well as I had hoped. For now, I must decide whether I have set a good course and should continue as I have, or whether I should change direction, if even just a little bit. **Ace of Pentacles.** I am a child of the earth. I am in the here and now, my feet firmly planted deep in the ground, my spirit channeling light from the heavens. The earth cares for me and nurtures me, providing all I need with astonishing abundance. I have nothing to fear, for I know who I am, where I belong, where I come from, and where I am going. I am part of something much greater than myself. This connection with all creation is the foundation of my being.

Toon Tarot   Adam Stoller, 1992

Toon Tarot   The artist of the Toon Tarot, Adam Stoller, describes his work as taking "a whimsical approach to the images and symbols of the Rider-Waite deck." The artwork was completed in 1992.

Melissa Townsend Tarot 1993

Melissa Townsend Tarot Melissa Townsend drew the designs of her tarot deck on the backs of business cards from El Teddy's, a friend's restaurant in Manhattan, where she was doing tarot card readings. "I was surprised by the light-hearted quality of the deck that I created—but pleased," the artist writes. "In my observation, most people tend to take readings too seriously. Even those who profess skepticism are often the ones most afraid of what they will hear. In all matters in life, a sense of humor is an invaluable asset. I did not need to be taught to take myself and my pursuits seriously. El Teddy's taught me to take myself lightly as well." The art was made in 1993.

Transitional Tarot Nora Scholin describes her tarot designs: "A Transitional Tarot card consists of three sections that correspond with three levels of interpretation." The three levels are spiritual, mental/emotional, and physical/material. The deck was designed circa 2000.

Tribal Tarot In the words of the artist Orryelle, "The Tribal Tarot depicts bohemians living tribal or semi-tribal lifestyles, secluded from the mainstream of the societies around them and largely independent of them, communities with their own subcultures amalgamated from a diverse range of current and historical/mythological influences. Most of the char-

Transitional Tarot
Nora Scholin, circa 2000
2 The High Priestess

acters depicted in the tarot deck are based on real people: modern primitives, neopagans, and eccentric romantics living now. My correlation of these spirited characters with the timeless archetypes of the tarot is a part of the creation of a contemporary mythology."

The deck, which includes Major and Minor Arcana cards, was finished in 1992.

Typology Tarot Rose Gwain based her tarot designs on Jungian self-actualization. The four suits are color-coded according to psychological function; blue represents swords and thinking; red is for wands and feeling (emotion); yellow is for cups and intuition; and green is for pentacles and sensation. An additional suit is white, spirit, and represents the integration of all the functions. The Major Arcana are abstract paintings. The deck was designed circa 1993.

Typology Tarot Rose Gwain, 1993

Tribal Tarot Orryelle, 1992   The captions are based on correspondence with the artist.

TOP ROW: **0 The Fool** is an adventurer who, uninhibited, hurls himself constantly into new and potentially dangerous experiences. **3 The Empress** represents womanhood in full bloom, fertilized by the male. Her shield is the full moon, and upon it is the symbol of Venus. **4 The Emperor** is a mature, wise man. He is the eagle who may prey upon weaker men to achieve status. **9 The Hermit** is matter within space. To him, all is void but for his own soul, as he turns within on a

journey of self-discovery. **20 Judgement** occurs at a point of change, rebirth.

SECOND ROW: **King of Swords** is an intellectual, a dark, authoritative figure. He is shown at the wheel of a ship, holding a saber. **Queen of Swords** is dreamy, good-natured, calm. **Nine of Swords** shows worry, fear, and anxiety, as a person sits up in bed, sleepless. **Eight of Swords** depicts inner turmoil with a woman whose belly is filled with a dragon. **Six of Swords** is a journey away from strife. A violin is pierced and shattered by swords.

Unity Tarot   Linda J. Franks, 1993

Unity Tarot "As graphic designer, artist, and student of the Mysteries, I began the creation of Unity Tarot in order to fill a personal need for a deck that avoids unnecessary bias and displays in vivid terms the universal nature of the system." Linda J. Franks began the artwork for her deck in 1993; some of the artwork was still in sketch form when sent for inclusion in the *Encyclopedia*.

THIRD ROW: **King of Staves** is a strong and admirable character. **Three of Staves** shows a figure who grasps the middle tree-staff, the archetypal Mother between Maiden and Crone. **Two of Staves** depicts dominion and leadership over a place and its inhabitants. **Queen of Cups** is an intuitive, dreamy, good-natured woman. **Seven of Cups** shows strange chalices of vision, especially of the fantastic spirit.

BOTTOM ROW: **Three of Cups** depicts a dance of gratitude for abundant harvests, harmony, and happiness. **Two of Cups** shows two young people building a foundation of love. **Ace of Cups** is the root of the water suit, representing feelings, emotions, and intuition. **Three of Pentacles** shows a craftsperson forging a pentacle. The smaller figures represent the energies that contribute to the best work: a sylph for air and intellect, an undine for water and emotions, a salamander for fire and creativity, and a gnome for earth and physical labor. **Two of Pentacles** shows the juggler, a balance of the Magician and the Fool.

Universal Doorway Tarot Alexander S. Holub designed a tarot "on the surrealistic line," as he describes it. The concept is based on cosmology, or "construction of the universe." Based on the premise of tarot being a vehicle of myth, and cosmology being a branch of myth, the artist says in the manuscript accompanying the art, "The way that our mind constructs our own universe and the way that the greater universe was constructed are much the same. Consequently, since there was much mythical reference in the early tarot trumps, they were probably a means of gaining an understanding of creation by passing down in mythical characters and symbols the underlying meanings of the stories associated with those characters and symbols…. By an understanding of the symbols, the individual could expand his awareness of himself, his created universe, and all of existence." The deck was created in 1991.

John Upton Tarot The tarot artwork by John Upton was mentored by his African Caribbean wife. It was completed in 1992.

Urban Tarot The Urban Tarot depicts scenes from contemporary life. The artist Morgana Abbey worked with Christopher Abbey on the designs, in 1996.

Urban Tarot: War and Peace in the Streets Graffiti artists Anatol Luthi and George Hogan created two tarot cards based on urban street life. The designs were made circa 2000.

Collection of the artist

Collection of the artist

John Upton Tarot 1992

Universal Doorway Tarot Alexander S. Holub, 1991 Descriptions are by the artist.

TOP ROW: **Fool** is the beginning and the end of all creation and represents the universal processes of Involution (birth), Evolution (existence), and Devolution (death). **IV The Emperor** represents the "opening" or "window" in Involution by which energy begins to take form and become matter. It is the potentiality for life. **V The Hierophant** illustrates the laws by which energy becomes matter. These laws are modes of action that determine the nature of things. **IX The Hermit** is the second stage of Evolution. It is the harmony and balance that is the root of Evolution. **XII The Hanged Man** represents the primeval life forms that have the potential for all the life forms that exist and eventually become a living system.

SECOND ROW: **XIII Death** portrays the point when groups of cells banded together to form more complex structures in order to increase their chances for survival. **XVI The Tower** is the point where congealed energies begin to transform into a higher vibrational rate, expanding

beyond their physical housing. **XVII The Star** shows the Devolving energies beginning to break the bonds of their physical housing and interacting with each other, transcending into higher levels. **XIX The Sun** shows the Devolving energies beginning to return back to their source—back to the ether, becoming Light. **XX Judgement** is the point where Devolving energies become Light. These energies are no longer attached to any sort of physicality existing without time and space.

BOTTOM ROW: **Knight of Swords** is the Refining or Purification of Thought. It is the area where a concept takes on a more definite form as a thought object. **Ace of Swords** shows the mental attitudes and ideas that cause us to react uniquely to situations. **10 Wands** is the identification with and accumulation of physical objects that weigh down the expansion to greater levels. **Ace of Cups** represents our purity of purpose, truth, and our emotions. It is our self-unity and knowingness on higher levels. **Back design.**

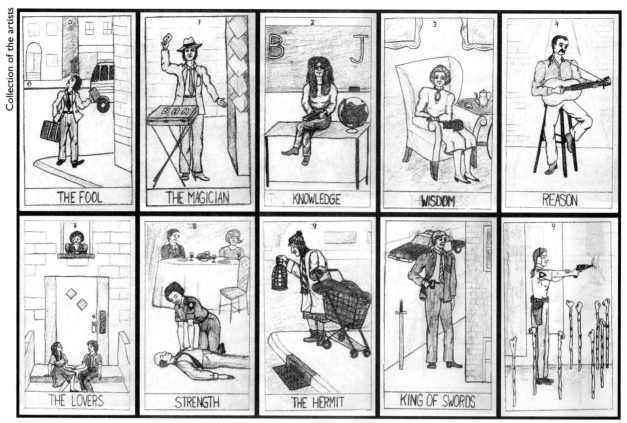

Urban Tarot   Morgana Abbey and Christopher Abbey, 1996

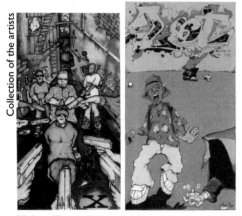

Urban Tarot: War and Peace in the Streets   Anatol Luthi and George Hogan, 2000   Ten of Swords. Ace of Pentacles.

"000 The Artist" from the Viggo Tarot   Viggo describes the card: "The definitively shamanistic and alchemical operations performed by artists, often using solvents and metals, puts them on a level with the Magician. Indeed the Tarot, itself a series of visionary images for augury and communication, has in every case been visually interpreted and created by artists."

Victorian Tarot   "Nothing captures the Victorian period more completely than the beautiful greeting cards, advertisements, and other paper ephemera which is known as Victorian scrap art," says Laurie Amato, artist of the Victorian Tarot. "These captivating color pictures of children, animals, and flowers were collected by Victorian ladies who created the popular pastime of pasting the scraps into decorative albums." The Victorian Tarot was created in 1996. Each card has a background of moire taffeta, bordered by antique lace and overlaid with ribbons, charms, and scrap art of the period.

Viggo Tarot   Bryon Wake, the Los Angeles artist and designer known as Viggo, designed a tarot deck in a pop expressionist style. The deck includes four extra Major Arcana: The Space Card, 00 Phone Man, 000 The Artist, and 0000 The Dreamer. A prototype of the deck was made in 1998. "The stylistic unity characterizing the imagery of this colorful deck balances a world of both urban and pastoral environments," says Viggo.

Collection of the artist

Victorian Tarot   Laurie Amato, 1996

TOP ROW: 0 The Fool. I The Magician. III The Empress. V The Hierophant.

SECOND ROW: VI The Lovers. VII The Chariot. VIII Strength. IX The Hermit.

THIRD ROW: XI Justice. XII Hanged Man. XIII Death. XIV Temperance.

BOTTOM ROW: XV Devil. XVIII The Moon. XX Judgement. XXI The World.

Viggo Tarot   Bryon Wake (Viggo), 1998   The bottom right card is The Space Card.

Eduoardo Vilela Tarot "Due to the chaos humanity faces at the end of this millennium, I decided there was a need to stimulate human beings to reflect on the reasons for this situation and what could be done to change it," says Brazilian artist Eduoardo Vilela. "Therefore, I got my inspiration from tarot's Greatest Arcana to do my work, trying to induce humanity to reflect upon the purpose and meaning of life." Vilela's tarot paintings were made in 1997.

Virgin Tarot The Virgin Tarot is named after the spiritual master of the Russian artist Alexander Egorov. About the designs, Egorov says, "It is a look into tarot from the point where all spiritual ways are joining, where there are no counteractions and animosities, there are no politics." The designs were made circa 1993.

Collection of the artist

Eduoardo Vilela Tarot 1997

Virgin Tarot
Alexander Egorov, circa 1993 Magician. Wheel of Fortune. Temperance.

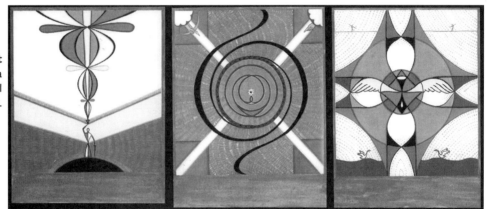

Collection of the artist

Ronald C. Waller Tarot Ronald C. Waller made black and white designs for the tarot in 1993.

Janet Wheeler Tarot Janet Wheeler's photo and art collage tarot designs were made circa 1996.

Carol Williams Tarot "These tarot cards are specially drawn using the power of color," Carol Williams writes, "a wish on the part of the artist that they may assist those who use them to gain a better understanding of self and the greater reality. The two main requirements to achieve these aims are ruthless self-honesty and a true desire to understand." The designs were made in 1987.

Paula Wittner Tarot Paula Wittner of Arizona painted the Fool in 1990.

Wonderland Tarot Children's book illustrator Jesse Spicer Zerner created images for a tarot based on fairytales. The Wonderland illustrations were made in 1991.

Collection of the artist

Ronald C. Waller Tarot 1993

Janet Wheeler Tarot Circa 1996

TOP ROW: 0 The Fool. 1 The Magician. 2 The High Priestess. 3 The Empress. 4 The Emperor. SECOND ROW: 5 The Pope. 6 The Lovers. 7 The Chariot. 8 Strength. 9 The Hermit. THIRD ROW: 10 Wheel of Fortune. 11 Justice. 12 The Hanged Man. 13 Death. 14 Temperance. BOTTOM ROW: 15 The Devil. 16 The Tower. 17 The Star. 18 The Moon. 19 The Sun.

Carol Williams Tarot 1987

Paula Wittner Tarot
1990 The Fool.

Wonderland Tarot Jesse
Spicer Zerner, 1991 The Fool.
The Empress.

Mercedes Letitia Yaeger Tarot 1998

Mercedes Letitia Yaeger Tarot Mercedes Letitia Yaeger drew on her experience in theater set design to create Major Arcana, using laser copies and card stock. "In my work, both in theater and art, I have always relied on unifying design themes," she says in a letter to Stuart Kaplan. The Washington state artist created her Major Arcana from 1996 to 1998.

PUBLISHED TAROT DECKS

The tarot decks in this chapter comprise artwork printed as decks and distributed in quantities that make them readily available, at least for the time that they are in print. This chapter also includes a special section devoted to Japanese tarot decks.

Adrian Tarot Swiss painter and designer Adrian Bernhard Koehli completed the Adrian Tarot with illustration software, using photographs as a basis for layers of figures and objects. The deck was created as a university project. Each Major Arcana has on it a Hebrew letter. When the cards I through X are laid out vertically, three across, with I at the top, the shadow figure of the man on VI The Lovers is revealed, symbolizing the Tree of Life. When cards XI through XIX are laid out in the same way, with XI at the bottom, a shadow figure of the woman on VI the Lovers symbolizes the Tree of Knowledge. The Minor Arcana, too, piece together to form the shadows of the man and the woman. The titles are in German and English. Adrian Tarot was published in 1997 by AGMüller, Neuhausen, Switzerland.

African Tarot: Journey into the Self The African Tarot features African scenes and people, in the context of the Rider-Waite Tarot's symbolism and composition. Fresh emotions and natural scenery color the cards, which are meant to be gentle and accessible to all. The artist of the deck is Marina Romito of South Africa. Denese Palm cowrote the text of the booklet accompanying the deck. The cards are small, measuring about 3 by 2.5 inches. The eighty-card deck includes a title card and introductory card. The packaging of the deck is unusual: a paper box with a lid of corrugated cardboard, with top and bottom labeled with a card glued on. The back design is

inspired by the culture of the Shangaan, a group indigenous to South Africa. The tortoise symbolizes the slow coming of justice, a reference to the election of Nelson Mandela as president in 1994, after many years of oppression. U.S. Games Systems, Stamford, Connecticut, published the African Tarot in 1997.

Alchemical Tarot The Major Arcana of the Alchemical Tarot, say authors Rosemary Ellen Guiley and Robert M. Place, "is a textbook for the Great Work and each card is a step in the process. The alchemist, represented by the Fool, begins with the *prima materia,* represented by the Magician, and culminates in merging with the Anima Mundi or God consciousness, represented by the World." The cards of the deck represent the principles and symbols of alchemy, described in mundane terms as the process of turning lead into gold, and in spiritual terms as the "path…to transcend the world of matter and rise into the world of spirit." The deck, illustrated by Robert M. Place, was published by Thorsons of London in 1995. The back design is a rose.

Alchemisten Tarot This Belgian tarot applies to the tarot antique engravings with alchemical subjects. The illustrations of the deck often show symbolic images of chemical procedures for creating desired substances. The creator of the deck is Guido Gillabel. The large cards (8.25 by 5.5 inches) are in black and white with Flemish titles. The decks were issued in a numbered edition of 250. Each deck comprises twenty-two Major Arcana plus a presentation card. The deck was also issued in a limited edition of 120. It was packaged in a wooden box and included an extra card and instruction booklet. De Hierofant published both editions of the deck in 1987.

Adrian Tarot   Adrian Bernhard Koehli, AGMüller, 1997
The descriptions are based on the images and on the booklet, by Miki Krefting, accompanying the deck.

TOP ROW: **0 THE FOOL** is young and, literally, green. The fossilized ammonite symbolizes change, the cycle of life, the rhythm of nature. **III THE EMPRESS,** in a dark red dress, sits like a brooding hen on an egg. **IV THE EMPEROR** straddles the sphere of his power, which is too large to hold. An ankh, Egyptian symbol of life, is in front of the sphere, and an eagle is above. **V THE HIEROPHANT** holds two keys on strings, the keys to heaven and earth. He is lifeless, resembling a puppet. **VI THE LOVERS** is a central card in the deck, as the figures of the man and the woman form a motif throughout the rest of the cards. The cloth that covers their loins wraps both of them. The scissors symbolize decision.

SECOND ROW: **VII THE CHARIOT. IX THE HERMIT. XI STRENGTH** shows a woman holding weights. A lion's face forms a golden disk before her. **XII THE HANGED MAN** smiles despite the crisis he is in. A rose window is superimposed behind his head and over his chest. **XIII DEATH** swings a scythe over a human skull. The skull denotes that only humans are aware of the passage of time and thus their own impermanence.

THIRD ROW: **XVI THE TOWER** shows a person wielding a lightning bolt. An ancient Egyptian-style eye, "the eye of God," is above him. **XVII THE STAR** shows "the good fairy." She taps the fountain of life. **XVIII THE MOON** is guarded by twin manifestations of the Egyptian god of the underworld, Anubis. The Moon stands for the unconscious. The danger of this realm is symbolized by the predatory fish that swim below the surface. Note that a corner of the face of the female Lover is in the upper left corner of the card. **XIX THE SUN** is a golden disk, observing with big eyes. The two children are twin girls from China, called "the land of smiles" in German. They are descendants of the Sun. **XXI THE WORLD** shows a green woman, the counterpart to the Fool, sitting atop the globe of Earth.

BOTTOM ROW: **ACE [of Swords]: CLARITY OF AIR. KING OF WANDS** is bathed in a fiery red glow. **QUEEN OF CUPS** appears in the outlines of a fountain. Her head is festooned with the roses of love, and her attention is turned inward. **ACE OF CUPS: HAPPINESS OF WATER** shows the water of life as a perfect drop entering the chalice. **KING OF DISKS** lives amidst plenty, as symbolized by the dark, sweet grapes, the gold disk behind him, and the disk he wears.

The Fool | The Magician | The High Priestess | The Empress | The Hierophant

The Lovers | The Chariot | strength | The Hermit | Wheel of Fortune

African Tarot: Journey Into the Self   Marina Romito, artist, and Denese Palm, U.S. Games Systems, 1997   Descriptions are based on the imagery and on the booklet accompanying the deck.

TOP ROW: **0 The Fool** represents the inner child. **I The Magician** represents the beginning of conscious, goal-oriented effort. **II The High Priestess** is surrounded by pomegranates, stars, and palm trees. She refers to the subconscious knowledge of deep inner mysteries, intuition, and imagination. **III The Empress** is surrounded by fruits and vegetables, the bounty of the earth. **V The Hierophant.**

SECOND ROW: **VI The Lovers** shows a man and woman who represent the equal union of male (conscious intellect) and female (subconscious knowledge). **VII The Chariot** represents the triumph of self-discipline, with a man who has two lions under his command. **VIII Strength** represents the mind-force, spiritual power. **IX The Hermit** is in a time of solitude and inner contemplation. **X The Wheel of Fortune** shows a rainbow between the hills as the sun shines and rain falls. On the wheel is written "ROTA," for wheel, and the Hebrew letters for the name of "the divine one," as A.E. Waite described it.

African Tarot (continued)   THIRD ROW: **XII The Hanged Man** represents the willingness to change perspective for a greater cause. **XIII Death** represents change. The card departs from the Rider-Waite symbolism to show a monk with corpse and mourner. The sun is between two pillars in the background. **XIV Temperance** means a harmonious state of consciousness. **XVII The Star** reveals inspiration, faith and hope. **XIX The Sun** shows happiness awakening the life force.   BOTTOM ROW: **Page of Swords** carries a spear. **Ace of Wands. VI of Cups. Ace of Cups. Queen of Pentacles.**

Alchemical Tarot   Rosemary Ellen Guiley and Robert M. Place, Thorsons, 1995   The description is based on those in the book accompanying the deck.

TOP ROW: **0 The Fool** represents the neophyte alchemist. His blindfold signifies ignorance of the basic principles of alchemy. He is unaware of the hare, an archetypal guide to the underworld of the unconscious, and of the guiding Platonic star, which, in Jungian terms, is the self. The feathers in his cap are sensors for the higher self. **II The High Priestess** makes a gesture of silence. In her moon boat, she becomes the gateway to the deepest parts of ourselves. **V The Hierophant** holds his book open; the secrets are to be read by all. His triple crown represents the kingdoms of animal, vegetable, and mineral. The small figures represent the Emperor and the Empress, who are being joined in sacred

marriage. **VII The Chariot.** A young man sets off on the alchemical journey, a hero's journey. The vision before him is the solar wheel, or wheel of the year. In the center of the wheel is the alchemical trinity of mercury, salt, and sulphur, with the sun, representing the self, at its center. The alchemical process the charioteer represents is sublimation, whereby a substance, when heated, passes directly into a gaseous state, bypassing liquefaction, and ascends to the top of the alchemical vessel, where it condenses. Sublimation improves quality. **VIII Justice** weighs fire and water; she balances the masculine and feminine principles. Her alchemical process is called disposition, in which correct proportions are determined by weight before they are sealed in the retort. The hilt of her sword bears the symbol for vitriol, or "oil of glass," which is the secret fire.

SECOND ROW: **IX The Hermit** is a Saturnic figure representing lead. He rules the nigredo, the dark phase, signified by his black companion, the raven. His alchemical process is exaltation, in which the *prima materia,* now recombined and balanced, is dissolved into a purer or higher degree of itself. **X The Wheel of Fortune** shows a double ouroboros. It represents the fixed (the serpent at the bottom) and the volatile (the top serpent), each transforming into one another in an unending cycle. The Wheel of Fortune is an overview of the whole alchemical process, placed in the center of the trumps. **XI Strength** holds a flaming heart, symbol of love. The sun and moon pour the masculine and feminine liquids into the heart-shaped vessel. The alchemical process is fermentation, part of the process of exaltation, in which a ferment is incorporated with the matter, bringing it to a higher form—this is an analogy for the soul entering the body. The green lion refers to antimony, which can free gold from impurities. **XIII Death** stands chained to the alchemical vessel, which has been blackened in the furnace. At the center is a well-formed nigredo, which is also represented by the raven. In the process of mortification and putrefaction, the celestial element is separated, and the matter rots and putrifies. **XIV Temperance** represents time; the water pouring from one cup to another is a clock. The rose is symbol of perfection of the alchemical opus. Distillation extracts the material from its solution by forced evaporation.

THIRD ROW: **XV The Devil.** Hermes/Mercury is a red dragon on top of the same vessel shown on the Death card. Coagulation reduces matter to a solid state in a homogenous body, the Lovers united into the form of the hermaphrodite. They coagulate in the darkness while awaiting rebirth. **XVI The Tower** is the oven, the atanor, in which the elixir is prepared. The process is the second, or great, separation or dissolution. The power of the strike separates the solution into the masculine red and the feminine white. The man is the alchemist and the woman is the "mystic sister." **XVII The Star** shows a goddess whose body is literally the fountain of life. Her breasts stream blood and milk; with the sea water they form the alchemical trinity of sulphur, mercury, and salt. **King of Swords** is master of the intellect. **Two of Swords** shows swords crossed in opposition. Athena's owl is the symbol of wisdom and war.

BOTTOM ROW: **Five of Staffs** shows the creative hand of an artist, inventor, scientist, or entrepreneur. **Ace of Staffs.** The salamander helps the substance under transformation give up its secret fire. **Four of Vessels** represents physical and emotional balance, the body in harmony with the emotions. **Ace of Vessels** shows a fish bearing the alchemist's retort. The blood from the heart is the water of life. **Two of Coins.** The lion represents the fixed in alchemy; it swallows an eagle, which represents the volatile. This is a fitting image for the earth suit, for it shows fixation in the material plane.

211

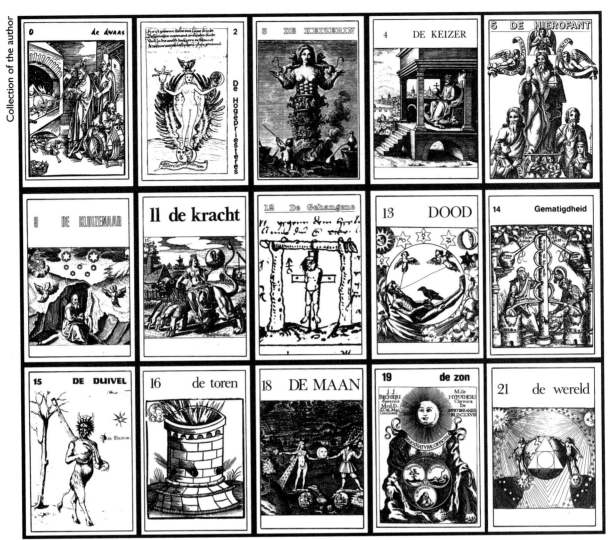

Alchemisten Tarot Guido Gillabel, De Hierofant, 1987

TOP ROW: **0 de dwaas** (The Fool) is "The Workshop of the Alchemist," from *Ship of Fools* by S. Brant, Basil, 1494. In the early Renaissance, the figure wearing ass' ears signified foolishness. **2 De Hogepriesteres** (The High Priestess) depicts "Philosophical Quicksilver" or Mercury. It is Parisian, from the sixteenth century. **3 DE KEIZERIN** (The Empress) is the title page of an alchemical work by Urbani Hierne, Stockholm, 1712. The figure of the Great Mother stands over the alchemical forge. **4 DE KEIZER** (The Emperor) is from *A Treatise on the Philosopher's Stone*, by Van Lambsprinck, 1678. **5 DE HIEROFANT** (The Hierophant) is from I.M.D.R., *Bibliothèque des philosophes chemiques*, Paris, 1741.

SECOND ROW: **9 DE KLUIZENAAR** (The Hermit) is from *Philosophia reformata* by Johann Daniel Mylius, Frankfurt,

1622. **11 de kracht** (Strength) is from *Philosophia reformata*. **12 De Gehangene** (The Hanged Man) is from *De Alchimia*, circa 1526. **13 DOOD** (Death) is from *Viridarium*, by Daniel Stolcius de Stolcenberg, Frankfurt, 1624. **14 Gematigdheid** (Temperance) is the titlepiece to *Liber de arte distillandi*, by Hieronymous Brunschwygt, Strassburg, 1507.

BOTTOM ROW: **15 DE DUIVEL** (The Devil) is an anonymous work from the fourteenth century. **16 de toren** (The Tower) is from *Coelum philosophorum* by P. Ulstadius, Strassburg, 1528. **18 DE MAAN** (The Moon) is a detail from *Musaeum hermeticum reformatum et amplificatum* by Janitor Pansophus, Frankfurt, 1678. **19 de zon** is the title page from *Actorum Laboratorii Chymici Monacensis, seu Physicae Subterranene*, by Johann Joachim Becher, Frankfurt, 1669. **21 de wereld** (The World) is from *Philosophia reformata* by Johann Daniel Mylius, Frankfurt, 1622.

Ananda Tarot German artist Ananda Kurt Pilz applied a surrealistic style to the tarot. His deck was published by Urania Verlag, Neuhausen, Switzerland, in 2001. The back design is an abstract rectangular pattern. The deck includes an advertising card and a card with a biographical sketch of Pilz. The suits are Schwerter (swords), Flammen (flames), Kelche (cups), and Kugeln (spheres).

Ancestral Path Tarot The introductory card of the Ancestral Path Tarot, by Julie Cuccia-Watts, describes the deck as one that "threads together the diverse beliefs of various cultures in order to find commonalities of experience between them. It examines the traditions of our ancestors through mythology to reclaim a personal spirituality that enables us to perceive the divine in ourselves and others." The images on the suit cards draw from races, geographical areas, and historical periods: swords are yellow/Japanese feudal era; staves are black/Egyptian nineteenth dynasty of Ramses II; cups are white/Arthurian Britain; and sacred circles (coins) are red/Native America after the Europeans landed. Legends and songs interweave throughout the suits. For example, the sacred circles tell a Menominee creation legend of Bear and Thunder Spirit, and a Winnebago medicine song. The court cards are deified ancestral figures. The Major Arcana are also founded on many different traditions. The back design shows a globe with an image of people on a hill reflected. The colors are blended blue and green. The deck includes a title card and an introductory card, and it was published by U.S. Games Systems, Stamford, Connecticut, in 1995.

Angels Tarot Rosemary Ellen Guiley, one of the creators of the Angels Tarot, was inspired to explore the presence of angels by dreams of a "glowing silvery woman" whom she named "The Silver Lady." Robert Michael Place, who co-created and illustrated the deck, grew up with angels, as it were, contemplating stained glass window depictions of them while attending mass as a boy and later exploring them at the Metropolitan Museum of Art in New York. He says in the book accompanying the deck, "Some religions focus on unity, and are therefore monotheistic; others focus on the many archetypal manifestations, and are therefore polytheistic. In our Western traditions angels bridge this gap; they allow the monotheistic traditions to bridge this gap and incorporate the innumerable archetypes." The Angels Tarot was published by HarperSanFrancisco, in 1995.

Animal Tarot Paula J. Gibby made the Animal Tarot using photocollage. The deck was published in 2001, in a handmade edition, by Sun Productions, New York.

Collection of the artist

Animal Tarot Paula J. Gibby, Sun Productions, 2001

TOP ROW: I DER MAGIER. II DIE HOHEPRIESTERIN. III DIE HERRSCHERIN. VII DER WAGENLENKER. VIII DIE GERECHTIGKEIT.

SECOND ROW: IX DER EREMIT. X DAS SCHICKSALSRAD. XI DIE KRAFT. XII DIE UMKEHR. XV DER TEUFEL.

THIRD ROW: XVI DER TURM. XVII DER STERN. XVIII DER MOND. XX DIE ZEITENWENDE. XXII DER NARR.

BOTTOM ROW: KÖNIGIN DER SCHWERTER. RITTER DER FLAMMEN. RITTER DER KELCHE. KELCHE VIII. KUGELN VIII.

Ananda Tarot   Ananda Kurt Pilz, Urania Verlag, 2001   TOP ROW: I Der Magier (The Magician). II Die Hohepriesterin (The High Priestess). III Die Herrscherin (The Empress). VII Der Wagenlenker (The Charioteer). VIII Die Gerechtigkeit (Justice). SECOND ROW: IX Der Eremit (The Hermit). X Das Schicksalsrad (The Wheel of Fortune). XI Die Kraft (Strength). XII Die Umkehr (The Reversal). XV Der Teufel (The Devil).   THIRD ROW: XVI Der Turm (The Tower). XVII Der Stern (The Star). XVIII Der Mond (The Moon). XX Die Zeitenwende (Change in Time [as in, the coming of a new age, the turn of the century]). XXII Der Narr (The Fool).   BOTTOM ROW: Königin der Schwerter (Queen of Swords). Ritter der Flammen (Knight of Flames). Ritter der Kelche (Knight of Cups). Kelche VIII (Eight of Cups). Kugeln VIII (Eight of Spheres).

Ancestral Path Tarot   Julie Cuccia-Watts, U.S. Games Systems, 1995   The description is based on Tracey Hoover's booklet, which accompanies the deck.   TOP ROW: **0 THE FOOL** has the tarot deck spread out before her. Puppets and jesters decorate her mirrored throne. **I THE MAGICIAN** appears to be in a cave with the Celtic fertility god Cernunnos and a horse painted on the wall. **III THE EMPRESS** is pregnant. Her foot rests upon a tiled crescent. **IV THE EMPEROR** wears a totemic headdress. A raven perches on his ankh staff. **VI THE LOVERS.** A snake is in the fruit trees behind the woman, and astrological symbols are in the tree behind the man.   SECOND ROW: **X THE WHEEL OF FORTUNE** shows the wheel of the zodiac. Below it are ancient standing stones and symbols. **XI STRENGTH. XII THE HANGED ONE** is an embryo, ourselves as ancestors with the potential to give birth to our own impact on human culture. **XVII THE STAR.** A woman pours water from pottery bearing designs of the Pacific Northwest of America. Behind her is a tree carved with astrological symbols. **XX JUDGMENT.** A woman seems to be pushing through the tissue of a dream. A sleeper lies below.   THIRD ROW: **XXI THE WORLD. KING OF SWORDS** is Izanagi, a creator deity of ancient Japan. **QUEEN OF SWORDS** is Izanami, also a creator deity of ancient Japan. **QUEEN OF STAVES** is Isis of ancient Egypt, goddess of the moon and magic. **TEN OF STAVES.**   BOTTOM ROW: **EIGHT OF STAVES. SEVEN OF CUPS** shows cups filled with various images, some religious, some of lovers. **ACE OF CUPS** is a wish-fulfilling cup with a fish, symbolic of Christ. A whale leaps in the background. **KING OF SACRED CIRCLES** is Grandfather Thunder of Menominee lore. **TEN OF SACRED CIRCLES.**

Adamel — The Fool Who Attained Knowledge

Abraxas — Angel of Magic

Gabriel — Angel of Revelation

Mary — Queen of Angels

Metatron — King of Angels

Raphael — Angel of Healing

Cherubiel — Chief of the Charioteers

Michael — Champion of Justice

Orifiel — Angel of Wilderness

Abaddon — Angel of Death

Barakiel — Lightning of God

Moon — Angel of Dreams

Uriel — Regent of the Sun

Shekinah — Soul of the World

Knight of Spades

Lady of Clubs

Lady of Diamonds

Angels Tarot   Rosemary Ellen Guiley and Robert Michael Place, HarperSanFrancisco, 1995

TOP ROW: **Adamel: The Fool Who Attained Knowledge** is the first man of Hebrew cosmology, his name in angelic form. The Hebrew suffix "el" means "shining one." His nudity symbolizes his return to his original innocence. The apple in his hand symbolizes disobedience to God, and it also symbolizes knowledge. **I Abraxas: Angel of Magic** has a human torso, symbolizing articulated thought, a cock's head, for watchfulness, and serpentine legs, for power tempered by prudence. The whip he holds stands for relentless driving power. The shield has on it letters representing the name of God, and it represents the wisdom that guards warriors. The sun and the moon above are for the union of opposites: dark and light, masculine and feminine. **II Gabriel: Angel of Revelation** is shown in the classic pose of the annunciation, the announcement to Mary that she would be mother of God. With his right hand, he beckons all to listen. The lily symbolizes purity. **III Mary: Queen of Angels** stands atop a crescent moon that has the radiance of the sun. Her hands radiate to beings love and compassion. **IV Metatron: King of Angels** stands huge, towering over the earth. His sword indicates the power of death. The orb is the power of life. He is the mightiest angel of Kabbalistic lore.

SECOND ROW: **V Raphael: Angel of Healing** holds the snake-twined healing staff of Asclepius, Greek god of medicine. He holds the books he gave Noah. The fish on the ground is the one he gave to Tobit, when teaching the mortal how to use fish for healing and exorcisms. **VII Cherubiel: Chief of the Charioteers** is chief of the Cherubim, the charioteers of God. The flame at his crown is the fire of God. The flaming, many-eyed wheels at his feet are the ophanim, thrones, or chariots of God. Their eyes symbolize all-seeing wisdom. **VIII Michael: Champion of Justice** tramples evil, with the scales of truth and justice in his left hand and the sword of victory in the other. **IX Orifiel: Angel of Wilderness** holds a staff symbolic of his role as wandering philosopher. In Kabbalistic lore, Orifiel is linked with Saturn, called in Greek Kronos, who rules the passage of time. **XIII Abaddon: Angel of Death** is shown as the traditional "Grim Reaper." In some lore, he is considered king of demons, and in other versions he is considered the agent of God who holds Satan in Hell.

THIRD ROW: **XVI Barakiel: Lightning of God** prepares to destroy a tower with his sword of lightning, which represents enlightenment and the destruction of illusions. **XVIII Moon: Angel of Dreams. XIX Uriel: Regent of the Sun** is based both on the traditional image of Uriel and on a vision had by the illustrator. The sun in which he stands is enlightening. The fire he holds can punish sinners and is also connected with alchemy, which he gave humanity. Uriel is also credited with giving people the Kabbalah. **XXI Shekinah: Soul of the World** is enclosed in a mandorla symbolizing the gateway to the mysteries. Her nudity symbolizes uncovered truth. She holds the sword of truth and power and the heart of life. The creatures in the corner represent, among other things, the four evangelists of the New Testament. **Knight of Spades** holds a shield emblazoned with a cloud, representing air.

BOTTOM ROW: **Ace of Spades. Lady of Clubs** holds a shield decked with a salamander, representing fire. **Seven of Clubs. Nine of Hearts. Lady of Diamonds** has a shield on which a rabbit symbolizes earth.

Animal-Wise Tarot   Ted Andrews created the Animal-Wise Tarot from stock photographs. Each card features a different animal that exemplifies tarot symbolism, and a tarot title, the name of the animal, and a few key words of meaning. The back design is a silhouette of a griffin. The intention of the artist in creating the deck was "to help align us with the intimate wisdom of animals for insight, self-knowledge and even divination, opening a window for us to the language and wisdom of animals." The Major Arcana have traditional titles, but the Minor Arcana have suits that parallel with different kinds of animals and beliefs about them. Traditional wands are the ancient ones and feature reptiles and salamanders. Swords are the winged ones and feature birds. Cups are the shapeshifters and depict insects and arachnids. Coins are the four-leggeds and show mammals. Animal-Wise Tarot was published in 1999 by Dragonhawk Publishing, Jackson, Tennessee.

Anonymous Dutch Tarot   A full tarot deck with Dutch titles is unidentified except for the artist's sigil in the lower right corner. The deck probably dates from the 1930s, judging by the style, the age of the paper, the back design, and the coarse printing screen used. The symbolism is traditional, and yet the cards show original thought and in-depth study of the occult significance of the tarot. Nontraditional numbering is on cards XVIII Temperance, XIV Judgment, XX The Tower, and XVI The Moon. The figures of the Minor Arcana show dwarves for swords, sylphs for staves, mermen and mermaids for cups, and children for pentacles.

Anonymous French Tarot   This deck went through a few collectors, remaining anonymous at each change of hands. It was originally sent to the manager of a French playing card club, as a sample. The collector did not maintain a record of the artist's name and never heard further from him or her. The deck was then sold to another French collector. It is now in a private American collection. It was most likely rendered circa 1980 as linoleum or woodcut block prints, then hand-colored in mauve, orange, and green. It is in a paper box with the Hermit and the Sun on the cover.

Tarocchi dell'Apocalisse (Tarot of the Apocalypse) The deck by Raffaello Mori comprises the Major Arcana. In disturbing, Boschean scenes, the Italian artist interprets the tarot with grinning, sinister figures and muted colors. The originals were painted in oil, and the cards are printed on paper that has the texture of fine fabric. The artist was born in Firenze in 1934. Lo Scarabeo of Turin, Italy, published the deck in 1990.

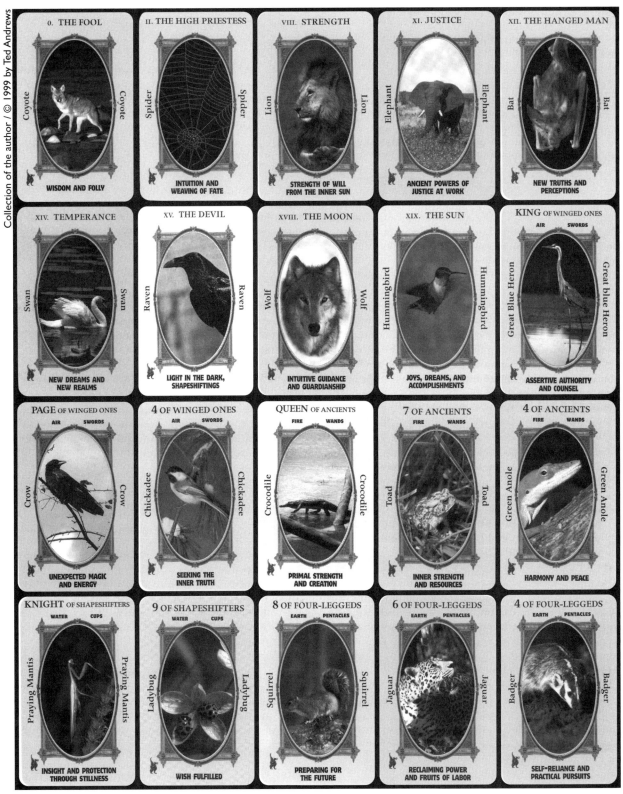

Animal-Wise Tarot   Ted Andrews, Dragonhawk Publishing, 1999

Anonymous Dutch Tarot Artist and publisher unknown, circa 1935

TOP ROW: XXII. DE DWAAS (The Fool). I. DE MAGIER (The Magician). II. DE HOOGE PRIESTERES (The High Priestess). V. DE HIEROPHANT (The Hierophant). VI. DE LIEFDE (The Lover).

SECOND ROW: IX. DE PELGRIM (The Pilgrim). X. HET RAD VAN FORTUIN (The Wheel of Fortune). XI. KRACHT (Strength). XII. DE GEHANGENE (The Hanged Man). XIII. DE DOOD (Death).

THIRD ROW: XV. DE DUIVEL (The Devil). XVI. DE MAAN (The Moon). XVIII MATIGING (Temperance). XIX. DE ZON (The Sun). XXI. DE WERELD (The World).

BOTTOM ROW: ZWAARDEN - 7 (Seven of Swords). STAVEN - 8 (Eight of Staves). BEKERS - 9 (Nine of Cups). PENTAKELS - PAGE (Page of Pentacles). PENTAKELS - 2 (Two of Pentacles).

Anonymous French Tarot   Circa 1980

Tarocchi dell'Apocalisse   Raffaello Mori, Lo Scarabeo, 1990

TOP ROW: **0 IL MATTO** (The Fool) is in a cauldron. He holds the United States flag in his left hand. Coming out of the cauldron are skewered frogs. Grinning faces cluster around him. **I IL BAGATTO** (The Magician) is hunched over an ovoid object. Birds are behind him. **II LA PAPESSA** (The Popess) regards herself in a mirror. Birdlike creatures surround her. **III L'IMPERATRICE** (The Empress) is in a mob of women. **IV L'IMPERATORE** (The Emperor) is in a subdued crowd of men bearing white banners.

SECOND ROW: **VI GLI AMANTI** (The Lovers) embrace behind a wall, with faces peering over. **VII IL CARRO** (The Chariot) is a winged vehicle driven by a winged, horned creature. Angelic beings are in the sky. **VIII LA GIUSTIZIA** (Justice) holds the traditional scales and sword. On the ground are faces pierced and bleeding. **XIII LA MORTE** (Death) is pregnant or bloated with her feast. **XIV LA TEMPERANZA** (Temperance) kneels in a flowered meadow, holding a vase into which water pours. This is one of the few cards in the deck that has tranquil imagery.

BOTTOM ROW: **XV IL DIAVOLO** (The Devil) shows bodies stuck in cauldrons of flame, behind a horned, crowned devil. **XVI LA TORRE** (The Tower) cracks and topples as angelic figures play trumpets in the sky. **XVIII LA LUNA** (The Moon) is connected to earth by a long ladder. A United States flag is planted on it. **XIX IL SOLE** (The Sun) shines on a man sprawled by a pond. Flowers and animals crowd the ground. The sun seems to be sinking in water. **XX IL GIUDIZIO** (Judgment) shows three angels blowing trumpets as bodies emerge from the ground.

Tarocchi Art Nouveau Antonella Castelli created Tarocchi Art Nouveau based on the turn-of-the-century art style, with its organic curves and floral motifs. The cards are titled in English, French, German, Spanish, and Italian. The deck features a title card and an advertising card. The back design is a double-ended rendition of 0 The Fool, in monotone purple. The deck was published by Lo Scarabeo, Turin, in 1998.

Art of Tarot The deck that accompanies the book *The Art of Tarot* was commissioned for the set. Liz Dean, author of the book, writes, "The cards in your new tarot deck have been specially commissioned to reflect both longstanding tarot imagery and to aid modern evaluation. Both the Devil and the Death cards in the Major Arcana have been re-interpreted, as their traditionally ghoulish appearance, particularly in the novice, can color one's judgment of a reading. Death, for example, appears not as the poised grim reaper, but as a dying tree and a new tree, representing the symbolic death of a particular phase of one's life." The illustrations by Emma Garner recall romantic Victorian prints. Fragments of printed text appear on the clothes of the figures. The back design shows a tree holding the four suit symbols. The deck was published by Cico Books, London, and Barnes & Noble Books, New York, in 2001.

Arthurian Tarot The images of the Arthurian Tarot are not so much the medieval images usually associated with King Arthur, but rather the "so-called Dark Age Arthur," as authors Caitlin and John Matthews explain. "The Arthurian mythos is like a great tree planted in ancient soil: although everyone sees the branches, it is the roots which channel the earth's nourishment to the leaves and fruit upon it." The deck was illustrated by Miranda Gray and published by the Aquarian Press of London in 1990, and reprinted by Thorsons of London in 1995. The back design shows "the Goddess of the Land herself, with the empowering objects of the Quest: the sword, spear, grail, and stone." The deck includes two advertising cards.

Artists Inner Vision Tarot NoMonet coordinated the creation of the Artist's Inner Vision Tarot. Twenty-six artists each made three cards and, for the book that accompanies the deck, three rubber stamp designs. Most of the artists are members of the Capolan mail art swap. The deck was published in 1999 by NoMonet Full Court Press, in a print run of 4,750 decks, with a special limited, numbered edition of 250 containing the deck of cards with each card signed by the artist and a hand-made book with original hand-stamped and screened art. Several of the artists, for example, Arnell Ando and Sarah Ovenall, have had their own decks published. The back design is a collage by NoMonet. The deck includes an extra card listing the artists who participated.

Atavist Tarot Sally Annett created most of the images of the Atavist Tarot with acrylic paint, with photographs on some of the cards, and computer graphics used to combine the media. The deck was published by W. Foulsham of England in 2003. Rowena Shepherd authored the text that accompanies the deck.

Atavist Tarot
Sally Annett and
Rowena Shepherd,
W. Foulshalm, 2002

Tarocchi Art Nouveau   Antonella Castelli, Lo Scarabeo, 1998

Art of Tarot   Emma Garner, Cico Books/Barnes & Noble Books, 2001

Arthurian Tarot   Miranda Gray, artist, and Caitlin and John Matthews, Aquarian Press, 1990   The description is based on that in the book *The Arthurian Tarot: A Hallowquest Handbook.*

TOP ROW: **0 The Seeker** is the one who embarks on the quest for the Holy Grail, the Hallowquest. **I Merlin** has a map of Britain before him. The four suit symbols, and symbols of the Hallowquest, are the sword, the spear, the grail, and the stone chessboard. **II The Lady of the Lake** is Morgan, sister and foster mother of King Arthur. **III Guinevere** was not an unfaithful wife, in the earliest legends, but rather a manifestation of the harmony between king and land.

SECOND ROW: **IV Arthur** is in the role of the Dark Age battle king, under a dragon standard. **V Taliesin** is a poet, a guardian of tradition, who is able to impart knowledge. **VI The White Hart** shows Enid with her champion Gereint. The White Hart represents spiritual adventure and the purity of love. **VII Pryowen** is Arthur's ship sailing into the Underworld to get a sacred cauldron.

0 the seeker	I merlin	II the lady of the lake	III guinevere
IV arthur	V taliesin	VI the white hart	VII prydwen
IX the grail hermit	XI sovereignty	XII the wounded king	XIII the washer at the ford
XXI the flowering of logres	spear nine	grail queen	stone king

(continued from facing page) THIRD ROW: **IX The Grail Hermit** helps seekers, admonishing the lazy, explaining the wonders encountered, and providing food and shelter. **XI Sovereignty** shows the Queen of the Hallows holding the four-sided cup of truth. The stream runs black with the dark drink of forgetfulness, white with the milk of fostering, and red with the drink of lordship. **XII The Wounded King** cannot be healed until the cup of the Grail is attained. Meanwhile, the land is barren. **XIII The Washer at the Ford** is seen washing bloody linen of warriors who will die in battle.

BOTTOM ROW: **XXI The Flowering of Logres** shows the Seeker of card 0 dancing with children. The land has been restored by successful completion of the Quest. **Spear Nine. Grail Queen. Stone King.**

225

Artist's Inner Vision Tarot NoMonet, et al., NoMonet Full Court Press, 1999 The descriptions are extracted from statements by the artists, whose names are in parentheses.

TOP ROW: **0 THE FOOL** (Red Dog Scott). "I wanted to capture his naivete and perhaps the bit of clownishness he embodies, so when I came across the image of the slightly off-kilter dancing man, I knew I was heading in the direction I wanted to go.... I located an old map of Italy to use as the background to make sure the aspect of his being a traveler was made clear. Butterflies are a well-known representation of new beginnings, metamorphosis, so the images of the butterflies with clownlike bodies added the finishing touches...." **I MAGICIAN** (Julie Hagan Bloch). "The figure is deliberately ambiguous as to gender (because gender in a shaman is irrelevant). The scene depicts a time just after the elements and directions have been invoked/invited and awareness of the contact is made deeper. **II HIGH PRIESTESS** (Alexandra Genetti). "This card is comprised of several paintings...united with the aid of additional silver paper and touches of pen and colored pencil." **III EMPRESS** (Teesha Moore). "I used a combination of collage, rubber stamps, paint, photocopies, and hand drawing.... I am highly inspired by medieval and renaissance images and am really drawn to images of the Madonna as a source of strength." **IV THE EMPEROR** (Dennis Jordan). "After a review of the meaning of the card, its history and past designs, I used a thesaurus to assist with the alternate meanings of the word Emperor to obtain images. The whole time I imagine images for each term....During card development I will constantly go back to these words, reviewing images in my mind, logging them in my journal, drawing around the 'word tree.'"

SECOND ROW: **V HIEROPHANT** (Becky Ericsen). "I needed a benevolent-looking wise face for the Hierophant, the educator and spiritual leader. I searched for a rather nondescript man and woman to depict opposites as well as people in general...." **VI THE LOVERS** (Michele Monet). "The card was done in Photoshop.... The images of the people started out as photographs, which I took and converted into black and white line art. The background consisted of royalty-free clip art and stock photography." **VII CHARIOT** (Sarah Ovenall). "The stone archway came from a clip art Pictorial Archive book on medieval stonework and was lightly tinted with copper colored pencil. The background layer is from a sheet of marbleized paper....The laurel leaves were clipped from a shrub in my back yard, painted gold, then color photocopied to size." **IX THE HERMIT** (Tracy Moore). "This card was created with collage of two old photographs (one is simply the eye), computer-generated text, and rubber stamps." **X WHEEL OF FORTUNE** (Rosalyn Stendahl). "All elements were composited electronically using Photoshop masking and blending techniques. The title was computer generated."

THIRD ROW: **XI Strength** (Ricë Freeman Zachery). "The photograph is of me as a child, a much-loved child who wielded a great deal of power in her tiny universe and could have tamed lions as easily as her parents tamed her with their love and compassion." **XII Hanged One** (Renee Pearson). "Before beginning the work on the art, I spent time writing out my personal interpretation of the card meaning. I wrote very quickly and almost automatically.... Sometimes I will photograph something myself if I can't find an image I want. I also scan actual objects whenever I want to give more texture and add dimension to the work." **XV The Devil** (Sandra McCall). "The background is composed of cut and torn pieces of paper. The devil is an eraser cut that I liked so much I remade it into a rubber stamp. The people are clip art." **XVI The Tower** (Susan Rene Tomb). "This card was designed in Photoshop." **XVIII THE MOON** (Mart Jetton). "This card was created using colored pencils with some sponging.... I added the curves partially for my benefit and partially to inflame those who are sensitive to objectifying the female form."

BOTTOM ROW: **XIX SUN** (Keely Barham). "This card was done as a watercolor with some computer graphics printed over. It was inspired by some design work I had seen that involved creating font styles." **FOUR OF SWORDS** (NoMonet). "I saw a photograph of a tree that had an unusual branching...a 'woman tree.' I drew it and turned it into a stamp.... I drew two versions of the babies and made them into stamps as well. The babies were stamped first in dark purple with a round egg-shaped mask around them to emulate the birth sac.... I added the blue leaves in with watercolor for extra definition and to bring the color forward in the card a bit." **SEVEN OF WANDS** (Tracy Cutts). "I tried to think of all the types of wands we have in our lives: guns and rifles, knives and tools, even pens and pencils.... I played around with different backgrounds and I liked the juxtaposition of feathers and swords. They seemed both one and the same and yet also at odds, the very antithesis of each other." **ACE OF CUPS** (Tracy Cutts). "I have always loved Venice, and it's one of, if not the most romantic city on earth, so this picture seemed perfect." **QUEEN OF COINS** (Amy McClure). "The Queen is a softly shaded pencil drawing, juxtaposed and overlapped with cut decorative paper and illustrative collage that creates a feeling of movement.... Strong colors and gold pigment were used to give the image a feeling of substance and weight."

Ator Tarot   Robin Ator, GlowInTheDark Pictures, 2002

Ator Tarot   The Ator Tarot is based on the Rider-Waite Tarot, but "translated into a thick-and-thin-lined, brightly colored cartoon version," says the artist, Robin Ator. "It's intended as a less visually intimidating alternative to the familiar cards, yet still containing all the expected substance and symbology. Childlike, but not childish, this deck works well for more lighthearted readings and for introducing children to the tarot." The deck was published in 2002 by GlowInTheDark Pictures LLC. The deck includes two extra cards: one with the title of the deck and an angel and yinyang symbol; the other with the angel over the globe and the words "As Above, So Below."

Aura-Soma Tarot A distinctive aspect of this deck is that the backs are each different from each other; there is not a fixed back design. Aura Soma is a New Age healing technique that incorporates bottles containing mineral and gemstone essences, herbal extracts and the essential oils of flowers. The bottles are colored to reflect their properties. The client selects "Equilibrium bottles," which are considered to have vibrations that will restore one's soul to balance and harmony. The bottles are numbered 0 through 97.

Each card of the Aura-Soma tarot corresponds to a bottle. One side of each card is a tarot image, while the other side shows the corresponding bottle and a symbolic image. The extra twenty cards (beyond the seventy-eight traditional tarot cards) repeat twenty of the Major Arcana, though with different images. The artwork of the deck is by Phyllis Mahon with assistance from Rory Baxter and Andy Quick. The deck was published by Aura-Soma, Lincolnshire, England, in 1997.

Aura-Soma Tarot Phyllis Mahon, Rory Baxter, and Andy Quick, Aura-Soma, 1997 The cards illustrated are arranged in tarot order. Descriptions are from the booklet accompanying the deck.

TOP ROW: **1 The Magician:** Blue/Deep magenta; Physical Rescue - communication with the being within. **Bottle 1** (Reverse side of 1 The Magician). **79 The Magician:** Orange/Violet; Ostrich Bottle - A deep healing from within for a shock situation. **3 The Empress:** Blue/Green; Heart Bottle/Atlantean Bottle - nurturing communications of the heart. **81 The Empress:** Pink/Pink; Unconditional Love - Compassion and understanding. The need for love.

SECOND ROW: **4 The Emperor:** Yellow/Gold; Sunlight Bottle - Knowledge and wisdom; the thinker, the student, the teacher. **82 The Emperor:** Green/Orange; Calypso - The space to connect with the insight from within. Deep bliss from the heart. **88 The Wheel of Fortune:** Green/Blue; Jade Emperor - The communication from the depths of peace through one's feeling. **88** (Reverse side of 88 The Wheel of Fortune). **89 Strength:** Red/Deep Magenta; Energy Rescue - The Time Shift.

BOTTOM ROW: **96 The Moon:** Royal Blue/Royal Blue; Archangel Raphael. **97 The Sun:** Gold/Royal Blue; Archangel Uriel. **32 Five of Wands:** Royal Blue/Gold; Sophia - A message of good things for the future. **39 Knight of Cups:** Violet/Gold; Egyptian Bottle II - The Puppeteer. **66 Queen of Pentacles:** Pale Violet/Pale Pink; The Actress - Unconditional love in the service of others.

Tarocchi Aurei   Roberto Granchi, Il Mosaico Gruppo Editoriale De Agostini, 1997   TOP ROW: IL MATTO (The Fool). I IL MAGO (The Magician). II LA SACERDOTESSA (The High Priestess). III LA GRANDE MADRE (The Great Mother). IV L'IMPERATORE (The Emperor).   SECOND ROW: V IL PONTEFICE (The Pontiff). VI L'AMORE (Love). VII IL CARRO (The Chariot). VIII LA GIUSTIZIA (Justice). IX L'EREMITA (The Hermit).   THIRD ROW: X LA RUOTA (The Wheel). XI LA FORZA (Strength). XII L'APPESO (The Hanged Man). XIV LA TEMPERANZA (Temperance). XV IL DIAVOLO (The Devil).   BOTTOM ROW: XVI LA TORRE (The Tower). XVII LA STELLA (The Star). XIX IL SOLE (The Sun). XX IL GIUDIZIO (Judgment). XXI IL MONDO (The World).

Tarocchi Aurei The Major Arcana deck, Aurei Tarot, accompanies the book *I Tarocchi Aurei*, by Giovanni Pelosini. The artwork was painted by Roberto Granchi. The cards feature Italian titles, runes, and astrological sigils. The book and cards were published in 1997 by Il Mosaico Gruppo Editoriale De Agostini.

Australian Animal Tarot Ann Williams-Fitzgerald of Australia created a tarot illustrated by Tracy Hinschen with animals of her native continent. "The world around us is our living classroom," Williams-Fitzgerald says in the booklet accompanying the deck. "The animals that surround us and cross our paths are all part of our 'lessons' of the process of becoming wiser about who and what we are, and the choices we have in this lifetime." The deck was published by AGMüller of Neuhausen, Switzerland, in 2000, and it includes an advertising card and a guarantee card. The back design is of a starry sky.

Collection of the author / © 2000 by AGM AGMüller

Australian Animal Tarot Ann Williams-Fitzgerald and Tracy Hinschen, AGMüller, 2000

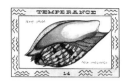

Animals and the Tarot

Whether as domestic companions or creatures of the wild, animals inspire artists of the tarot by their appearance, names, and attributes. Tarots in volume III that feature animals are:

Animal Tarot
Animal Wise Tarot
Australian Animal Tarot
Cani del Mondo (Dogs of the World)
Tarot for Cats
Gatti (The Cats) 22 Arcani
Gufi della Buona Fortuna
 (Owls of Good Fortune)
Hugobian Tarot

Marine Tarot
Pet Tarot
Shell Tarot
Spirit of the
 Animals Tarot
Tarot Taurin
Teddy Tarot
Tiny Bug Tarot

Australian Contemporary Dreamtime Tarot The illustrations in the Dreamtime Tarot are by Keith Courtenay-Peto. The booklet accompanying the deck, written by Daicon Courtenay-Peto, relates that the artist encountered an Aboriginal spiritual mentor while on a hunting and prospecting expedition in Australia.

The booklet explains, "The Australian Aboriginal word for the Dreamtime is more closely translated as the 'eternal Dreamtime' for it is believed to have only a beginning and will never end as long as the world is in existence. The dreaming is always 'now'—our ancestral spirits or guides are with us always, looking over us while residing in rocks, trees, animals, people and all things that are part of our life." The dotted backgrounds, drawn from Aboriginal art, are called songlines and represent the tracks left by the ancestors during creation. The titles of the cards derive from various Aboriginal dialects spoken throughout Australia.

The cards have black borders, and the back design is of a red circle on orange. The suits are muggils (stone knives), kundas (decorated digging sticks), coolamons (cups), and wariats (stones). Courts are tribal elder, earth mother, hunter, and maiden. The numbers are shown with a small dot signifying one and a larger dot signifying five. Other symbols, including astrological and elemental signs, are featured on the cards. The deck was published in 1991 by Goldrope Pty. Ltd. It includes a title card and a card that reads, "Collectors Limited Edition Signed by the Artist/Brisbane Australia," with the signature and the hand-written date "Feb 91." Nothing with the deck, however, indicates how many copies were printed for the edition.

Avalon Tarot Avalon Tarot draws from the legends of the Round Table of the court of King Arthur. Artist Joseph Viglioglia used the style of science-fiction/fantasy art to illustrate the medieval tales, creating a compelling dissonance in the images, a reflection of the Christian and pre-Christian influences that created dissonance in the milieu of King Arthur. Titles of the deck are in English, Italian, French, Spanish, German, and Dutch. The deck includes a title card and an advertising card. The back design is an angel with a sword. The Avalon Tarot was published by Lo Scarabeo, Turin, Italy, in 2000.

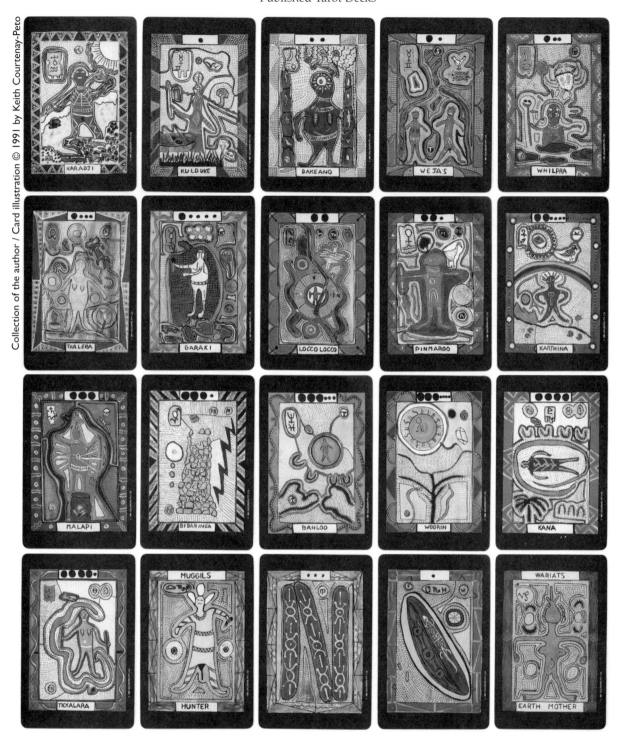

Australian Contemporary Dreamtime Tarot Keith Courtenay-Peto, artist, and Daicon Courtenay-Peto, Goldrope, 1991 Traditional tarot titles are drawn from the booklet accompanying the deck.

TOP ROW: 0 KARADJI (Fool). 1 KULDUKE (Magician). 2 BAKEANO (High Priestess). 6 WEJA'S (Lovers). 7 WHILPRA (Chariot).

SECOND ROW: 8 THALERA (Strength). 9 GARAKI (Hermit). 10 LOCCO LOCCO (Wheel of Fortune). 11 PINMAROO (Justice). 14 KARTHINA (Temperance).

THIRD ROW: 15 MALAPI (Devil). 16 BIBARINGA (Tower). 18 BAHLOO (Moon). 19 WOORIN (Sun). 20 KANA (Judgment).

BOTTOM ROW: 21 TICKALARA (World). HUNTER MUGGILS. Three Kundas. One Coolamons. EARTH MOTHER WARIATS.

Avalon Tarot   Joseph Viglioglia, Lo Scarabeo, 2000

TOP ROW: **0 THE FOOL** is Percival, who was raised in seclusion and so was unaware of the mores of society. **I THE MAGICIAN** is Merlin, the wizard and counselor to King Arthur. **II THE HIGH PRIESTESS** is Morgana, a sorceress who was King Arthur's half-sister. **III THE EMPRESS** is Guinevere, King Arthur's wife, and lover of Lancelot. **IV THE EMPEROR** is King Arthur.

SECOND ROW: **V THE HIEROPHANT** is Bishop Josephus, the first Christian bishop of Sarras and keeper of the Grail, the cup containing the blood of Christ. **VII THE CHARIOT** depicts Lancelot of the Lake, who was considered the greatest knight of the Round Table, but betrayed his liege lord by his adulterous affair with Guinevere. **IX THE HERMIT** is the wise man who guides Galahad, Percival, and Bors closer to the Grail. **XIII DEATH** is described in the flyer accompanying the deck as "one of the protagonists which appears the most often in the legends of the Round Table." **XIV TEMPERANCE** is Vivien, the Lady of the Lake. She fostered Lancelot and delivered the sword Excalibur to King Arthur.

THIRD ROW: **XVI THE TOWER** is inhabited by the usurper Vortigern. It collapsed because of two dragons at its foundations. **XVIII THE MOON** reflects the vision Arthur and his companions had of the white deer and four lions, Christ and the four evangelists. **XIX THE SUN** is Galahad, the greatest knight of all time and the only one with the purity to see the Grail. **XX JUDGEMENT. XXI THE WORLD.**

BOTTOM ROW: **9 SWORDS** shows Percival. He resists the temptation of lust by remembering his mother's teachings. **6 WANDS** shows the poisoned fountain that almost killed Lancelot. **6 CHALICES** depicts Lancelot's experience in prison, when he saw a rose outside his window that reminded him of Guinevere. **KNAVE OF PENTACLES** is Gundebald, a scholarly cleric of the magic arts. **4 PENTACLES** shows Uther Pendragon, King Arthur's father, driving Excalibur into the stone with the command that only the true king would be able to extract it.

Samantha Bale Tarot   The deck and book set titled *Tarot* has a book by Sasha Fenton and a deck illustrated by Samantha Bale. The set was published by Smithmark Publishers, New York, in 1998.

Baphomet: The Tarot of the Underworld   Baphomet Tarot is a collaboration between Swiss artist H.R. Giger and occultist Akron. Giger is best known for the visuals in the movie *Alien*, for which he won an Academy Award. Akron is the pseudonym for occultist C.F. Frey. The symbolic person of Baphomet is called in the booklet accompanying the deck "the pictorial manifestation of the self-recognizing God," a shadow figure, the "light in hell." The images of the deck are monochromatic, in silver and sepia, complex and dark, bringing the nightmares of Bosch into the age of science fiction.

The deck comprises twenty-two Major Arcana, titled in English. H.R. Giger painted the images between 1973 and 1992. The Baphomet deck and book set was published by AGMüller, Neuhausen, Switzerland, in 1993. A special edition of the deck included a CD by the rock group Epilepsy. The deck was published in 2000 by Taschen America as the H.R. Giger Tarot; this edition included a spread poster and Akron's book.

Tarot of Baseball   "Baseball is life, and life is baseball," says Robert Kasher, creator of the Tarot of Baseball. Kasher, with artist Beverly Ransom, created a seventy-eight-card deck that plays on the terminology and culture of that great American sport, baseball. The "Major League" cards have two titles: a traditional Major Arcana title and a baseball equivalent. For example, XII the Hanged Man is also The Hung-Up Man, representing a player who gets caught stealing bases. The suits of the "Minor League" are balls (swords), bats (wands), gloves (cups), and caps (coins). The court cards are umpire (page), pitcher (knight), coach (queen), and manager (king). The composition of the cards resembles that of the Rider-Waite deck. For example, the Eight of Balls shows a "visitor" as the "sitting duck" for a dunk tank, and the Rider-Waite Eight of Swords shows a woman bound and blindfolded amidst swords. The back design is a double-ended arrangement of caps, bats, balls, and gloves. The deck includes a title card and an introductory card. The booklet accompanying the deck weaves baseball into the symbolism and divinatory meanings of the tarot. It was published by U.S. Games Systems, Stamford, Connecticut, in 1996.

Baseball Tarot   Mark Lerner and Laura Philips took the experience of baseball and turned it into a tarot deck, with illustrations by Dan Gardiner. The cards cover all the players, from Major League to Little League. Each card is titled and includes a key word, from baseball lingo, that connects with the traditional tarot meaning. Minor Arcana suits are balls (swords), bats (wands), mitts (cups), and bases (coins). The Minors are numbered one through twelve, with only two courts: coach and MVP (most valued player). The back design shows baseballs against a starry sky. The deck was published by Workman Publishing, New York, in 1999.

Basic Tarot   "Like religions and other esoteric doctrines, tarot represents a model of reality, a philosophy in images.... Here, we can only provide one of the many possible ways of approaching and interpreting the tarot; there are many others." Gudrun Dobratz created the Basic Tarot by manipulating artwork with computer software. A monochrome frame with feathered inside edges gives consistency to the deck, but the images layered within the frames range from pencil drawings to expressionistic paintings to photographs to ink washes. The cards are titled in German and English. The backs show an image of a seated putto in aqua. The Basic Tarot was published in 1997 by AGMüller, Neuhausen, Switzerland.

0 — The Fool	1 — The Magician	2 — The High Priestess	3 — The Empress	4 — The Emperor
6 — The Lovers	7 — The Chariot	8 — Strength	9 — The Hermit	10 — Wheel of Fortune
11 — Justice	12 — The Hanged Man	13 — Death	14 — Temperance	17 — The Star
18 — The Moon	19 — The Sun	21 — The World	Queen of Swords	2 — Cups

Samantha Bale Tarot   Samantha Bale, Smithmark Publishers, 1998

Baphomet: The Tarot of the Underworld   H.R. Giger, artist, and Akron, AGMüller, 1993   The caption gives the Self-expression of the card (in quotes) and the Principle, from the book that accompanies the deck.

TOP ROW: **0 THE FOOL.** "I become." Metamorphosis. **I THE MAGICIAN.** "I am." Attainment of ego. **II THE HIGH PRIESTESS.** "I conceive." Ego devotion. **III THE EMPRESS.** "I give birth." Motherhood. **IV THE EMPEROR.** "I rule." Law and order.

SECOND ROW: **V THE HIEROPHANT.** "I teach." The spiritual authority. **VII THE CHARIOT.** "I am victorious." Sturm und drang. [*Sturm und drang* is a German phrase denoting turmoil of mind and spirit.] **VIII STRENGTH.** "I copulate." The sexual instinct. **IX THE HERMIT.** "I seek." The hidden truth. **XI JUSTICE.** "I pass judgement." The verdict.

BOTTOM ROW: **XIV ALCHEMY.** "I sublimate." Transformation. **XVI THE TOWER.** "I destroy." The illusion of matter. **XVIII THE MOON.** "I dream." The reflected light of the unconscious. **XIX THE SUN.** "I create." The creative will. **XXI THE UNIVERSE.** "I crown." Creative energy.

Tarot of Baseball   Beverly Ransom, artist, and Robert Kasher, U.S. Games Systems, 1996

Collection of the author / Illustrations © 1999 by Dan Gardiner

Baseball Tarot   Dan Gardiner, artist, Mark Lerner, and Laura Philips, Workman Publishing, 1999
TOP ROW: 0 The Rookie. I The All-Star. II The Coach. III The Natural. IV The Legend.
SECOND ROW: V The Manager. VI The Team. VII Control. VIII Power. XIV The Hero.
THIRD ROW: XV The Goat. XVIII The Catcher. XIX The Pitcher. XX The Rule Book. XXI World Series.
BOTTOM ROW: MVP of Balls: Intellectual Accomplishments. Eleven of Bats: Switch-Hitter. Twelve of Mits: Circus Catch. Seven of Bases: On Deck.

Basic Tarot   Gudrun Dobratz, AGMüller, 1997

Basque Country Tarot (Tarot de Euskaherria)   Alfredo Fermin Cemillán Mintxo, artist, and Maritxu Eranz de Güler, Naipes Heraclio Fournier, 1991

Basque Country Tarot (Tarot de Euskaherria)   The Basque Country Tarot was issued in 1991 as part of the celebration of the seventy-fifth anniversary of the Museo Fournier de Naipes (Fournier Playing Card Museum). Under direction of Maritxu Eranz de Güler, artist Alfredo Fermin Cemillán Mintxo painted the deck. The Minor Arcana pips include flora of the Basque region and plants reputed to have magical properties, including mandragora and belladonna. Eranz de Güler says, "The tarot is a live construction, a pure and integral path. It represents ourselves, it represents the universe…. The tarot holds the key for every single situation; it encompasses the scheme not only of the collective evolution of humanity, but also of the individual's evolution." The deck is dedicated "To all women so that they can wisely interpret the tarot."   The Major Arcana are titled in Spanish, Basque, and English; the Minor Arcana are untitled. The deck includes two presentation cards and is packaged with a book. The back design shows the earth encircled by flying people, with the sigils of Jupiter and Pisces at the bottom. Naipes Heraclio Fournier of Vitoria, Spain, published the deck in 1991.

241

| II *Mystery* | III *of Nature* | VII EXPERIENCE | VIII *Assessment* | XVIIII *Enlightenment* |

William Blake Tarot Triumphs Ed Buryn (T.A.R.O.T. edition) **II Mystery** is *Mary at Her Distaff Watched Over by Two Angels*. **III Nature** is *Mirth*. **VII Experience** is *God Judging Adam*. **VIII Assessment** is an illustration for the Edward Young poem "Night Thoughts." **XVIIII Enlightenment** is *As if an Angel Dropped Down from the Clouds*.

Bella Vista Tarot Chilean artist Tito Calderón painted the Bella Vista Tarot following the directions of tarotist Pedro Engel. The deck is named after a neighborhood in Santiago, Chile, and was published by the artists in 2002. The backs show yellow starbursts on a blue background.

Tarô da Bíblia de Gustave Doré (Tarot of the Bible of Gustave Doré) Martius Americano do Brasil prepared woodcuts by Gustave Doré as a tarot deck. The artist used complete illustrations, resorting to montage only when compelled by the symbolism of the card. The cards are black and white, with titles in French, English, and Portuguese. The Minor Arcana have the same images for each number or court, with only the suit sign varying. For example, the kings all show the same image of Jesus, with a different suit sign inset. The back design is a black stipple pattern. The deck was published in 1990 by Thot Livraria e Editora Esotérica of Brazil. Two extra cards with the name of the publisher are included.

Bildteppich Tarot (Tapestry Tarot) Yvonne G. Jensen's tarot first appeared in *The Encyclopedia of Tarot*, volume III, as the Heel de Mens Tarot (The Entire Person Tarot). At the time the deck was unpublished. Jensen created the cards with fabric, paint, and objects such as beads, trim, and string. Besides seventy-eight traditional cards, the deck includes 22 Die Erde (The Earth) and 23 Das All (Everything), a title card, and a card with a short biography of the artist. Major Arcana 1 through 12 have in the side margins astrological correspondences of body, sign, and house. The Minor Arcana, except for the man and woman of each suit also have astrological attributions. Bildteppich Tarot was published by Carta Mundi of Belgium under license of U.S. Games Systems in 1995.

Black Tarot The Black Tarot shows "the beauty and the beast that we all carry inside," according to Luis Royo, who worked with Pilar San Martin in creating the cards. The deck includes a title card and a card naming the creators. The back design shows a skull burning in green flames and surrounded by a snake. Titles are in Spanish, English, French, and German. The Black Tarot was published in 1998 by Naipes Heraclio Fournier, Spain.

William Blake Tarot Ed Buryn drew from the work of the visionary poet and artist William Blake (1757–1827) to create the William Blake Tarot. In an April 1992 letter to Stuart Kaplan, Buryn writes, "Much of Blake's work in both art and poetry can be viewed as his attempts to create a vehicle for metaphysical truth, and this deck began when I realized that tarot is, of course, such a vehicle…. The motif I chose for the deck is the Soul's Journey, which not only works well to portray Blake's ideas and vision, but also presents a spiritual message that seems to me very much needed today." Buryn's interest in tarot was sparked by his wife, tarotist Mary K. Greer.

Buryn does not claim any direct relationship between Blake and the tarot. In fact, he points out, "all foreign-made cards had been banned [from England] a century before, isolating England from tarot developments on the continent." Nevertheless, Buryn feels that "Blake, a natural mystic and symbolist, working from the same sources and impulses as the original Renaissance designers of the tarot, repeatedly invented and illustrated his own functional equivalents of it."

Buryn published the deck in 1991 through his own imprint T.A.R.O.T. (Tools And Rights Of Transformation). The cards measured 8.5 inches by 5.5 inches; the illustrations are in blue and sepia. The deck comprised Triumphs (cards 0 through XXI, 00 Eternity, and 001 Eternity), a title card, and a card giving sources of the illustrations. The backs showed seven angels, from "the Seven Eyes of God," and William Blake's signature. The deck came with a booklet by Buryn. The T.A.R.O.T. edition decks were wrapped in a piece of silk stamped in blue with the name of the deck and a Blake illustration.

A full deck was published in 1995 by HarperCollins, with Triumphs (parallel to Major Arcana) and Creative Process Suits (parallel to Minor Arcana). Some of the images used for the cards differ from those in Buryn's original deck. Approximately a fifth of the cards are based on uncolored designs by Blake, which Buryn painted using colors drawn from other works by Blake.

The Creative Process Suits are painting, "The Embodiment of Inner Vision" (corresponding to pentacles); science, "The Path of Self-Understanding" (swords); music, "The Celebration of Life Force" (cups); and poetry, "The Expression of Eternal Truth" (wands). Blake said, "In Eternity, the four arts: Poetry, Painting, Music and . . . Science, are the four faces of man." The "person" cards are man (king), woman (queen), angel (knight), and child (page).

Bella Vista Tarot   Tito Calderón and Pedro Engel, published by the artists, 2002

Tarô da Bíblia de Gustave Doré (Tarot of the Bible of Gustave Doré)   Martius Americano do Brasil, Thot Livraria e Editora Esotérica, 1990

244

Bildteppich Tarot (The Tapestry Tarot) Yvonne G. Jensen, Carta Mundi/U.S. Games Systems, 1995 Titles given are translations of the German titles on the cards. TOP ROW: III THE EMPRESS; lungs and hands, Gemini. XII THE HANGED MAN; feet, Pisces. 13 DEATH; Saturn. 15 THE DEVIL, Mars. SECOND ROW: 16 THE TOWER; Dragon Castle. 18 THE MOON. 20 RESURRECTION; Jupiter. 22 THE EARTH. THIRD ROW: TWO OF SWORDS: INNER CONFLICT. PAGE OF WANDS: NEWS. THREE OF WANDS: THE PASSWORD. WOMAN OF CUPS. BOTTOM ROW: KNIGHT OF CUPS: WEAKNESS. SEVEN OF CUPS: UNCERTAINTY. 10 OF PENTACLES: LUXURY. ACE OF PENTACLES: BEAUTY.

Black Tarot   Luis Royo, artist, and Pilar San Martin, Naipes Heraclio Fournier, 1998

William Blake Tarot   Ed Buryn, HarperCollins, 1995   The description is based on the book that accompanies the deck.

TOP ROW: **0 Innocence** shows Tharmas reacting to "the beauty and terror of material existence." **00 Eternity** shows "Jacob's ladder," the visionary path from heaven to earth, on which angels walk. **II Mystery** portrays Enitharman, symbolic of the point at which the soul assumes gender and becomes sexual. **VI Knowledge** shows Adam, Eve, and the archangel Raphael, as the angel appeals to the couple to obey God's commandment. **VIII Assessment** shows Luvah, the prince of love in Blakean lore.

SECOND ROW: **IX Imagination** recalls the quote by Blake, "Man is all imagination: God is man & exists in us & we in him." **XI Energy** shows Tharmas, "filled with renewed energy of life." Tharmas's connection with the animals around him shows understanding and love of bodily instincts and physical capabilities. **XII Reversal** represents the upset of reason and the overturn of old views. **XIII Transformation. XIV Forgiveness** shows Jesus as symbol of the human imagination, the divine power in man.

BOTTOM ROW: **XV Error** shows Satan enthroned. Satan represents "reasoning and doubting," which Blake equated with spiritual fear. **XVII Stars** depicts the poet John Milton, who wrote the epic poem *Paradise Lost.* Although he is under the earth, he communes easily with the stars. **XIX Sun** shows a spiritual Eden, where ignorance and experience are joined in a symbolic archway. **XX Liberty** shows at its center a figure of Jerusalem, ascending on a plume of flame. **XXI Union** portrays Albion, Blake's figure for self. He has been regenerated through sacrifice of himself for Jesus.

William Blake Tarot (*continued*)
8 of Poetry. 3 of Music. Man of Science. 3 of Science. 8 of Painting.

Blue Moon Tarot Blue Moon Tarot features dramatic artwork by Julie Cuccia-Watts, artist of the Ancestral Path Tarot (published by U.S. Games Systems). The twenty-two-card deck features Major Arcana images linked to Wiccan holy days, including lunar and solar events and special days such as Beltane (May day) and Lammas (August eve). The deck was published in 1999 as greeting cards, with the title "T.A.R.O. Ancient Wheel of Wisdom." It was published as the Blue Moon Tarot deck in 2000 by New Moon Trading Company, Wisconsin.

Blue Rose Tarot Paula J. Gibby used photocollage to create the Blue Rose Tarot. The deck was produced in 2000 in a handmade edition by Sun Productions, New York City.

Blue Rose Tarot Paula J. Gibby, Sun Productions, 2000

Blue Moon Tarot   Julie Cuccia-Watts, New Moon Trading Company, 1999

Bosch Tarot Artist A. Alexandrov Atanassov based his seventy-eight-card tarot deck on the work of Flemish painter Hieronymus Bosch (1450–1516). The accompanying flyer by Riccardo Minetti says, "The realism of Bosch's lines goes hand in hand with the rawest monstrosity and the most disturbingly grotesque…. Modern man calls them fears and anxieties. The Bosch Tarots are intended to be a window on that world to be used carefully to explore it and in doing so to explore the things we fear." In creating the deck, Atanassov modified fragments of Bosch's work, including adding symbols of the suits to make the Minor Arcana cards. Titles are in English, French, German, Spanish, and Italian. The double-ended back design shows six scenes from the Minor Arcana in black and white. The Bosch Tarot was published by Lo Scarabeo, Turin, in 2000.

Buckland Romani Tarot Raymond Buckland, whose father was gypsy, created the Romani Tarot with artist Lissane Lake. "As a child, on visits to my grandparents, I was always fascinated by the fact that my grandmother spent so many hours with the cards," Buckland writes in the book accompanying the deck. "She had an ancient deck that was made up of handcrafted Major Arcana cards together with an old poker deck serving as the Minor Arcana. I say the handcrafted ones were Major Arcana cards, but the scenes on them were unlike any other cards I have ever seen…. I, myself, learned to read the tarot in the early 1960s. I started with the Rider-Waite deck and, over the years, purchased and used many other decks, doing hundreds of readings for a wide variety of people."

On the process of making the deck, Buckland writes, "Much as Arthur Edward Waite worked with Pamela Colman Smith, so I worked with Lissanne Lake, directing her and explaining exactly what I wanted. The symbolism of our deck closely follows that of the Rider-Waite deck, yet with certain departures. For example, in the Buckland Romani Tarot the Magician is female. This is because, in Gypsy life, the majority of "magicians" (wise ones, witches, or *shuv'hanis*) are female. Another departure from the Rider-Waite deck shows the Priestess as the *puridai,* the matriarch of the tribe, and Justice as the Romani *kris,* or court…. The back of each card shows a representation of the romani flag: divided horizontally with blue (sky) above and green (earth) below, with a sixteen-spoke wagon wheel on that background." In keeping with his father's kin, Buckland represented the culture of the English Gypsies in his deck. The Major Arcana are titled *Boro Lil* (Big Book), and the Minor Arcana are titled *Tarno Lil* (Little Book). Suits are chiv (knife), symbol of strength and power, though it may also indicate difficulties; kosh (rod), for fertility and creativity; koro (cup), for love, and also passion and openness; and boler (wheel), signifying mobility. The Major Arcana cards are numbered only and do not have titles.

Buckland Romani Tarot was published by Llewellyn Publications, St. Paul, in 2001.

Tarocchi del Buongustaio A food-lover's delight, the Major Arcana Gourmet Tarot deck depicts characters who represent various aspects of cuisine. Spiced with humor and literary allusions, the twenty-two-card "succulent tarot deck" is presented by Ando Gilardi and designed by Cosimo Musio. Not all the cards correspond to the traditional Major Arcana; those that do offer piquant views on eating. For example, 13, traditionally the Death card, is titled "The Vegetarian." 15, traditionally the Devil, is "The Hot Pepper." 16, The Tower, shows "The Gluttons." 20, traditionally Judgment, shows "The Dishwasher," perhaps a reference to the fact that the humble dishwasher is the one who sees what comes back uneaten on the plates. Last but not least, 21 "The Bill" apparently asks the World of the shocked couple who have received it. The backs of the cards are double-ended, with a black and white illustration of a tureen. The deck was published circa 1998 by Lo Scarabeo, Turin, Italy.

Cani del Mondo 22 Arcani (Dogs of the World 22 Arcana) Osvaldo Menegazzi has dogs acting out the Major Arcana in the Cani del Mondo 22 Arcani. The deck was issued in a limited, miniature edition of 2000 numbered decks. The cards have Italian titles and blank backs. The deck was published by Edizioni Il Meneghello, Milan, in 1991.

Mauro Capitano Triumphs The tarot cards by Mauro Capitano of Italy are large and printed on heavy cardboard. The deck was published in 1997 as a limited edition of 99, and each card is signed and numbered by the artist. The back design is red and gold marbled. The deck includes an introductory card and a booklet.

Caring Psychic Family Tarot The Major Arcana Caring Psychic Family Tarot was produced by Vision Telemedia in 1998 in order to promote a "dial-a-psychic" program. The artist is not identified.

Tarot of Casanova Casanova, or Giacomo Casanova, wrote memoirs that gave him the reputation of being the world's greatest lover. Casanova was born in Venice in 1725 and died in what is now the Czech Republic in 1798. The Tarot of Casanova, by Luca Raimondo, is as much about Venice as about Casanova's erotic adventures. To anyone who has visited or lived in Venice, the vistas and scenes will be familiar, basically unchanged since the time of Casanova. Many of the cards do not show specific characters from Casanova's memoirs, but rather people who reflect the milieu in which Casanova lived. The cards are titled in Italian, English, French, German, and Spanish, and the deck was published by Lo Scarabeo, Turin, Italy, in 2000.

Bosch Tarot   A. Alexandrov Atanassov, Lo Scarabeo, 2000

Buckland Romani Tarot Raymond Buckland and Lissane Lake, Llewellyn Publications, 2001   Descriptions are based on those by Raymond Buckland.

TOP ROW: **0** depicts a young Gypsy, well-dressed, with a *putsi*, or pouch, decorated with a rose. A white *diklo* (scarf) and blue cummerbund show sincerity, truth, patience, and understanding. The vest, though black, is edged with white, a yin-yang of positive and negative. The red color of his hat and pants shows courage, health, and vigor, with the ability for great sexual love. A *lurcher* (Gypsy dog) tries to get his attention. **1.** A *shuv'hani,* or Gypsy witch/female magician, stands with a *chiv* (knife) and a whip in her hands. On a tree stump behind her lie a cup and saucer resting on a *boler* (wheel). She wears a crown bearing the sign of infinity, for her knowledge and wisdom are without end. Her bracelet shows by its pentagram engraving that she is a priestess of the Old Religion. The serpent coiled around her waist is a symbol of wisdom and healing. A necklace of large blue beads shows patience, understanding, and tranquility, while amber beads hanging from her arms suggest fire and energy, life and nature. Tiny bells hang from the fringe of her dress, symbols of communication with divinity. The roses and lilies around her are for passion, purity, and fertility. **2.** The *puridai*, matriarch of the Gypsy tribe, sits in a chair on the footboard of her *vardo* (wagon), smoking a pipe. In her arms she holds a *tikni* (or *tikno*, a girl or boy child). The tribal council is made up of men, but they will not finalize a decision without first clearing it with the *puridai*. She is considered the font of wisdom, the holder of the tribal records, the arbitrator of disputes. The child represents the future. The blue dress and pink blanket show that the child could be male or female. The *puridai's* head is draped with a blue *diklo,* or scarf, edged with gold coins. Gold is the color of charm, persuasion, protection, and confidence. Her blouse is green for fertility, finance, healing, and good luck. The large amber necklace is for energy, the blue beads for patience, understanding, and tranquility, the red beads suggest strength, courage, health, and sexual love, and the necklace of silver and turquoise combines neutrality and understanding with patience and communication. The pipe is symbolic of contemplation and cogitation. **3.** A Gypsy woman, a *juvvel,* sits on the footboard of a *vardo*. The door to her dwelling is always open for those who need her. Her embroidered green shirt suggests the earth with its colorful flora. **4.** The Gypsy king, or *kralis*, sits on his throne. He wears the black-stoned ring of his office. Behind him is a tent hung with the wheel reminiscent of the Romani and symbolic of travel. Leaders of the tribe must constantly make judgements, advise their people, and negotiate with *gaujos*, non-Gypsies.

SECOND ROW: **5.** The *petulengro*, or farrier, is held in awe by many cultures. He is a man of great strength, yet possesses gentleness when necessary. He can dominate, or he can caress and cajole. His green work pants reflect his role as healer. His *diklo* is red, showing health and strength. His blue striped shirt symbolizes the patience and understanding it takes to work with animals. **7.** A Gypsy drives a flatcart with a raised accommodation. This kind of cart is a vehicle of great maneuverability, speedy and easily controlled. The cart and harnesses are blue. The accommodation top is a yellow-orange tarp of protection, adaptability, and stimulation. The Rom driver wears a red shirt and dark vest decorated with coins. The white horse in command wears blinders; the black horse is without. **8.** The *juvvel* who holds the mouth of the bear is the same seen in 1 and 21. The tent repeats the motifs seen on 4, with the addition of the magical lemniscate. **9.** The Rom is surrounded by nature in the dead of night, yet he has the brilliance of the lantern to comfort him. He is far from camp, his shelter a solitary bender tent. **10.** The wheel from a showman's wagon is carved and painted to represent a Wheel of Fortune. Its twelve white spokes show signs of the zodiac. On the tent canvas is depicted a crow, often associated with bad luck, but also a harbinger of good luck; a rooster, a proud bird and fearless fighter; and a swan for strength, beauty, purity, sincerity, and truth. A fox in the foreground pounces on a hedgehog. The fox can be clever, tenacious, and loyal. The hedgehog seems unafraid, since it has not rolled into a self-protective ball.

THIRD ROW: **11.** The *kris* is the Gypsy court of justice. The tribe's leader makes the final judgement. The leader raises the *chiv* of justice. In his left hand, he holds the silver-topped cane of his office. Beside rests a *koro* (cup), behind him is a *boler*. The *boler* is the wheel of the year, of time; the knife shows that something or someone may be hurt. **14.** A *rakli*, Gypsy girl, pours water from a churn into a large water jack. Wild azaleas bloom at her feet. The scene is one of fertility. The *rakli* wears jewelry of aventurine and turquoise. Aventurine is found in India and is worn to bring one into alignment with one's center, to increase perception and create insight. The turquoise is for peace of mind, communication, emotional balance, and creative expression. The *rakli* also wears a large necklace of copper or gold, hung with hearts, a symbol of love, affection, attraction, and confidence. **15.** A *beng*, or devil, takes the form of a satyr, a woodland creature. He has pulled away a *kavvi-saster* (kettle iron), allowing the contents to fall into the fire. He rolls on the ground, helpless with laughter at his own prank. **18.** A *lurcher* and a fox howl beside a stream. Two *vardos,* a Reading wagon and an Open Lot, stand on opposite banks. The crustacean in the stream represents early stages of spiritual insight, and also something dark and sinister lying in wait. The dog and fox are aspects of humankind—tamed and wild. **20.** A Gypsy Rom stands with his wife and child in the surf, beneath a bright light. Behind them is the mundane world, seemingly solid castles standing battered by the waves.

BOTTOM ROW: **21.** A Gypsy woman dances with a *baulo tek* (tambourine) in each hand. She is the same *shuv'hani* seen in 1 and 8, but her shawl is now brilliantly colored with flowers, herbs, leaves, and berries, elements of Mother Nature. Around her are a rabbit, or *shushi*, who lives in the earth, passing easily between the world and the underworld; a bird, or *chirikli,* bringer of news from afar; a fox, clever, sometimes deadly, but capable of deep affection and loyalty; and a snake, *sap*, at home in the water and on the land, symbol of great and ancient wisdom and of healing. The daylilies are plants of forgetfulness. The red and white carnations are symbolic of marital bliss and fecundity. **2 of Chiv. 4 of Koshes. King of Koros. 9 of Bolers.**

Tarocchi del Buongustaio (Gourmet Tarot)   Ando Gilardi and Cosimo Musio, Lo Scarabeo, circa 1998
TOP ROW: 0 IL RISTORANTE (The Restaurant). 1 IL CUOCO (The Cook, a man). 2 LA CUOCA (The Cook, a woman). 3 IL MENU (The Menu). 4 IL VINO (Wine).   SECOND ROW: 5 GLI ANTIPASTI (The Appetizers). 6 IL CONSOMMÉ (Broth). 7 IL PRIMO (The First Course). 8 L'ARROSTO (The Roast). 10 I CROSTACEI (Shellfish).   THIRD ROW: 11 I LEGUMI (The Vegetables). 13 IL VEGETARIANO (The Vegetarian). 14 IL PIATTO DELLA CASA (House Special). 15 IL PEPERONCINO (The Hot Pepper). 16 I GHIOTTONI (The Gluttons).   BOTTOM ROW: 17 IL DOLCE (Dessert). 18 LA FRUTTA (Fruit). 19 IL CAFFÈ È L'AMARO (Coffee and Bitters). 20 IL LAVAPIATTI (The Dishwasher). 21 IL CONTO (The Bill).

Collection of the author

Cani del Mondo 22 Arcani (Dogs of the World 22 Arcana)   Osvaldo Menegazzi, Edizioni Il Meneghello 1991

TOP ROW: 0 IL MATTO (The Fool). 1 IL BAGATTO (The Magician). 3 L'IMPERATRICE (The Empress). 4 L'IMPERATORE (The Emperor). 5 IL PAPA (The Pope).

SECOND ROW: 6 L'AMORE (Love). 7 IL CARRO (The Chariot). 8 LA GIUSTIZIA (Justice). 9 L'EREMITA (The Hermit). 10 LA FORTUNA (Fortune).

THIRD ROW: 11 LA FORZA (Strength). 12 L'APPESO (The Hanged Man). 13 LA MORTE (Death). 14 LA TEMPERANZA (Temperance). 16 LA TORRE (The Tower).

BOTTOM ROW: 17 LE STELLE (The Star). 18 LA LUNA (The Moon). 19 IL SOLE (The Sun). 20 IL GIUDIZIO (Judgment). 21 IL MONDO (The World).

Mauro Capitano Triumphs   Mauro Capitano, published by the artist, 1997

Caring Psychic Family Tarot   Anonymous, Vision Telemedia, 1998

Caselli Tarot   The deck illustrated by Giovanni Caselli was part of a book and deck set called *Beginner's Guide to Tarot.* The book was by Juliet Sharman-Burke. The set was published by St. Martin's Press, New York, in 2001. The Major Arcana are unnumbered. The back design is deep magenta with a silver frame and a copyright notice printed on it.

Tarot for Cats   "Tarot cards serve as signposts to direct your soul's journey through all nine of your lives." So advises the book that accompanies the Tarot for Cats deck. The book is by Regen Dennis, and the artwork is by Kipling West. The deck comprises twenty-two Major Arcana, all featuring cats in various poses, with symbols that would appeal to felines. The back design is a blue double-ended image of a cat amidst swirling flora and stars. The book accompanying the deck is written from the point of view of a cat, complete with sample readings—for cats. The Tarot for Cats was produced by becker&meyer!, ltd., and published by MacMillan, New York, in 1996.

C.D. Tarot (Didactic Tarot)   The C.D. Tarot comprises twenty-six cards: twenty-two Major Arcana and four Minor Arcana, the aces of each suit. An explanatory card accompanying the deck says, "The origin of the C.D. cards can be found in the Tarot symbols of the Middle Ages. Furthermore, they revive the use of animals as symbols." Each card is framed with an inner band whose color denotes whether or not the card is favorable in a divination. For example, the seven cards with an inner gray band are considered unfavorable. A heart and a crook indicate answers for questions about love and health, respectively. The cards include astrological symbols at the tops and divinatory meanings in English (the deck is also available in French and Dutch). The box labels the deck as "26 Didactic Tarot Cards"; however, the deck is called C.D. cards in the instructions. The deck was created by Christiane Dhooge and published in 1995 by Aldez Belgium.

Celestial Tarot   Artist Kay Steventon and Brian Clark interwove mythic images and tarot symbolism with astronomy and astrology to create the Celestial Tarot. The Celestial Tarot was made to be both a handbook of the heavens and an oracular guide to the inner life. It was published in 2004 by U.S. Games Systems, Stamford, Connecticut.

Celestial Messages of Light Tarot   H. Alan Roe created the Celestial Message of Light Tarot with help from Delia Moreno. The artwork was over twenty years in the making. The artist describes the deck as "a Christ Consciousness and Angelic Order deck," and many of the cards carry images of Jesus Christ. The play of light and structures of light are the predominating artistic motif. The deck, which comprises twenty-two Major Arcana, was published by the artist in 1995.

Celtic Tarot (by Davis)   Courtney Davis illustrated the Celtic Tarot using gouache and ink. Helena Paterson's book, which accompanies the deck, says, "The Celtic Tarot has been devised in order to re-establish a lost legacy of Celtic art and mythology within the ancient wisdom of the tarot. Courtney Davis…was inspired by the revival of Celtic thought and vision." Recurrent patterns in the deck are spirals and knots. "The spiral symbols represent eternal life, and the intricate knotwork spiritual growth." The deck was published by Aquarian Press in 1990, reprinted by Thorsons in 1995, and then by Element Books in 2002. The back design shows a central diamond and knotted creatures in the four corners.

Celtic Tarot (by De Burgh)   The Celtic lore of Ireland is illustrated by Mary Guinan in the tarot deck by Julian De Burgh. The deck was published in 2000 by Rider Books, London, and St. Martin's Press, New York. The back design shows dogs and birds knotted in Celtic style on a yellow background. The Major Arcana are unnumbered.

Tarot of Casanova   Luca Raimondo, Lo Scarabeo, 2000
TOP ROW: **0 The Fool** is in a mask for Carnival. **I The Magician** shows Casanova and the Marquise of Urfé, whom he exploited mercilessly with promises of enabling her to take birth as a man. **II The High Priestess. IV The Emperor. V The Hierophant.**
SECOND ROW: **VII The Chariot** shows the elopement of Barbaruccia, for which Casanova was blamed. **IX The Hermit. X The Wheel** depicts the spiral staircase of the Palazzo Contarini dal Bobolo. **XII The Hanged Man** depicts Casanova's famous escape from the prison of Venice. **XV The Devil.**
THIRD ROW: **XVI The Tower** is part of the Church of Santa Maria Formosa. **XVII The Stars** shine on the Rialto Bridge. **XVIII The Moon** is a vista of the Grand Canal with the Church of Santa Maria della Salute in the background. **XIX The Sun**. It's dawn, and Casanova is returning home from a night of love. **XXI The World** depicts Casanova writing his memoirs at the castle of his friend the Count von Waldstein.
BOTTOM ROW: **Four of Swords** portrays Casanova in prison. **Eight of Wands** depicts a gondola in the Lagoon, with the tower of St. Mark in the background. **Seven of Wands** shows the duel in which Casanova seriously wounded Count Xavier Branicky. **Two of Cups** shows the Villa Carrara, where Casanova lived, in the city of Salerno, artist Luca Raimondo's city of birth. **Five of Pentacles** depicts a blind and lame beggar, as the accompanying literature says, "with respect for eyes which saw and now no longer see, for he who went far afield and now has come to a halt."

Caselli Tarot   Giovanni Caselli, St. Martin's Press, 2001

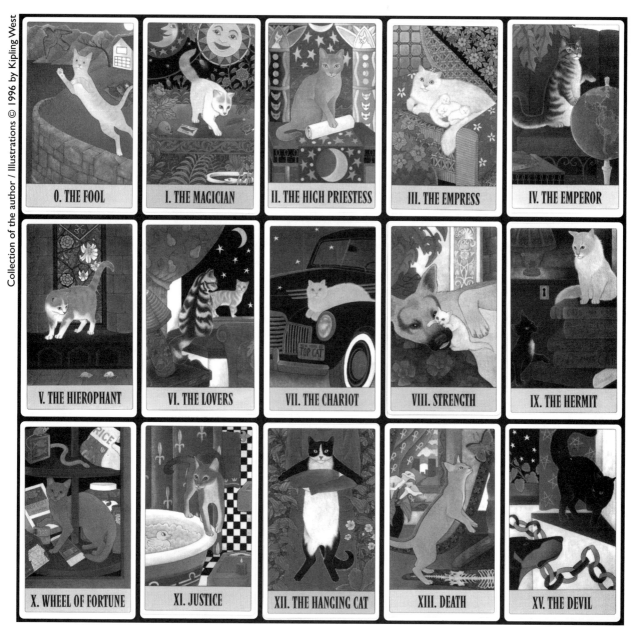

0. THE FOOL	I. THE MAGICIAN	II. THE HIGH PRIESTESS	III. THE EMPRESS	IV. THE EMPEROR
V. THE HIEROPHANT	VI. THE LOVERS	VII. THE CHARIOT	VIII. STRENGTH	IX. THE HERMIT
X. WHEEL OF FORTUNE	XI. JUSTICE	XII. THE HANGING CAT	XIII. DEATH	XV. THE DEVIL

Tarot for Cats Kipling West, artist, and Regen Dennis, MacMillan, 1996 Captions are based on the book accompanying the deck.

TOP ROW: **0. THE FOOL.** A kitten leaps at a red bird of desire. In the background are toys she no longer needs. **I. THE MAGICIAN.** A Turkish Van prowls among the symbols of the elements: mouse for earth, fish for water, feather for air, and matches for fire. **II. THE HIGH PRIESTESS** is an Abyssinian with her paw on the scroll of natural law. The fish behind her and the stars symbolize the cycle of life: meal after meal, nap after nap. **III. THE EMPRESS** is a lush Chinchilla with her kittens in luxurious surroundings. **IV. THE EMPEROR** is a powerful Maine Coon cat atop a leather couch studded with the symbol of Aries. He spins the globe. The ankhs that border the table symbolize life.

SECOND ROW: **V. THE HIEROPHANT** exemplifies choice, as a British shorthair contemplates the two mice: to take one (which one?), neither, both? The stained glass windows symbolize duality, with red roses of desire and yellow lilies of spiritual thought. Three crowns indicate dominion over the creative, formative, and material worlds. **VI. THE LOVERS.** A silver tabby gazes at her lover, who is perched on a wall, demonstrating the dangers and uncertainty of love. **VII. THE CHARIOT** is a Golden Longhair in regal sphinx-like pose atop a 1939 Studebaker Champion. **VIII. STRENGTH** is exemplified by a kitten licking the nose of a big dog. **IX. THE HERMIT** is an old Asian Longhair teaching a young kitten. He perches atop a pile of books, indicating disdain for human attempts to explain felines.

THIRD ROW: **X. WHEEL OF FORTUNE.** A Russian Blue is on a lazy susan filled with food. Warnings lurk in the snake, on the top shelf, and in Anubis, Egyptian god of death, on the bag of rice. **XI. JUSTICE.** An Abyssinian Blue balances gracefully between wetness and the safety of the floor. **XII. THE HANGING CAT** is an American Shorthair who symbolizes temporary surrender to forces beyond control. **XIII. DEATH.** An Abyssinian chases a live butterfly that contrasts with the skeleton. The nine ankhs on the curtain symbolize the cat's nine lives. **XV. THE DEVIL** is a Doberman Pinscher who has cornered a British Black Shorthair. The paper chain symbolizes bondage, but the loose open links imply that some bonds are imagined.

Tarot for Cats (*continued*) **XVI. THE TOWER** portrays a Lilac Point Siamese who watches as its favorite catnip mouse is about to be vacuumed up. The terrifying sound of the machine and the storm outside show instability. **XVII. THE STAR** shows a Tortoiseshell contemplating koi fish with awe. The fish in the pond represent the waters of life that are constantly creating and sustaining life. The eight stars above are the path of illumination to good fortune, and the bird signifies the soul. **XVIII. THE MOON** shines on a Tiffany, perched out of reach of the dog, but aware of lurking danger. **XIX. THE SUN** depicts a White Calico in the deep contentment of a sun-drenched nap. The scarlet pillow symbolizes the desire for material happiness. The sunflowers, symbols of the four elements, face the cat as center of the universe. The prancing horses on the drapes signify childlike play. **XX. JUDGMENT** shows six playful kittens in a pet shop window. They perform for the onlookers, knowing that their behavior could earn them a home.

Collection of the author / © 1995 Christiane Dooghe

C.D. Tarot (Didactic Tarot)   Christiane Dooghe, Aldez Belgium, 1995

Celestial Tarot Kay Steventon, artist, and Brian Clark, U.S. Games Systems, 2004 The illustrations are of the artwork alone. The published deck has numbers and titles on the cards. TOP ROW: 0 The Fool. 1 The Magician. 2 The High Priestess. 3 The Empress. SECOND ROW: 4 The Emperor. 5 The Hierophant. 6 The Lovers. 7 The Chariot. THIRD ROW: 8 Strength. 9 The Hermit. 11 Justice. 12 The Hanged Man. BOTTOM ROW: 14 Temperance. 15 The Devil. 16 The Tower. 18 The Moon.

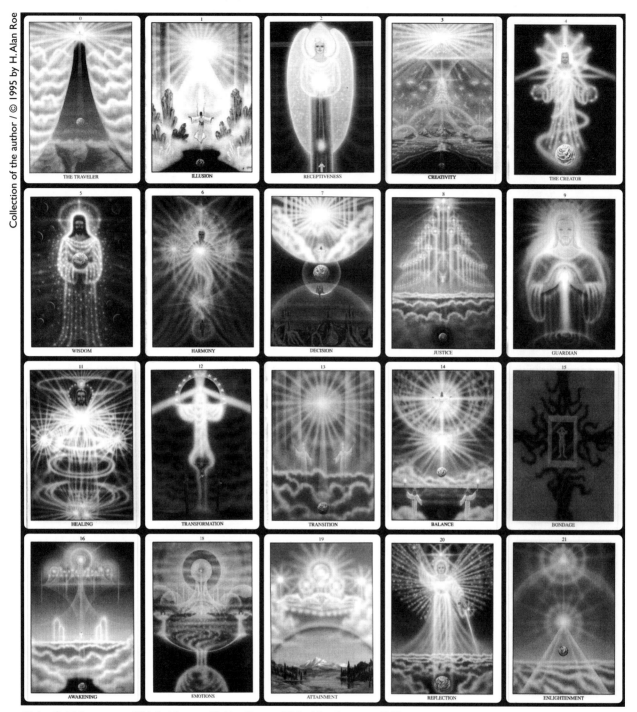

Celestial Messages of Light Tarot H. Alan Roe, published by the artist, 1995

Celtic Tarot   Courtney Davis, Aquarian Press, 1990; reprint Element Books, 2002   Descriptions are based on those by Helena Paterson.

TOP ROW: **0 The Fool** can be linked to the "Great Fool," Dalua, of the Celts. The card is also linked to the Spring festival represented by the goddess Brigantia. **I The Magician** is the Archdruid. The symbols shown within the zodiacal wheel are the energies controlled by the six-pointed Star of David, symbol of the evolved man or Magus. **II The High Priestess** is associated with the goddess Ceridwen of the Lake of Tegid, who first created the Sacred Cauldron of Inspiration. **VI The Lovers** celebrate their union as the man offers a drinking horn of wine to the woman.

SECOND ROW: **XII The Hanged Man** is associated with Arianrhod, a lunar spider goddess. He dangles by a thread, taking in a spider's vision of the world. The gold disk around his head is a solar symbol of a sacrificed god. **XIII Death** is

a skeletal spectre who arrives by boat, wrapped in the cloak of Manannan, a sea god who conveys the dead to the Land of Youth. The figurehead of the boat is Janus, god of the underworld. The mermaid swimming alongside the boat is like the Lady of the Lake, raising her hand to greet King Arthur. **XIV Temperance** connects with the Holy Well of St. Keyne, who was renowned for her strength of purity and radiant beauty. **XVIII The Moon** has two interlocking circles that represent the waxing and waning of the moon. The young goddess holds symbols of the new moon and full moon. The old goddess covers her face to hide her vast age. She is surrounded by a circle of chasing hounds.

THIRD ROW: **XIX The Sun** rises in the form of Lugh, the god of light. The women and two children represent the birth of light and new hope. **Queen of Swords. King of Wands. VII of Coins.**

265

The Fool • The Magician • The High Priestess • The Empress • The Emperor

The Druid • The Chariot • The Hermit • Death • Temperance

The Devil • The Star • The Moon • The Sun • Judgement

The World • Ten of Swords • Three of Wands • Ten of Cups • Ten of Pentacles

Celtic Tarot Mary Guinan, artist, and Julian De Burgh, Rider Books/St. Martin's Press, 2000 The following descriptions are based on the book by Julian De Burgh, which accompanies the deck.

TOP ROW: **The Fool** shows Cú Chulainn, whose strength made him a favorite in the king's court. In defending himself against a dog, he killed the animal, and to make up for it, he served its master by assuming the dog's duty for five years. **The Magician** is Mog Ruith of Munster, said to be the most powerful Druid in Ireland. **The High Priestess** is Morrigu, whose gift

Celtic Tarot (Tarocchi Celtici, by Gaudenzi and Tenuta) The Major Arcana of I Tarocchi Celtici were created by Giacinto Gaudenzi, while the Minor Arcana are by Saverio Tenuta. Both draw from the fantasy genre in different ways. Gaudenzi's art reflects a style that is found more in book illustration, whereas Tenuta's art recalls fantasy comic book art. The Major Arcana's images are from the folklore and fairytales of Northern Europe. For example, "Little Red Riding Hood" is shown on XVIII The Moon. The Minor Arcana are based on the Rider-Waite Tarot in composition and symbolism. Cards are titled in Italian, English, French, German, and Spanish. The back design, by Tenuta, is a double-ended image of a king holding a cup. The deck was published by Lo Scarabeo, Turin, Italy, in 2000.

Celtic Tarot (by Gonzalez Miranda) The Celtic Tarot is called Celtic after the style that artist Manuel Gonzales Miranda used. The back design is based on a Celtic motif and "the style of the illustrations on the front of the cards complies with the Celtic preference for the use of only straight or only curved lines." The Major Arcana images are based on those of the Tarot of Marseilles, and the titles are in French. The Minor Arcana include human figures. The box of the deck says "No. 1973," but the booklet accompanying the deck says "PIATNIK Game no. 1913." The deck was published by Piatnik, Vienna, Austria, in 1990.

Celtic Tarot (Tarocchi dei Celti, by Jacovitti) A satirical take on the "mysterious world" of the Celts is offered by Italian artist Benito Jacovitti in the twenty-two-card deck Tarocchi dei Celti. The deck comprises Major Arcana with a back design of a Celtic knot in white on a green ground. It was published in 1991 by Lo Scarabeo of Turin, Italy.

Celtic Tarot (Tarocchi dei Celti, by Lupatelli) The cards of Antonio Lupatelli's Celtic Tarot draw their titles from figures of Celtic lore. The old tales are interpreted with gentle humor in twenty-two Major Arcana. The back design is of intertwined animals. The deck was published by Lo Scarabeo, Turin, Italy, in 1991.

Celtic Tarot (Tarots Celtiques, by Tuan) The cards of L. Tuan's Celtic tarot deck were illustrated by M. Ameli, and the deck was published by Editions De Vecchi, Paris, in 1998. The Major Arcana show the name of a deity (center) and an astrological symbol at top and bottom corners. Key meanings are also given. The Minors are not traditional, though they are divided into four sections corresponding to the four elements. The cards are large and printed on heavy, textured paper; the back design is lightly marbled in green.

Celtic Dragon Tarot Fantasy illustrator Lisa Hunt painted the Celtic Dragon Tarot according to descriptions by author D.J. Conway. Said Conway of the designs, "Determined that the deck should be unique, we decided to avoid all New Age looks and designs, striving instead for an atmosphere and symbolism that blended perfectly with dragons—that of the Celts who used so many spiritual symbols. We chose to use only landscapes from the Celtic countries of Ireland, Scotland, and Wales. It seemed natural that medieval clothing and castles should be part of the Celtic, almost otherworldly atmosphere." The pictures on the cards are loaded with dragons great and small—some even quite cute. The deck was issued in 2001 by Llewellyn Publications, St. Paul, Minnesota.

---

of prophecy was used to forewarn her allies of battle. **The Empress** is Brigit, the goddess of fertility. **The Emperor** is the Dagda who was a god called the "All-Father."

SECOND ROW: **The Druid** is part of a priestly caste, interpreters of secret knowledge. **The Chariot** shows Laeg mac Riamgabra, Cú Chulainn's charioteer. **The Hermit** seeks solace among the stone idols on the lonely landscape of the Plain of Mag Slecht. **Death** represents Badb, who is often linked with the Banshee, as her wail warns of the death of someone close. **Temperance** shows the goddess Bean Naomha, goddess of wisdom.

THIRD ROW: **The Devil** is Cernunnos, a stag god representing fertility, and a consort of the Great Mother. **The Star** shows Angus mac Og searching for the goddess of sleep and dreams, Caer Ibormeith. **The Moon** illuminates a dark landscape in which a stone circle stands. **The Sun** shows Lugh, the sun god. **Judgement** shows the Brehon laws being administered by the *breitheamh*, lawgivers or judges of the Druid sect.

BOTTOM ROW: **The World** shows a hermaphrodite as a symbol of inner healing and completion, as two disparate parts are brought together. **Ten of Swords** shows the Battle of Mag Tuired, when Bres became king after King Nuadu's arm was severed. **Three of Wands** portrays Fionn mac Cumhaill standing guard on the tower of the Hill of Tara, ready to fight the Goblin whose music disarms his foes. He is armed with a fairy spear that breaks the spell. **Ten of Cups** depicts the poet Oisín with his great love, Niamh, in their celestial home. **Ten of Pentacles.** King Tigernmas ruled Ireland for seventy-seven years, starting in 1618 BCE.

Tarocchi Celtici   Giacinto Gaudenzi and Saverio Tenuta, Lo Scarabeo, 2000

Celtic Tarot   Manuel Gonzales Miranda, Piatnik, 1990

Tarocchi dei Celti   Benito Jacovitti, Lo Scarabeo, 1991

TOP ROW: 0 Il Matto (The Fool). I Il Ciabattino (The Cobbler). II La Sacerdotessa (The High Priestess). III L'Imperatrice (The Empress). IV L'Imperatore (The Emperor).   SECOND ROW: V Il Druido (The Druid). VI Gli Amanti (The Lovers). VII Il Carro (The Chariot). VIII La Giustizia (Justice). XI L'Eremita (The Hermit).   THIRD ROW: XI La Forza (Strength). XII L'Appeso (The Hanged Man). XIII La Morte (Death). XIV La Temperanza (Temperance). XV Il Diavolo (The Devil).   BOTTOM ROW: XVI La Torre (The Tower). XVII Le Stelle (The Star). XVIII La Luna (The Moon). XIX Il Sole (The Sun). XXI Il Mondo (The World).

Tarocchi dei Celti   Antonio Lupatelli, Lo Scarabeo, 1991

TOP ROW: **0 FINTAN MAC BOCHRA** depicts the first chronicler of Ireland. **I LUG** draws divinatory powers from an affinity with deities and animals. **II BRIGH** is associated with the yearly Pagan festival of purification. **III MORRIGAN** is supplicated in battle. The crow, carrion bird of the battle field, is on her shoulder. **V DIAN CECHT** is supplicated by herbalists.

SECOND ROW: **VIII OGMA** has powers of war, magic, and eloquence. **X BOADB** governs the fate of men with her wand. **XI CONCHOHAR** is associated with both fertility and war. **XII CU CHULAINN** is a hero of the Ulaid people. His death—and the end of the strength of the Ulaid—is shown. **XIV ACHTAN** is shown with the baby Cormac, who prevailed not through force but rather through wisdom.

BOTTOM ROW: **XV FINN MAC CUMAILL** is shown as an infant being instructed in the secrets of nature by a female druid. Cernunnos, the fertility god, is in the background. **XVIII OISIN** is a magical child who rides a sacred deer. **XIX BRAN MAC FEBAL. XX MANANNAN MAC LER** rules the after-life paradisiacal island. **XXI ERIU** shows Ireland surrounded by animals sacred to the Celts.

271

Tarots Celtiques   M. Ameli, artist, and L. Tuan, Editions De Vecchi, 1998

1 - The Magician | 2 - High Priestess | 3 - The Empress | 4 - The Emperor | 6 - The Lovers

7 - The Chariot | 8 - Strength | 9 - The Hermit | 10 - The Wheel | 13 - Death

14 - Temperance | 15 - Chains | 16 - The Tower | 17 - The Star | 18 - The Moon

Celtic Dragon Tarot   D.J. Conway and Lisa Hunt, artist, Llewellyn Publications, 2001

TOP ROW: **1 The Magician** has a dragon-topped wand. The half-formed images of dragons in the smoke indicate psychic abilities beginning to form. **2 High Priestess** stands between a dragon of Chaos and a dragon of Light, indicating the need to embrace and balance opposites. **3 The Empress** patiently waits to give birth, just as the dragon near her patiently broods on its eggs. Her bouquet of red roses symbolizes new cycles in life and rebirth of the self. The small dragon on her shoulder is her intermediary with astral beings. **4 The Emperor** is in the garden of regeneration and renewal. He watches over the children, symbolic of the power of the mystical center of each being, and the little dragons, which signify new magical endeavors. **6 The Lovers** shows a forest dragon, symbolizing analytical powers, and a water dragon, symbolizing creative powers.

SECOND ROW: **7 The Chariot.** Two dragons hold a crystal ball, in perfect balance with each other. The smaller dragons are events needing balance and resolution. **8 Strength.** A dragon emits a gust of fire. The spiritual seeker, a young woman, is unafraid. Her red rose symbolizes her accomplishments. **9 The Hermit** is an ancient dragon studying texts of wisdom. Vague dragon and human faces are teachers from the astral plane, and signify past lives. **10 The Wheel.** *The Grimoire of Life* is held open by a dragon's claw. The Wheel on the left page signifies fate. The quill signifies truth. **13 Death.** A dragon sheds its old scales and skin to emerge new and transformed. A ray of light breaks through the storm to illuminate the triumph.

BOTTOM ROW: **14 Temperance.** Three dragons intertwine. The red dragon is for life energy and sex drive; the green is for the productivity of mind; and the blue dragon is for emotions. Twining among them is the gold line of spirituality. **15 Chains.** A couple immersed in self-pity does not realize that the chain that binds them is broken. A dragon of chaos holds the chain in its claws. **16 The Tower,** symbolic of human ego, is destroyed by two black dragons of chaos. **17 The Star.** Seven gold-red dragons dance through the cosmos. **18 The Moon** is the backdrop for a silvery-white dragon dancing a celestial dance.

273

| 20 - Judgment | Four of Swords | Six of Wands | Four of Cups | Page of Pentacles |

Celtic Dragon Tarot (continued)

20 Judgment shows a dragon caring for a man who is struggling in the agony of renewal. The medallion the dragon wears has the triple spiral of life, death, and rebirth. The Celtic tree at the window symbolizes life past, present, and future. **Four of Swords** shows a woman and a dragon, exhausted, yet with four swords at the ready. **Six of Wands** shows a woman with a dragon on her shoulder and a crown

of spiritual enlightenment. The wands in the vase symbolize will power that can bring things into manifestation. **Four of Cups** depicts a woman who lives in false, empty dreams, as signified by the empty cups. The four dragons are the emotional abundance and love she could have if she would but choose. **Page of Pentacles** is a boy with his guardian dragon. The cat and the tiny dragon touching noses show similar ideas in different forms.

Celtic revival

Tarot is a looking glass of culture; the Celtic revival of the 1990s was reflected in tarot decks, published and unpublished, that drew from the images and traditions of Celtic Europe. Celtic-inspired decks featured in Volume IV are:

Arthurian Tarot
Avalon Tarot
Celtic Tarot (by Courtney Davis)
Celtic Tarot (by Julian De Burgh and Mary Guinan)
Tarocchi Celtici (by Giacinto Gaudenzi and Saverio Tenuta)
Celtic Tarot (by Manuel Gonzales Miranda)
Celtic Wisdom Tarot
Tarocchi dei Celti (by Benito Jacovitti)
Tarocchi dei Celti (by Antonio Lupatelli)
Tarots Celtique (by L. Tuan)
Celtic Dragon Tarot
Tarot of Celtic Legends
Druid Tarot
Faery Wicca Tarot
Glastonbury Tarot
Greenwood Tarot
Tarot of the Holy Grail
Kyle Tarot
Legend: The Arthurian Tarot
Merlin Tarot
Merryday Tarot
Tarot of the Northern Shadows
Tarot of the Old Path
Sacred Circle Tarot

Celtic Wisdom Tarot   "The immortality of the soul was a central tenet of druidic belief," says Caitlin Matthews, author of the Celtic Wisdom Tarot, "and the track of the soul through many lifetimes had its own distinct shape and pattern.... The Celtic Wisdom Tarot follows the track of the soul's path through the 22 Wisdom Cards. The 56 Story Cards reveal the more mundane features of life, depicting the rich variety of human experience through the tales and legends of the Celtic storytellers." The suits are battle (swords), skill (wands), art (cups), and knowledge (coins). The deck was illustrated by Olivia Rayner and published by Godsfield Press, U.K., and Destiny Books, Rochester, Vermont, in 1999. The back design is three spirals in red on orange.

Celtic Wisdom Tarot   Olivia Rayner, artist, and Caitlin Matthews, Destiny Books, 1999   The caption is based on the book accompanying the deck.

TOP ROW: **0 THE SOUL** is shown as a young traveler on the path of his destiny. His *riocht* or spirit body goes forth in a dream to visit the immensities of the Celtic cosmos contained within the cauldron. **I THE DECIDER** shows Dagda, the Great God of the Druids. He governs willpower and intention. **II THE GUARDIAN** is the Goddess Brigantia, the Mistress of Truth, who guards the land by truth, health, and creativity. Her *crios*, a woven triskele of rushes, is a protective emblem that is placed in many households in Ireland today. **VI THE LOVER** shows Nemetona, the Goddess of the Sacred Grove, with her suitors. In Celtic tradition, love and rivalry are closely combined. The Rowan tree, around her, has a long tradition of being a magical tree that is used in spells but protects from sorcery.

SECOND ROW: **VIII THE EMPOWERER** shows Andraste, Goddess of Victory. "She Who Is Unconquerable" was invoked by queen Boudicca in her insurrection against

0 THE SOUL

I THE DECIDER

II THE GUARDIAN

VI THE LOVER

VIII THE EMPOWERER

XI THE BALANCER

XII THE DEDICATOR

XIV THE MINGLER

9 REVELATION OF BATTLE

7 ADVENTURE OF SKILL

QUEEN OF ART

3 COURTSHIP OF KNOWLEDGE

the Romans. **XI THE BALANCER** is the Goddess of Safe Passage, Nehelania, invoked by all travelers, especially seafarers, and by those transacting business. Here she is Elen, the Goddess of the Ways, depicted as a dancer. **XII THE DEDICATOR** is the Goddess of Sacrifice from the Gundestrup Cauldron. Many stories speak of sacrificial cauldrons that restore life to the dead, who return to fight again but are unable to speak, or of the cauldrons of initiation that utterly change those who drink. **XIV THE MINGLER** shows Coventina, Goddess of the holy spring at Carrawburgh, which seems to have been popular with women who left offerings in return for safe delivery from childbirth.

BOTTOM ROW: **9 REVELATION OF BATTLE** depicts Deirdriu, whose lover was killed by King Conchobar, who wished her to be his own wife. **7 ADVENTURE OF SKILL** is a mouse who is really the pregnant wife of Llwyd ap Cilcoed, an Otherworldly man who had worked a series of enchantments on a kingdom. The mouse is kept as hostage until the enchantments are lifted. **QUEEN OF ART** is Brighid, matron of healers, smiths, and poets. **3 COURTSHIP OF KNOWLEDGE** shows the poet Amairgin visiting the goddesses of Ireland, Banba, Fotla and Eriu, so that the Milesians can be successful in their invasion of Ireland.

Ceremonial Magic Tarot The Ceremonial Magic Tarot cards are designed for both divination and use in magical rituals. The Major Arcana are taken from the "Talismans of the Sage of the Pyramids," presented by A.E. Waite in *Ceremonial Magic*. Forty-four of the Minor Arcana comprise the "Planetary Seals" of the Greater Key of Solomon, and the other twelve depict various pentacles, pentagrams, seals, and accouterments associated with ceremonies in the Greater Key of Solomon. The numbering is not traditional; for example, the Fool is card 1 of the Major Arcana, Judgement is number 21. The black and white deck was published in 1992 by the designers, Marianne Peterson and Priscilla Schwei.

Tarot of Ceremonial Magick The images of the Tarot of Ceremonial Magick are based on illustrations originally made for the book *Sex Magic, Tantra, and Tarot: The Way of the Secret Lover,* by Lon Milo DuQuette and Christopher S. Hyatt (New Falcon Publications, Tempe, Arizona, 1991). The book illustrations, black and white line drawings by David P. Wilson, follow Aleister Crowley's "Ritual of the Secret Lover." The Tarot of Ceremonial Magic, by Lon and Constance DuQuette, was published in 1994 by U.S. Games Systems, Stamford, Connecticut.

The authors say, in the booklet accompanying the deck, "The tarot is the most perfect representation of the Qabalistic fundamentals and is the common denominator between all the various Hermetic arts. One could even say that the tarot is the DNA of the Qabalah.... The Tarot of Ceremonial Magick is the only tarot deck ever created that accurately incorporates the key elements of the two most popular and widely practiced varieties of Qabalah-based magick: the Enochian magick of Dr. John Dee, and Goetia."

Each Major Arcana includes at the bottom border (left to right) the "magical seals of the Geniis (spirits) of the Domarum Mercurii (House of Mercury)," an elemental or astrological sigil and a Hebrew letter, and the "magical seals of the Geniis of the Carcerorum Qliphoth (Prison of the Shells)." "If evoked with skill, these spirits can serve as guides, counselors, and agents of the forces and dimensions represented by the trumps."

The aces and courts have at the bottom right a meditation symbol originating from Hinduism, and at the bottom left "the appropriate square from the Enochian Tablet of Union (the Spirit Tablet)." At the upper left of the courts are I Ching hexagrams and at the upper right the astrological position of the card. Also on the courts is "the appropriate Enochian subangle" (bottom center). On each ace, the entire elemental tablet for the element of each suit is displayed at the upper left, and the Enochian seal of the element is at the bottom center.

The sigils of the seventy-two spirits of Goetia are displayed on the lower left and right of numbered cards 2 through 10, which are called the Small Cards by the authors. The spirits of Goetia are described in some texts as "fallen angels." "The modern magician, however, does not view the spirits in the same sinister light. Rather, they represent imbalanced and heretofore uncontrolled aspects of the magician him/herself, which, if properly called forth, controlled and directed, can be of immeasurable benefit, especially in mundane and material matters." Above the Goetic seals are the "names of the Angels of the Shemhamphorash (divided Name of God)...the traditional Qabalistic rulers of the 36 Small Cards. Ruling in pairs, the angels can be called upon to bestow greater insight upon the inner meanings of each card, or can be evoked to manifest the energy represented by the cards."

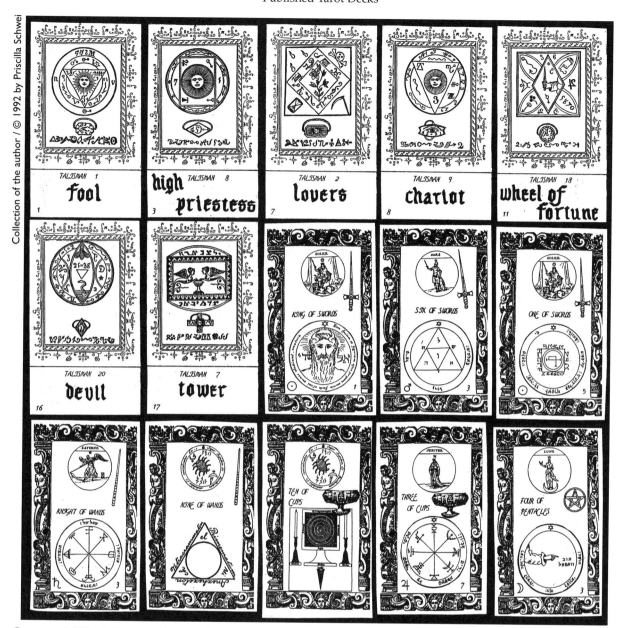

Collection of the author / © 1992 by Priscilla Schwei

Ceremonial Magic Tarot   Marianne Peterson and Priscilla Schwei, published by the artists, 1992

TOP ROW: **1 FOOL** conjures infernal or celestial spirits. **3 HIGH PRIESTESS** creates personal invisibility and the power to penetrate everywhere unseen. **7 LOVERS** is for success in love. **8 CHARIOT** enables the possessor to travel instantly to different places. **11 WHEEL OF FORTUNE** gains luck in gambling.

SECOND ROW: **16 DEVIL** is a shield against just such forces as the card represents in divination. **17 TOWER. KING OF SWORDS** commands the spirits of the sun. **SIX OF SWORDS** shows a pentacle used to gain military success. **ONE OF SWORDS** enables the possessor to be transported to distant places.

BOTTOM ROW: **KNIGHT OF WANDS** conjures spirits. **NINE OF WANDS** is the Triangle of Solomon, used to contain or confine any spirits conjured. **TEN OF CUPS** is the Mirror of Solomon, used to conjure visions. **THREE OF CUPS** signifies success and abundance. **FOUR OF PENTACLES** is used for protection in travel.

Tarot of Ceremonial Magick   Lon and Constance DuQuette, U.S. Games Systems, 1994

Children Tarot "Once upon a time, there was a tarot deck designed as if people had never grown up and all of the adults remained children forever...." Such is the premise printed on the box of the Children Tarot, and indeed the characters on the cards look as if they are playing at being in a tarot deck. The cards were illustrated by Lele Luzzati, using a technique of hand-coloring and applying patterned paper. The seventy-eight cards feature Italian, English, French, Spanish, and German titles, and the deck includes a title card and an advertising card. The backs have a monochrome double-ended design of four birds in purple. The Children Tarot was published by Lo Scarabeo, Turin, circa 2001.

Christian Bible Tarot Leslie Lewis created the Christian Bible Tarot "to help those who use tarot cards for the purposes of divination and take the subject seriously, to know that when justly used, and used correctly, it is easy to come to full terms with their own Christian teachings and upbringing." The artwork and design of the cards is by Sharp Studios of Liverpool, England, and the deck was published by the artist in 1995.

Each card, titled in English, features an image along with divinatory meanings and a quote from the Old or New Testament. The Major Arcana include Hebrew letters. They are traditionally numbered and titled, except that the Emperor and the Star are switched. Suits are spades, clubs, hearts, and diamonds. The deck comprises seventy-eight cards and two blank cards, and it includes an instructional leaflet. The back design is a cross, with the New Testament quote, "Father, into thy hands I commend my spirit" (Luke 23:46). One edition has a blue cross on a red background; the other has a red cross on a blue background.

Tarocchi del Cinema (Cinema Tarot) Tarocchi del Cinema evokes the great movies of the twentieth century. The films and stars depicted range from Hollywood to high art, comedy to horror. The artwork is by Sesar (Sergio Sarri). The deck has Major Arcana, with a double-ended back design portraying the artist in vintage style. A title card and a descriptive card are included, all in Italian, as are the titles. Tarocchi del Cinema was published by Lo Scarabeo, Turin, Italy, in 1995.

Tarô Clássico Nei Naiff The seventy-eight cards painted by Thais de Linhares under direction of Nei Naiff are based on the Tarot of Marseilles. The cards are symbolically coded by color. The Major Arcana cards are yellow (1, 2, 3, 4, 5), pink (6), green (7, 8, 9, 10, 11), gray (12, 13, 14, 15, 16), blue (17), purple (18, 19, 20, 21), and purple/yellow (Fool). Minor Arcana cards are green (pentacles), yellow (swords), blue (cups), and red (wands). The deck was published in 2002 by Distribuidora Record de Serviços de Imprensa, Rio de Janeiro, Brazil. The illustrations were first printed in the book *Curso completo de tarô*, by Nei Naiff, published by Record/Nova Era in 2002.

Tarocchi Clizia The artist Clizia produced Major Arcana using intaglio printing. The images were printed in 1985, in portfolio form by Pheljna Edizione of Turin, Italy. The images were attached to each other and accordion folded at their edges. The art is black and white, except for Il Folle (The Fool), which is also signed by the artist. The edition was of 1000 numbered copies.

Tarocchi dei Colori Elena Assante created Tarocchi dei Colori with bold areas of color that form the figures and objects of the Major and Minor Arcana. The cards are titled in Italian, German, Spanish, English, and French. The back design is wavy stripes in various colors, and the deck includes a title card and a card describing in Italian the artistic conception. The deck was published in a limited edition of 3000 numbered sets by Italcards, Bologna, Italy, in 1991.

Tarô Clássico Nei Naiff Thais de Linhares, artist, and Nei Naiff, Record/Nova Era, 2002

Children Tarot Lele Luzzati, Lo Scarabeo, circa 2001

Christian Bible Tarot Leslie Lewis and Sharp Studios, published by Leslie Lewis, 1995

Tarocchi del Cinema (Cinema Tarot)   Sesar, Lo Scarabeo, 1995

TOP ROW: **0 IL MATTO** (The Fool). The Marx brothers, with Groucho at top. **I IL MAGO** (The Magician). Werner Krauss as the creepy hypnotist in *The Cabinet of Dr. Caligari* (1921). **2 LA PAPESSA** (The Popess). Greta Garbo in *Mata Hari* (1932). **3 L'IMPERATRICE** (The Empress). Marlene Dietrich in *The Scarlet Empress* (1934). **6 GLI AMANTI** (The Lovers). Rudolph Valentino in *The Sheik* (1921), with co-star Agnes Ayers. This role made Valentino a heart-throb all over the world. SECOND ROW: **7 IL CARRO** (The Chariot). John Wayne as "Ringo Kid" in *Stagecoach* (1939). **8 LA GIUSTIZIA** (Justice).

Tarocchi Clizia   Clizia, Pheljna Edizione, 1985

Alfred Hitchcock on the set of the movie that changed forever the experience of taking a shower, *Psycho* (1960). **10 LA RUOTA** (The Wheel). The space station in Stanley Kubrick's *2001: A Space Odyssey* (1968). **11 LA FORZA** (Strength). The giant ape, King Kong, with "co-star" Fay Wray in the 1933 classic set in New York City. **13 LA MORTE** (Death) was played by Bengt Erkrot in the 1957 Ingmar Bergman arthouse classic *The Seventh Seal*. The knight he shadows was played by Max von Sydow.

THIRD ROW: **14 LA TEMPERANZA** (Temperance) depicts the troubled gossip-columnist (Marcello Mastrioanni) in Federico Fellini's decadent Rome as sex fantasy, *La Dolce Vita* (The Sweet Life; 1960). **16 LA TORRE** (The Tower) stars Boris Karloff in *Frankenstein* (1931). **17 LA STELLA** (The Star). Marilyn Monroe, in the famous Manhattan sidewalk scene in *The Seven Year Itch* (1955). **18 LA LUNA** (The Moon). *La Belle et La Bete (*The Beauty and the Beast) made in 1946 by Jean Cocteau and starring Josette Day and Jean Marais. **21 IL MONDO** (The World). Charlie Chaplin in *The Great Dictator* (1940).

Tarocchi dei Colori   Elena Assante, Italcards, 1991

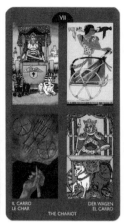

Comparative Tarot Developed by Valerie Sim; artwork by Robert De Angelis, Silvana Alasia, Sergio Toppi, Claude Burdel, 2002 (Lo Scarabeo)

Tarocchi nei Colori della Toscana (Colors of Tuscany Tarot) The Major Arcana deck by Amerigo Folchi depicts buildings from different cities of Tuscany. The buildings appear on abstract backgrounds, with figures from the Tarot of Marseilles. The deck was produced for the clock company Swatch; wristwatches are on each card, and outlines of seven wristwatches comprise the back design. The deck was published by Italcards in 1992, in a numbered edition of 3,333. The deck includes a title card and a card that has the back design on face and back. The cards are titled in English and Italian, and include the name of the town and the building featured.

Comparative Tarot Each card of the Comparative Tarot shows an image from the Universal Tarot, by Roberto De Angelis; the Tarot of the Sphinx, by Silvana Alasia; the Tarot of the Origins, by Sergio Toppi; and the 1751 Claude Burdel Tarot of Marseilles. All the decks are published by Lo Scarabeo of Turin, as was the Comparitive Tarot itself. The Comparitive Tarot method was developed by Valerie Sim, author of the booklet accompanying the deck. The method deepens understanding of tarot images by study of different interpretations of each card. The deck was conceived by Riccardo Minetti and published in 2002.

Connolly Tarot The Connolly Tarot deck was created by Eileen Connolly with artwork by her son, Peter Paul Connolly. The vividly colored art was rendered in colored pencils, with the intention to be reminiscent of medieval stained glass windows. The booklet accompanying the deck says that the tarot "eliminates all unnecessary and negative symbolism." Card 13 is re-titled "Transition," and card 15 is re-titled "Materialism." The Connolly Tarot was published in 1990 by U.S. Games Systems of Stamford, Connecticut. It includes a title card and a card picturing a door and the words "Gateway to Meditation." The back design is of white marble.

Corte dei Tarocchi (Court of the Tarots) Anna Maria D'Onofrio used aquatint to create the Corte dei Tarocchi, which was published by Edizione Il Meneghello of Milan

in 1999. The deck was issued in 1,100 numbered sets, and includes a presentation card. The back design shows an owl against a pattern of runes, with the artist's name and title of the deck at the bottom of the design. The cards are printed on thick, textured cardboard, and the package bears the seal of Osvaldo Menegazzi, publisher.

Cosmic Tarot The Cosmic Tarot was created by German artist Norbert Lösche. The deck combines images of celebrities and tarot symbolism to create a deck that can be read traditionally, and yet is re-interpreted for a contemporary audience. The deck was published by U.S. Games Systems in 1998. The back design is of a star with an English rose in the center.

Cosmic Egg Tarot The Cosmic Egg Tarot was first published as the Kosmisch Ei Tarot by its artist Guido Gillabel in 1987. The Major Arcana black and white deck was issued in a limited edition of 99 signed and numbered decks, each including a presentation card. Gillabel, a Belgian teacher of tarot, says, "The inspiration to draw this deck arose in the period around Easter. The egg, which plays an important role in Easter tradition, became the starting point of each card…. Every card is based on the philosophy of the Holy Trinity." Carol Herzer painted the images and published them, printed on silver-backed photopaper, in an edition of 333 numbered copies, signed by both Herzer and Gillabel and packaged in a cloth pouch. In addition to 22 Major Arcana, the color deck includes a presentation card, an edition card, and a card giving background for Herzer and Gillabel.

Cosmic Egg Tarot Guido Gillabel, 1987

Tarocchi nei Colori della Toscana (Colors of Tuscany Tarot)   Amerigo Folchi, Italcards, 1992

Connolly Tarot   Eileen Connolly and Peter Paul Connolly, artist, U.S. Games Systems, 1990

Corte dei Tarocchi (Court of the Tarots)   Anna Maria D'Onofrio, Edizioni Il Meneghello, 1999

Cosmic Tarot   Norbert Lösche, U.S. Games Systems, 1998

Cosmic Egg Tarot Guido Gillabel and Carol Herzer, published by the artists, 1987

Cosmic Tribe Tarot The Cosmic Tribe Tarot, by Stevee Postman, celebrates the body as "the birthplace of awareness." Eric Ganther, who wrote the book accompanying the deck, says, "The naked human figure is a primary component of Stevee's imagery, evoking our deepest sense of self.... The Cosmic Tribe reunites our amazing minds with our beautiful bodies at the point where internal exploration meets the universal energies that called it into being." The illustrations were made digitally, using photographs of the artist's friends. "Technology is an extension of our bodies, not an externality but another system used by the superorganism to express and adorn itself. Technology merely reflects the useful beauty of the world and enhances our ability to appreciate it. This vision is called technopaganism." Eyes are a strong motif; "these eyes represent your highest capacity for awareness—the point where you collapse time and space and become the eyes of the universe." The back design shows an eye at the center of the four suit symbols. Three versions of 6 The Lovers are in the deck, which was published by Destiny Books of Rochester, Vermont, in 1998.

Cosmo Deck The Cosmo Deck by Carol Herzer is very similar to one featured in volume III of *The Encyclopedia of Tarot*, the Cosmotarot, but the paintings have differences. (The artist has since renamed that deck Astrotarot.) Rarely do human figures enter the deck; birds are frequent motifs. The Cosmo Deck was issued in 1988 as a signed, numbered edition of photographs of Herzer's paintings, with a silver backing. The deck includes four instructional booklets. About the tarot, Herzer says, "I see the tarot as a work of art that has been evolving collectively, and I am totally involved in the process of developing and revealing the tarot as art." The deck has twenty-two Major Arcana and an extra card, 23 Nemesis, named after the Greek goddess who "represents collective karma."

Carol Herzer created **Cosmic Jewel** by assembling photographs of the Cosmo Deck

Cosmos Tarot California artist Maria Sky drew and painted the Tarot de Cosmos under direction of author Nicolas Tereshchenko. The deck was sold together with the book *Les Trésors du Tarot* (The Treasures of the Tarot), by Tereshchenko. The deck comprises twenty-two traditional Major Arcana plus four extra Arcana. The deck was published by Editions Atlas/Guy Tredaniel, Paris, with the book in 1986.

Cosmic Tribe Tarot 6 The Lovers "One of the most important issues in modern times involves the freedom to choose whom we fall in love with.... The objects of our love represent uniquely individual choices. Only cruelty would prevent love from flourishing wherever it would grow." (from *The Cosmic Tribe Tarot* book, by Eric Ganther)

0 Fool	1 Magician	3 Empress	5 Hierophant
6 Lovers	8 Balance	14 Art	16 Tower
17 Star	18 Moon	19 Sun	21 Universe
10 Wands	3 Wands	Princess of Cups	Princess of Disks

Cosmic Tribe Tarot Stevee Postman, Destiny Books, 1998

Cosmo Deck   Carol Herzer, published by the artist, 1988   Titles are from the book accompanying the deck.

TOP ROW: 0 The Wave. 2 The Goddess. 3 Love. 4 The Ego. 5 The Initiate.

SECOND ROW: 6 The Path. 7 Will. 8 Perfection. 9 The Guide. 10 The Wheel.

THIRD ROW: 11 Kundalini. 12 The Unconscious. 13 Ego Death. 15 The Veil of Illusion. 16 Awakening.

BOTTOM ROW: 18 The Threshold. 19 The Sun. 20 Generation. 21 Heaven World. 23 Nemesis.

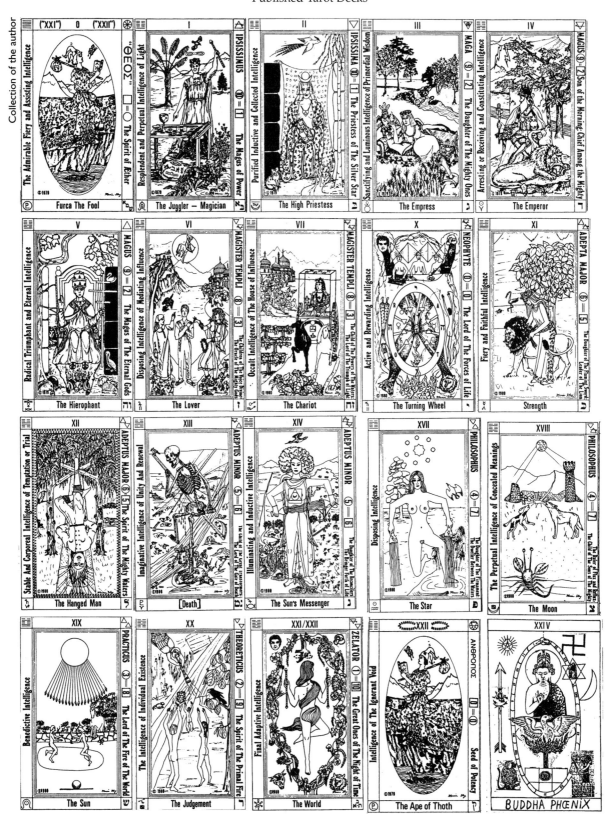

Cosmos Tarot Nicolas Tereshchenko and Maria Sky, 1986

Each card features, at the top, from left to right: the I Ching hexagram, the traditional number of the card, and elemental symbols. At the bottom from left to right are: the astrological correspondence and the alchemical attribute; the title of the card; the corresponding Hebrew letters. On the right side, from top down, are the "magical grade"; the number combination of the "magical grade," as used by the Hermetic Order of the Golden Dawn; and the "magical title" of the card. On the left side, from bottom up, are the kabbalistic Intelligences of the Sephirah and Path.

Crisse Tarot Belgian fantasy artist Crisse (pseudonym of Pierre Joassin) created an eighty-card tarot deck, which was published by Gibraltar, France, in 1998. The deck was also published in portfolio form by Pegasus, and several of the cards appeared in another portfolio, Erotic Fantasy. The court cards are identical, regardless of suit; for example, the queens of all the suits show the same image, with the only variation being the suit sign in the lower corner. The pips show a large number and the suit sign. Two extra cards are untitled. Titles are in French and Flemish, and the double-ended back design shows a woman wearing a starry cape, in blue on white.

Tarot of the Crone Ellen Lorenzi-Prince self-published the Tarot of the Crone in 2001 in a limited edition. The deck, she says, "is inspired by the myths, folktales, and magic of ancient goddesses, sorceresses, and wise-women throughout the world."

Crow's Magick Tarot "The crow is king" in this deck, as the artist Londa Marks writes. The bird takes on different forms, sometimes taking the body of a man, sometimes giving wings to other creatures, mostly North American animals. The artwork was drawn on computer in shapes that often have a metallic sheen, on black backgrounds. Each Major and Minor Arcana card features a title in English, plus key words and astrological symbols. The deck comprises Major and Minor Arcana plus a title card and an introductory card. The back design is double-ended red crows silhouetted against a black background. The deck was published by U.S. Games Systems, Stamford, Connecticut, in 1998.

Crystal Tarots Elisabetta Trevisan rendered the Crystal Tarots in tempera paints and pastels. The seventy-eight Minor and Major Arcana have kaleidoscopic images, with areas defined by intricate pattern and color. The cards are titled in English, French, German, Spanish, and Italian. The back design is a blue line drawing of a bird amidst foliage and landscape fragments. The deck includes a title card and instruction cards. The Crystal Tarots was published by Lo Scarabeo in 1995.

The Major Arcana of the deck were first published by Lo Scarabeo as Tarocchi di Vetro, with a purple back design, in 1990, and as Glass Tarots, with a green back design, in 1991. The Glass Tarots had English titles, and included a title card and a card offering a poetic musing: "Drops of colour sprinkled in the air / by the puff of a rainbow, / a tapestry of clouds, flower petals / and a finger-nail moon. / A patient hand has built / with tiny pieces of glass / the vault of heaven, and carved out / the roads of the world. / A hermit / recounts the tale of two smiles / that once upon a time invented / the Spring."

Curious Tarot The characters of the Curious Tarot, by Michelle Cohen, were made by collaging human bodies with the heads of animals and statues. The artist's studio, Curious Arts, issued the deck as a signed and numbered edition of 100 decks. The deck comprises twenty-two Major Arcana, sixteen court cards, and a presentation card, accompanied by a handmade instruction booklet on black paper, also signed and numbered, and dated. (The deck in the author's collection is dated "5/18/02.") The back design is the title of the deck around a sea urchin on a black background.

Glass Tarots, later re-named Crystal Tarots, by Elisabetta Trevisan, Lo Scarabeo, 1991.

Collection of the author

295

Crisse Tarot   Crisse, Gibraltar, 1998

Tarot of the Crone   Ellen Lorenzi-Prince, published by the artist, 2001 Descriptions are by the artist.

TOP ROW: **II The Priestess** is a standing stone among a circle of such stones. Her eyes glow with the light of the waning moon above her, and she transmits energy into a green land. **VIII Justice** is Spider Grandmother, who weaves the web of life and understands balance in all things. **XI Strength** portrays the serpent of kundalini, a power both sexual and spiritual. **XII Sacrifice** depicts Weeping Woman, whose empty eyes shed oceans of tears. Her reflection in the water is smiling. **XVII The Star** shows the Queen of Heaven haloed by the moon. She opens her cloak of stars to create the night sky.

SECOND ROW: **XVIII The Moon** is the Queen of the Ghosts. She smiles mysteriously, standing amid frozen crying faces etched into the desolate landscape and the wrap she wears. **XXI The World** shows the Crone as the sum of all who have come before and the key to a bright new world.

Grandmother of Swords (corresponding to the Queen) is a storyteller. The children of her community gather to her to hear of their culture and world. **Nine of Swords** represents Proof. The image is of a figure seated in meditation on a bed of sharp points. **Beast of Wands** (corresponding to the Page) is shown as a stalking cat.

BOTTOM ROW: **Nine of Wands** represents Power. A figure stands between the sun and the moon, with all her chakras alight. **Ace of Wands** represents Will. The image is a single pointed finger with a blazing tip. **Two of Cups** represents Desire. The image is two figures drawn together, opening their cloaks to one another to reveal and to connect their inner selves. **Nine of Disks** represents Community. The image is nine unique but unified homes upon a hill under the arch of the sky. **Three of Disks** is the Family. The image is three people holding hands as they journey down the road together toward the sun.

Crow's Magick Tarot   Londa Marks, U.S. Games Systems, 1998

| THE FOOL / LE FOU | 0 | DER NARR / EL LOCO | THE MAGICIAN / LE BATELEUR | I | DER MAGIER / EL MAGO | THE PRIESTESS / LA PAPESSE | II | DIE HOHEPRIESTERIN / LA SACERDOTISA | THE EMPRESSE / L'IMPERATRICE | III | DIE HERRSCHERIN / LA EMPERATRIZ |

IL MATTO — IL BAGATTO — LA PAPESSA — L'IMPERATRICE

| THE LOVERS / LES AMANTS | VI | DIE LIEBENDEN / LOS ENAMORADOS | STRENGTH / LA FORCE | XI | DIE STÄRKE / LA FUERZA | THE HANGED MAN / LE PENDU | XII | DER GEHÄNGTE / EL COLGADO | THE STARS / LES ETOILES | XVII | DER STERN / LA ESTRELLA |

GLI AMANTI — LA FORZA — L'APPESO — LE STELLE

| JUDGEMENT / LE JUGEMENT | XX | DIE MEINUNG / EL JUICIO | KNIGHT OF WANDS / CHEVALIER DE BATONS | | RITTER DER STÄBE / CABALLO DE BASTOS | KING OF CHALICES / ROI DE COUPES | | KÖNIG DER KELCHE / REY DE COPAS | PENTACLES / DENIERS | 5 | MÜNZEN / OROS |

IL GIUDIZIO — CAVALIERE DI BASTONI — RE DI COPPE — DENARI

Crystal Tarots   Elisabetta Trevisan, Lo Scarabeo, 1995

Curious Tarot Michelle Cohen, published by the artist, 2002

Cyber Deck   Diane Rinella, Brett Harrison, Matt Manson, and Ujvári Gabor, InVision Games, 1994

Cyber Deck   The Cyber Deck was created using computer-generated artwork by Diane Rinella with Brett Harrison, and contributing artists Matt Manson and Ujvári Gabor. Rinella explains, "The Cyber Deck is unique in design and contains forty-two Major Arcana cards. It was created in the popular, futuristic 'cyber' style, and creates many new cards while keeping or restructuring many time-tested traditional cards." The deck has no Minor Arcana. The back design is a white eye of Ra (the ancient Egyptian sun god) on a black background. A title card and advertising card are included in the deck, which was issued in 1994 by InVision Games.

Czech Tarot (První Ceské Taroty; First Czech Tarot) The Czech Tarot was created by Karel Filipu of the Czech Republic and published in 1993 by Svatá Mahatma. The deck comprises twenty-two Major Arcana. The back design is mauve and purple, with four eyes within a triangle. Each card includes a Hebrew letter and an astrological sign, and the titles are in Czech. The deck includes a credits card and a presentation card in black and white showing a bee over a pentagram.

Czech Tarot (První Ceské Taroty; First Czech Tarot)   Karel Filipu, Svatá Mahatma. 1993

Dance of Life: An Intimate Tarot "You dance to the rhythm of your life—to the rhythm of the streets, to the rhythm of your partners and friends, to the rhythm of your body and emotions, and to the calling of a higher power. You dance to the best of your ability to whatever is going on in your world." Audrey Savage created the Dance of Life Tarot, working with artist Paula Scott Frantz. The suits are self (wands), health (cups), money (swords), and the material world (pentacles), with courts of sage, lover, dancer, and muse. The deck was published in 2000 by Book Weaver Publishing of Indianapolis.

Dance of Life Tarot   Audrey Savage and Paula Scott Frantz, artist, Book Weaver Publishing, 2000

Dante Tarot Fluid, surrealistic forms illustrate the Dante Tarot, named after the Italian poet Dante Alighieri (1265–1321). The titles of the Major Arcana reflect the Renaissance list of virtues and qualities, and ranks of celestial authority, with cards such as II Philosophy and XXI Principalities. The suits of the Minor Arcana are flames, lights, clouds, and bricks; Lo Scarabeo's catalog indicates that they "describe the poet's life and narrate the stops along the supernatural journey through Hell, Purgatory, and Paradise including contemplation of Eternal Light." Flames illustrate the Inferno; bricks illustrate scenes from Dante's life; clouds show scenes from Purgatory; and light shows the ascension into Paradise. The artist of the deck is Andrea Serio. The deck includes a title card and advertising card, and the back, in shades of blue and green, shows on one end the poet writing, and on the other end a horse. The Dante Tarot was published by Lo Scarabeo, of Turin, Italy, in 2001.

David's Tarot David's Tarot, by David Chastain, is a seventy-eight-card deck rendered in brush and ink on stark white backgrounds. The images are often abstract, especially in the suit cards, which utilize simple and expressive brushwork to imply meaning. Structurally, the cards follow the Rider-Waite deck, with some deviations and references to earlier tarot traditions (for instance, The Hanged Man has been replaced with the Traitor). Says Chastain, "The images are intentionally spare and ambiguous, intended as catalysts for imaginative exploration rather than literal interpretation."

The artist published the deck in 1996 as laser copies on heavy stock. Chastain also issued t-shirts featuring some of the designs of the deck.

Tarocchi del Decamerone (Decameron Tarot) The Decameron Tarot by Giacinto Gaudenzi is described on the packaging as "Adults Only." The erotic images do not specifically match scenes from *The Decameron,* written circa 1350 by Giovanni Boccaccio, in the Tuscan dialect. Rather, they illustrate the milieu of the time. The oversized Major Arcana plus presentation card were published in 1993 by Ideogramma Arte Editoriale of Turin, in an edition limited to 300 copies. The back design shows two images of a couple making love, in green on a white background.

Jonathan Dee Tarot The tarot accompanying the book by Jonathan Dee has illustrations that resemble woodcut prints. The art is by Shirley Barker. The book and deck set was published by Parragon of London in 1996, and by Barnes & Noble Books, New York, in 1998.

Cartes du Destin (Cards of Destiny) Elsa Dax made the Cartes du Destin as a Major Arcana deck for limited distribution. The artwork is in a naïve style. The deck was made circa 2001. The back design is white with the artist's name at the bottom. Dax has been part of the "Stuckism" art movement, which originated in London. Among other (loosely held) tenets, Stuckism champions paintings on canvas, art shows outside of white-walled galleries, and art as a quest for self-discovery. The name originated when British artist Tracy Emin allegedly said to another artist, "Your paintings are stuck! You are stuck! Stuck! Stuck! Stuck!"

Dewa Tarot The Dewa Tarot was published by AGMüller, Neuhausen, Switzerland, in 1999. The seventy-eight-card deck features oval images in the center of each card. The pictures are from the Arcus Arcanum Tarot (see *The Encyclopedia of Tarot,* volume III), made by Hansrudi Wäscher under direction of Günter Hager, and published by AGMüller in 1986. Surrounding the image are the title and interpretations of the card, in German, under the headings Beziehungen (relationships), Allgemein (general), Beruf (job), and Anregung (emotions). The deck was developed by Melomoon Verlag of Nuremberg, Germany.

Tarot Divinatoire de L'Etoile Rana (Divinatory Tarot of the Rana Star) The Tarot Divinatoire de L'Etoile Rana comprises twenty-two Major Arcana plus a card titled "the star rana." The pastel originals by Regine Faudot have a naïve visionary style. The back design is an orange Star of David on blue. No publication information is given with the deck; presumably the artist published it herself. It dates from circa 1999. Titles are in English and French.

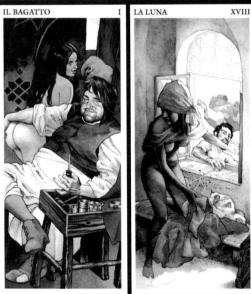

Collection of the author / © 1993 by Ideogramma s.a.s, di Pietro Alligo & Co.

IL BAGATTO I

LA LUNA XVIII

Tarocchi del Decamerone (Decameron Tarot)
Giacinto Gaudenzi, Ideogramma Arte Editoriale, 1993

Dante Tarot Andrea Serio, Lo Scarabeo, 2001

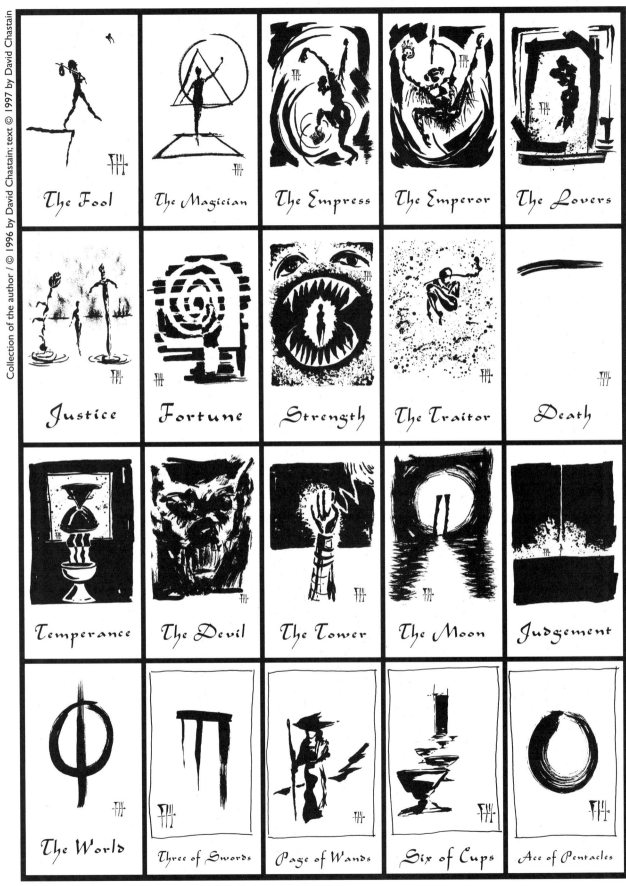

The Fool | The Magician | The Empress | The Emperor | The Lovers

Justice | Fortune | Strength | The Traitor | Death

Temperance | The Devil | The Tower | The Moon | Judgement

The World | Three of Swords | Page of Wands | Six of Cups | Ace of Pentacles

David's Tarot   David Chastain, published by the artist, 1996

Jonathan Dee Tarot   Shirley Barker, artist, and Jonathan Dee, Parragon, 1996; Barnes & Noble Books, 1998

Cartes du Destin (Cards of Destiny)   Elsa Dax, published by the artist, circa 2001

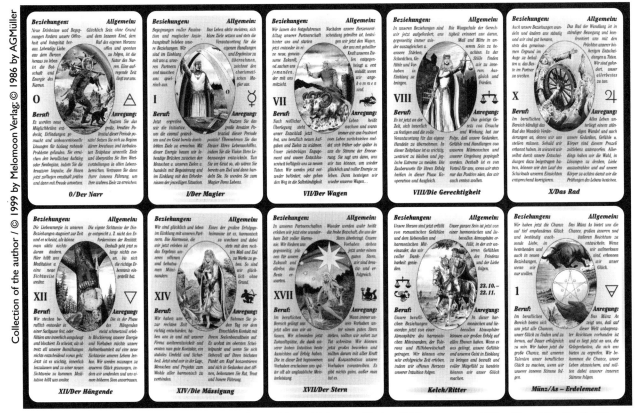

Dewa Tarot   Hansrudi Wäscher, artist, and Günter Hager, Melomoon Verlag, 1999   TOP ROW: 0/Der Narr (The Fool). I/Der Magier (The Magician). VII/Der Wagen (The Chariot). VIII/Die Gerechtigkeit (Justice). X/Das Rad (The Wheel).
SECOND ROW: XII/Der Hängende (The Hanged Man). XIV/Die Mässigung (Temperance). XVII/Der Stern (The Star). Kelche/Ritter (Knight of Cups). Münz/As - Erdelement (Ace of Coins - Earth Element).

Tarot Divinatoire de L'Etoile Rana (Divinatory Tarot of the Rana Star)   Regine Faudot, published by the artist, circa 1999

Dragon Tarot   Peter Pracownik, artist, and Terry Donaldson, U.S. Games Systems, 1996   The descriptions are based on the booklet accompanying the deck.

TOP ROW: **0 THE FOOL** stands on a black and white floor, representing the light and dark in life. In one hand he holds a die, for chance, and in the other a jester's head, for humor. The harp on the floor is that of Orpheus, who went into the underworld. **I THE MAGICIAN** is on a stage, as if performing. Around him are the suit and elemental symbols; above him is the lemniscate of infinity. **II THE HIGH PRIESTESS** stands between pillars of secret knowledge and initiation. One is topped with Earth, and the other with the yin-yang symbol, indicating constant change. She holds the Torah, written in runes, and a rainbow descends from her other hand into the cauldron, symbolic of seven initiations. **III THE EMPRESS** holds a newly hatched dragon. She is

Dragon Tarot Dragons are protagonists, symbols and artwork in the Dragon Tarot. Illustrated by Peter Pracownik under direction of Terry Donaldson, the deck is in the style of the Visionary Movement, the utopian and fantastical art that evolved from the psychedelic art of the 1960s. Each of the Major Arcana bears in the lower left and right corners astrological, alchemical, or other symbols, such as a heart on the Lovers card. The lower corners of the Minor Arcana bear symbols of the elements. The deck includes a title card and a presentation card. The deck was published in 1996 by U.S. Games Systems, Stamford, Connecticut.

Dreampower Tarot The Dreampower Tarot has seventy-eight cards, with twenty-two trumps, forty number cards, and sixteen court cards. However, the images, titles, and suits are not traditional. The number cards, which show only the suit sign with a numeral and a key word, are divided into suits of air, fire, water, and earth, and the suits do not correspond to tarot suits. The court cards are ranked king, queen, warrior, and child, and they have their own suits of spirits (fire), messengers (air), souls (water), and ancestors (Earth). Two extra cards diagram the Tree of Life and the trump cards according to the three realms of consciousness described by Stewart as stone (relative being), pearl (consciousness), and whirlpool (power).

The deck was painted by Stuart Littlejohn under direction of R.J. Stewart. The book, by Stewart, that accompanies the deck explains the intriguing origin of the cards. "In 1989 I was working on a book of visualization and transformative techniques, and it suddenly occurred to me, perhaps discovering the obvious, that tarot decks are full of people, both in the Trumps and the minor cards.... What intrigued me was a simple question: what kind of tarot might these people use?... The inspiration was that there was another set of trumps and courts to be found within the universal elemental cycle of tarot, and the key was in asking the tarot images that I might come to know what cards they might use." The back design shows an inverted tree, "an image used in faery, Underworld, alchemical, and other mystical traditions....This one grows in reverse, with its roots in our outer world, reaching through the Underworld, with its crown in the mysterious Realm of universal being deep below or within all forms." The Dreampower Tarot was published by Aquarian Press, London, in 1993.

Druid Tarot The Druid Tarot was self-published by the artist James Bluth in black and white. The square-cornered cards have solid black backs that are varnished, while the fronts of the cards are unlacquered, perhaps to permit coloring the faces. There are eighteen Major Arcana for eighteen Druid runes, which appear at the top of each Major Arcana card. In the lower left corner of each Major Arcana is a planetary sign. The number of the card is on the lower right. The titles are in English. Most of the titles are traditional tarot titles, but the numbering of the deck varies from the traditional order. The Minor Arcana are numbered 1 through 14, with the court cards numbered page 11, knight 12, queen 13, and king 14. The suits are swords, rods, cups, and stars. The deck was issued in 1985.

somewhat warlike, ready to defend her offspring. **IV THE EMPEROR** holds Martian symbols of orb and arrow. He is red for blood, fire, and the basic element of energy.

SECOND ROW: **VI THE LOVERS** are two dragons interlaced, gazing at each other. They each hold a heart. **VII THE CHARIOT** shows a rare golden dragon drawn across the sky by two smaller dragons, who scout the ground below. **VIII STRENGTH** displays a lion and a dragon playing in the sky. Between them is a caduceus, symbol of life processes. **IX THE HERMIT** is near human habitation, indicating that he is no longer part of his family, clan, or tribe. The shape above him recalls the pyramids, which were built to draw the energy of the constellation Draconis. The compass below recalls measurement and exactitude. **X THE WHEEL OF FORTUNE** shows the great Dragon Ourobouros coiled around a glyph of the zodiac. His tail is in his mouth, demonstrating self-sustaining creative force. A compass on the ground hints of the earth's cosmic lines of force, called ley lines or dragon lines.

THIRD ROW: **XI JUSTICE** shows a balance on one side of which rests a feather, symbolizing truth, and on the other side of which is the sun, for solar consciousness. The scales rest on Earth. **XIII DEATH** shows a skeletal dragon. In the mists behind it are stones of an ancient circle. An hourglass reminds us of impermanence, while an egg symbolizes rebirth. **XIV TEMPERANCE** shows a dragon absorbed in its own reflection. The hands of the Temperance angel are above, one bearing a symbol of fire and the other bearing a symbol of water. **XVIII THE STAR** shows a blue water dragon filling a jug from a waterfall. Distracted by a falling star, the dragon spills the water back into the stream. **XVIII THE MOON** shines on a dragon of interplanetary flight, resting between the towers of initiation.

BOTTOM ROW: **XIX THE SUN** rests on the body of a red fire dragon, who is on a yin-yang symbol. Stonehenge, a cosmic calendar in giant stone, is on the right. A rune for *siegel*, meaning "sun," is on the lion's forehead. **XXI THE WORLD** shows a huge dragon coiled around the world. Symbols of the four fixed signs of the zodiac are around it. **KING OF SWORDS. ACE OF WANDS. TEN OF CUPS.**

Collection of the author / Paintings © 1993 by Stuart Littlejohn

Dreampower Tarot Stuart Littlejohn, artist, and R.J. Stewart, Aquarian Press, 1993 Descriptions are based on those in the book, as are tarot equivalents of the cards (in parentheses).

TOP ROW: **The Choir** (The Magician) shows allies, spiritual creatures that energize us and work with us, rather than forces over which we seem to have no influence. **The Sleeper** (The Priestess) is close to the earth, and his or her finger naturally falls into a position that tells us that we may find truth, light, regeneration within the sacred land. **The Raptor** (The Emperor) is the liberating power of rapture and exaltation that arises from within ourselves. **Division** (The Lovers) embodies ideas of union, separation, and multiplication. **The Maker** (Strength) embodies the appearance of form out of formlessness. The card reveals the deepest creative and formative powers of the individual and often implies great energy for specific tasks.

SECOND ROW: **Becoming or Vanishment** (The Hermit). The being is approaching reality, becoming consciously transparent and vanishing willingly into the entirety of Being, into the Void. **The Stairway** (Justice) is within one of the megalithic Underworld chambers of the ancestors. This is the middle or balance Trump of the deck, and it can link upwards or downwards. The spiralling stair is a major image for entering and leaving the underworld. It is the trump of the womb or the tomb. **The Opener** (Death) shows the false or foolish Opener holding a key in blissful ignorance. The figure with the silver ax is the true Opener, who may destroy the false Opener or may be revealed to us by the false Opener, if we seek within. The ship that cannot be seen is the vessel of our true or universal being. **Conjunction** (Temperance) shows the fusion of polarities, which leads to further patterns, new life-forms. **The Tangler** (The Devil). Our inner liberation is clouded over by conditions and habits that accumulate in our surface life. Curiously, we only know of inner potential through our sense of being entangled, so the Tangler liberates through confusion, rather than suppresses or dominates.

BOTTOM ROW: **The Maze** (The Tower) is on the threshold between form and formlessness, for it is a seemingly closed pattern that holds a mysterious potential. **The Seed Pearl** (The Sun) is a card of illumination from within. **The Observatory** (Judgment) indicates a change of perception; at its most profound this change is from the transpersonal to the universal. **Herald of Messengers. Child of Spirits.**

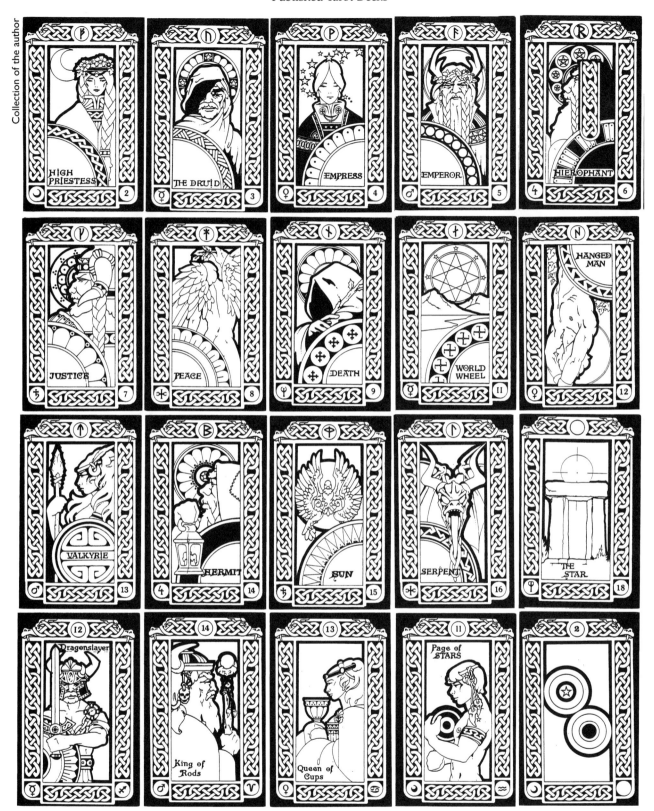

Druid Tarot   James Bluth, published by the artist, 1985

Tarocchi Dürer Italian artist Giacinto Gaudenzi turned his talents to creating a tarot inspired by the the etchings of the medieval German artist Albrecht Dürer. The deck comprises twenty-two Major Arcana, inked in brown on a cream background, and have traditional tarot titles in Italian. The Dürer Tarot was published by Lo Scarabeo, Turin, Italy, in 1991.

Tarocchi Dürer Giacinto Gaudenzi, Lo Scarabeo, 1991 Each card features an animal, even if a very tiny one, such as the butterfly on a pan of the scale of VIII La Giustizia (Justice). Dürer, too, used animals symbolically. The cat appears on VI Gli Amanti (The Lovers), as it does in Dürer's work, as a symbol of lust.

Egorov Tarot The tarot cards by Russian artist Alexander Egorov are rendered in the traditional style of Russian miniatures, with colorful figures on a black ground. The cards are bordered in gold. The titles of the Major Arcana, in English, German, and French, are interpretive, rather than traditional. The back design is double-ended, of two golden phoenixes on a black ground. The deck was published in 1992 by Piatnik of Vienna.

Tarot 88 Tarot 88 is accompanied by a descriptive card hand-written by the artist Johannes Dörflinger: "Tarot 88 / The 22 Major Arcana for Oskar Schlemmer / Edition 100 sets 12 colors / Original silkscreen / Handprinted 1988 / at the studio of /A. Diesterheft / Stuttgart / Signed and numbered / Johannes Dörflinger (signed)." Oskar Schlemmer, 1888–1943, was an artist of the Bauhaus school, which advocated a simple, geometric, functional style and led into Art Deco. The artist's card also includes the number of the deck. Titles are hand-written in English. The cards are large: approximately 6.25 inches wide by 8.75 inches tall. The board is light gray-brown, and the borders and figures on the cards are printed in layers of white, with black stars, blue squares, red circles, and yellow triangles. 0 The Fool and I The Magician are signed and numbered. Another card that accompanies the deck gives German translations of the card titles.

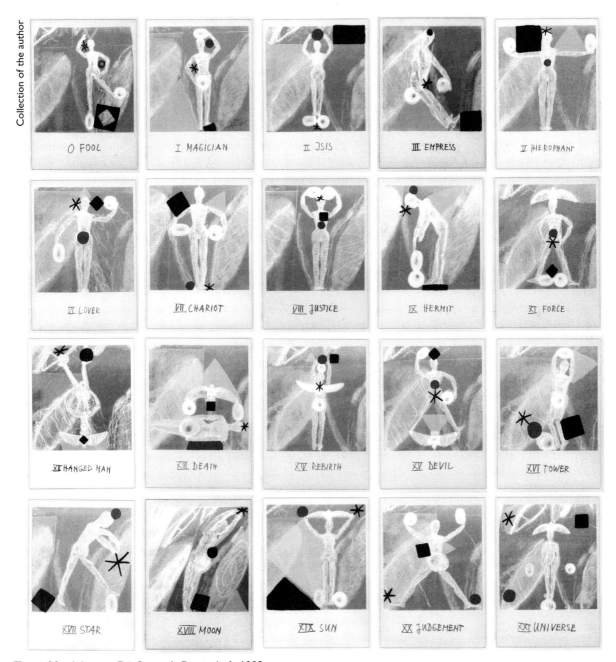

Collection of the author

Tarot 88 Johannes Dörflinger, A. Diesterheft, 1988

Egorov Tarot   Alexander Egorov, Piatnik, 1992

Electric Tarot Mystic Eye, artist and publisher, 1996

Electric Tarot The theme of electricity is pondered in the leaflet that accompanies the Electric Tarot. In a fictive story, a young man "ever questing for the key to the universe, a reason for his existence, a goal to strive for, decided the answer must lie in power...." A flash of lightning destroys his notes on power, which he was just about to save in his computer. "Even as the pattern of the last bolt was still sizzling on his retinas, he gazed out the window, considering long ago fictional tales of Frankenstein monsters, of history's Ben Franklin flying his kite, of biblical tales of the Arc of the Covenant, holy yet deadly. All these things, yes, yes, electricity, that was it, that was the key...." The twenty-two-card Electric Tarot was published in 1996 by Mystic Eye of Chicago.

Element (Dreamers) Tarot Staci Mendoza and David Bourne, Anness Publishing, 1999; Element Books, 2002
TOP ROW: Cards from the Element Tarot. SECOND AND BOTTOM ROW: Cards from the Dreamers Tarot.

Element (Dreamers) Tarot Staci Mendoza and David Bourne designed the Element Tarot to accompany their book *Tarot: Your Destiny Revealed in the Secrets of the Cards* (Southwater Publishing). The artists stated their aim was "to create a set of strong archetypal images associated with dream states. The bold colors, together with the mystical and fairytale imagery, are used in order to unlock the deeply seated subconscious feelings we all hold within us from childhood." The backs of the cards have a black and white pattern. The deck was first published as Dreamers Tarot, by Anness Publishing, London, in 1999, with a black and white pattern back design. The deck was republished by Element Books, London, in 2002.

Elle Tarot   Wun Wu, *Elle* magazine, 2002

Elle Tarot   The January 2002 Hong Kong issue of *Elle* magazine included a bonus pack of tarot cards, illustrated by Wun Wu. Lorraine R. Sharkey-Dolan and Jeannette K. Roth of Tarot Garden point out that the illustrations rely on the Renaissance Tarot by Jane Lyle and Helen Jones. The back design says "Elle Tarot Cards" in white on maroon. The deck is accompanied by an instructional leaflet in Chinese.

Six of Cups from the Renaissance Tarot by Helen Jones and Jane Lyle

Enchanted Tarot (Tarocchi Incantati) Beautiful and grotesque, earthy and mysterious, the Enchanted Tarot evokes the spooky and comical world of dreams, fantasy, fairies, and sprites. The artwork recalls that of the 1920s English artist, Cicely Mary Barker, with Barker's little fairy children of the flowers all grown up. Artist Giacinto Gaudenzi rendered the deck in ink and watercolor. The back design is an elfin couple on one end and a fairy on a swing on the other end.

Lo Scarabeo of Turin issued the deck in several editions:

- In 1990, a twenty-two-card deck, sold as Tarocchi dell'Alba Dorato (Tarot of the Golden Dawn), was printed on uncoated stock, with Italian titles, square corners, and back designs in green on white.

- In 1991, a twenty-two-card deck, sold as Tarots of the Golden Dawn, was printed on coated stock, with English titles, round corners, and back designs in green on white. This deck was accompanied by a title card and a card with a poem: "He who has gazed on the morning / of the Golden Dawn / holds within his secret heart / a wistful memory / of the fairy of the woods / and the mystery, pale blue light / that in a magic moment of Spring / brought the song of life / into the world."

The twenty-two-card decks have nontraditional titles. For example, 0, usually The Fool, is called The Imaginary.

- In 1995, a deck of seventy-eight cards plus a title card and instructional cards, was printed on coated stock and sold as Tarots of the Golden Dawn, with titles in five languages and sepia on white back designs. This deck was also sold under the title Tarot of the Hidden Folk.

- In 2000, a seventy-eight-card deck was sold as Enchanted Tarot (Tarocchi Incantati) and printed on coated card stock with titles in six languages and full-color back designs. It is accompanied by an instructional leaflet. The leaflet describes the Major Arcana as "Keepers of the Universal Power," defined as "temporary psychological states." The court cards are "'Governors,' or 'dignitaries,' who act directly on the four fundamental parts of nature." The suits are everlasting fire (wands), eternal wind (swords), water of life (chalices), and mother earth (pentacles).

Energy Tarot The twenty-two-card Energy Tarot augments the Tarot of Marseilles with symbols from Indian tantric symbolism. Indian tantric physiology holds that the human body has chakras, or energy centers. The main seven chakras are located along a central channel that runs from the base of the spine to the crown of the head. It is believed that tapping into these energy centers raises spiritual abilities and can also give one super-physical powers. The authors of the Energy Tarot, Pia Vercellesi and Giampaolo Gasparri, explain in correspondence with Stuart Kaplan that they created the deck so that people could access information on chakras through a familiar tool, the tarot. The deck was published and packaged with a book, *Tarocchi e Chakra* (Tarot and Chakra), by Xenia Edizioni of Milan, in 1999.

The back design is primarily blue and green and shows a meditator with chakras highlighted.

Engel-Tarot "The Angel Tarot introduces the mysterious world of heavenly archetypes," says the box of the Engel-Tarot deck. The tarot was painted by German artist Alois Hanslian and published as large cards, circa 1995, by Aquamarin Verlag. The backs of the cards are plain white and unvarnished. The deck comprises a title card and twenty-two Major Arcana. The cards are unnumbered, with German titles.

Equinox Celebration Tarot The Equinox Celebration Tarot was created by Amir Bey as a set of sculptures, which were photographed in black and white and published in 1993 as cards with gold borders. The "celebrants," as the artist calls the figures, were all carved from one stone, "like facets of one gem." The figures were then cast in bronze. Bey wrote, "Each of the 36 celebrants is bringing a gift or an attribute to observe the spring equinox."

The thirty-six-card deck is divided into three suits of suns, moons, and stars. Individual cards correspond to certain cards in the suits of swords, wands, cups, and coins. The numbering is based on the decans of astrology. (There are three decans per astrological sign, equaling thirty-six in all.) Each card shows a suit symbol, and a set of three numerological symbols, with the left one representing the celebrant preceding, the middle one the celebrant, and the right the celebrant to come. The box in which the cards are packaged shows all the sculptures arranged on a three-level pyramid. The back design gives the title of the deck, the artist's signature, and an abstract symbolic design in black on gold.

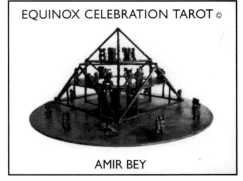

EQUINOX CELEBRATION TAROT ©

AMIR BEY

1 L'ABILITÁ	2 LA SAPIENZA	3 L'INTELLIGENZA	4 LA VOLONTÁ	6 LA FERTILITÁ
MEDITATION 9	FATE 10	ENERGY 11	EXPIATION 12	METAMORPHOSIS 13

Enchanted Tarot (Tarocchi Incantati) Giacinto Gaudenzi, Lo Scarabeo TOP ROW: From the 1990 deck, Tarocchi dell'Alba Dorato. SECOND ROW: From the 1991 deck, Tarots of the Golden Dawn. THIRD ROW: From the 1995 deck, Tarots of the Golden Dawn; Tarot of the Hidden Folk. BOTTOM ROW: From 2000 deck, Tarocchi Incantati; Enchanted Tarot.

Energy Tarot Pia Vercellesi and Giampaolo Gasparri, Xenia Edizioni, 1999 The seven chakras are indicated along the top, with the chakras that correspond to the card highlighted in color. A line above the chakras shows the kind of energy applied by the card; a line on the left is for "heavy" energy, the middle is "medium" energy, and the right is "subtle" energy. A tao (yin-yang) sign at the top left indicates that the meanings apply to all life situations. A plus sign at the top right indicates positive energy; a minus sign indicates a blockage of energy; an equal sign represents the "double polarity" of the card.

322

Collection of the author

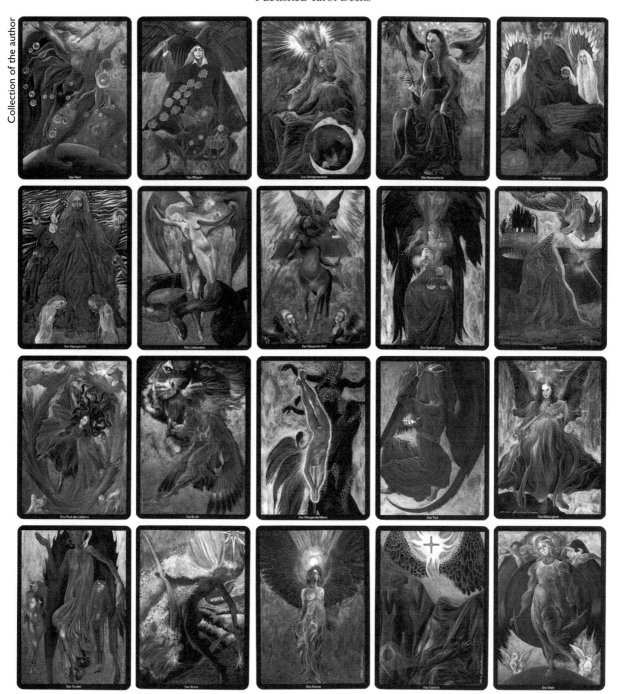

Engel-Tarot Alois Hanslian, Aquamarin Verlag, circa 1995

TOP ROW: Der Narr (The Fool). Der Magier (The Magician). Die Hohepriesterin (The High Priestess). Die Herrscherin (The Empress). Der Herrscher (The Emperor).

SECOND ROW: Der Hierophant (The Hierophant). Die Liebenden (The Lovers). Der Wagenlenker (The Chariot Driver). Die Gerechtigkeit (Justice). Der Eremit (The Hermit).

THIRD ROW: Das Rad des Lebens (The Wheel of Life). Die Kraft (Strength). Der Hängende Mann (The Hanged Man). Der Tod (Death). Die Mässigkeit (Temperance).

BOTTOM ROW: Der Teufel (The Devil). Der Stern (The Star). Die Sonne (The Sun). Das Gericht (Judgment). Die Welt (The World).

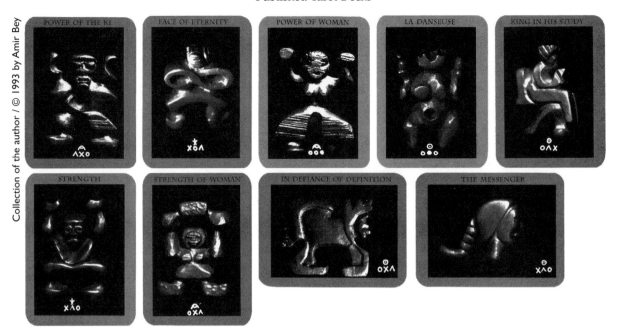

Equinox Celebration Tarot   Amir Bey, published by the artist, 1993   The caption text is from the booklet by Amir Bey.

TOP ROW: **POWER OF THE KI** (Eight of Moons; Ten of Swords) All sections and spaces of the celebrant's body find their center in Ki. **FACE OF ETERNITY** (Seven of Stars; Three of Swords) A face rests on the infinity symbol as a pair of legs carry it tirelessly. **POWER OF WOMAN** (One of Moons; Three of Wands) A woman with raised arms moves forward. **LA DANSEUSE** (Twelve of Suns; Two of Wands) The celebrant frees itself from the bonds of winter through vigorous dance. **KING IN HIS STUDY** (Nine of Suns; Eight of Cups) A king sits in his study, immersed in meditation.

SECOND ROW: **STRENGTH** (Three of Stars; Eight of Coins) The celebrant's upper and lower halves of its body are united, giving it strength. **STRENGTH OF WOMAN** (Four of Moons; Six of Coins) A woman with a small but strong frame. She is lifting a weight above her head with ease. **IN DEFIANCE OF DEFINITION** (Four of Suns; Three of Coins) It is difficult to fathom the direction as well as the character of the celebrant. **THE MESSENGER** (Three of Suns; Two of Coins) A friendly woman's profile.

Erde Tarock (Earth Tarot)   The Erde Tarock was created by Sieghard Dittner for Cartorama, a German retailer of playing and tarot cards, in a limited edition of 500 copies, signed and numbered by the artist on the sleeve of the package. The deck was printed by Wolfgang Schuboth in Malchow, Germany, in 1995, in black, green, blue, and pink. The cards feature double-ended designs, titled in German on one end and English on the other. The deck includes a presentation card and a blank card. The backs have a pattern of stylized rosettes in green.

Tarocchi Ermetici (Hermetic Tarot)   The Tarocchi Ermetici are new renderings of Oswald Wirth's Major Arcana, which were first published as art prints in 1926, then as illustrations in Wirth's book *Le Tarot, des Imagiers du Moyen Age,* in 1927. The Milanese artist, Sergio, kept the basic symbolism of Wirth's deck (for example, a cat instead of a dog on the Fool card). However, escaping from the rather static poses of the Wirth figures, Sergio's characters spring to life. The cards are titled in Italian; the backs feature an ornate symmetrical design in purple on white. The deck is accompanied by a title card and an instructional leaflet in Italian, and it was published by Lo Scarabeo, Turin, Italy, in 2000.

Tarot Erotica   "Do you know what people want to know when you read for them?" asks artist Lori Walls on the Q.E.D. Games website. "Their love life. Is their lover faithful? Is marriage in their future? Will they get laid? More than career, family, health, people want to know about The Heart. Maybe it's different in other circles, but I suspect not." Hence, Walls created the Tarot Erotica. The suits of the deck are swords, rods, cups, and stars, and the seventy-eight cards have titles in English, Spanish, and German. One variation in the Major Arcana is that XX is titled The Universe, and XXI is titled Judgement. The subtitle of Judgement, given in the booklet accompanying the deck, is "The Spiritual Universe." The back design is double-ended, showing a pink flower on a dark blue background. The deck was published in 1999 by Q.E.D. Games of New York City.

Etruscan Tarot   Riccardo Menetti conceived the Etruscan Tarot, which was illustrated by Silvana Alasia. Menetti describes the Etruscans, in the leaflet accompanying the deck, as a people living in ancient Tuscany before the rise of the Roman Empire. The two cultures eventually merged, but the remains of the Etruscan culture can be found in their funerary art. The deck was published by Lo Scarabeo, Turin, in 2002. The back design shows a pattern in white on orange. The cards have orange borders and titles in six languages.

Erde Tarock (Earth Tarot)   Sieghard Dittner, Cartorama, 1995

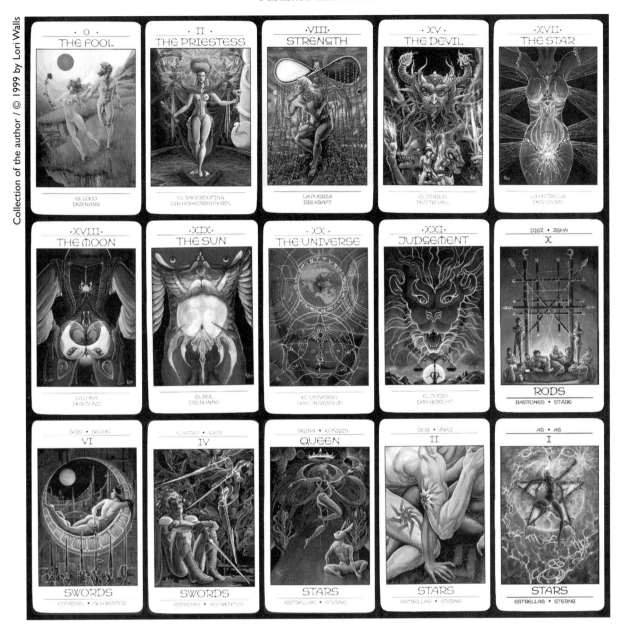

Tarot Erotica   Lori Walls, Q.E.D. Games, 1999

Tarocchi Ermetici (Hermetic Tarot)   Sergio, Lo Scarabeo, 2000

TOP ROW: 0 IL MATTO (The Fool). 1 IL BAGATTO (The Magician). 2 LA PAPESSA (The Popess). 4 L'IMPERATORE (The Emperor). 5 IL PAPA (The Pope).

SECOND ROW: 6 L'INNAMORATO (The Lover). 7 IL CARRO (The Chariot). 8 LA GIUSTIZIA (Justice). 9 L'EREMITA (The Hermit). 10 RUOTA DELLA FORTUNA (Wheel of Fortune).

THIRD ROW: 11 LA FORZA (Strength). 12 L'APPESO (The Hanged Man). 13 LA MORTE (Death). 14 LA TEMPERANZA (Temperance). 15 IL DIAVOLO (The Devil).

BOTTOM ROW: 17 LA STELLA (The Star). 18 LA LUNA (The Moon). 19 IL SOLE (The Sun). 20 IL GIUDIZIO (Judgment). 21 IL MONDO (The World).

Etruscan Tarot   Silvana Alasia, artist, and Riccardo Menetti, Lo Scarabeo, 2002

Experimental Tarot "Life to me is like a scientific experiment," says artist Gunnar Kossatz, "thus the naming of this tarot play. Within a given framework, its outcome is unknown and undetermined, free will being exercised at all times." Kossatz used mostly CorelDRAW clip art and computer-based drawing tools to compose the illustrations. The cards include astrological symbols, German and English titles, and key words. The back design is a shimmering disk. The deck was published by AGMüller of Neuhausen, Switzerland in 1995.

Experimental Tarot   Gunnar Kossatz, AGMüller, 1995

Faery Wicca Tarot The Faery Wicca Tarot was created by Kisma K. Stepanich and illustrated by Renée Christine Yates. It is based on Irish lore of pre-Christian times. This cycle describes Eiré (now Ireland) as ruled by the goddess Brigid and the three gods of Dana, who were Brian, Iuchar, and Iucharba. The deities were believed to come from the "other world" where there were four cities of learning: Falias (knowledge), Gorias (science), Findias (prophecy), and Muirias (magic).

Stepanich divides the deck into five groups: forty Element cards, which correspond to the numbered cards of the Minor Arcana; sixteen Helper cards, which correspond to the court cards; twenty-two Ancient Ones, which correspond to the Major Arcana; the Power Card, numbered 00 and titled The Tree of Life; and four Gift of Faery cards.

Each suit of the Element cards represents one of the "other world" cities, with aer for Gorias (swords), tine for Findias (wands), uisce for Muirias (cauldrons, or cups), and domhan for Falias (coins). The Gift of Faery cards each correspond to a city, as well as representing qualities that allow one to traverse the faery realm. The Ancient Ones cards have in each corner oghams, or sigils, of Celtic significance, and they and the Helper cards are titled in English and Gaelic. The deck was published by Llewellyn Publications, St. Paul, Minnesota, in 1999.

Fairy Tarots (Tarocchi dei Folletti) Antonio Lupatelli rendered the original artwork of the Fairy Tarots in tempera. The deck was issued in three versions:

- A Major Arcana deck, printed on coated stock with rounded corners, was a joint venture of GES: Gruppo Editoriale Sirio and Lo Scarabeo (undated).

- Another Major Arcana deck is slightly larger and printed on textured, uncoated stock with square corners. This deck was published by Lo Scarabeo in 1992.

- A seventy-eight-card deck, titled in five languages, was published by Lo Scarabeo in 1998. It includes a title card and an advertising card. The suits are leaves (swords), acorns (wands), hearts (cups), and bells (coins). The pip cards 2 through 10 are reproductions of antique artwork by other artists.

Some of the Major Arcana titles differ between the twenty-two-card decks and the seventy-eight-card deck. For example, II has the Italian title La Papessa in the seventy-eight-card deck, and the title La Sacerdotessa in the twenty-two-card deck.

The instructional leaflet that accompanies the seventy-eight-card deck touches on both the realm of the fairies and that of the gnomes, which was illustrated by Lupatelli in the Gnomes Tarot. The leaflet describes how the Great Magician of the Fairies met with Sichen, the Great Wizard of the Gnomes, who showed him the tarot deck that "described, through beautiful images, many aspects of the life of the Gnomes," and who gave lavish advice on ethics.

Fantastical Tarot French artist Nathalie Hertz created the Fantastical Tarot as a reflection of "a world at the edges of the senses, a dreamscape barely reachable by the mind." The deck was published in 1999 by U.S. Games Systems, with a presentation card and an introductory card. The cards have metallic gold borders, and the back design is a double-ended image of a dragon.

Fairy Tarots (Tarocchi dei Folletti) Antonio Lupatelli, Lo Scarabeo

Minor Arcana cards from the seventy-eight-card deck

Faery Wicca Tarot Kisma K. Stepanich and Renée Christine Yates, artist, Llewellyn Publications, 1999 The words in parentheses are translations of the Gaelic title, where that title differs from the English title.

TOP ROW: **00 The Tree of Life** represents the structure of the Faery realm and the highest attainment of the spiritual voyager. **0 The Seeker. 2 The High Priestess** (The High Priestess Brigid). **4 The Father God** (Father God Dagda). **5 The Guide.**

SECOND ROW: **6 The Beloved** (Beloved Deirdre and Naoise). **8 Poetical Justice** (Poetical Justice of Macha). **12 The Hangman** (Hangman Amorgen). **13 The Banshee Crone** (The Banshee Cailleach). **14 The Holy Waters.**

THIRD ROW: **15 The Old One** (Cernunnos the Old One). **18 Old Witch Moon Hill. 19 The Sun Child. 21 The Weaver Goddess. The Apple Branch** connects to the mythological cycle of Tuatha de Danann, and represents thought.

BOTTOM ROW: **The Hazel Wand** is connected to the Fenian cycle, the fianna and medieval faery, and represents feeling. **Seven of Tine** shows the champion's wheel. **Ard Ri of Uisce** (High King of Uisce). **Five of Uisce. Ten of Domhan.**

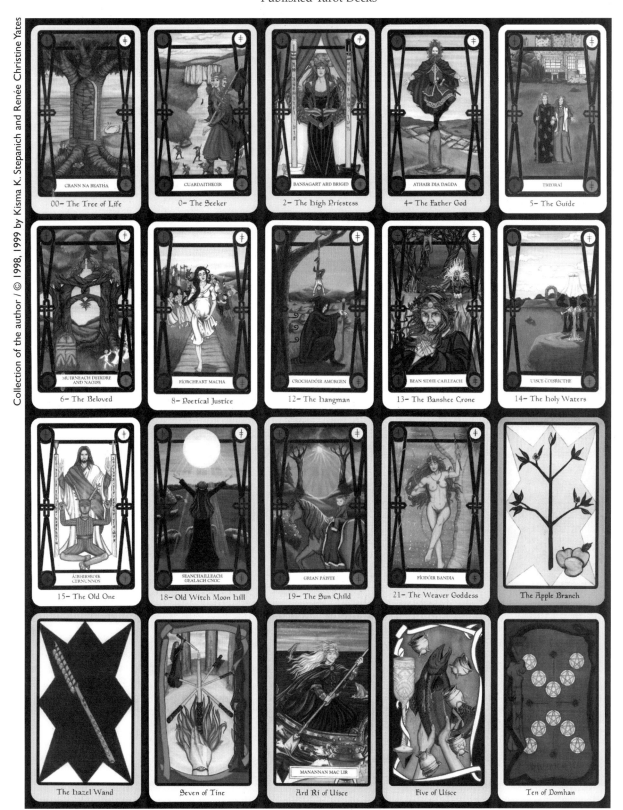

00– The Tree of Life   0– The Seeker   2– The high Priestess   4– The Father God   5– The Guide

6– The Beloved   8– Poetical Justice   12– The hangman   13– The Banshee Crone   14– The holy Waters

15– The Old One   18– Old Witch Moon hill   19– The Sun Child   21– The Weaver Goddess   The Apple Branch

The hazel Wand   Seven of Tine   Ard Rí of Uisce   Five of Uisce   Ten of Domhan

Fairy Tarots (Tarocchi dei Folletti) Antonio Lupatelli, Lo Scarabeo, 1990s TOP ROW: (From the twenty-two-card undated deck) 0 IL FOLLETTO (The Fairy). I IL MAGO (The Magician). II LA SACERDOTESSA (The High Priestess). III LA REGINA (The Queen). IV IL RE (The King.) SECOND ROW: V IL GEROFANTE (The Hierophant). VI GLI INNAMORATI (The Lovers). VIII LA DRIADE (The Dryad, a fairy that lives in an oak tree). IX L'EREMITA (The Hermit). X L'OREADE (Oread, a spirit of luck). THIRD ROW: XI LA FORZA (Strength). XII L'APPESO (The Hanged Man). XIV LA SILFIDE (The Sylph, a spirit of the air). XVII LA NAIADE (The Naiad, a spirit of brooks, springs and fountains). XVIII LA LUNA (The Moon).

Fantastical Tarot   Nathalie Hertz, U.S. Games Systems, 1999

Il Bagatto	La Papessa	L' Imperatrice	L' Imperatore	Il Papa
L' Amore	Il Carro	La Giustizia	L' Eremita	La Ruota della Fortuna
La Forza	L' Appeso	La Morte	Il Diavolo	La Torre
Le Stelle	Il Sole	L' Angelo	Il Mondo	Il Matto

Fantastico Viaggio di un Manichino da Pittore (Fantastic Voyage of an Artist's Mannequin)   Osvaldo Menegazzi, Edizioni Il Meneghello, 1993

Fantastico Viaggio di un Manichino da Pittore (Fantastic Voyage of an Artist's Mannequin) Osvaldo Menegazzi captured in a Major Arcana deck that figure so familiar to artists and art students everywhere: the wooden, jointed mannequin. The deck was issued in a signed, numbered edition of 800, and includes a presentation card. The cards measure 8.25 inches by 4 inches.

The book that accompanies the deck, by Pina Andronico Tosonotti, pays homage to Menegazzi's mannequins. "Rare is it to meet a mannequin with feminine characteristics. But one day, in the back of the studio of Osvaldo Menegazzi, She appeared, through the work of this artist, manifesting the eternal feminine principle, the most desired one…." Menegazzi's paint-spattered mannequin women float in a Daliesque world. The book includes a poem for each card of the deck. The back design is of a fingerprint in white on brown. The deck was published by Edizioni Il Meneghello, Milan, in 1993.

Tarocchi di Federico II: Lo Sguardo dell'Aquila (Tarot of Frederick II: The Glance of the Eagle) Ernesto Solari created the Tarocchi of Federico II in commemoration of Frederick II, who lived from 1194 to 1250, and was Holy Roman Emperor from 1215 to 1250. The twenty-two-card deck was published by the author in 1994, for the 800th anniversary of Frederick II's birth, as gray line art on cream cards. The back design is double-ended, showing a crowned eagle atop a globe.

Feng Shui Tarot The Feng Shui Tarot was created by Eileen Connolly and Peter Paul Connolly, a mother-and-son team. The deck draws on the principles of Form School Feng Shui. This school works with elements of the physical environment, such as the shape of a building, location of doors and windows, bodies of water, and so on, to create harmony and auspiciousness. The deck is not intended for Feng Shui analysis or arrangements in an environment. Rather, the traditional tarot meanings are illustrated in terms of Feng Shui. The Minor Arcana suits are named after animals: white tigers (swords), black tortoise (wands), red phoenix (cups), and green dragon (coins). The back design shows an auspicious symbol in red. The Feng Shui Tarot was published by U.S. Games Systems, Stamford, Connecticut, in 2001. The deck includes a title card and an introductory card.

Fey Tarot "The Fey creatures seem what they are, they are what they seem. Joy, sadness, pain, wisdom, happiness…are reflected in their bodies, clothing, and even their posture. Each of them acts as the mirror of a mood, a point of view, a way of being, going beyond the image which comes from what surrounds it." Thus Riccardo Minetti writes in the booklet that accompanies the deck. The artwork is by Mara Aghem, and the deck was published by Lo Scarabeo of Turin in 2002. Titles are in five languages. The back design shows the picture on VI The Lovers in purple on lavender. The deck includes a title card and an advertising card.

Tarocchi di Federico II Ernesto Solari, published by the artist, 1994 Information in the caption was provided by the artist.
I IL BAGATTO (The Magician) shows the love of Frederick II for knowledge. Of this quest, he wrote, "Before assuming the duties of the sovereignty, I inclined to knowledge and I breathed balsamic scents." **II LA PAPESSA** (The Popess). **III L'IMPERATRICE** (The Empress). **IV L'IMPERATORE** (The Emperor). **V IL PAPA** (The Pope).

L'AMOROSO VI	L'EREMITA IX	LA RUOTA X	LA FORZA XI	L'APPESO XII
LA MORTE XIII	LA TEMPERANZA XIV	IL DIAVOLO XV	LA TORRE XVI	LA STELLA XVII
LA LUNA XVIII	IL SOLE XIX	IL GIUDIZIO XX	IL MATTO XXI	IL MONDO XXII

Tarocchi di Federico II *(continued)*

TOP ROW: **VI L'AMOROSO** (The Lover) shows the difficult relationship of man with nature, based on the eternal conflict of overwhelming love. **IX L'EREMITA** (The Hermit). **X LA RUOTA** (The Wheel) refers to Frederick's interest in astrology. The eagle glares at the changeable course of events, which it wants to unmask. **XI LA FORZA** (Strength) shows the eagle clutching its quarry with a cruelty that symbolizes energy, the consciousness of its own strength revealed through action. **XII L'APPESO** (The Hanged Man).

SECOND ROW: **XIII LA MORTE** (Death) shows the meditative and philosophical nature of the emperor, at the lonely hermitage of Castel del Monte. **XIV LA TEMPER-ANZA** (Temperance). **XV IL DIAVOLO** (The Devil) symbolizes the emperor saving the Saracen from the flames of hatred. **XVI LA TORRE** (The Tower) indicates that the safety of Frederick was perpetually precarious. **XVII LA STELLA** (The Star) symbolizes the success of Frederick.

BOTTOM ROW: **XVIII LA LUNA** (The Moon) symbolizes Frederick's love of esoteric doctrine. **XIX IL SOLE** (The Sun) refers to the crusades, which he won by allying with the king of Egypt rather than by fighting. **XX IL GIUDIZIO** (Judgment) shows the eagle as symbol of St. John the Evangelist and of the resurrected Jesus Christ. **XXI IL MATTO** (The Fool) shows the eagle's eye, ever watchful, inquisitive, restless, and even disquieting. **XXII IL MONDO** (The World) is the perfect balance, the final success, a sign of harmony within Frederick and with all around him.

Feng Shui Tarot   Eileen Connolly and Peter Paul Connolly, U.S. Games Systems, 2001

Fey Tarot   Mara Aghem, Lo Scarabeo, 2002

Tarocchi delle Fiabe (Fairy Tales Tarot) Twenty-two different artist contributed to I Tarocchi delle Fiabe, just as different fairy tales are represented on each card. The cards are titled in Italian, and each card includes the title and author of the fairy tale, and the artist's name in the lower left margin. The deck was published in 1997 on the occasion of the fourteenth Festival Internazionale di Teatro Figura (International Festival of Puppet Theater), held in San Miniato, Italy. The Fairy Tales Tarot was published by Lo Scarabeo, Turin, Italy, in 1997.

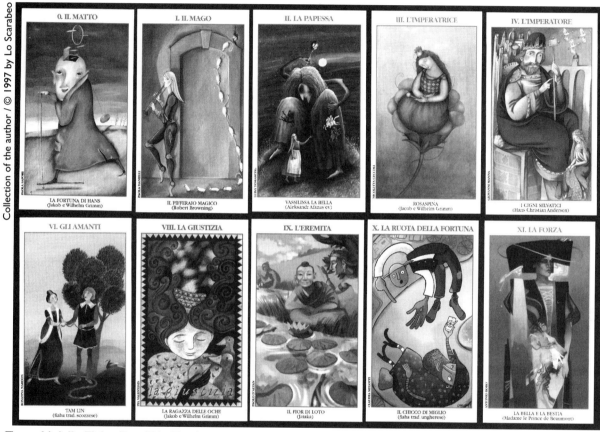

Tarocchi delle Fiabe (Fairy Tales Tarot) Various artists, Lo Scarabeo, 1997

TOP ROW: **0 IL MATTO** (The Fool; Paolo Sapori). "Hans in Luck," or "Foolish Hans," exchanges a lump of gold for a horse and continues trading down until he is joyful at his lack of burdens. **I IL MAGO** (The Magician; Paolo Danielli). "The Pied Piper" lures away the children of Hamlin when he is not paid for luring away the mice with his magic flute. **II LA PAPESSA** (The Popess; Luisa Tomasetig). "Vassilissa La Belle." **III L'IMPERATRICE** (The Empress; Nicoletta Ceccoli). "Little Briar-Rose," or "Sleeping Beauty," is a princess who falls asleep when pricked by a bewitched spindle and wakes at the kiss of a prince. **IV L'IMPERATORE** (The Emperor; Giovanni Manna). "The Wild Swans" is about a young girl whose brothers are transformed into wild swans. She undergoes trials, including weaving them shirts of nettle, to free them from the spell.

BOTTOM ROW: **VI GLI AMANTI** (The Lovers; Rosanna Nardon). "Tam Lin" is a Scottish tale of a youth who is captured by faeries and rescued by a young woman. **VIII LA GIUSTIZIA** (Justice; Pia Valentinis). "The Goose Girl" is a princess who was later restored to her rightful state. **IX L'EREMITA** (The Hermit; Paolo d'Altan). "The Lotus Flower," is one of the Jataka tales, which tell about previous incarnations of the Buddha. **X LA RUOTA DELLA FORTUNA** (The Wheel of Fortune; Claudia Melotti). "The Grain of Millet" is a Hungarian tale. **XI LA FORZA** (Strength; Antonio Bobo). "The Beauty and the Beast" tells how a man trapped in the body of a beast is freed by the love of Beauty.

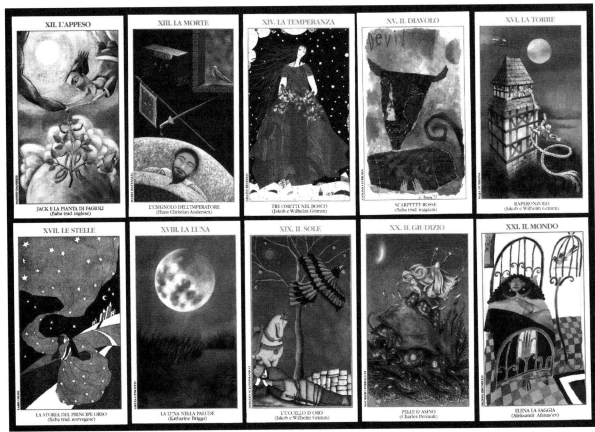

Tarocchi delle Fiabe (*continued*)

TOP ROW: **XII L'APPESO** (The Hanged Man; Fausto Danielli). "Jack and the Beanstalk" is about a boy who gains riches by facing the dangers of climbing a giant beanstalk. **XIII LA MORTE** (Death; Maria Bataglia). "The Emperor's Nightingale" banished death with its song at the emperor's bed. **XIV LA TEMPERANZA** (Temperance; Grazia Restelli). "The Three Little Men in the Woods" help a woman overcome evil relatives to become a queen. **XV IL DIAVOLO** (The Devil; Antonio Ferrara). "The Red Slippers" compel a girl to dance continuously when she puts them on in defiance of mourning her foster-mother. **XVI LA TORRE** (The Tower; Maja Dusikova). "Rapunzel" is locked in a tower; the only way up is to climb her long hair.

BOTTOM ROW: **XVII LE STELLE** (The Star; Fabio Dose). "The Story of Prince Orso" is a traditional Norwegian tale. **XVIII LA LUNA** (The Moon; Greta Cencetti). "The Moon of the Marsh" is by Katharine Briggs, who, with her daughter Isabel Briggs Myers, developed the Myers-Briggs psychological type indicator. **XIX IL SOLE** (The Sun; Donato Sciannimanico) "The Golden Bird" is about a youth whose quest for a golden bird leads him on a series of magical adventures that end, of course, with his marriage to a beautiful princess. **XX IL GIUDIZIO** (Judgment; Maurizio Ferracuti). "Donkey Skin" is about a Princess who, helped by her Fairy Godmother, hides under a donkey skin to escape marriage. She is found by a prince and they get married. **XXI IL MONDO** (The World; Filippo Brunello). "Elena the Wise" is a Russian tale.

Flying Hearts Tarot The Flying Hearts Tarot is by the art collective Flying Hearts. The collage deck draws from different cultures for images that convey traditional tarot symbolism in often humorous ways. Tarotist K. Frank Jensen identifies the designers of the deck as disciples of Rajneesh, the spiritual leader who was known as Osho (see *Manteia,* issue one, and also the Osho Zen Tarot). The deck breaks free of tarot tradition in its Major Arcana titles and Minor Arcana suits. An extra Major Arcana card is included. The suits are master, Luft (air), Feuer (fire), Wasser (water), and Erde (earth). The elemental suits have ten cards each, and the master suit has fifteen cards. Many of the cards are printed horizontally. Flying Hearts Tarot was published by Verlag Hermann Bauer in 1988. The back design shows a flying heart in an architectural frame.

Flying Hearts Tarot Flying Hearts art collective, Verlag Hermann Bauer, 1988

TOP ROW: **Der Spieler** (The Player). **2 Intuition. 3 Freude** (Joy). **4 Der Lebemann** (The Swinger). **5 Der spirituelle Meister** (The Spiritual Master).

SECOND ROW: **7 Geist der Rebellion** (Spirit of Rebellion). **8 Samba. 9 Allein-Sein** (Solitude). **11 Gleichmut** (Equanimity). **15 Pan.**

BOTTOM ROW: **20 Freiheit** (Freedom). **21 In der Welt, doch nicht von dieser Welt** (In the World, yet not of this World). **Master Zehn: Quelle der Meditation** (Ten of Master: Source of Meditation). **Luft Acht: Berg und Tal** (Eight of Air: Mountain and Valley; Switchback). **Feuer Zwei: Gebet** (Two of Fire: Prayer).

Tarocco di Amerigo Folchi   Amerigo Folchi, Italcards, 1991

Tarocco di Amerigo Folchi   Italian artist Amerigo Folchi has designed several tarot decks. The deck that bears his name as title was issued in 1991 in a numbered, limited edition of 3,000 by Italcards of Bologna. The bottom of the box has a paper pasted to it that indicates the number of the deck. The seventy-eight-card deck includes a title card and a presentation card. Titles are in Italian, German, English, and French.

Tarocchi della Follia (Tarot of Folly)   Alessandro Baggi created the Tarot of Folly in 1987, and the deck was published in 1988 by Lo Scarabeo in a numbered, limited edition of 595 decks. The deck comprises 22 Major Arcana and 12 cards, one for each sign of the zodiac, plus a title card and a presentation card. The images are influenced by many artistic styles, including Symbolist, Decadent, Orientalist, and Jugendstil/Art Nouveau. The cards, titled in Italian, are printed in dark blue on white. The back design is a floral pattern in light blue. The deck includes an instructional leaflet by Piero Alligo. Some of the decks came packaged in black matte boxes, others in white glossy boxes, both with silver printing.

Tarocchi della Follia (Tarot of Folly) Alessandro Baggi, Lo Scarabeo, 1988 TOP ROW: I IL BAGATTO (The Magician). II LA PAPESSA (The Popess). III L'IMPERATRICE (The Empress). IV L'IMPERATORE (The Emperor). VI L'INNAMORATO (The Lover). SECOND ROW: VII IL CARRO (The Chariot). VIII LA GIUSTIZIA (Justice). X LA RUOTA DELLA FORTUNA (The Wheel of Fortune). XI LA FORZA (Strength). XII L'APPESO (The Hanged Man). THIRD ROW: XIV LA TEMPERANZA (Temperance). XV IL DIAVOLO (The Devil). XVII LE STELLE (The Star). XIX IL SOLE (The Sun). XX IL GIUDIZIO (Judgment). BOTTOM ROW: XXI IL MONDO (The World). XXII ARIETE (Aries). XXVIII BILANCIA (Libra). XXIX SCORPIONE (Scorpio). Title card.

Forest Folklore Tarot Kessia Beverley-Smith created this mystical deck by combining watercolor technique with photography. The enchanting seventy-eight cards are inspired by a unique area of the United Kingdom called New Forest, where the artist lives. These historical woodlands are lush with wildlife and legends. The characters honor the people who call this area their home. The Minor Arcana bring to life forest folklore filled with imps, fairies, nymphs, and dwarves. Each ace shows an animal native to New Forest. The deck, including a booklet of instructions, was published by U.S. Games Systems of Stamford, Connecticut, in 2004.

Fradella Adventure Tarot The Fradella Adventure Tarot features the heroes and villains of the iHero Universe™, created by Frank Fradella. Artist JP Dupras drew and colored the artwork for the deck. The adventure series started as an Internet e-zine (electronic magazine) called *Cyber Age Adventures,* and later became available in print. The deck was published by U.S. Games Systems of Stamford, Connecticut, in 2003. It includes a title card. The back design is two red Fs intertwined on a starry background. The suits are blades (swords), staves, masks (cups), and discs.

Tarot Elisabeth Frolet Roman artist Elisabeth Frolet made her tarot using linoleum prints colored in gouache. The cards are printed on gray stock, with russet ink on the faces and a pattern of blue diamonds on the backs. The deck was made, according to the presentation card (translated from French), "in Rome in December 1992, the day before the anniversary of Mithra, by Luciano Trina for the Compte de Serge Plantureux." Luciano Trina is a performance artist; Serge Plantureux is a book collector and seller. The deck was issued in a signed, numbered edition of ninety-nine, and it includes a title card and a presentation card. Some of the copies have hand-painted gold accents.

Tarocchi del Futuro (Future Tarot) The Major Arcana tarot deck Tarocchi del Futuro is based on the Italian comic book character Nathan Never. The series takes place in a grim future in which nature has been nearly annihilated by technology. The hero, Nathan Never, is an ex-policeman turned detective. Never works for a private investigation firm called Agenzia Alfa (Alfa Agency). The comics are published by Sergio Bonelli Editore. The creators of the comic books and the tarot deck are Michele Medda, Antonio Serra, and Giuseppe Vigna, with the tarot deck colored in tempera by Nicola Mari. The deck is accompanied by a title card and an index of the characters illustrated on the cards. The deck was published by Lo Scarabeo, Turin, in 1992.

Tarocchi di Gambedotti Mario Gambedotti's style captures the playful side of food and drink in the tarot deck he created under license from Club della Buona Carta. The suits of the deck are knives (swords), rolling pins (batons), ewers (cups), and coins. The deck was pub-

lished in 1986 by Priuli & Verlucca of Ivrea, Italy. The back design, in red on cream, shows foliage and the publisher's name.

Gatti 22 Arcani (Cats 22 Arcana) Osvaldo Menegazzi turns his prolific tarot imagination to cats with the Gatti 22 Arcani. The deck was issued in a limited, miniature edition of 2000 numbered decks. The cards have Italian titles and blank backs. The deck was published in 1990 by Edizioni Il Meneghello, Milan.

Tarot of Gemstones and Crystals The Tarot of Gemstones and Crystals features photographs of minerals. Each card has a tarot title and the name of the mineral. The photographs are very clear and well-lit, and furnish an excellent means of studying and identifying minerals. Many of the cards feature the minerals in both their raw state and cut for jewelry. The booklet by Helmut G. Hofmann, which accompanies the deck, provides interpretations of the properties of the minerals featured, including the powers of the minerals to act on body and mind. The Major Arcana cards are unnumbered, but the book provides numbering. The back design is plain light green with a white border. The deck was published in 1996 by AGMüller, Neuhausen, Switzerland.

Tarot of Gemstones and Crystals VI The Lovers: Ruby. The ruby brings harmony into love. People who lack self-love or love for others should use the ruby to meditate on love.

Gendron Tarot Melanie Gendron created her tarot deck "inspired by The Sacred Feminine…an offering with a desire to help you become the God/dess you are." Each Major Arcana card is associated with a goddess from each of the four directions and includes a Hebrew letter and a planetary sigil. Animal mythology enriches the symbolism. The artwork combines original paintings with photographs through computer imaging. The deck includes an instructional booklet, a title card, and a presentation card with a poetic introduction by the artist in the "voice" of the Sacred Feminine. The Gendron Tarot was published by U.S. Games Systems of Stamford, Connecticut, in 1997.

Forest Folklore Tarot Kessia Beverley-Smith, U.S. Games Systems, 2004 The artwork shown here is from before publication as a deck. The cards of the published deck have numbers and titles.

TOP ROW: 0 The Fool. I The Magician. II The High Priestess. III The Empress. IV The Emperor.

SECOND ROW: V The Hierophant. VI The Lovers. VIII Strength. IX The Hermit. XI Justice.

THIRD ROW: XII The Hanged Man. XIII Death. XIV Temperance. XV The Devil. XVI The Tower.

BOTTOM ROW: XVII The Star. XVIII The Moon. XIX The Sun. XX Judgment. XXI The World.

Fradella Adventure Tarot Frank Fradella, with art by JP Dupras, U.S. Games Systems, 2003   Captions are from the book with the deck.

TOP ROW: **0 THE FOOL.** Arachnid takes the first step from his homeworld to Earth. He was persecuted on his own planet, because he was born with only four arms, while the rest of his people were born with six. **I THE MAGICIAN** is Pulsar, master of the engineering marvel.

When he's not in armor, Pulsar is billionaire Ben Holliday. **III The Empress** is Aura, wife of Ben Holliday/Pulsar. **IV The Emperor** is the Minuteman, first among superheroes. **VI The Lovers.** Lung Tao Kai, or Jade Tiger, faces Lexicon, the Chinese representative of the U.N. Peacekeepers. She can understand any language. The goddess Xi Wang-mu looks down on them.

SECOND ROW: **X Wheel of Fortune.** Rush, a teenager,

346

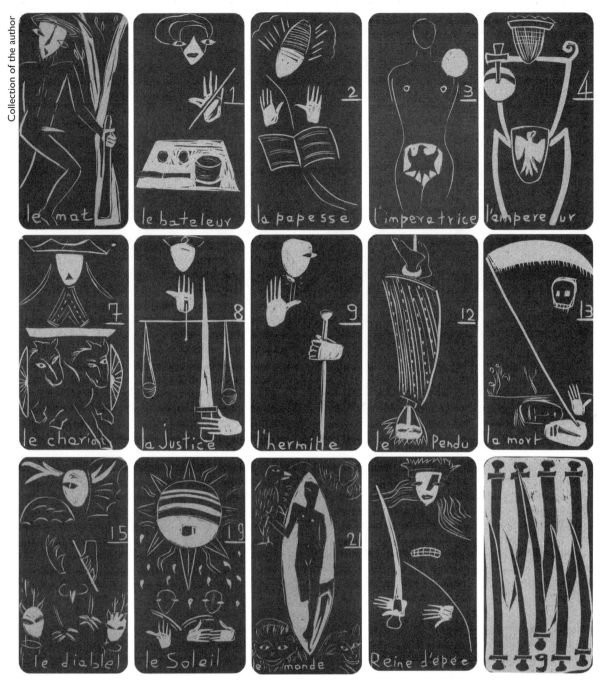

Tarot Elisabeth Frolet   Published by the artist, 1992

can run at fantastic speed, but the quicker he runs, the quicker he ages. **XI JUSTICE.** Patriot, the U.S. representative of the U.N. Peacekeepers, holds the scales of justice and the U.S. Constitution. **XII THE HANGED MAN** is Eclipse of the Misfits. He is a former Soviet operative who can control the Oblivion Force, a substance capable of creating anything he imagines. **XIII DEATH.** Terrance Scott bonds an ultradense alloy onto his own DNA, transforming his body. **XIV TEMPERANCE.** Monarch, a villain, warps the masks of comedy and tragedy from one to the other.

THIRD ROW: **XV THE DEVIL.** Fallout and his bearded Russian counterpart lock hands in the towering shadow of nuclear missile. Neither will surrender, though the land suffers from their conflict. **XVII THE STAR.** Permafrost generates water and ice. **XVIII THE MOON.** The merman

Naiad gazes into the sky, faced by the silhouette of Sphere, backlit by Luna herself. Both Sphere and Naiad are outsiders. **XIX THE SUN.** Ben Holliday plays with Aura's and his children. **XX JUDGMENT.** Thessaly and Trey Xavier were abducted by aliens and returned forty years later, without having aged and infused with wondrous powers.

BOTTOM ROW: **TWO OF BLADES.** Bao Chou's name means "revenge." **KNIGHT OF STAVES.** Riding a steed of solid rock and holding a staff of molten lava, Fahrenheit of the Misfits charges. **PAGE OF STAVES.** Desert Fox calls to the troops who are on maneuvers. **EIGHT OF MASKS.** Aquarius, an amphibious hybrid, is the last of his people. He leaves behind the masks of his abandoned brethren. **SEVEN OF DISCS.** Michael Tremere, known as Chimaera, searches for the cure to his odd genetic disposition.

Tarocchi del Futuro (Future Tarot)   Michele Medda, Antonio Serra, Giuseppe Vigna, and Nicola Mari, Lo Scarabeo, 1992
TOP ROW: **0 IL MATTO** (The Fool; Mac). **I IL MAGO** (The Magician; Sigmund Baginov). **II LA PAPESSA** (The Popess; Sada). **III L'IMPERATRICE** (The Empress; Legs Weaver). **IV L'IMPERATORE** (The Emperor; Nathan Never).   SECOND ROW: **V IL PAPA** (The Pope; Reiser). **VI L'AMORE** (Love). **VII IL CARRO** (The Chariot). **IX L'EREMITA** (The Hermit; Father Omero). **X LA RUOTA DELLA FORTUNA** (The Wheel of Fortune; the orbiting base).   THIRD ROW: **XI LA FORZA** (Strength; Exoskeletal Power). **XII L'APPESO** (The Hanged Man; The Mutant). **XIII LA MORTE** (Death; Athos Than). **XIV LA TEMPERANZA** (Temperance; Li-Xiaolong). **XV IL DIAVOLO** (The Devil; Skotos).   FOURTH ROW: **XVI LA TORRE** (The Tower; headquarters of the Alfa Agency). **XVIII LA LUNA** (The Moon). **XIX IL SOLE** (The Sun). **XX L'ANGELO** (The Angel). **XXI IL MONDO** (The World; "The City," where the story takes place).

Tarocchi di Gambedotti   Mario Gambedotti, Priuli & Verlucca, 1986

Gatti 22 Arcani (Cats 22 Arcana)   Osvaldo Menegazzi, Edizioni Il Meneghello, 1990

TOP ROW: 0 IL MATTO (The Fool). 1 IL BAGATTO (The Magician). 2 LA PAPESSA (The Popess). 4 L'IMPERATORE (The Emperor). 5 IL PAPA (The Pope).

SECOND ROW: 6 GLI AMANTI (The Lovers). 7 IL CARRO (The Chariot). 8 LA GIUSTIZIA (Justice). 9 L'EREMITA (The Hermit). 10 RUOTA DELLA FORTUNA (Wheel of Fortune).

THIRD ROW: 11 LA FORZA (Strength). 12 L'APPESO (The Hanged Man). 13 LA MORTE (Death). 14 LA TEMPERANZA (Temperance). 15 IL DIAVOLO (The Devil).

BOTTOM ROW: 17 LE STELLE (The Star). 18 LA LUNA (The Moon). 19 IL SOLE (The Sun). 20 IL GIUDIZIO (Judgment). 21 IL MONDO (The World).

Tarot of Gemstones and Crystals   Helmut G. Hofman, AGMüller, 1996   Caption information is from the booklet by Helmut G. Hofmann.

TOP ROW: **0 The Fool: Silex** is an activating stone that connects with the earth and calms the mind. **I The Magician: Herkimer Diamond** or quartz is a double-ended crystal. It imparts clarity and strengthens self-esteem. **IV The Emperor: Purpurite** intensifies the visualization of new plans and provides the resolution to put them into action. **V The Hierophant: Diamond** imparts clarity and illumination. We experience our relationship to the cosmos with it, and feel harmony and closeness to God. **VIII Justice: Tourmaline Quartz** is the connection of black and white, earth and heaven, shadow and light.

SECOND ROW: **X Wheel of Fortune: Alexandrite,** with its changing color play of green to red, brings harmony, joy and happiness. **XIII Death: Amethyst** promotes humility and philanthropy. It brings light into problems, and so helps us in the transformation from the mental to the spiritual level. **XIV Temperance: Rose Quartz.** Its delicate pink can heal the wounds inflicted to the heart and comfort us. Rose quartz imparts a loving vibration, which allows us to be trusting and to love our fellow human beings. **XVII The Star: Moldavite** helps us to perceive the lost purpose in life and release constricting thought patterns. **XIX The Sun: Sunstone,** by activating vital energy, supports self-development and allows us to understand wider correlations.

BOTTOM ROW: **Ace of Swords: Quartz Crystal,** through its clear, energetic vibration, shows us the path to perception and harmony. **Knight of Wands: Iron** represents courage (weapons of iron), protection (iron armor, cars), and desire for action (tools). **Seven of Wands: Zoisite with Ruby** activates the development of the self, clears the mind, and expands the consciousness. **Eight of Cups: Malachite** resolves repressed emotions and promotes understanding of ourselves and our fellow human beings. **Queen of Coins: Agate** connects us with the earth, the material world, and reality.

Gendron Tarot   Melanie Gendron, U.S. Games Systems, 1997

Gill Tarot The Gill Tarot is based on the Kabbalistic Tree of Life, which is illustrated on the back of the cards. Ace through ten of the Minor Arcana correspond to the spheres as noted on an extra card labeled "Layout Guide." Each of the Minor Arcana has a key word. Elizabeth Josephine Gill, the author of the deck, likens tarot cards to "clews," balls of string that guide one through a labyrinth. "As the clew unwinds and snakes ahead, the seeker may find his/her way through the impenetrable forest by following it. The clew of the old symbolic stories unravels of its own volition, suggesting that it is self-regulating, a guide with greater knowledge and ability than the follower. When you use the Gill Tarot as a mirror, you will find within it ancient clews, which if followed through your unique forest can help you towards your center." The deck was published in 1990 by U.S. Games Systems. It includes a title card and the "Layout Guide" card.

Gill Tarot   Elizabeth Josephine Gill, U.S. Games Systems, 1990

Giotto Tarot The Giotto Tarot was inspired by the art of Ambrogio da Bondone, the medieval Italian artist known as Giotto. Giotto lived from circa 1276 to 1337 in Florence. Italian artist Guido Zibordi translated Giotto's visual allegories and symbolism to tarot, demonstrating the medieval roots of tarot. The cards are titled in English, Italian, French, Spanish, German, and Flemish. The deck includes a title card and advertising card. The back design is a double-ended rendition of the 3 of Chalices in purple. The Giotto Tarot was published by Lo Scarabeo, Turin, Italy, circa 2000.

Tarots des Gitans M. Ameli illustrated the Tarots des Gitans under direction of I. Donelli. The large cards are printed on heavy, textured stock. Each has a border of animals, plants, and objects traditionally associated with Gypsy culture. The Major Arcana have titles in Romani and French, and all the cards have upright and reversed divinatory meanings. The deck was published in 2000 by Editions De Vecchi, Paris.

Glastonbury Tarot Lisa Tenzin-Dolma, who lives in Glastonbury, England, created the Glastonbury Tarot as oil paintings. In *The Glastonbury Tarot: Timeless Wisdom from The Isle of Avalon,* the artist writes, "The illustrations depict the history of the area through Pagan, Christian, and Arthurian figures, reflecting the marriage of belief systems in this small area of land which is a melting pot of ideas and ideologies, a cauldron of inspiration which feeds all who come here."

The suits are swords, staffs, chalices, and vesicas. The back design shows a hilltop tower silhouetted by the sun. The tower is the ancient Tor of Glastonbury, atop a five-hundred-foot-high hill. The site has been sacred to succeeding waves of Glastonbury inhabitants. The deck and book were published in 1999 by Gothic Image Publications of Glastonbury and Samuel Weiser, York Beach, Maine.

Gnomes Tarot (Tarocchi degli Gnomi) The Gnomes Tarot was published in several different sizes, as twenty-two- and seventy-eight-card decks, with different sleeves, and even with two different artists' names given: Antony Moore and Antonio Lupatelli.

Decks with Antony Moore given as the artist's name are two miniature twenty-two-card decks (undated) and a large twenty-two-card edition (1990).

- The miniature decks are numbered and titled in Italian and include a presentation card and instructional leaflet. The deck that has Il Ciabattino (The Cobbler, used for Major Arcana I) on the front cover has an abstract brown and green back design. The deck that has Il Carro (The Chariot) on the cover has an abstract green and white back design.

- The large deck features Italian titles only and has a double-ended back design of gnomes drinking, in black-green on white. It is printed on textured paper. The large deck includes a title card, presentation card, and instruction card.

Miniature **Gnomes Tarot** "The smallest tarot deck in the world" (I Tarocchi piu' Piccolo del Mondo), actual size.

Decks issued with Antonio Lupatelli given as the artist's name are:

- "The smallest tarot deck in the world" (Tarocchi piu' Piccolo del Mondo; 1991).

- "The Gnomes Tarot," a standard-sized Major Arcana deck (1991). Titles are in English and Italian, and the back design is the same as the large twenty-two-card deck, of gnomes drinking. The deck includes a title card and a card with the inscription in English: "Tiny, industrious gnomes / wrest gems and other treasures / from the bosom of the earth, / yet hold within their most secret casket / the secret of a smile, / the richest of all riches."

- A miniature seventy-eight-card edition (1993) with titles in Italian and a back design of Celtic knots in olive green. It includes a title card and a card describing the deck.

- "Tarots of the Gnomes," a standard seventy-eight-card deck (1995). The Major Arcana cards include personal names. Titles are in Italian, English, French, German, and Spanish. The double-ended back design is of two gnomes shaking hands under a tree. The deck includes a title card and instruction cards in five languages. A flyer reveals that Il Matto (The Fool) is Sichen, the greatest wizard of the gnomes. He revealed the history of the gnomes to the artist, to be rendered as tarot cards.

The artwork is tempera and watercolor. The Gnomes decks were published by Lo Scarabeo, Turin, Italy.

Goblin Tarot Unabashedly ugly, the Goblin Tarot has twenty-two Major Arcana plus a title card signed and numbered by English artist Peter Wood. The deck was published in a limited edition of two hundred by Wood in 2001. The paper band holding the cards and the envelope package are also signed and dated by the artist.

Goddess Tarot The Goddess Tarot, according to the artist Kris Waldherr, is a "celebration of the Divine Feminine." "My intention in creating the art and design for The Goddess Tarot was to create a tarot deck that would speak directly to women using our stories, while incorporating the archetypal power and symbols of the tarot." The art reflects the Rider-Waite deck, especially in the Minor Arcana, so that the deck is easily accessible and familiar to readers. The four suits are associated with the goddesses Freyja (staves), Isis (swords), Venus (cups), and Lakshmi (pentacles). The back design is gold foliage on blue. The deck was published by U.S. Games Systems, Stamford, Connecticut, in 1998.

Giotto Tarot Guido Zibordi, based on the paintings of Giotto, Lo Scarabeo, circa 2000

Tarots des Gitans M. Ameli, artist, and I. Donelli, Editions De Vecchi, 2000 Descriptions are based on the book by Donelli.

TOP ROW: **L'URSARO: LE MAT** (Bear Tamer: The Fool). **I LE ZAHORI: LE BATELEUR** (The Geomancer: The Magician). **III ANA: L'IMPÉRATRICE** (Ana: The Empress). Ana is queen of the Kechali, the fairies who live in the valleys and fix the fate of humans. **IV LE FORGERON: L'EMPEREUR** (The Blacksmith: The Emperor). **V LE GRAND MARÉCHAL-FERRANT: LE PAPE** (The Great Farrier: The Pope).

SECOND ROW: **VI LE FLAMENCO: L'AMOUREUX** (The Flamenco: The Lovers). **VII LE ROTARO: LE CHARIOT** (The Charioteer: The Chariot). **VIII LA MATAORA: LA JUSTICE** (The Matriarch: Justice). **IX LE SECRET: L'ERMITE** (The Secret: The Hermit). **X L'OUROBOUROS: LA ROUE DE FORTUNE** (Ourobouros: The Wheel of Fortune).

THIRD ROW: **XII LE JOUR DE L'OMBRE: LE PENDU** (The Day of Shadow: The Hanged Man). In spring, an effigy dressed in old clothes is hung by a red cord from a tree in the center of the encampment. The effigy is beaten, then burned, in symbolic vanquishment of winter and sterility. **XIII LA POMANA: LA MORT** (The Pentecost: Death). The Feast of the Pentecost is a day on which the gypsies acknowledge Death and renewal by hanging bones from a tree. **XIV L'OURME: LA TEMPÉRANCE** (The Fairy: Temperance). The beneficent fairy, seen only by magicians, brings peace to families and promotes sobriety and moderation. **XVIII LES NIVACI: LA LUNE** (The Fairies: The Moon). The magician can draw fairies both benevolent and malevolent, as well as the spirits of the dead, represented by the black cat and white dog. **XIX MITHRA: LE SOLEIL** (Mithra: The Sun). Mithra is the sun deity, celebrated with joyous music and colorful dances.

BOTTOM ROW: **XX LE BUTYAKENGO: LE JUGEMENT** (Butyakengo: Judgment). Butyakengo is a guardian angel. People receive messages from the angel by putting the left little finger in the ear. **NEUF D'EPÉE** (Nine of Swords). **CAVALIER DE BÂTON** (Knight of Batons). **ROI DE COUPE** (King of Cups). **DAME DE DENIER** (Queen of Coins).

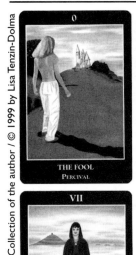

Collection of the author / © 1999 by Lisa Tenzin-Dolma

ons on his tunic represent the victory of the Britons over the Saxons. **V THE HIEROPHANT: JOSEPH OF ARIMATHEA** was a tin merchant and uncle of Jesus Christ. Business took him to the British Islands, and legend has it that Jesus came with him and walked on England's soil. After Jesus' death, Joseph retired to England. The round hut behind him was a church built by him and his followers. **VI THE LOVERS: CREIDDYLAD AND GWYTHYR** represent the union of earth goddess and sun god. They stand against a springtime sunset, the moon rising behind them. Their arms form the rune of transformation, in the shape of a butterfly, and the rune of a gift or kiss, in the shape of an x.

SECOND ROW: **VII THE CHARIOT: THE BARGE OF AVALON** carries Vivian, a lady of the Lake, from Glastonbury to Avalon. She directs the boat using the power of her will, as there is no physical way into Avalon. At the prow is a crescent waning moon, the dark of the moon when dreams and visions can be at their most potent. **VIII JUSTICE: ARVIRAGUS** was king of Britain in the first century CE. Although he was a druid, he bequeathed Joseph of Arimathea the land on which to live and build Christian churches. He holds two bowls in balance. The silver bowl is lunar for the ability to follow intuition and to know truths from the depths of feelings. The golden bowl is solar for the ability to deduce logically and to calculate the rights and wrongs in a situation.

Glastonbury Tarot Lisa Tenzin-Dolma, Gothic Image Publications and Samuel Weiser, 1999 Captions are based on descriptions of the card by the artist.

TOP ROW: **0 THE FOOL: PERCIVAL** was brought up innocent of the ways of the world. He beholds the castle of the Grail which, through his ignorance and shyness in asking questions, he did not identify. Although naïve and foolish at first, he was with Galahad and Bors when the quest of the Holy Grail was achieved. **I THE MAGICIAN: MERLIN,** a clairvoyant and magician, was King Arthur's advisor. He stands in a sacred grove of oaks. His hair radiates the vivid light of a brilliant and powerful mind at work. **IV THE EMPEROR: ARTHUR,** king of the Britons, sits in a throne at the roots of a tree in Wickhollow, Glastonbury. The drag-

IX	XII	XIII	XIV	XV
THE HERMIT St. Collen	THE HANGED MAN The Fisher King	DEATH Gwyn Ap Nudd	TEMPERANCE Brigit	THE DEVIL St. Dunstan

XVI	XVIII	XIX	XXI	
THE TOWER The Tor	THE MOON Chalice Hill	THE SUN The Grail	THE WORLD The Phoenix	10 OF SWORDS Rebirth

ACE OF STAFFS The Glastonbury Thorn	8 OF CHALICES Renewal	KING OF VESICAS

DUNSTAN was born near Glastonbury in 909 CE. He holds red-hot tongs to ward off his spiritual adversary. The devil has taken the form of a seductive woman to tempt him to break his monastic vows. A great spiral of energy, clutched by malicious claws, is ready to suck them into its vortex.

THIRD ROW: **XVI THE TOWER: THE TOR** rises out of reach of the waves that try to destroy it. A phoenix behind it symbolizes the indestructible lifeforce of man/woman, which dies only to be reborn. **XVIII THE MOON: CHALICE HILL** shows a lime (linden) tree on the small, beautiful Chalice Hill, near the Tor. The linden represents protection and healing. The full moon means that the seeds of contemplation, planted in the dark of the moon, are now rising to the light. **XIX THE SUN: THE GRAIL** is the cup Joseph of Arimathea brought to England. By legend, Jesus and his disciples drank from it at their last supper, and Joseph used the cup to catch drops of Jesus' blood at the crucifixion. The cup is also the Cauldron of Inspiration and Plenty. The face is that of the goddess of sovereignty, who nourishes all life. **XXI THE WORLD: THE PHOENIX.** A beautiful, abstract phoenix rises. From her body emerges the Egg-Stone, which exists at Glastonbury and is a symbol of the center of the world, the source of life itself. She clasps a round mirror, which reveals the true face of the gazer. **10 OF SWORDS: REBIRTH.** A man floats above the ground, looking up at a mirror image of himself in the sky.

BOTTOM ROW: **ACE OF STAFFS: THE GLASTONBURY THORN** derives from a staff planted by Joseph of Arimathea. **8 OF CHALICES: RENEWAL** shows a woman wearing a cloak of many layers, symbolizing her vast potential. She holds a lowered mask, indicating that she no longer needs to hide from the world. **KING OF VESICAS** stands at the entrance to Ebbor Gorge. The winter trees, with rootlike branches, symbolize his connection to earth.

Glastonbury Tarot (continued)

TOP ROW: **IX THE HERMIT: ST. COLLEN** was a Welsh saint who retired to a cave in Glastonbury. He stands at the top of the Tor. Around his neck is a silver cross, and he holds a pewter vessel of holy water. Silhouetted against the setting sun is the round hut, the first Christian church. St. Collen leaves it behind for a life of solitude and contemplation. **XII THE HANGED MAN: THE FISHER KING** rules Corbenic, where the Holy Grail is kept. Blood drips from a wound to his groin, which will not heal; his lands are infertile as well. His ancient, ghostlike father is in the background. Percival watches a procession of maidens carrying the grail and other holy relics, but asks no questions—and therefore does not consummate the quest that would heal the Fisher King. **XIII DEATH: GWYN AP NUDD** is King of the Faeries and Lord of the Underworld. He rides across the sky to gather the souls of the dead. His black cloak flies behind, as if it would darken the entire sky. **XIV TEMPERANCE: BRIGIT** was an Irish saint who moved to Glastonbury. She stands at the foot of Chalice Hill. Her red hair signifies a connection with the goddess Bridie, patron of fire, of the forge, of holy wells, and of healing. The thorn branches above represent a "wishing tree"; one makes a wish while tying a ribbon to a branch. **XV THE DEVIL: ST.**

358

Gnomes Tarot (Tarocchi degli Gnomi) Antony Moore/Antonio Lupatelli, Lo Scarabeo, 1990–1993
Cards are shown at forty-five percent of their actual size. TOP ROW: From the Moore large deck SECOND ROW: From the Moore miniature deck THIRD ROW: From the twenty-two-card Lupatelli deck BOTTOM ROW: From the seventy-eight-card Lupatelli deck

Goblin Tarot   Peter Wood, published by the artist, 2001

Goddess Tarot   Kris Waldherr, U.S. Games Systems, 1998
The caption is based on the descriptions in the booklet
accompanying the deck.

TOP ROW: **0 BEGINNINGS: TARA** is a protective goddess of Tibet. **II WISDOM: SARASVATI** is a Hindu goddess of wisdom and culture. **IV POWER: FREYJA** is the
Norse goddess of creativity, love, and beauty. **V TRADI-
TION: JUNO** is the Roman patroness of marriage and
other rites of passage in women's lives. **VI LOVE: VENUS**
is the Roman goddess of love, described by many as queen of
pleasure and passion.

SECOND ROW: **VII MOVEMENT: RHIANNON** is a British horse goddess who symbolizes the unceasing force of movement which pulls all of life along with it. **VIII JUS-TICE: ATHENA** is a Greek goddess, depicted with an owl as a symbol of enlightenment. **X FORTUNE: LAKSHMI** is the Hindu goddess of fortune and prosperity. **XI STRENGTH: OYA** is the Yoruba goddess of the Niger river, and a patroness of female leadership and strength. **XII SACRIFICE: KUAN YIN** is honored as the holy mother of compassion in China. Instead of allowing herself to enjoy the delights of the heavenly Pure Lands, Kuan Yin vowed to remain on earth until all beings are liberated from suffering.

THIRD ROW: **XIII TRANSFORMATION: UKE-MOCHI** is the Japanese food goddess, whose body was transformed into food upon her death. **XIV BALANCE:**

YEMANA is the Santeria goddess of the ocean, often called upon to provide rain. **XVI OPPRESSION: THE WAWALAK** are the Australian sister goddesses who were swallowed by the Great Rainbow Serpent. They wept until they were reborn from Yurlungur back into the light. **XVII THE STAR: INANNA** is the great Middle Eastern goddess of the Bronze Age. **XIX THE SUN: THE ZORYA** are Russian goddesses attendant to the sun god.

BOTTOM ROW: **XX JUDGMENT: GWENHWYFAR** is the Welsh first lady of the islands and sea. Praised for her judgment and wisdom, it was believed that no man could rule Wales without her by his side. **XXI THE WORLD: GAIA** was the personification of the earth in ancient Greece. **PRINCESS OF SWORDS. FOUR OF STAVES. NINE OF PENTACLES.**

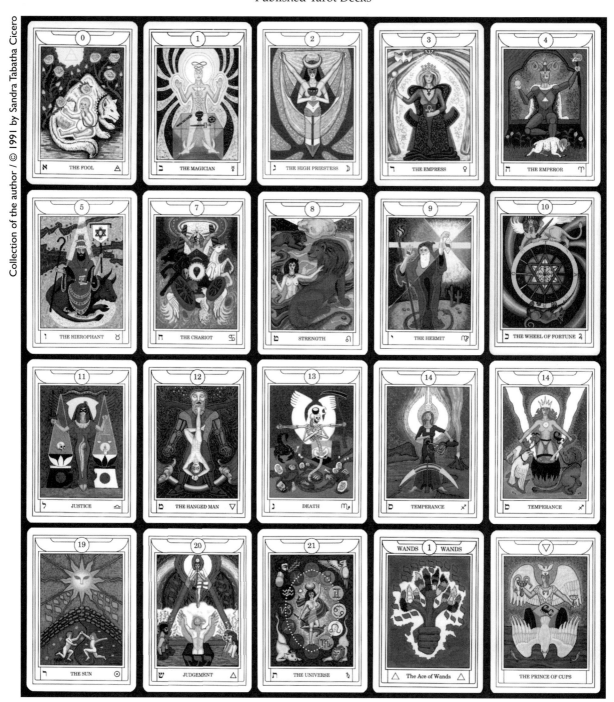

Golden Dawn Magical Tarot Sandra Tabatha Cicero and Chic Cicero, Llewellyn Publications, 2000 The caption is based on the book *Golden Dawn Magical Tarot.*

TOP ROW: **0 THE FOOL** shows an innocent child as Harpocrates, god of silence. He holds a dangerous wolf on a leash. **I THE MAGICIAN** is Hermes-Thoth. The four elemental weapons are on an altar before him. **2 THE HIGH PRIESTESS** is veiled and crowned with the crescent moon. She holds a cup of water. **3 THE EMPRESS** holds an ankh, symbol of life, and a scepter. A dove is at her right. **4 THE EMPEROR** wears ram's horns and holds a ram-headed scepter, symbolizing the zodiacal sign Aries.

SECOND ROW: **5 THE HIEROPHANT** wears a triple crown. The bull that is his seat stands for Taurus. **7 THE CHARIOT** enthrones an armored driver and is pulled by a black horse and a white horse. **8 STRENGTH** shows a woman touching a red lion, with a green lion in the background. **9 THE HERMIT** is an old and wise master magician. Cacti in the background recall Israel Regardie's Sedona, Arizona, home. **10 THE WHEEL OF FORTUNE** supports the sphinx at the top. Beneath is Cynocephalus, the dog-faced ape.

THIRD ROW: **11 JUSTICE** is represented by the Egyptian goddess Maat. A jackal is at her feet. **12 THE HANGED MAN** dangles from a structure that is part tree, part god. **13 DEATH** is part snake, part human skeleton. At

362

Golden Dawn Magical Tarot Romanian edition, 1998

Golden Dawn Magical Tarot The Golden Dawn Magical Tarot was created by Sandra Tabatha Cicero. Chic Cicero, who co-wrote the book accompanying the deck, describes how the work came into being. The couple visited occultist Israel Regardie. "After viewing several of my wife's sketches of the Major Arcana, he was impressed enough to commission her to paint the deck for the Order [of the Golden Dawn]. Although Regardie died ten days later on March 10, 1985, work on the deck continued for another four years." Each Major Arcana card includes a Hebrew letter and an elemental or astrological symbol. Two versions of the Temperance card are given. The court cards show element symbols; the pips show astrological and elemental symbols. The back design is a white triangle containing a sun design, surmounted by a red cross. The deck, published by Llewellyn Publications, was first issued in 1991 as the New Golden Dawn Ritual Tarot and reissued in 2000 as the Golden Dawn Magical Tarot. The 1991 edition was not printed on card stock, and the images on the cards are not square with the edges. The 2000 edition is printed on card stock with alignment of the images corrected.

A Romanian version, possibly unauthorized, was published in 1998 by Editura Ananta, Bucharest. This edition substitutes astrological signs for the Hebrew letters on the bottom left corners of the Major Arcana cards. The borders are also changed somewhat. The numbering

of Strength and Justice is switched from the Llewellyn version. Only one version of the Temperance card is given. Most of the images on the cards are the same as those in the Llewellyn deck. The Hanged Man, however, is substantially altered. Also, the Star of David, on Major Arcana 5, is replaced with a cross.

Golden Tarot "Golden Tarot is a celebration of tarot's heritage," says Kat Black, the creator of the deck. "It has been collaged completely from artwork of the late Middle Ages and early Renaissance. Poignant images of a gentle beauty and human frailty came from a time of violence, pestilence, and oppression. They speak of a truth that is timeless, and a hope that flowers even in the darkest conditions."

Part of Black's motive for creating the deck was to gain recognition for paintings that have been mostly only in churches. She chose paintings that are relatively obscure, discovering many by Internet. The deck comprises digital collages, with fragments from several artworks used for each card. "Each picture is composed of about twenty layers, and each layer has been manipulated to make it match the whole composition as much as possible." The booklet included with the deck names the original sources for the objects on each card. The Golden Tarot was published in 2004 by U.S. Games Systems, Stamford, Connecticut.

Golden Tarot of the Tsar The Golden Tarot of the Tsar is based on the art of Russian religious icons. Such images were created according to a strict code of composition and appearance. The leaflet accompanying the deck says that, in order to avoid offending the precepts of the Orthodoxy, Bulgarian painter Atanas Atanassov "avoided reproducing the 'acheropitus' images, that is, the icons that are said to have appeared miraculously without human intervention.… Atanassov did not reinterpret the tarot or modify the icons, but rather adapted the tarot to the icons by associating the traditional meaning of each card to a biblical subject or the portrait of a saint." The background of the cards is embossed metallic gold, with red borders. The deck was published by Lo Scarabeo in 2002. The double-ended back design shows an icon of Jesus Christ.

---

its feet are beings, including human fetuses. **14 TEMPERANCE** is a giant feminine angel standing on earth and water, mixing fire and water. A volcano is in the background, and a bow and arrow represent Sagittarius. **14 TEMPERANCE** shows a woman pouring water into a cauldron while holding a torch. A white eagle and red lion are chained to her waist.

BOTTOM ROW: **19 THE SUN** shines brilliantly on a boy on the earth and a girl in the water. Two groups of Hebrew yods fall on either side of the sun. **20 JUDGEMENT** shows the archangel Michael descending. The candidate for initiation

rises from the tomb on which is the Hebrew letter shin. **21 THE UNIVERSE** shows the goddess Isis holding wands of negative and positive power. Around her are symbols of the twelve houses of the zodiac. **The Ace of Wands** shows an angelic hand issuing from clouds, grasping a heavy club with three branches ending in multi-colored flames. Twenty-two flaming yods surround the club. **THE PRINCE OF CUPS** is drawn by an eagle. Calm water is under the wheels of his vehicle.

Golden Tarot   Kat Black, U.S. Games Systems, 2004

Golden Tarot of the Tsar   Atanas Atanassov, Lo Scarabeo, 2002

TOP ROW: **V THE HIEROPHANT.** The apostle Peter. **VII THE CHARIOT.** The ascension of Elijah. **VIII Justice.** The Archangel Michael. **IX THE HERMIT.** Saint John the Baptist. **X THE WHEEL.** The Archangel Gabriel.

SECOND ROW: **XI STRENGTH.** Saint George and the dragon. **XIII DEATH. XIV TEMPERANCE.** Saint Sophia. **XV THE DEVIL. XVI THE TOWER.** Saint Simeon the Stylite.

BOTTOM ROW: **XVII THE STARS.** The Holy Nativity. **XX JUDGEMENT.** The Final Judgement. **QUEEN OF SWORDS. SIX OF WANDS. SEVEN OF CUPS.**

Gothic Tarot   Mystic Eye, Mystic Eye, 1995

Gothic Tarot (by Mystic Eye) Mystic Eye created a Gothic Tarot focusing on the "undead," vampires and supernatural creatures. The Vampire Chronicles of novelist Anne Rice seem to have been an influence, as the leaflet that accompanies the deck describes a vampire consumed by jealousy and loneliness, who goes underground for renewal, only to claw his way up again to seek company. The deck was published in 1995 by Mystic Eye. A dedication on the box says, "The Gothic Tarot was originally created as a birthday gift for a dear friend after discussing her ideas for a Vampire Tarot." The twenty-two-card deck is described as the first ever created by Mystic Eye. Each card has a title and a few words of description, from the vampire's point of view.

The back design is double-ended of red griffins, skulls, and foliage.

Gothic Tarot (by Wendell) Leilah Wendell combined photographs of funereal sculpture from cemeteries around the world with sky, flowers, and other images, and hand-colored the resulting collages. Contributors to the deck are George Higham, Janelle Smith, and Daniel Kemp. The back design is a black and white abstract pattern. The deck includes a title card and presentation card. The twenty-two-card deck was published by Westgate Press, New Orleans, in 1998, in a numbered and signed limited edition of 1,000 decks.

Gothic Tarot   Leilah Wendell, Westgate Press, 1998

Granny Jones Australian Tarot   "Granny Jones lives in Tasmania with her cats and dogs in an historic little cottage covered in jasmine vines," says the preface of the book that accompanies the deck. Granny Jones is the nom de plume of Rebecca Jones. The artwork on the cards, naïve in style, depicts Granny Jones and her friends and animals in a variety of situations. Key words give interpretations of each card. The back design shows Granny Jones, with her signature below the picture. In 1992, the artist self-published a small run of decks mostly for friends. The deck was published again in 1994 by Kangaroo Press Pty Ltd, of Australia.

Gran Tarot de los Tattwas   J.A. Portela designed a tarot deck based on tattwas, geometric signs used for meditation. Tattwas originated in India. The double-ended back design is of a yellow star on blue. The deck includes a title card and a credits card. The deck was published circa 1999 by Nostradamus, Barcelona. Portela and Gloria de la Varga designed another deck featuring the tattwas, with different artwork (see Tattwas Tarot).

Graphik Tarocchi   Zoltan Tamassi is a Hungarian artist known for his poster art. The art for his tarot deck was rendered in tempera in 1990. Each card is titled in Italian and includes a poem by Gianni Brunoro. The double-ended back design, in red on white, shows a hand surrounded by the alphabet. The deck includes a title card and was published by Lo Scarabeo, Turin, Italy, in 1992.

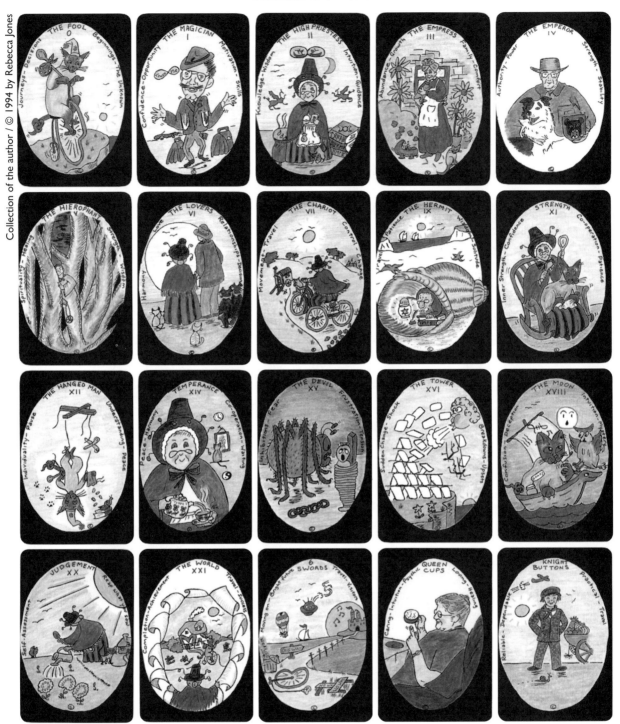

Granny Jones Australian Tarot   Rebecca Jones, Kangaroo Press, 1994   The caption is based on *Granny Jones Australian Tarot Book.*

TOP ROW: **0 THE FOOL** is portrayed by a cat, and cats, particularly Siamese, are always seeking new adventures. **I THE MAGICIAN** is a sharp salesman, with sample cases at his side. Wads of money are in his pocket, and a flashy car awaits him. **II THE HIGH PRIESTESS** stands with the tools of her trade and her faithful Siamese cat, Tom, at her side. Behind her is the cauldron of intuition, belonging to Ceridwen, Celtic goddess of wisdom. The three droplets gave Gwion Bach knowledge of everything, so that he later

became the poet Taliesen. **III THE EMPRESS** is Granny Jones in her garden, cuddling a cat, a baby at her feet. **IV THE EMPEROR** holds a shield illustrated by a bear, show-ing his strength. His leadership is indicated by the collie, whose intelligence and control keep the flocks in order. He portrays the artist's late husband Lloyd Fenton Jones.

SECOND ROW: **V THE HIEROPHANT** is at one with nature. He holds a Celtic triquetra, or trinity, for body, mind, and spirit. **VI THE LOVERS** depicts Granny and Grandpa Jones with their family of cats and dogs. **VII THE CHARI-OT** is Granny Jones' adult-sized tricycle. The gypsy caravan and the tricycle indicate change and movement. The cats in

Gran Tarot de los Tattwas J.A. Portela, Nostradamus, circa 1999

the basket of the tricycle indicate victory, as they tricked Granny into giving them a ride. **IX THE HERMIT** is in a shell on the beach. His pen and books indicate that he is an academic. **XI STRENGTH** shows Granny Jones brushing her cat, showing perseverance, as well as cooperation.

THIRD ROW: **XII THE HANGED MAN.** The cat of The Fool card is cut from puppet strings, showing he will not be manipulated. The money spilling from his pockets indicates that he doesn't care for material things; the books indicate inner knowledge. The snail shows a slow phase; the pawprints indicate a pause (paws). **XIV TEMPERANCE.** Granny Jones pours a nice cup of tea for you, indicating harmony and cooperation. The cat gazing in the mirror indicates a time of reflection. **XV THE DEVIL** is a huge, hairy spider, stifling influences. **XVI THE TOWER** depicts breakdown with the collapse of a house of cards, and sudden, possibly traumatic, change as two people fall from a cliff. **XVIII THE MOON** illustrates the poem "The Owl and the Pussycat." The cat got the bird out in the boat by trickery; now they will both have to use intuition to get out of the situation.

BOTTOM ROW: **XX JUDGEMENT.** Granny Smith waters her garden of good deeds. **XXI THE WORLD.** Granny Smith has broken through a paper hoop and is able to see beyond the dull side. She sees a bright garden and the Fool on his pennyfarthing bicycle, ready to start on new adventures. **6 SWORDS.** Obstacles and a difficult phase are at an end. **QUEEN CUPS** reads tea leaves in a cup. **KNIGHT BUTTONS** wears a knotted silk scarf called a "king's man." His costermonger barrow is piled high with fruit, showing his connection with earth. The spider indicates patience, and the snail indicates a slow, but steady pace.

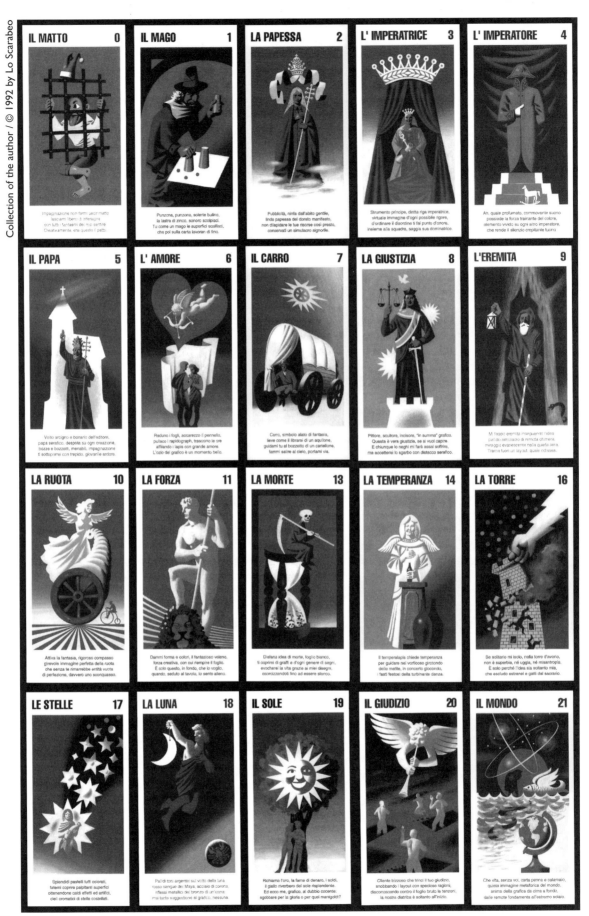

Graphik Tarocchi   Zoltan Tamassi, Lo Scarabeo, 1992

Greenwood Tarot Mark Ryan and Chesca Potter delve into the lore and myth of the forest in the Greenwood Tarot. "The forest is both a metaphor for life and for the unknown and sometimes shadowy aspects of it," Ryan says in *The Greenwood Tarot,* the book that accompanies the deck. "Within the forest mythos every human trait and condition is stored and cherished for future explorers to wander along the path, absorb, study and meditate upon as they choose. What better basis for a tarot pack than this?"

Pre-Christian British lore is the vehicle for the deck. The Major Arcana are structured on "The Wheel of the Year," a diagram of which is included as a small black and white poster with the deck. The Major Arcana cards themselves are unnumbered, and the numbers given in the book do not always correspond to the traditional Major Arcana. Some titles are changed from the traditional; where there is a correspondence with the traditional, the book gives it. Ryan explains, "The Greenwood Tarot seeks to strip back the archetypes to their basic form and remove the political and sexual attributes that were added in later years." The deck was published in 1996 by Thorsons/HarperCollins of San Francisco.

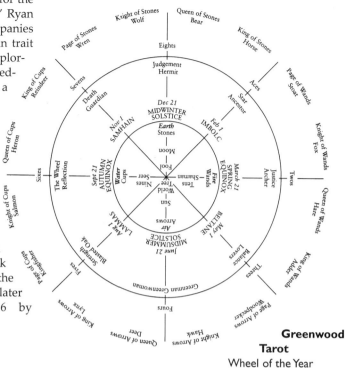

Greenwood Tarot
Wheel of the Year

The Fool | The Ancestor | The Pole Star | The Archer | Justice

Greenwood Tarot Mark Ryan and Chesca Potter, Thorsons/HarperCollins, 1996 Descriptions are based on the book accompanying the deck.

0 The Fool stands on the white chalk cliff poised to step into the abyss. The Wheel of the Year turns behind him. Unconsciously, the white hart, symbol of the spirit of the Fool, has already made the leap. **I The Ancestor** is a creature of myth, half-animal, half-human, but carries the wand of wisdom and the drum that summons all who can hear to gather and watch the sun rise. His coat is of white winter fur and evergreen leaves. The gateway formed by the silver birch trees either side of the path marks a new commitment and a point from where you cannot turn back. **2 The Pole Star** illuminates the dark void of the universe. The swirling clouds of stellar dust that formed the heart of the Star spiral outward into infinity and turn with the cycle of the universe. **3 The Archer** (The Chariot) holds the broad longbow poised in the act of release. The bow is of the Meare longbow design, the fletchings are of goose feather, taken from the right wing, and the arrowhead is of flint. The Meare bow dates from 2300 BCE and was a vital tool for survival and defense. **4 Justice** is personified by a stag, forest king and guardian, verdant with greenery. The ax is a manifestation of the human will to change the environment. The shield, bearing the Major Oak in Sherwood Forest, reminds us that we must preserve and protect our natural resources.

Balance	Greenwoman	The Blasted Oak	Strength	The Guardian
Death	Judgement	The Seer	The Moon	The Shaman
The World Tree	Deer	Stoat	Attraction	Protection
	Queen of Arrows	Page of Wands	Two of Cups	Four of Stones

Greenwood Tarot *(continued)* TOP ROW: **6 Balance** (Temperance) is based on the Pictish (ancient Scottish) symbols of entwined red and white horses, whose colors represent the basic color of a primal world-blood: fire and iron are red; milk, ash, and bone are white. The green mound is the healthy land. At its center is the universal egg of creation. The yellow iris represents the concept that two energies become one living entity with three separate but co-existing parts. **8 Greenwoman** (The Empress) is crowned with ferns and roses and breathes the divine word of life. Around her neck, the golden Celtic gorget represents the sun throughout the year. The amber cup holds the milk of love and nurturing, and the *sheela-na-gig* holds a sun disk, the life-force of woman. The green dragon, the life-force of the land, stands sentinel. **9 The Blasted Oak** (The Tower/The Hanged Man). A figure falls from the severed branch of the lightning-struck oak. Flames catch the hair and burn the bonds that appear to have tied the person to the branch. **10 Strength.** A human hunter, wearing a lion mask and holding a bloodied spear, balances with the cup of giving, intoxication, and compassion. On the spear shaft is an ivory statuette found in Europe, a lion-headed human thought to be 30,000 years old. In the background, Silbury Hill symbolizes the harvest aligned to the sunrise at Lammas. **13 The Guardian** (The Devil) is the skeleton of a great cave bear. He guards a cave that is filled with stalactites. Beyond is an unknown and untrodden path.

SECOND ROW: **14 Death.** A reindeer skull has been picked clean by a flock of ravens. The raven's beak is bloody. The bird waits both as a guardian and as a guide, its unblinking eye all-seeing and unafraid. **16 Judgement.** The initiate has been laid to rest in a mound between two yew trees, covered with earth and stone, both elements of the northern quadrant, waiting to be reborn. The shamanic sentinel of the mound is a polar bear. **17 The Seer** (The High Priestess) wears the owl's cloak of wisdom, which is decorated with animals of power and their shamanic spirits. She stands before the World Tree, studying the roots deeply embedded in the earth. On her staff is a crane bag and from her cloak hang runes. **18 The Moon** illuminates a dark winter sky. The primal egg lies submerged in the nutrient-rich swamp, full of potential energy and creative power. A lone auroch (horned animal) moves across the mysterious landscape. **19 The Shaman** (The Magician) is wrapped in a bearskin adorned with Paleolithic paintings of animal spirits, taken from La Caverne des Trois Frères, Arièges, France. He holds four tools representing the elements: a roebuck skull rattle (air), a stone knife (earth), a smoking bundle (fire), and a hollow antler cup (water).

BOTTOM ROW: **21 The World Tree** (The Universe) stands as the symbol of the conscious bridge between the living macrocosm and the inner universe of the human psyche. To gain access to the tree, one must walk the labyrinth at its base. **Queen of Arrows. Page of Wands. Two of Cups. Four of Stones.**

Tarot de Gruyères The Château de Gruyères, in Switzerland, is not only of historical significance. Since 1990, it has housed the Centre international de l'Art fantastique. The original pen-and-ink drawings of the Tarot de Gruyères, by José Roosevelt, have been on display in the castle's gallery. The Major Arcana deck was published in 1993 by the Commission Administrative du Château de Gruyères. It was accompanied by a booklet with poetic text by Marie-Claire Dewarrat. The double-ended back design shows the castle in red on white.

Gruyères Tarot back design is the Château de Gruyères as rendered by José Roosevelt

Tarot de Gruyères José Roosevelt, Commission Administrative du Château de Gruyères, 1993

Gufi della Buona Fortuna
Osvaldo Menegazzi, Edizioni Il Meneghello, 1990

Gufi della Buona Fortuna
Osvaldo Menegazzi took owls as his subject for the Good Luck Owls tarot deck. The deck was published in 1990 by Edizioni Il Meneghello.

Haindl Tarot The paintings by Hermann Haindl draw on various traditions to make a tarot deck with layers of symbolism. The Major Arcana feature Hebrew letters, astrological symbols, and runes. The inner borders are white for air, blue for water, red for fire, or yellow for earth. The Minor Arcana represent ancient Egypt (swords), Hinduism (wands), ancient northern Europe (cups), and Native America (stones). Each of the numbered Minor Arcana includes an I Ching hexagram. The court cards are father, mother, son, and daughter. The deck was published in 1990 by U.S. Games Systems of Stamford, Connecticut. The back design shows a single eye.

Halloween Tarot "Whatever the season, jump into the festive, if slightly freakish, old-time Halloween world of Kipling West, and let the tarot cards help you take a closer look at what may be lurking in the shadows of your life." So reads the presentation card of the Halloween Tarot. Pamela Colman Smith, the artist of the Rider-Waite Tarot, might have enjoyed this take on her deck, since she loved to tell ghost stories herself.

Artist Kipling West drew images from horror movies and old circus posters, and from the German "vegetable people," dolls made from harvest bounty, popular in 1920s America as Halloween toys and decorations. The four suits are bats (swords), imps (wands), ghosts (cups), and pumpkins (pentacles). The deck is accompanied by an instructional brochure by Karin Lee, and includes a title card and a presentation card. The double-ended back design shows the ubiquitous black cat haunted by a spider, surrounded by Halloween motifs. The Halloween Tarot was published by U.S. Games Systems, Stamford, Connecticut, in 1996.

Tarot of Hellen The Tarot of Hellen features plants as symbols of the tarot. The paintings, by Valérie Bernard, show individual plants for each Major Arcana card and, for the suits, branches (swords), leaves (wands), flowers (cups), and grains (coins). The back design shows a rodent with its tail wrapped around a tree. The Tarot of Hellen was published by AGMüller of Neuhausen, Switzerland, in 1999.

Tarot in de Herstelde Orde The Minor Arcana of Tarot in de Herstelde Orde are based on the Minor Arcana of the Rider-Waite Tarot. The Major Arcana, however, show variations. The numbering differs from the traditional. There are two extra Major Arcana: De Intuitie (Intuition), intended to follow card 5 The High Priest, and De Waarheid (Truth), following card 15 The Devil. 18 The Star shows a nude male figure, rather than the usual female figure. The top of each card features an arrangement of the letters TARO. The deck was created by Onno and Rob Docters van Leeuwen, with titles in Flemish. The deck was published by Uitgeverij Servire, Utrecht, Belgium, in 1995.

Hudes Tarot The tarot deck created by Susan Hudes draws from medieval art and the symbolism of mythology. "Themes of alchemy and astrology suggest the magical nature of medieval thought," says the introductory card, "the same ideas that initiated the art of tarot reading…. Antique maps, constellation charts, and marbled paper are some of the elements used to complete the look of the deck." U.S. Games Systems, Stamford, Connecticut, published the deck in 1995 and included with it a title card and an introductory card. The double-ended back design is a Celtic-style knot and two faces.

Haindl Tarot Hermann Haindl, U.S. Games Systems, 1990 Descriptions are based on the booklet, by Rachel Pollack, that accompanies the deck.

TOP ROW: **0 The Fool** is a medieval jester, required to entertain but also to speak truths that no one else would care to express. The wounded swan represents the fall from grace. **III The Empress** stands before a door representing culture. The arch suggests a church, religion. The woman's scepter is wrapped with the snake of transformation and enlightenment. A golden bird flies toward her ear, as if bringing the word of heaven. **IV The Emperor** stands in front of Yggdrasil, the world tree of Scandinavian myth. The diamond over his head contains the colors of humanity. **V The Hierophant** shows a grandfather, a father, and a boy. The three generations indicate the positive value of patriarchal religion and Judaism, the "father" of Christianity and Islam. The book and key represent the Torah.

SECOND ROW: **VII The Chariot** is a wheeled boat. Its red color is of energy, and a red glow surrounds the figure riding the boat. In the sky, a beast part wolf, part boar signifies our deepest fears, unnameable and wild. **XII The Hanged Man** is Odin of Scandinavian myth. The rainbow implies water and its colors correspond to the chakras (energy centers) of Odin's body. Odin's hair seems to root into the earth. The two ravens signify thought and memory, and also death and transformation into the "other world." **XIII Death** shows a boat, an image of death and birth. The trees and grass signify plants; the bones, minerals; and the birds, the animal world. The ferryman is of the human world. The peacock's eye signifies looking at the truth in regard to death. The bird also symbolizes the soul and the divine potential in each person. **XV The Devil** is organized around a diagonal line broken by a crystal, which transforms the aggressive instinct of the Devil. The snake is an image of rebirth and the visionary experience, and of evil.

The Fool

The Empress

The Emperor

The Hierophant

The Chariot

The Hanged Man

Death

The Devil

The Star

The Sun

Success
Ten of Cups

Ace of Stones in the West

BOTTOM ROW: **XVII The Star** shows a woman at the bottom of a bare rocky hill where water splashes into a pool. She is washing her hair, an act of unity with the earth. Her hair blends into the water. Her dress suggests age. She is Gaia, the Mother of Life. Only water and rock, earth's oldest forms, are around her. **XIX The Sun** is a labyrinth of spirals; the trees line up with an order never found in nature; and the rose appears as dreamlike. We have not returned to the ordinary world, but have moved to another level of myth. **Ten of Cups: Success** has hexagram 46 Pushing Upward. Stones push from the sea. An ancient rock has a dark hole at its center, signifying mystery. **Ace of Stones in the West.** The eagle landing on the rock shows the joining of earth and sky, ordinary reality and spiritual reality, masculine and feminine. The sky, earth, and rainbow are beauty and gifts.

Halloween Tarot   Kipling West, U.S. Games Systems, 1996

0 Centaury	*I* Pansy	*II* Rose	*IIII* Angelica	*VI* Mandrake
VII Monkshood	*VIIII* Orchis	*X* Thyme	*XI* Snapdragon	*XIIII* Waterlily
XV Rue	*XVIII* Meadow Saffron	*XVIIII* Saint-John's-Wort	*Two* of Flowers	*As of Grains* the Cornucopia

Tarot of Hellen Valérie Bernard, AGMüller, 1999 TOP ROW: **0 Centaury** was claimed by medieval magic books to induce hallucinations when mixed with lamp oil. **I Pansy** is the flower of initiative. **II Rose** symbolizes the sacred, and divine secrets revealed step by step. Its thorns warn of trouble. **IIII Angelica** is the flower of the archangel. **VI Mandrake** is the most powerful plant of love.

SECOND ROW: **VII Monkshood** is like a helmet to put on before embarking on an adventure. It is highly poisonous. **VIIII Orchis** is a wild mountain orchid. The small speckles symbolize the wounds of life, which are more bearable when we understand and accept them. **X Thyme** is said to cure wounds and sprains, and even to prevent poverty. **XI Snapdragon** is able to withstand austere conditions. **XIIII**

Waterlily warns us with the tale of Deianeira, the wife of Heracles. To gain back his love, she soaked a shirt in the poison blood of the centaur Nessos. When Heracles died on putting on the shirt, she took her own life and was reborn in the form of the waterlily.

BOTTOM ROW: **XV Rue** is used to purify, to combat magicians and witches, to repel parasites, and to exorcise places. **XVIII Meadow Saffron** flowers are poisonous, but contain the hidden wealth of saffron. **XVIIII Saint-John's-Wort** is harvested on Saint John's Day at noon. It was believed to concentrate the sun's energy. **Two of Flowers** has the names of the artist and the publisher. **As [ace] of Grains: the Cornucopia.**

Tarot in de Herstelde Orde   Onno and Rob Docters van Leeuwen, Uitgeverij Servire, 1995

TOP ROW: 4 DE GELIEFDEN (The Lovers). DE INTUÏTIE (Intuition) portrays the Roman goddess of earth, Juno. 6 DE KEIZERIN (The Empress). 10 DE WERELD (The World). 11 DE KRACHT (Strength).

SECOND ROW: 12 DE GEHANGENE (The Hanged Man). 13 DE GEMATIGDHEID (Temperance). 14 DE DOOD (Death). DE WAARHEID (Truth) portrays the Roman god of lightning, Jupiter. 18 DE STER (The Star).

BOTTOM ROW: 19 DE ZON (The Sun). 20 DE LAATSTE OORDEEL (The Last Judgement). 21 HET UNIVERSUM (The Universe). PAGE VAN ZWAARDEN (Page of Swords). 4 of Pentacles.

Hudes Tarot   Susan Hudes, U.S. Games Systems, 1995

I Am One Tarot The I Am One Tarot was painted in oils by Israeli artist Maya Britan. It reflects the imagery of the 1968 New Tarot for the Aquarian Age (also known as Book of T and New Tarot), painted by Rosalind Sharpe (see *The Encyclopedia of Tarot*, volume I). Maya Britan relates that she continued the "unfinished project" of the New Tarot after a meeting with Rosalind Sharpe.

About the deck, the artist says, "The I Am One Tarot is an invitation to ones who are ready to join The Enlightened Brotherhood of the Universal Order, from a place where true understanding of 'free will' is made clear. It is a school program, given in 22 Universal Laws of the Major Arcana. The artwork is on a deep psychological level that takes the reader on the red path of initiation, consciously and subconsciously, to where he becomes one with the One Will of his Creator." The art for the Major Arcana was completed circa 1996.

I Am One Tarot
Published card

I Am One Tarot was published as a full deck in 2002 with titles and key phrases in English, Spanish, and French by Saint-Art.com. It includes an advertising card, a card with an affirmation verse, an instructional booklet, and a small poster giving a card spread. The Major Arcana have black borders, and the suits' borders are variously colored: the curved blade (blue), two-headed serpent (red), pear of tears (green), and stone of age (orange). The back design is a black and white image of stars with the word "One" in the center.

Tarot of the Imagination The Tarot of the Imagination, by Ferenc Pinter, is subtitled "fragments of perception." It contains images that are familiar from photography and art, just beyond definite identification, leaving our imagination to fill in the context. The brochure explains, "It would appear that the mind can contain an unreal landscape, consisting of symbols and sensations which can filter reality, softening it into a recognizable form. More than a dream landscape, it is a symbolic representation of reality without a precise landscape."

The Tarot of the Imagination was published as a Major Arcana deck by Lo Scarabeo, Turin, Italy, in 1991, in both a standard size and in a larger size, with Italian titles. The back design is abstract, in blue. The standard deck includes a title card and a card with a poem on it. The larger size includes a title card (the poem is printed on the inside sleeve of the package) and is printed on matte paper lightly embossed in a pinstripe. A seventy-eight-card version was published by Lo Scarabeo in 2000, with English, Italian, French, Spanish, German, and Flemish titles. The back design shows a woman prying open the jaws of a huge, fanged beast.

Tarot of Initiation The intricate Major Arcana Tarot of Initiation was drawn in pen and ink by Emmett Brennan of Portland, Oregon. Steven Marshall wrote descriptions of the cards, noting that they are based on "the rich symbolism of the Western esoteric tradition." The deck was published by Marshall in 1984. The back design shows a cross and circle superimposed on a starburst, with the title of the deck at the top.

Intuitive Tarot The Intuitive Tarot was first self-published by Dirk Gillabel, using the pseudonym Medicator, as black and white drawings. Carol Herzer painted the cards, preserving the original line art but adding shading, color, "energy fields," and so on. Dirk Gillabel's brother, Guido Gillabel, has also created tarot decks that Herzer painted. Photographs of the paintings were mounted on black adhesive backing, and published by Herzer as a numbered Major Arcana deck. Cards 19, 20, and 21 are combined into one. A booklet by Herzer is included with the deck.

Of the Intuitive Tarot deck, Dirk Gillabel says (on the website soul-guidance.com), "I was born in 1959. The sixties passed me by; I was too young to understand what was happening. I had heard the songs of the Beatles, but it wasn't until 1990 that I first heard [the song] 'The Fool on the Hill.' It absolutely entranced me. The Tarot door flew open and inspiration came in to create a new Major Arcana. It was a pure pleasure to create the images. All are representative of my mood at that time, which was influenced by the Beatles' songs. Only three images are directly related to the Beatles. Card 0 is the 'Fool on the Hill.' Card 12 is a compilation of the four Beatles and the songs 'Yellow Submarine' and 'Lucy in the Sky with Diamonds.' Card 19.20.21 is 'the girl with the sun in her eyes' (from 'Lucy in the Sky with Diamonds')."

Nigel Jackson Tarot The magical images of Nigel Jackson's tarot deck have their roots in Symbolist illustration. He says in the book accompanying the deck, "The truth about the development of the deck over the last 2,000 years, resulting in the formalized woodcut packs produced in the eighteenth and nineteenth centuries at Marseilles, Besançon, and elsewhere in Europe, reveals a much more complex, subtle, and intricate picture of diverse esoteric influences cross-fertilizing and cohering over many centuries around the now-familiar Greater and Lesser Trumps of Tarot. These symbols, once treasured in the courts of fifteenth-century Italian nobles and carried through many lands in the painted caravans of Romany sorcerers and fortunetellers, have never lost their appeal to the imagination and speak as beguilingly today with their voice of enchantment as they ever did in days gone by. Once known, they are quite unforgettable. This is because they resonate within us as a true 'psychic language,' epitomizing the original timeless archetypes within the Deep Mind." The Nigel Jackson Tarot was published by Llewellyn Publications, St. Paul, Minnesota, in 2000. The back design is of a circle with a lemniscate in its center, bordered by stars on a blue ground.

I Am One Tarot Maya Britan, published by the artist, 2002 The images shown are from photographs of the original artwork; titles and commentary are from the published deck.

TOP ROW: **I The Changer.** I Am Master Communication. **3 The Feeler.** I Am Master Motion. **4 The Actor.** I Am Master Power. **8 The Donor.** I am Master of The Law.

SECOND ROW: **10 The Royal Maze.** I Am Master Destiny. The Cup of Wine. **12 The Hanging Man.** I Am Master Redeemer. **13 The Renewer.** I Am Master Transformation. **16 The Citadel.** I Am Master Perfection.

BOTTOM ROW: **18 The Reacter.** I Am Master Pattern. **20 The Knower.** I Am Master of Soul-Consciousness. **21 The Virgin.** I Am Master of Free Will. The Cup of Light. **22 The Nameless One.** I Am Master Recorder.

Tarot of the Imagination   Ferenc Pinter, Lo Scarabeo, 2000

0	1	3	4
THE FOOL	THE MAGICIAN	THE EMPRESS	THE EMPEROR
5	6	8	9
THE HIEROPHANT	THE LOVERS	STRENGTH	THE HERMIT
11	12	14	19
JUSTICE	THE HANGED MAN	TEMPERANCE	THE SUN

Tarot of Initiation   Emmett Brennan, artist, and Steven Marshall, published by Steven Marshall, 1984

Collection of the author

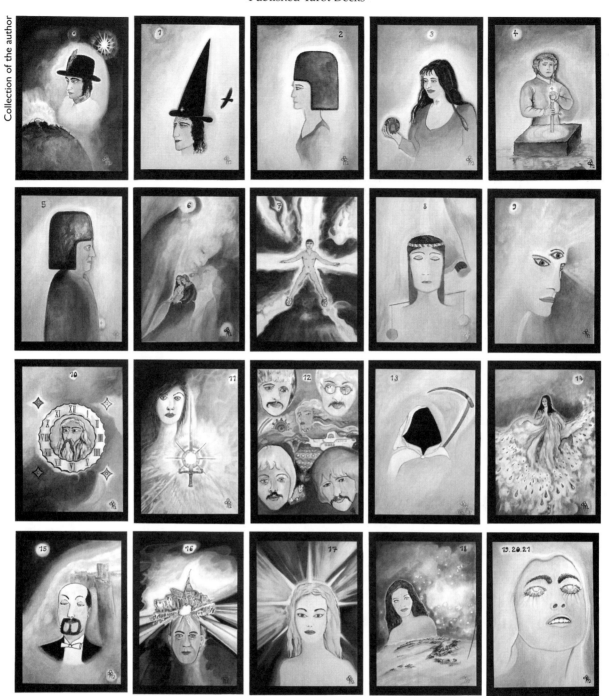

Intuitive Tarot   Dirk Gillabel, published by the artist, 1990

Nigel Jackson Tarot Llewellyn Publications, 2000 The caption is based on descriptions in the book with the deck.

TOP ROW: **0 The Fool** walks along a high precipice in the early morning brilliance with his cat at his heels, bearing a staff twined about with the vine and grapes of ecstasy and an air-filled bladder. He can be interpreted as the youthful Dionysus-Zagreus with his panther and thyrsus wand, as "Green George" the medieval Woodrose or Wildman, and even as the mysterious "Green Wanderer" of Arab lore, Al-Khidir. **I The Juggler** is a mountebank, trickster, and magician, causing things to appear, disappear, and reappear. In his hat is the feather of a magpie, a bird sacred to Gemini. **III The Empress** is in front of the Venus Mountain, entrance to the magical Other World, womb of the Great Mother, Dame Nature. She is the green-robed goddess of fecundity, love, beauty, and the bountiful earth. The Mystical Rose is her emblem. **VI The Lovers** represents the "Alchemical Wedding" of Male and Female Principles. Cupid, mischievous Love-God, fires gold-tipped arrows of infatuation into mortal hearts. **VII The Chariot.** A knightly, armored man bearing a halberd steers the horse-drawn "Triumphal Chariot." The seven stars of Ursa Major are on the front of the vehicle.

SECOND ROW: **VIII Justice** epitomizes the balance of the eight spheres of the planets and the fixed stars around the earth. **IX The Hermit** fares by the beams of his lantern on his lonely pathway above the world of men. **XI Fortitude.** A maiden masters a lion. The mythical nymph huntress Cyrene was seen by Apollo overpowering a lion on Mount Pelion. **XII The Hanged Man** represents the river-waters between worlds, through which the initiate must pass. **XIII Death** cuts away surface appearances, stripping the world down to the bones prior to regeneration and resurrection.

THIRD ROW: **XIV Temperance** mingles the waters of the higher self into the waters of the lower, for the winged figure is the Divine Genius, Holy Angel, or "Good Daimon" set over each person. **XV The Devil** is in the traditional form of a goat holding a trident. This image lies in the classical cults of the great god Pan-Faunus and the horned Dionysus-Zagreus, the "One of the Black Goatskin," whose mystic drama forms the heart of the Orphic Mysteries. **XVI The Tower** bears the emblem of the Tower of Babel, which was destroyed, according to some accounts, when its builder Nimrod tried to shoot an arrow from its summit into the "eye of god." **XVII The Star** depicts the "Evening Star," Venus. She pours forth the waters of purification and psychic renewal. **XVIII The Moon** casts ghostly rays over the sinister Gate-Towers of Hades, guarded by ever-watchful hounds. A crustacean emerges from the waters of the unconscious.

XXI THE WORLD · NINE OF SWORDS · KING OF STAVES · ACE OF CUPS · THREE OF COINS

Nigel Jackson Tarot (continued)
XXI The World depicts a goddess dancing amidst starry space, bearing a laurel wreath and wand. She is naked as the symbol of release, spiritual freedom, and ultimate reality, liberated from all veils. **Nine of Swords. King of Staves. Ace of Cups. Three of Coins.**

Jaśniak Black and White Tarot Aleksandra Jaśniak's black and white tarot deck has titles in English and Polish. The deck was published in two editions. One was printed by Chemigraph of Chicago in 1990 and has hand-lettered titles on the Major Arcana and court cards. The other was printed in Poland and has typeset titles. The back design is the artist's monogram. The Polish-printed deck includes a card with a blank face and a stamped back.

Polish tax stamp circa 1990 (with part of back design on the right)

Jaśniak Color Tarot Aleksandra Jaśniak created a tarot with bright, almost psychedelic colors and patterns. The deck was printed in Poland in 1993, accompanied by a book. The titles are in English and Polish, and the back design is double-ended, with the letter J in gold on black.

Tarot of the Journey to the Orient The Tarot of the Journey to the Orient features the scenes, customs, dress, and ritual described by the Venetian explorer Marco Polo (1254–1324). Each of the Major Arcana has two scenes, Western and Eastern. The titles are in five languages. The double-ended back design shows Marco Polo at the Great Wall of China. The deck, with artwork by Severino Baraldi, was published in 2002 by Lo Scarabeo of Turin, Italy. It includes a title card and an advertising card, and a booklet by Pietro Alligo and Riccardo Minetti.

Jungian Tarot Robert Wang, artist of the Jungian Tarot, calls the deck "a set of precisely interrelated images designed on Jungian principles for a method which Jung described as 'active imagination.'" Based on a Jungian tenet that "everything is based on opposites, male and female," Wang portrayed the Magician as "the totality of Self, a unity which is the potential for male and female." The rest of the deck, except for the Fool, "shows aspects of one or the other, like separate facets of two crystals which have been broken from a single primordial crystal…. When we meditate on a given tarot card, we deal with a specific aspect of ourselves. With the Empress we address first our own Mother, and then the pure Mother aspect of our own being; the Emperor brings us to consider first our own father and then the pure Father in each of us. The ultimate aim is the reintegration of our own opposites, a return to the pristine spiritual state of The Fool."

Each of the Major Arcana has at its base a mandala. "The Mandala, a 'magic circle' used as an aid to contemplation in the East, is a more graphic way of suggesting the energies of the many archetypes connected to each card."

The Jungian Tarot was published Urania Verlag in Neuhausen, Switzerland, in 1988, and republished by Marcus Aurelius Press of Columbia, Maryland, in 2001. The cardstock on the 2001 edition is lighter, and some of the color tones are slightly different.

Kalevala Tarot Kalervo Aaltonen was inspired to create the Kalevala Tarot by the Finnish epic compiled by Helsinki University professor Elias Lönnrot and published in 1835. The epic was a blend of Finnish, Karelian, and Estonian poems, songs, and stories about the adventures of the Kalevala people. It tells the story of two warring tribes, the Kalevala and the Pohjola, and in doing so encompasses cosmology, shamanism, love, culture, and battles between good and evil—the breadth of life. Names of characters from the epic are below the titles of the Major Arcana cards. The suits of the deck are swords, stakes (wands), dishes (cups), and loaves (coins). The Kalevala deck was illustrated by Taina Pailos. The back design is a four-sided design of deer and abstract patterns in black on gold, and includes a title card and an introductory card. U.S. Games Systems of Stamford, Connecticut, published the deck in 1996.

Jaśniak Black and White Tarot   Aleksandra Jaśniak, Chemigraph, 1990

Jaśniak Color Tarot   Aleksandra Jaśniak, publisher unknown, 1993

Tarot of the Journey to the Orient Severino Baraldi, Lo Scarabeo, 2002

Jungian Tarot   Robert Wang, Urania Verlag, 1988; Marcus Aurelia Press, 2001   Descriptions are extracted from the book *Tarot Psychology,* by Robert Wang.

TOP ROW: **The Fool: Spirit: The Source.** A young man, carrying the spark of life symbolized by a flaming rose, is about to step off into a starry sky. The act will create a universe to eventually be destroyed by the panther at his right. At his left is the Orphic Egg in which the Cosmos is nurtured. The Crown above refers to that which is the unified source of All, that which directs and controls the framework of consciousness at all levels. **The Magician: The Son.** The Magician is the celestial alchemist, the ultimate director of the quest for Self. He is the author of Sun and Moon. He is at once the potential for all opposites and the means for their reconciliation. As Mercurius he is the "Messenger of the Gods." **The High Priestess: The Daughter.** Anima is the inner self of a man. She is eternal woman who, as The High Priestess, holds a book symbolizing the ultimate secrets of the unconscious, most frequently represented by water. As the Moon, she creates the universal tides of consciousness. **The Empress: The Mother.** The Empress is seated on a throne amidst a profusion of foliage. She holds a golden cup symbolizing the yoni, the female generative organ. Behind the Empress is a lake symbolizing the unconscious, and referring to her "Virgin" phase as the High Priestess. But in these waters swims a deadly serpent, meaning that destructive aspect of the Mother. The dove in the leaves at her feet is that of Venus, goddess of Love; the cave at bottom left suggests that, as Mother Earth, she also rules the Underworld.

SECOND ROW: **The Hierophant: The Father as Law-Giver.** The card relates to the Gnostic concept of Demiurge, which supposes that the illusions of the material condition are created not by a Supreme Deity but by a Lesser Creator. In the Hierophant's right hand is a small figure representing Original Man, the potentially perfected Self which will evolve within the restriction of the earth, a condition created by the Hierophant. **Hanged Man: The Son Self-Sacrificed.** The Hanged Man is generally agreed to represent a state of consciousness called sammadhi, a condi-

tion where the center of consciousness is reversed, and subject becomes object. One looks "down" from the unconscious to the conscious. In Christian terms, this may be described as a mystical "Crucifixion in Space." **Death: The Mother as Gateway.** The "Grim Reaper" crosses a bridge. Although the bridge is collapsing behind him to symbolize the end of a phase, it is certain that he will reach a new shore and a new beginning. A woman behind him is death in Jungian terms, described as a return to the Mother. **Temperance: The Conciliatory Daughter.** The card depicts a young girl, to suggest the importance of absolute innocence (lack of prejudice) in the active and ongoing process represented here. On a natural stone "altar" water is poured onto a fire, and fire is immersed in water, meaning that one opposite is tempered, or mediated, by the other. The twelve candles in the background suggest the twelve signs of the zodiac, which, in psychological terms, symbolize the variety and totality of human experience.

THIRD ROW: **The Devil: The Dark Son.** The Devil represents enslavement of consciousness by the illusion of matter. One must be immersed in the material condition to this extreme before release is possible. The fish points clockwise toward manifestation, i.e., toward the earth. **The Tower: The Father as Avenger/Protector.** The figure behind the Tower is the Emperor. His task is to sweep away institutions that have become useless in our lives. A sword in one hand destroys utterly, but the other hand holds a rose of peace and conciliation. **Judgment: The Son Who Judges.** Judgment represents the Archetype of Rebirth. It shows a pause, a momentary turning inward and looking back, before the beginning of something entirely new. **The World: The Daughter Who Conceals Herself.** The World contains all of the elements that were unexpressed in The Magician. The dancing figure is the wave action of Spirit activating matter. The mask represents the public self, or Persona, that each individual develops to deal with society.

BOTTOM ROW: **Seven of Swords: Love. Ten of Wands: Control over Others. Princess of Cups: The Ambitious Daughter. King of Pentacles: The Responsible Father.**

Kalevala Tarot Kalervo Aaltonen and Taina Pailos, artist, U.S. Games Systems, 1996 TOP ROW: 0 The Fool: Lemminkäinen is a Kalevala hero with great passions—where he has been chaos reigns. I **The Magician: Ilmarinen** is the companion and helpmate of Väinämöinen. At his smithy, iron is melted and wrought. **3 The Empress: Louhi. 5 The Pope: Väinämöinen** is a wise man, old and steadfast, and from his belt poems are born. **6 The Lovers: Rakastavaiset.**

SECOND ROW: **7 The Chariot:** Isäntä. **8 Force:** Kyllikki. **11 Justice:** Aiti. **12 The Hanged Man:** Tiera. **14 Temperance:** Ainikki.

THIRD ROW: **16 The Falling Tower:** Tammi. **17 The Star:** Marjatta. **18 The Moon:** Mielikki. **19 The Sun:** Son. **20 Judgment:** Ukko.

BOTTOM ROW: **21 The World:** Luonnotar. **Six of Swords. The Princess of Stakes:** Kalervo's sister. A Passive Companion. **Eight of Dishes. Ace of Loaves:** The Fields of Pohjola.

Kazanlar Tarot Dr. Emil Kazanlar brought his heritage and talent together to create the profound illustrations of the Kazanlar Tarot. "I was born in Iran, of a father of mixed Turkish and Persian origin and a Hungarian mother, and lived in the home countries of my parents, who were followers of different religions. It became clear to me that the God of my Asian relations was the same as the God of my European relations. After studying painting, philosophy, and general linguistics, I discovered that the tarot is an applied system of art and meditation for the purpose of ecumenical improvements. This then is my ecumenical tarot which I now pass on to you…."

The Kazanlar Tarot has gold borders and is titled in German, English, Hungarian, and French. The Minor Arcana suits focus on different symbolic worlds: the suit of swords focuses on ancient Egyptian symbolism; wands on India, including the Hindu and Moslem aspects; cups on Hungary; and coins on Persia. At the top of each Minor Arcana card is a Kabbalistic "angelic" Sephirah; at the bottom is the inverted or "demonic" Sephirah. The sides show, on the left, astrological symbols and, on the right, the rank, suit, and element of the card. The deck includes a booklet by the artist and two extra cards that depict the artist's parents. The back design in an arabesque mandala on blue. The Kazanlar Tarot was published in 1996 by AGMüller, Neuhausen, Switzerland.

Kinder-Tarot (Children's Tarot) The Kinder-Tarot has two identical sets of Major Arcana, for use with non-divination card games such as SchnippSchnapp and Memory. The deck is intended for use by children, with illustrations of childlike characters. The art is by Klaus Holitzka, and the deck was published in 1997 by Schirner Verlag, Darmstadt, Germany. An advertising card and a card giving brief divinatory meanings are included. The back design is of a smiling sun face.

Tarocchi Lanzichenecchi Artist Giorgio Trevisan created Tarocchi Lanzichenecchi as a reflection of the spirit of the mercenary troops of the sixteenth century, whose career reached a climax with the sacking of Rome. The original art was executed in watercolor. The twenty-two-card deck was published in 1988 by Lo Scarabeo of Turin in a limited edition of 909. It includes a presentation card signed by the artist. The deck was also issued in a miniature size. The back design shows a male's bust, in a double-ended portrait in brown. The cards are titled in Italian. The deck was republished as a seventy-eight card deck in an unlimited edition, with titles in English, French, German, and Italian. The English-language box titles the deck "The Tarots of the Renaissance." The deck also includes a title card and nine cards that with publication information and directions for divination.

Kazanlar Tarot Two extra cards in the deck portray the heritage of the artist, his Hungarian mother and his Turkish-Persian father.

Legend: The Arthurian Tarot The Legend Tarot was created and illustrated by Anna-Marie Ferguson. The deck, also known as the Avalon Tarot, was published by Llewellyn in 1995, with a second edition in 1999. The back design shows the labyrinth of Chartres Cathedral in gold on purple. The suits are swords, spears, cups, and shields, and the courts are king, queen, knight, and page, with the page cards featuring symbolic animals rather than people. The deck includes an extra card on which is a dragon, totem of Pendragon, Arthur's male lineage.

Tarot: Lekarz Duszy (Tarot: Physician of the Soul) A set of Major Arcana was bound into the Polish book *Tarot: Lekarz Duszy,* by Manuela Klara Olszewska, with the intention that the cards would be cut out. The deck was painted by Jadwiga Kalmus. The book was published in 1998 by Studio Astropsychologh of Poland. The back design is a red starburst on black. The cards include astrological signs at the bottom.

22 Arcani di Leonardo Italian artist Ernesto Solari created the Arcana of Leonardo as interpretations of paintings by Leonardo da Vinci (1452–1519). The original art was woodblock prints. The artist published the deck circa 1990 as russet-inked cards on cream stock, in a signed, numbered edition 150 sets. The backs are blank.

Tarocchi di Leonardo The Major Arcana deck inspired by the genius of Leonardo da Vinci was rendered in colored pencil by Iassen Ghiuselev under the direction of Giordano Berti. The Tarocchi di Leonardo was published in 1992 by Lo Scarabeo of Turin. The cards are titled in Italian, and include titles in "mirror-writing," imitating Leonardo's hand. The deck was made in honor of the exhibition "Leonardo and Venezia" at the Palazzo Grassi, Venice, in 1992.

Der Magier   1.   A Mágus
The Magician   Le Magicien

Die Herrscherin   3.   A Czászárnő
The Empress   L'Impératrice

Der Prophet   5.   A Próféta
The Prophet   Le Prophète

Die Liebenden   6.   A Szerelmes
The Lovers   Les Amoureux

Die Kraft   11.   Az Erő
Strength   La Force

Die Mäßigkeit   14.   A Mértékletesség
Temperance   La Tempérance

Der Teufel   15.   Az Ördög
The Devil   Le Diable

Der Mond   18.   A Hold
The Moon   La Lune

Die Sonne   19.   A Nap
The Sun   Le Soleil

Die Welt   21.   A Világ
The World   Le Monde

Der Narr   22.   A Bolond
The Fool   Le Fou

König der Schwerter   Ozirisz
King of Swords   Le Roi des Épées

Sechs der Stäbe   Budha
Six of Wands   Le Six des Bâtons

Zwei der Kelche   Kukorica Jancsi
Two of Cups   Le Deux des Coupes

Sechs der Münzen   Aladin
Six of Coins   Le Six des Disques

Kinder-Tarot (Children's Tarot)   Klaus Holitzka, Schirner Verlag, 1997

TOP ROW: 0 Der Narr (The Fool). 1 Der Zauberer (The Magician). 2 Die Mondfee (The Moon Fairy). 3 Die Prinzessin (The Princess). 4 Der König (The King).

SECOND ROW: 5 Der Lehrer (The Teacher). 6 Die Freunde (Friends). 8 Die Meisterin (The Master Craftswoman). 10 Die Glücksfee (The Lucky Fairy). 11 Die Waage (Balance).

THIRD ROW: 12 Der Träumer (The Dreamer). 13 Der Abschied (The Departure). 14 Der Schutzengel (The Guardian Angel). 15 Der Teufel (The Devil). 16 Der Turm (The Tower).

BOTTOM ROW: 17 Die Sternenfrau (The Star Lady). 18 Der Mondmann (The Man in the Moon). 19 Die Sonnenkinder (The Sun Children). 20 Die Heimkehr (The Homecoming). 21 Die Welt (The World).

Kazanlar Tarot   Emil Kazanlar, AGMüller, 1996

Tarocchi Lanzichenecchi   Giorgio Trevisan, Lo Scarabeo, 1988

Legend: The Arthurian Tarot   Anna-Marie Ferguson, Llewellyn Publications, 1995

Tarot: Lekarz Duszy (Tarot: Physician of the Soul)   Jadwiga Kalmus, Studio Astropsychologh, 1998

22 Arcani di Leonardo   Ernesto Solari, published by the artist, circa 1990   The caption gives the work of Leonardo to which the card corresponds.   TOP ROW: **1 MACROCOSMO** (The Macrocosm); *The Last Supper.* **2 LA PAPESSA** (The Popess); *The Annunciation.* **3 IMPERATRICE** (Empress); *Leda and the Swan.* **4 IMPERATORE** (Emperor); *Bacchus.* **5 IL PAPA** (The Pope); *Saint Peter.*   SECOND ROW: **6 L'AMOROSO** (The Lover); *Saint Philip.* **7 IL CARRO** (The Chariot); *Saint Andrew.* **8 LA GIUSTIZIA** (Justice); *St. Matthew.* **10 IL DESTINO** (Destiny); *Saint James the Great.* **11 LA FORZA** (Strength); *Saint Girolamo.*   THIRD ROW: **12 L'APPESO** (The Hanged Man); *Saint Jude.* **13 LA MORTE** (Death); *The Virgin of the Rock.* **15 DEMONIO** (Demon); *Saint Simon.* **16 LA TORRE** (The Tower); *Saint Bartholomew.* **17 LA STELLA** (The Star); *Saint Anne with the Virgin and Child.*   BOTTOM ROW: **18 LA LUNA** (The Moon); *Saint Thomas.* **19 IL SOLE** (The Sun); *Saint John.* **20 GIUDIZIO** (Judgement); *The Virgin of the Rock.* **21 DEMIURGO** (Demiurge); *Saint John the Baptist.* **22 IL MONDO** (The World); *Mona Lisa.*

Tarocchi di Leonardo Iassen Ghiuselev, artist, and Giordano Berti, Lo Scarabeo, 1992 TOP ROW: 0 MATTO (Fool). I BAGATTO (Magician). II PAPESSA (Popess). III IMPERATRICE (Empress). IV IMPERATORE (Emperor). SECOND ROW: V PAPA (Pope). VI AMANTI (Lovers). VII CARRO (Chariot). VIII GIUSTIZIA (Justice). IX EREMITA (Hermit). THIRD ROW: X RUOTA (Wheel). XI FORZA (Strength). XII IMPICCATO (Hanged Man). XIII MORTE (Death). XV DIAVOLO (Devil). BOTTOM ROW: XVI TORRE (Tower). XVII STELLA (Star). XIX SOLE (Sun). XX GIUDIZIO (Judgment). XXI MONDO (World).

Light and Shadow Tarot   The Light and Shadow Tarot comprises seventy-eight large cards in black and white. The original artwork was executed by Michael Goepferd as linoleum block prints. An edition of the deck was published in 1994 by the artist as the Contrast Tarot. Destiny Books published the deck as Light and Shadow Tarot in 1998, with titles on the cards.

The images make magic of simple lines and contrast, with images and details metamorphosing as the cards are studied. For example, the Hierophant's legs and feet form an ox's head, and a complex of stars is over his body. Artist and author Brian Williams co-authored with Goepferd the book that accompanies the deck, based on interviews with the artist.

Sadly, Michael Goepferd did not live to see his work reach publication with Destiny Books, although he worked closely with the publishers and Brian Williams on the project. Williams describes the creation of the deck, based on his conversations with the artist. "It embodies the contrast between light and dark, heavy and light, feminine and masculine, expressed in a lively, linear idiom of black-and-white graphics. This contrast, though, does not mean a Manichean duality of good battling evil, order against chaos, darkness striving to drive out the light. Instead, Light and Shadow celebrates the balance and synthesis of contrasting forces. It honors the significance and interplay of both extremes."

Linol Tarot   German artist Gerhard Haack published the Linol Tarot in a limited edition of 150 sets in 1988. The box of the deck is signed and numbered by the artist. The deck was printed as linoleum block prints in five colors. It includes seventy-eight cards plus a blank card and an untitled card that shows a man with a club and a shield. The back design is a white cross with the suit signs. About tarot, the artist says, "Tarot lives in its images, and that is its fascination. One can let the thoughts go free, and get new insights on life situations."

Tarot Marita Liulia   Finnish multimedia artist Marita Liulia created a tarot deck as "an interactive net community." The artwork was made with photographs altered and recomposed on backgrounds, using computer software. The back of the booklet that accompanies the deck bears a code that allows the user of the deck access to Liulia's website maritaliulia.com, which includes additional information about the cards and instructions so that "you can create a personal Tarot history based on your personal card." The artist's imprint, Medeia, in Helsinki, published the deck in 2003. The cards are titled in English; the booklet is in English, French, and Italian.

Londa Tarot   "Londa's characters appear in a state of theatrics; all in their own personal play, acting out their divinations." In that sentence, the booklet accompanying the Londa Tarot captures the dramatic quality of the characters on the cards, both self-absorbed and inviting the viewer into their world. The figures recall waifish anime cartoons mixed with Goth sensibilities.

The deck is accompanied by a title card and a card that asks, "Who are you really?" "You might have a sec-

ond thought about putting the top card aside when using Londa Tarot," says Londa Marks in the booklet accompanying the deck. "Although it is not a part of the tarot itself, you may find it interesting in how it affects some readings. And the fact will always remain that we should consider what we are really about when making important decisions." The Londa Tarot was published by U.S. Games Systems in 1993. The back design is double-ended, of a circled cross in gold on black.

Lord of the Rings Tarot   The Lord of the Rings Tarot was illustrated by Peter Pracownik under direction of Terry Donaldson. The deck was based on the epic by J.R.R. Tolkien, *The Lord of the Rings*. Donaldson identifies the most important character in the epic as Gandalf, the wizard who guides the others in their quest. "Gandalf is a Merlin archetype," he says, "that interconnecting link of guide and teacher between the realm of mortals and the kingdom of the gods which we find in every culture, spiritual tradition, time, and region. In creating The Lord of the Rings Tarot, we have felt, at the ragged edges of our own reality, the occasional presence of this 'archetype': it is playful as well as full of great teaching."

Each card includes a brief description of the episode it illustrates and has in its upper right corner a symbol. A star disk is for "Free Peoples," Gandalf and the forces of good in Middle Earth. A shield with an eye is the symbol of the "Dark Forces," Sauron and the forces of evil. The "Neutral" symbol is a square with both shield and star. The "One Ring" symbol appears only on X The Wheel of Fortune. The symbols are used in the game invented by Mike Fitzgerald and described in the booklet accompanying the deck. In the artwork, wands are symbolized by torches, and coins by round labyrinths. U.S. Games Systems, of Stamford, Connecticut, published the Lord of the Rings Tarot in 1997.

Love Tarot (by Lada)   The February 1998 issue of *YM: Young and Modern* magazine featured a Major Arcana insert called Love Tarot. Elizabeth Lada created the artwork. The deck was printed as one page on heavy paper, to be detached from the magazine and broken along perforations into the individual cards. The back design has the letters YM in the center. The cards are unnumbered, and Death and The Devil are not included, so there is a total of twenty cards.

Love Tarot (by Tolford)   Collage artist Nancy Tolford designed the Love Tarot to accompany the book of the same name by Sarah Bartlett. The set was published in the U.K. by Rider/Ebury Press in 1995, and in the U.S.A. by Bullfinch Press/Little Brown & Company in 1998. The deck comprises twenty-two Major Arcana created as collages of artwork with classical and mythological themes. The back design shows gold stars on blue. Bartlett describes the tarot in her book: "Tarot cards are like mirrors of our emotions and of our being. They are like reflections on a pond where the visual images remain the same, yet move with the wind, with the moment. Tarot moves with you."

Light and Shadow Tarot Michael Goepferd, Destiny Books, 1998   The descriptions are based on Brian Williams' interviews with the artist.

TOP ROW: **0 The Fool** follows the path of the butterfly, symbol of beauty and the ephemeral. A monkey, symbolic of the intellect, clutches his ankle. **I The Magician** juggles fish, with the greater devouring the lesser, showing the food chain and chain of existence. At his trunk a tiny figure of Mother Earth jumps into a chalice, like sperm fertilizing the egg. **4 The Emperor** holds the scepter of power and spirituality, and the orb of the earth. **5 The Hierophant.** The tiny figure at his heart shows that humanity is his charge. **6 The Lovers** are inspired by an image of Adam and Eve, by Tamara de Lempicka. The couple touch but are drawn inward.

SECOND ROW: **8 Justice** holds the balance and the sword of executive power, of punishment but also of obstacles to clarity. **12 The Hanged Man.** The tree grows between night and day, deep into the earth and into the heavens. **13 The Endless Dance of Death** has at its center the Tree of Life. Towering over the tree are the dancing figures of Death and Humanity. Faces of rebirth and renewal spring from corn. **14 Temperance** depicts the archangel Michael mixing the holy waters of spirituality. **15 The Devil** holds a mirror of deception, and an hourglass showing that he is the lord of time.

THIRD ROW: **16 The Tower** warns against arrogance, while showing the human striving toward godhead. The falling person plunges into dangerous waters of oblivion that yet are also the matrix of renewal and rebirth. **17 The Star** guards a brilliant star in her hands. Radiance emanating from her head becomes wings. **18 The Moon** shines on an empty bed, home of sleep. The wolf and the dog show two sides of humanity, the wild and the tame. **Four of Swords. Ace of Swords.**

BOTTOM ROW: **Four of Wands. Prince of Cups. Seven of Cups. Prince of Pentacles. Two of Pentacles.**

Linol Tarot   Gerhard Haack, published by the artist, 1988

Tarot Marita Liulia   Marita Liulia, Medeia, 2003

Londa Tarot   Londa Marks, U.S. Games Systems, 1993

Lord of the Rings Tarot   Peter Pracownik, artist, and Terry Donaldson, U.S. Games Systems, 1997

ELIZABETH LADA

Love Tarot   Elizabeth Lada, Y&M, 1998

Love Tarot   Nancy Tolford, Bullfinch Press/Little Brown & Company, 1998

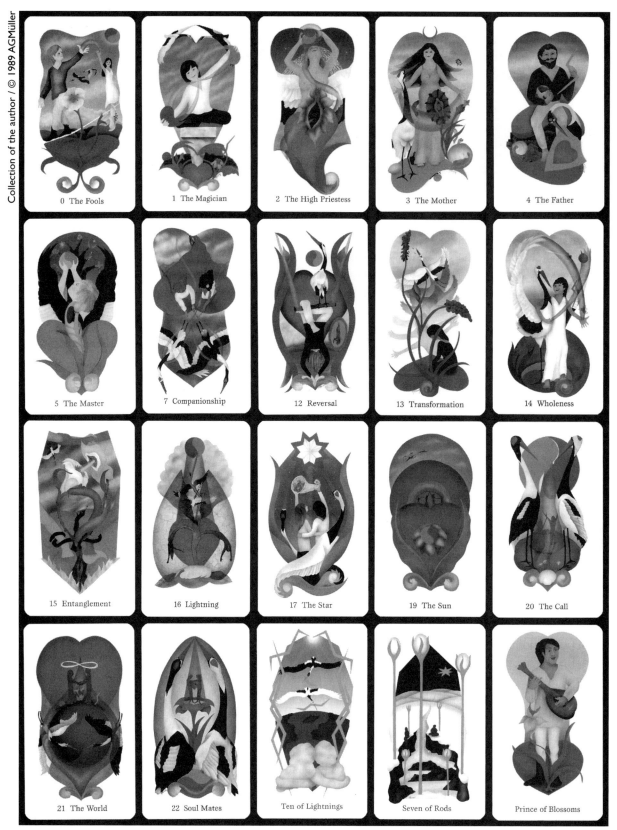

0 The Fools   1 The Magician   2 The High Priestess   3 The Mother   4 The Father

5 The Master   7 Companionship   12 Reversal   13 Transformation   14 Wholeness

15 Entanglement   16 Lightning   17 The Star   19 The Sun   20 The Call

21 The World   22 Soul Mates   Ten of Lightnings   Seven of Rods   Prince of Blossoms

Tarot of Love Marcia Perry designed the Tarot of Love under guidance from psychotherapists Wulfing von Rohr and Gayan S. Winter. The tarot focuses on relationships, with many of the Major Arcana retitled in order to reflect real-life concerns. For example, 7 is Companionship and 15 is Entanglement. An extra Major

Tarot of Love Marcia Perry, artist, and Wulfing von Rohr and Gayan S. Winter, AGMüller, 1989

Arcana card is 22 Soul Mates. The deck was published in 1989 by AGMüller of Neuhausen, Switzerland. The double-ended back design is hearts around a world globe.

H.P. Lovecraft Tarot back design: a portrait of Lovecraft

H.P. Lovecraft Tarot The American master of grotesque fiction, H.P. Lovecraft, is honored by the tarot deck illustrated by Daryl Hutchinson. The deck was published in 2002 by Mythos Books LLC. It includes a title card and a card whose face shows the back design: a photograph of Lovecraft in a tombstone format. A booklet by Eric C. Friedman accompanies the deck. The cards' titles are drawn from the names of characters, cults, and phenomena that occur in Lovecraft's fiction. The Major Arcana are called the "suit of Primal Powers." The Minor Arcana comprise the suits of man, artifacts, tomes, and sites. They are numbered I through XIV, with no court cards.

Lovers' Tarot The twenty-two-card Lovers' Tarot, illustrated by Oliver Burston, was created to accompany the book *The Lovers' Tarot,* by Jane Lyle. The cards are a collage of European paintings in a large format, 8.75 by 5 inches. The back design shows two gold cupids on a dark blue background. The deck was published in a set with the book by St. Martin's Press, New York, in 1992.

Lover's Path Tarot The Lover's Path Tarot, by Kris Waldherr, features classic love stories and myths from around the world. Each Major Arcana card has a tarot title and the names of the lovers whose story exemplifies the card. The double-ended back design shows a crowned, winged heart on a dark red background. The deck was published in 2004 by U.S. Games Systems of Stamford, Connecticut.

Ludvig Tarot The Ludvig Tarot, with art by Ludvig Zsuzsa, was published by Offset Nyomda in 1998. The deck has seventy-eight cards plus two blank cards. Titles are in Hungarian.

Macondo Tarot Andrés Marquinez Casas, the artist of the Macondo Tarot, was "inspired by the magic of Colombian reality," as he says in the booklet accompanying the deck. The deck was a final project for a Graphic Arts degree as well as part of a tribute to Gabriel García Marquez, author of the novel *One Hundred Years of Solitude.* It was chosen to represent Colombia for the "New Designers 1998" international exhibition in London. "The Macondo Tarot deck is the result, in graphic form, of research based on real stories and archetypal personalities from the coast of Colombia…a fusion of universal and local elements, by means of which I hope to place the old arcana in the context of our Latin American medium, and show the magic power that is ever present in daily life, as reflected in our literature,

art, dance, and tradition." The artist chose to use oval frames in the cards "to evoke the religious prints, medallions, and relics that are so traditional in our culture.… The oval frame denotes the mirror and its reflection, giving the impression that the characters represented in the scene are ourselves, and not mere caricatures." The suits of the Minor Arcana are tears (swords), flowers (wands), butterflies (cups), and fish (coins). The back design is a green and gold abstract pattern. The Macondo Tarot was published by Naipes Heraclio Fournier of Vitoria, Spain, in 1999. It is accompanied by two introductory cards in Spanish, Portuguese, French, and English.

Mage: The Ascension Tarot The imagery of this deck frequently recalls in composition and symbolism the Rider-Waite deck. The resemblance departs into edgy, urban imagery and fantasy or, in the words of the authors, "Gothic-Punk." The Major Arcana have traditional titles, but the suits are renamed.

The deck was designed by Nicky Rea and Jackie Cassada and executed by different artists. The Major Arcana are by Joshua Gabriel Timbrook, the suit of questing (wands) by Alex Sheikman, the suit of primordialism (cups) by John Cobb, the suit of dynamism (swords) by Larry McDougall, and the suit of pattern (coins) by Dan Smith.

The deck was created for use in "Mage: The Ascension" role-playing games set in a fantastical world, and is accompanied by a book explaining the way in which the cards are used. Mage Tarot was published by White Wolf, Clarkston, California, in 1995.

Manara: The Erotic Tarot The Erotic Tarot features illustrations by Italian artist Milo Manara, who is famous for his erotic comic book adventures. Some of the women of Manara's books appear on the cards. The cards include titles in English, German, French, Spanish, and Italian, as well as astrological and elemental correspondences. The suits are air, fire, water, and earth. The Manara deck was published by Lo Scarabeo of Turin, Italy, in 2000. It includes a title card and an advertising card. The double-ended back design shows a woman sitting on a park bench with two men.

Mandala Astrological Tarot The cards of the Mandala Astrological Tarot have a square shape as a reflection of astrological angles. The creator, A.T. Mann, explains, "The four angles of the ascendant, descendant, midheaven, and *immum coeli* (bottom of the heavens) are primary points that refer to, respectively, the personality, the not-self or partner, the ego, and the [Jungian] shadow or center of the unconscious." The way in which the cards fall in a reading would reflect the source of the influence indicated by the card's meaning.

Each card of the deck has astrological correspondences indicated, and the Major Arcana also include Hebrew letters. The deck was published, in a set with a book by A.T. Mann, by Harper & Row Publishers in 1987.

H.P. Lovecraft Tarot Daryl Hutchinson, Mythos Books, 2002

Lovers' Tarot Oliver Burston, St. Martin's Press, 1992

Lover's Path Tarot Kris Waldherr, U.S. Games Systems, 2004 The artwork shown is from before publication as a deck, and titles were not yet added. Titles in the caption are from the manuscript accompanying the deck.

TOP ROW: 0 Innocence. I Magic. IV Power. V Tradition.

SECOND ROW: VI Love. VII Desire. XIII Transformation. XV Temptation.

THIRD ROW: XVII Grace. XIX Awakening. XXI Triumph. Princess of Arrows.

BOTTOM ROW: Two of Arrows. King of Staves. Ace of Cups. King of Coins.

Collection of the author

A vándor	I — A bűvész	II — A főpapnő	III — A császárnő	IV — A császár
V — A főpap	VI — A szerelmesek	VII — A kocsi	IX — A remete	X — A sorskerék
XI — Az erő	XII — Az akasztott	XIII — A halál	XV — Az ördög	XVI — A torony
XVII — A csillag	XVIII — A Hold	XIX — A Nap	XXI — A világ	A botok lovagja

Ludvig Tarot   Ludvig Zsuzsa, Offset Nyomda, 1998

Macondo Tarot   Andrés Marquinez Casas, Naipes Heraclio Fournier, 1999

TOP ROW: **0 El Hombre** (The Man) is Francisco, a mythical character who defeated the Devil in a duel by reciting the Creed backward. **I El Gitano** (The Gypsy) harks back to the arrival of the gypsies, despite a royal decree forbidding their presence. They presented themselves as men capable of doing amazing acrobatic tricks and reading the future, and sold all kinds of trinkets and gadgets. **II La Beata** (The Devout Woman) is the prototype of the over-pious woman, wrapped up in herself and seeing death as the only escape from her bitterness. **III La Matrona** (The Matron) is the matriarch at the heart of the household. With her feet firmly planted on the ground, she bears the absurd world of the men. **IIII El Coronel** (The Colonel) represents the vice of eternal war, using up the most fervent and purest of ideals, until the motive of the struggle is forgotten.

SECOND ROW: **VI Los Amantes** (The Lovers) is a triangle of the man, his family that he presents to society, and his girlfriend. **VII El Avance** (Progress) shows that, in the life of the villages, a new invention is a great popular attraction that lasts as long as the novelty does. **VIIII La Soledad** (Solitude) shows a person living on the edge of the community. Such people are considered idiots, crazy, witches, or at best, absent-minded sages following their ideas or hiding some valuable treasure. **X El Apetito** (The Appetite)

reflects a readiness for celebrations in an atmosphere in which any scene, however excessive, seems normal. **XI La Fuerza** (Fortitude) shows a woman who, in the middle of a male-dominated universe, ends up winning the man and keeping him at her feet.

THIRD ROW: **XII El Caido** (The Fallen Man) is undeserving of a wife because he is not willing to work hard, or is not well off or even from a good family. **XIII La Muerte** (Death) is in ordinary clothes, a part of life everywhere. **XIIII La Piedad** (Piety) shows generosity, hospitality, and solidarity fused with compassion and piety. **XV El Errante** (The Wanderer) is feared by peasants, as calamity goes with him. **XVI La Torre** (The Tower) demonstrates that people resort to their religious faith when natural disasters occur.

BOTTOM ROW: **XVII La Espera** (Hope), along with optimism, a passion for life, and dreams, lives on despite the hard realities of everyday life. **XVIII El Olvido** (Oblivion) is as serious for a people as for individuals. **XVIIII Los Compinches** (The Accomplices) are those who share everything. The only things sacred to them are the family and secrets—those who give them away are spurned and given the nickname of "Toad." **Sota de Lágrimas** (Page of Tears). **Reina de Mariposas** (Queen of Butterflies).

THE FOOL.   THE MAGE.   THE EMPRESS.   THE EMPEROR.   THE HIEROPHANT.

Mage: The Ascension Tarot   Nicky Rea and Jackie Cassada, designers, Joshua Gabriel Timbrook, Alex Sheikman, John Cobb, Larry McDougall, and Dan Smith, published by White Wolf, 1995   Quotes are from the book accompanying the deck.

0 THE FOOL is called "the child of Dreaming." A sword is in his right hand and a wilted rose in his left. **I THE MAGE** grasps the "wand of Prime, closing the link between the energy that gives him the power of Magick and the tools that lie before him on the table of the world." The tools

include the sigils of the four suits of the deck. **III THE EMPRESS** is Heasha Morninglade, enthroned upon the World Tree. Her scepter is of the moon, which channels to her the feminine principle of cyclic movement. The cauldron holds the red fluid of birth and rebirth. **IV THE EMPEROR** is the lord of reason, Caeron Mustai. His sword symbolizes the power of active will, and the mountains behind him symbolize logic. **V THE HIEROPHANT** has at his waist the keys to conscious and unconscious thought. Two men kneel before him, one holding a rose, the other holding a lily.

THE LOVERS.   STRENGTH.   DEATH.   TEMPERANCE.   THE STAR.

LUNA.   THE SUN.   GAIA.   QUEEN OF DYNAMISM.   KNIGHT OF DYNAMISM.

PAGE OF QUESTING.   KNIGHT OF PRIMORDIALISM.   QUEEN OF PATTERN.

Mage: The Ascension Tarot *(continued)*   TOP ROW: **VI THE LOVERS** flank a hookah from which an angelic spirit rises. **VIII STRENGTH** shows a burly woman wrestling a dragonish beast in a pool of slime. The animal represents the bestial and tainted sides of her nature. **XIII DEATH** depicts an elegant couple behind a board holding chess pieces. Behind the curtain is a stormy landscape. **XIV TEMPERANCE** depicts Saulot "tempering the essence of life with the flow of conscious and unconscious wisdom." The fluid that flows between the cups is half red and half blue. **XVII THE STAR** shines on the "eternal maiden" pouring the blue water of inspiration into the pool of the unconscious and the red essence of the five senses onto the earth. In the background is the "meditative phoenix, representative of instinct and the indestructible soul."

SECOND ROW: **XVIII LUNA.** A woman sinks into a pool that may be "the blood of her inner beasts" or "the depths of imaginative vision." Two apelike dogs are near the "swords of matter and spirit." **XIX THE SUN,** one of the brighter cards of the deck, shows a child naked and unafraid. On the grass is a toy horse and a wizard's hat and wand. **XXI GAIA** is the unity of the material world with the spiritual. **QUEEN OF DYNAMISM** is called Medea. The sword before her is a "vision of her bloody past." The green figures swirling about her are "her airy messengers of thought." **KNIGHT OF DYNAMISM** "visits destruction upon the pitiful fruits of prideful creation."

BOTTOM ROW: **PAGE OF QUESTING** is "The Apprentice," with the bones of her past life. Her robes mean pure intent, and the bones symbolize triumph over the limitations of mortality. **IV (of Questing).** A creature part man, part skeleton plays "the song of celebration" on a flute. The arch bones are old ideas; they merge with the contents of the cups, the rose of purity and the flowers of sensation. **KNIGHT OF PRIMORDIALISM** submerges itself and others into dreams and nightmares of emotion and desire. **QUEEN OF PATTERN** wears the "mask of enlightened sight, intimately connected to the throne through which her power flows." **II (of Pattern)** shows a "willworker" maintaining spiritual and physical in equilibrium.

Manara: The Erotic Tarot   Milo Manara, Lo Scarabeo, 2000

Mandala Astrological Tarot   A.T. Mann, Harper & Row, 1987   Descriptions are based on the book by A.T. Mann.

TOP ROW: **0 FOOL** shows a circular "jacket" and a wheel of fortune joined to create the symbol of infinity. The sun and the moon show the male and female qualities in everyone. **II HIGH PRIESTESS** has a color motif of blue and indigo, symbolic of the moon. The horns and orb of Isis, the arch of the lunar cycle, the white and black pillars, the lotus, the crab, and the camel are all lunar symbols. **III EMPRESS** has a shield bearing a regal eagle of rebirth, symbolic of the earth mysteries, and a crown of twelve stars, showing that she produces all souls. The red robe in front is covered with all-seeing eyes. The harvested sheaf and the upturned lunar crescent show that leaving the womb is a sacrifice required in order to dominate the baser instincts of life during the spiritual quest. **VI LOVERS.** A circle of twelve flaming apples indicates temptations of desire. The white rose and the red rose, and the symbols beneath them, symbolize a virgin and a temptress.

SECOND ROW: **VII CHARIOT** is driven by the mind, drawn by two sphinxes of the emotions. The walled city shows that past patterns result in stagnation. **IX HERMIT.** A striped staff bridges the space between a barren tree and a fruitful tree. The rainbow veil of the illusory pictures of the world hangs from the staff. **XII HANGED MAN.** An inverted triangle and cross represent the element of sulphur and spiritual humanity trapped by, and suspended from, reality. The arched zodiac is time, which contains and limits one. **XIII DEATH** shows the triangle of growth, maturity, and decay that governs all life, within which the lotus of wholeness grows from a skull atop a turtle, symbol of the soul's resurrection.

THIRD ROW: **XIV TEMPERANCE.** The spiraling snake of time enwraps the winged Venusian love symbol, showing the eternal nature of true love. The transforming Aquarian fluid poured between vessels represents the fertilizing energy passing from male to female. **XVI TOWER** shows the top of the phallic tower sheared off. The falling figures show that the desire to keep issues of duality within leads to separation and breakdown. The streaming eyes are the

Tarocchi Marvel The superheroes of the Tarocchi Marvel are based on the characters of the Marvel comic book studios. Artist Claudio Villa drew the cartoons, which he and Luca Poli colored in. The twenty-two-card deck is accompanied by a title card and a card giving the names of the heroes on each card. Tarocchi Marvel was published by Lo Scarabeo of Turin in 1995. The backs show a double-ended picture of Dr. Strange, who is also pictured on I Il Mago.

Masquerade Tarot In the Masquerade Tarot, the only face "deprived" of a mask is that of the artist, Martin, whose profile is shown in the suit of coins. As the booklet accompanying the deck says, "The faces without features or expression and covered by the same masque signify that it is up to the Questioner…to decide which features will be given to each character and, consequently, to his or her own destiny. Behind a mask is actually whatever each Questioner wants to find out, good or evil, feeling absolutely free to make his or her own choice." U.S. Games Systems of Stamford, Connecticut,

published the Masquerade Tarot in 1995. The deck includes a title card and an introductory card. The back design is a harlequin pattern in red, white, and black.

Master Tarot "This is a work for the Master Jesus," says the booklet that accompanies the Master Tarot, "not an exercise in Christianity, or in Gnosticism, or any other religion, whether 'new age' or traditional." The twenty-two Major cards of the Master Tarot are often, but not always, parallel to the traditional Major Arcana. Instead of Minor Arcana, the deck has forty Minor cards and sixteen People cards. The Minor cards are based on sayings of Jesus; People cards each express "a psychological, physiognomic, cultural, and spiritual type." The back design is blue speckled with white, and the deck includes two advertising cards and a booklet by Mario Montano. The Master Tarot was illustrated by Amerigo Folchi, whose signature appears on each card, under direction of Mario Montano. It was published by AGMüller of Neuhausen, Switzerland, in 1996.

Masquerade Tarot　Martin, U.S. Games Systems, 1995

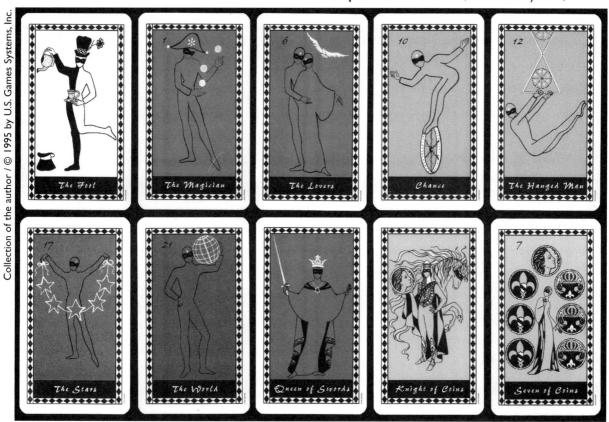

archetypal world of the divine as twenty-two ways of seeing the next stage of the quest. **XVIII MOON** indicates a sensitivity to moral choices, indicated by the black and white dogs within the pyramids of prejudice and convention. **XIX SUN.** Sunflowers follow the sun's movement across the sky, as the spiritual path must be followed for life to be full. The Gemini symbol is squared in the circle of the integration of

opposites, and is itself within a circular wreath of the yearly process of nature governed and fueled by the sun.

BOTTOM ROW: **XX JUDGEMENT** shows fire, the energy of heaven, shattering structures in order to unite humanity. In the coffin, symbols of male, female, and a central child, unity, float on the unconscious. **WAND FIVE. CUP FOUR. PENTACLE KING.**

Tarocchi Marvel Claudio Villa and Luca Poli, Lo Scarabeo, 1995

TOP ROW: 0 IL MATTO (The Fool; Wolverine). I IL MAGO (The Magician; Dr. Strange). II LA PAPESSA (The Popess; Storm). III L'IMPERATRICE (The Empress; Invisible Woman). IV L'IMPERATORE (The Emperor; Mr. Fantastic).

SECOND ROW: V IL PAPA (The Pope; Professor X). VI GLI AMANTI (The Lovers; Spiderman and Mary Jane). VII IL CARRO (The Chariot; Ghost Rider). VIII LA GIUSTIZIA (Justice; Daredevil). IX L'EREMITA (The Hermit; Silver Surfer).

THIRD ROW: X LA RUOTA (The Wheel; Longshot). XI LA FORZA (Strength; Hulk). XII L'APPESO (The Hanged Man; Nightcrawler). XIV LA TEMPERANZA (Temperance; Scarlet Witch). XVI LA TORRE (The Tower; Baxter Building).

BOTTOM ROW: XVII LA STELLA (The Star; Dazzler). XVIII LA LUNA (The Moon; Moon Knight). XIX IL SOLE (The Sun; Thor). XX IL GIUDIZIO (Judgment; The Punisher). XXI IL MONDO (The World; Captain America).

420

O	I	II	III	IV
Der Komet The Comet	Der Menschensohn The Son of Man	Der Engel The Angel	Die Mutter The Mother	Der Vater The Father

V	VII	IX	X	XI
Der Tempel The Temple	Magdalena Magdalen	Die Jünger The Disciples	Das Wunder The Miracle	Vergebung Forgiving

XII	XIV	XV	XIX	XXI
Die Peitsche The Whip	Liebet einander Love one another	Der Kuss The Kiss	Der Geist The Spirit	Die Galaxis The Galaxy

Master Tarot   Amerigo Folchi, artist, and Mario Montano, AGMüller, 1996   The caption is based on the booklet by Mario Montano.

TOP ROW: **0 The Comet** is carrier of a divine seed, cosmic announcer of good news to come. **I The Son of Man** is the promise of our own divinity. **II The Angel** is guidance from a higher dimension. **III The Mother** is Mary, who is in us when we unconditionally give. **IV The Father** is Joseph, simple, yet deeply intelligent, our trusted guide, our faithful friend.

SECOND ROW: **V The Temple** has at its door two soldiers, a priest, and a merchant. It is the power of institutions, of society, to coerce and condition. **VII Magdalen** stands for the whole journey from Eros to unconditional Love. **IX The Disciples** come when touched by the love of the Master and when ready to learn and grow. **X The Miracle** shows a blind man who can suddenly see; healing occurs when the sufferer no longer sees any value in

pain. **XI Forgiving** shows the adulteress chased by the mob, and shown mercy and forgiveness. Forgiving is the very melting of sin before the warmth of love.

BOTTOM ROW: **XII The Whip** refers to the story of Jesus driving the merchants and money-changers from the temple. It's time for a confrontation with a "religion" that has betrayed its Master. **XIV Love one another** shows Jesus washing the feet of his disciples, demonstrating the commitment to serve others. **XV The Kiss** is the kiss of Judas, which he used to betray Christ to the Roman soldiers. It symbolizes the ego, which betrays us through self-deception and impossible guarantees of control and independence and safety. **XIX The Spirit** shows the spirit of God descending as flames. It is the time of fulfillment of our spiritual search into an experience of transpersonal oneness. **XXI The Galaxy** is the symbol of the greater whole that surrounds us.

| Die Lilien | Liebe deinen Feind | Der Geliebte | Barabbas | Der Nächste |
| The Lilies | Love Your Enemy | The Beloved | Barabbas | The Neighbour |

Master Tarot (*continued*)   **1 The Lilies** refers to Luke 12:29: "Consider the lilies of the field, how they grow: they toil not, neither do they spin, yet I say to you that Solomon in all his glory was not arrayed like one of these." **16 Love Your Enemy** illustrates Matthew 5:44: "Ye have heard it said, Thou shalt love they neighbor and hate thine enemy. But I say unto you, Love your enemies…" **The Beloved** is at once the archetype of the Lover, the Disciple, and the Mystic. He imbibes the Master's every word. **Barabbas** is the archetype of the criminal whom the crowd loves and absolves. He is a symbol of the crowd's utter senselessness and of its short-lived illusion of power. **The Neighbour** is the Good Samaritan of the Parable. He is the one who feeds us when we're in need, loves us when we cannot love ourselves, gives us of his life when our life is withering, of his energy until we get back our own and doesn't ask for gratitude.

Tarot Médiéval   The Tarot Médiéval was illustrated by Pal Degome under direction of Nina Montangero. Degome says, "Creating a tarot has been a dream of mine since I was a child. For it, I put myself in the skin of a painter of the middle ages. I made a voyage to the châteaux of the Loire, Venice, Seville, Switzerland, France, etc." Many of the pips are also inspired by the Rider-Waite Tarot. Montangero chose to create a medieval tarot because, "For me, the medieval epoque is mysterious…. Also, the châteaux have always fascinated me, as well as the clothes people wore in that period."

The deck was published by Editions Indigo-Montangero in Montreaux, Switzerland, in 2002. The backs show an abstract design in white on brown. The deck includes two versions of Major Arcana II and a blank card, and is packaged with a book by Montangero.

Medieval Cat Tarot   Lawrence Teng celebrates the glory of felines with Renaissance flair in the seventy-eight cards of Medieval Cat Tarot. The ornate deck seeks to bridge the gap between past and present by blending classical and contemporary ideologies along with artistic styles. The result is an aristocratic deck with a humorous twist. The deck includes a booklet of instructions. It was published in 2004 by U.S. Games Systems of Stamford, Connecticut.

Merlin Tarot   The Merlin Tarot is drawn from medieval manuscripts of the British tales of Merlin. The main sources were Geoffrey of Monmouth's *Vita Merlini* (Life of Merlin) and the twelfth-century *Prophecies of Merlin*. The Major Arcana are renumbered. The suits are birds (swords), serpents (wands), fishes (cups), and beasts (pentacles). Pips two through ten have line drawings of the suit sign in Celtic style. The deck was conceived by R.J. Stewart and illustrated by Miranda Gray. It was first published in 1992 by Aquarian Press of England, and reprinted by Element Books, London, in 2002.

Merlusine Tarot   The Merlusine Tarot was designed by Charles Pasino and hand-printed by Moretti Editeur, Paris. The full title of the deck is "Le Vrai Conte Merlusine Jeu du Tarot" (The True Merlusine Fairy Tale Game of Tarot). The coloring is done by stencil, recalling antique Tarot of Marseilles decks. Merlusine (Melusine, Melusina), in the tale, was transformed once a week into a creature half-woman, half-fish. She wed a man, under condition that he not look at her the night of her transformation, or she would have to leave him. Of course, this being a tale of destiny, he broke his promise, and the couple were split. The deck has French suits and is intended, the presentation card says, for the game of tarot. It was issued in 1996 in a signed and numbered limited edition of 300. The maker's or artist's name appears on VII, X, King of Spades, Knight of Clubs, and Knight of Diamonds.

Merlusine Tarot title card and presentation card

Tarot Médiéval Pal Degome, artist, and Nina Montangero Montangero directed Degome to make two versions of Major Arcana II: La Papesse (The Popess) and La Gitane (The Gypsy). "For me, she brings out in us the 'Gypsy,' the side that is feminine, sensual, charming, the side that is provocative."

Medieval Cat Tarot   Lawrence Teng, U.S. Games Systems, 2004

I MOON	II SUN	III STAR	IV FORTUNE	V JUSTICE
VI JUDGEMENT	VII FOOL	VIII MAGICIAN	IX CHARIOT	XIII HANGED MAN
XV INNOCENT	XVI TEMPERANCE	XVII EMPEROR	XVIII STRENGTH	XIX EMPRESS
XXI PRIESTESS	Suffering	ACE	FISHES	BEASTS

Merlin Tarot   Miranda Gray, artist, and R.J. Stewart, Element Books, 2002

Merlusine Tarot   Charles Pasino and Moretti Editeur, published by the artists, 1996

Merryday Tarot Louisa Poole, Jackie and Rick McCabe, 1997

Merryday Tarot The intricate and colorful illustrations of the Merryday Tarot are by Louisa Poole. The deck blends various traditions in its symbolism. The suit of swords is Oriental, wands are African, cups are Native American, and pentacles are European. The Major Arcana draw from the magical culture of unicorns and dragons, as well as North American images. The deck was published in 1997 by Jackie and Rick McCabe of Salem, Massachusetts.

Millennium Tarot The Millennium Tarot by Amerigo Folchi was published by Altenburger und Stralsunder Spielkarten (ASS) Verlag of Germany. The Major Arcana, courts, and aces depict people who had an impact on the (mostly Western) world during the millennium of 1000 to 2000 CE. Some of the associations are baffling, such as Mozart for XV The Devil and Louis Pasteur for V The Hierophant. Leonardo da Vinci gets two cards: I and VI (The Lovers as Mona Lisa). The designs are based on the Rider-Waite Tarot. The cards are titled in German, and the back design is a double-ended rendition of 0 The Fool. The artist is not credited on the packaging, but was identified by K. Frank Jensen by the style and the initials in the lower right corner of most of the cards. The deck includes two advertising cards.

Tarocco Mitologico (Mythological Tarot) Amerigo Folchi illustrated the Mythological Tarot with figures from classical Greek and Roman mythology. The figures, rendered in pale colors, are silhouetted against abstract backgrounds. The deck was published by Italcards of Bologna in 1988, in a limited edition of 3,000 numbered copies. An interesting feature of the deck is the fabric-covered box and sleeve. The cards are titled in Italian and English. The deck includes an advertising card and a presentation card, as well as a booklet in Italian and English. The back design is double-ended, showing an Ionic column and the maker's name.

Other decks by Amerigo Folchi
in *The Encyclopedia of Tarot*, volume IV, are:
Tarocco di Afrodite • Colori della Toscana
Tarocco di Amerigo Folchi • Fontane Divinitore
Master Tarot (with Mario Montano) • Millenium Tarot
Tarocco Mitologico • Tarocco del Mondo Nuovo
Omaggio a Galileo Chini • Tarocchi di Sissi
Folchi decks featured in volume III are:
Happiness Tarot (Tarocco della Felicita)
Homage to Erté (Ommagio a Erté)
Pistoia Tarot (Tarocco storica del Palio di Pistoia).

Tarocco del Mondo Nuovo (Tarot of the New World) "I began my life as a sailor at a very early age, and have continued to live as a sailor up to this day. Those who lead this profession are driven by a desire to know the world's secrets." Amerigo Folchi uses this quote from Christopher Columbus to parallel the explorer of the "new world," the Americas, with "the reader confronting these magical cards, placing himself before them in a querying frame of mind and undertaking a fascinating new voyage which will lead him toward knowledge." Folchi goes on to say, "The navigator who explores that infinite and unknown ocean is himself the guide, the hermit who has abandoned dogma, dedicating himself in great faith to the search for truth."

The Major Arcana feature allegorical figures and the "conquistadors" of the American continents. The suit of swords focuses on the European coats of arms; the wands on maps of the world; the cups on animals, especially marine; and the coins on pre-Columbian artifacts. The deck was published by Italcards in 1991 and includes a title card, a presentation card, and a descriptive leaflet by the artist. Titles are in Italian, Spanish, English, and French. The back design shows a coat of arms on blue and "ITALCARDS" at top and bottom.

Tarot of a Moon Garden "From time immemorial, humanity has gazed at the changing phases of the moon and imagined magical seas and gardens on its surface," reads the booklet that accompanies Tarot of a Moon Garden. "…From these magical images, the whimsical symbols used in the Tarot of a Moon Garden have emerged." The paintings are by Karen Marie Sweikhardt. A title card and a card reading "Welcome to a Realm where Myth and Magic Are the Reality," are included. The deck was published in 1993 by U.S. Games Systems, Stamford, Connecticut. The double-ended back design shows a garden in the moonlight.

Millennium Tarot   Amerigo Folchi, Altenburger und Stralsunder Spielkarten, 1999

O · IL MATTO	I · IL BAGATTO	II · LA PAPESSA	III · L'IMPERATRICE	IV · L'IMPERATORE
THE FOOL	THE MAGICIAN	THE HIGH PRIESTESS	THE EMPRESS	THE EMPEROR

VI · L'INNAMORATO	VIII · LA GIUSTIZIA	IX · L'EREMITA	X · LA RUOTA DELLA FORTUNA	XII · L'APPESO
THE LOVER	JUSTICE	THE HERMIT	THE WHEEL OF FORTUNE	THE HANGED MAN

XV · IL DIAVOLO	XVI · LA TORRE	XVII · LA STELLA	XVIII · LA LUNA	XIX · IL SOLE
THE DEVIL	THE TOWER	THE STAR	THE MOON	THE SUN

XX · IL GIUDIZIO	XXI · IL MONDO	SEI DI SPADE	SETTE DI COPPE	SEI DI DENARI
JUDGMENT	THE WORLD	SIX OF SWORDS	SEVEN OF CUPS	SIX OF PENTACLES

Tarocco Mitologico (Mythological Tarot)   Amerigo Folchi, Italcards, 1988 The caption is based on the booklet, by Andrea Gamboni, that accompanies the deck.

TOP ROW: **0 The Fool.** Dionysus is symbol of nature's energy. **I The Magician** is Narcissus, symbolizing the child who believes that he is all-powerful and self-sufficient. **II The High Priestess.** Medea dismembers her brother Apsyrtus. **III The Empress.** Rhea, shelters the child Zeus from his destructive father Cronos. **IV The Emperor.** Prometheus steals fire to benefit the human race.

SECOND ROW: **VI The Lover.** Paris chooses Aphrodite as the most beautiful goddess. **VIII Justice** is Athena; her shield with the head of Medusa shows victory over beastly instincts. **IX The Hermit** is Theseus looking into the darkness of the labyrinth. **X The Wheel of Fortune.** Tyche, goddess of fortune, steers the boat of life. **XII The**

Tarocco del Mondo Nuovo (Tarot of the New World)   Amerigo Folchi, Italcards, 1991

Hanged Man. Prometheus must suffer an eagle tearing his innards, in punishment for stealing fire from the gods.

THIRD ROW: **XV The Devil.** The Minotaur lives in the labyrinth and eats young men and women. **XVI The Tower** depicts Bellophoron thrown by Pegasus. He is trying to reach Olympus. **XVII The Star** shows Venus led to trysts by the star Esperus. **XVIII The Moon** is Selene, who goes every

night to see her beloved asleep in a cave on Mount Latmos. **XIX The Sun** shows Apollo, god of intellect and of beneficial human activity.

BOTTOM ROW: **XX Judgment** shows Eos, goddess of dawn. **XXI The World** is carried by Atlas. Two lovers are enclosed in it. **Six of Swords. Seven of Cups. Six of Pentacles.**

Tarot of a Moon Garden   Karen Marie Sweikhardt, U.S. Games Systems, 1993

Collection of the author / © 1989 by Ignacio Garcia

Tarot Murciano Ignacio Garcia, Ars Gratia Artis, 1989

Tarot Murciano The Tarot Murciano draws from the landmarks, culture, mythology, and history of the Murcia region of southeast Spain, on the Mediterranean Sea. The twenty-two-card deck was illustrated by Ignacio Garcia, and is accompanied by a book by Santiago Delgado. It was published in 1989 by Ars Gratia Artis in a limited edition of 3,000. The titles are in regional dialect. The back design shows a flower vase in silver on red.

Mystic Meg Tarot "Mystic Meg" worked with illustrator Caroline Smith to create the tarot deck that was packaged with her book, *Mystic Meg Tarot: Predictions Made Easy by the World's Best-Known Fortune-Teller*. The deck and book were published in 1997 by Carlton Books, England. The double-ended back design is purple on purple, with birds and the letters "MM." The suits are air (swords), fire (wands), water (cups), and earth (coins). The court cards are king, queen, prince, and princess.

Mystic Meg Tarot   Caroline Smith, artist, and Mystic Meg, Carlton Books, 1997

Tarot Namur   The Tarot Namur was created by Marta Leyrós under direction of Namur Gopalla. The Major Arcana deck was produced in Brazil in 2000 by Academia de Cultura Arcana. The back design shows an N in curved brackets. Two extra cards with the back design printed on both sides are included.

Napo Tarot   The folkways of Argentina are illustrated in the Napo Tarot, created by Betty Lopez with artwork by Napo, both of Argentina. Betty Lopez describes Argentina as "brimming with esoteric possibilities. Our aboriginal mythology, rich and profound, always skirts around mystery, destiny, and hope." The figures are drawn from folk life and archetypes: "The Magus is a 'gaucho,' dressed in rich clothing, living in the country but well established; the Hierophant is the exact figure of the Old Vizcacha, a character from the book *Martin Fierro* by José Hernández, considered as a 'Gaucho Bible'…. In the Death card, the skeletal figure wears vestiges of Indian drawing and the typical clothing of northern Argentina. The face cards get their grace and harmony from the typical representations of the 'show-off,' a character more urban than rural, who handled both the dagger and feelings with the same rapidity." The back design is based on the constellations Three Marias and Southern cross and shows four gold stars on a blue ground. The Napo Tarot was published by U.S. Games Systems of Stamford, Connecticut, in 1998, and the deck includes a title card and an introductory card.

Navigators Tarot of the Mystic SEA   The Navigators Tarot of the Mystic SEA is based on the Order of the Golden Dawn's interpretation of the Kabbalah. The back design is the Tree of Life. The Major Arcana are unnumbered. According to the booklet accompanying the deck, "The sequence of these potent cards has never been adamantly fixed." The sigil of the artist, Julia Turk, is in the lower right corner of each card, with numbers that give the year in which the card was completed. The artist's website states: "In 1988, once again divorced, Julia was involved in a single car off-road wreck, and in gratitude for being unhurt, offered her life to cosmic forces, who instructed her in the form of the Navigator to design a new tarot deck. Julia took up her art again, and used her knowledge of philosophy and magical symbols to write an accompanying book." The deck was published by U.S. Games Systems of Stamford, Connecticut, in 1996. A title card and a card with a poem accompany the deck.

Necromantic Tarot   In celebration of the fifteenth anniversary of Westgate Press, New Orleans, Leilah Wendell, with George Higham, created the Necromantic Tarot. The Major Arcana deck was issued in 1994, in a limited edition of 1,000 decks signed and numbered by the artist. It includes a presentation card.

New Orleans Voodoo Tarot   The New Orleans Voodoo Tarot is illustrated with the practitioners, rites, and metaphysical beings of voodoo as practiced in New Orleans. Louis Martinié collaborated with artist Sallie Ann Glassman to create the deck, which was published in 1992 by Destiny Books of Rochester, Vermont. The deck has seventy-eight card, plus a "Wild Card." The suits of the Minor Arcana are of the three "nations," or traditions of voodoo, plus Santería. Petro, common in Haiti, corresponds to fire; Congo corresponds to water; Rada corresponds to air. Santería, a separate tradition, derives from the Yoruba people of Africa, whereas voodoo looks to the Fon-speaking people of Dahomey, Africa.

The religion of voodoo centers around the *loa*, spirits that traveled from Africa with the people who were enslaved in the New World. The practitioner works to establish close contact with the *loa* so that the spirits will help them. "In New Orleans the *loa* thrived under the general title of Voodoo," says the book accompanying the deck. "Voodoo Tarot is an invocation of the Mysteries or Spirits which are the Voodoo. This Tarot is a tool we offer to these Great Mysteries. Through it They can begin to exercise their powers to teach, advise, and initiate into their deep and ancient wisdom. This Tarot is also a tribute to New Orleans, the Crescent City, at whose steamy breast the essence of Voodoo found nourishment and a link with the postindustrial presence."

Tarot, Death, and the Undead

Many tarot artists choose to give card 13 more "upbeat" titles, such as
Rebirth, Transformation, Reincarnation, and so on.
A few artists, however, prefer to plunge wholeheartedly
into the macabre, not only on card 13, but for the entire deck.
Tarot decks, in this volume, dedicated to death and the undead include:
Clavicle Tarot   •   Dark Shadows Tarot   •   Tarot of the Dead
Death's Tarot   •   Gothic Tarot (Wendell)   •   Gothic Tarot (Mystic Eye)
Gothic Tarot of Vampires   •   Halloween Tarot   •   Haunted Tarot
Londa Tarot   •   H.P. Lovecraft Tarot   •   Necromantic Tarot
Skeleton Tarot   •   Vampire Tarot

Tarot Namur   Marta Leyrós and Namur Gopalla, Academia de Cultura Aracana, 2000

Napo Tarot   Betty Lopez and Napo, artist, U.S. Games Systems, 1998

emanation

FOOL

encapsulation

MAGIAN

conception

EMPRESS

propulsion

EMPEROR

intuition

HIEROPHANT

discrimination

LOVERS

exaltation

HERMIT

rotation

FORTUNE

revelation

STAR

gratification

MOON

organization

SUN

consecration

UNIVERSE

decomposition

PAGE OF SWORDS

cohesion

THREE OF WANDS

seclusion

EIGHT OF CUPS

foundation

THREE OF PENTACLES

Navigators Tarot of the Mystic SEA   Julia Turk, U.S. Games Systems, 1996   The cards are arranged in traditional order.

Necromantic Tarot   Leilah Wendell and George Higham, Westgate Press, 1994
   TOP ROW: 0 Innocence. 1 The Magician. 2 The High Priestess. 3 The Empress. 4 The Emperor.
   SECOND ROW: 5 The Hierophant. 6 The Lovers. 7 The Chariot. 9 The Hermit. 10 The Wheel.
   THIRD ROW: 11 Justice. 13 Death. 14 Temperance. 15 Deception. 16 The Tower.
   BOTTOM ROW: 17 The Star. 18 The Moon. 19 The Sun. 20 Judgement. 21 The World.

New Orleans Voodoo Tarot Louis Martinié and Sallie Ann Glassman, artist, Destiny Books, 1992

TOP ROW: **0 WORLD EGG** forms the center of the Crossroads, the point from which all creation takes its measure. It is the offspring of the holy serpents Ayida Wedo and Damballah Wedo. **I DR. JOHN** was a voodoo practicioner and sacred drummer during the 1800s. His aspect is that of a fierce, free African whose face is tattooed with red and blue lines in the form of snakes. **II MARIE LAVEAU** lived in New Orleans from 1794 to 1881. She is still famous as being among the greatest of Voodoo queens. **XIV TI BON ANGE** (Small Good Angel) is diving into a *canari*, or clay jar, carried by a woman. Each person has a *Ti Bon Ange*, which can be sheltered in a *canari*, in care of a priest or priestess, as protection against malevolence and mishaps. **XVIII MAGICK MIRROR** is surrounded by stars, rising from the blue Waters. Deception and true sight play on its surface, and the *loa* reach out from its depths.

BOTTOM ROW: **SANTERÍA 4: OBATALÁ** is the Orishà (Santería for spirit) of the white road. A wise male elder has the attributes of compassion and coolness. Snails, sacred to Obatalá, crawl on his arm. **CONGO: HOUNSIS** is the wife of a spirit or a male or female voodoo initiate. The *hoursis* provides a spirit with entrance to the safe abode of the *govi*, an earthen vessel used to house *loa* or spirits of the dead. The waters rush and swirl into the *govi*, and a spirit, perhaps that of a dead husband or lover, looks out from the entrance. **PETRO 1: DAMBALLAH LA FLAMBEAU** is a fire-breathing serpent. **RADA 9: MASA** are spirits of the air. They spin the star web that reaches between worlds. **WILD CARD: LES BARONS** belong to and lead the family of Guedeh spirits. They are not spirits of the dead, but the spirit of Death itself. It is traditional that the first male buried in a cemetery be regarded as the Baron, and that the first female be regarded and Manman Brigitte, a powerful *loa*, judge, and lawyer.

New Palladini Tarot David Palladini, the artist of the popular Aquarian Tarot, created the New Palladini Tarot about twenty-five years after his first deck. The images were rendered in magic marker, ink, and pencil on rag paper. He says on the introductory card accompanying the deck, "The cards can only be a tool of introspection, a mirror for one's own development, an occasional counsel and help. That is the spirit in which I wish my decks to be used. Not as a substitute for spirituality, but as an enhancement of belief and faith." The richly colored images have a resemblance to the form of Russian icons, with the features of the people set in static costumes and backgrounds. The symbolism and composition are based on the Rider-Waite deck, with different cultures and backgrounds incorporated. The New Palladini Tarot was published by U.S. Games Systems of Stamford, Connecticut, in 1996. The deck includes a title card and introductory card. The double-ended back design shows a snake, in the form of a figure eight, biting its tail.

New Palladini Tarot David Palladini, U.S. Games Systems, 1996

441

Collection of the author / © 1989 by Clive Barrett

Norse Tarot   Clive Barrett, Thorsons, 1989

Norse Tarot   The gods, sagas and runes from the lives of the Vikings are illustrated in the Norse Tarot, by Clive Barrett. Runes appear at the bottom center of each card. The Major Arcana portray Norse gods, and the Minor Arcana focus on the lives of people. Courts are King, Queen, Prince, and Princess. The deck was published in 1989 by Thorsons of England. It was accompanied by a book by Barrett.

Tarot of Northern Shadows   Sylvia Gainsford, the artist of the Tarot of Northern Shadows, describes her work in the booklet accompanying the deck. "This tarot portrays the roots of Norse and Celtic belief along with the traditions and tales whose origins are lost in the mists of time—shadows of a familiar dream." The court cards of swords portray characters from British Celtic and Continental legend; rods portray Norse gods and goddesses; cups show the heroes from the epic saga *The Mabinogion;* and disks picture Irish Celtic people. The cards also portray friends and family. For example, the King of Discs is Mannan Maclir, the Celtic god of seafarers, and also the artist's father James Gainsford, with the castle of Tonbridge in the background. The deck was published in 1997 by AGMüller of Neuhausen, Switzerland, with titles in German and English. The back design is a black and white Celtic knot.

Tarot Nova   The Tarot Nova was illustrated by Julie Paschkis and designed by Paul Kepple, under direction of Dennis Fairchild. The deck is part of a set that includes a book on palmistry and a booklet on reading the tarot, both by Dennis Fairchild. The cards of the deck are small with charming, naïve pictures. An extra card gives publishing and art credits. The double-ended back design shows a person shuffling cards amidst floral designs, with a sunburst at the center. The set was published in 1996 by Running Press, Philadelphia.

Tarot of Northern Shadows Sylvia Gainsford, AGMüller, 1997

Tarot Nova   Julie Paschkis, artist, Paul Kepple, designer, and Dennis Fairchild, Running Press, 1996

Old English Tarot   Maggie Kneen, artist of the Old English Tarot, used as reference a fourteenth-century manuscript, the *Luttrell Psalter*. The manuscript, which was written and illuminated for a wealthy landowner named Sir Geoffrey Luttrell, provides details of everyday life in medieval times, as well as images of the fantastical creatures of myth. The seventy-eight-card Old English Tarot was published in 1997 by U.S. Games Systems of Stamford, Connecticut. The back design features a lozenge pattern in red and gold.

Tarot of the Old Path   The Tarot of the Old Path is subtitled "A Handbook of Female Wisdom." The name refers to Wicca, or witchcraft, which, the authors say in the booklet accompanying the deck, "should not be confused with Satanism or black magic. It is a beneficial, nature-based religion and philosophy which aims to improve the quality of life." The artwork is by Sylvia Gainsford, in collaboration with Howard Rodway head-

ing the project and with consultants Margot Adler, Lois Bourne, Patricia Crowther, Janet and Stewart Farrar, Aislinn Lester, Pauline Newbery, and Kim Tracey contributing ideas to specific cards. The back design is double-ended, a picture of entwined foliage in green on white. The deck was published by AGMüller, Neuhausen, Switzerland, in 1990.

Olympus Tarot   The mythology of ancient Greece illustrates the Olympus Tarot. The artwork is by Luca Raimondo, and the deck was created and conceived by Manfredi Toraldo.   Titles are in five languages. The Minor Arcana suits are associated with heroes (swords), creatures (wands), places (cups), and objects (pentacles). The Olympus Tarot was published by Lo Scarabeo of Turin, Italy, in 2002. The back design is a blue and white image of a battle scene. A title card and an advertising card are included in the deck.

Old English Tarot   Maggie Kneen, U.S. Games Systems, 1997

Tarot of the Old Path   Howard Rodway, et al, and Sylvia Gainsford, artist, AGMüller, 1990

Olympus Tarot   Luca Raimondo, artist, and Manfredi Toraldo, Lo Scarabeo, 2002   According to the leaflet accompanying the deck, "In the Major Arcana, each archetype [of the tarot] was linked with an Olympic deity.... For example, in the original interpretation of the myth, Zeus was a patriarch but most importantly a man who knew how to adapt to situations and knew how to let his charisma dominate the other gods. Zeus is a transformist, a god who in many cases, in order to follow his own will, did not hesitate to take back his word or deceive his fellow man and put on numerous masks in order to satisfy his carnal and earthly desires. Because of this game of masks and deceit, which is in any case supported by undeniable personal power, Zeus represents the first card of the Major Arcana, The Magician."

447

One World Tarot   The One World Tarot was created by Crystal Love with artwork by her son Michael Hobbs. Hobbs used computer imaging to create the cards. The colors are associated by Love with the planets and signs of the zodiac, and the vivid colors reflect the symbolism of the cards. The court cards show people who blend the races of the world. The back design is a geometric pattern representing the zodiac, in black and white and blue. The One World Tarot was published by U.S. Games Systems in 1999. It includes a presentation card and an introductory card. The book and deck set includes a poster "The Astrological Spread: Reference Card."

Oracle de Giselle Flavie   "This oracle was channeled by Giselle Flavie through inner flashes of insight," says the booklet accompanying the Oracle of Giselle Flavie deck. "All of the Major Arcana are the expression of pure inspiration, painted by an Initiate who has scrupulously reproduced Giselle Flavie's visions in her drawings." The painter is Russian expatriot artist Aniram (Marina spelled backwards) Makowsky. The Major Arcana deck was published by FJP: France Jeux Production, Paris, circa 1997. The deck includes two extra "talisman" cards, which are meant to be cut in half and carried on one's person.

Collection of the author / © 1999 by U.S. Games Systems, Inc.

One World Tarot   Crystal Love and Michael Hobbs, artist, U.S. Games Systems, 1999

Oracle de Giselle Flavie   Giselle Flavie and Aniram Makowsky, artist, FJP: France Jeux Production, circa 1997

Tarot of the Origins   Tarot of the Origins depicts native people who seem intrinsically part of the earth that surrounds them. Sergio Toppi created the deck. The four suits are given colors which "refer to different meanings and messages in an essential, instinctive world," as the leaflet accompanying the deck explains. The soul suit (cups) is blue for night: dreams, meditation, and spirituality. The jewels suit (pentacles) is yellow for the radiance of daylight, energy, and material existence. The nature suit (wands) is green for harmony, tranquility, and life. The blood suit (swords) is red for aggressiveness, survival, instinct, and action. The court cards are man, woman, animal, child. The deck includes a title card and advertising card, and the cards are titled in Italian, French, Spanish, English, German, and Flemish. The full deck was published by Lo Scarabeo, Turin, Italy, in 2000.

Lo Scarabeo issued Tarocchi delle Origini as a larger Major Arcana deck in 1989, with titles in Italian and a title card. A smaller, English-language Major Arcana deck, accompanied by a title card and a card with a poem printed on it, was published in 1991.

Tarot of the Orishàs   The Tarot of the Orishàs was created by Zolrak and illustrated by Dürkön. It is based on the African-Brazilian religion of Santería. The Orishás are animist spirits or deities of the Yoruba religion, brought by enslaved Africans to South America and blended, or syncretized, with Roman Catholic saints. Zolrak, in the book accompanying the deck, distinguishes Santería from Voodoo: "The primary difference between the two religions is that Santería is against black magic." Although the imagery and rites are similar, "Santería does not have chaotic or evil forces in its pantheon." The deck is not traditional, but many of the cards correspond to traditional tarot decks. There are twenty-five Principle cards, many of which correspond to Major Arcana cards. The suits are named for the four elements, with cards numbered ace through ten and two more cards: element and messenger. Titles are in English, Spanish, and Portuguese. The deck was published by Llewellyn Publications, St. Paul, in 2000.

Osho Zen Tarot   The Osho Zen Tarot is based on the teachings of Osho, also known as Rajneesh (1931–1990). An extra card with the deck, titled Master, is a portrait of Osho. The book accompanying the deck says, "Ultimately, Osho concentrates on transmitting the unique wisdom of Zen, because, he says, Zen is the one spiritual tradition whose approach to the inner life of human beings has weathered the test of time and is still relevant to contemporary humanity." The illustrations are by Ma Deva Padma. The deck was originally published by Boxtree of Great Britain, and was republished by St. Martin's Press, New York City, in 1994.

Tarot of Oz   David Sexton illustrates in the Tarot of Oz the adventures of Dorothy, from the books by Frank Baum, written between 1900 and 1920. The story begins when Dorothy is taken by a cyclone from her small Kansas farm to the magical land of Oz. Of the parallel between the Baum stories and the tarot, Sexton writes, "Though much has been made of her destination—usually the Emerald City, capital of Oz—the point of these stories is the lessons she learns along the way. The tarot, like the Yellow Brick Road, is another form the path of enlightenment may take." The back design is a monogram of Oz with the four suit signs. The Major Arcana and court cards show the names of the characters they portray in addition to the tarot title. The Tarot of Oz was published by Llewellyn Publications, St. Paul, Minnesota, in 2002. The deck is accompanied by a book by David Sexton and includes two cards showing the "Yellow Brick Road Spread."

Tarot of Oz   Some of the most well-known characters are: **0 The Fool: Dorothy** heads down the perilous and powerful path of yellow bricks with her beloved dog Toto right behind her. **4 The Emperor: The Tin Woodman** was originally Nick Chopper, a human, but is replaced by tin as an ax cursed by a witch chops off parts of him. As the Tinman he has no heart until the Wizard restores it to him, and he becomes Emperor of the Winkies, who revere him as a kind and strong ruler. **8 Strength: The Cowardly Lion** is a huge and powerful beast, but without courage, sheer brute force is useless.

Pagan Tarot   The Pagan Tarot, also called Tarot 2000, has illustrations by Rosemarie Lewsey, made under direction of Robin Payne. The tarot was created under inspiration of Renaissance tarot and minchiate decks, which featured ancient Greco-Roman deities on the *triumphi*. The book accompanying the deck gives a sonnet for each Major Arcana card. The set was published in 1999 by Alexander Associates of Cornwall, England.

Tarot of the Origins Sergio Toppi, Lo Scarabeo, 2000

Tarot of the Orishàs Zolrak and Dürkön, artist, Llewellyn Publications, 1994 The correspondences of the cards to Major Arcana are found in the book that accompanies the deck.

TOP ROW: **The Babalorisha** (The Magician) is a priest. He controls the elements through the power conferred by his guardian angel. **Oshun** (The Priestess) is known as the "Great Magician," because she is able to plead successfully with her father, Oshala. **Oshala** (The Emperor) is the father of all the saints. **The Couple** (The Lovers). **Oba** (The Chariot) cut off one of her ears to feed her husband, against his wishes. She is syncretized with Joan of Arc.

SECOND ROW: **Elebba** (Strength) is the patron of all doors and of roads. Therefore, the magic keys to open the

Osho Zen Tarot   Ma Deva Padma, artist, and Osho International Foundation, St. Martin's Press, 1994

most inviolable locks and the permits to walk the different paths that humanity will travel belong to him. **Xapana-Shapana** (The Hermit) is known as the saint who cures plagues and smallpox. They say that he covers his body so completely because of the marks left by eruption pustules. **Oshumare** (Wheel of Fortune) represents the union of sky, earth, and water. She therefore meddles with all three, and has the power of transmutation and change. **Shango** (Justice). His power resides in the stones, and he is as imperturbable as they are. This would appear to give him certain

rigidity, but law or justice, while it must be tolerated, is also rigid in its scale of values, where ethics plays a leading role. **The Enslaved Prisoner** (Hanged Man) represents any person who has been persecuted because of his or her ideas or thinking.

THIRD ROW: **Iku** (Death). **The Guardian Angel** (Temperance). **The Sun. The Earth** (The World). **The Fire Element.**

BOTTOM ROW: **Salamanders. IX of Fire. III of Water. Messenger from Earth. IV of Earth.**

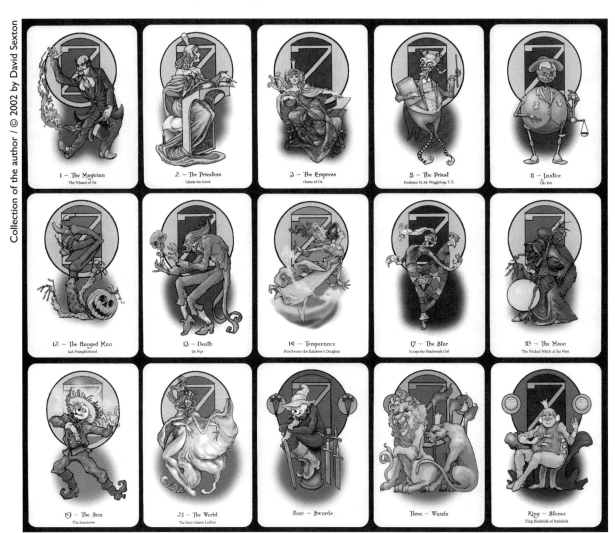

1 – The Magician
The Wizard of Oz

2 – The Priestess
Glinda the Good

3 – The Empress
Ozma of Oz

5 – The Priest
Professor H. M. Wogglebug, T. E.

11 – Justice
Tik-Tok

12 – The Hanged Man
Jack Pumpkinhead

13 – Death
Dr. Pipt

14 – Temperance
Polychrome the Rainbow's Daughter

17 – The Star
Scraps the Patchwork Girl

18 – The Moon
The Wicked Witch of the West

19 – The Sun
The Scarecrow

21 – The World
The Fairy Queen Lurline

Four ~ Swords

Three ~ Wands

King ~ Stones
King Rinkitink of Rinkitink

Tarot of Oz David Sexton, Llewellyn Publications, 2002
The descriptions are based on those in David Sexton's booklet, which accompanies the deck.

TOP ROW: **1 The Magician: The Wizard of Oz** is Oscar Zoraster Diggs, a charlatan who becomes a real magician. Oftentimes the act of imagining ourselves as something new is the most powerful form of magic. **2 The Priestess: Glinda the Good** is the ruler of Quadling Country. Her Great Book of Records shows every event that takes place in Oz and elsewhere. She is immensely powerful, but she rarely intervenes in the sights she sees in her book. **3 The Empress: Ozma of Oz** was designated to rule Oz, but the witch Mombi transformed her into a boy. After she regains her rightful form, she appears to be a little girl, but rules with a wisdom far beyond her years. **5 The Priest: Professor H.M. Wogglebug, T.E.** began life as a lowly bug, but one day he crawled up on a projection screen. When the screen projected him giant-sized on the wall, he stepped off as an amazing new creature and earned his title H.M.: Highly Magnified. The T.E. stands for "Thoroughly Educated." **11 Justice: Tik-tok** is a mechanical man.

SECOND ROW: **12 The Hanged Man: Jack Pumpkinhead,** though not the brightest resident of Oz, is one of the sweetest, and he has sacrificed himself many times to save his friends. Whenever harm befalls him he has only to carve himself a fresh head and he's good as new. **13 Death: Dr. Pipt** is an evil magician who is yet responsible for giving life to many of the most beloved beings of Oz, including Patchwork Girl and Jack Pumpkinhead. That an evil magician would be responsible for such good is a paradox, not unlike the paradox represented by the Death card itself. **14 Temperance: Polychrome the Rainbow's Daughter** often dances off the rainbow to accompany Dorothy and her companions. She uses her abilities to heal her comrades. **17 The Star: Scraps the Patchwork Girl** was created by the wife of Dr. Pipt to be a mindless servant. However, she received extra brains just before she was brought to life and ended up escaping servitude to become one of the most famous residents of the Land of Oz. **18 The Moon: The Wicked Witch of the West** ruthlessly pursues Dorothy in vengeance for the killing of her sister and the theft of the magic shoes. She blocks Dorothy from following the Yellow Brick Road; so the Moon challenges us to step off the more obvious paths and learn from the dark forests that surround our yellow brick roads.

BOTTOM ROW: **19 The Sun: The Scarecrow** realized his intellectual limitations as a scarecrow hanging in a field, when he pondered the mysteries of life. Once he received his "official" brain, he became the most consulted person in Oz. **21 The World: The Fairy Queen Lurline** is the mythical creator of Oz. **Four - Swords. Three - Wands** shows the cowardly lion with Gugu the panther king. **King - Stones: King Rinkitink of Rinkitink** is the jolly ruler of a kingdom across the Deadly Desert from Oz.

Pagan Tarot   Rosemarie Lewsey, artist, and Robin Payne, Alexander Associates, 1999

Tarocchi di Paracelso The Tarot of Paracelsus was designed by Arrigo Pecchioli, executed by ltalo Curzio and Mario Rivosecchi, and published by Antonio Delfino Editore of Rome. The deck was issued in 1993 in an edition limited to 1,000 copies and intended primarily for distribution to the medical establishment.

The deck commemorates the fifth centenary of the birth of Theophrastus Phillippus Aureolus Bombastus von Hohenheim, known as Paracelsus. He lived in Germany from 1493 to 1541, and was a medical doctor, surgeon, philologist, astrologist, botanist, alchemist, theologist, and magician. His mentor was Johannes Tritheminus, an alchemist and scholar of the "cursed sciences," as they were called by some.

Paracelsus lived when classical rationalism co-existed with the belief that unseen forces and essences could be harnessed to serve humans. "Traditional alchemy did include a belief in the transmutation of the base metals to gold, but more important was the separation by chemical means of the pure essence of a substance from its impurities. Through such processes (frequently through distillation) the true divine signatures impressed on earthly things by the Creator for their proper use (and then lost at the time of the Fall) might be rediscovered. In this fashion we would learn more of our Creator while recovering His gifts through our labor. Surely we could expect to find substances of medicinal value in this way." (From "Paracelsus and the Medical Revolution of the Renaissance," by Dr. Allen G. Debus, University of Chicago.)

The Major Arcana are renderings of the alchemical symbols in the 1532 Salomone Trismosin manuscript *Splendor Solis*. The Minor Arcana pips feature suit symbols, and the courts show representations of the rank. The deck includes a title card and a card showing a black and white line drawing of Paracelsus. The double-ended back design shows black, red, and white birds intertwined on a background of gold, with a monogram of the publisher in the center.

Tarot de Paris "The Tarot de Paris is the progeny of a twenty-one-year gestation period, compiled from more than 3,500 photographs taken during hundreds of miles of trekking back and forth across the city." J. Philip Thomas began the Tarot de Paris in 1981.

Thomas was inspired to create the tarot one morning when he faced the Grand Palais. "I was momentarily stunned by an intense light that was streaming out through a wreath held high by a female statue, riding in a horse-drawn chariot that seemed to be leaping right off the façade of the building…. In that flashing moment I had a vision of all the Major Arcana cards as a sequence of statues, located somewhere in Paris."

The first set of Paris Major Arcana designs was featured in volume III of *The Encyclopedia of Tarot*. Thomas stopped work on the deck during the early 1990s, but resumed in 1999, when he received a grant to extend the deck to seventy-eight cards. He used computer imaging to complete the designs, as opposed to the manual paste-up and airbrush techniques of the first set. Many of the

images are different from those on the original cards.

The full seventy-eight-card deck was published by St. Martin's Press, New York, in 2002. It is accompanied by a book, by the artist, that gives meanings for the cards and identifies the artworks and buildings on each card. The boxed set also includes a silk cloth printed with the rose window that appears as a back design on the cards.

Parrott Tarot The Parrott Tarot was painted by Margaret Parrott with the guidance of her son Thom Parrott. It was published in 1996 by S.S. Adams Company, New Jersey. The artist says, "I think in color, and I wanted to use vivid colors to express the excitement and potential for knowledge and growth that the tarot represents. The parrot is included [at the bottom of each card] as a personal symbol and because to understand the tarot, as well as each other, there must be verbal communication." The cards include elemental, astrological, and kabbalistic symbols. Four extra cards are in the deck: a mentor for each suit. The titles of the Minor Arcana are from Aleister Crowley's Book of Thoth Tarot.

Pet Tarot The Major Arcana Pet Tarot is illustrated with computer-composed collages starring animals. Mystic Eye, the Chicago-based author and publisher, asks in the leaflet accompanying the deck, "Do the cards hold the key to unlock the mysteries of your animal friend's other side? Just how multi-faceted might they really be?" The 1998 deck includes a title card and a blank card. The back design is abstract designs, including a pyramid.

Phantasmagoric Theater "Envision Phantasmagoric Theater Tarot as a doorway into your life," says artist Graham Cameron. "The curtains open, revealing the Fool, who invites us on a journey of spiritual fulfillment." The large cards of the Phantasmagoric Theater Tarot are childlike, macabre, and humorous, with Cameron's personal symbolism sprinkled amidst traditional tarot symbolism. A puzzle piece in the lower right corner of many of the Major Arcana cards indicates whether the card has a masculine, feminine or mixed influence. Each suit corresponds to an element and mode: swords are air, labyrinth; wands are fire, circus; cups are water, desert; coins are earth, village. The back design features a puzzle piece, the number 56, which is the artist's "own chosen number," a dice, which represents fate, and the question mark. "There are many questions that remain unanswered, and many of my paintings contain hidden interpretations that, once uncovered, unlock subconscious doorways." The Phantasmagoric Theater Tarot was published in 1999 by U.S. Games Systems, Stamford, Connecticut, and features a presentation card and an introductory card.

Phantasmagoric Theater A puzzle piece in the lower right corner of each Major Arcana card, except the Fool, indicates whether the card has a masculine *(left)*, feminine *(middle)* or mixed *(right)* influence.

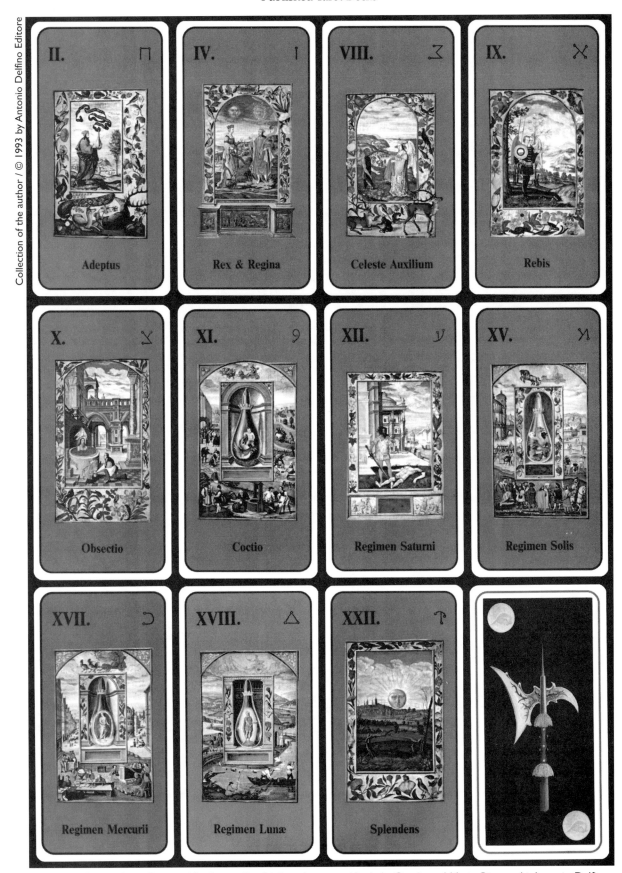

Tarocchi di Paracelso   Designed by Arrigo Pecchioli, and executed by Italo Curzio and Mario Rivosecchi, Antonio Delfino Editore, 1993

Tarot de Paris   J. Philip Thomas, St. Martin's Press, 2002

Parrott Tarot Margaret Parrott and Thom Parrott, S.S. Adams Company, 1996

The Fool | The Magician | The High Priestess | The Empress | The Emperor

The Hierophant | The Lovers | The Chariot | Strength | The Wheel of Fortune

Justice | The Hanged Man | Death | Temperance | The Devil

The Tower | The Star | The Moon | Judgement | The World

Pet Tarot Mystic Eye, Mystic Eye, 1998

Phantasmagoric Theater   Graham Cameron, U.S. Games Systems, 1999

Pictogram Tarot The Pictogram Tarot is by Medicator, pseudonym of Guido Gillabel. The black and white Major Arcana were issued in 1987 by the Belgian artist in a numbered, limited edition of 120 examples. The deck includes a title card and a blank card, and a booklet by Medicator in Flemish and English. The backs are blank.

Tarocchi di Pinocchio (by Valcauda) A Major Arcana deck from Italy illustrates the Italian children's classic *Pinocchio: The Adventures of a Puppet.* The book by Carlo Collodi, published in 1883, describes the adventures of a wooden puppet who becomes a boy.

Armando Valcauda's Major Arcana show the influence of Walt Disney as well as classic fantasy and horror films. The deck was published by Lo Scarabeo, of Turin, Italy, in 1988, in a limited edition of 888. The deck includes a presentation card signed by the artist and numbered.

Tarocchi di Pinocchio (by Ghiuselev) In 1994 Ideogramma of Turin also published a deck illustrating *Pinocchio.* The Major Arcana deck by Iassen Ghiuselev was issued in a limited edition of 300. It includes a presentation card, and each Major Arcana has an excerpt from Collodi's book.

Tarocco di Sandro Pipino When Italian artist Sandro Pipino first considered creating a tarot deck, he was apprehensive that his designs would be repetitive of the tarot of Oswald Wirth, whose work he studied. However, it was Wirth's own words that encouraged him

to embark on the project: "When employing symbols, which are windows open to infinity, our interpretations may only have a suggestive value, and never exhaust the subject."

Pipino describes cards I through XI of the Major Arcana as "symbol of the Doric way, the rational, male, solar course, man's voyage towards the discovery of his outer Self." Cards XII through XXI are "symbol of the Ionic way, the emotional, female, lunar course, man's voyage towards the discovery of his inner Ego." 0 The Fool "acts as a link." Pipino further describes the Minor Arcana: "If the Major Arcana are the 'paths' leading to the nucleus of our 'Ego,' the Minor Arcana represent the 'cities' we encounter along the way during our quest." The numbering of the Major Arcana is according to the esoteric scheme, with Strength as 8 and Justice as 11. Pipino switches the numbering of the Hermit and the Wheel of Fortune, giving the Hermit 10 and the Wheel 9.

The deck was published in a numbered, limited edition of 3,000 by Italcards in 1991. It includes a title card, a blank card, a leaflet in English, and a paper giving the number of the deck and signed by the artist. The back design is of a blue, green, red, black, and yellow compass star on a black background. The cards are titled in Italian, German, Spanish, English, and French.

P.J. Tarot The Major Arcana deck by Judit Pállfy was drawn in pencil. The deck was published by Módia Bt. of Budapest in 1998. The images are in black and white, with borders in maroon and gray. The back pattern is interlocking circles in maroon on black.

Pictogram Tarot Medicator (Guido Gillabel), published by the artist, 1987 The descriptions are from the booklet by Medicator

TOP ROW: **0.** Cypher, nought and zero. The primitive waters above which spirit floated. The Ouroboros. **I.** The vertical line represents the phallus, lingam, fire, spirit, the staff of the magician, energy, will, connecting above with below. **II.** Both vertical lines are the pair of opposites, inseparably connected with each other by an oblique junction, which is the cause that opposites are each other's reflection. **III.** The serpent is the third, which combines the opposites (the two coils of the serpent) or is rather the common essence of

both. **V.** An antenna receives ethereal information and transmits it to the material world.

BOTTOM ROW: **VI.** A symbol partly formed from the symbol for Venus and partly from the symbol of life, the ankh. **VIII.** Two links that grip each other give the idea of a chain, the universal laws by which man has been fettered in the material. **IX.** The flame of the candle is the interior light of man, which is in the body, represented by four horizontal lines. The light vivifies the body; the reversed ankh represents its quality. **X.** The eight-spoked wheel of the universe. **XIII.** Death transforms old forms, which must decay in order to generate new life forms.

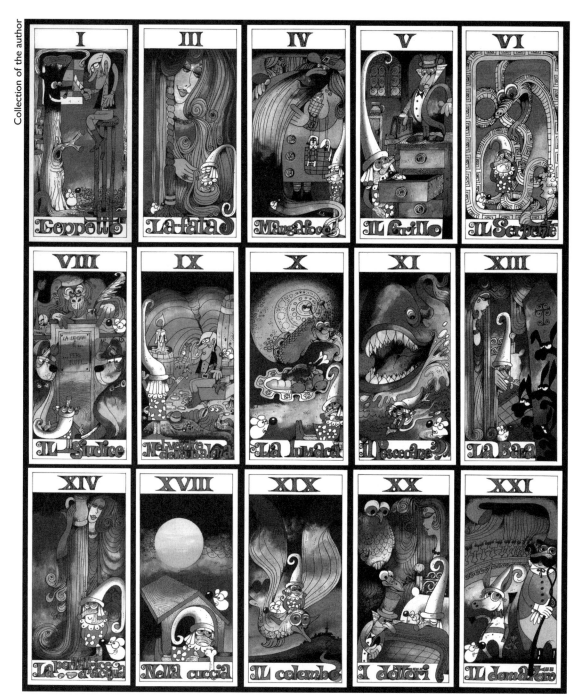

Tarocchi di Pinocchio   Armando Valcauda, Lo Scarabeo, 1988

TOP ROW: **I Geppetto** is the woodcarver who created Pinocchio. **III La fata** (The Fairy) is the beautiful Blue Fairy who rescues Pinocchio when he gets in trouble. **IV Mangiafoco** (Fire-eater) nearly puts Pinocchio on the fire to cook his dinner. **V Il Grillo** (The Cricket) attempts to give Pinocchio good advice, but only gets smashed by the puppet. **VI Il Serpente** (The Serpent) blocks the road home, but fortunately for Pinocchio, it ends up dying of laughter when the puppet gets stuck in the mud.

SECOND ROW: **VIII Il Giudice** (The Judge) is an ape who imprisons Pinocchio for getting robbed, because he is in the town of "Trap for Blockheads." **IX Nel ventre della Balena** (In the Belly of the Whale) is where Pinocchio finds his father, Gepetto. **X La Lumaca** (The Snail) brings

Pinocchio food that, unfortunately, is made of plaster. **XI il Pescecane** (The Dogfish) is the creature that swallows Gepetto, then Pinocchio. **XIII La Bara** (The Coffin), carried by four black rabbits, encourages Pinocchio to take his medicine, which he has refused.

BOTTOM ROW: **XIV La portatrice d'acqua** (The Water Carrier) is the Blue Fairy. **XVIII Nella cuccia** (In the dog-house) is where Pinocchio ends up after trying to steal some grapes. He is forced to take the place of the farmer's watch-dog. **XIX Il colombo** (The Dove) takes Pinocchio in search of his father Gepetto. **XX I Dottori** (The Doctors) are an owl, a crow, and a cricket, who are called by the Blue Fairy after she rescues Pinocchio from the noose. **XXI Il domatore** (The Trainer) uses Pinocchio as a show animal, after Pinocchio became a donkey from living in the "Land of the Boobies" for five months.

Tarocchi di Pinocchio Iassen Ghiuselev, Ideogramma, 1994 TOP ROW: 0 Il Pescatore Verde (The Green Fisherman). I Geppetto. III La Fata Turchina (The Blue Fairy). VII Il Carro (The Chariot). SECOND ROW: XII L'Impiccato (The Hanged Man). XIII La Bara (The Coffin). XIV La Portatrice d'Acqua (The Water Carrier). XV Il Gatto e la Volpe (The Cat and the Fox). BOTTOM ROW: XVII L'Osteria (The Tavern). XVIII La Luna (The Moon). XX Il Burattino (The Puppet). XXI Il Circo (The Circus).

Tarocco di Sandro Pipino   Sandro Pipino, Italcards, 1991

P.J. Tarot   Judit Pállfy, Módia Bt., 1998

Collection of the author

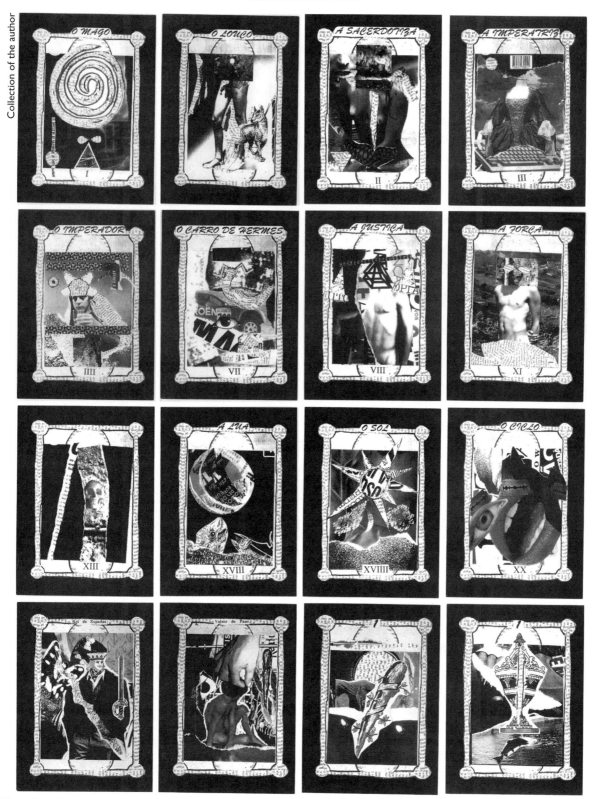

Tarot Poético   Almeida e Sousa, Edição Mandrágora, circa 2000

Tarot Poético   Portuguese artist Almeida e Sousa created the Tarot Poético as a collage of printed material,
including words set in type. The faces are printed in
brown, and the back design is in green. The deck was
published by Edição Mandrágora circa 2000.

467

Polish Tarot   Anonymous, KZWP Trefl, 1997

Polish Tarot   A deck with Polish and English titles was published by KZWP Trefl of Krakow, in 1997. The back design is of a sunburst on green, surrounded by stars.

Mag The Magician / le Bateleur	**Kapłanka** The Priestess / la Papesse	**Cesarzowa** The Empress / l'Impératrice	**Cesarz** The Emperor / l'Empereur	**Papież** The Pope / le Pape
Rydwan The Chariot / le Chariot	**Sprawiedliwość** Justice / la Justice	**Pustelnik** The Hermit / l'Ermite	**Koło Fortuny** The Wheel of Fortune / la Roue de Fortune	**Moc** Strength / la Force
Wisielec The Hanged Man / le Pendu	**Śmierć** Death / la Mort	**Umiarkowanie** Temperance / la Tempérance	**Diabeł** The Devil / le Diable	**Księżyc** The Moon / la Lune
Słońce The Sun / le Soleil	**Głupiec** The Fool / le Mat	**Król Mieczy** King of Swords / Roi d'Épée		**Walet Monet** Page of Coins / Valet de Deniers

Tarot Polski (Polish Tarot) Anna Ligero created a tarot deck that was published by Wydawnictwo Siedmioróg of Wroclaw in 1998. Titles are in Polish, English, and French. The deck includes two extra cards with no image

Tarot Polski (Polish Tarot) Anna Ligero, Wydawnictwo Siedmioróg, 1998

(only the black and white border), and the back design is black and gold with the word "TAROT" in white.

469

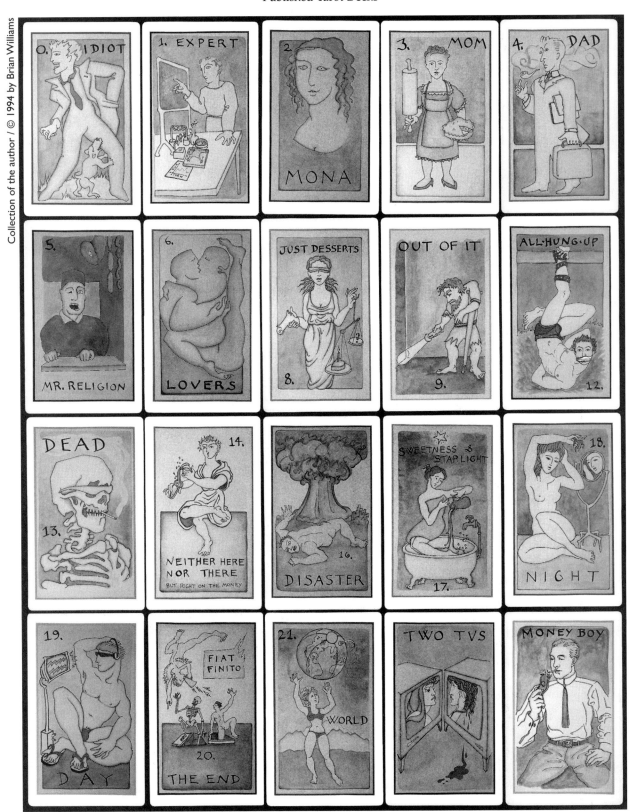

PoMo Tarot "PoMo is a reductionist abbreviation for the term Postmodern," says the artist Brian Williams in the book accompanying his deck. "…Postmodernism, via PoMo Tarot, offers a deconstructional divinational semiotics to the sophisticated researcher. Here is a message-rich medium with which to plumb the zeitgeist on the threshold of the millenial spring-cleaning house party, the incipient bang and/or whimper." The Major Arcana, aces and courts of the PoMo Tarot interpret the tarot with late-twentieth century icons, such as Mom and Apple Pie, and the pips two through ten spring from artworks from the nineteenth and twentieth centuries. The suits are TVs (swords), guns (staves), bottles (cups), and money (coins). The back design is double-ended and shows a fountain statue bearing the four suit symbols, in lavender on purple.

The PoMo Tarot was published by HarperSanFrancisco in 1994.

Poslednja Ljubav u Carigradu Tarot (Last Love in Constantinople Tarot) The Major Arcana both illustrate and determine the plot movement of Serbian writer Milorad Pavic's novel, *Last Love in Constantinople*. Twenty-two cards are bound into the book, and each corresponds to a chapter. The deck can be shuffled to determine the order in which to read the chapters, or it can be used for divination. The novel takes place in Serbia at the turn of the nineteenth century and is about the military and romantic adventures of two Serbian families. The artwork, also by Milorad Pavic, blends the styles of Russian icons and folk art. The book was published in Belgrade, Yugoslavia, in 1993.

PoMo Tarot Brian Williams, Harper San Francisco 1994 Descriptions are based on those by the artist in the book accompanying the deck.

TOP ROW: **0. Idiot** wears the modern jester's costume: the designer suit suitable for office or discothèque, the red power tie. His foolery kicks up a crazy wisdom, whether we are ready for it or not. **1. Expert** points a significant finger at arcane calculations on a blackboard. His lab coat is tabula rasa white. Instruments and experiments lie on his work table. The Expert is indeed a kind of late-modern magician; his knowledge means recourse to real power. **2. Mona** half-smiles in her familiar way. Leonardo's creation has become an emblem and deep-rooted cultural icon of—what?—the feminine mystique, perhaps, the cerebral, the sublime. **3. Mom** holds a pie and rolling pin like a monarch's orb and scepter. Benevolent is her smile and threatening is her gesture. **4. Dad** strides with pipe in hand (or not quite in hand), business files under arm, briefcase in tow. In PoMo Tarot, the Emperor has been particularized into an attaché-wielding paterfamilias. It may seem something of a comedown after the supreme, universal political suzerainty of the Emperor to end up as mere Dad. Remember, though, how looming a presence fathers can have.

SECOND ROW: **5. Mr. Religion** owes his demeanor to the paintings of Francis Bacon, which were in turn inspired by Velázquez portraits of Pope Urban VIII. In homage to Bacon's paintings of sides of beef and such, and in honor of his cognomen, salamis and other sausages hang behind Mr. Religion. He is another manifestation of the male principle, here in its old-fogey role…a storehouse of priceless memories and, when unburdened of his geriatric complaints, font of much avuncular or grandfathular kindness and wisdom. **6. Lovers** shows everything stripped down to its essential, and down to the essential act. **8. Just Desserts** shows Justice aiming a pistol in one hand and holding her scales in the other. Hanging in the balance are a question mark and a heart-shaped cake, a play on the card's title. **9. Out of It** shows an old man aiming a flashlight into an empty corner. His electric torch searches out a path in the darkness, a bit of truth from obscurity. **12. All Hung Up** reminds us, that which is postponed is not abandoned.

THIRD ROW: **13. Dead** shows a skeleton looking cool in shades and puffing a butt. **14. Neither Here nor There but Right on the Money** shows a figure of indeterminate gender pouring one test tube into another, as bubbling beakers are mixed in scary movies. Swirl a little yin into your yang, the character seems to say, for a balanced psychosexual cocktail. **16 Disaster** show a naked figure who gestures in alarm and horror at that emblematic invention of the modern age, a mushroom cloud, billowing behind. **17. Sweetness & Starlight** shows our stellar bathing beauty stepping into a bubble bath, pouring a pitcher of bath salts or who-knows-what into the mixture. **18. Night** sits before a mirror, eternal symbol of femininity both frivolous and profound.

BOTTOM ROW: **19. Day** is a blond youth preening under a sun lamp, armed with sunglasses, headphones, and bathing costume. The Day is a triumph of technology and the male principle. **20. The End** comes right from the standard church images of the Last Judgment, Armageddon, Apocalypse, the final curtain on history. **21. World,** a great big beach ball, soars into the air at the hand of a bikinied woman, presumably Dame Nature, or Anima Mundi. **Two TVs** refers to Aubrey Beardsley's 1892 illustration *Salomé*. The grisly-glamorous Salomé is about to kiss the lifeless lips of the decapitated John the Baptist. **Money Boy** is based on the 1912 painting *Arrow Collar Man*, by J.C. Leyendecker. As Money Boy, he is the picture of aristocratic (or *nouveau riche*) wealth, lighting a cigarette with a burning bill and sporting a dollar-sign belt buckle.

Poslednja Ljubav u Carigradu Tarot (Last Love in Constantinople Tarot)   Milorad Pavic, 1993

Tarot selon Prinner   Anton Prinner issued a portfolio, measuring 12.5 inches high by 9.75 inches wide, containing reproductions of a hand-written text and artwork for the Major Arcana. The originals of the text and art were made in pencil. The artwork includes Latin titles and explanations in French. Prinner cites his sources as *Amulettes, Talismans et Pantacles,* by Jean Marquès Riviè (Edition Payot, Paris); *Episodes de la Vie Esotérique 1780–1824* (Paul Derain, Lyon); and the Bible. The text was bound; the artwork is printed on single sheets of heavy paper. The artwork includes a title card and "the 23rd page of the tarot." The title card reads (translated from French): "The Esoteric and Poetic Tarot of Prinner and the scientific, poetic, anecdotal development of cartomancie," with a quote from the New Testament, John 18:37, "And I came into the world to witness to the truth." The text is dated by Prinner "Paris, 1971."

Pythagorean Tarot   The Pythagorean Tarot is, in the words of its creator, "rooted in ancient Greek paganism and esoteric doctrine." John Opsopaus writes in the book accompanying his deck, "Twenty-seven hundred years ago, the Pythagoreans formed an esoteric society built on the traditions of the Orphics, Babylonians, Phoenicians, and Egyptians, among others.... The Pythagorean Tarot is unique in using authentic Pythagorean numerology as the principal interpretive framework for both Major and Minor Arcana." The illustrations are by Rho.

The sequence of the Major Arcana is based on the anonymous *Sermones de ludo cum aliis,* circa 1500, the oldest known listing of the Major Arcana. They have titles in Greek and English, and on each is a letter of the Greek alphabet. Each Minor Arcana card has at its top elemental glyphs that correspond to the suit. The double-ended back design shows a red pentagram with ten blue globes arranged at its center, all on a green background.

The Pythagorean Tarot was published by Llewellyn Publishers, St. Paul, Minnesota, in 2001.

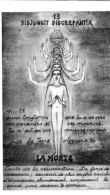

Le Tarot selon Prinner   Anton Prinner, published by the artist, 1971

Pythagorean Tarot   John Opsopaus and Rho, artist, Llewellyn Publications, 2001   The descriptions are based on those in the book by John Opsopaus.

TOP ROW: **0. Idiot** moves to the left, the unconscious. He whistles because he represents the spirit of vitality. He carries the thyrsus and grapes of Dionysos. A panther bites him—attacking or marking him. The snake in the Idiot's path indicates regeneration. A fig tree is over him. **I. Magician** wears a fringed mantle characteristic of shamans. The mask represents the custom of dressing in costumes at Saturnalia

Quest Tarot Joseph Ernest Martin used computer graphics to illustrate the Quest Tarot. The Daliesque scenes have figures that look as if they are made of glass or metal, "to try to make the cards as universal as possible without rendering an ethnic type as dominant," says Martin in the book accompanying the deck. The framework of each card includes symbols that vary according to the value of the card. Gems stud the borders. Astrological signs are in the upper left corner of all the cards, except the courts. The courts have daggers that mean yes, no, or maybe, depending on how they are pointing, and on left and right indications of the physical features of a person involved with the reader. I Ching hexagrams are on the pips, and Hebrew letters and Celtic runes are on the Major Arcana. Roman letters near the titles allow divination through spelling out words that are formed in a spread. The four aces bear symbols of the four seasons. Besides the traditional seventy-eight cards, the deck includes "the mysterious blank card," which is framed but has no image, and an additional 0 card titled "The Multiverse: Unbound."

The deck was published by Llewellyn Publications in 2003. The backs of the cards show four gold symbols around an eye in blue and purple, on a blue background.

Quester: The Journey of the Brave Mike Giddens, in partnership with Patricia Beattie, illustrated a tarot deck with a Native American theme. The deck includes twenty-three "Life Path" cards, with all but one, Warrior, corresponding to Major Arcana. The suits, called "Totem" cards, correspond to the elements. Eagles are air, wolves are fire, bears are water, and buffalos are earth. Court cards are patriarch, matriarch, warrior, maiden, and an extra, dancer. The deck was published by Element Books of England in 1999, with a book by Patricia Beattie.

Raczkowska Tarot Malgorzata Raczkowska of Poland drew in pen and ink a tarot deck that was published as seven sheets of cardboard by Stowarzyszenie Radiestezyjne (Radiesthetic Society) in Bydgoszcz, Poland, in 1989. The back is plain, gray cardboard with a maroon crosshatch.

Radical Wirth Tarot Carol Herzer recolored the illustrations of Oswald Wirth's Tarot. Herzer painted the Radical Wirth Tarot in 1989, a century after the Wirth Tarot was first issued as a limited edition of prints titled *Le Livre de Thoth.*

Tarocchi del Re Sole (Tarot of the Sun King) Paolo Piffarerio based the line drawings of his tarot deck on Alexander Dumas' *The Three Musketeers,* which was set in the reign of France's "Sun King," Louis XIV. The suit of swords is associated with D'Artagnan, batons with Porthos, cups with Aramis, and coins with Athos. The deck was issued in 1986 by Lo Scarabeo Azzuro of Turin in a limited edition of 936 decks, comprising two versions: 530 decks have faces printed in black and the backs printed in blue; the remaining 406 decks have faces and backs printed in brown. The decks include a title card and a presentation card. The back design shows a woman amidst scrolls. Titles are in Italian.

and Carnival. The cock is symbol of vigilance. **II. Empress** suggests all the ideas of Mothers, positive and negative. The peacock of Juno is at her side. She wears a gown decorated with pomegranates and a girdle embroidered with myrtle. **III. Emperor** wears a deep red mantle decorated with green foliage and seven golden flowers. He holds a stylized thunderbolt in his right hand. A ruby eagle is at his feet. **V. High Priest** sits in a golden chariot pulled over the ocean by two hippocamps. He holds a pruning saw and a golden vase, from which he pours wine into the ocean.

SECOND ROW: **VI. Love** shows two lovers facing each other in a forest clearing. The man holds a spear; at his heel is a scorpion. The woman wears a crescent and holds a cup. Her clothes hang drying over a fire in the background. A winged cupid points a silver arrow at the man's heart. **VII. Temperance** shows an androgynous-looking young woman pouring light-colored liquid from a golden wine jug into the reddish fumes that rise from a silver dish. Her gown is iridescent. **VIII. Victory** flies winged and in purple robes over the Hero, who sits in the chariot with a dog or wolf. **VIIII. Fortitude** shows a woman in an uncultivated field holding open the jaws of a lion. She has set aside her sword as ineffective for taming the beast. **X. Fortune** shows Fortuna at the center of the wheel. Each of the figures around the wheel is labeled: the blond one at Fortuna's right has *Io Altum tollor,* "I am raised on high"; the top has *Nimus exaltatus,* "Exalted too much"; the left has *Descendo minoratus,* "I descend diminished"; and the bottom one has *Funditus mortificatus,* "Utterly destroyed."

THIRD ROW: **XI. Old Man** carries a sickle and an hourglass in the twilight. Asphodels grow on the ground at his feet. **XIII. Death** holds an empty dish and a cornucopia that may also be empty. He wears a key around his neck. A dark river flows behind him, and further is a tomb. **XVI. Star** shows a young woman who pours water from a gold and a silver drinking horn. A lion-headed bird is in the cypress nearby. **XVII. Moon** shines on the edge of a dark sea. Glowing white and red tears fall from the crescent. A scorpion crawls from the salt-edged tide. **XVIII. Sun** is a disk that is over twins who dance within a ring of reddish mushrooms in a garden.

BOTTOM ROW: **XXI. Cosmos** shows an androgynous figure dancing in an oval surrounded by four heads. The figure holds a golden key that points to heaven and a silver key that points to earth. **Knight of Swords** is Athena, goddess of wisdom, as Maid of Air. **Queen of Wands** is Hestia, goddess of the home, as Lady of Fire. **King of Cups** is Poseidon, god of the sea, as Lord of Water. **Ace of Pentacles.**

Quest Tarot   Joseph Ernest Martin, Llewellyn Publications, 2003

BRAVE · HEYOKAH · KEEPER · CORNMOTHER · CHIEF

SHAMAN · AWAKENING · TRAIL MAKER · TWISTED HAIR · SUN RITUAL

SHADOW DANCER · IMAGE SHATTERER · GRANDFATHER SUN · THE CALLING · VILLAGE

WARRIOR · EIGHT OF EAGLES · WOLF PATRIARCH · EIGHT OF BEARS · BUFFALO DANCER

Quester: The Journey of the Brave Mike Giddens, Element Books, 1999

Raczkowska Tarot   Malgorzata Raczkowska, Stowarzyszenie Radiestezyjne, 1989

Radical Wirth Tarot   Recolored by Carol Herzer from the Osward Wirth Tarot, published by the artist, 1989

Tarocchi del Re Sole (Tarot of the Sun King)   Paolo Piffarerio, Lo Scarabeo, 1986

Reise ins Licht (Journey in Light)   The Journey in Light Tarot is part of a board game described as "a game for heart and soul." The players move over the spaces according to the roll of a dice. They draw cards as they go along. According to the square they land on, they draw one of the ninety-eight "task" cards, which set tasks for the players, or one of the twenty-two "wisdom" cards, or Major Arcana, which are used to answer personal questions. The game was created by Rolf Herkert, and the artwork on the twenty-two wisdom cards is by Anna Maximilian-Leon. It was published by CBD Spiele of Frankfurt in 1990.

Reise ins Licht (Journey in Light)   Rolf Herkert, and Anna Maximilian-Leon, artist, CBD Spiele, 1990

Renaissance Tarot Helen Jones used bas-relief to illustrate the cards of the Renaissance Tarot, which was packaged with a book by Jane Lyle. The back design is a blue and gold lozenge pattern. The set was published by Simon & Schuster, New York, in 1998.

Collection of the author / © 1998 by Helen Jones

Renaissance Tarot   Helen Jones, Simon & Schuster, 1998

Tarot Révélé   The Major Arcana by Suzanne Kloster first illustrated the book *Le Tarot Révélé,* by Valentin Bresle, published in Paris in 1949. In 1989 Carol Herzer painted the images and issued them as photos mounted on light backing.

Tarot Révélé   Suzanne Kloster and Valentin Bresle, 1949; painted by Carol Herzer, published by Carol Herzer, 1989

The Rider-Waite Tarot

Many editions and copies of the Rider-Waite Tarot have been published since the deck first appeared in December 1909. The deck was designed by Pamela Colman Smith under direction of Arthur Edward Waite. It is the best-selling tarot deck in the world.

Original Rider-Waite Tarot Pack The Original Rider-Waite Tarot Pack, published by U.S. Games Systems, is a facsimile of a very early edition Rider-Waite Tarot. The back design is a blue and white checkerboard pattern of roses and lilies. Other early editions feature the rose and lily design in brown and red, or a craquelure back design in brown. The exact back design used for the very first print run is unknown. The facsimile deck was published in 1999.

Rose and lily back design
Waite described the rose, which also emblazons the banner of death, as "the Mystic Rose, which signifies life."

Rider-Waite Glow in the Dark Tarot U.S. Games Systems, 1999

Rider-Waite Glow in the Dark Tarot The Major Arcana deck includes a presentation card and three cards giving instructions for divination. The cards are printed in black, with a greenish background that glows in the dark (after being first exposed to light). As the packaging says, "Now tarot doesn't have to end when the lights go out!" The Glow in the Dark deck was published by U.S. Games Systems of Stamford, Connecticut, in 1999.

Rider-Waite Tarot in non-English Languages The Rider-Waite Tarot is available in several different languages, including a five-language edition (Dutch, English, French, German, and Italian), French, German, Spanish, Czech, Slovak, and Turkish. Although Turkish has words for "Fool," the term Joker was used, probably

Rider-Waite Tarot TOP ROW: Czech, Slovak
BOTTOM ROW: Spanish, Turkish

Jesset's Rider-Waite Greeting Cards 1990

Collection of the author / Rider-Waite Tarot © 1971 by U.S. Games Systems, Inc.

in connection with the Joker of regular playing card decks. The Turkish deck was issued in a smaller size.

Jesset's Rider-Waite Greeting Cards Jesset's of New Jersey printed several of the cards from the Rider-Waite deck as greeting cards. The images were recolored in vivid colors. The inside of the card has a verse expressing the sentiment of the occasion (birthday, anniversary, etc.), and the back has a brief description of the tarot image. The cards were produced in 1990.

Fantasy Workshop Rider-Waite Tarot
For tarotists who live in doll houses, Marilyn's Miniatures / Fantasy Workshop produced a tiny deck, circa 1999, printed on photo paper scored to come apart. The deck is not a full one, but an assortment of Major and Minor Arcana cards. The deck in the author's collection has forty-nine cards. Backs are plain white.

Original Rider-Waite Tarot Pack Pamela Colman Smith under direction of Arthur Edward Waite, 1909; circa 1920 edition; reprint U.S. Games Systems, 1999

COLOR AND THE RIDER-WAITE TAROT

The original artwork from Smith's hand is lost, although she mentions the possibility of selling it in a letter to Alfred Stieglitz: "I've just finished a big job for very little cash! a set of designs for a pack of Tarot cards 80 designs. I shall send some over—the original drawings as some people may like them! I will send you a pack—(printed in colour by lithography)—(probably very badly!) as soon as they are ready—by Dec. 1—I think."

Illuminated Rider-Waite Tarot   Artwork by Pamela Colman Smith under direction of Arthur Edward Waite, 1909; recolored by Carol Herzer, 1988 (unpublished)

The "original drawings," may have been uncolored, made with brush or pen and black ink. The designs first appeared in print as uncolored line drawings in the December 1909 issue of *The Occult Review,* accompanying an article by A.E. Waite. The early printed decks do not reflect the usual delicacy of Pamela Colman Smith's color treatments.

When the Rider-Waite deck was published, commercial printers used zinc plates for lithography (originally, lithography, as the name indicates, was done with stone plates). The process remained much the same throughout the twentieth century.

Ink for large areas (as opposed to a letter or line drawing) was applied not as a wash of color, but as a pattern of dots or lines called a screen. From reading distance, the screen creates an illusion of solid color. The denser the screen's dots or lines, the darker the shade. For example, a light grey requires a "thirty percent" screen (dots over thirty percent of the color area). Colors are applied using three to five different colors of inks, with each color plate called a "separation." The separations are "layered" to create additional colors. For example, red printed over yellow makes orange.

Photolithography was in use when the Rider-Waite deck was printed. This technique uses photo filters to create separations of the art work that, when combined, can create a reasonably faithful reproduction of the original. The colors cyan, magenta, yellow, and black (CMYK) are usually used as separations (hence the term "four-color" printing).

The lack of subtlety in the colors of the early Rider-Waite decks indicates that photolithography was not used, which means that line drawings were used for the printing process. (The drawings might have been colored for sale after the plates were made.) Jeff Hill, an artist and ardent fan of Smith's work, proposed that Smith "used basic black line drawings with an 'onion skin' tissue system of overlays. The overlays were also rendered in black with marginal notes as to what basic colors, tints [screen percentages], and overprints she desired."

A close look at early decks indicates that the inks were most likely blue, yellow, and red, applied in that order, with black applied last. If Smith directed the overlays, she would have had to analyze the colors. For example, for the skin tone of her figures, she would have had to determine the correct screen percentages of red and yellow that would make pale flesh color.

A high-quality result using this overlay process required more ink colors (for example, a custom tint for skin), and hence more plates and more runs through the press—and more expense. Smith's pessimism about the quality of the printed deck was likely based on the prospect of a rather coarse screen and a limited number of colored inks to be used. If she herself created the overlays, she might also have had doubts about her own control of the process, especially if the illustrations she sold to other publishers were separated by print professionals, and she was unused to creating overlays.

Different artists have grappled with recoloring the Rider-Waite Tarot, sometimes for aesthetic reasons, sometimes for interpretive reasons, or a combination. The Rider-Waite deck has been issued in several recolored editions. The Radiant Rider-Waite Tarot and the Universal Waite Tarot feature cards that were redrawn and newly colored, copying the artwork by Pamela Colman Smith.

Albano-Waite Tarot (German and French editions)   The Albano-Waite Tarot features colors that are heavier and more vivid and saturated than the original printings. The Albano-Waite deck was originally issued in 1968 by Tarot Productions, Inc., directed by Frankie Albano. U.S. Games Systems reissued a facsimile of the Albano-Waite deck in 1987.

Diamond Tarot   The Diamond Tarot features the images of the Rider-Waite Tarot, by Pamela Colman Smith. Artist Marie-Louis Bergoint recolored the cards and added kaleidoscopic borders. The borders express the moods of the cards through color and shape. The back design is double-ended, a rainbow of concentric flower-petals. The Diamond Tarot was published by U.S. Games Systems, Stamford, Connecticut, and AGMüller, Neuhausen, Switzerland, in 1987.

Albano-Waite Tarot (German and French editions)   Artwork by Pamela Colman Smith under direction of Arthur Edward Waite, 1909; recolored by Tarot Productions, 1968; reprint U.S. Games Systems, 1987

Rider-Waite Tarot   Artwork by Pamela Colman Smith under direction of Arthur Edward Waite, 1909; recolored by Stewart Tabori & Chang, 1996

Illuminated Rider-Waite Tarot   Carol Herzer hand-colored black and white images of the Major Arcana of the Rider-Waite Tarot by Pamela Colman Smith. In correspondence with Stuart Kaplan, Herzer explains, "If you lay them out next to the corresponding cards from my decks, the Astrotarot and the Cosmo deck, you will see similarities. The reason the Fool is in a dark sky is because he is Zero, the Void, the black hole, an eclipse, the infinite. The edge of the mountains is the wave of my card, The Wave, 0."

Although Herzer painted within the original line art, she added interpretive elements, such as rays of light, haloes and starry skies. The hand-drawn titles and numbers were replaced by typeset numbers on the borders, "giving a totally clean look to the paintings," the artist says. "This also makes the deck universal; there is no language problem." The Illuminated Rider-Waite Tarot was completed in 1988.

Radiant Rider-Waite Tarot Virginijus Poshkus was commissioned by U.S. Games Systems to make the Radiant Rider-Waite Tarot. The deck is redrawn from the original Rider-Waite Tarot, with colors based on those used in the printed deck. The titles and numbers of the cards are typeset and placed in the borders of the cards. The back design shows tiny gold stars on a blue background. The deck includes a title card, an introductory card and an instructional booklet by Stuart R. Kaplan. It was published by U.S. Games Systems of Stamford, Connecticut, in 2003, in collaboration with Miss Sybil Waite and Rider & Company, London.

Tabori & Chang version The Rider-Waite Tarot was issued by Stewart Tabori & Chang in heavy colors with a beige background. This version of the Rider-Waite deck was published in 1996.

Diamond Tarot   Artwork by Pamela Colman Smith under direction of Arthur Edward Waite, 1909; recolored, with new borders, by Marie-Louis Bergoint, U.S. Games Systems and AGMüller, 1987

Radiant Rider-Waite Tarot   Artwork by Pamela Colman Smith under direction of Arthur Edward Waite, 1909; redrawn and recolored by Virginijus Poshkus, U.S. Games Systems, 2003

Universal Waite Tarot U.S. Games Systems commissioned Mary Hanson-Roberts to recolor the Rider-Waite deck. The artist had already published with the company the Hanson-Roberts Tarot deck (see *The Encyclopedia of Tarot,* volume III). Hanson-Roberts carefully redrew the line art and colored it in pencil. The Universal Waite Tarot was published in 1991 by U.S. Games Systems. It includes a presentation card, which features original art by Hanson-Roberts and text by Stuart Kaplan, and a title card. The deck is available in several languages and as the "Tiny Universal Waite Tarot." The artwork also appears on other products.

Collection of the author / © 1991 by U.S. Games Systems

Tiny Universal Waite Tarot (actual size) The Tiny Tarot is packaged in a small plastic box that can serve as a keychain.

Tarot Affirmations The Tarot Affirmations cards feature images from the Universal Waite Tarot, with artwork by Pamela Colman Smith re-colored by Mary Hanson-Roberts, along with text by Sally Hill. In the booklet accompanying the deck, Hill says, "I began serious work with tarot in 1990, when I encountered a difficult period during my graduate studies in psychology. I had run out of energy and had lost sight of the vision that sent me back to graduate school at the age of forty-seven."

Hill began study of Angeles Arrien's *The Tarot Handbook.* "From Arrien, I learned that all tarot cards, no matter how negative they may appear to be at first glance, carry a positive message.… One morning, when I was feeling particularly drained, I wrote an affirmation down on an index card and carried it with me through the day. I had no idea then what those index cards would inspire. I knew only that the words I wrote helped me to get through the day and began to slowly restore my vision."

Tarot Affirmations was published by U.S. Games Systems in 2001. The double-ended back design is of an angel blowing a trumpet. The deck includes a presentation card and an instructional card "Reading the Cards."

Epicurean Tarot The Epicurean Tarot is a set of recipe cards featuring the Universal Waite Tarot deck. Each card includes an image from the deck and a recipe based on the interpretation of the card. Corrine Kenner wrote the text and researched the recipes. The connections made between food and the tarot are often humorous. The Epicurean Tarot was published by U.S. Games Systems in 2001.

Quick and Easy Rider-Waite Tarot This deck features interpretations for upright and reverse meanings on the face of each card. The deck includes a title card and a card giving instructions for divination. The artwork is from the Universal Tarot. The text is by Ellen Lytle. It was published in 1999 by U.S. Games Systems, Inc.

Quick and Easy Rider-Waite Tarot Artwork from the Universal Tarot; text by Ellen Lytle, U.S. Games Systems, 1999

Tarot Affirmations Artwork from the Universal Waite Tarot; text by Sally Hill, U.S. Games Systems, 2001

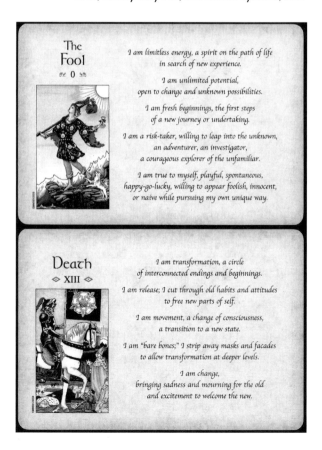

Universal Waite Tarot Pamela Colman Smith under direction of Arthur Edward Waite, recolored by Mary Hanson-Roberts,
U.S. Games Systems, 1991   The card at bottom right of the illustration is a presentation card with original artwork by Mary
Hanson-Roberts.

Epicurean Tarot
Artwork from Universal Waite Tarot; recipes by Corrine Kenner, U.S. Games Systems, 2001

THE KING OF SWORDS' LONDON BROIL

1 two-pound flank steak
3 tablespoons olive oil
2 cloves garlic, pressed
1 1/2 tablespoon red wine vinegar
1 teaspoon salt
1/2 teaspoon pepper

Butter sauce:
1/4 cup butter
1 tablespoon lemon juice
1/2 teaspoon salt
1 tablespoon dried parsley
(if fresh, use 3 tablespoons)

Trim any excess fat from the meat and score it on both sides with a sharp knife.

In a zippered plastic bag, combine the oil, garlic, vinegar, salt, and pepper. Add the beef, seal the bag, and shake gently to ensure that all sides are covered. Refrigerate for at least three hours or overnight, turning once or twice.

Remove the meat and throw the used bag and marinade away.

Broil the steak on high heat under a broiler or on the grill, for five minutes on each side. The steak will be rare; you can cook it longer if your tastes differ from the king's.

Let the steak "rest" for a few minutes while preparing the butter sauce. Melt the butter, remove it from the heat, and whisk in the lemon juice, salt, and chopped parsley.

Slice the steak very thinly, on the diagonal across the grain, and drizzle it with the butter sauce.

The manly King of Swords is not afraid of conflict. In fact, he's the first to defend anyone who faces injustice or oppression. He likes his meat red, rare, broiled, and sliced thin against the grain.

XIII · DEATH'S STUFFED MUSHROOMS

1 pound medium or large mushrooms
1/4 cup olive oil
1 clove garlic, pressed
1/4 cup green onions, finely chopped

1/2 cup white wine
1 teaspoon lemon juice
1 cup bread crumbs
1/2 cup chopped parsley
salt and pepper to taste

Wipe the mushrooms clean with a damp paper towel and gently pull out the stems.

Chop the stems and sauté them in olive oil, along with the garlic and green onions.

Take the sautéed mixture off the heat, add the wine and the lemon juice, and stir in the bread crumbs and parsley.

Season with salt and pepper to taste.

Dip the mushroom caps in olive oil and put them in a shallow, lightly greased baking dish, hollow side up.

Spoon the filling into the hollow of the mushroom caps, drizzle the entire dish lightly with oil, and bake them uncovered in a preheated 350°F oven for 10 minutes.

What could be more fitting for Death's favorite dish than the perpetual flower of decay, the mushroom? Just be sure you pick yours in the safety of your grocer's market.

Collection of the author / Universal Waite Tarot deck © 1991 by U.S. Games Systems, Inc.;
Epicurean Tarot © 2001 by U.S. Games Systems, Inc.

Tarocchi di Robot (Tarot of the Robot)   The Tarot of the Robot was created in 1987 by Massimo Borrelli, a computer artist on the staff of Giugiaro Design, Turin, Italy. The humanoid robots are in keeping with Giugiaro Design's main product: industrial design, where human needs meet factory production. The deck was published by Lo Scarabeo, Turin, Italy. The suits of the deck are nulla (nothing), laser, luci (light), and scarabei (scarabs).

Collection of the author / © by Lo Scarabeo

Tarocchi di Robot (Tarot of the Robot)   Massimo Borrelli, Lo Scarabeo, 1987

Rock and Roll Tarot "These artists and performers are from the first fifty years of Rock & Roll music history," artist Chris Paradis says of the figures in his tarot. "They reside in the temple of the Juke Box, their lyrics invoke love, thought, passion, and comforts. The lyrics taken out of context give each card its meaning (stichomancy). The images on the tarot cards (cartomancy) invoke what that individual or Band contributes to the energy behind the words and a new Archetype presents itself."

Each card shows a rock and roll artist and a line of lyrics by that artist. Paradis composed the images using Adobe Photoshop. Suits are guitars (swords), voice (wands), muse (Cups), and albums (coins). The deck comprises seventy-eight cards, plus six alternate Major Arcana and two alternate Minor Arcana, an "Introduction" card, an "Acknowledgements" card, a card signed and numbered by Paradis, two cards listing the Major Arcana, one card listing the alternate cards, a card printed with scraps of lyrics, a title card, and eight cards describing the Minor Arcana.

The deck was first published in 2000, in a limited edition of 500 that did not include the alternate cards. The second edition was also limited to 500 copies, and the cards are smaller. Rock and Roll Tarot was published by no parking productions. The back design shows a juke box.

Rock Art Tarot Jerry Roelen, artist of the Rock Art Tarot, based the images on the marking and images left on rocks by people all over the world. The interpretations he makes are his own. He says in the introductory card accompanying the deck, "It is easy to speculate on their true meaning, but only the original artists know their importance and purpose. Over the years I've photographed and sketched many panels of images, and my spirit has been touched by the past. I began to have visions and dreams that were dominated by the Rock Art images. Psychic messages came to me when I was at a site or at home reviewing my sketches. The result of these experiences is the Rock Art Tarot deck." In correspondence with Stuart Kaplan, Roelen adds, "The deck is about prehistoric petroglyphs and pictographs of different continents and cultures. They express a mystical concept, a metaphysical journey. This unique art form reveals a higher spiritual understanding, and is similar to the esoteric teachings of the tarot." The Minor Arcana suits are intellect, intuition, emotions, and sensations, with guardian spirit cards in place of courts: mankind, womankind, peacemaker, and defender. The deck was published by U.S. Games Systems, Stamford, Connecticut, in 1996. It includes an introductory card and a presentation card, and the back design is a double-ended rock image on a green background.

Röhrig Tarot German artist Carl-W. Röhrig used airbrush to paint the cards for his tarot deck. The large cards feature complex images with hand-written titles and meanings in different languages, mostly German and English. A typeset title is also included on each card. The back is a swirling design in blue. The deck was published in 1995 by Bluestar Communications of Woodside, California, and it includes a booklet by Francesca Marzano-Fritz.

Tarocchi di Romagna The Tarocchi di Romagna, by Luigi E. Mattei, portrays folktales of the Romagna, or Emilia-Romagna region of Italy. The Major Arcana deck was issued in 1984, in a signed and numbered edition of 3,000, by Cassa di Risparmio in Bologna, an art and history museum. The back design has a black and white drawing of a winged horse and the logo *Al passo con i tempi* (In step with the times).

Romantic Tarots The Romantic Tarots, painted in acrylics by Giorgio Trevisan, were published as Major Arcana decks by Lo Scarabeo, of Turin, in 1991. An edition with English-language titles, and a larger edition with Italian titles (called Tarocchi Romantici) were issued. The English-language edition includes a title card and a card with a verse on it. The Italian edition includes a title card and a descriptive leaflet. The verse is on the flap of the packaging. It has a line that the translation into English misses. The back design on both decks is a foliage pattern in blue on white.

Roots of Asia Tarot Writer Thaworn Boonyawan and artist Amnart Klanpracher based the Roots of Asia Tarot on Buddhist dharma (teachings). Of the artist, Boonyawan says, "Amnart Klanpracher…has devoted all his life in search of understanding the truth through art, which he believes is not only the reflection of one's state of mind, but also a channel for the oneness to be unveiled." The deck was published by AGMüller of Switzerland in 2001. The back design is a whirling image of light and other figures that compose a face and hands in meditational posture.

Royal Thai Tarot Sungkom Horharin based the Royal Thai Tarot upon Thai customs, traditions, art, culture, literature, history, beliefs, and religion. The seventy-eight-card deck includes a booklet of instructions. It was published in 2004 by U.S. Games Systems, Stamford, Connecticut.

Rock and Roll Tarot Chris Paradis, no parking productions, 2000 TOP ROW: 0 The Fool (alternate): Lou Reed. I The Magician: Frank Zappa. I The Magician (alternate): ELO. III The Empress: Annie Lennox. SECOND ROW: III The Empress (alternate): Tori Amos. IV The Emperor: Elvis Presley. IX The Hermit: Bob Dylan. XI Justice (alternate): Marvin Gaye. BOTTOM ROW: XVII The Star (alternate): Joni Mitchell. Princess of Guitars: Sheryl Crow. 10 of Voice: Bob Marley. Prince of Muse: NIN.

Rock Art Tarot   Jerry Roelen, U.S. Games Systems, 1996

The Fool

The Magus

The High Priestess

The Emperor

The Hierophant

The Lovers

The Chariot

Strength

The Hermit

Death

Temperance

The Devil

The Tower

The Star

The Sun

The Judgment

Queen of Swords

Virtue

Princess of Cups

Prudence

Röhrig Tarot Carl-W. Röhrig, Blue Star Communications, 1995

Tarocchi di Romagna   Luigi E. Mattei, Cassa di Risparmio, 1984

TOP ROW: 1 il Mago (The Magician). 2 la Prosperità (Prosperity). 4 l'Imperatore (The Emperor). 5 il Papa (The Pope). 7 il Carro (The Chariot).

SECOND ROW: 8 il Passatore (The Shepherd). 10 la Fortuna (Fortune). 11 La Fortezza (Strength). 13 la Morte (Death). 14 l'Operosità (Industry).

BOTTOM ROW: 15 l'Esorcismo (Excorcism). 16 la Torre (The Tower). 17 la Stella (The Star). 18 la Luna (The Moon). 21 il Mondo (The World).

Romantic Tarots   Giorgio Trevisan, Lo Scarabeo, 1991   The verse accompanying the deck is, translated from the Italian, "The fantasy of a boy populates the world with fairy people, invincible forces, and dream-shaded colors. In the castle's empty rooms echoes the flight of a carriage that takes away forever the incandescence of a festivity where, one time, we met."

0 THE FOOL	1 THE MAGICIAN	2 THE POPESS	3 THE EMPRESS	4 THE EMPEROR
5 THE POPE	6 THE LOVERS	7 THE CHARIOT	8 JUSTICE	9 THE HERMIT
10 THE WHEEL	11 FORTITUDE	12 THE HANGED MAN	14 TEMPERANCE	15 THE DEVIL
16 THE TOWER	17 THE STAR	18 THE MOON	20 JUDGEMENT	21 THE WORLD

O THE FOOL	I THE MAGICIAN	II HIGH PRIESTESS	V THE HIEROPHANT	VI THE LOVERS
VII CHARIOT	VIII STRENGTH	X THE WHEEL	XI JUSTICE	XII HANGED MAN

Roots of Asia Tarot Amnart Klanpracher with Thaworn Boonyawan, AGMüller, 2001 Descriptions are based on the booklet by Boonyawan.

TOP ROW: **0 The Fool** represents the foundation from which existence arises. To understand the Fool, one must look deep into the furthest recess of the mind and find the origin that reveals the interconnectedness and unity of all. **I The Magician.** Those who understand the Magician possess a keen awareness of the interdependence essential to existence and have the ability to balance their own emotions while spreading compassion to those around them. **II High Priestess** has the ability to use power for positive or negative reasons. She stands in the middle of the water of change and transformation. **V The Hierophant** indicates good action. When the lotus grows up from the humus of the earth and blooms for everyone to see, there will be understanding of the results of good action. **VI The Lovers** sym-

bolizes the embrace and kiss of heaven and earth, of the marriage of the human and the divine.

BOTTOM ROW: **VII Chariot.** Centered in the inner power of patience, mindfulness, concentration, and wisdom, we are able to move forward and face the world. **VIII Strength** indicates the lion that exists in our mind and heart that demands to be fed. The food of the lion hides in the deepest part of our hearts, in our sensitivities, doubts, and false self. **X The Wheel** indicates the continually changing and unexpected situations of life. **XI Justice** makes us aware of the laws of karma and justice. The scales of justice are reflected back to the one who is mindful. If you have faith, strength, and self-sufficiency, and choose right action, goodness will come into your heart by the fact of the act itself. **XII Hanged Man** indicates our willingness and courage to surrender oneself and hang over the abyss that is inside the self.

| XIII DEATH | XVII THE STAR | XVIII THE MOON | XIX THE SUN | XXI THE UNIVERSE |
| KING OF SWORDS | FIVE OF SWORDS | SIX OF WANDS | FOUR OF CUPS | TEN OF PENTACLES |

Roots of Asia Tarot *(continued)*

TOP ROW: **XIII Death** indicates that we have found the evil within us. This death is not the ending of things. **XVII The Star.** When we see the value of all things in creation, creativity is released. **XVIII The Moon.** The creativity is strong with this card; however, others wish to squelch this positive energy. The heaviness of illusion tries to push us down. **XIX The Sun** is the supreme stage of existence. When the sun comes to us, we are reminded of the value of giving without thought of receiving anything in return. The eyes of the sun sun look down on all of creation and give full mercies and unconditional love. **XXI The Universe** indicates the oneness of all of creation. Union with the divine is reached.

BOTTOM ROW: **King of Swords.** To become a positive King of Swords, one must develop wisdom and insight, a foundation in truthfulness, detachment from results, and tranquility and peace of mind. **Five of Swords:** Causation of Loss. The root causes of loss become the obstacles of our mind that prevent us from solving our problems. **Six of Wands:** Right Perception. We can develop right perception through the six supreme experiences: supreme sight, supreme hearing, supreme gain, supreme training, supreme service and ministry, supreme memory. **Four of Cups:** Development of Mindfulness. The four things asked of us to develop mindfulness are: contemplation on the body, contemplation of feelings, contemplation of the mind, and contemplation of the objects of mind/ideas. **Ten of Pentacles:** Basis of Meritorious Action. The foundation of the path to goodness is built by acquiring merit.

Royal Thai Tarot   Sungkom Horharin, U.S. Games Systems, 2004   The illustrations are of the artwork before publication as a deck. The published cards have numbers and titles.

TOP ROW: 0 The Fool. I The Magician. II The High Priestess. III The Empress.

SECOND ROW: IV The Emperor. VI The Lovers. VII The Chariot. IX The Hermit.

THIRD ROW: X Wheel of Fortune. XI Justice. XIV Temperance. XVI The Tower.

BOTTOM ROW: XVII The Star. XVIII The Moon. XIX The Sun. XXI The World.

Russian Tarot   Victor Bakhtin, 1993

Russian Tarot   A tarot deck from Krasnoyarsk, Russia, features elaborate imagery on the Major Arcana and court cards. The pips have symmetrical arrangements of the suit signs. The artist of the deck is Victor Bakhtin.

The cards of the 1993 edition have images framed in black with gold borders and titles in Russian and English. One side of the box reads, in English, "Magical Cards for cartomancy and patience" and "Taro." A 1992 edition has titles in Russian only, and the images are framed in light purple. The back design is a black and gold pattern with an eight-pointed geometric figure in the center. One side of the 1992 box reads, "Magic Fortune Telling and Meditation Cards."

Sacred Circle Tarot "The Sacred Circle Tarot is a seventy-eight-card deck drawing on the Pagan heritage of Britain and Ireland, its sacred sites, and symbolic imagery from the tradition," says Anna Franklin, author of the deck and its accompanying book. "We have tried to make this a truly Pagan deck and remove some of the Cabalistic and Christian iconography that has crept into the tarot over the centuries.… We have tried to restore the Celtic Pagan imagery in a way that speaks to, and is of use to, modern Pagans."

Paul Mason, who illustrated the deck, describes his process. "The tarot was produced using a combination of photographs (scanned into the Kodak PhotoCD format), pencil drawings colorized and enhanced by computer, and elements drawn and constructed directly in computer graphics applications. This combination of media was then assembled in Adobe Photoshop, and the color, contrast, and density of each element adjusted to produce a more harmonious whole. When the composition was completed, I applied a filter to give a more painterly appearance, varying the degree of effect to different parts of the picture. At this stage, I also applied lighting effects, such as stars and rays of light. The final aim was to produce a tarot that had some of the naturalism of photography, but also had a magical realism that did justice to the subject." The deck, which includes two advertising cards, was published by Llewellyn Publications, St. Paul, in 1998.

Sacred Circle Tarot Anna Franklin and Paul Mason, artist, Llwewellyn Publications, 1998 The descriptions are based on those in Anna Franklin's book.

TOP ROW: **3 The Lady** is Mother Nature. The apple bough in the border of the card represents immortality, the passage of time, the turning of the wheel, and the mysteries of the goddess. Silbury Hill, near Avebury in Wiltshire, was constructed about 4,600 years ago and represents the womb of the Goddess. **4 The Lord** is the Lord of the Animals, sometimes called Cernunnos, Kerne, or Herne. It is early summer, and leaves appear on the apple, hawthorn, elder, birch, honeysuckle, and oak. Gathered around him, their rivalry forgotten under his benign influence, are the stag, the hare, and the badger. **5 The Druid** is at the evening of the midwinter solstice, which we call Yule. He wears a garland of oak and holly leaves. A wren perches on one corner of the card, and a robin on the chalice. The robin and the wren are totem birds of winter and summer. The dawn sun rises behind him through the stones of Stonehenge. The evergreen holly represents continuing life; its berries may represent blood and sacrifice. **6 The Lovers** are the May King and Queen about to undergo their ritual marriage. They dance around a maypole of birch wood. The background shows a hawthorn in full bloom, and in the foreground is a cuckoo pint. A dove circles in the sky. The flowering of the hawthorn signals the start of the fire festival of Beltane—which means "bright-fire"—a May celebration of life and fertility.

SECOND ROW: **8 The Warrior** is the British warrior woman Scathach, who trained the Irish hero Cuchulain. Her name means "the Shadowy One." She readies herself for the Lughnasa games. A borage plant grows at her feet, and she is accompanied by her familiar, the badger, one of the strongest woodland animals. The Celts steeped borage leaves in wine; the mixture resulted in a very significant rise in the blood adrenaline level. **9 The Shaman** is clad in deerskin. He lives in the forest with only his familiar, the wolf, for company. His brew of inspiration will enable him to travel to the spirit world. Some of the ingredients, including vervain, lie on the ground. Beating his drum, the *bodhran,* he calls to the spirits. **11 The Web** shows the Weaver Goddess in an autumnal clearing. At the corners of the card are juniper berries, associated with purification and also sacred to the spirits of divine vengeance as sent by the gods to administer justice; hazelnuts, symbol of wisdom that can create or destroy; and a spider in a web. She is Arianrhod, mistress of the Spiral Castle of death, initiation, and rebirth. **12 Sacrifice** shows a man of corn or corn dolly, which represents the life of the corn spirit sacrificed so that humankind might eat. The corn dolly was made up of the last sheaf of grain that was harvested. In the border are poppies and cornflowers, the fruit of the Underworld womb of the Harvest Mother; blackberries, which provide the wine at the autumn equinox; and a harvest mouse, regarded as an Underworld animal.

THIRD ROW: **14 The Underworld** shows King Gwyn ap Nudd in his Underworld domain of Annwn. He is in purple and wears a crown of lead and onyx. A white pig with red ears is with him. The border of the card shows a green dragon and a red one, with branches of yew. The station of this card is Samhain, or Halloween, the start of winter and the Celtic New Year Festival. **19 The Sun** shows the bright face of the sun god at the height of his powers, at the midsummer solstice. Lizards bask in the heat, and bees pollinate the flowers of St. John's wort. Lizards, sun-loving creatures, are associated with light, as well as wisdom and divination. Bees are also considered wise creatures with special knowledge of the future. St. John's wort, a sacred herb of midsummer, is the plant of the sun and magically encompasses the sun's energy. **20 Rebirth** shows the sun, reborn as a babe of Ceridwen after the winter solstice, rising through a domen arch that is inscribed with spiral patterns and decorated with holly and ivy. **21 The World Tree** is a giant oak that links the Three Realms of Being: the Underworld, the Middle Earth, and the heavens. Mistletoe, symbol of life through death, hangs on its branches. An eagle, associated with authority and royalty, soars in the air. A snake, associated with the entire cycle of the year, is at its roots.

BOTTOM ROW: **7 of Swords: Diplomacy.** The Uffington White Horse, in Oxfordshire, England, was made circa 1400 BCE. Horses were sacred as enabling humankind to perform previously impossible tasks, and as symbolic of travel to the Otherworld. **King of Wands: Fire.** The King is crowned with golden oak leaves. Behind him is Stonehenge in midsummer. **Queen of Cups: Intuition.** The Queen holds a gold cup as she rises from the center of a lake. A kingfisher flashes across the water. In the background is Glastonbury Tor, Somerset. By following the spiral path to the summit of the Tor, one is said to gain access to the Otherworld, the fairy realm. **Queen of Discs: Expression.** The Queen sits in a winter landscape in Kerry, Ireland. She is like the ivy around her throne, alive and vital whatever the season.

| The Lady | The Lord | The Druid | The Lovers |
| 3 | 4 | 5 | 6 |

| The Warrior | The Shaman | The Web | Sacrifice |
| 8 | 9 | 11 | 12 |

| The Underworld | The Sun | Rebirth | The World Tree |
| 14 | 19 | 20 | 21 |

| Diplomacy | Fire | Intuition | Expression |
| 7 of Swords | King of Wands | Queen of Cups | Queen of Discs |

Tarot of the Saints Robert M. Place, Llewellyn Publications, 2001 The description is extracted from the book *A Gnostic Book of Saints,* by Place.

TOP ROW: **St. Francis: The Fool.** The card illustrates St. Francis "foolishly" preaching to the birds, much to the amusement of observers. Their amusement turned to amazement when the birds flew away in the formation of a cross.

II St. Mary Magdalen: The Papesse. Mary Magdalen, in Gnostic belief, was the beloved of Christ and leader of the Apostles. She embodies the individual visionary experience.

Tarot of the Saints   Robert M. Place created the Tarot of the Saints following a suggestion from artist Rosemary Guiley, and then a visionary dream. He describes the dream in his book, *A Gnostic Book of Saints.* In the dream, he found a corpse in a ruined church. He took it home and cooked it, and to his amazement, it tasted of chocolate. He realized that the corpse was a relic, and that the taste of chocolate was a reflection on the Latin name for the cacao bush, which means "food of god." He was also inspired by holy cards, which show saints on cards approximately the size of tarot cards. The Major Arcana and court cards portray saints. The pips show objects or scenes, some Biblical, that reflect the traditional symbolism of the cards.

Place bases many of his interpretations of the saints largely on texts by the Gnostics, various mystics who flourished from the second to the fourth centuries after Christ. What they had in common was a yearning for *gnosis,* union with God. Usually the term Gnostic refers to Christian, but there were Hermetic, Jewish, and Pagan Gnostics as well.

The deck was published by Llewellyn Publications, St. Paul, in 2001. The back design shows an eye, a dove, and a heart in purple on white.

Santa Fe Tarot   The Santa Fe Tarot is based on Navajo sand paintings. The creators of the deck are sisters Holly Huber and Tracy LeCocq. The suits of the deck are lightning (swords), rainbows (wands), water (cups), and buffalos (disks). The deck includes a title card and an introductory card. The back design is double-ended, a geometric pattern in green, black, and orange, with snakes at the ends. The Santa Fe Tarot was published by U.S. Games Systems, Stamford, Connecticut, in 1993.

VI St. Valentine and the Lovers. According to the legend, Valentine was a priest in Rome under the reign of Emperor Claudius II. The emperor ordered all soldiers to remain unmarried so that they would be free of attachments. Valentine defied the emperor and secretly married soldiers. **VII St. Christopher: The Chariot.** St. Christopher was a man of great strength. He carried a child across a river, but with every step the child grew heavier and the river rougher. He persevered, and when they reached the other shore, the child revealed that he was Christ. **VIII St. Michael: Justice.** Michael is an angel who cast Satan into a fiery pit. He brandishes sword and holds the scales of justice. He protects souls, and also rescues them from hell.

SECOND ROW: **IX St. Anthony of Egypt: The Hermit.** St. Anthony lived in the desert as a hermit for twenty years, then founded the first Christian monastic committee. The pig in the picture represents the lust he overcame, and the saint's bell drives evil away. **XII St. Blandina: The Hanged One.** Blandina of Lyon was a slave and a Christian serving a Christian master. She was arrested with her master and others, and all were tortured. Her faith withstood the torments, which included being hung by her feet in an arena to be eaten by wild animals, who refused their meal. **XIV St. Benedict: Temperance.** St. Benedict lived for a while as a hermit; it is said he was fed by a raven, which is shown at his feet. He eventually established twelve monasteries. He used the waterclock, symbolized by the water-driven hourglass, to regulate all aspects of a monk's life. **XV St. Margaret and the Devil.** Margaret was turned out of her home, when she converted to Christianity, and became a shepherdess. The governor of Antioch was taken by her beauty and tried to seduce her, but she refused. In his anger, the governor fed her to a dragon. She burst open its belly and stepped out triumphant. **XVI St. Barbara: The Tower.** Barbara was the daughter of a rich Pagan, so she kept her Christianity secret. She was very beautiful, and to protect her from suitors, her father locked her in a tower. She had three windows made in the tower to symbolize the trinity, and when her father

asked about them, she acknowledged that she was Christian. The prefect of the province sentenced her to death, and her father beheaded her in the tower. However, as he carried out the sentence, a bolt of lightning struck him dead.

THIRD ROW: **XVIII St. Mary: The Moon.** Mary stands on the moon as Queen of Heavens. From her hands, she radiates God's grace, love, and forgiveness. **XIX Christ: The Sun.** Blessed Faustina Kawalska, a Polish nun, had a vision in which she beheld Christ with two rays streaming from his heart. One, stemming from the right side, was red, symbolizing the blood that he shed to atone for our sins, and the other, from the left, was white, symbolizing the water of baptism. **XXI St. Sophia: The World.** In Gnostic creation myths, Sophia was an emanation of the true God and the mother of all the angels. She became trapped in the world of matter and transmigrated into different female bodies, suffering various indignities. Eventually her love of the light of lights was restored, and she became the mystical bride of Christ. In the picture, Sophia, which means wisdom, stands on a globe, and in front are the symbols of the three Christian virtues, her daughters Faith (the cross), Hope (the anchor), and Charity (the heart). **St. Joan: Queen of Swords** was a visionary French girl who helped restore Charles VII to the throne. **Three of Swords.** Three swords pierce the immaculate heart of Mary. Through suffering, one learns to empathize with the suffering of others. In this light, suffering is love, symbolized by the roses.

BOTTOM ROW: **Five of Staffs.** The hand bears the stigmata, a wound duplicating one of Christ's wounds. It symbolizes the spirit working through the hands. **St. John: Knight of Cups.** John was ordered by an emperor to drink a cup of poisoned wine. When he picked up the cup, the poison departed in the form of a snake. **Ten of Cups.** In St. Mark 10:14, Christ says, "Suffer the little children to come unto me, and forbid them not, for of such is the kingdom of god." **Six of Cups.** Christ washes St. Peter's feet. **Six of Coins** shows a pelican, which has the legend of drawing blood from its own breast in order to feed its young.

Santa Fe Tarot Holly Huber and Tracy LeCocq, U.S. Games Systems, 1993 The descriptions are by the artists.

TOP ROW: **0 The Fool: Rainboy** dances with snakes coming from his feet, showing he travels to many unusual places. He holds crooked lightning and a wand to give him power and vision. From the wand hand dangle rattles which grant him joy and dreams. Guardian bats protect him, and they flank a barred rainbow headdress with many small corn people showing Rainboy's ability to please and entertain. Because the headdress does not actually touch Rainboy, his dreams may be distant. **2 The High Priestess: Corn-Cloud Woman.** Butterflies guardians signify Corn-Cloud Woman's beauty and her transformation. In her right hand is a weasel pouch to indicate her wisdom and perception. In her left is a medicine pouch adorned with feathers, signifying intuition and far-reaching thought. She wears a feathered headdress, and the rainbow border surrounding her is capped and underscored with feathers. **4 The Emperor: Father Sky** is one of the few male *yeis* to have the square head normally assigned to female deities. (A *yei* is a powerful being that gives knowledge on living in beauty and harmony.) Like his mate, Mother Earth, Father Sky wears a horned headdress, but his mask is the yellow and black of the warrior. Inside him, the sun, moon, and stars depict his influence over all he sees. His hands hold the earth and all its elements, and his rainbow border is adorned by the feathers of intuition colored with war colors. Sun and Moon guardians offer him protection day and night. **5 The Hierophant: Holy Man.** As a powerful *ha'atathli,* Holy Man traveled far and wide to learn the powers of many different peoples, until he himself became a *yei*. He wears a horned headdress, signifying his wisdom, and a feathered mask to show his adherence to old ways. Curved rainbows extend from his hands and feet, showing his powerful nature and his innate kindness. He carries a crooked spear and a bull-roarer and medicine wand. A butterfly and a frog serve as his guardians, lending him both beauty and cunning. His dress is dark and warriorlike, giving him a somber, oppressive air. **6 The Lovers: White Corn Man-Yellow Corn Woman** seem eternally apart here, and yet are forever linked by Corn-Beetle who interrupts the separation. Depicted here in their *yei* form, both have many ears of ripe corn, waiting to be plucked, and large feather headdresses showing idealism and faith. In the four corners are the tipi, clouds, fish, and hearth, representing the four elements.

SECOND ROW: **7 The Chariot: B'Ganaskiddy,** also known as the Hump-backed *yei* or the Navajo God of Plenty, is on a continual journey with many perils. His hump is a deerskin bag carrying seeds. He holds a medicine pouch and a double bull-roarer. The mountains beneath his feet show the distances he must walk. His headdress is traditional Mountain Sheep horns. **8 Strength: Monster Slayer.** Nayenezgani, or Monster Slayer, is armed with crooked lightning given to him by his father, the Sun. His dress is decorated with crooked lightning, and crooked lightning crosses him, pointing in all directions His guardians are twin suns, dark and light. He stands on a double-headed lightning bolt. **9 The Hermit: Pollen Boy on the Sun.** Pollen Boy took his place so that the sun might not be lonely and could take a rest, allowing the People to escape the burning heat. He

stands upon the Sun's mouth, flanked by two short rainbow bars. His hands seem to cup the Sun's eyes. The Sun is huge, with red and black eagle feathers and black, lightning-decorated horns. **10 Wheel of Fortune: Whirling Rainbow.** A single, right-sided Rainbow *yei* with black and white face and blue feathers borders eight Whirling Rainbow *yeis* all connected and spinning clockwise. Crooked lightning of different lengths and heights float in between the Whirling *yeis* and all are just out of grasp. **12 The Hanged Man: Blue Whirlwind Boy** pestered one and all until caught by the Thunders and forced to contemplate his existence. His whirlwind rattles are in warrior colors, and crooked lightning spills from his hands. Trapped suns serve as his rattles and hang above his head. Snake guardians, which would ordinarily flank his head, run from his feet instead. An unarmed, non-headdressed Rainbow *yei* serves as his border.

THIRD ROW: **13 Death: Big Endless Snake.** In Navajo tradition, Death disrupts balance and harmony. Nowhere in sand paintings or myth does any *yei* represent Death. However, Big Endless Snake represents transformation, the eternal change with no beginnings, no endings. Big Endless Snake curls in the center of the card, as though ready to strike—or to transform. It is accompanied by four smaller Endless Snakes, black and yellow on the left, white and green on the right. A large guardian snake marked with deer tracks borders the painting. Two cloud guardians highlight the way to the future. **16 The Tower: Red Thunder Yei.** Red Thunder *Yei* is depicted headless, with crooked lightning shooting across four feathers. Warlike yellow crooked lightning forks from yellow-tipped open hands with small black circles showing the world already taken. Two male and female *yeis* peer fearfully from each level on each side of the wings as they are about to be spilled out. Fanged snakes approach each foot instead of drawing away from them. **18 The Moon: The Moon,** considered a pale twin brother of the Sun, wears two broad, striped horns with dangling feathers and beads indicating superior status. Dyed eagle feathers as headdress and collar reveal intuition and sometimes artifice. His cheeks are masked with short rainbow bars while an inverted tipi adorns his forehead and a true tipi, his chin. He is protected by a thick rainbow border with three feathers, and his guardians are twin snakes. **19 The Sun: The Sun.** Father of the Twin War Gods—represented here by the two inverted and fringed medicine pouches—the Sun is a powerful god who affects most of life. He has a horned headdress with long feathers and beads and wears cloth-and-bead earrings. His headdress is crowned with tremendous feathers and shafts of spears while his collar is comprised of eagle feathers with sand and seeds painted on them. The central feather of the collar holds the bean plant. He is protected by four rainbow bars. **20 Judgment: Water Creatures.** Balancing the waterways of the world are four Water Creatures, two linked above and two touching hands below. The waterways are twisted and confused. These *yeis* are all female in nature. A tri-colored rainbow border with two feathers protects the Water Creatures in their difficult task.

BOTTOM ROW: **21 The World: Emergence Place.** In the Creation Story, the People had to pass through several levels before arriving in the present world. The way through to this world is the Emergence Place. A yellow-masked and

0 THE FOOL Rainboy	2 THE HIGH PRIESTESS CORN-CLOUD WOMAN	4 THE EMPEROR FATHER SKY	5 THE HIEROPHANT HOLY MAN	6 THE LOVERS WHITE CORN MAN—YELLOW CORN WOMAN
7 THE CHARIOT B'GANASKIDDY	8 STRENGTH MONSTER SLAYER	9 THE HERMIT POLLEN BOY ON THE SUN	10 WHEEL OF FORTUNE WHIRLING RAINBOW	12 THE HANGED MAN BLUE WHIRLWIND BOY
15 DEATH BIG ENDLESS SNAKE	16 THE TOWER RED THUNDER YEI	18 THE MOON THE MOON	19 THE SUN THE SUN	20 JUDGMENT WATER CREATURES
21 THE WORLD EMERGENCE PLACE	NINE OF LIGHTNING	ACE OF RAINBOWS	QUEEN OF WATER WATER WOMAN	TWO OF BUFFALO

skirted rainbow *yei* borders the world, offering fierce protection. The world, depicted with sand in it, has corn-cloud rays stretching out from it. Two cloud tiers are capped with Buffalo People, the other two with Bird People. Crooked

lightning lies in between the tiers but doesn't follow a particular pattern. **Nine of Lightning. Ace of Rainbows. Queen of Water. Two of Buffalo.**

509

Collection of the author / © 1993 by U.S. Games Systems, Inc.

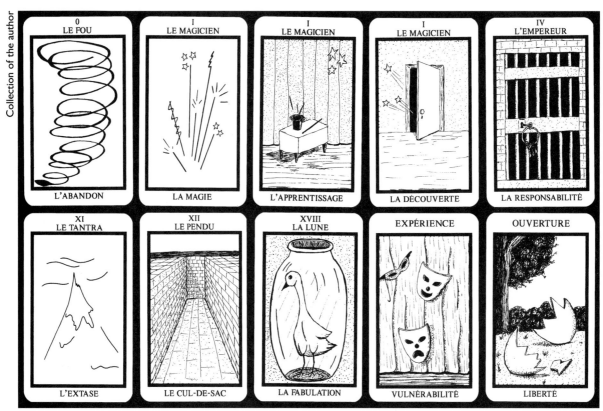

Tarot de Sati Hélèle Lavoie-Sati, Sati International, 1991

Tarot de Sati Hélèle Lavoie-Sati created the Tarot de Sati as a guide to everyday life. The deck has a Major Arcana that includes three versions of I Le Magicien (The Magician). The four suits are energy (with orange backgrounds), emotions (pink backgrounds), matter (blue backgrounds), and intellect (yellow backgrounds). Instead of courts, the suits have ouverture (opening), intérieur (interior), expérience, and choix (choice). The deck was published by Sati International (previously C.R.I. Publications) of Quebec in 1991. The back design is black and white, with the words "Le Tarot de Sati" under a circle in a triangle.

Scented Tarot Witta Jensen created the Scented Tarot with small drawings color-photocopied and attached back to back (to make the face and back of each card), then cut round. "The illustrations are based on my picture-Diary of a Danish Housewife," Jensen says in the folding flyer that accompanies the Scented Tarot. There is no back design; rather, the backs of the cards correspond in meaning to their faces. The decks were packaged in tins that originally held scented candles, hence the name and fragrance of the decks. At the bottom of the tin is glued a photograph of the artist. The artist's full name, given in the flyer, is Georgine, Margareta Witta Kiessling Smith Jensen. The artist cites many inspira-

tions, including cards by Tracy Moore and Sandra McCall, which she calls "inspirators." Jensen issued the deck in a signed, numbered edition of 35, circa 2000. The flyer accompanying the deck refers to two versions each of 0, I, II, and III. The deck in the author's collection has two versions of I, II, and III, and no X card.

Tarocchi dei Segretti (Secrets Tarots) "This Land is a magical world, inhabited by angels and devils, peopled by enchanted beasts and extraordinary characters, whose deeds become important exemplary events." The Secrets Tarots, by Marco Nizzoli, illustrates a journey by a "tramp, a young idle," who accidentally discovers the Secret Land. His journey through it and adventures there are an allegorical story of self-development described in the leaflet accompanying the deck. The four suits correspond to the the Kingdom of Sorrow (swords), the Kingdom of Human Work (wands), the Kingdom of Pleasure (chalices), and the Kingdom of Riches (pentacles). The deck was published by Lo Scarabeo of Turin, Italy, in 1997. It includes a title card and an advertising card. The double-ended back design, in blue, shows a man sitting at a window. The cards are titled in English, German, French, Spanish, and Italian.

Scented Tarot   Witta Jensen, published by the artist, 2000   The caption gives the words written on the cards, which did not reproduce successfully, since the lettering is dark on dark backgrounds.

TOP ROW: 0 The Fool / Ideas • Abiss. 0 (back). I The Magician / Mind Expansion • Eternity. I (back).

SECOND ROW: I The Magician / Originality • Flexibility. I (back). II The High Priestess / Withdrawn Phantom. II (back).

THIRD ROW: II The High Priestess / Mysticism • Serious. II (back). III The Empress / Natural Grace • Action. III (back).

BOTTOM ROW: VI The Lovers / Shallowness • Puerility. VI (back). XIII Death / Transformation • End. XIII (back)

Tarocchi dei Segretti (Secrets Tarot)   Marco Nizzoli, Lo Scarabeo, 1997

Tarot of the Sephiroth   Artist Dan Staroff created the Tarot of the Sephiroth with the intention to "break through the veils and shadows of traditional Tarot images, and to interpret them for a new era in which accessibility to the concepts and constructs of the Qabalah was key." The Major Arcana cards correspond to the paths that connect the Sephiroth. The numbered Minor Arcana correspond to the Sephiroth, or spheres, of the Kabbalistic Tree of Life. They are shown with circular borders in symbolic colors. "Additionally," the artist describes, "in an overlay of the twos, threes, sixes, and tens, the borders of these cards will align with the appropriate sphere formed by the joining of the Court cards into their respective spheres." The artist's use of clear colors and flowing lines free this deck of the rigidness that often characterizes decks based on symbolic or philosophical systems. The deck, which includes a presentation card and an introductory card, was published by U.S. Games Systems in 1999. The back design is of white stars on a blue background.

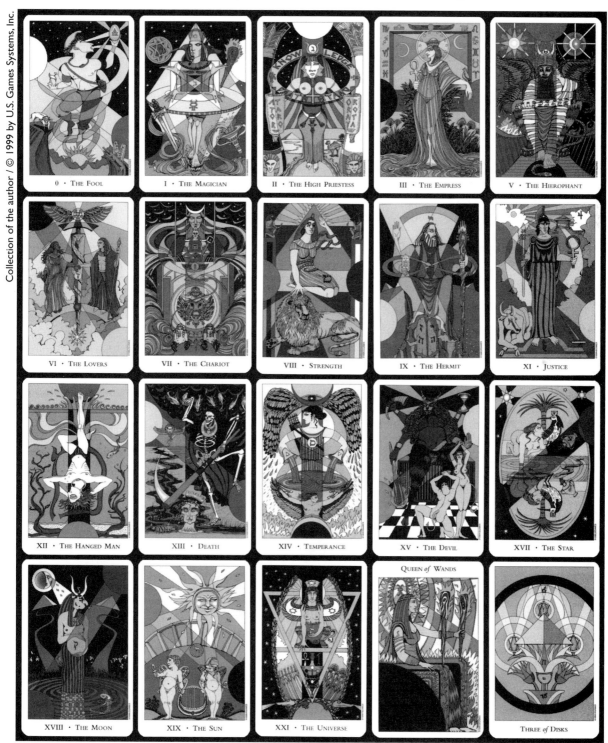

0 · The Fool | I · The Magician | II · The High Priestess | III · The Empress | V · The Hierophant

VI · The Lovers | VII · The Chariot | VIII · Strength | IX · The Hermit | XI · Justice

XII · The Hanged Man | XIII · Death | XIV · Temperance | XV · The Devil | XVII · The Star

XVIII · The Moon | XIX · The Sun | XXI · The Universe | Queen of Wands | Three of Disks

Tarot of the Sephiroth   Dan Staroff, U.S. Games Systems, 1999

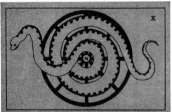

Serpent-Dragon Tarot Medicator is the pseudonym of Dirk Gillabel, the artist who created the Serpent-Dragon Tarot. The deck was issued by his brother Guido Gillabel in an edition of seventy-seven copies, in 1989. Another edition, with black background and white line art, was issued in 2001 by Soul Guidance, the company of Dirk Gillabel and Carol Herzer. The 2001 deck, made with laser prints backed with vinyl and laminated, includes a twenty-page booklet.

The cards have black line art on gold backgrounds. The back design reads "Medicator" in the middle, with "Slang Draak Tarot" in the upper right corner and "Serpent-Dragon Tarot" at the lower left. The deck comprises Major Arcana plus two cards showing a diagram of the Kabbalistic Tree of Life, one in English and the other in Flemish. The artist says of the deck, "The Serpent-Dragon Tarot combines world-wide symbolic images of serpents and dragons, the Hebrew alphabet, and the traditional meaning of the tarot cards. The basis of each card is a Hebrew letter, around which a serpent or dragon is woven to enhance the meaning of the card." Many of the images are from alchemical texts.

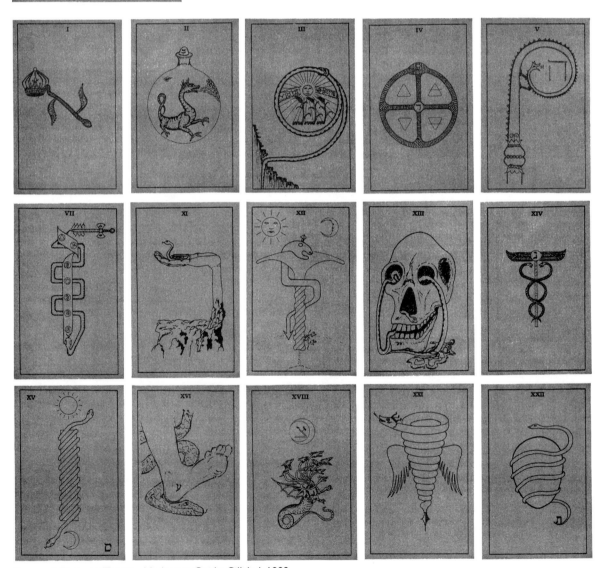

Serpent-Dragon Tarot Medicator, Guido Gillabel, 1989

Tarot Settanni All of the models photographed by Pino Settanni for the Major Arcana of his tarot deck are women, with the exception of 22 The Fool, who is Mario Scaccia, an Italian actor. The models wear mostly bold colors of red, blue, yellow, and green, and appear against a black background. XVI The Tower is the only Major Arcana that does not show an actual model, but only a set. For the rest, only the simple set and figures can be seen. Jean-Louis Victor's book, which accompanies the deck, does not say whether the models were posed against the black or if the figures were composed by computer on the black background. Only on The Fool is any hint of background features visible. The court cards feature one dominant color, depending on the suit, and even the makeup on the models is in that color. For example, the models of the suit of coins have yellow lips. The pip cards are artist's puppets colored in red, green, yellow, and blue and posed on the suit sign. The images are bordered in red and gold. Titles are in German and English. The back design shows a square of red, blue, green, and yellow, on gold with a purple border. The overall appearance of the cards is simple, but much ingenuity and craftsmanship went into the design and construction of the costumes and the sets, as well as in the photography itself. Settanni shot the deck using a Mamiya RZ67 camera with Kodak Ektachrome 64 film. The deck was published by Urania Art, Neuhausen, Switzerland, in 1995.

Shakespeare Oracle "No one understands human nature as does the eternally popular William Shakespeare," says the packaging of the Shakespeare Oracle. "His immortal works abound with countless insights into the human condition, while encompassing the full range of human emotion. Who better to advise us as we struggle to navigate our own lives? Just as tarot cards mirror a moment in time and offer clues to your inner world, Shakespeare's famed theater mirrored every situation of his day."

The suits of the Shakespeare Oracle are quills (swords), sceptres, chalices, and coins, with courts of king, queen, lord, and lady. Each of the Major Arcana and courts features a Shakespearian character. The pips show the suit signs and a scroll with an appropriate quote from Shakespeare. A. Bronwyn Llewellyn created the Shakespeare Oracle, with paintings by Cynthia von Buhler. The deck-and-book set was published in 2003 by Fair Winds Press, Gloucester, Massachusetts. The back design is of a coin with the letter S on a black background.

Shakespeare Tarot (Tarocchi di Giulietta e Romeo) Veronese artist Luigi Scapini brings his rich imagination and chaotic symbology to Shakespeare. Although the Italian title of the deck is the Tarot of Romeo and Juliet, the scenes on the cards range from all the works of Shakespeare. In the booklet accompanying the deck, Scapini explains, "I have a clear preference—also because I am from Verona—for Romeo and Juliet. They loved and died at the beginning of the fourteenth century, and what does it matter if they were historical personages or merely characters from someone's imagination? Because of this choice, characters, architecture, objects, coins, references to this period dominate my work." The artist's comments reveal his mix of realism and fantasy. "In my references I have tried to be as precise as possible, since I believe the more hypothetical a world is, the richer it must be in details of the real world, so that it may acquire a projective and at the same time autonomous essence; in other words, it must be real!"

The background of the Major Arcana scenes and the back design are gold-figured, in reference to the Renaissance cards of Northern Italy. As Scapini says, "I have kept in mind the ancient cards of the Veneto so as to create a pack with which the two lovers of Verona, between one amorous game and another, would not have thought beneath them to play."

The deck was published by Dal Negro Spa of Treviso, Italy, around 1990, and is accompanied by a descriptive book by the artist, in Italian and translated into English by Susanna Corradi. Titles on the cards are in Italian and English.

Shakespeare Oracle A. Bronwyn Llewellyn and Cynthia von Buhler, artist, Fair Winds Press, 2003

Collection of the author / Paintings © 2003 by Cynthia von Buhler

Tarot Settanni   Pino Settanni, Urania Art, 1995

Shakespeare Tarot (Tarocchi di Giulietta e Romeo)   Luigi Scapini, Dal Negro, circa 1990   Quotes are from the book accompanying the deck.

TOP ROW: **0 The Fool** is the Fool of King Lear, based on the 1767 painting by John Runciman, *King Lear in the Storm.* "If the Fool in vain blows his meaningless individual soul into the face of cosmic revolutions, the alms sack he carries upon his shoulder, like the Fool in Claude Burdel's tarot, is torn, and from the bottom flies out the winged maid of the world, anima mundi of the tarot, sealing up the wheel of the Major Arcana cards, which open with the Fool and end in the World." [Burdel was an eighteenth-century Swiss cardmaker.] **I The Magician** is "the magic stage director…William Shakespeare himself. He holds the strings of Romeo's and Juliet's lives, who are about to act out their own script in a puppet Theatre of the World, a lilliputian Globe. [The Globe was the theater in which many of Shakespeare's plays were first performed.] But it's uncertain whether the theatre is a miniature, or the puppeteer a mighty giant.…" **II The Popess** is "a papist popess to face an obvious rival, the lawful queen, Elisabeth Empress." Mary Stuart was the Catholic contender to the English throne, and Elizabeth's half-sister.

She was eventually executed. **III The Empress** is "Elisabeth Tudor in her prime. This is the self-same dress she wore the day History put a crown upon her head." **IIII The Emperor** is Albert I, of the House of Hapsburg, head of the Holy Roman Empire. The dog that ripped the Fool's back fawns at the Emperor's feet.

BOTTOM ROW: **VI The Lovers** are, of course, Romeo and Juliet. They are being wed by Friar Lawrence. **VII The Chariot** is driven by the defeated Coriolanus. "I feared my world in miniature would collapse when, reading over *Coriolanus,* I had to face a loser, rather than the proud charioteer of a platonic chariot. Yes, there's the patrician's noble death and his decorous funeral.…" **VIII Justice** "comes from the allegory of Justice illuminated on a later copy of the statues of Domus Mercatorum in Verona.…" The double-faced figure at the bottom shows the feuding patriarchs, Capulet and Montague. Above is the double-faced figure of Romeo and Juliet. **VIIII The Hermit** is Friar Lawrence, gathering the herbs that will send Juliet into her fateful swoon. **XI Force** depicts Orlando, of *As You Like It.* He struggles with a lioness that represents his spiteful brother Olivier.

Shakespeare Tarot (*continued*)   TOP ROW: **XII The Hanged Man** is Hamlet, and he is a self-portrait of the artist, though "I dyed my hair to a fair mane and in conscious vanity did rejuvenate myself!" From Hamlet's ankle depends the skull of Yorick, the jester, and below, Ophelia floats upon her outspread gown. **XIII** is "An arcanum without a name." The skeletal figures represent "Romeo's death, rising up, yang, and Juliet's, squatting down, yin." **XIIII Temperance** is Cordelia of *King Lear*. "The pitiful daughter restores her thirsty father with a liquor so thin it can disobey the laws of gravity and return from down here to our heavenly father in the sky." **XV The Devil** is Richard the Third. In Shakespeare's drama, he had the child princes Edward and Richard killed in the Tower of London. The wicked daughters of King Lear, Regan and Goneril, hold the babies up to him. **XVII The Star** depicts Miranda, from *The Tempest*. She holds the cup from which she taught the "hag seed" Caliban to

drink. "Perhaps the lucky log bearing Miranda's weight is what's left of the Hanged Man's willow, once it has been chopped down."

BOTTOM ROW: **VIII The Moon** is the famous scene in *Romeo and Juliet*, in which Romeo comes to make love to Juliet, scaling the wall to the balcony outside her room. "A nightingale—not a lark!—is in the foreground." **Queen of Swords** is the cruel and power-hungry Lady MacBeth. The three witches of the moor are at the lower right. Scapini's image is after J.P. Sargent's painting of actress Ellen Terry on the opening night of *King Lear*, December 29, 1888. **Four of Wands** depicts Mrs. Ford and Mrs. Page, in *The Merry Wives of Windsor*, plotting revenge on the fat John Falstaff. **Seven of Cups** shows Puck at the center, directing the show of *A Midsummer Night's Dream*. The poppy juice in the cups has sent the cast to sleep. **Ace of Coins** depicts Teodomiro dal Negro, who commissioned the Shakespeare Tarot.

Shakespearian Tarot Dolores Ashcroft-Nowicki, together with artist Paul Hardy, aspired to create a deck "to show that behind the playwright was a mind that encompassed the Hidden Art as well as a vast knowledge of his fellow man." Each card of the deck shows a scene illustrating the quote that appears on the card. The back design is a trompe l'oeil design of a floral motif carved in wood. The deck was published by Aquarian Press, London, in 1993.

Shapeshifter Tarot Lisa Hunt illustrated the Shapeshifter Tarot under direction of D.J. Conway and Sirona Knight. The full deck includes two extra Major Arcana, numbered 23 and 24. The deck draws from

Celtic lore of shapeshifters, people who can assume the forms of animals. "There are many Celtic legends about the power of shapeshifting, all written as if the person practicing it physically became another creature. However, physically speaking, this doesn't happen. The shamanistic talent is really the assuming of a certain creature's characteristics, traits, and talents for a limited time." The images of the deck show people symbolically taking on the forms of animals and plants. The total of eighty-one cards in the deck refers to an oath taken by eighty-one knights. The oath was to bring light back into the dark land. The deck was published by Llewellyn Publications of St. Paul, Minnesota, in 1998. The back design shows a Celtic medallion in yellow on blue.

0 THE FOOL
"I am but a fool, look you"
TWO GENTLEMEN OF VERONA

I THE MAGICIAN
"Now does my project gather to a head"
THE TEMPEST

II THE HIGH PRIESTESS
"I have immortal longings in me"
ANTONY AND CLEOPATRA

III THE EMPRESS
"What wisdom stirs amongst you?"
A WINTER'S TALE

IV THE EMPEROR
"I am as constant as the northern star"
JULIUS CAESAR

VII THE CHARIOT
"He doth bestride the narrow world"
JULIUS CAESAR

VIII STRENGTH
"O, I am fire and air..."
ANTONY AND CLEOPATRA

IX THE HERMIT
"Blow winds, and crack thy cheeks"
KING LEAR

X THE WHEEL OF FORTUNE
"The wheel hath come full circle"
KING LEAR

XI JUSTICE
"The quality of mercy is not strained"
THE MERCHANT OF VENICE

XIII DEATH
"And if I die no soul shall pity me..."
RICHARD THE THIRD

XIV TEMPERANCE
"One foot in sea, and one on shore"
MUCH ADO ABOUT NOTHING

XVII THE STAR
"A star danced, and under that I was born"
MUCH ADO ABOUT NOTHING

XVIII THE MOON
"Ill met by moonlight proud Titania"
A MIDSUMMER NIGHT'S DREAM

XIX THE SUN
"This chosen infant... bright sun of heaven"
KING HENRY THE EIGHTH

XXI THE WORLD
"All the world's a stage..."
AS YOU LIKE IT

TWO OF SWORDS
"A plague on both your houses, I am spent"
ROMEO AND JULIET

EIGHT OF SCEPTRES
"I'll promise you calm seas"
THE TEMPEST

SIX OF CROWNS
"Crowns in my purse have I..."
THE TAMING OF THE SHREW

SIX OF ORBS
"...to dew her orbs upon the green"
A MIDSUMMER NIGHT'S DREAM

Shakespearian Tarot Paul Hardy, artist, and Dolores Ashcroft-Nowicki, Aquarian Press, 1993

0 Initiation   2 Sorceress   3 The Mother   4 The Father   5 Knowledge

8 Courage   9 The Seer   13 Rebirth   14 Balance   15 Choice

Shapeshifter Tarot   Lisa Hunt, artist, D.J. Conway, and Sirona Knight, Llewellyn Publications, 1998   The descriptions are based on those in the book accompanying the deck.

TOP ROW: **0 Initiation.** The powerful dragon energy is working within the initiate, giving him the spiritual strength, determination, and courage to face his inner self. **2 Sorceress** has half-shifted into an owl, the bird of mystical wisdom and ancient knowledge of the powers of the moon, which is at her feet and behind her. Ancient standing stones circle her head, representing her ability to access forgotten wisdom through the subconscious mind. A crow is the messenger of the Goddess. **3 The Mother.** As the divine mare drinks from the pool of knowledge, the pregnant Mother stands with her feet immersed. She holds a ripe pomegranate and a triskelion amulet necklace. Her green robes, decorated with the cosmic web, signify her close relationship with nature and the green world. **4 The Father** has a powerful body, symbolizing his perfect balance in both nature and spirit. His green belt establishes his eternal reign, with the Mother, over all forms of reproduction. The antler crown is a sign that he is in complete control of himself and all his emotions and energy. His left hand holds a globe, the material world, and his right calls down and catches bolts of lightning, the divine spark of life. **5 Knowledge** shows a woman shapeshifting into an elephant, symbol of action, power, and long life. The trefoil on her green robe symbolizes the threefold: positive, neutral, and negative. The open book symbolizes an open mind and conscious awareness.

BOTTOM ROW: **8 Courage.** Part bear and part human, the woman stands undaunted by life. Her half-shifted daughter is at her side, secure in the shelter of her mother's arm. The bear-woman holds a ball of brilliant light, symbolic of the guiding spiritual light in her life. The green snake at her feet is symbol of the mystical labyrinthine patterns of the seeker's path. **9 The Seer** is a shapeshifter eagle-man standing alone in a lush woodland. Associated with lightning and with powers that control rain and thunder, the eagle, just as the Seer, understands the power of the elements. One of the eagle-man's hands is outstretched in a creative gesture, holding a large shining crystal that looks like a beacon, lighting his path. **13 Rebirth.** the raven-woman embodies Rebirth as the full moon shines. Images of a scorpion (survival on an earthly plane) and the beetle (eternal life) flow before her. She is drinking in the moment, the eternal now. A band of roses covers her, the mystic red rose signifying life and sexuality. **14 Balance.** The woman and her children float effortlessly in the primal ocean of creative energy and the life force. About them swim their guardians and guides, the dolphins. The spiral sea shells represent the constant presence of the Great Goddess. **15 Choice.** Standing at the threshold of a great henge of stone, the satyr-woman and the minotaur-man become the Lady and Lord of the Gates of Matter. Loosely connected at the ankles by a spiral of divine light, the woman and man are joined together in sacred union. He holds the torch of creative vision and passion.

17 The Star   18 The Moon   20 Transcendence   21 The Double   22 The Journey

23 The Dreamer   24 Oneness   Fire Element (Swords) 12 Warrior of Fire   Air Element (Wands) 5 Struggle   Water Element (Cups) 8 The Quest

Shapeshifter Tarot *(continued)*

TOP ROW: **17 The Star.** The spider-woman weaves the fabric of life and personifies the daughter of the firmament. Her web is woven like an eight-pointed star representing the Wheel of Life and the path of the sun. Green (earth), gold (air), crimson (fire), and blue (water) dragons coil through the star web in the four directions. Seven smaller stars represent the seven veils of spiritual awareness and the Seven Sisters, the Pleiades. **18 The Moon.** The woman (a white timber wolf) and the man (a black timber wolf) are allowing complete flow of power from the animal allies (Otherworld helpers) to pour through them. The twisted tree behind them represents the World Tree, the cosmic bridge to the Otherworld. **20 Transcendence.** The seekers have come to the point when their spiritual seeking has opened their eyes to the reality of all levels of existence. The woman, half shifted into a butterfly, has freed herself from the cocoon of limited physical thinking. The man has freed himself from the cocoon of common stultifying images of males and is expressing his softer, creative side through music. The harp itself represents the bridge between the Upperworld and Earth. **21 The Double.** Part human, part fox, the woman shapeshifter moves and doubles out between dimensions of the continuum at will. The red fox symbolizes the vital and active energy of Oneness. Wearing a single ruby ring and spiral disks as earrings, the woman stands in a star-filled pool of water that ripples outward in tiers, like veils of awareness. **22 The Journey.** The initiate has taken the form of a house, a Goddess creature whose keen senses of inner sight and smell will aid the initiate in traversing the labyrinth of life in his search for the Divine Center. Accompanying him are cats

(symbols of independence, resourcefulness, and wisdom) and mice (representations of stealth, caution, and cunning). Faces of his past lives peer out from the tree trunks; he has delved into his past lives and learned from them so that they no longer hold any fear, shame, or glory except as physical learning stations along the eternal journey.

BOTTOM ROW: **23 The Dreamer.** Standing in the Goddess position with arms stretched upward, the swan-woman holds the full moon lightly in her hands. Birds (ideas) fly freely in the distance, representing the boundless potential of the Dreamer's mind. **24 Oneness.** Various members of the human family are pictured within a great globe. The globe itself represents the world-soul and wholeness, the goal of every true spiritual seeker and magician. **12 Warrior of Fire.** Part brown bear, part human, a radiant young shapeshifter with amber eyes and curling golden hair stands ready. In one hand, he carries a magickal golden sword, while the other hand is a fully extended bear claw. **5 Struggle: Air Element (Wands).** It is a stormy, wet, icy, snowy night. The moon (emotions) is a waning crescent, and in the background are dark silhouettes of jagged mountains (obstacles). A master of disguise and cunning, a lone, large gray wolf paws at the snow (frozen action and energy), and a large black raven (symbol of the threefold Goddess) flies over the wolf's head. **8 The Quest: Water Element (Cups).** Disembodied faces float in the rushing waters of a mountain stream. Their emotions have been disengaged from reality, and they float in a dream-world of illusion. They ignore the mountain (gateway to the realm of spirit), and even ignore the flowers of renewal closer at hand.

The FOOL
0

The HIGH PRIESTESS
2

The EMPRESS
3

The EMPEROR
4

The CHARIOT
7

8 Strength

9 The Hermit

12 The Hanged Woman

13 Death

15 The Devil

17 The Star

19 The Sun

20 Awakening

21 The World – Shining Woman

4 of Birds

10 of Trees

2 of Stones

Shining Tribe Tarot (Shining Woman Tarot) Rachel Pollack writes of the tarot, "All of us who work with tarot form a kind of tribe, one whose roots go back many thousands of years before the actual appearance of tarot cards. This is the tribe of diviners, those special magicians, shamans, psychics, and visionaries who use cards, or sticks, or trees, or stones, or shells to communicate with the Gods." She drew from the symbols and archetypal images of sacred traditions around the world to create the naïve-style drawings of her deck.

The suits of the deck are trees (wands), rivers (cups), birds (swords), and stones (coins). The cards that are usually court cards are called vision cards. Each suit has vision cards of knower, speaker, gift, and place.

Although the vision cards do not depict people, the speakers can be compared to kings, and the knowers to Queens. The place and gift cards do not have court equivalents.

The deck was first published as the Shining Woman Tarot by Aquarian Press in 1992, with white borders. The back design shows the four suit signs contained within a diamond shape. It was reissued as the Shining Tribe Tarot in 2001 by Llewellyn Publishers of St. Paul, Minnesota. The Llewellyn edition has light orange borders and, while the cards are slightly larger than those of the Aquarian Press edition, the titles are smaller. The double-ended back design is of a light orange figure on a brown background.

Shining Tribe Tarot (Shining Woman Tarot) Rachel Pollack The first row shows cards from the Shining Woman Tarot (Aquarian Press, 1992); the rest of the cards shown are from the Shining Tribe Tarot (Llewellyn Publications, 2001). The caption is based on Pollack's book, *The Shining Tribe Tarot: Awakening the Universal Spirit.*

TOP ROW: **0 The Fool** is carried by the bird of instinct. The three middle left hills form a figure of the Great Goddess, what a child sees on emerging from the womb: the mound of the mother's belly framed by two breasts. The mountains at the back symbolize the unknown Spiritworld. The Fool's robe of braided colors symbolizes the complexity and wonder of experience. **2 The High Priestess** wears robe and mask derived from Kono, Guinea, in Africa. The cowrie shells link to divination. The Priestess sits between the pillars of duality, forming the middle pillar on the Kabbalistic tree, the pillar of balance. The coiled snake leads to inner peace and revelation. The fish brings myths and dreams from the unconscious to awareness. **3 The Empress** follows a figure from a prehistoric vase painting, 4,500 years old, discovered in Romania. Mountains form her arms and together create the form called Winged Artemis. On either side are trees with the roots in the River of Being. **4 The Emperor** is based on a photo of a shaman encountered by Tsar Nicholas II on a journey across Siberia. He wears a blue crescent to symbolize his connection to the Triple Goddess of the moon. His red hands and eyes, as well as the red stripes on his green robe signify the complex issues of blood and maleness—the blood of sexual erections as well as the blood of war and violence. The city behind him is the image of civilization. The bull is from the caves of Lescaux, an image 17,000 years old. **7 The Chariot** comes from the Book of Ezekiel, when the prophet witnessed a heavenly chariot of fire, and from the myth of the Indian god Shiva, who used the power of all the gods to create a chariot from all parts of existence. The front of the chariot is a mask which has broken open, revealing a country hidden within.

SECOND ROW: **8 Strength** symbolizes the release of desire. A lion stands before the Tree of Life on a rounded hill that is like an egg. The lion extends a paw forward to new beginnings, while looking back to her past experiences. **9 The Hermit** shows a semiabstract figure joyously mounting the hill, seeking enlightenment. The staff was inspired by a ceremonial staff from Angola, while the form of the Hermit derives from a style of rock art found in many lands, especially Africa and Australia. The dark doorway leads to the astral world. The tortoise within the hill begins a journey from the sun to the moon, symbolizing the journey to the inner world. **12 The Hanged Woman** is the reverse of the Shining Woman on card 21. She hangs from the Tree of Life, its roots in the formless sea, its branches in the heavenly stars. Her red body symbolizes vitality, while her golden hair signifies revelation. **13 Death** is an image of a goddess of death from a belt buckle found in France and dated to the sixth or seventh century CE. The fish in the sea is a symbol of the soul returning to the Great Mother.

THIRD ROW: **15 The Devil** presses his hands at his sides and yet has a certain seductiveness, for that suppressed energy builds power. He stands in darkness, a symbol of fear. **17 The Star** maiden is the goddess Persephone, from the Greek Eleusinian Mysteries of life and death. When she was abducted by the god of the underworld, Hades, winter came, and when she returned to earth, spring came. **19 The Sun.** The sunwheel on the card derives from a Native American rock carving from Klikitat County, Washington. The layers of color suggest a pulsating movement through conscious and unconscious energy to emerge into life. The bull hints at masculine energy, but its head also resembles the shape of the uterus and fallopian tubes. **20 Awakening** shows a man, woman, and child, and a birdlike Spirit in an urban setting. The twenty-two windows, for the Major Arcana, shine with light. The people celebrate the Spirit, who fills their world with joy.

BOTTOM ROW: **21 The World - Shining Woman** dances on one foot, recalling the Hanged Woman. Her arms bear double-headed snakes, symbol of a unified consciousness. The double spirals on her breasts derive from the path the sun takes through the course of a year. The bird of instinct is above her heart. The fish, creature of the soul, and the tortoise, symbolic of the world's endurance, are on her legs. Waves of energy fill the four corners of the card. **4 of Birds** shows the healing meditation of a woman recovering from illness. She is resting on her way to an encounter with the Spirit, her hand cooling in a pot of water. It is at this moment, though she does not actively seek or call for it, the vision comes. Three birds swirl down to her side; she has become the fourth. **10 of Trees.** The tree stands in a series of circles representing the solar system. At the top of the tree, the branches transform into spirits. **2 of Stones** shows the tortoise as yin, or feminine, and the frog as yang, masculine. They do not flow into each other, but rather show a distinct choice between one quality or the other.

Ship of Fools Tarot The last published work of artist and writer Brian Williams was the Ship of Fools Tarot. "Why a Ship of Fools Tarot?" Williams asks rhetorically in his introduction to the deck. "The Fool…is understood as a kind of Everyperson: the human personality in its sweetest, simplest, most innocent, most impetuous, most courageous state.…The Fool's Journey is also the name given to a favorite approach to the tarot, as the trump sequence is seen as a path of lessons, obstacles, and pleasures that the Fool encounters on life's adventure." The line illustrations were inspired by the work of the 1494 German book *Das Narrenschiff* (The Ship of Fools), by Sebastian Brant. "The Narrenschiff images and text function as a kind of encyclopedia of the human soul, with special emphasis on humanity's capacity for foolish-ness." Many of the Major Arcana are images copied almost directly from the book, while some are assembled from several images. For the Minors, Williams created scenes inspired both by Brant's work and by the Rider-Waite Tarot. The deck was published by Llewellyn Publications, St. Paul, Minnesota, in 2002. Two extra cards in the deck give spreads. The back design shows the suit signs.

Brian's last message in the introduction to his last tarot work captures the tarotist's quest in the endlessly entertaining, edifying, and ultimately unknowable tarot universe: "Seriousness and joy need not be mutually exclusive states! It should be possible to be the Fool—one hopes—and not be an idiot!"

Ship of Fools Tarot Brian Williams, Llewellyn Publications, 2002 Descriptions are based on those in the book accompanying the deck.

TOP ROW: **0 The Vagabond.** As the Ship of Fools Tarot is made up almost entirely of such characters [fools], our card stresses the tarot Fool as traveler, pilgrim, adventurer, and vagabond. **1 The Montebank** is taken from a *Narrenschiff* illustration that depicts "Ritter Peter" and "Doctor Griff," a pompous old nobleman and the wise fool who admonishes him and tweaks his ear. **4 The Emperor** stands on a cliff above the sea. A fool seems to mock or challenge him. **5 The Pope** stands in disputatious gesture with the kneeling fool before him, who holds out his cap and seems to be laughing. Two other fools chatter and observe from a high wall. The image is from a Brant illustration, "Of the Decline of Faith." **6 Love** shows Venus holding ropes that bind two fools, a friar, a seated monkey, a standing donkey, and even her own blindfolded child.

SECOND ROW: **7 The Cart** carries a bunch of fools on their way to fleets that will carry them to far-off Narragonia, a fictional land of fools. **8 Justice.** The fool renders Justice blind in the sense of depriving her of her rightful role. In Brant's book, it describes the folly of those who recklessly take their every dispute before a judge. **10 The Wheel of Fortune** shows asses and men ascending and descending the Wheel. A tomblike ditch is below the unlucky fools, and the handle of the wheel is turned by a hand from heaven. **12 The Hanged Man** illustrates the foolishness of one who reaches for the too-high bird's nest. **13 Death** shows a shocked fool accosted by the skeletal figure of Death. The fool holds a sort of bouquet of little bells; Death hoists the fool's coffin.

THIRD ROW: **14 Temperance** shows a fool spilling the pitcher's contents onto a flower that grows between his feet. Temperance, as portrayed in the tarot, is properly female and she does not spill her water and wine, for she tempers them instead within her containers, as she tempers extremes in the individual soul. **15 The Devil.** A fool strains on his leash toward a cache of discovered loot, heedless of the danger to his soul in keeping ill-gotten gains, unconcerned at his bondage to the Devil. **16 The Tower** shows a half-timbered house engulfed by flames, and a fool who has thrust his head apprehensively from an upstairs window. House and head are about to be struck by the hammer of heaven. Brant's illustration accompanies the verses that warn of "vaunting luck." **18 The Moon** shows a fool holding a compass. For Brant it is folly to pursue the measurement of land and sea while neglecting to take the measure of one's own soul. **19 The Sun** is taken from the illustration in which the fool is mocked who would compete with the sun by building a fire in daytime.

BOTTOM ROW: **20 Judgment.** A lone fool gestures in consternation as a plague of locusts and frogs is sent down on him from Heaven. Moses and Samuel look on from heaven, unmoved by the fool's pleas for mercy. **Queen of Swords** drags a fool's cap along the floor. Brant's illustration (which showed a male youth instead of a woman) was about bad manners. **Queen of Staves** holds leashes that bind a bird, a sheep, and a bull. A fool pulls on the tails of the latter two animals. Brant's figure is a personification of slavery to sensual appetite. **Queen of Cups** smiles and holds up her cup, as if offering it to the fool, who covers his face. A cat has caught one mouse and chases three others. In the Brant illustration, the woman is a straying wife whose husband, a fool, turns a blind eye. **Five of Coins.** A wealthy fool paws through a chest full of treasure, while outside an old beggar sits with his crutch and begging bowl.

0 The Vagabond   1 The Mountebank   4 The Emperor   5 The Pope   6 Love

7 The Cart   8 Justice   10 The Wheel of Fortune   12 The Hanged Man   13 Death

14 Temperance   15 The Devil   16 The Tower   18 The Moon   19 The Sun

20 Judgment   Queen of Swords   Queen of Staves   Queen of Cups   Five of Coins

Silicon Valley Tarot The Silicon Valley Tarot is a witty take on computer culture. The artist, Thomas Scoville, says of the deck, "Every card in the Silicon Valley Tarot is a slice of experience, a fragment of the Silicon Valley existence, that maze of cubicles and marketing decisions and undocumented compromises at the core of the Information Age." The number of each Major Arcana card is given as a binary number in the upper right cor-ner. The suits are hosts, networks, cubicles, and disks. Court cards are nerd, marketeer, salesman, and CIO (chief information officer). The double-ended back design has the title in white on a black and green background of schematics. The "consultant in a box" tarot was published by Steve Jackson Games in 1998. It includes two extra cards that give instructions for a game called RAM, by S. John Ross.

Silicon Valley Tarot Thomas Scoville, Steve Jackson Games, 1998

Tarocchi di Sissi Amerigo Folchi made the Tarocchi di Sissi in honor of Empress Elizabeth of Austria, who was called "Sissi." The Empress was wife of Franz Joseph of Hapsburg, the last Austrian emperor. The Major Arcana are based on the murals in the Hofer Hall, Relais Club des Alpes, at Madonna di Campiglio, Austria. (The artist who painted the murals was named Hofer.) A gold star in purple square is at the bottom center of each illustration of the Major Arcana.

The deck was published by Bagaglino Hotels, in two limited, numbered editions: 1,000 were stamped Bagaglino Hotels; 3,000 are without the hotel's stamp. The printer was Italcards of Bologna, Italy. Publication date is circa 1999. The back design is a green, purple, and yellow geometric floral pattern, with Italcards on each end. The deck includes two title cards.

Tarocchi di Sissi Amerigo Folchi, Italcards, 1999

Soul Tidings Tarot Susan Marais and Lou Henning, artist, Revolo, 1999

TOP ROW: **0 The Sinner. I Voice in the Wilderness** depicts John the Baptist, who heralded the coming of Jesus. **II The Door** is based on the scripture, "I am the gate, whoever enters through me will be saved." (John 10:9) **III A New Creation** shows a fountain of water, flowers, and light. It is based on John 3:5, "Unless a man is born of water and the Spirit, he cannot enter the kingdom of God." **XVI Confusion** depicts the Tower of Babel, the construction of which was seen as arrogant and disobedient, so that God caused confusion and a diversity of language among people.

BOTTOM ROW: **XVII Hope** is compared to a rose in its fragrance of life and beauty. **XVIII False Prophets** shows a being with the face of a man but the body of a snake. **XIX Mary, Mother of Jesus. 2 of Doves: Love** depicts Mother Theresa, who aided the sick and dying poor of India. **I of Doves: Joy.**

Sliva Tarot The Major Arcana Sliva Tarot was designed by Tomas Sliva and Kveta Maryskova of the Czech Republic. It was published by Sliva in 1993. The card titles are in Czech, English, German, French, and Italian. The back design shows a sun and moon design on each end, with the word TARO in a circle at the center. The deck includes two blank cards.

Songs for the Journey Home New Zealand artists Catharine Cook and Dwariko von Sommaruga created a round tarot deck that reflects their experience as devotees of Bhagwan Shree Rajneesh. "Songs for the Journey Home visually portrays the experience of listening to an inner sound—perhaps a voice—that draws us ever closer to living more and more frequently in harmony with our own personal sense of 'being on the right track.'" The deck was published in 1993 by the artists' company Alchemists & Artists, Devonport, New Zealand.

Soul Tidings Deck The Soul Tidings Deck is based on the Old and New Testaments, described by the artist as "a Christian alternative to tarot cards," intended not for divination, but rather for spiritual and educational use. It was designed by Susan Marais and illustrated by Lou Henning, both from South Africa. Says Marais, "The Bible Tarot brings the Bible to people in a simple and refreshing form. Covering a spectrum of life issues, it gives hope, advice, wisdom, and encouragement, with-

out prescribing a particular religious branch of the Christian faith." The Major Arcana are called the Major Revelations, and the Minor Arcana, called the Guidance Revelations, have suits of doves, for words of comfort; thorns, for trials and difficulties; eagles, for law and principles; and figs, for fruits of the spirit. The court cards are priest, priestess, deacon, and deaconess. The deck was published in 1999 by Revolo.

Tarot of the Southwest Sacred Tribes Violeta Monreal created the Tarot of the Southwest Sacred Tribes as "an aesthetic introduction to Southwestern Native art, revealing the beauty of the traditional mediums, materials, and creations: feathers, pottery, garments, costumes, houses, baskets, rugs, jewelry, and all kinds of landscapes. The spiritual qualities of the people are further represented through the use of organic features, geometric trimmings, and most importantly, ceremonial tools and instruments, all of them filled with symbolism." The Major Arcana draw from Native nations Apache, Pueblo, Rio Grande Pueblo, and Navajo. The suit of swords was inspired by Apache ceremonial swords; wands is based on Hopi ceremonial clubs; cups draws from traditional Rio Grande-Pueblo pottery; and coins shows Navajo sand paintings. The back design is a double-ended design of owls and foliage. The deck was published in 1996 by U.S. Games Systems, and it includes a presentation card and an introductory card.

Sliva Tarot Tomas Sliva and Kveta Maryskova, published by Tomas Sliva, 1993

529

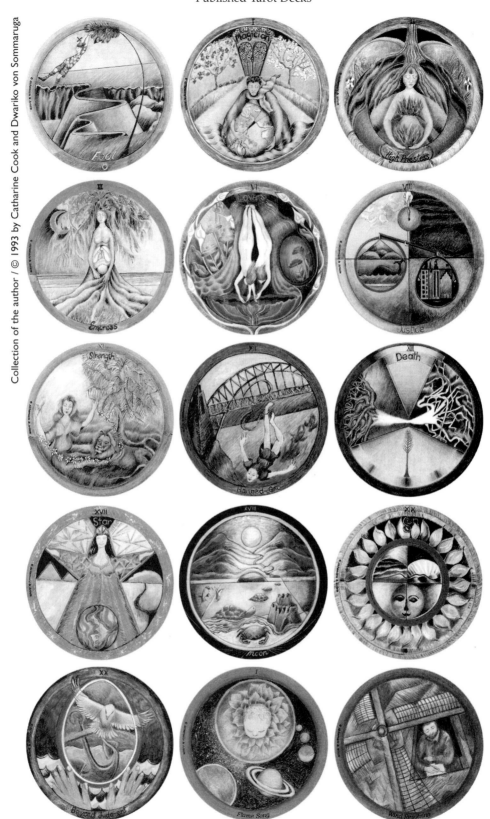

Songs for the Journey Home   Catharine Cook and Dwariko von Sommaruga, Alchemists & Artists, 1993   The Major Arcana are collectively called life songs, and the suits are wind songs (swords), flame songs (wands), wave songs (cups), and earth songs (coins). The court cards are innocence (page), awakening (knight), creating (queen), and resolving (king).

Tarot of the Southwest Sacred Tribes Violeta Monreal, U.S. Games Systems, 1996

TOP ROW: 0 The Fool (Pueblo). I The Magician (Pueblo). III The Empress (Pueblo). IIII The Emperor (Pueblo). V The Hierophant (Navajo). SECOND ROW: VII The Chariot (Apache). VIIII The Hermit (Pueblo). X Wheel of Fortune (Navajo). XI Strength (Apache). XII The Hanged Man (Pueblo). THIRD ROW: XIII Death (Apache). XV The Devil (Navajo). XVIII The Moon (Rio Grande Pueblo). XVIIII The Sun (Rio Grande Pueblo). XX Judgement (Apache). BOTTOM ROW: XXI The World (Pueblo). King of Swords. Knight of Wands. Two of Cups. Page of Coins.

Spheres Tarot Atle Vere and Jarle Vere, Virtual Magic, 1997

Spheres Tarot Spheres is "the strategy tarot game" created by Atle Vere and Jarl Vere. "The theme of Spheres is spiritual warfare," says the booklet accompanying the deck. "Players place cards from their own tarot decks into their own tarot layouts. Each layout represents a player's spiritual power in the world." The object of the game is to take over the other players' layouts and to be the last player left. The cards accompanying the deck are traditional tarot, but the numbers are not the tarot numbers, but rather "the Ten Spheres of Being...part of the world view of the mystics who invented the tarot during the Renaissance." The deck was published by Virtual Magic in 1997. The back design shows the figure of the Magician on a red background. Three extra cards come with the deck: Phases of Turn, Card Rituals, and Relic Spells.

Spiele der Weisheit (Game of Wisdom) The Spiele der Weisheit was created by Uli Lorenz and Michael Schlosser for self-development and Bible meditation. The Major Arcana are not numbered and titled traditionally, but many correspond to traditional tarot cards. The four suits are Stern (star), Tropfen (drops), Stein (stone), and Monde (moons). In place of court cards, there are Leuchter (candleholder), Anker (anchor), Fisch (fish), and Vogel (bird). The deck was published jointly by Kösel Verlag of Germany and Urania Verlag of Switzerland in 1995. The back design shows a bird and a woman's face on a red background. Two extra cards come with the deck. The "Grundsymbole" (basic symbols) card describes the symbolism of the suits and courts. The "Grundfragen" (basic questions) suggest questions for meditation.

Spiele der Weisheit (Game of Wisdom)   Uli Lorenz and Michael Schlosser, Kösel Verlag/Urania Verlag, 1995
TOP ROW: 0 Wirrsal (Confusion). 1 Schöpfung (Creation). 2 Kind (Child). 3 Prophet. 4 Bund (Government).
SECOND ROW: 5 Stern (Star). 6 Entscheidung (Decision). 7 Stille (Silence). 9 Anmassung (Accumulation). 10 Engel (Angel).
THIRD ROW: 12 Liebende (Lovers). 14 Weg (Way). 18 Festgenagelt (Firmly Nailed). 19 Tod (Death). 20 Paradies (Paradise).
BOTTOM ROW: 21 Einklang (Harmony). Vogel der Tropfen: Moses (Bird of Drops). Anker der Sterne: Sara (Anchor of Stars).
Vier der Monde: Maria (Four of Moons). Sieben der Steine: Petrus (Seven of Stones: Peter).

Collection of the author

Grote Arcana van Doetie Spinder Published by the artist, 1997 TOP ROW: 0 The Fool. 1 The Magician. 2 The High Priestess. 3 The Empress. 5 The Hierophant. SECOND ROW: 6 The Lovers. 9 The Hermit. 10 The Wheel of Fortune. 12 The Hanged Man. 14 Temperance. BOTTOM ROW: 17 The Star. 18 The Moon. 19 The Sun. 20 Judgement. 21 The World.

Grote Arcana van Doetie Spinder (Major Arcana by Doetie Spinder) The Major Arcana by Dutch artist Doetie Spinder grew from her fascination with drawing mandalas. As in her mandala drawings, strong symbolism mixed with an intuitive process of creating imagery. The sequence in which she drew the cards was determined by drawing a card from the Crowley/Harris Book of Thoth Major Arcana. The artist would research the tarot card, and then draw, blending personal and traditional symbolism. The internet art gallery by eCompany Audio Group notes, "Doetie Spinder considers the images of the Major Arcana as archetypes: ancient principles of the collective subconsciousness as they are described by C.G. Jung. The depiction of these archetypes is not fixed, because they are individually experienced."

The black and white cards are dated 1997, although according to the gallery the artist completed the art in 1995. The bottom right margin gives the artist's initials, the year, and the number of the card. Included is an unnumbered design and a card listing the titles in Dutch and English. The artist self-published the set of cards.

Spiral Tarot Kay Steventon created the Spiral Tarot in dedication to her Celtic grandmother. "As a child, I gained my first education into the mysteries of the tarot from my grandmother, who used to 'read' the playing cards. I took this procedure for granted and had no idea I would develop a deep involvement with the cards and their complex meanings much later in my life. My grandmother promised she would try to reach me 'one way or another' after her death. I have the feeling she has been behind me all through this process, guiding my thoughts. Thus I chose the late 1800s as the period to depict the Minor Arcana cards in honor of her birthday."

The deck presents scenes of magical realism, with people in every stage and station of life. The original artwork, oil paintings, is studded with glittering notions and faux gems. The deck was published in 1997 by U.S. Games Systems, Stamford, Connecticut. It includes a title card and an introductory card and an instructional booklet. The back design is of a double-spiral in gold on blue.

The artist states that "the ultimate aspiration is to be like the Tarot Fool, not allowing past experiences to hold us back, but embracing the new cycle with open heart and mind, each time with a little more wisdom."

Spiral Tarot   Kay Steventon, U.S. Games Systems, 1997
The caption is based on the book, by Kay Steventon, *Spiral Tarot*.

TOP ROW: **0 The Fool.** Young Perceval wears the simple homespun garment his mother made for him. Around his waist he wears a belt of laurel leaves, reminding us of the victories won in life; attached to the belt is a small bag containing courage, optimism, loyalty, and fearlessness. This bag also contains the memory of many lifetimes and many journeys that lie just below the surface of consciousness. He looks in wonder and awe at the grail image, symbol of his quest. An angel watches over him. **I The Magician** is Hermes, holding the caduceus aloft, making divine energy manifest. This is represented by a fertile tree bearing fruit. The symbols of the suits are on his cape. He has one foot in the inner world, the unknown unconscious realm, and the other foot in the world of the manifest. Thus, he bridges both worlds. **III The Empress** sits in a paradise where growth flourishes, trees bear fruit, and the grain is plentiful. She holds a spiral, indicating the secrets of the seasons and of the life/death process (the thread of life). Her garden is flourishing; in fact, it might revert to jungle if the Emperor does not come along soon to do a little pruning. **X The**

Wheel of Fortune. The Moirae, also known as the Fates, were the triple goddesses of fate and destiny. The Triple Fates were Clotho, the Spinner, who spins the thread of life; Lachesis, disposer of lots, who determines life's length; and Atropos, inflexibility, who cuts life's thread at death.

SECOND ROW: **XII The Hanged Man.** Dionysus hangs suspended in time, symbolic of unfulfilled yearnings and longings. His red shirt is the color of life and sacrifice; his black pants, the color of fertilized winter earth before rebirth (spring). A rainbow bridge connects the two rocky cliff faces. **XIV Temperance.** The goddess Iris is symbolic of the alchemical union of opposites, like the mixing and blending of her many colors. The divine water flowing between the cups is the water of life, carefully poured back and forth with never a drop wasted. **XV The Devil.** Lucifer is relaxed and confident, for his role is to seduce and enlighten us. In the mirror, a woman has caught a glimpse of reality and she doesn't like what she sees. She wants the image to go away; the light bringer has given her the gift of seeing herself as she really is. **XVII The Star.** Isis is the naked star maiden, who comes to replenish the waters of life with her tears. Her vessels contain gifts to renew the shattered dreams of humanity, after times of strife.

XVIII The Moon | XX Judgment | XXI The World | Two of Swords

Princess of Wands | Ace of Cups | Three of Pentacles | Ace of Pentacles

Spiral Tarot (*continued*)

TOP ROW: **XVIII The Moon.** The Triple Moon goddess has been worshiped from earliest times. The three phases of the moon, new, full, and dark, represent the three faces of the goddess. The goddess Hera, of the full moon, holds an embryo contained within an egg. The egg represents creative potential; the embryo, the yet unformed creation, the seed for new growth. It is the gift from the unconscious. **XX Judgment.** The sleeping hero is reawakened. Out of nowhere a divine source arouses us to continue the quest. An angel blows his trumpet, loud and clear. Human beings, of all ages and genders, rise to respond. The red equal-armed cross on the angel's trumpet symbolizes the crossroads we come to in life, and the choices we must make. **XXI The World** unites all the elements of the tarot. We see the androgynous figure spinning, emulating the macrocosmic creative dance of the Lord of the Universe, Shiva, and his female counterpart, Shakti. She emulates the revolution of the planets, the dance of the atoms, and the dance of the whirling Dervish, whose spirit spirals up through the celestial heavings to unite with the divine. The figure is helped along by the four winds. The dancing figure is wreathed by the Ouroboros, the World Serpent, who wreaths the figure in an egg-shaped space, symbolically re-enacting the first act of creation. **Two of Swords.** A vulnerable young girl walking a tightrope is trying to balance opposing forces within herself, and is caught up in so much emotional turmoil that she is afraid to remove the blindfold in case she topples into the sea.

BOTTOM ROW: **Princess of Wands.** The young princess and the baby dragon (or salamander) look in wonder at the new leaf sprouting on the wand. This princess promises the new seed for projects and ventures. **Ace of Cups.** A forest fairy discovers the Well of Happiness, known in myth as the Grail, the fountain of youth, and the cornucopia of plenty. The earthenware pot reminds us of our mortality, while the fountain represents divine love. An ancient spiral design symbolizes the continuum of the life/death cycle. **Three of Pentacles.** A prima ballerina is receiving acknowledgment for her achievement. She has had to work hard to reach the top of her profession and now is reaping the reward for her efforts. **Ace of Pentacles** is represented in the Spiral Tarot by the World Tree. Earth Mother goddess reaches out to the heavens. Her branches are laden with life while her feet are rooted in the ground.

Tarot of the Spirit "The tarot is only one of the many paths to enlightened understanding," says Pamela Eakins in the book accompanying the Tarot of the Spirit. "Yet it is comprehensive and provides a marvelously magical and mystical journey that spirals through the innermost layers of the mind to the very heart of being. This is possible because the tarot has every key element for enlightenment which has become known to humankind in its age-old quest for wisdom. The tarot arranges these elements as stepping stones that carry the player forward." The paintings by Pamela Eakins' mother, Joyce Eakins, recall those of Lady Frieda Harris for the Book of Thoth Tarot, with human figures in symbolic settings. The suits of the deck are wind, fire, water, and earth, with courts of father, mother, brother, and sister. The deck was published in 1992 by U.S. Games Systems, Stamford, Connecticut, and includes a title card. The back design is an oval image on black.

Spiritual Tarot Marie-Claire Wilson created and published the twenty-two-card Spiritual Tarot with titles in English and an accompanying booklet in English, Greek, and French. The cards also feature interpretations. The back design shows a Grecian man and woman in profile on a turquoise background. The deck was issued in 1993.

Stained Glass Tarot Laurie Amato used the art of stained glass in creating a full tarot deck. The glassworks range from medieval to contemporary. Most of the cards have images layered from different works to create the tarot card. The cards are untitled, but usually are easily identified, as Amato skillfully adapted the glass works to fit the tarot archetypes. The deck was printed out in color laser copies, then laminated, and published in a numbered, signed edition. The deck includes a signed presentation card. It was created circa 1999.

Star that Never Walks Around Tarot Stella Bennett created a round deck based on Native American traditions and legends passed to her by her grandmother. The title is the name the Plains people had for the North Star (Polar Star), so-called because it is a fixed guide star that doesn't move around as the other stars seem to do. The deck was published by Red Wheel/Weiser, Boston and York Beach, Maine, in 2002. The back design is a textile art image of a star in cream on blue.

Collection of the author / © 2002 by Stella Bennett

Star that Never Walks Around Tarot Stella Bennett, Red Wheel/Weiser, 2002

Tarot of the Spirit   Pamela Eakins and Joyce Eakins, artist, U.S. Games Systems, 1992

Spiritual Tarot   Marie-Claire Wilson, published by the artist, 1993

Stained Glass Tarot Laurie Amato, published by the artist, 1999 TOP ROW: 0 The Fool. 3 The Empress. 4 The Emperor. 8 Justice. SECOND ROW: 12 The Hanged Man. 13 Death. 18 The Moon. 20 Judgement. THIRD ROW: Three of Swords. Two of Swords. Queen of Batons. Knight of Cups. BOTTOM ROW: Two of Cups. King of Coins. Six of Coins. Two of Coins.

Tarocchi delle Stelle: La Porta Celeste (Tarot of the Stars: The Celestial Door   Giorgio Tavaglione   The Major Arcana are structured according to the map in Tavaglione's booklet:

1. Roman numeral for the card
2. (For Magician only) The lemniscate of eternity
3. Wheel of the zodiac, showing symbols for each astrological sign, corresponding planet, and three decans
4. Celestial letter, alchemical sign, and zodiacal symbol
5. Latin, Sanskrit, and Hebrew letters
6. Astrological aspects: opposition, trine, and square
7. The main figure of the card
8. Hebrew letter
9. Above: zodiacal symbol; below: Latin letter
10. Arabic numeral for the card
11. Traditional title
12. Meanings

Tarocchi delle Stelle: La Porta Celeste (Tarot of the Stars: The Celestial Door)   Giorgio Tavaglione's intricate illustrations are based on astrological correspondences to tarot cards. The figures are contained in an elaborate frame of ornament and symbolism. The deck was published by Dal Negro, Milan, in 1991, and includes a thick booklet written and illustrated by Tavaglione. The large-sized deck includes a title card and an introductory card. The back design is a symmetrical blend of astrological symbolism, heraldic motifs, and classical ornaments on a blue background.

Sternenmädchens Wahrsagespiel Tarot (Starmaiden's Fortuneteller Tarot) German artist Peter Geitner designed the Sternenmädchens Tarot under direction of record producer Rolf-Ulrich Kaiser, founder of the label Kosmische Musik (Cosmic Music), also called Sun Courier. Kaiser's wife, Gille Lettman, was known as the Sternenmädchen and was the inspiration for the deck. The deck, published in 1975, comprises twenty-two Major Arcana, plus three extra cards, one promotional, one with an introduction, and one with instructions for games and fortunetelling. (In 1973, Kosmische Musik released an album by Walter Wegmüller called *Tarot,* which was packaged with the first edition of Wegmüller's Zigeuner/Tsigane/Gipsy Tarot. See volume III, *The Encyclopedia of Tarot,* for illustrations.)

Tarot Stones Timothy Hanley, creator of the Tarot Stones, relates his inspiration in a booklet accompanying the Stones. "One evening, after I retired, I was summoned in the spirit. A tall slender man in a white robe greeted me with open arms standing in the center of a long and narrow corridor. As we began our journey down this mysterious hallway, the man spoke. 'This tunnel is symbolic of your life. The time has come for you to increase your awareness.' We stepped through a doorway and entered a very large dome-shaped room. It was made of black marble stones inlaid with ivory. Twenty-two stone mirrors, obviously sculptured by the grandest of all Stone Masters, were positioned on the wall around the room. I discovered they were mirrors when I stood in front of them, as each one reflected an aspect of my life. When I returned from the dream I sculpted similar images to those I had seen. The man informed me that enlightenment comes only to those who teach about enlightenment. It is my hope that these stones might aid you, as you teach others to teach others, too." The Tarot Stones are made from cultured marble and were produced by Worldcomm in 1995.

Tarot Stones   Timothy Hanley, 1995
The Tarot Stones are shown at full size.

Collection of the author / © 1995 by Timothy Hanley

Tarocchi delle Stelle: La Porta Celeste (Tarot of the Stars: The Celestial Door)   Giorgio Tavaglione, Dal Negro, 1991
TOP ROW: 0 Matto (Fool). 1 Mago (Magician). 4 Imperatore (Emperor). 5 Papa (Pope).
SECOND ROW: 9 Eremita (Hermit). 10 Ruota della Fortuna (Wheel of Fortune). 14 Temperanza (Temperance). 17 Stelle (Star).
BOTTOM ROW: 19 Sole (Sun). Ace of Swords. Knight of Batons. Two of Coins.

Sternenmädchens Wahrsagespiel Tarot (Starmaiden's Fortuneteller Tarot)   Peter Geitner, artist, and Rolf-Ulrich Kaiser, Kosmische Musik, 1975

Tantra Tarot Leah Levine and Bertram Wallrath took sacred images from Islam, Buddhism, and Hinduism to make the Tantra Tarot. The images are apparently taken from works in museums and private collections, but no provenance is given in the book accompanying the deck, and the descriptions in the book do not provide context. For example, a Tibetan Buddhist meditational icon on Major Arcana XXI is described as showing the Hindu deity "Shiva dancing in paradise." A siddhi, or realized yogi, is described on the Prince of Cups as an "attractive young man." Benevolent and sacred beings of different religions are sometimes identified as "demons." The back design shows Krishna dancing with his consort. The deck and book were published by Urania Verlag, Neuhausen, Switzerland, in 2002.

Tarocki The Tarocki is dedicated to rock and roll, with each card of the Major Arcana deck picturing a rock and roll artist or group. The back design features "the King," Elvis Presley. The artwork is by Massimo Galloni, and the concept by Paola De Filippo. The deck was published in 1995 by Lo Scarabeo of Turin, Italy. The deck includes a title card and two descriptive cards.

Tarokado Robert Cadot describes his large-sized tarot deck as being "simply the result of intuitive, pictorial, and poetic explorations of the tarot." The Major Arcana are in color, and the Minor Arcana are in black and white, with suits of etoiles (stars; swords), soleils (suns; wands), lunes (moons; cups), and terres (earths; coins). The deck is accompanied by a booklet by Cadot and poet José Acquelin. It was published by Editions de Mortagne, Québec, circa 1990. The artist worked on the paintings for the deck from 1986 to 1990. The back design is a blue geometric pattern.

Tartessos Tarot The Tartessos Tarot, rendered by Violeta Monreal, is named after the civilization that flourished in the first millennium BCE, on the Iberian peninsula. The deck is part of a tetralogy called *Las Huellas de Hispania,* "The Footprints of Hispania." Archeological findings indicate that the late Bronze Age culture was a wealthy trade center. The designs on the Major Arcana derive from fertility and solar cult images of a female deity who ruled over life and death. The Tartesian alphabet is in the background. The Minor Arcana represent various characters portrayed in the Carambolo archeological findings. The backgrounds of the pip cards recreate the mysterious funeral stelas engraved on stones and monoliths in the area. The back design is an orange, patterned block on blue. The deck includes two introductory cards in four languages, and it was published by Naipes Heraclio Fournier of Vitoria, Spain, in 1997.

Tattwas Tarot Tattwas are ancient geometric signs used for mental yoga, or meditation. They are believed to represent all the energies of nature in simple, direct form. Their shape and color and their relations to each other determine their influence. The Tattwas Tarot, say the authors, "represents not only the universe, but also all the beings, in their different planes and dimensions, who are carrying out the process of self-development and evolution. Each card shows a combination of symbols that synthesizes pure ideas or subtle energies, which result in a concrete appearance or in individual awareness. Meditation on or contemplation of the cards produces an understanding of who we are and why we are here. Its wave forms are extremely beneficial and energetical. The Tattwas Tarot is the key which opens the doors of the crystal palace of the subconscious, where the true roots are found which are capable of solving all the mysteries and discovering all the secrets." The deck was designed and drafted by J.A. Portela, and the final drawings are by Gloria de la Varga. The deck was published in 1992 by Edita Orbe and Fourlabor of Madrid. The deck was also issued in an undated edition by N.E.G.S.A. Naipes Comas of Barcelona. The back design is a five-pointed star with tattwa shapes at its points and center, in white on a blue background.

Collection of the author

Tantra Tarot Leah Levine and Bertram Wallrath, Urania Verlag, 2002

Tarocki   Massimo Galloni, artist, and Paola De Filippo, Lo Scarabeo, 1995

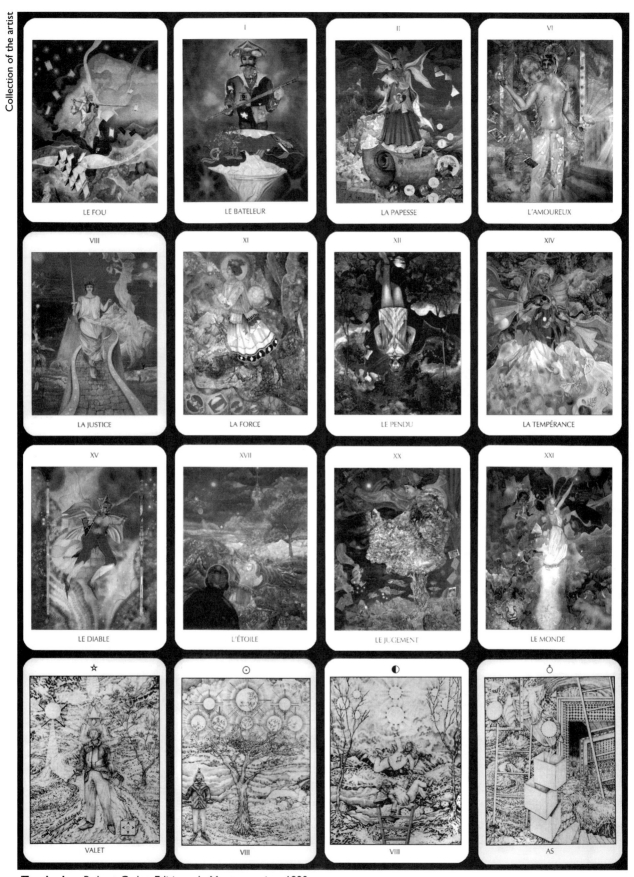

Tarokado   Robert Cadot, Editions de Mortagne, circa 1990

Tartessos Tarot Violeta Monreal, Naipes Heraclio Fournier, 1997

Tattwas Tarot   J.A. Portela and Gloria de la Varga, Edita Orbe and Fourlabor, 1992

Templar Tarot The Knights Templar was founded in 1118 as the Order of the Poor Knights of Christ and the Temple of Solomon. Their mission was to keep Palestine safe for Christian pilgrims. In time, they grew in wealth and status, but made powerful enemies. In 1306, King Philippe IV of France destroyed the Knights Templar, accusing them of Satan worship, desecration of the cross, and sodomy. Many scholars believe that Philippe feared their power and wealth. Because they gave succor to the Cathar "heretics" and were connected with Palestine, many perceive them as having secret mystical leanings.

The booklet by Daria Kelleher, accompanying the Templar Tarot, notes, "Over the centuries their mystical image has only intensified. They've been called adepts, magicians, and sorcerers. It's known that they had secret ceremonies but not what the ceremonies were or what they meant." The book describes various theories as to the origin of tarot, including the following: "A persistent belief is that the Tarot was the invention of the Knights Templar. The order of warrior monks was believed to have created the cards to hide secret knowledge they brought into Europe from the Middle East—knowledge deemed heretical and forbidden by the Church."

The creator and painter of the Templar Tarot is Allen Chester. It was published by Inspire by Design, Newport News, Virginia, in 2001. The back design is a Templar cross in brown on a white background. The deck includes a title card.

The last card Allen Chester painted for the **Templar Tarot** was a twenty-third Major Arcana card called "The Magic Flute." In an interview with Alex B. Crowther of Aeclectic Tarot (www.aeclectic.net), he says, "This is not an extra card but it is a necessary card. I thought the last painting was Death completing the deck and my creative journey with this project. Everything was being put together, and I was starting a new painting. This new painting was not a commissioned piece of work so the image was not preconceived. I usually paint this way; I stare at the blank canvas, and it stares back at me. Music playing, incense burning, hours go by. The brush touches the paint then touches the canvas. An unclear image appears. Over the next several painting sessions the image becomes clearer. The paint speaks and sings to me, and I am able to finish. The Piper is here. It belongs. The Piper plays a tune for you and me. Only you know what tune it is. The project is now complete."

Tarot Terapia Slowem (Instant Therapy Tarot) The Polish deck Tarot Terapia Slowem has eighty cards; 5 (The Hierophant) and 15 (The Devil) each have two versions. The deck was painted by Jadwiga Kalmus and published in 1999 by Studio Astropsychologh of Poland, packaged with a book by Manuela Klara Olszewska. The back design shows a head wearing a winged helmet. The margins of the cards have elemental signs on the left, and the Major Arcana include astrological signs at the bottom. The suits are idea (swords), percepcia (perception; wands), uczucie (emotions; cups), and materia (material; coins).

Terrestrial Tarot Ara Gerhardt and Ad Zeeuwen collaborated to make the Terrestrial Tarot. The introductory card accompanying the deck says, "Ara is an artist and Ad is experienced in the world of energy and powers…. In their basic form, these images are compositions from the structures of living material, mainly from the animal world. These basic compositions have been worked with a variety of techniques to create the image which rightly represents and expresses the power that is embedded in that particular form. The resulting images can serve as gateways to a direct contact with these powers." The full deck includes four extra cards, called level, or phase cards, each featuring the element of fire, water, earth, or air. A title card and an introductory card also come with the deck. The back design is five round, gold patterns on black. The deck was published by U.S. Games Systems in 1996.

Tarocchi Tharbon Fantasy artist Roberto Bonadimani used pen and ink to create the grotesque but charming characters of the Tarocchi Tharbon. Each Minor Arcana card has a tarot title at the bottom and character names at the top. The deck was issued in 1987 in a numbered, limited edition of 1,001 copies by Lo Scarabeo Fantastico of Turin, Italy. The deck includes a title card and a presentation card, and a card warning that the uncoated cards do not lend themselves to frequent handling. The back design is green on white, with floral motifs in the corners.

Templar Tarot Allen Chester, Inspire by Design, 2001 TOP ROW: Fool. Magician. High Priestess. Emperor. SECOND ROW: Priest. Lovers. Hermit. Wheel of Fortune. THIRD ROW: Hanged Man. Tower. Star. Page of Swords. BOTTOM ROW: 6 of Swords. 5 of Staves. 3 of Cups. Knight of Pentacles.

Collection of the author / © 2001 by Allen Chester

Tarot Terapia Slowem (Instant Therapy Tarot) Jadwiga Kalmus, Studio Astropsychologh, 1999 TOP ROW: 0 Fool. 1 Magician. 3 Empress. 4 Emperor. 5 Hierophant. SECOND ROW: 5 Hierophant (a). 6 Lovers. 8 Justice. 12 Hanged Man. 13 Death. THIRD ROW: 15 Demon. 15 Demon (a). 18 Moon. 19 Sun. 20 Last Judgment. BOTTOM ROW: 21 World. Five of Swords. Three of Wands. Page of Cups. Knight of Coins.

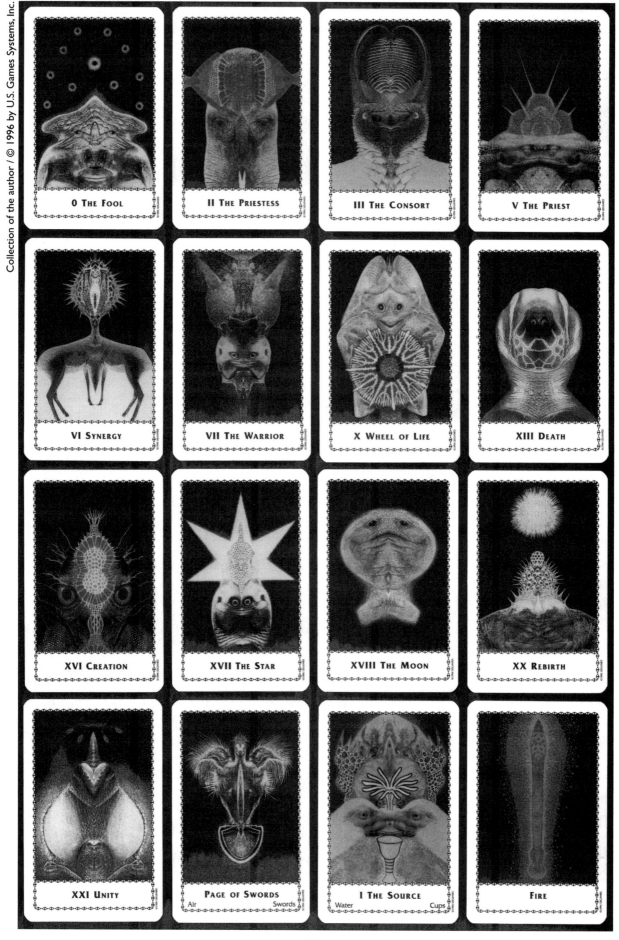

0 THE FOOL

II THE PRIESTESS

III THE CONSORT

V THE PRIEST

VI SYNERGY

VII THE WARRIOR

X WHEEL OF LIFE

XIII DEATH

XVI CREATION

XVII THE STAR

XVIII THE MOON

XX REBIRTH

XXI UNITY

PAGE OF SWORDS
Air   Swords

I THE SOURCE
Water   Cups

FIRE

Tarocchi Tharbon   Roberto Bonadimani, Lo Scarabeo, 1987

Terrestrial Tarot   Ara Gerhardt and Ad Zeeuwen, U.S. Games Systems, 1996

Tarot of the III Millennium "This deck, which offers a possible key to understanding the Third Millennium, could be imagined as nothing other than a great puzzle," says the brochure accompanying the Tarot of the III Millennium. The deck has four main layers of symbolism, which appear particularly in the Minor Arcana. Medieval and classical images "recall the spiritual part of man, his age-old, immortal soul, free from traditional values and conventions." The technological images—web addresses, schematics, and so on—are "an obsessive component of our times."

The images of the Minor Arcana are, individually, fragments of larger pictures. For example, the aces can be assembled to form an image of a scholar or monk—poisoned? drugged? "The puzzle is never complete, and meditating on the part which does not appear could at times be more useful than concentrating one's perception on that which does."

Only the court cards and the mini Tarot of Marseilles cards on the Minor Arcana are colored. The monochromatic color scheme for the rest of the deck "indicates the difficulty with which man perceives the profoundness of things."

The titles on the Major Arcana are in English, French, German, and Spanish. A Hebrew letter is in the upper left corner of each Major Arcana card. The deck also includes a title card and an advertising card. The back design is an image of the Fool (not exactly the same as the Major Arcana Fool) in purple.

The seventy-eight-card Tarot of the III Millennium was drawn by Iassen Ghiuselev and published in 2000 by Lo Scarabeo, Turin, Italy. In 1992 Lo Scarabeo first issued the deck as a twenty-two-card deck, printed on matte paper, with a double-ended back design of the figure on Justice and a planetary or elemental symbol in the upper right corner of each card. The Major Arcana deck includes a title card and a leaflet in Italian.

Tiny Bug Tarot The Tiny Bug Tarot is a sheet of tarot cards. The cards each have the name of the bug and a tarot title. The sheets were copied in black and white, then hand-colored in watercolor. The deck was issued in 2001 by the artist, Peter Wood, in a signed, numbered edition of 100 copies.

TM Tarot The TM Playing Cards Manufacturing Co. of Mumbai, India, made a tarot deck using scanned and clip art. For example, the central image on 10 Wheel of Fortune is from the Rider-Waite deck. 21 The World is assembled from clip art of *Venus*, by Botticelli, and a Christmas wreath of holly. The images are placed on backgrounds of floral patterns, with cherubs in the corners. The back designs are red and blue plaid. The deck was published circa 2001.

Tarot of the Trance "The Tarot of the Trance deck was created during a trance state," says Eva Maria Nitsche, artist of the deck. "On this absorbed conscious level of the imagination, I encountered an entire submerged world of forms and figures, full of symbolism and wisdom." The world depicted on the deck is at once playful, sinister, bizarre, complex, and childlike. The figures seem to dance in a shimmering world of color, objects, and shapes. The booklet accompanying the deck gives interpretations of the cards as well as instructions for entering a "light trance state" and, for each Major Arcana card, an "imagination exercise" to be done while contemplating the card in a trance state. For example, the imagination exercise for 0 The Fool is: "You go on a trip around the world. As luggage, you have a little sack which contains objects that give you magical protection. What are these objects?"

The Tarot of the Trance was published by U.S. Games Systems, Stamford, Connecticut, in 1998. A title card and introductory card are included. The back design is a kaleidoscopic blue pattern.

Transcendental Tarot The Russian Transcendental Tarot totals eighty-five cards; in addition to twenty-two Major Arcana there are two versions of 12, 13, 15, 16, 18, and 20, and two more cards numbered 22 and 0. Some of the cards are not in traditional order. For example, The Hermit is card 6 and The Lovers is card 9; 18 is Judgement and 20 is The Moon; 21 is The Fool and 22 is The World. The deck was designed by A.V. Zaraev and published in 1999.

Tarot of the III Millennium The aces form an image when put together. In this composite, the borders of the cards are cropped to show the image more clearly.

Tarot of the III Millennium   Iassen Ghiuselev, Lo Scarabeo, 2000

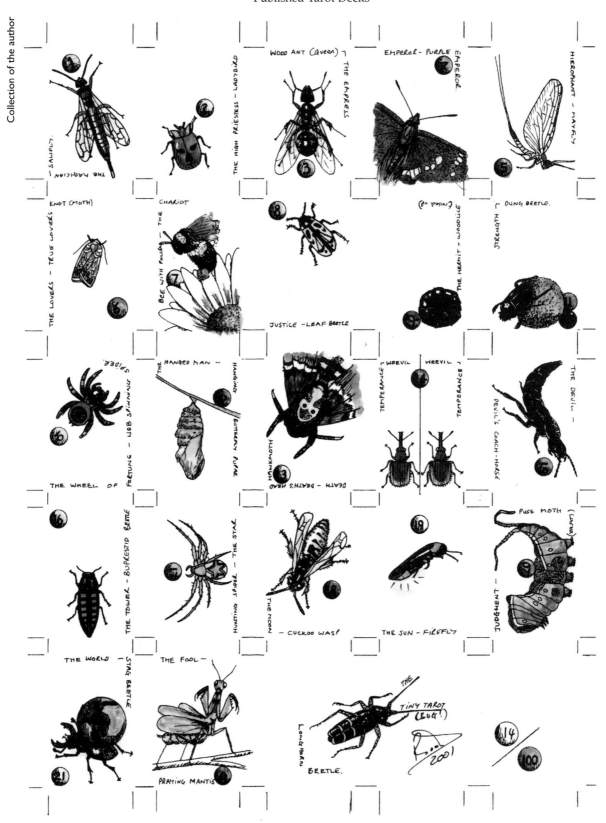

Tiny Bug Tarot   Peter Wood, published by the artist, 2001

Collection of the author

TM Tarot   Anonymous, TM Playing Cards Manufacturing Co., circa 2001

Tarot of the Trance   Eva Maria Nitsche, U.S. Games Systems, 1998

Transcendental Tarot   A.V. Zaraev, publisher unknown, 1999

Tarot of Transformation Willow Arlenea and Jasmin Lee Cori intend their tarot to "stay true to an underlying thread central to the traditional meaning of each card, while often approaching it from a slightly different angle...." Of the tarot, Cori writes, "Each of the seventy-eight cards represents some kind of archetype or energy pattern; together they form a map of consciousness. The Major Arcana are thought to illustrate the spiritual journey in a concise way, while the Minor Arcana and court cards round out the picture and bring it into everyday life." The cards each have a title at the bottom, with an interpretation at the top.

Arleana illustrated the deck, and Cori wrote a text to accompany the cards. The suits are traditional, but the courts are master, healer, teacher, and server. The back design is a purple motif. The designs were begun in 2000 and published in 2002 by Red Wheel/Weiser of Boston. An extra card gives publishing information.

Transformational Tarot The cards of the Transformational Tarot are collages created mostly from photographs of paintings, with some original work and photographs by the artist, Arnell Ando. The deck was issued by the artist in a signed and numbered edition of 1,000 decks in 1995. The deck was re-issued by U.S. Games Systems of Stamford, Connecticut, in 2005.

In *ITS News* (International Tarot Society), the artist says, "Creating a personal deck gave me the opportunity to put myself in each of the cards and reflect on how I felt, thought, and reacted to the possibilities presented in the cards.... It's rather like a pictorial autobiography."

Ando used a photograph of herself on XV The Devil. She describes the card in the September/October 1997 issue of *Arcanum*. She alludes to the "Spider Woman," an archetypal self that protected her psychologically when she feared exploitation and hurt. "I have depicted myself in the guise of Spider Woman, who has a man entangled in a web beneath her. To the right of this image is the stereotypical Devil of my dreams, ravishing women and feeding off their illusions, in much the same manner as Spider Woman did with her men. Directly below these two images is a fiery, red beast: the raw, uninhibited 'id,' representing an intimidating figure who appears to be fierce and forbidding, but whose true nature is to watch over and protect that which is vulnerable."

Transformational Tarot Arnell Ando, published by the artist, 1995 The cards here are from the limited edition deck.

Tarot of Transformation   Willow Arlenea, artist, and Jasmin Lee Cori, Red Wheel/Weiser, 2002

Transformational Tarot   Peggy Gotthold, artist, and Shirley Gotthold, Foolscap Press, 1995

Transformational Tarot The Transformational Tarot Major Arcana comprise twenty-two cards, based on the Rider-Waite Tarot, and six new cards. The Minor Arcana are similar to the Rider-Waite Tarot, but includes new courts: teacher-student, reformer, oracle, and sage.

The deck was created by Shirley Gotthold and illustrated in watercolor by her daughter Peggy Gotthold. The author explains, in the book accompanying the deck, "The Transformational Tarot deck expands the total number of cards…so that the Tarot appropriately reflects the expanded opportunities now available for our personal development and insight, opportunities available because we are moving out of the Piscean Age into the Aquarian Age." The deck is packaged with a separate, full-color chart showing thumbnails of all one hundred cards. The Transformational Tarot was published by Foolscap Press, Berkeley, California, in 1995. The back design is of a jester in gray and white.

Triple Goddess Tarot The Triple Goddess Tarot comprises twenty-six Alchemy cards and seven Chakra cards. The Alchemy cards are based on the traditional Major Arcana with four cards added, and the Chakra cards "represent the seven power points of the body that energize the vital life force of the human being." The deck was illustrated by Mara Friedman, working together with Isha Lerner. "The Triple Goddess Tarot book/deck set is designed to offer an experience that will connect the realm of archetypal cosmology with the female body and feminine sensibilities," says the book accompanying the deck. "If we know how to read Her, the Triple Goddess in Her various manifestations can shed light on the fundamental birth, death, and rebirth mysteries of life." The deck was published in 2002 by Bear and Company, Rochester, Vermont. The backs of the cards have the image of the Trinity card in purple for the Alchemy Cards and in green for the Chakra cards.

Tarot 22 Artist Michael Román created the 22 Tarot "simple enough for anyone to use," and to make tarot "accessible and applicable to modern society." Each card was painted in oil on canvas during the waxing and full phases of the moon. The deck was issued by Gypsy Arts in 2000 as a signed, numbered edition limited to 300.

22 Artisti Liguri in 22 Arcana in una Libera Interpretazione su Cristoforo Colombo (22 Ligurian Artists in 22 Arcana in a Free Interpretation of Christopher Columbus) Osvaldo Menegazzi of Edizioni Il Meneghello coordinated twenty-two artists to create a set of Major Arcana illustrating the life and exploits of explorer Christopher Columbus. The large cards were published in 1992 in a numbered edition of 2,000 decks. The deck includes a presentation card and a card with text by Paolo Emilio Taviani, of the committee to celebrate the fifth centennial of Columbus' discovery of America. Each card bears its artist's name. The backs are blank. The deck also includes a booklet by Angelo Valcarenghi and a leaflet with divinatory meanings of the cards.

22 Artisti Liguri in 22 Arcana in una Libera Interpretazione su Cristoforo Colombo
2 The Popess
by Pier Canosa

La Papessa

22 Pittore in 22 Arcani Edizione il Meneghello of Milan gathered twenty-two artists to create twenty-two Major Arcana with an intriguing range of interpretation and artistic style, from fantasy to surrealism to illustrative to cartoon. The original works were shown at Galleria il Torchio di Porta Romana in Milan in April 1989, then published as a deck of 2,000 numbered copies by Edizione il Meneghello. The backs are plain brown.

Unicorn Tarot The unicorn is the theme of every card in the deck by Suzanne Star and artist Liz Hilton. The mythical animal has long been a symbol of purity, and its horn (called an alicorn) is reputed to have healing powers. The unicorn is occasionally said to represent evil, but the Unicorn Tarot adheres to the more popular, positive mythology of the beast. The deck was published in 1995 by U.S. Games Systems, Stamford, Connecticut. The back design is double-ended, of a unicorn's head.

Universal Tarot Maxwell Miller drew from the entire spectrum of world mythology and religion in creating the Universal Tarot. From alchemy to ancient Egyptian myth, to Hinduism, to Sufism, the lore and symbolism are blended on the cards. Some of the titles of the Major Arcana are not traditional, and each suit has only three courts: king, queen, and knave. It includes a book by the artist. The cards are bordered by a photograph of marble, and the back design is of the same marble picture, with an inset of the symbols of male and female combined. Nine "appendix cards" giving divinatory meanings of the cards, and another extra card gives the title, copyright, and publishing information. The deck was published in 1995 by Samuel Weiser of York Beach, Maine.

Triple Goddess Tarot
Card 25 Trinity, in the deck by Mara Friedman and Isha Lerner. "The source image for the Triple Goddess Tarot was a painting I did in 1997 entitled Trinity," Friedman says. "Trinity is an image in which all the elements seem to unite perfectly, fulfilling my longing to express the Sacred Feminine."

Triple Goddess Tarot   Mara Friedman, artist, and Isha Lerner, Bear and Company, 2002   TOP ROW: 0 Flying into Spring. 1 Song of Creation. 3 Fullness of Life. 5 Blossoming Spirit.   SECOND ROW: 6 Open Heart. 8 Strength. 10 Womb of Potential. 11 Tree of Life.   THIRD ROW: 16 Kundalini Rising. 17 Initiation. 19 Dancing with the Sun. 20 Alchemy.   BOTTOM ROW: 21 Awakened Aphrodite. 22 Infinite Bliss. First Chakra. Seventh Chakra.

Tarot 22   Michael Román, Gypsy Arts, 2000

22 Artisti Liguri in 22 Arcana in una Libera Interpretazione su Cristoforo Colombo (22 Ligurian Artists in 22 Arcana in a Free Interpretation of Christopher Columbus) Osvaldo Menegazzi, et al, Edizioni Il Meneghello, 1992 Names given after the card titles are those of the artist. TOP ROW: 0 Il Matto (Attilio Cassinelli). 1 Il Bagatto (Rosita Isopo). 3 L'Imperatrice (Gabriella Grosso). 4 L'Imperatore (Antonio Contrada). SECOND ROW: 6 Gli Amanti (Umberto Zonari). 9 L'Eremita (Giovanni Scarsato). 10 Ruota della Fortuna (Adriana Desana). 11 La Forza (Beppe Diena). BOTTOM ROW: 12 L'Appeso (Luigi degli Abbati). 17 Le Stelle (Tina Caliandro). 19 Il Sole (Osvaldo Menegazzi). 21 Il Mondo (Serena Boccardo).

Il Matto	Il Bagatto	La Papessa	L'Imperatore	Il Papa	Gli Amanti
Il Carro	L'Eremita	La Fortuna	La Forza	L'Appeso	La Morte
La Temperanza	Il Diavolo	La Luna	Il Sole	L'Angelo	Il Mondo

22 Pittore in 22 Arcani   Osvaldo Menegazzi, et al, Edizioni Il Meneghello, 1989

TOP ROW: **0 Il Matto** (The Fool) by Giovanni Scarsato. **I Il Bagatto** (The Magician) by Piero Alligo. **2 La Papessa** (The Popess) by Davide Noti. **4 L'Imperatore** (The Emperor) by Gino Mazzotta. **5 Il Papa** (The Pope) by Sandro Bellenghi. **6 Gli Amanti** (The Lovers) by Galeazzo van Mörl.

SECOND ROW: **7 Il Carro** (The Chariot) by Giorgio dall'Aglio. **9 L'Eremita** (The Hermit) by Paolo Giorno. **10 La Fortuna** (Fortune) by Coca Frigerio. **II La Forza** (Strength) by Alessandra Titti Cusatelli. **12 L'Appeso** (The Hanged Man) by Domenico Balbi. **13 La Morte** (Death) by Pina Andronico Tosonotti.

BOTTOM ROW: **14 La Temperanza** (Temperance) by Giuliano Spagnul. **15 Il Diavolo** (The Devil) by Marisa Bello. **18 La Luna** (The Moon) by Gianni Meloniski. **19 Il Sole** (The Sun) by Osvaldo Menegazzi. **20 L'Angelo** (The Angel) by Gianni Maiotti. **21 Il Mondo** (The World) by Elio R. Silvestri.

Unicorn Tarot   Suzanne Star and Liz Hilton, U.S. Games Systems, 1995

THE FOOL

I. THE MAGICIAN

V. THE HIEROPHANT

VI. THE LOVERS

XI. KARMA

XII. THE HANGED MAN

XIV. TIME

XV. THE DEVIL

Universal Tarot Maxwell Miller, Samuel Weiser Books, 1995 The descriptions are based on those in the book accompanying the deck.

TOP ROW: **The Fool** breathes into the flute and creates the music of the spheres. The archway is supported by the spirits of the wind, servants of Shu, Egyptian god of the air. The crocodile is also a godlike creature; Horus took the form of a crocodile as he searched for his lost father, Osiris, in the Nile. The Fool's leap from the precipice is like Zarasthustra's metaphorical descent from the mountain into the world. **I. The Magician** is surrounded by a crystal landscape, referring to the use of crystals by shamans and healers. The Magician's necklace is a reminder of the great "circle of self," the totality of his consciousness. He stands with one arm raised and the other pointing downwards; his energy is passing down to earth from a higher level. The snowflake's hexagonal form expresses the four directions, dissected by the vertical line, symbol of movement from lower world to upper world, or from darkness to light. **V. The Hierophant** has a musical instrument at his left side as a symbol of the ability of music to penetrate and break the confines of normal consciousness which prevent "other worldly" experiences. At his right stand the books of his learning, of his analytical ability to formulate coherent scriptures from abstract intuitional knowledge. The mask of white feathers is the element of air, or intellect, which he can adopt or dispense with at will, without attachment. He wears the shaman's drum. The crucifix of Christianity is pulled over his heart, symbolic of esoteric Christianity based on love and the intuitional worlds. The archway has symbols of Sufism, astrology, Judaism, and the I Ching. **VI. The Lovers** deals with messages that come via the heart or intuition. The bottle in which the Lovers dance contains the alchemical blending of male and female, sun and moon. The fertilized egg is the result of natural love and attraction between opposite sexes.

SECOND ROW: **XI. Karma** depicts Tara of the Buddhist tradition. All is mirrored, as the nature of karma implies that for every action there is an equal reaction. Tara has numerous, all-seeing eyes, most particularly the eye of enlightenment in her forehead, and the eyes of mercy on her palms, which balance the sword of detachment wielded by the Egyptian goddess Maat. **XII. The Hanged Man** is suspended over water, indicating the initiation of baptism. The coins falling are a symbol of detachment from material wealth. The inverted triangle surmounted by a cross is symbolic of the descent of light into darkness in order to redeem it. Nailed to the gibbet is the sign of Osiris, a sacrificed god. **XIV. Time** shows Thoth, in ibis-headed form, as the lord of time and keeper of the Akashic records, patron of healers, and ruler of herbal remedies and natural medicine. His wings imply his ability to soar to great heights. The alchemical fluids flow from cup to cup, symbols of the womb. The pyramid stands for evolution of the soul through time. The two glyphs in the smaller pyramids are the cross, signifying the four elements in balance and the intersection of space and time, and the sign of Sagittarius, representative of the perception of time, speed, and movement. **XV. The Devil** enchains in matter by causing identification with the material body. The Lovers are chained in the picture, an expression of the aspect of the card that means enslavement. Baalzebub was called by the Canaanites the Lord of the Flies. It was thought that individual souls took the form of flies between incarnations as they passed from one body to another, and that when a woman swallowed a fly, it was the soul of her unborn child taking material form inside her.

XIX. THE SUN — XXI. THE UNIVERSE — King of Swords — Knave of Cups

Five of Cups — Knave of Disks — Ten of Disks — Eight of Disks

Universal Tarot (continued)

TOP ROW: **XIX. The Sun** shows Ra, the Sun God, sailing in his barge across the firmament. The musicians are his four sons. They are in harmony with each other, as different parts of the self harmonize to express the fully integrated personality. The sign of the eight-pointed star crowning the triangles is the Babylonian symbol of the sun god. **XXI. The Universe** shows a whirling dervish absorbed in his cosmic dance, at the center of a universe whose heavenly bodies spin in their orbits of perfection. The elements, expressed as the zodiacal fixed signs, and represented by the lion, eagle, man, and bull, are in balance. **King of Swords** has at the base of the picture a banner reading "Rex Quondam Et Futuris," meaning, "The Once and Future King." This king returns in a time of need, to restore order and harmony. He blends male and female elements, as indicated by the two convergent triangles on the shield. **Knave of Cups** and the cup he carries are completely blue, symbolizing that he is ruled by water, the element of the emotions. His mask is not successful in hiding his feelings. He almost totally surrounds

himself in yellow, the color of the rational world. The red form behind him, though, his passion, is still clearly seen.

BOTTOM ROW: **Five of Cups. Knave of Disks** represents Taurus, and his highest aspect is reflected in the path of the Sufi brotherhoods, who placed great emphasis on skills and crafts such as masonry, pottery, and carpet weaving. He wears the blue, patched robe often associated with the Sufis. His disk bears the heptagram of the sevenfold law, which permeates all aspects of his world. **Ten of Disks** shows yantras, tantric meditative forms that are used to focus meditation on different aspects of the Divine Mother. The birds are the crows of Dhumavati, the witchlike goddess whose form is repulsive to those caught in the illusion of worldly wealth, but is a channel of subtle illumination for those on the spiritual quest. **Eight of disks** shows a rose surrounded by symbols of different religions. The rose has for centuries been a symbol of the female reproductive organ, of the life-creating uterine blood and of female self-knowledge. At the heart of exoteric religious dogma lies matriarchal wisdom.

Tarocchi Universali (Universal Tarots) The Major Arcana deck by Sergio Toppi was published in several editions by Lo Scarabeo of Turin. A limited edition in a large size was issued in 1988. It included a leaflet and a presentation card, and had Italian titles. The back design was lavender, with an I Ching hexagram. Another edition was issued with English titles and in a smaller size

in 1991, and it included a title card and a card with a poem. The double-ended back design showed the bird from the Magician card. A miniature edition was published circa 1991, with Italian titles and a green and brown back design of a woman looking at a star. It included a title card. The set was also issued as postcards, circa 1991.

Tarocchi Universali (Universal Tarots)   Sergio Toppi, Lo Scarabeo, 1988

Collection of the author

0 THE FOOL	I THE MAGICIAN
II THE HIGH PRIESTESS	III THE EMPRESS
IV THE EMPEROR	VI THE LOVERS
VIII STRENGTH	IX THE HERMIT
X THE WHEEL	XV THE DEVIL
XVI THE TOWER	XVII THE STAR
XVIII THE MOON	XIX THE SUN
XX JUDGEMENT	XXI THE UNIVERSE

Tarot of the Universe   Rafael Trelles, Antakarana, 1988

Tarot of the Universe   The leaflet in the Tarot of the Universe describes the process of Rafael Trelles: "His creative process did not consist in recreating an image as complete as possible, in order to 'pass it on' later to canvas, but in letting himself flow before the cloth, without knowing exactly what he was going to do, as if to say 'rising to what he knew, without previously or intellectually realizing it.'" The Major Arcana deck was published in 1988 by Antakarana, Canary Islands, Spain.

Vampire Tarot   Nathalie Hertz, U.S. Games Systems, 2000

Vampire Tarot   As gory as any vampire could wish, the Vampire Tarot features the blood-sucking undead that have haunted human legend for centuries. The deck, by French artist Nathalie Hertz, was published by U.S. Games Systems in 2000. The back has a red and black design. The booklet describes Hertz's method: "to first create a mental picture of an image or concept, and then to draw it." Humans and animals are, for her, an inexhaustible source of inspiration. When drawing, she always uses music to foster a creative atmosphere.

Tarocchi Veneziani Maria Cristina Venditti describes her Major Arcana tarot deck, as "the kind of card deck that was produced in Venetian print shops in the fourteenth century."

The deck was produced in 1995 in the Bottega del Tintoretto print shop in Venice, Italy. The drawings were made using a direct engraving technique, called dry point, on cardboard matrices. Each card was printed individually, by hand, on an eighteenth-century press. Because the matrices are fragile and printing each card individually takes a great deal of time, the edition is lim-

ited to fifty decks. To obtain the hardness of a real card, the papers were treated with a special glue, handmade using an old process.

The style of each image is intentionally archaic with titles in the Venetian dialect. The backs of the cards were printed with an old wood engraving that was used for printing fabric around the turn of the century. The pack for the deck is made of jute, cord, and sealing wax. The deck has twenty-two Major Arcana plus a presentation card signed and numbered by the artist.

Tarocchi Veneziani Maria Cristina Venditti, Bottega del Tintoretto, 1995 Descriptions of the card are by the artist.

TOP ROW: **EL MATO** (The Fool): THE MAN THAT RUNS AWAY. He is a misfit who has lost his bearings, running from the world with his baggage of joy and pain, hounded by his own nightmares (the dog). He represents the journey, the movement, the escape, living without a base. Though cards in this deck are not numbered, if they were, this would be the only card without a number. **EL BAGATO** (The Magician): THE MAN THAT SEARCHES. He is the creative alchemist, inventing, and producing. He represents creativeness, work, and everything that is just born. He experiments to discover the philosophers' stone, that is, the meaning of life. **EA PAPESSA** (The Popess): THE WOMAN THAT FEELS. She is the spiritual side of femininity, the intuition, the mystic intellect of women, the mother of the ancient Greek, Roman, and Egyptian temples. She expresses the wisdom of sacred texts and has the symbols of the night and mystery tattooed on her skin. **L'IMPERATRICE** (The Empress): THE WOMAN THAT BEARS. She is the material side of femininity, the maternal, earthly, solar strength of women. She holds a flower, which is Nature, and a sword, which is strength, that she uses to defend the fruit of the earth. Fertility, Mother Earth. **L'IMPERADOR** (The Emperor): THE MAN THAT DECIDES. He is the material side of masculinity. Seated on a throne of power, he represents decisive energy. His sword is for attack and his shield for defense.

SECOND ROW: **EL PAPA** (The Pope): THE MAN THAT UNDERSTANDS. Depicted as the Doge di Venezia. Seated on a throne of wisdom, he symbolizes the spiritual side of masculinity. He represents holiness, patience, understanding, and forgiveness. His cane is old age and experience. **I MOROSI** (The Lovers): THE CHOICE OF AMOR. The card of love and passion, but also of choosing. This card is duality. It represents the opposites of female and male looking at each other, each mirroring the other, and doing this they recognize themselves. **EL CARO** (The Chariot): THE PATH. The journey in a mystic sense, the journey of life, the road, the beginning of a path that brings experience and growth. The charioteer directs the horses and looks out onto the horizon to see what he is going to achieve. **LA JUSTISIA**

(Justice): EQUILIBRIUM. The Law, the balance of the essential cosmic duality. The Natural justice that through karma levels everything. Also human justice. Legal affairs and business. **EL REMITO** (The Hermit): THE MAN THAT MEDITATES. Introspection, thought, meditation, the internal path, spiritual growth, silence. The resting place where the walking stick is put aside and you stop to look inside yourself. The lantern is for lighting the dark.

THIRD ROW: **EA RODA DE LA FORTUNA** (The Wheel of Fortune): DESTINY. The card of destiny, of the unpredictable, the unexpected. The wheel's gears turning and fitting one in the other is the mysterious arcane symbolism of the mechanism of destiny. **EA FORSA** (Strength): ENERGY. The energy, the courage, the spiritual strength that dominates the material. The logic that rules the instinct. The other side of strength can be oppressive and tyrannical. **L'IMPICCA** (The Hanged Man): THE SACRIFICE. The sacrifice, the wait, the hanged man looks at the world from another perspective, everything is upside-down and, at the same time, is no-where. This card represents a state of suspension in which one must wait because he cannot move. **EA TEMPERANSA** (Temperance): MEDIATION. The art of diplomacy, compromise. Recycling, while the angel decants water, life is cleansed and regenerated. **EL DIAVOLO** (The Devil): ANIMAL INSTINCT. Temptation, envy, passion, lust, sex, the senses, instinct. The wild side of the human being. A human relation that is controlling and possessive.

BOTTOM ROW: **EA TORE** (The Tower): COLLAPSE. The destruction, the tempest, the collapse of something that may have been built in the wrong way. Failure. **LE STELLE** (The Stars): HOPE. Hopes and dreams for the future, the seed longing to grow, the light at the end of the tunnel illuminating the way. An adolescent sleeps protected by the sky. **EL SOL** (The Sun): REALIZATION. Light, clarity, warmth, success. His energy gives life to the fruits of the earth. **EL GIUDISIO** (The Last Judgment): RECOGNITION OF THE PAST. The universal judgment, redemption from darkness, the reward for what you have done, the past is reviewed, the trumpet of the last day. **EL MONDO** (The World): THE WHOLE. Everything, the whole, the union of duality as one, complete total realization.

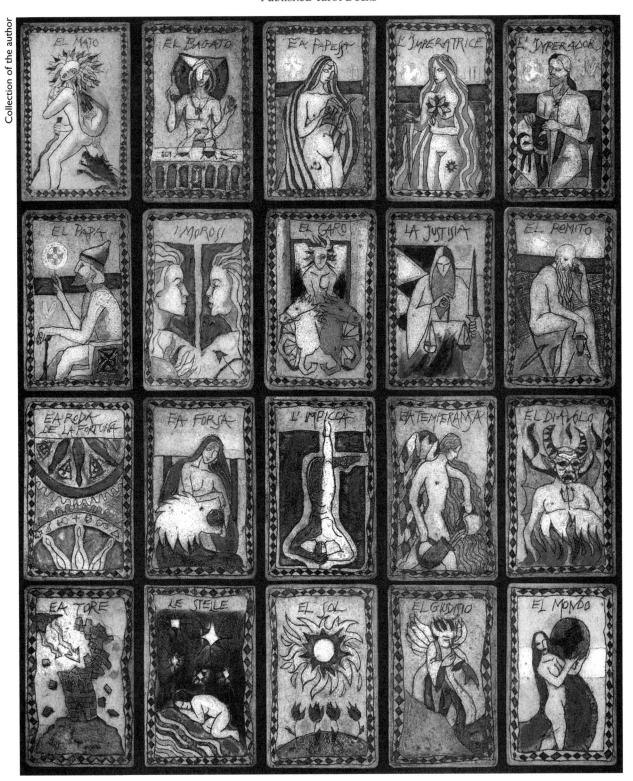

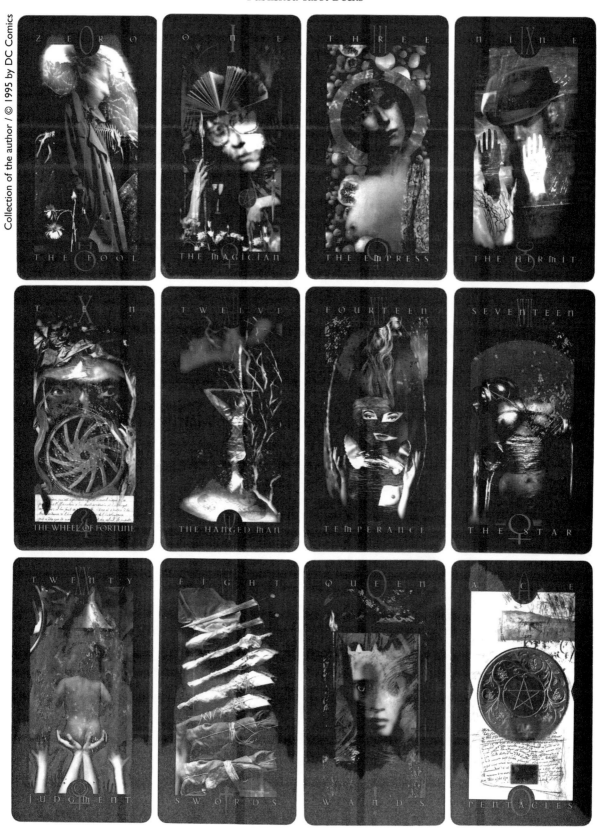

Vertigo Tarot The Vertigo Tarot features characters from the DC Comics series of "comics and books for the mature reader." The illustrations by Dave McKean were composed on computer. Rachel Pollack collaborated with the artist on the deck and wrote a book to accompany the deck. The back design on the cards is a swirling nautilus composition, with the title of the deck in the center. The deck-and-book set, published by DC Comics, New York, was issued in a limited edition of 5,000 in 1995. The 1995 edition includes Pollack's book in hardcover, and the cards measure 3 by 5.5 inches. In 2001 another edition was issued, with smaller cards and the book in paperback.

computer graphics

From the earliest extant decks, when gold leaf was applied to tarocchi cards, to now, tarot artists use all the techniques at their command. In the late twentieth century, computer graphics software made possible new techniques for interpreting the tarot. Beyond scanning original artwork and applying titles and numbers, artists use computer software to create new works. Photographs are altered, and clip art is assembled into tarot designs, illustrations are drawn with mouse or stylus. Tarot designs in volume IV that were created primarily through software include:

Antoni Tarot
Basic Tarot
Chaos
Cosmic Tribe
Cyber Tarot (InVision)
Cyber Tarot (Johnstone)
Deck of the Dreamers
Electric Tarot
Experimental Tarot
Gendron Tarot
Gothic Tarot (Mystic Eye)
Gnostic Tarot (Dengel)
Ernie James Tarot
Teresa Knezek Tarot
Liulia Tarot
Tarot of Maud
New Millenium (Varis)
One World Tarot
Paul O'Meara Tarot
Pet Tarot
Quest Tarot
Razor's Edge Tarot

Reincarnation of Adam and Eve
Tarocchi di Robot
Sacred Circle Tarot
Seasons of the Tarot
Share Tarot
Silicon Valley Tarot
Simple Tarot
Southwestern Tarot
Tarot of the Storm
TarotPro
Terrestrial Tarot
3D Tarot
3DCG Tarot
Three-Dimensional Tarot
Tiffany Tarot
Tarot of Timeless Truth
TM Tarot
Vertigo Tarot
Vision Tarot
Wicca Tarot
Woowoo Tarot

Vertigo Tarot Dave McKean, artist, and Rachel Pollack, DC Comics, 1995 Descriptions are based on those in the book, by Rachel Pollack, that accompanies the deck.

TOP ROW: **0 The Fool** (John Constantine, from "Hellblazer") On this card, the sun has become a kind of nuclear explosion, the flowers have wilted, and the animal has become a skeleton piercing the Fool's body. **I The Magician** (Tim Hunter, from "Books of Magic") Light shines in Tim's face and reflects off his glasses—the classic image of a nerd. The book in front of his forehead suggests all the tedious study necessary to become a mage. **III The Empress** (Titania, Queen of the Fairies, from "Books of Magic") The Empress stands in a universe of ripe fruit. Around her head is a kind of cracked halo, as if she has descended from heaven to rule our imperfect world. **IX The Hermit** (The Phantom Stranger) stares at his hands. They appear disembodied, as if he cannot connect himself (or his feelings) to any of the things he does.

SECOND ROW: **X The Wheel of Fortune** (Destiny, from "Sandman") The face of Destiny looms large behind the Wheel, as if he himself sets it spinning. The spiraling spokes make it appear to turn hypnotically. **XII The Hanged Man** (Shade, the Changing Man) hangs upside down, because he has reversed the values most people live by, seeking Strength and Justice rather than personal profit or power. He hangs above a map of the cosmos. **XIV Temperance** (Delirium, from "Sandman") carries the message of liberation, coming after Death. Here, we see her almost completely bound. One provocative breast shows. We see her eyes and mouth, but they appear out of place. To be delirious is to feel like your body has come apart and will fly off in all directions. **XVII The Star** is unconnected with any Vertigo characters. Urns are bound to a woman's body, as if to attach her inexorably to her function.

BOTTOM ROW: **XX Judgment** shows the imagery of new life, a baby born in the wash of its mother's blood. **Eight of Swords** shows a sword confined, concealed, disguised. **Queen of Wands** looks out at us intensely, even though swirls of green and red cover one eye. The insignificant place of the wand shows that she does not seem to need props or tools. **Ace of Pentacles.** The element of earth, that of pentacles, means realization, and writing is the most realized of the arts, the most didactic, the most explicit and concrete in its messages.

Tarocco delle Vetrate (Stained Glass Tarot) Luigi Scapini worked with his daughter Giulia to create the Stained Glass Tarot. The artist had created several tarot decks, as well as stained glass artworks; as a professor of art history, he was also familiar with the symbolism of both tarot and Gothic stained glass windows. "Cabala, deeply imbued with Neoplatonism since the Middle Ages, is the basis of the esotericism of tarot cards; in it Marsilio Ficino [Florentine philosopher, 1433–1499] saw one of the connecting elements between Neoplatonism and Aristotelianism."

Scapini describes three primary kinds of energy represented: yod (called IOD in the booklet), which is active, positive, and strengthening. The energy of heh (HE in the booklet) reflects and holds yod, and is connected with the world of feeling. Vau joins yod and heh and connects with the world of balance.

The Stained Glass Tarot was published by Dal Negro, Italy, in 1997. The back design shows a window set with clear glass rounds. The deck includes a title card and a card with the back design printed on both sides.

Tarocco delle Vetrate (Stained Glass Tarot) Luigi Scapini and Giulia Scapini, Dal Negro, 1997 Descriptions are based on those in the booklet accompanying the deck.

TOP ROW: **0 IL MATTO** (The Fool). The left column is made of fire and has a lion on its capital and a salamander at the base; the right column is scaly and has an eagle and a dragon. The columns represent, respectively, the active and passive principles. The azure clouds stand for his vau energy. **I IL BAGATTO** (The Magician). While the sun is shining, behind the great juggler stands the tree of life. With compasses on his yod table, he invents and sets in order the elements of the cosmos. **II LA PAPESSA** (The Popess) is pure heh, green branches bursting with sap. The tree of life has become a book; the popess has the key that opens up the mysteries of the word. **III L'IMPERATRICE** (The Empress) balances the creative energy of the Magician with the absolute reaction of the Popess. All takes place throughout the twelve months of the year, the twelve hours of the day, the authority of the twelve Patriarchs, in the twelve sweet regions of the world, with the purity of the lily (at her feet), the knowledge of the eagle (her shield), and the perfection of the pearl (decorating her headdress). **IIII L'IMPERA-TORE** (The Emperor) is in the center of the four directions and has the power of the four elements, protecting and building the world of human beings.

SECOND ROW: **V IL PAPA** (The Pope). The dove of the Holy Ghost inspires the Pope's authority. He bridges the gap between the worlds represented by the two men in prayer—contemplation and action. **VI L'INNAMORATO** (The Lover). Beauty, love, universal attraction balance the Emperor's power and the Pope's authority, and reflect the Empress's perfection. Cupid shoots his arrow, and the woman's womb miraculously transmutes; this is the mystery of the three blue flowers. **VII IL CARRO** (The Chariot) is another link of the chain and carries us from heaven to earth. **VIII LA GIVSTIZIA** (Justice) is as patient as a good mother resolving the contradictions of existence; she is vested with the image of Alchemy in the northern rose-window of Laon. **IX L'EREMITA** (The Hermit) fights against the dark dragon through the energy of vau. He is the old and wise Lord of Time, and he fights with care and love.

THIRD ROW: **XI LA FORZA** (Strength) has power over the sulphurous, all-immobilizing dragon through the heh force of loving reaction. The maiden wears the Magician's cap, but is allied to the Popess. **XII L'IMPICCATO** (The Hanged Man) is judged by foolish people who do not realize that he has the same spontaneous charm as natural phenomena, which are not polluted by human pretentiousness. **XIII LA MORTE** (Death) takes us from the heh world of men, where the heart suffers, to the world of Mother Nature where, as the followers of the Enlightenment movement will never understand, there is neither good nor evil, and death is the highest vital force. The bodies of kings, popes, and murderers return to the great Mother's womb, where the universal transformation principle will have new, wonderful possibilities to continue its game. **XV IL DIAVOLO** (The Devil) nails us in the material world, the world of passion, through the fatality of destiny. From within the inertia of the elements, he lulls us to sleep with ignorance, dims our mind with passion, deceives us with pride. **XVI LA TORRE** (The Tower) represents, at least for man, the negative aspect of transformation force, implying destruction of what went before.

BOTTOM ROW: **XVII LA STELLA** (The Star). The maiden pouring out her liquids into the river of life knows well that we are made of stardust and that we travel along with the stars towards a certain aim. **XVIII LA LUNA** (The Moon). The crayfish knows that to reach the aim defended by the wolves, he must walk backwards. This is the lunar way, the way of reflection. **XXI IL MONDO** (The World) is the last great vau of the Major Arcana. The lovely maiden represents the soul of the world, which spins destiny, She holds in her left hand the secret of good and evil as she dances in a "mandorla" of juicy grapes. **Four of Swords.** The owl is a symbol of renunciation, loneliness, and asceticism. However, his big yellow eyes, which can see a mouse, tell us that concentration is born of asceticism, and it makes us find again true freedom, which throws us into the center of the cosmos. **Page of Wands** uses the heraldic imagery of the wild man, from a bas-relief at Thiers Chateau. The child's head on the staff suggests St. Christopher, who carried across a torrent a child who weighed as heavy as the world.

Via Tarot: The Path of Life The descriptive card that accompanies Via Tarot says that artist "Susan Jameson deliberately picks up the thread of the famous Thoth Tarot deck." Jameson executed the artwork in colored pencil. The book by John Bonner, which accompanies the deck, describes the artistic process. "The twenty-two trumps or Major Arcana of this pack derive from a 'channeling' experience resulting from a series of 'scryings' or 'spirit-visions' using a magical technology developed by Dr. John Dee and elaborated by the Hermetic Order of the Golden Dawn and others.... The cards were transmitted as short packets of compressed data, initially seeming the merest bubbles of light in the blackness of an obsidian sphere [the instrument used to scry].... In the Minor Arcana, Jameson has used fragments of dream and scrying imagery combined with her own understanding of the nature of each Atu and notes, some unpublished, made by Aleister Crowley." The back design shows a rose, cross, and septagram within a circle, with the four evangelist's creatures in the corner. The deck includes an introductory card and an advertising card, and it was published by AGMüller of Neuhausen, Switzerland, in 2002.

Via Tarot: The Path of Life Susan Jameson, AGMüller, 2002 Descriptions are based on those by John Bonner.

TOP ROW: **0 The Fool** is a naked, monkish individual. He has his head and right arm raised through the clouds of the great abyss to clarity in the realm of Negative Existence, which is Ain, Ain Soph, and Ain Soph Aur. He holds aloft double roses in the shape of human eyes. In his left hand is the caduceus attributed to Kether, the first Sephirah, suggesting that his thoughts are set on matters beyond the mundane. Thirty-two rays of light project from the roses, for the ten Sephiroth and the twenty-two Paths on the Tree of Life. A rabid dog attacking him is the unreasoning power of nature, or the unredeemed animal soul striving to destroy the elevated vision of its host. **I The Magus** performs a pentagram ritual. The pentagrams have traced a blaze around him, and he becomes himself "the flaming pentagram in the column of the six-rayed star." **II The High Priestess** sits armed within her NOX temple guarded by her hunting dogs. She holds the bow and quiver of Artemis, and is naked, crowned with the triple moons and bathed in light. The tails of her hounds entwine to produce the Vesica Pisces, the "fish bladder," a figure that symbolizes the womb and is one of the principal images of Binah. **III The Empress** wears a headdress of a turtledove, symbolic of the descending spirit.

SECOND ROW: **IV The Emperor** has arms upraised, forming the magical gesture of Shu and the element of air. In his right hand is a woman facing a lunar disk and in his left hand is a man in front of a solar disk. Above all blazes a disk of Venus, the astrological correspondence of Netzach. **V The Hierophant** shows an androgynous central figure. Arrayed on each side are the Daughters of the Daughters of Light, wearing white caps, and the the Daughters of Light, wearing black caps. The depiction of death and resurrection is reminiscent of the raising of the Priest in the Gnostic Mass from "a man among men" to one who is "worthy to administer the virtues" and the many initiations in which the candidate is symbolically killed in order to rise again perfected. **VII The Chariot** is drawn by three fierce tigers, notable for their maternal instincts and preparedness to sacrifice themselves for their young. The four pillars of the Chariot represent the four worlds of the Qabalah. The sea eagle symbolizes the watery nature of Cancer. The female charioteer holds a Japanese sword and guides the tigers by gripping their tails, forming the letter shin. **IX The Hermit** shows a solitary male standing atop a tall column bounded by a double-headed serpent. Streams of energy blaze from his hands, piercing the tails of the serpents, demonstrating that the world of matter is under control. Above hangs a figure nailed to a cross, from which sacrifice of self streams the power that energizes and sustains the Hermit in his interior work.

THIRD ROW: **XIV Art** consists of a full-face portrait of a woman with her hair blown backwards into what appears to be a solar storm against a deep blue star-flecked night sky. The figure looks at the viewer through its one human eye. More than half the face is composed of finely worked stone. This is a direct reference to the Enochian being who was in part responsible for the "channeling," or transmission, of the Major Arcana. The female figure is clearly breaking out of her stone carapace and beginning to sense the world in a much fuller manner. **XV The Devil** shows a skull fixed to a column. It stares out through its opened third eye, but otherwise seems completely dead. However, a yoni-like opening and the phallic column give hope that the creative process continues and new life may yet be brought forth. The image shows the extraordinary tenacity of the will to life, even in the most seemingly unpromising conditions. **XVII The Star** shows a young virgin moving down the rainbow steps of her domed temple, under the auspices of the sevenfold star of Babylon with a pentagram at its center. The temple is supported by ten pillars, for the ten Sephiroth. The Sun of Tiphareth blazes above her. **XXI The Universe** depicts the elements as whirling dervishes, recalling the "First Swirlings," out of which spin the creative energies that eventually form the manifest universe. The central figure is reflected by another, of indeterminate gender, who stands in the shape of the tau cross on the whole edifice. All takes place within an egg-shaped ring design surrounded by a serpent that is also a black lotus of one thousand petals.

BOTTOM ROW: **Seven of Swords. Ace of Wands. Princess of Cups. Eight of Disks.**

Victoria Regina Tarot Sarah Ovenall, the artist of the Victoria Regina Tarot, described her process of creating the cards as "very low-tech." In the fall 1997 issue of *Tapestry* magazine, she said of the work in progress, "I tried to use a computer, scanning the images and assembling the collages in Photoshop, but it just wasn't workable. Sometimes the tried and true methods are the best. All the images on the cards are Victorian steel engravings. For reference material, I use the Dover Pictorial Archive and original source material (mainly the *London Illustrated Times* from the last two decades of the 19th century). When I'm working on cards, I like to spread out several decks in front of me, with the different variations of each card together. Then I go through my books, looking for images that work for the card. When I find something that works, I make a sketch in my notebook and make note of the book and page number. I make sketches for a number of cards, a dozen or so at a time, then I take the books to the copy shop and photocopy them to the right size. Then it's just a matter of cutting out the images and pasting them together.... I print blank cards with the name and number on my laser printer, and then paste the collage onto that." The suit symbols are guns for swords, pens for wands, Mason jars for cups, and clocks for coins. The black and white deck was published by Llewellyn Publications, St. Paul, in 2002. The back design shows a bust of Queen Victoria in profile.

Vision Tarot Tim Thompson call his tarot deck "a visual atlas of human existence seen through the mind's eye of the medieval tarot artists." The deck's images are collaged photographs, with numbering and titles based on the Tarot of Marseilles. Carta Mundi of Turnhout, Belgium, published the deck under license by the artist

III The Empress from the Victoria Regina Tarot by Sarah Ovenall   The artist describes the Empress as her favorite card. "I guess it seems a little strange that the Empress in a deck called Victoria Regina would not be a portrait of Queen Victoria. But Victoria just doesn't represent the qualities of the Empress to me. I love the expression on the woman that I ended up using: her smile is feminine, but her eyes are direct and unafraid. Most women in steel engravings look down

3 · The Empress

'eyes modestly downcast,' or else up imploringly. Either way, the features express submission and inferiority. It's not easy to find a woman looking directly at the viewer. This Empress knows who she is and has supreme confidence in her femininity." For the final deck, Ovenall actually chose an image different from the one pictured in *Tapestry* magazine, but her description still applies.

in 1995. The French titles appear within the images, and English titles are in the black borders. The back design is black with four white sunbursts. The deck includes a title card and an introductory card.

Victoria Regina Tarot   Sarah Ovenall, Llewellyn Publications, 2002   The descriptions are from the book accompanying the deck, by Sarah Ovenall and Georg Patterson, and indicate the original sources of the images.

TOP ROW: **0 The Fool** was originally a beggar dancing in a group of three country bumpkins with a trained bear. The cliff is an enlarged crystal. **I The Magician** originally appeared as "Baron Sergius Von Holsten lecturing on the people and resources of New Ireland, before the Royal Geographical Society." The display of mounted bugs, the table and the objects to the left were part of the illustration. Instead of a pen, he originally held a large bone or horn. **4 The Emperor** represents a variety of cultures. The king is Hindu, his scepter Asian, and the stone archway is European. **5 The Hierophant** is an Eastern Orthodox patriarch. The background is from a sixteenth-century collection illustrating perspective.

SECOND ROW: **6 The Lovers** is mostly from an engraving illustrating a poem "Favored and Flouted." **8 Strength. 9 The Hermit. 12 The Hanged Man** is from the television series *Monty Python's Flying Circus*, where the character was a dancer in an animation segment.

THIRD ROW: **14 Temperance** shows a woman performing a magic show for children. The waves are the Whirlpool Rapids of Niagara, Canada. The sky is from an advertisement for Aspinall's Oxidized Enamel. **15 The Devil** is a clown who originally advertised Hovis brand bread and biscuits. The background image depicts the British Army destroying a slave encampment on the Mozambique Channel in an attempt to slow the slave trade. **17 The Star** shows an illustration of a Middle Eastern servant welcoming home the master of the house by washing his feet. **19 The Sun** wears the face of a tribal man with face paint and a ring in his lip.

BOTTOM ROW: **21 The World** shows the four suit symbols around a globe before which a woman floats. The woman could be flying or falling. **Prince Wands** is writer Oscar Wilde. The writing in the background is from *De Profundis*, a essay/letter he wrote while in prison. **Eight Wands** shows athletes, with the Crystal Palace in the background. **Four Coins** shows a Japanese man crouched in a martial arts pose.

0 · The Fool

1 · The Magician

4 · The Emperor

5 · The Hierophant

6 · The Lovers

8 · Strength

9 · The Hermit

12 · The Hanged Man

14 · Temperance

15 · The Devil

17 · The Star

19 · The Sun

21 · The World

Prince · Wands

Eight · Wands

Four · Coins

Vision Quest Tarot Sante Fe artists Gaylan Sylvie Winter and Jo Dosé created the Vision Quest Tarot with symbols "inspired by Native American wisdom." The suits are air, showing feathers and birds, for swords; fire, showing arrows, for wands; water, showing jars and bowls, for cups; and earth, showing vegetables and flowers, for pentacles. The back design is of a starry sky with a raptor flying. The deck was published by AGMüller of Neuhausen, Switzerland, in 1998.

Vivere una vita Tarot (To Live Life) Italian artist Dovilio Brero created the Major Arcana deck Vivere una Vita in two media: eighteen of the images are oil paintings and the four others are sculptures. Each image has a Hebrew letter in the design. The deck was published by Editions Centre d'Art Vaas of Vence, France, in 1995. It includes a presentation card and a booklet with a short poem for each Arcana card.

Waite-De Angelis Tarot Artist Roberto De Angelis reinterpreted the Rider-Waite Tarot, embellishing the art of Pamela Colman Smith. The New Waite-De Angelis Tarot has card titles in Italian, German, French, English, and Spanish. The deck includes a title card and cards with instructions for cartomancy in five languages. It was published in 1996 by Lo Scarabeo, Turin, Italy. The box of the deck distributed to English-speakers gives the title "Universal Tarots," but the title card reads "I Nuovi Tarocchi Waite-De Angelis" (The New Waite-De AngelisTarot).

Waking the Wild Spirit Tarot The book accompanying the Waking the Wild Spirit Tarot says, "The tarot pack celebrates the natural world and reaffirms our place within it, revealing our true Wild Self, our spiritual essence, putting us back in touch with our untamed core being, and connecting us to the wild within as well as without." The artist, Poppy Palin, used colored pencil to create images that draw from fairy tales, folklore, nature, and the traditional tarot. Suits are named after the elements, and several of the cards have new titles. For example, the traditional Emperor is called Lord of the Wild—Strong Spirit. The deck and book were published by Llewellyn Publishers, St. Paul, in 2002. The deck includes two extra cards giving spreads. The back design is double-ended, showing elven creatures around a four-sided design.

Wheel of Change Tarot Alexandra Genetti's tarot deck was ten years in the making. "I wanted this new tarot to express elements of the modern world of science and of our contemporary life, but also to relate to our history and evolution. I also knew it should be traditional…. I wanted the cards of the Major Arcana to be immediately distinguishable from the pip cards of the common deck, so I knew that there would be no human figures in the numbered cards." The deck includes an extra card show-

ing a flaming wheel. The back design is a white galaxy on purple. Wheel of Change Tarot was published by Destiny Books, of Rochester, Vermont, in 1997.

Wheel of Destiny Tarot Andrée Tessier designed the Wheel of Destiny deck to "bring the art of divination to within everyone's reach." Each card of the Major Arcana includes divinatory meanings that are color-coded; for example, a red dot beside the meaning indicates finances. The yellow bands on the Major Arcana show general meanings. The Minor Arcana comprise suits of obstacles, hearts, work, and money. The courts are illustrated with playing card courts, except for knights, which have new illustrations like those of the Major Arcana. The illustrations on the cards are by Brigitte Coulombe. The back design, printed in blue, is a sun face surrounded by stars, with the name of the deck. The deck was packaged with a poster on which to lay out the cards. It was published by A.S.T. Distributions in Quebec, Canada, in 1996.

Whimsical Tarot The subtitle of the Whimsical Tarot is "A Deck for Children and the Young at Heart." The images are based on nursery rhymes and fairytales, with the originals rendered in colored pencil by Mary Hanson-Roberts. The deck was published by U.S. Games Systems in 2000, and includes a presentation card and an introductory card. The back design is a flower in a square border.

Wicca Tarot "The Wicca Tarot deck celebrates Cosmic Energy and teaches us the path to it," says the brochure accompanying the deck. "The name is related both to the old English word *wicce* meaning 'wise woman' and to *wicca*, which, in Quechua, the language of the Incas, is the word used to invoke the secret powers of the earth. The meanings of the cards are those of Peruvian shamans who divine with the Tarot of Marseilles and the Cartas Españolas." The deck was designed on computer by K. Chauvin H. The black and white cards have titles and divinatory meanings in Spanish. The back design is floral motifs. The deck includes three extra cards giving spreads. The Wicca Tarot was published by the artist in 1993, in Lima, Peru.

Wild Flower Tarot The symbolism of wild flowers decorates the Major Arcana deck by Hilde Douchar. The black and white deck was published in 1995 by Guido Gillabel of Belgium in a limited edition of ninety-nine decks numbered and signed by the artist. The cards are titled in English, Flemish, and French. The deck includes a blank card, a title card, and a presentation card, a folding double-sized card giving the Latin names and the familiar names of the flowers in English and Flemish, and a booklet by Gillabel in English and Flemish. The back design is a floral arrangement printed in green.

Vision Tarot   Tim Thompson, Carta Mundi, 1995

0
Clown

I
Medicine Man

III
Grand Mother

VII
Spiritual Warrior

VIII
Balance

IX
Hermit

X
Small Medicine Wheel

XI
Life Force

XII
Vision Quest

XIII
Transformation

XIV
Integration

XV
Torment

XVI
Chaos

XVII
Star

IXX
Sun

XX
Spirit Guide

XXI
Big Medicine Wheel

Six of Air
Clarity

Father
of Fire

Four of Earth
Security

Vision Quest Tarot   Gaylan Sylvie Winter and Jo Dosé, AGMüller, 1998

Vivere una vita Tarot (To Live Life Tarot)   Dovilio Brero, Editions Centre d'Art Vaas, 1995

Waite-De Angelis Tarot (New Tarots; Universal Tarots)   Roberto De Angelis, Lo Scarabeo, 1996

Waking the Wild Spirit Tarot   Poppy Palin, Llewellyn Publications, 2002

Wheel of Change Tarot   Alexandra Genetti, Destiny Books, 1997   The descriptions are based on those in the book accompanying the deck.

TOP ROW: **The Fool** stands over a chasm, symbol of the descent into the unconscious that leads to self-understanding. He is upon two green plains, symbolizing that the journey begins in the spring. The fox at the lower right is symbol of the animal nature of the fool. The red roses symbolize wild joy and the primitive animal natures. The swirling stars and the solar eclipse symbolize the immediate nature of the Fool. **The Magician.** The temple was built by human hands and is the result of vision and work, and is a sacred space within which magic can unfold. The solar red and gold columns wrapped with a golden vine are symbolic of the potency of the masculine god and his phallus enclosed within the feminine. In the background, a path leads to the highest mountain, lit by the rising sun, symbolic of the Magician's path in life. **The High Priestess** is an old woman who has lived in her power for many years. She sits under willow trees, which are connected with water and hence to the female and the Goddess. They are shown in fall and winter aspects, and are the pillars to the aging Priestess. The dark blue of the Priestess's robe connects her to the night sky. **The Empress** is a pregnant woman from the fertile crescent between the Tigris and Euphrates rivers. She wears red, the color of her life blood. Her crown of twelve roses symbolizes passion for life. She holds an apple cut crosswise to reveal a five-pointed star. The apple is an ancient symbol of fertility and love.

SECOND ROW: **The Lovers** personify the sun and the moon, joined together in a partnership that defines their roles in the cosmos. Behind them are two oak trees, symbolizing the ancient polarity of the twin children of the Great Goddess. **The Chariot** shows the analogy between the larger heavenly cycles and the smaller wheels we create as we orbit throughout our lives and interact with people in pursuit of our goals. **Strength** shows a strong, beautiful woman

riding forward on a lion, holding a flag that proclaims the source of her power. She is naked because she feels pride in her womanly body. The spirals painted on her body tell of the cyclic nature of all life and give expression to her own menstrual cycle. **The Hermit** carries a lamp that symbolically lights up what is obscure and in darkness, and lets us see the fearsome creatures of the darkness to dispel our fear. He personifies the archetype of the wild old man who represents meaning and understanding. **Wheel of Fortune** shows the planets of our solar system, with the inner planets separated from the outer by the band of the wheel. The inner rocky planets symbolize all that is internal to us—our bodies, feelings, and perceptions—and the outer planets embody the spirit and what is external to us—our common ground such as religion and the law. The sun in the center is symbolic of the individual will and ego.

THIRD ROW: **The Hanged Man** shows the solar king turned on his head, ready to begin the journey back to the darkness he has come from. The solar wheel behind him is symbol of the ancient eight-year term of the solar king. **Temperance** shows the Goddess who pours from her hands fire and water. From her breasts pour milk and blood, the liquids of life. **The Devil** is the wild king of the autumn equinox. **The Star** is represented by a young woman who has harnessed her creative power to create the galaxy that swirls around her. As she pours the stars out of the cup in her left hand, her right hand pours the fiery star power back into her heart. **The Moon** shows the passageway of death, guarded by hounds who howl at the light of the moon.

BOTTOM ROW: **Judgment** shows a child emerging from the soil of a beautiful flower garden in a land shaped like a woman's body. **6 of Swords.** A fallen caribou gives its life to feed the people. **8 of Wands.** Tools of the artist bring the painting to life. **Ace of Wands.** The ribbons of the Maypole are ready for the dance. **4 of Cups.** A simple potter's studio filled with light.

Whimsical Tarot   Mary Hanson-Roberts, U.S. Games Systems, 2000

Wheel of Destiny Tarot   Andrée Tessier and Brigitte Coulombe, artist, A.S.T. Distributions, 1996

Wicca Tarot K. Chauvin H., published by the artist, 1993

Wild Flower Tarot Hilde Douchar, published by Guido Gillabel, 1995 TOP ROW: 0 The Fool (chickweed evergreen). I The Magician (rose). II The High Priestess (columbine). III The Empress (dog rose). V The Hierophant (lords-and-ladies). SECOND ROW: VI The Lovers (field bindweed). VIII Justice (mare's tail). IX The Hermit. X Wheel of Fortune (lesser celandine, corn poppy, meadow saffron, winter aconite). XI Strenght [sic] (snapdragon). THIRD ROW: XII De Hanged Man [sic] (alfalfa). XIII Death (coventry bells). XIV Temperance (cat's tail). XV The Devil (greater bindweed). XVI The Tower (Scottish thistle). BOTTOM ROW: XVII The Star (ground ivy). XVIII The Moon (rozette). XIX The Sun (sunflower). XX The Last Judgment (holly). XXI The World (wild strawberry).

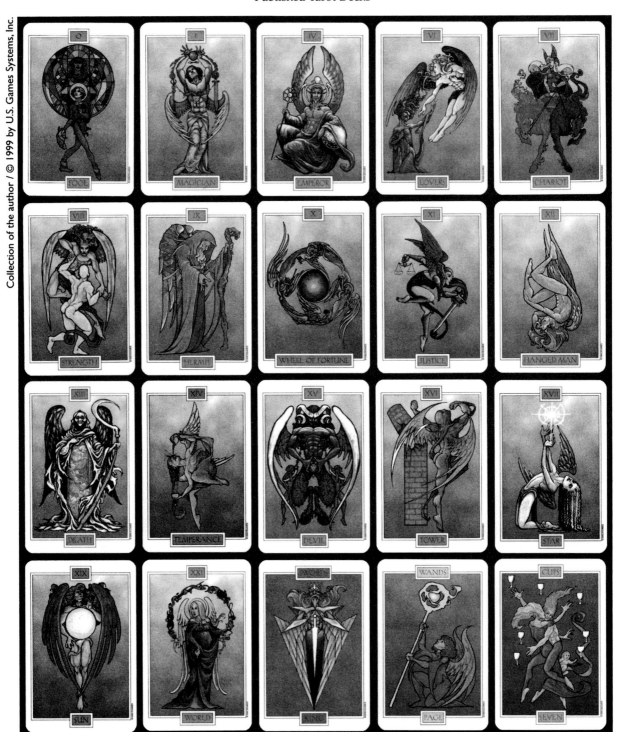

Winged Spirit Tarot "The chasm between human comprehension and the mysteries of the divine are enormous," says the introductory card to the Winged Spirit Tarot. "In spite of this gulf, humankind continues to reach into the unknown.... The winged spirit is dedicated to forming a bridge to two of these divine mysteries: the angels and the tarot." David Sexton used the figures of angels on the Major Arcana "to help us understand the will of the Higher Power." The Minor Arcana feature angels that are not named but rather are types who manifest in particular kinds of situations. The deck was published in 1999 by U.S. Games Systems. It features a presentation card and an introductory card, and a back design of wings and spheres arranged geometrically.

Witches Tarot The Witches Tarot was designed to blend the ideas of the tarot with kabbalistic symbolism in a way that would appeal to pagans and others. The Major Arcana move from tradition in numbering Justice XI and Wheel of Fortune X. The back design is of a silver pentagram on black. The deck was first issued by Llewellyn of St. Paul, Minnesota, in 1989, and reprinted in 2000. The 1989 edition has the publisher's name at the lower right corner of the back. Martin Cannon painted the deck under direction of Ellen Cannon Reed.

Wonderland Tarot The Wonderland Tarot is based on the illustrations by Sir John Tenniel for Lewis Carroll's classic fantasies *Alice's Adventures in Wonderland* and *Through the Looking Glass.* Lewis Carroll was the pen-name of Rev. Charles Lutwidge Dodgson, who lived from 1832 to 1898. The stories were originally told aloud to a child, who fortunately begged Carroll to write them down. The Wonderland Tarot was designed by Christopher Abbey and Morgana Abbey, with drawings by Morgana Abbey. The suits are Flamingos (swords), Peppermills (wands), Hats (cups), and Oysters (coins). The courts have playing card suit signs as well as tarot titles. (Knight is C for Cavalier.) The back design shows vines with red flowers. The deck was published by U.S. Games Systems, Stamford, Connecticut, in 1989. It includes two presentation cards—one in mirror writing.

Robin Wood Tarot The Robin Wood Tarot features illustrations drawn from European medieval and Celtic imagery. The deck, created by Robin Wood, was published by Llewellyn Publications, St. Paul, in 1991. The back design features a green and white knot pattern on black. The full-color deck was redrawn from a black and white Robin Wood Tarot, which the artist published as a coloring book (see *The Encyclopedia of Tarot,* volume 3).

Winged Spirit Tarot David Sexton, U.S. Games Systems, 1999 Descriptions are based on those in the booklet accompanying the deck.

TOP ROW: **0 Fool** shows Tobias watched over by the angel Raphael. The boy carries a flower, representing the freshness of youth, and a fish, representing lessons he will learn on his path. **I Magician** is Metatron. He represents the divine power within the mortal shell of a man, because he was once mortal himself. **IV Emperor** is the universal father, portrayed as the Gnostic angel Aeon, the Demiurge. One group of Gnostics believed that the Demiurge was actually the creator of the universe, since a perfect god could not create such a flawed thing. **VI Lovers** are Samiasa and Aholibamah, from a play by George Byron. Samiasa is an angel torn between his love for a mortal, Aholibamah, daughter of Noah, and his love of heaven. **VII Chariot** shows a Valkyrie, a Norse spirit who brings dead warriors to Valhalla in a chariot drawn by horses of fire and air.

SECOND ROW: **VIII Strength** shows the man Jacob in his epic wrestling match with the angel Uriel. Jacob wins the struggle, but is wounded in the thigh. **IX The Hermit** is Orifiel, the angel of solitude and the wilderness. He is depicted with his wings bound; he is in a period of withdrawal, learning the lessons of acceptance and patience. **X Wheel of Fortune** shows the Gnostic Aeons, creators of a flawed universe. **XI Justice** is Nemesis, whose role in Greek mythology is one of divine retribution. **XII Hanged Man** is Azazel, sent by God to teach mankind righteousness. His lust for women corrupted him, and in penance, he flung himself into the heavens, where he hangs from one foot.

THIRD ROW: **XIII Death** is Azrael. He alone of the four archangels succeeded in bringing back to God a handful of dust with which to create humankind. Thus, he was also charged with returning man to dust and is the angel of death. **XIV Temperance** shows Bethesda. Her legend describes her as coming to earth and touching the ground, giving birth to a healing fountain. **XV Devil.** Lucifer rebelled against God in order to gain power, and was exiled to darkness. His disciples are chained loosely, indicating that they are chained by their own choice. **XVI Tower** shows Abaddon, the angel of destruction, with wings of lightning and veiled eyes symbolic of the random nature of disaster. **XVII Star** is Phanuel, "the face of God." She is the angel of hope and penance. As the Star, she represents the ability to see the face of God through the darkest of trials.

BOTTOM ROW: **XIX Sun** shows the angel Galgaliel. He leads a chorus of angels in singing the celestial song, which illuminates the universe. **XXI World** is Shekinah, the female aspect of divinity. She is surrounded by the symbols of the Major Arcana. **King of Swords. Page of Wands. Seven of Cups.**

Witches Tarot   Ellen Cannon Reed and Martin Cannon, Llewellyn Publications, 1989

Wonderland Tarot Christopher Abbey and Morgana Abbey, based on the illustrations by Sir John Tenniel, U.S. Games Systems, 1989   TOP ROW: 0 THE FOOL (Mad Hatter). I THE MAGICIAN (Lewis Carroll). II THE HIGH PRIESTESS (Alice). IV THE EMPEROR (Cheshire Cat). V THE HIEROPHANT.   SECOND ROW: VI THE LOVERS (Tweedledee and Tweedledum). IX THE HERMIT (Dormouse). X WHEEL OF FORTUNE (The caucus race of the Dodo, Mouse, Owl, Eaglet, and Guinea Pig). XI JUSTICE (Father William). XIII DEATH (Queen of Hearts).

THIRD ROW: XIV TEMPERANCE (Haigha, the messenger). XV THE DEVIL (Jabberwock). XVI THE TOWER (the White Rabbit and Bill, with Alice's hand reaching for them). XVII THE STAR (the Gryphon). XVIII THE MOON (the Walrus and the Carpenter, ready to feast on oysters).   BOTTOM ROW: XX JUDGEMENT (the White Rabbit heralding the trial for the Knave of Hearts). XXI THE WORLD (Alice). KING OF FLAMINGOS. PAGE OF PEPPERMILLS. TEN OF CUPS (Alice).

Robin Wood Tarot   Llewellyn Publications, 1991

Woo-Woo Tarot   Mystic Eye, artist and publisher, 1998

Woo-Woo Tarot   The Woo-Woo Tarot, from Mystic Eye, Chicago, is accompanied by a leaflet with a story hinting at how the Major Arcana deck came into being. A schoolgirl, Beverly, invites her friends to brave with her a sinister abandoned house. They go to the house and hold a séance, and the rest of the girls are frightened off when "an old Indian woman" appears. Beverly stays, and the woman presents to her a deck of cards with "bright colors, American Indian symbols, a touch of romanticism, some modernism." The deck was published in 1998. The deck includes a title card and a blank card.

601

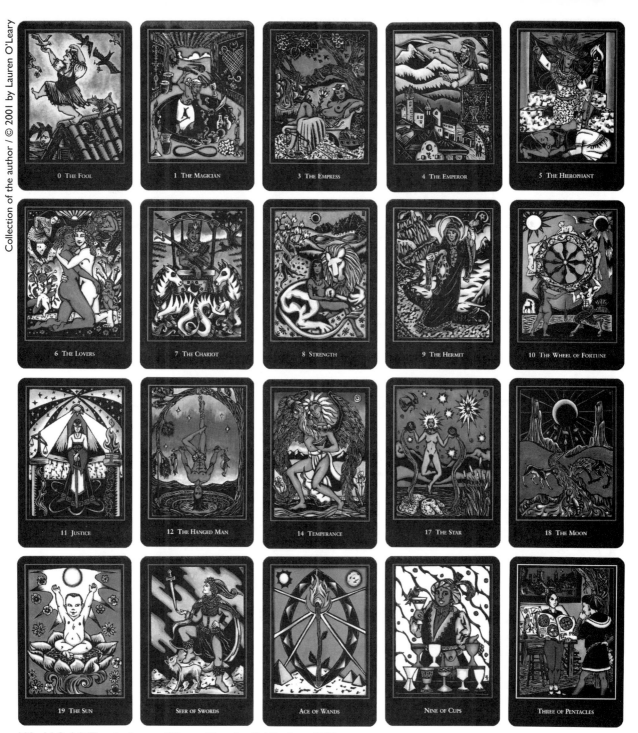

World Spirit Tarot   Lauren O'Leary, Llewellyn Publications, 2001

World Spirit Tarot The artwork of the World Spirit Tarot draws from that by Pamela Colman Smith, who created the Rider-Waite Tarot, and that by Frieda Harris, who painted the Book of Thoth Tarot, under direction of Aleister Crowley. The artist, Lauren O'Leary, also added many other elements and for some cards created new scenarios in order to make a globally oriented deck. The deck is accompanied by a booklet written by Jessica Goding and Lauren O'Leary. The court cards are Seers, Seekers, Sybils, and Sages. Although they correspond to the traditional courts of Page, Knight, Queen, and King, "they are not meant to be hierarchical," as explained in the booklet accompanying the deck, "rather, they speak to different stages of development." The book describes the courts: "The Seers are students, curious about the world around them…. The Seekers interact more dynamically with the world, questing for answers and challenges, taking risks, and trying to get things done…. The Sibyls are the mature embodiment of their suits…. The Sages are accomplished in the world. They bring a broad perspective gained by age and responsibility, and they possess great authority." The illustrations were created as hand-colored linoleum block prints. Llewellyn Publications of St. Paul issued the deck in 2001. The deck includes two identical title cards. The back design shows an hour glass, with night and day at right and left.

Fleeing Nazis · Munich · The British Empire · Sir W.S. Churchill · Harry S. Truman · Generalissimo and Madame / Chiang Kai-shek · R.A.F. · Charles De Gaulle · Stalingrad · Auschwitz, Treblinka...

World War II Tarot   Helene Bouboulis, published by the artist, 1994   Descriptions are from the flyer accompanying the deck.

TOP ROW: **Fleeing Nazis** An undetermined number of Nazis managed to flee to South America and the Middle East, some with Vatican passports given to them by the CIA that used them to infiltrate communist parties in Europe, others through the SS Odessa organization set up before the end of the war. **1 Munich.** Scene of the meeting of September 29, 1938, when the rights of Czechoslovakia were to be signed away to Hitler by Italy, France, and Britain. **3 The British Empire.** Except for Ireland, all British colonies and dominions participated in World War II. The Empire broke up after the war, when colonies obtained independence. **4 Sir Winston S. Churchill** (1874–1965). Prime Minister of Britain from 1940 to 1945, and again from 1951 to 1955. His defiant speeches and courageous example made him an inspiring war leader. **5 Harry S. Truman** (1884–1972). President of the U.S. from 1945 to 1953. Made the decision to use the atomic bomb against Japan. After the war, he guaranteed American aid to any free country resisting communist propaganda and infiltration.

SECOND ROW: **6 Generalissimo and Madame**

Chiang Kai-shek. Chiang Kai-shek was a Chinese leader from 1926 to 1949. He was driven out in 1950 by Communists to the island of Formosa (Taiwan). His wife Sung Mei-ling played an important political role by his side. **8 R.A.F.** (Royal Air Force). Headed by Lord Dowding, the R.A.F. saved Great Britain from German invasion in 1940. From 1943, the R.A.F. dominated the skies, thanks to American help. **9 Charles de Gaulle** (1890–1970). De Gaulle was leader of the Free French in London from 1940. He was recognized leader of France after the liberation of Paris in August 1944, and he retired in 1946. He was president of the French Republic from 1958 to 1969. **10 Stalingrad.** The city in Russia was under siege from August 1942 until February 2, 1943. The heroic defense of the city was lead by general (later marshal) Vassili Chuikov, who would later conquer Berlin. Stalingrad, with the battles of Midway and El Alamein, was a turning point in the war, the first major setbacks suffered by the Axis (Germany, Italy, Japan). **13 Auschwitz, Treblinka...** Some thirty concentration camps were set up by the Nazis in Germany and occupied countries between 1940 and 1945. As many as twelve million people died in them, among whom were six million Jews, as well as Gypsies and Slavs.

World War II Tarot   Helene Bouboulis describes in a letter to Stuart Kaplan how she created the World War II Tarot: "All the participants, events, and countries were selected on one hand according to the impact they had on the war and sometimes on the world later on. On the other hand, the choice was also firmly guided by how close they came to representing the symbolism of tarot. Some important characters, events, and countries were regretfully set aside also due to the limited number of cards."

The back design shows the Mae Klong Bridge, the thousand-mile Japanese railway between Burma and Thailand, built in over a year by 61,000 Allied prisoners. The deck was published by the artist in 1994, and it includes an advertising card and a card describing the suits of the deck: the American flag is on the suit of coins; the rising sun of the Japanese is on the suit of wands; the Nazi swastika is on the suit of swords; and the red star of the Soviets is on the suit of cups.

World War II Tarot *(continued)*   TOP ROW: **15 Heinrich Himmler** (1900–1945). Named Reichsführer of all the SS Corps by Hitler in 1929. In 1934 he became Chief of the Gestapo, and by 1944 he controlled all the organs of surveillance and repression in the Third Reich. Organized mass exterminations, concentration camps, administered Waffen SS divisions of the Field Army. **16 Hiroshima–Nagasaki.** On August 6 and 9, 1945, these Japanese cities suffered an atomic bomb attack ordered by President Truman after the negative Japanese response to the Potsdam Ultimatum. The attacks led to the capitulation by Japan on September 2, 1945. More than a 100,000 were killed outright. 15,000 went missing. More than 40,000 were seriously injured. **17 The Star.** The Jews in Germany and occupied territories were required to wear the yellow Star of David in a visible way at all times. The big blue star with two blue stripes became the national flag of Israel on May 14, 1948. **18 Iwo Jima.** Along with the Bonin Islands, Iwo Jima Island was assaulted by American forces in February 1945. Of 22,000 Japanese troops, only 212 chose to surrender in March. 6,891 Americans got killed, 18,700 wounded. **20 Nüremberg, Tokyo.** Venues of the international tribunals on war crimes, where German and Japanese leaders were tried and sentenced after the war.

BOTTOM ROW: **21 U.N.O.** (United Nations Organization) The charter was signed in San Francisco on June, 26, 1945, by the 51 nations at war against the Axis. It was designed to maintain peace and security in the world. **Page of Swords. G.P. Goebbels** (1897–1945) Nazi Minister of Propaganda since 1933. Died with wife and children in Führer bunker after Hitler's suicide. **Ace of Batons.** The rising sun of Japan. **King of Disks. F. D. Roosevelt** (1882–1945) President of the United States from 1933 to 1945. Took part in Yalta and Teheran meetings with Stalin and Churchill where they drew up the new map of Europe and their zones of influence, died three weeks before German surrender. **Queen of Disks. B29 Superfortress** was used in the Pacific. Cheesecake and pinup pictures of women were painted on the forward fuselage until religious groups protested to Air Force headquarters and "nose art" was all together banned.

I Les Magiciennes	*III L'ordre*	*V La Porte sacrée*	*VI La Fiancée*	*VII Les Jumelles*
XIV La Fécondité	*XV La Diablesse*	*XVI Le Feu*	*XIX La Reine du ciel*	*XXII L'acrobate*
XXIII La Grande prêtresse	*La Gloire du ciel*	*I Le soleil*	*La Gloire de la terre*	*YUMI*

Tarot de Yumi   Yumi, B. P. Grimaud, 2002

Tarot de Yumi   French artist Yumi created a forty-five-card deck that is not traditional tarot but shares many of the same cards. All of the figures in the deck are female. The Major Arcana comprise twenty-four cards, and the Minor Arcana comprise suits, called joyaux (joys), of océan (ocean), terre (earth), feu (fire), and ciel (sky). Each suit has four numbered cards and a card called the La Gloire (Glory). The deck was published in 2002 by Grimaud, France.

Zerner Farber Tarot   Artist Amy Zerner created the designs of the Zerner Farber Tarot in collaboration with her husband, writer Monte Farber. The collages combine textile, embroidery, paper, and found objects to make visionary images. The deck was published as the Enchanted Tarot by Eddison-Sadd Editions of London (American edition by St. Martin's Press) in 1990. It was republished by the authors as the Zerner Farber Tarot in 1997. The two editions vary slightly. For example, the title treatment differs, and the Enchanted Tarot was packaged with a book by Monte Farber.

Zerner Farber Tarot   Amy Zerner, artist, and Monte Farber, published by the artists, 1997

Enchanted Tarot   Amy Zerner, artist, and Monte Farber, Eddison-Sadd Editions, 1990

Oreste Zevola Tarots Oreste Zevola, B.P. Grimaud, 1989

Oreste Zevola Tarots Oreste Zevola, from Naples, created a tarot with elongated designs that often veer to grotesque and sinister. The deck was published by L'Aire du Verseau and ACL Construction, printed by Grimaud of France, in 1989, in a limited edition of 2,500 copies. The back design is a white drawing on gray.

Zukunfts Tarot "The variety of cultures and races in the world, of kingdoms in nature (plants, animals, angels), of elements (fire, water, air, earth, ether), is the basis for this universal tarot deck," says the description by Alika Lindbergh, artist of the Zukunfts Tarot. "Created as a tool for divination and guidance, the Zukunfts Tarot also points the way towards humanity's evolution into planetary consciousness—a time of balance between mind and body, masculine and feminine, society and individual—and new partnership with the whole earth." Lindbergh was inspired by the author and psychic Maud Kristen. The original artwork was done as oil paintings. The deck was published in 2001 by Urania Verlag of Neuhausen, Switzerland, and it includes an advertising card and a card about Lindbergh and Kristen.

Zukunfts Tarot   Alika Lindbergh, artist, and Maud Kristen,
Urania Verlag, 2001   The original oil paintings are the basis
for the illustrations here.

Published card
from the Zukunfts Tarot

TAROT DECKS FROM JAPAN

Most Japanese tarot decks are Major Arcana only, packaged with a book. Titles of the decks are often given in English, even when the accompanying packaging and book are in Japanese.

Many Japanese decks are based on popular manga and anime characters. *Manga* (pronounced monga) is the term for Japanese comic strips; *anime* (pronounced animay) refers to animated cartoons. Manga has its roots in Ukiyoe art, but the genre solidified in the 1950s. Its commercial appeal exploded internationally in the 1980s. Many genres and subgenres in anime/manga exist, and many artists specialize.

Popular anime/manga series generate a huge variety of products, such as trading cards, video games, magazines, clothing, posters, feature movies, and music recordings. Tarot is a natural spin-off, because the medium favors visual art and strong characters, and because anime/manga loves fantasy and the supernatural, with characters of gods, angels, demons, and, most popular, schoolchildren endowed with magical powers.

Anime/manga characters have childlike faces, big eyes, tiny mouths, and tousled hair. Walt Disney productions were obviously a strong influence. Costumes are of supreme importance. Above all, the characters must be *kawaii*, or cute, whether the content is for children or "for adults only."

The artists of decks based on manga/anime are often difficult to identify. Manga/anime products are generally created by a team of artists including character designers, writers, colorists, inkers, and letterers. Also, one artist will initiate a manga series, and the characters and scenarios are taken up by other artists as well as anime studios and so on.

This section also includes Chinese copies or spinoffs of Japanese originals. Japanese tarots usually have titles in English and sometimes in French, whereas Chinese versions are usually titled in Chinese.

Some manga/anime terms that apply to tarot are:
Doujinshi artists are basically "fan artists." They create their own stories and artwork using the characters and settings of an already published manga. Doujinshi art often takes a satiric or erotic turn from the original.

Shoujo artists make anime/manga for women and girls. Shoujo tarot decks often depict female figures in place of traditionally male figures, such as the Emperor. Interestingly, though, the Hanged Man is nearly always male.

Uranai, frequently part of the title of a deck, means "fortune-telling" or "divination."

Japanese tarot decks featured in this chapter are:

Age of Mythology Tarot
Ah! My Goddess Tarot
Amano Tarot
Amazing Tarot
Anan Tarot
Angel CLAMP Tarot
Angel Mithra Divination Tarot
Angel of Tarot Divination
Angel Sanctuary Tarots (2)
Angelique Tarots (2)
Angelique Innocence Tarot
Animal Tarot
Arcana Tarot
Astrologic Tarot
Astrology Egyptian Tarot
Atelier Elie Tarot
Basara Gold Tarot
Big Arukana Tarot
Blade of Arcana Tarot
Blue Moon Tarot
Cardcaptor Sakura Tarot
Cats World Tarot
CLAMP Tarot
CLAMP X Tarot
Cocktail de Tarot
Crystal Tarot
DiGi Charat Tarot
Divination Tarot
Divination for Love Tarot (2)

Divinatory Tarot of Destiny
Dr. Rin Tarot
Dr. Rin Special Happy Tarot
Egiptian Tarot 22
Encounter your Destiny with Tarot
End Sector Tarot
Fairy Tarot
Tarot Fairy
La Fillette Revolutionaire Tarot
Foreseeable Future Tarot
FOX Tarot
Galaxy Angel Tarot
Gensomaden Saikyuki Tarot
Ghost Sweeper Tarot
Good Luck Tarot
Gundam Wing Tarot
Happiness Tarot (2)
Happiness and Love Divination Tarot
Heterophony Tarot
Iris Lam Tarot
Kabbalah Tarot
Kabbalah: Tarot of Love
Keishobou Tarot
Love Tarot
Lucky Tarot
Luna Original Tarot

Magic Story of Misa Tarot
Meditation Tarot
Megu Manga Gundam Wing Tarot
Miracle Tarot
Mirai O Tsugeru Tarot
Miraiwo Hiraku Arcana Tarot
Moon Dawn of Crystal Tarot
Moonprincess Tarot
Moonprincess Himiko Tarot
Morinaga Hi-Crown Original Tarot
Naruto Tarot
Non No Tarot
Orizinaru Tarot
Pandora's Tarot
Passion Tarot
Pierre Tarot
Planet Girls of the Solar System Tarot
Pocketable Tarot
Renaissance-style Tarot
RG Veda Tarot
Ribon Furoku Tarot
Rise No Miracle Tarot

Romance Tarot
Sailor Moon Tarot (German)
Sentimental Journey Tarot
Shigeru Mizuki Tarot
Sho Comi Tarot
Sol Bianca: The Legend Tarot
Starlot Tarot
Studio Takama/Nukadaya Kouriten Tarot
Tarot World Tarot
Texthoth Ludo Tarot
Tokyo Nova: The Revolution Tarot
Twelve Constellations Divinatory Tarot (2)
Uru Q Tarot
Vision of Escaflowne Tarot
Weiß Kreuz Tarot
Wirth Tarot
Yu-Gi-Oh Tarot

Age of Mythology Tarot (Megami Tensei Tarot; also known as Mega Ten World Tarot), Atlus (publisher), circa 1990   Atlus is a video game developer, and the games in the series *Megami Tensei* are based on classical Greek and Roman mythology, with Biblical and Shin supernatural figures as well.

Ah! My Goddess Tarot   AIC studio (designer), Kodan-sha/Movic (publisher), 1998   *Ah! My Goddess* is about a college student living in a temple with three goddesses. The manga series was created by Kosuke Fujishima in 1988. In 1993, a television series of it was made.

Amano Tarot (also called Shiwase o Tsukamu Uranai [Finding Happiness with Tarot Fortune-telling]) Yoshitaka Amano (artist), Narumdio Shuppan / Seibido Shuppan (publisher), 1991 Yoshitaka Amano created the beautiful and intricate designs of a seventy-eight-card deck. The double-ended back design shows a flower with a face in it, on a black background. The book accompanying the deck is by Emile Scheherazade.

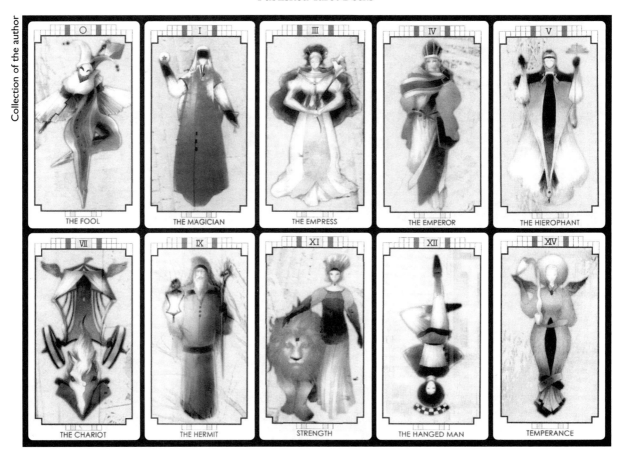

Amazing Tarot   Kao, 2002

Anan Tarot   2002

Anan Tarot *(continued)*

Angel CLAMP Tarot   CLAMP studio (artists), circa 1999   CLAMP is a shoujo manga studio. The Angel CLAMP Tarot shown here has eighty-one cards. The three extra cards are untitled and unnumbered, with illustrations. Another Angel CLAMP tarot was published in China circa 2002, with different illustrations.

Angel Mithra Divination Tarot (Love Tarot of Mithras; Tenshi Mitora no Renai Tarot Uranai)   Naoko Okano (artist), Kokushokankoukai (publisher), 1996   Major Arcana only, packaged with a book by Masato Tojo.

Angel of Tarot Divination   Marie Primavera (artist), Seibido Shuppan (publisher), 1995

Collection of Laurie Amato

	愚者
I	魔術師
IV	皇帝
VII	戰車
X	命運之輪
XI	正義
XII	倒吊男
	節制

Angel Sanctuary Tarot   Kaori Yuki, 1990s   The eighty-one-card Angel Sanctuary Tarot is based on the manga series by Kaori Yuki. The story is of reincarnated angels and their romances and wars. The three extra cards are unnumbered and untitled.

Collection of Laurie Amato

Angel Sanctuary Tarot Kaori Yuki, 1990s Seventy-eight-card deck based on manga by Kaori Yuki.

Collection of Laurie Amato

Angelique Tarot Yura Kairi (character designer), Koei Co. (publisher), 1994

The Angelique Tarot decks are based on the video game series by shoujo manga artist Kairi Yura. The games were produced by Koei Co., Ltd.

Angelique Tarot Kairi Yura (character designer), Koei Co. (publisher), 2000

Angelique Innocence Tarot Marumi Yamamoto (artist), 2000 Major Arcana only, packaged with a book by Mimu

Angelique Innocence Tarot *(continued)*

Animal Tarot   Artist and publisher unknown, 1995

Arcana Tarot   Ciel (publisher), 2000

Astrologic Tarot Sosei Fujimoto (artist), Natsume-sha (publisher), 1989 Twenty-two Major Arcana plus two extra cards: Head of Dragon and Tail of Dragon. Packaged with a book by Shurei Etoile.

Astrology Egyptian Tarot Futami Shobo (publisher), circa 1997 The Astrology Egyptian Tarot was originally published in 1974, printed in black on white (see Egyptian Japanese Tarot in *The Encyclopedia of Tarot*, volume III). The 1997 edition is a negative of the 1974 deck.

Atelier Elie Tarot Designs based on a game with graphics by Ouse Kohime; deck developed and published by Gust Co., Ltd./Imagineer Co., Ltd., 1997

Basara Gold Tarot Yumi Tamura (artist), 2000 The deck is based on the anime series *Basara*. The card faces are etched gold foil. Major Arcana only.

Big Arukana Tarot (Shinpi no Tarot Uranai)   Kazumi Niikura (artist), Jitsugyo-no Nihon-sha (publisher), 1999   Packaged with a book by Mondo Oki and Mei Unasaka.

Blade of Arcana   Aspect (publisher), 1999   The deck is based on a manga series, *Blade of Arcana*. It comprises Major Arcana plus eight cards created for use with a role-playing game. The cards were included as a punch-out set (four to a sheet) in an envelope attached to the inside back cover of the instruction manual.

Blue Moon Tarot   Anonymous, circa 1995

Collection of Laurie Amato

Collection of the author

Cardcaptor Sakura Tarot   CLAMP, 1990s   *Cardcaptor Sakura* is a manga story about a ten-year-old girl, Kinomoto Sakura, who has to use magic to collect *clow* cards that have escaped from a magical book. The cards can take the form of various objects, some of which are very powerful. Sakura must get all of the cards in order to prevent a world disaster. She has the help of her best friend and the guardian of the cards, Cerberu (Kero-chan), who is pictured as The Fool. The original Cardcaptor manga is by CLAMP studio. Several tarot decks based on the series were published.

0 THE FOOL 愚者	
2 THE HIGH PRIESTESS 女教皇	
3 THE EMPRESS 女帝	
4 THE EMPEROR 皇帝	
5 THE HIEROPHANT 法皇	
9 THE HERMIT 隠者	
12 THE HANGED MAN 吊るされた男	
13 DEATH 死	
17 THE STAR 星	
20 JUDGEMENT 審判	

Cats World Tarot (Kyattsu Waarudo) Helen Miu (artist), Tokyodo Shuppan (publisher), 1997 Cats World Tarot, with titles in English and Japanese, features people with the ears and tails of cats. The back design is a hexagram surrounded by cats. Major Arcana only.

0 愚者	I 魔法師	V 教皇
LE.FOV	LE.BATELEUR	LE.PAPE
XIV 節制	XIX 太陽	銭幣騎士
I.A.TEMPERANCE	LE.SOLEIL	KNIGHT.OF.PENTACLS

CLAMP Tarot CLAMP studio (artists), 1990s

CLAMP X Tarot CLAMP studio (artists), 1990s *X* is the name of one of the comic book series created by CLAMP. The cover of each comic in the series was a tarot card; the plan was to publish a deck after all issues were published. The CLAMP X Tarot was published in China, possibly as a "pirate" product, before the series was complete, with images from the comics to fill out the seventy-eight-card deck. The deck includes two extra cards: one is labeled "Major Arcana: The Seven Seals," and the other is "The Minor Arcana: The Seven Angels." Another edition of the CLAMP X Tarot was also published in China, with three extra cards and titles in Chinese.

Cocktail de Tarot Shimmei (artist), published by the artist, 2000 The Major Arcana artwork was made using computer graphics. The back design shows a Star of David on a blue, gray, and green pattern.

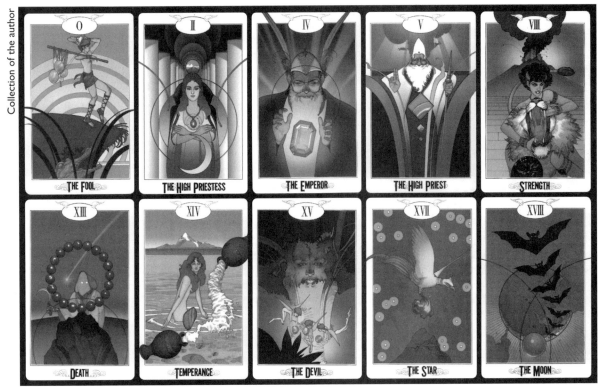

Crystal Tarot Mokuseioh (artist), Seitosiya (publisher), 1991 The Crystal Tarot was packaged with a book and a CD titled *Original Psychic Sound*. The double-ended back design has the title of the deck with ornamentation in white on red. The deck includes two blank cards and a round card showing the Kabbalistic tetragrammaton.

DiGi Charat Tarot Circa 2000 The DiGi Charat is based on the illustrations by Kage Donbo. The character was created in 1998 for the company Brocolli, makers of computer games, trading card games, character merchandise, and anime, to use as the mascot for their Gamers chain of stores. The protagonist's name was derived from the store name: Digital Character Total Shop Gamers.

Collection of Laurie Amato

Collection of the author / © 1990 Enishi Gen

Divination Tarot (Tarot Uranai) Jun Kozima (artist), Natsume-sha, Tokyo (publisher), 1999 The deck is accompanied by a book by Enishi Gen. The back design of the Major Arcana deck is a Star of David within a pattern in white on pink.

Divination for Love Tarot (Ai no Tarot Uranai)   Mari Mihori (artist), Nihon Bungei-sha (publisher), 1990s   The deck is accompanied by a book by Mari Mihori. The numbering on cards II, III, IV, IX, and XI through XIV is nontraditional.

Divination for Love Tarot (Ai no Tarot Uranai)   George Domon (artist), Natsume-sha (publisher), 1989

Divinatory Tarot of Destiny (Unmei ga Meiru Tarot Uranai)   Mari Mihori (artist), Narumido Shuppan (publisher), 2000
Major Arcana deck packaged with a book by Tomoko Taguchi. The back design is doubled ended, of a white feature on a black background. The order of the Major Arcana is not traditional for cards 2 through 4 and 9 through 14.

Dr. Rin Tarot (Akuma-Kun Tarot) Bandai (publisher), 1989 An unusual feature of this deck is the inclusion of a plastic device that shoots cards across the room. The deck includes two extra cards showing pictures of a castle. The back design shows a Star of David within a circle in yellow on purple. Dr. Rin is a fortuneteller in a manga series.

Dr. Rin Special Happy Tarot Kiyoko Arai (artist), 2001

KHNUM
The Magician

HATHOR
The High Priestess

THE LOVERS

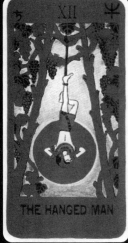

THE HANGED MAN

ANUBIS Death

SATURN
The Devil

Egiptian Tarot 22 Yoshio Karashima (artist), Tokyodo Shuppan (publisher), 1987

Encounter Your Destiny with Tarot (Unmei no Deai ga Meiru Tarot) Moris Chacosy (artist), Kagakusho Kanoukai (publisher), 1998 The artwork for this seventy-eight-card deck is largely based on paintings, from Renaissance to modern. Several of the Major Arcana are renamed. The suits are wind (swords), fire (wands), aqua (cups), and earth (coins). The images of the Minor Arcana draw from the Rider-Waite deck, although the numbering may be different. For example, the Five of Wind resembles the Rider-Waite Three of Swords, showing a heart pierced with swords. The pips also draw from the Medieval Scapini deck. For example, the Seven of Earth shows coins whose images are found on the Medieval Scapini Four of Coins and Five of Coins. The background shows a cross within a Star of David with wings in two corners.

Joker 0

Magic I

Self II

Fight VII

Energy VIII

Dream XVII

Moon XVIII

Universe XXI

Five of Fire

King of Fire

THE FOOL | THE HIEROPHANT | THE LOVERS | WHEEL OF FORTUNE

TEMPERANCE | THE SUN | JUDGEMENT | THE WORLD

End Sector Tarot ASCII Corporation, 1998 This deck accompanied a video game.

Fairy Tarot Anonymous, circa 1995

Tarot Fairy Yo Su-Lan, 1990s Taiwanese shoujo artist Yo Su-Lan created the Major Arcana Tarot Fairy. The deck is accompanied by an instructional book written in the character of Fang Ya, a college witch, from the artist's humorous love story "Scorpion Magic."

La Fillette Revolutionaire Tarot (Shoujo Kakumei Utena)   1990s   This doujinshi deck is based on the anime TV show
Utena: La Fillette Revolutionaire, or *Revolutionary Girl Utena*.

Foreseeable Future Tarot   Anonymous, 1988   The style of the art strongly resembles that of the Moonprincess Tarot, by
Kiyoko Tsuchiya

F.O.X. Tarot   Jonseky (publisher), 2001

Galaxy Angel Tarot   2001   The manga series on which the deck is based was created by Brocolli studio, illustrated by Kanam, and published by Dragon Jr.

Gensomaden Saiyuki Tarot Minekura Kazuya (artist), Saiyuki Project, TV Tokyo (publisher), 2000 Based on a Japanese manga character, Saiyuki, by artist Minekura Kazuya. The Major Arcana deck includes a title card and booklet in Japanese. The back design is crosses in blue on blue.

Ghost Sweeper Tarot Reiko Mikami (artist), Movic (publisher), 1990s *Ghost Sweeper* is a supernatural comedy television show about a team that deals with getting ghosts out of places people want to be.

Good Luck Tarot (Omajinai Tarot) Anonymous, 1990s This deck may be related to Mio Odagi's manga, *Magical Mates,* published in English by Antarctic Press. The three characters of the series, schoolgirls, use the tarot to help solve problems.

Gundam Wing Tarot: Gundam on the After Colony UGEPPA studio (artists), Movic (publisher), 1990s Gundam Wing is an elite unit of warriors in a futuristic world. The teenaged warriors have robot mounts, called Gundams. The double-ended back design has the words "The Gundam on the After Colony / Gundam Wing Tarot" with a Star of David in the center, in gold on black. The anime series is produced by Sunrise Productions/Asahi TV.

Happiness Tarot   Anonymous, 1990s

Happiness Tarot (Shiawasewo no Mai Tarot)   Keiko Sugimoto (artist), Tsuchiya Books (publisher), 1989   Marina Oka wrote the accompanying book.

Happiness and Love Divination Tarot (Shiawasewo Yobu Ai no Tarot Uranai)   Beline (artist), Nittoshoin (publisher), 1990

Heterophony Tarot Dendan Hashimoto (artist), 1990s

Iris Lam Tarot Iris Lam, 2002 (published in China)

Iris Lam Tarot *(continued)*

Kabbalah: Tarot of Love　Miss Persephone and Noma Araki (artists), Teresis Network (publisher), 1996

Kabbalah Tarot   Kazumi Akutsu (artist), Gakushu Kenkyu-sha (publisher), 1992   The seventy-eight-card deck is accompanied by two books by Keiichi Saito. One book is about the cards themselves, and the other is about reading the cards. The numbering of the Arcana is not traditional. The images on the cards have an overall yellowish tint and are unified by a circular motif. The back design is pink with a geometrical design in black.

Keishobou Tarot   Gaichi Muramatsu (artist), Keishobou (publisher), 1973   The Keishobou Tarot is one of the earliest tarot decks published in Japan. The deck is based on the Tarot of Marseilles, with details from the Western esoteric tarot tradition. I The Magician departs completely from the imagery of the Tarot of Marseilles, though it retains the woodcut look. A copyright notice, "© 1973 GAICHI," is printed on each card.

Love Tarot   Anonymous, circa 1990

Love Tarot *(continued)*

Lucky Tarot　Mokuseio (artist), 1978　The Lucky Tarot, in reverse from most Japanese decks, is a Minor-Arcana-only tarot.

Luna Original Tarot　Aki Horiuchi and Ryuji Kagami (artists), Bun Ka-sha (publisher), 2002　The deck was issued as sheets with perforations between the cards.

Collection of Laurie Amato

Magic Story of Misa Tarot (Misa no Mahou Monogatari)   Takada Akemi (artist), Sammy, Inc. (publisher), 1998   This deck accompanied a video game, with characters drawn by Takada Akemi.

Talisman card from Meditation Tarot
Meditation Tarot   Mondo Oki and Mei Unasaka (artists), Jitsugyo-no Nihon-sha (publisher), 2000   The Meditation Tarot comprises Major Arcana and two talisman cards. The back design is double-ended of blue dragons on a gold background. The book accompanying the deck is by Mondo Oki and Mei Unasaka.

Meditation Tarot *(continued)*

Megu Manga Gundam Wing Tarot   Anonymous, 1990s   Deck based on the *Gundam Wing* series, included in a 1996 Japanese magazine.

0	I	IV	V	VI	IX
THE FOOL	THE MAGICIAN	THE EMPEROR	THE HIEROPHANT	THE LOVERS	THE HERMIT
X	XI	XII	XIII	XIV	XVI
WHEEL of FORTUNE	JUSTICE	THE HANGED MAN	DEATH	TEMPERANCE	THE TOWER
XIX	XXI	PAGE of SWORDS	KING of WANDS	KNIGHT of CUPS	QUEEN of PENTACLES
THE SUN	THE WORLD	PAGE of SWORDS	KING of WANDS	KNIGHT of CUPS	QUEEN of PENTACLES

Miracle Tarot Reiko Shimitsu (artist), Angel Playing Card of Higashi-Osaka, 1994 The backs of the Miracle Tarot show a Beaux Arts-style design in silver on black. The full deck includes six blank cards.

Fantasy Tarot Miracle Tarot was also published with Chinese and English titles, under the name Fantasy Tarot. The Fantasy Tarot edition includes fifteen additional Major Arcana, whose illustrations appear to be taken from the CLAMP X tarot.

VII戦車	VIII力量	X命運之輪
THE CHARIOT	STRENGTH	WHEEL of FORTUNE

Collection of Laurie Amato

Mirai O Hiraku Arcana Tarot   Artwork attributed to Le Pro or Freija, Gijyutsu Hyoron-sha (publisher), 1995

Collection of Laurie Amato

Mirai O Tsugeru Tarot (Gypsy Fortune-telling Tarot)   Takeshi Nanjo, 1989   This deck comprises Minor Arcana plus two extra cards showing a "gypsy witch"—no Major Arcana. It was first published in 1979 with less elaborate, black and white artwork, with the title Gypsy Witch Tarot.

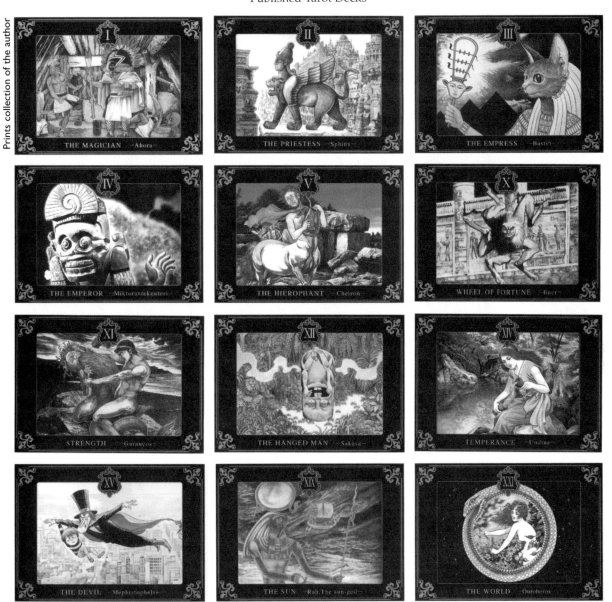

Shigeru Mizuki Tarot 2002 Shigeru Mizuki (born 1924) is an immensely popular manga artist. Before he broke through to success, however, many considered him eccentric due to his connection with the *yokai,* the spirits. He grew up with the tales of the local spirits of Japan, and he credits his success to their guidance. "The older I get, the more I feel like I'm becoming one of them," Mizuki told the audience at the sixth annual Sekai Yokai Kaigi (International Spirits Convention) in 2002. In turn, folklorists of Japan credit him with helping revive interest in the world of the *yokai.* The tarot designs he made are peopled with the beings of world religion, myth, and folklore.

Moon Dawn of Crystal Tarot Masanori Miyamoto (also called Myamo, artist), published by the artist, 1999 The deck draws some of its imagery and style from Etteilla decks as well as the Oswald Wirth and Rider-Waite tarots. It was rendered in pen and ink and colored pencil. The back design shows a mandala in blue on lavender.

Moonprincess Tarot Kiyoko Tsuchiya (artist), 1989 Moonprincess Himiko authored the book accompanying the Major Arcana deck.

Moonprincess Himiko Tarot (Ai to Shinpi no Tarot Uranai; Divinatory Tarot of Love and Mystery)   Ayumi Kasai (artist), Seibido Shuppan (publisher), 1993   Moonprincess Himiko is the author of the book accompanying the deck. The seventy-eight-card deck features intricate, illustrative designs. The double-ended back design shows a face and butterflies on black.

Morinaga Hi-Crown Tarot Riyoko Ikeda (artist), Morinaga (publisher), circa 1995 Riyoko Ikeda's manga novel, *The Rose of Versailles,* brought her renown in 1972. Most of her work revolves around romantic legends of Europe. Her tarot deck was created on commission; Morinaga is a Japanese food manufacturer, and Hi-Crown is one of their chocolate products. Morinaga also commissioned a tarot deck by Susumu Matsushita, six cards of which were featured in *The Encyclopedia of Tarot,* volume III.

Naruto Tarot Anonymous, 1990s The Naruto Tarot is *yaoi,* a subgenre of manga that features erotic romance between men. The deck is probably not related to the manga series of the same name. In style and mood it resembles the Angel Sanctuary deck.

Non No Tarot Anonymous, 1990s Based on the Rider-Waite Tarot.

Orizinaru Tarot Anonymous, 1990s Major Arcana deck featured as a supplement to a Japanese magazine.

Pandora's Tarot Chen Shu-Fen (artist), P&S Studio, China (publisher), 2002 Seventy-eight-card deck. Chen Shu Fen and her husband Ping-Fan are Taiwanese artists well-known for illustrations for the covers of romance novels. The book accompanying the deck is by Emile Scheherazade and Stella Bon Voyage.

Pandora's Tarot *(continued)*

Passion Tarot   Kao Yung (artist), published in China, 1997   The Passion Tarot comprises Major Arcana plus two blank cards. The back design is white lilies on a blue and green background.

Collection of the author

Pierre Tarot   Onon (publisher), 1997   The Pierre Tarot is a reprint of the Major Arcana of the Pierpont-Morgan Bergamo deck, published by U.S. Games Systems, adding gold borders, numbers, and Japanese titles. The back design is a red and gold lozenge pattern of flowers. Pierre is author of the book accompanying the deck.

Collection of Laurie Amato

Planet Girls of the Solar System Tarot   Anonymous, 1991   Planet Girls Tarot is probably a *doujinshi* product based on Sailor Moon, the magical girl whose group of Sailor Senshi (warriors) wield powers related to different planets. All of the characters in the deck are female.

Pocketable Tarot   SYU Creation, 1997   SYU Creation is a toy company. Many of the cards are clearly inspired by the Hanson-Roberts Tarot.

Renaissance-style Tarot   Anonymous, 1978

Collection of Laurie Amato

| 0 | 愚者 | II | 女祭司 | V | 祭司 | VII | 戰車 |

| VIII | 力量 | XI | 正義 | XII | 倒吊男 | XV | 惡魔 |

RG Veda Tarot CLAMP studio, circa 1995 RG Veda, which started as a manga series, was the first major product of CLAMP studio. The characters of the story were based on the gods of the Hindu sacred text *Rig Veda*, but the storylines are not connected with the original scripture.

Ribon Furoku Tarot   *Ribon* magazine, 2002   A *furoku* is a promotional item offered in conjunction with another product. The Ribon Furoku Tarot was a free Major Arcana deck offered in a 2002 issue of *Ribon* magazine. The deck includes a title card and an "Omamori" card, as well as a sheet with instructions for reading the cards. The cards measure only 2.5 by 1.75 inches. The back design is a pattern of stars and fleurettes in pink on white.

Rise no Miracle Tarot   Emiko Sugi (artist), Shojo Comic (publisher), 1999   Sugi is known as a *shoujo* artist; Shojo Comic is a manga house.

Collection of Laurie Amato

Romance Tarot Anonymous, 1990s

Collection of the author / © 1992, 1999 by Naoko Takeuchi, Kodansha Ltd., Toei Animation Co. Ltd.

Sailor Moon Tarot Kodansha Ltd. and Egmont Ehapa Verlag (publishers), 1999 The *Sailor Moon* anime series became internationally popular, with videos and books translated into many languages. The writer of the original *Sailor Moon* manga is Naoko Takeuchi. Sailor Moon Tarot, in German, was issued as a magazine with inserts of Major Arcana cards and a box printed on heavy stock to be punched out and assembled. The deck includes a title card and a card giving key words to each of the Major Arcana. The back design shows the heroine, a fourteen-year-old who was given superpowers by a magical black cat that she rescued.

Sentimental Journey Tarot   Kumi Horii (artist), 1999   Horii is known as an anime character designer.

Sho Comi Tarot   Chie Shinohara (artist), Sho Comi (publisher), 1997   *Sho Comi* (short for Shoujo Comic) is a magazine that runs manga stories. The tarot deck was offered as a *fukuri* (promotional offer) with the magazine in 1997. The artwork is childlike, although the magazine's audience is primarily adult women.

Sho Comi Tarot *(continued)*

Sol Bianca: The Legend Tarot Pioneer Entertainment (publisher), 1999 The *Sol Bianca* anime series is Japanese, but Sol Bianca: The Legend Tarot was published in the United States to promote the American release of the video. Sol Bianca is the name of a pirate spaceship. AIC studio created the series. The deck comprises Major Arcana plus two blank cards.

Starlot Tarot   Jun Kozima (artist), Natsume-sha (publisher), 1998   The deck was accompanied by a book by Enishi Gen.

Studio Takama/Nukadaya Kouriten Tarot   Haruka Ikusabe, 1998   Ikusabe is a well-known *doujinshi* artist.

Collection of Laurie Amato

Tarot World Tarot Toko Miyagi (artist), 2000 *Tarot World* was published as a comic book that includes an insert of cards on heavy paper intended to be cut apart and used as a Major Arcana deck, as well as full-page color illustrations of the cards.

Collection of the author / © 1997 Pai, © 1997 Falcon

Texthoth Ludo Tarot Pai (artist), Falcon (publisher), 1997 Texthoth Ludo is based on a Sega Saturn video game. Characters from the game illustrate the twenty-two cards. The deck, which was packaged with the game, is also known as the Arukana Wars Tarot.

Tokyo NOVA: The Revolution Tarot Anonymous, 1990s Tokyo NOVA: The Revolution is a video game from Japan. The Major Arcana deck includes two extra cards that read: 1 Safe / Alright / SURE OK / TRUST ME and 2 Chance (with writing also in Japanese).

Twelve Constellations Divinatory Tarot (Sensei Jyutsu Tarot) Keichii Konno (artist), Tsuchiya Books (publisher), 1990 The deck has seventy-eight cards plus two "dragon" cards. The book accompanying the deck is by Shurei Etoile and Etowauru. The set was first published in 1988 by Tsuchiya Books. A Major Arcana edition was published as Juni Seiza Tarot Uranai in 1990.

Twelve Constellations Divinatory Tarot (Sensei Jyutsu Tarot)   Will and Shigeyuki Ozawa (artists),
Ikeda-shoten (publisher)

Japanese tarot decks featured in volume III of
  The Encyclopedia of Tarot **are:**
Buddhistic Fantasy Tarot
Egyptian Japanese Tarot (Astrology Egyptian)
Entropy Tarot
Susumu Matsushita Tarot (Moringa Hi-Crown Tarot)
Mineo Maya Tarot
Medical Fantasy Tarot
Nature Tarot
Newwave Tarot
M. Oki and M. Unasaka Tarot (Derakkusu ban Hihou;
  Secret Methods; Gorgeous Secrets)
Sawaki's Tarot
Waite J.K. Tarot

Uru Q Tarot   Nami Akimoto (artist), *Nakayosi* monthly magazine (publisher), 2001   The Uru Q Major Arcana tarot has two extra cards showing girls holding cards. The *Uru Q* manga series, also known as *Cutie N,* is about girls who were fighting over boys but end up becoming friends.

Collection of Laurie Amato

Vision of Escaflowne Tarot (Tenkû no Escaflowne Tarot)
Kimitoshi Yamane (artist), Bandai (publisher)   The *Vision of Escaflowne* was a twenty-six-episode television anime series. Every episode started with a tarot card. The Vision of Escaflowne Tarot has twenty-two Major Arcana plus four Minor Arcana cards based on the Merlin Tarot. The titles on the cards are copied from Italian and often misspelled. The deck was issued with the video game based on *Vision of Escaflowne*.

Collection of Laurie Amato

Vision of Escaflowne   Yashiro Yuzuru (artist)   Yuzuru created this deck for a shoujo manga version of the story. The titles are in English.

Collection of Laurie Amato / © Project Weiß

Weiß Kreuz Tarot (White Cross Tarot)   Movic (publisher), 1990s   This manga/anime with a German title has countless spinoffs and products. The tarot deck was published by Movic. *Weiß Kreuz* is an ongoing story about four young men who are part of a group called "Weiss," after a Japanese pop group. The characters are florists by day and assassins by night.

Oswald Wirth Tarot U.S. Games Systems (publisher), 1997 The Major Arcana deck was accompanied by a book, *Tarot Card Fortune Telling,* by Chen.

Yu-Gi-Oh Tarot Anonymous, 2001 The children's anime series *Yu-Gi-Oh* features a boy named Yugi Moto as the main character.

Deep bows to collector and tarotist Laurie Amato, and to Jeanette Roth and Lorraine Sharkey-Dolan of Tarot Garden (tarotgarden.com) for identifying many of these decks. Extra thanks to Laurie Amato for sending photos of many of the decks featured here.

III

ANTIQUES AND ANCIENTS

This chapter highlights decks and facsimiles of tarot decks printed before the twentieth century, arranged in order of their first known printing. A special section is devoted to the Tarot of Marseilles. Another section, "The Ancient Egyptian Temple," comprises tarots inspired by ancient Egypt, from the late eighteenth century on.

Visconti-Sforza Tarot The cards of the Visconti-Sforza Tarot (also known as the Pierpont Morgan-Bergamo Tarot) are among the oldest extant tarot cards. They were created circa 1450. The artists to whom the deck has been attributed are Bonifacio Bembo, Michelino da Besozzo, Antonio Cicognara (cards XI, XIV, XVII, XVIII, XIX, XXI), Marziano da Tortona, and the Zavattari brothers.

The original cards from the deck are split among the collections of the Pierpont Morgan Library, New York; L'Accademia Carrara, Bergamo; and the Colleoni family. Two Major Arcana cards that are now considered an integral part of the tarot are missing from the original set: XV The Devil and XVI The Tower. Two cards from the Minor Arcana are also missing from the original.

U.S. Games Systems published in 1975 a facsimile edition of the deck, with the four missing cards recreated by Veronese artist Luigi Scapini (see *The Encyclopedia of Tarot*, volume I).

Edizioni Il Meneghello of Milan published an edition of the deck in 1996. Miniaturist Giovanni Scarsato of Milan recreated the four missing cards. The deck was published in a numbered edition of 1,000 decks. Andrea Vitali, of the Associazione Cultura "Le Tarot", wrote a booklet to accompany the deck. The backs of the cards are plain reddish brown.

Gertrude Moakley, who died in 1999, was one of the great scholars of the tarot. She researched tarot in the context of art history, authoring *The Tarot Cards Painted by Bonifacio Bembo for the Visconti-Sforza Family*, in 1966. She was also instrumental in inspiring a scholarly interest in the work of Pamela Colman Smith. Her article "The Waite-Smith Tarot," in 1954, traced references to the deck in T.S. Eliot's poem "The Waste Land."

An amusing sign (at right) was created when Gertrude Moakley gave a presentation on tarot cards, in 1987, at the retirement home where she lived. The tarot cards on the sign were hand-drawn by Charlie Hoddenott. About the sign, Moakley said, tongue-in-cheek, "Italy is nonfactual, but allowed to stand." The presentation was a great success. The organizer wrote in a note to Moakley, "Nobody wanted to go home! An hour later everyone in the lobby was still talking about it."

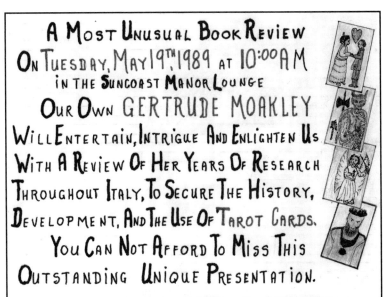

A Most Unusual Book Review On Tuesday, May 19th, 1989 at 10:00 AM in the Suncoast Manor Lounge Our Own GERTRUDE MOAKLEY Will Entertain, Intrigue And Enlighten Us With A Review Of Her Years Of Research Throughout Italy, To Secure The History, Development, And The Use Of Tarot Cards. You Can Not Afford To Miss This Outstanding Unique Presentation.

Lo Scarabeo published in 1997 a deck titled Tarocchi dei Visconti, with backgrounds in gold foil. The back design is double-ended, of architectural foliage motifs. Atanas Alexandrov Atanassov touched up the artwork and re-created the four missing cards. The edition adds a black border with numbers, and titles in Italian, English, German, French, and Spanish in the left margin. The original borders are cropped off. The deck includes a title card and nine cards with instructions for divination in four languages. A book by Giordano Berti and Tiberio Gonard was written to accompany the deck.

Visconti-Sforza Tarot The Devil, The Tower and the Page of Coins recreated by Luigi Scapini, for the deck published by U.S. Games Systems, 1975

Tarocchi Visconti-Sforza Cards recreated by Giovanni Scarsato, for the deck published by Edizioni Il Meneghello, 1996

Tarocchi dei Visconti Cards recreated by Atanas Alexandrov Atanassov for the deck published by Lo Scarabeo, 1997

Tarocchi dei Visconti With art touched up by Atanas Alexandrov Atanassov, Lo Scarabeo, 1997

Ferrara Chariot card

Anonymous, circa 1450; reproduction, Musée Français de la Carte à Jouer, 1995 (see also the color plates in this volume)

Ferrara Chariot card

The Musée Français de la Carte à Jouer (French Museum of Playing Cards) in Ville d'Issy-Les Moulineaux, France, presented a Renaissance Chariot card on the cover of invitations to a gala 1995 New Year's party. The card is of the Ferrara school, and dates from around 1450. The paper card was prepared with gesso, then stamped in gold, with the figures painted as the top layer. The artist is unknown.

Sola-Busca Tarot (Tarocchi Illuminati)   The Sola-Busca Tarot published by Lo Scarabeo of Turin as Tarocchi Illuminati reproduces a copy of the Sola-Busca Tarot that was made in the early twentieth century and is now in a private collection in Turin. The reproduction deck was also packaged as Illuminating Ancient Tarot and Enlightened Ancient Tarot.

The original artwork of the Sola-Busca Tarot was engraved on copper in the late fifteenth century, then hand-colored later. In 1934, A.M. Hind of the British Museum photographed a complete deck owned by the Sola-Busca family. Hind believed that the engraver was from Ferrara and the illuminator from the Veneto region. (See *The Encyclopedia of Tarot,* volume II, pages 297–302.) The originals that Hind photographed unfortunately are lost, although individual cards survive in several museum collections. The early twentieth-century copy appears to be not engravings, but ink renderings.

Lo Scarabeo's Sola-Busca Tarot was published in 1995, with card titles on the Minor Arcana in English, French, German, Spanish, and Italian. The double-ended back design shows in maroon the head of the warrior on the four of batons. The deck includes a title card and nine explanatory cards in five languages, including one side that gives credits for publication of the deck.

Sola-Busca Tarot   Anonymous, late fifteenth century; reproduced in black and white in the early twentieth century; color reproduction by Lo Scarabeo, 1995

Mantegna Tarot The Mantegna artwork does not actually make a traditional tarot deck. However, no lover of tarot would have the heart to exile the deck from the tarot world. Some of the images bear a striking resemblance to the images of the tarot, and it is not unreasonable to see a connection.

Despite its sobriquet, the deck's artwork is unlikely to be by the Paduan artist Andrea Mantegna (1431–1506), though it was issued circa 1470 in Northern Italy. They may have been intended as study tools for Renaissance boys and girls. They divide into five classes of ten figures each: class A: The Planets and Celestial Spheres; class B: Cosmic Principles and seven Virtues; class C: Liberal Arts; class D: Apollo and the Muses; class E: Conditions of Humanity. (For more information on the Tarot of Mantegna, see *The Encyclopedia of Tarot,* volume I, pages 35, 37–40.)

Bulgarian artist Atanas Atanassov reproduced Mantegna's designs in color. In 2000, Lo Scarabeo of Turin, Italy, printed the deck with metallic backgrounds, giving a very rich effect. Titles are in five languages, and the class of each card is in the bottom left corner. The fifty Mantegna designs are accompanied by twenty-five cards that give a thumbnail and brief description of each design in six languages, as well as three cards giving simple divination instructions in six languages, a title card, and an advertising card. The descriptive leaflet includes instructions for a game of divinatory solitaire, "The Chessboard Game," created by Giordano Berti of Lo Scarabeo.

Giacomo Zoni Tarot (Ancient Tarots of Bologna) The Ancient Tarots of Bologna deck is a facsimile of a deck made by Giacomo Zoni of Bologna, Italy, circa 1780. A few traits indicate that the deck was most likely intended for export: the French titles and the fact that trumps II through IV are traditional, as opposed to the "four Moors" favored by Bolognese cardmakers of the time. The deck has a naïve charm, in scenes showing frolicking dogs on XVIII and a pleasantly smiling devil on XV. An interesting vestige from an earlier time shows in the feather-cap, rather than coxcomb, of 0 Le Fol. The woodcuts are simple but elegant; however, the heavy-handed stenciled color obscures much of their detail and finesse. The facsimile includes a title card and nine instruction cards in four languages. The reproduction was published as Ancient Tarots of Bologna by Lo Scarabeo of Turin, Italy, in 1995.

Mantegna Tarots Anonymous, circa 1470; reproduction by Atanas Atanassov, Lo Scarabeo, 2000

Giacomo Zoni Tarot   Giacomo Zoni, circa 1780; reproduction: Ancient Tarots of Bologna, Lo Scarabeo, 1995

Etruria Minchiate (Ancient Minchiate Etruria) The Minchiate deck reproduced by Lo Scarabeo of Turin in 1995 is wonderfully illustrated with hand-painted engravings. The title card that comes with the reproduction gives the date of 1725, but that date may be early. The deck was made with the same engraving plates as an uncut sheet in the author's collection (see *The Encyclopedia of Tarot,* volume I, page 52), and a deck in the Cary-Yale collection, dated by William B. Keller circa 1790. The deck reproduced by Lo Scarabeo is probably later than the Cary-Yale deck and the uncut sheet, since numerals in scrolls were added so that all the non-suit cards are numbered, except the Fool. The painter of the deck also thought to add a modest touch to card XXXV (Gemini) by painting hair (beyond the engraving) over one of the women. The original of the Lo Scarabeo deck, in a private collection in Turin, has on card XXIIII (Libra) a tax stamp that was in use circa 1800.

Its back design is a woodcut of a standing woman. The inscription ETRURIA, at the bottom, refers to the region of Italy just north of Rome, famous for the ancient ruins left by the Etruscan civilization. It was printed on a separate sheet of thin paper, with the border folded over the edge of the card and glued to the face of the card.

The reproduction is titled Ancient Minchiate Etruria, and it includes a title card, a card giving publication credits and a leaflet, "Fortune Telling with the Florentine Minchiate."

Tax stamp, Florence, circa 1800
From Etruria Minchiate deck, reproduced by Lo Scarabeo of Turin

Ferdinand Gumppenberg circa 1810 Tarot (Tarocchi Lombardi) Lo Scarabeo of Turin, Italy, issued a facsimile of a Gumppenberg deck from circa 1810. The deck is from the same plates as the deck from which Edizione del Solleone made a full facsimile, Tarocco Neoclassico Italiano, in 1980 (see *The Encyclopedia of Tarot,* volume II, page 347). The original Gumppenberg deck is hand-colored engravings.

Lo Scarabeo issued the facsimile, titled Tarocchi Lombardi, circa 1995. The deck was published as a twenty-two card miniature deck and as a full seventy-eight-card deck. The miniature has square corners and includes a title card. The back design is green with a gold pattern of sunbursts and dots. The full deck has rounded corners and includes a title card and nine cards with instructions for divination, with a presentation on a side of one of the cards. The back design is white with a red pattern of sunbursts and dots.

Two different tax stamps are on the Ace of Swords; they date from the Austrian restoration of Lombardy and span the years 1816 to 1823.

Gumppenberg Aces of Swords and Cups Circa 1810
Two very distinct tax stamps are on the Ace of Swords (LEFT); they date from the Austrian restoration of Lombardy. The top one is for 25 centesimi and was in use from 1816 to 1818. The other is for 60 centesimi and was in use from 1818 to 1823.

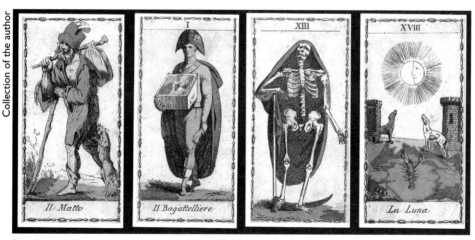

Collection of the author

Ferdinand Gumppenberg Tarot Circa 1810; reproduction: Tarocchi Lombardi, by Lo Scarabeo, circa 1995

Etruria Minchiate deck   Anonymous maker, circa 1800; reproduction: Ancient Minchiate Etruria, Lo Scarabeo, 1995   The back design is shown at bottom right.

Teodoro Dotti Tarot Editions de Vecchi of Paris published in 1994 a large facsimile of a tarot deck made by Teodoro Dotti, a cardmaker of Milan who lived from 1805 to 1855. The faces of the deck seem to have been made from the same plates as the faces of the deck by Edoardo Dotti (see *The Encyclopedia of Tarot*, volume II, page 374), who lived from 1836 to circa 1865. The decks differ in the following details: Edoardo's deck has a pictorial back design, and its edges wrapped around to the front of the card, while Teodoro's has a simple dot pattern and is printed on the card itself (not printed separately and wrapped around); Edoardo's deck has the medallion for the tax stamp on the Ace of Coins, and Teodoro's deck has the medallion on the King of Batons; the shield on the Empress is blank on Edoardo's deck, whereas on Teodoro's deck an imperial eagle shows. Teodoro's deck is also more finely colored. Edoardo's deck has Italian titles, while the reproduction of Teodoro's has added French titles and changed the title

of Edoardo's trump XIV, which was called "L'Intemperanza" (Intemperance), to La Temperance. The corners of the reproduction are square in order to accommodate the irregular shape of the original cards; the originals had rounded corners.

Ferdinand Gumppenberg circa 1835 Tarot (Tarocchi Classici) The Classical Tarot is a 1999 facsimile of a deck published by the famous early nineteenth-century cardmaker Ferdinand Gumppenberg of Milan. The deck was printed with steel engravings by Carlo Dellarocca, then hand-colored. The elegant, flowing lines of the art are in contrast with the rough woodcuts of the French Tarot of Marseilles decks of the time. Card XIII is untitled, perhaps in superstition.

In accordance with the tax laws of the time, the King of Batons (Re di Bastoni) bears the name of the maker and the tax stamp of Lombardy. The tax stamp shows the steel crown of Lombardy and the crown of Holy Roman Emperor Rudolf I, symbols of the Austrian Empire, which ruled Lombardy at the time. The initials "F.I." stand for Franz I, Austrian ruler. "C. 70," is 70 centesimi, the rate at which the deck was taxed. The tax stamp was valid from November 1, 1823, to January 26, 1840. The engraver's name, "C. Dellarocca inc." is beneath the tax stamp. Under the picture is "Faba. di Gumppenberg, Milano," Made by Gumppenberg, Milan.

The back design of the reproduction features a doubled ended design of the figure of XVII The Star in sepia monochrome (probably, the original back design featured an advertisement of the maker). The publishers of the reproduction, Lo Scarabeo, date the original deck to 1835. The reproduction adds Italian, French, English, and German one-word interpretations, along the left edge, to the original Italian titles. The deck includes a title card and an advertising card.

Teodoro Dotti Tarot
Circa 1830 to 1855;
reproduction: Editions de Vecchi, 1994

Ferdinand Gumppenberg Tarot Circa 1835; reproduction: Tarocchi Classici (Classic Tarot), Lo Scarabeo, 1999

Lattanzio Lamperti Tarot (Tarocchi Lombardi) The circa 1995 Lo Scarabeo facsimile of a Lattanzio Lamperti deck is a miniature edition of the Major Arcana only. The deck was issued as Tarocchi Lombardi. With the King of Batons absent, no tax stamp shows to help date the deck. However, the coat of arms on the Empress and the Emperor cards indicates that the deck dates from the mid-nineteenth century when the Austrian eagle ruled Lombardy. The same woodcuts were used after 1859 by Lamperti (see *The Encyclopedia of Tarot*, volume 2, page 370) when Lombardy became part of the Kingdom of Sardinia, but with the Austrian arms replaced by the white cross of Savoy, which ruled Sardinia. The back design is of a lyre with a glowing head over it.

Giovanbattista Guala Tarot (Tarocchi Piemontesi; Ancient Tarot of Liguria-Piedmont; Antichi Tarocchi Divinatori) Giovanbattista Guala worked in Ghemme, a Piedmont town. A deck was made circa 1860 by Guala from woodblocks and colored using stencils. The face of each card was stamped with a round stamp of a four-part coat of arms, topped by a crown. The stamp does not indicate value (as in a tax stamp) or date. It is possibly a mark of the printer, who seemed anxious to be credited with the deck; his name appears on all the court cards, on the Two of Cups, Il Pazzo, I Il Bagatto, and XXI Il Mondo. The deck shows a regional flavor in details such as the double-ended numbers, the double line borders, the apron worn by Il Bagatto, and the style of the maker's imprint on the Two of Cups. (See *The Encyclopedia of Tarot*, volume II, to compare with Piedmontese contemporaries of Guala: Giro. Montalenti, page 368, Fantini, page 379, Antonio Rossi, page 380.)

Lo Scarabeo published reproductions of the deck, as a full deck and as Major Arcana only. The Major Arcana deck, issued circa 1995, is a miniature facsimile of the original and was published as Tarocchi Piemontesi (Piedmontese Tarot) and later as Tarocchi Piemontesi Mignon (Miniature Piedmontese Tarot). The full deck was published as Antichi Tarocchi Divinatori (Antique Divinatory Tarot), with divinatory meanings in Italian added at the bottom of each card. It includes a title card and nine instruction cards in four languages (with a presentation on one side of a card). Another edition of the seventy-eight-card deck was published in 2000 with the title Ancient Tarot of Liguria-Piedmont and titles in English, French, German, and Italian instead of divinatory meanings. The original deck belongs to a private collection in Turin.

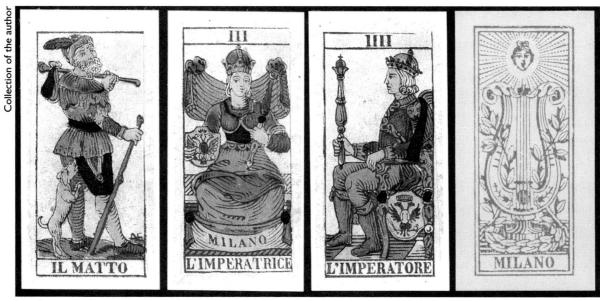

Collection of the author

Lattanzio Lamperti Tarot Circa 1850; reproduction: Tarocchi Lombardi, Lo Scarabeo, circa 1995 The back design is on the right.

Collection of the author

Giovanbattista Guala Tarot Circa 1860; reproduction: Tarocchi Piemontesi (Piedmontese Tarot) of Major Arcana in miniature, Lo Scarabeo, circa 1995

Giovanbattista Guala Tarot Circa 1860; reproduction of full deck: Antichi Tarocchi Divinatori
(Antique Divinatory Tarot), Lo Scarabeo, 1995

Avondo Brothers–Cartiera Italiana Tarot (Ancient Italian Tarot; Tarocchi Serravalle Avondo) The original of the tarot deck reproduced by Lo Scarabeo dates from circa 1880, as indicated by the tax stamp on the Ace of Coins, and the extra tax stamp, dated 1880, toward the top of the card. The extra stamp is in black, indicating that the deck was for domestic markets (as opposed to export). Contrary to custom on other Piedmontese decks, the maker's name is not to be found on the Two of Cups. Rather, the Ace of Coins reveals the maker as Cartiera Italiana, owned by brothers named Avondo, in the town of Serravalle-Sesia.

A facsimile of the full deck was published by Lo Scarabeo, Turin, Italy, in 2001, under the title Ancient Italian Tarot. Lo Scarabeo also issued in 2001 a facsimile

of the Major Arcana only, with the title Tarocchi Serravalle Avondo. The Major Arcana deck includes a card that reads (in Italian) "Faithful reproduction in reduced form of the 22 Major Arcana of the Tarocchi Avondo stamped Serravalle Sesia circa 1880."

Avondo Brothers Tarot
Two tax stamps are on the Ace of Coins. The central stamp dates from the late 1870s. The stamp above is dated 1880.

Bordoni Tarot (Tarocchino Milanese) Edizione Il Meneghello of Milan published a reproduction of a deck made by the Milanese cardmaker Bordoni. The Major Arcana and courts are double-ended. The back design shows a lancer on horseback; on the original deck, the back was printed on a separate sheet and glued to the card, with the edges wrapped around to the front. The engravings for the cards are fairly refined, but the coloring is roughly stenciled.

One interesting and unusual detail is the windows in the background of the Queen of Cups. The courts almost always show only the figure, the suit sign, and the ground and throne.

Osvaldo Menegazzi dates the deck circa 1880; however, the date stamp on the Ace of Coins seems to read [18]90, and Bordoni is known to have worked from 1887 to 1900. The tax stamp on the Ace of Coins came into use in the mid-1880s. Tax stamps don't give a completely reliable way of dating decks, as they may be applied years after the deck was first published. The designs are similar to but not the same as those of the Bordoni deck dated circa 1891 (see *The Encyclopedia of Tarot,* volume II, page 388).

The reproduction was published as a numbered edition of 2,000 decks, in the year 2000. The box for the reproduction has the seal of Il Meneghello and an Italian postage stamp "postmarked" by Il Meneghello.

Osvaldo Menegazzi Tarot decks The publisher of Edizioni Il Meneghello, Osvaldo Menegazzi, created a set of miniature tarot decks, some historical and some previously published separately by his company. The six decks, contained in a sleeve papered with tarot designs, were issued circa 1999. The titles of the decks, as written on the spines of their individual sleeves, are: Il Tarocco di Besançon, Classico Tarocco di Marsiglia, Minchiate Florentine Gioco di Tarocchi di 97 carte - Sec XIX, Tarocco Popolare Ligure Piemontese, Tarocco con Personaggi Napoleonici, Tarocco della Musica. The latter two decks were originally published by Il Meneghello; the rest are reproductions of historical decks. The cards in all of the decks except Tarocco Popolare have black edges. The backs are blank. (Tarocco con Personaggi Napoleonici and Tarocco della Musica are featured in *The Encyclopedia of Tarot,* volume III. The Tarocco di Besançon and Classico Tarocco di Marsiglia are illustrated in the section in this chapter, "The Tarot of Marseilles.")

Giovanni Vacchetta Tarot Giovanni Vacchetta lived from 1863 to 1940. A facsimile of his tarot deck, originally published in 1893, was first produced in black and white by Edizioni del Solleone in 1976 (see *The Encyclopedia of Tarot,* volume I, page 166).

In 2001 Il Meneghello of Milan produced a facsimile in color. This edition makes it tempting to see in Vacchetta's artwork the roots of comic book design. For example, XV Il Diavolo is like a carnival ride with a devil frightened by his own fanged tail, and the suit of cups is ruled by a tipsy king. The deck was published as a numbered edition of 1,500. The back design reproduces the original dot pattern.

In 2002 Lo Scarabeo of Turin reprinted the deck as the Tarot of the Master, colored by Michela Gaudenzi. The back design of the Lo Scarabeo edition shows I Bagat printed in green. The cards have borders giving meanings of the cards in five languages. The deck includes an advertising card. The Two of Swords, Two of Batons, Two of Cups, and Ace of Coins bear the maker's name and city, and the date of publication.

Bordoni Tarot Circa 1890; reproduction: Tarocchino Milanese, 2000 Back design. Ace of Coins with tax stamp.

Avondo Brothers–Cartiera Italiana Tarot   Avondo brothers, circa 1880; reproduction: Ancient Italian Tarot, Lo Scarabeo, 2001

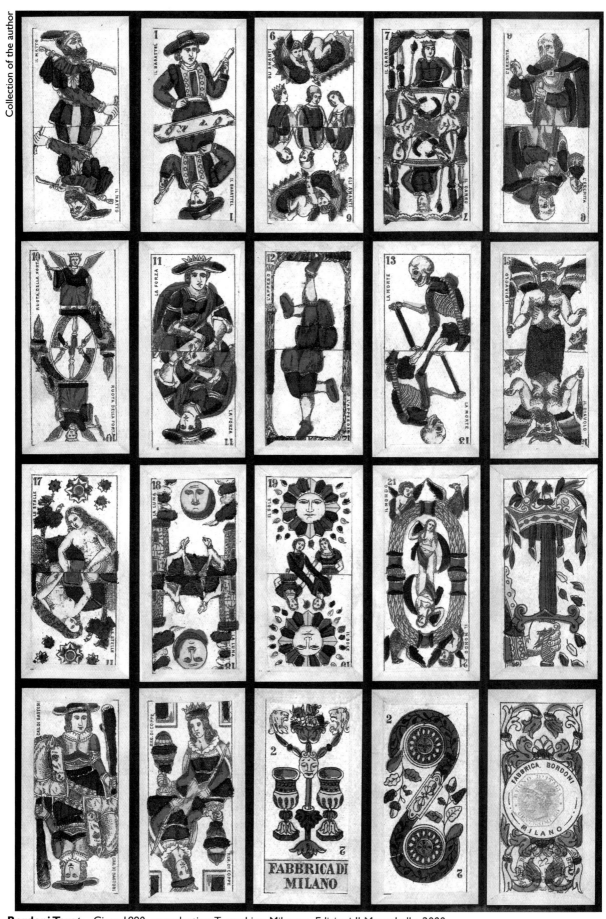

Bordoni Tarot   Circa 1890; reproduction: Tarocchino Milanese, Edizioni Il Meneghello, 2000

Osvaldo Menegazzi Tarot decks   Osvaldo Menegazzi, Edizioni Il Meneghello, circa 1999   Cards are shown at actual size.

(TOP & SECOND ROWS) **Minchiate Florentine Gioco di Tarocchi di 97 carte - Sec XIX** (Florentine Minchiate, nineteenth century). The tax stamp on the Ace of Coins is dated 1852.

(BOTTOM) **Tarocco Popolare Ligure Piemontese** (Popular Ligurian Piedmontese Tarot) Circa nineteenth-century deck. Unfortunately, the medallion on the Ace of Coins, which usually identifies the maker, is blank.

Giovanni Vacchetta Tarot Original published in 1893 TOP AND SECOND ROW: Reproduction: Tarot of the Master, colored by Michela Gaudenzi, Lo Scarabeo, 2001. THIRD AND BOTTOM ROW: Reproduction: Il Meneghello, 2000.

THE TAROT OF MARSEILLES

The type of tarot deck that came to be called the Tarot of Marseilles, or Tarot de Marseille, was not always made in Marseilles, but the name stuck because of Marseilles' prominence as a cardmaking center during the seventeenth and eighteenth centuries.

The patterns of the Tarot of Marseilles likely migrated from Italy, through trade or through traffic from royal inter-marriages and conquest. The patterns "returned" to Italy in the nineteenth century, as can be seen in decks by cardmakers such as Guala and Zoni, which have characteristics of the Tarot of Marseilles.

This section includes reproductions of Tarot of Marseilles decks as well as decks redrawn and recolored.

Jean Noblet Tarot Jean Noblet was a cartier working in the mid-seventeenth century. Though he worked in Paris, his decks conform to the Tarot of Marseilles style. A few interesting distinctions of the Noblet Tarot housed in the Bibliothèque Nationale are the man and woman (instead of two children) on XIX The Sun, and a woman wearing a cape and wreath (instead of wearing a banner) on XXI The World. A deck with similar details was made in the early eighteenth-century by Swiss cartier François Heri (collection of the Schweizerisches Landesmuseum). Noblet's original deck is pictured in *The Encyclopedia of Tarot,* volume II, page 309; Heri's deck is illustrated in volume I, page 318.

Jean-Claude Flornoy, tarot historian and cartier of Sainte-Suzanne, France, recreated the Noblet Major Arcana to "conform to the originals as they probably were when young." The deck was published in 2002 in a numbered, limited edition of 650. Flornoy redrew the Noblet deck that is housed in the Bibliothèque Nationale, Paris.

Flornoy hand-stenciled the cards, creating a depth and richness to the colors that machine-printed decks cannot rival. In choosing the colors for the Noblet and other Tarot of Marseilles reproductions, Flornoy referred to the magnificent stained-glass windows of Chartres Cathedral, in order to see the primary colors "favored by Europeans centuries ago" unfaded by the process of aging paper and inks.

The deck was packaged with a paper band around the cards, printed with cards I and 0 and Flornoy's name and location. A booklet by Flornoy that accompanied the deck relates the "legend of the tarot," connecting the Tarot of Marseilles to the Templars. The box of the deck shows the number of issue. The back design is a pattern of crosses within hexagons, in black and white.

Jean Dodal Tarot (Carta Mundi) Carta Mundi of Belgium issued a Tarot of Marseilles "based on the deck published by Jean Dodal (also known as Dodali) in Lyon around 1700." An interesting aspect of the deck is the male Christ-like figure on XXI The World. The figure resembles that of the Jean Payen deck of 1713, with its dancing pose. (See *The Encyclopedia of Tarot,* volume 2, pages 178–181 for more on the iconography of The World card, and pages 314 and 316 for the Payen deck.)

Carta Mundi recolored the deck to reflect the original, which has faded with time, and added English titles. The back design is a starburst pattern in red on white. The deck was published in 1996. It includes a title card, a card explaining the provenance of the deck, and an instructional booklet. The same deck, including the instructional booklet and extra cards, was sold packaged by U.S. Games Systems, of Stamford, Connecticut.

Jean Dodal Tarot (Flornoy) Jean-Claude Flornoy (see Noblet Tarot) recreated a Dodal Major Arcana deck, issued in 2002 in a limited edition of 650. Flornoy dates Dodal's work between 1701 and 1715, in keeping with other tarot historians. As with the Noblet Tarot, Flornoy's Dodal deck is not a facsimile, but rather a redrawing, and it shows some idiosyncrasies, such as the bare breasts of the figure on XIV Temperance.

The deck, colored by hand using stencils, was packaged with a paper band around the cards, printed with cards I and 0 and Flornoy's name and location. A booklet by Flornoy that accompanies the deck has essays on the game of tarot, the Tarot of Marseilles, and the color symbolism of the cards. The box of the deck shows the number of issue. The back design is a pattern of black sprigs on white.

Collection of the author

Jean Noblet Tarot Circa 1650; re-drawing by Jean-Claude Flornoy, 2002

Jean Dodal Tarot of Marseilles Original 1701 to 1715; reproduction Carta Mundi, 1996

Jean Dodal Tarot   Original 1701 to 1715; recreated by Jean-Claude Flornoy, 2002

Claude Burdel Tarot of Marseilles   1751; reproduction, Lo Scarabeo, 1987

Claude Burdel Tarot   Lo Scarabeo of Turin published a Tarot of Marseilles based on the woodcut deck made by Claude Burdel in 1751 (see *The Encyclopedia of Tarot,* volume II, page 328). Lo Scarabeo describes Burdel as working in Schaffhausen, German Switzerland; other authorities locate him in Fribourg, French Switzerland. In place of the original numbering, Lo Scarabeo placed an Italian title, and the original French titles are replaced by the number and titles in English, French, German, and Spanish. The double-ended back design shows mytho-logical motifs in red on pink. Burdel's initials remain on the Two of Cups and on the shield of VII The Chariot, but the Two of Coins shows "EDIZIONI D'ARTE LO SCARABEO TORINO 1987." The deck includes a title card and nine extra instructional cards in five languages.

Nicolas Conver Tarot   Several reproductions of tarot decks by Nicolas Conver have been made. Conver worked in Marseilles from 1760 to 1803.

Boechat Heron of France issued a facsimile of a Conver deck around 1980 (see *The Encyclopedia of Tarot,* volume III, page 594). The Boechat Heron edition was a facsimile of a deck in the collection of the Bibliothèque Nationale, Paris.

Around 1965, **Camoin** of Marseilles issued a facsimile of a Conver deck (see *The Encyclopedia of Tarot,* volume I, page 149).

In 1995 **Lo Scarabeo** of Turin issued a facsimile of a Tarot of Marseilles originally made by Nicolas Conver. The original cards of the Lo Scarabeo edition were heavily inked and stenciled. The Lo Scarabeo edition includes a title card and nine cards with instructions for divination, with a presentation on a side of

Life-sized Conver Tarot cards, by Jean-Claude Flornoy

Nicolas Conver Tarot of Marseilles   1760; reproduction, Lo Scarabeo, 1995

Collection of the author

one of the cards. The back design is an olive green checkerboard on white.

The originals of these three decks seem to have been printed from the same woodblocks over a number of years. As the woodblocks were used, they deteriorated, and gaps in the line art show up. Judging from the deterioration of lines in the three facsimiles, the original decks are, from oldest to youngest, Camoin, Lo Scarabeo, and Boechat Heron.

Nicolas Conver Tarot paintings (Flornoy)   Artist and cartier Jean-Claude Flornoy created an exhibition of Conver's Tarot, "life-sized." "The scale chosen corresponds to an average man's height, and so Le Bateleur measures nearly six feet." The exhibit was mounted in Andouillé, France, in 1998.

Anonymous 1797 Tarot of Marseilles (Divination Tarot)   The Divination Tarot is a reproduction of a deck from 1797, republished by Naipes Comas of Barcelona, Spain, in 1988. The Major and Minor Arcana are traditional Tarot of Marseilles designs. The Major Arcana are titled in English and Spanish; the court cards in Spanish only; and the pips are untitled. The deck includes a presentation card and a card referring to the instructions that are included with the deck. The back design is a mottled brown and yellow. The Two of Coins includes the original year of the deck's publication and the name of the present-day publisher.

Tarocco di Besançon   In 1999, Oswaldo Menegazzi published a set of five miniature decks. One is a facsimile of a deck by J.B. Benois of Strasbourg, circa 1818. (For more examples of work by Benois, see volume II of *The Encyclopedia of Tarot*.) Besançon tarots are a subcategory of Marseilles tarots. Their main distinction is in the substitution of Junon and Jupiter for Popess and Pope.

Anonymous 1830 Italian Tarot of Marseilles (Tarocchi Marsigliesi)   The twenty-two Major Arcana of an antique Tarot of Marseilles were produced as a miniature facsimile by Lo Scarabeo, Turin, Italy, circa 1995. The deck is dated circa 1830 by Lo Scarabeo. However, it closely resembles a deck that Giuseppe Lando of Turin made circa 1760. Some points in common are: on card I, the arrangement of objects on the table and the spelling of the title as Le Batelleur; the coats of arms on III and IV; on card VII, the angle at which the Charioteer holds his wand, and the spelling of the title as Le Cariot; on card X, the title spelled La Rou de Fortune; the title L'Ange for card XX. The anonymous deck is crudely cut and colored, and was most likely made by a cardmaker of the Turin area. The back design of the facsimile is a gold-on-green checkered pattern.

Anonymous 1797 Tarot of Marseilles Reproduction: Divination Tarot, Naipes Comas, 1988

Tarocco di Besançon (Besançon Tarot). Facsimile of a deck by J.B. Benois of Strasbourg, circa 1818. Edizioni Il Meneghello, circa 1999

Anonymous 1830 Italian Tarot of Marseilles   Original circa 1830;
reproduction: Tarocchi Marsigliesi, Lo Scarabeo, circa 1995

Fournier Tarot of Marseilles   Naipes Heraclio Fournier, miniature edition circa 1995

Fournier Tarot of Marseilles   A recolored copy of the traditional Tarot of Marseilles was commissioned by Naipes Heraclio Fournier circa 1980, and published again, in miniature, circa 1995. The illustrations of the miniature deck are slightly stretched horizontally, presumably to fit the format. The Two of Cups credits Maritxu de Guler as "specialist in tarot" and A. Aymerich for "artistic creation." "Heraclio Fournier / Vitoria / Made in Spain" is typeset on the Five of Swords. Each pip card except the aces is numbered on left and right and at the bottom. The back design is a pattern of flowers and trapezoids in olive green.

Tarot de Marseilles (anonymous)   Two editions of a facsimile or redrawing of a deck resemble a deck made by Gassman of Geneva, Switzerland, around 1873 (see *The Encyclopedia of Tarot,* volume I, page 163). The striped, man-made gibbet and the profile rendering of the victim on XII The Hanged Man are most distinctive.

Le Véritable Tarot de Marseille was accompanied by the book, *Votre Destinée par les Tarot,* written by Louise Beni. The set was published by Editions de Vecchi, Paris, in 1987. The seventy-eight-card deck was printed on textured paper and has a gray pebbled back design. It includes a title card.

In 1999, Oswaldo Menegazzi published **Classico Tarocco di Marsiglia** as part of a set of five miniature decks.

The main differences between the two decks are size, and the black borders and slightly heavier printing of Menegazzi's deck. Neither edition gives information as to the artist, or whether the decks are new artwork modeled on old decks or are actual facsimiles.

Classico Tarocco di Marsiglia (Classic Tarot of Marseilles) Edizioni Il Meneghello, circa 1999   Cards are shown at their actual size.

Le Véritable Tarot of Marseilles (True Tarot of Marseilles)   Editions de Vecchi, 1987

Marseilles Astrological Tarots   J.A. Portela, unpublished, circa 1995

Marseilles Astrological Tarots   J.A. Portela designed tarot cards using the Tarot of Marseilles as an inset with astrological and Kabbalistic symbolism. The designs were made circa 1995. Another deck designed by J.A. Portela around the same time is round, and each card features the wheel of the zodiac, along with interpretive words, with a Tarot of Marseilles figure in the center.

Tarot Marsylski (Tarot of Marseilles) Heleny Starowieyskiej redrew and added Polish titles to the Tarot of Marseilles, most likely modeling the deck on the Conver version. Three of the cards have Hebrew lettering added: the shield on VII Chariot, the base of the throne on the King of Swords, and the lower left corner on the Page of Cups. The back design is a pattern of interlocking stars. The deck was published in 1996 by Wydawnictwo HSJ, Warsaw.

Tarot Marsylski (Tarot of Marseilles)   Heleny Starowieyskiej, Wydawnictwo HSJ, 1996

Véritable Tarot de Marseille (True Tarot of Marseilles) Kris Hadar, Les Editions de Mortagne, 1996 "In V The Pope, the two acolytes are not standing. The one on the left is in prayer, and the one on the right is seated on a bench; this expresses that knowledge is received inwardly by communion (the one on the left) or by words (the one on the right).…The King of Swords is not seated on a throne, but rather on a tombstone. His companion, the Queen of Swords, pregnant, hides under her robe [at the hem] a spiral staircase, symbolizing the descent to the depths of oneself (= infancy + stairs) to die and be reborn (= the tomb of the king)." (From the booklet, by Kris Hadar, that accompanies the deck.)

Véritable Tarot de Marseille (True Tarot of Marseilles) Kris Hadar, in a letter to Stuart Kaplan, explains how his project came into being. "Two years ago [in 1995], my publisher, Les Editions de Mortagne, asked me to research the Tarot of Marseilles, in order to restore it to its original form. The task was almost impossible, since no one knows who invented the tarot, but through existing tarots, such as the Conver, the Païen [Payen], the Dodal, the Italian tarots, and with the study of history, and of the habits and customs of the Middle Ages, the Tarot of Marseilles is restored.… One of the reasons…is that I was able to trace back its era, its date of birth, and the circumstances surrounding its development. It does not originate from Italy, nor is it inspired by the game of Naïb, but would be a creation from Occitanie [Occitane, south of France], in the twelfth century." The deck was published by Les Editions de Mortagne of Quebec, Canada, in 1996. The back design is a carpet-like pattern, mostly in blue.

Astrologie Tarot In 1998, the German astrology magazine *Die Geheimnisvolle Welt der Astrologie* included tarot cards with the magazine, offering several cards per issue. The deck featured is based on the Tarot of Marseilles. The magazine is published by Astrologie Bestell-Service.

Camoin and Jodorowsky Tarot of Marseilles In 1993, Alexandre Jodorowsky and Philippe Camoin met in Paris and decided to work together to restore the Tarot of Marseilles to its original form. Both had studied tarot extensively. Philippe Camoin is the direct heir of the Camoin family, whose cardmaking factory was founded by Nicolas Conver. Jodorowsky is a writer of *bandes dessinées,* published as Alexandro or Alejandro Jodorowsky.

Jodorowsky and Camoin created a "restored" Tarot of Marseilles by analyzing and synthesizing the imagery of many different Tarot of Marseilles decks, using computer enlargements and overlays. The deck was issued in 1997 by Camoin of Marseilles, France, and includes an introductory card by Philippe Camoin and a booklet in French. The deck was reissued in 1999 with some alterations in the symbolism and a booklet in six languages.

Nouveau Tarot de Marseille FJP France Jeux Production published a tarot deck based on the Tarot of Marseilles, with modern drawings that recall the tarot designs of Oswald Wirth. The maker's name and city "FJP Paris" appear on the left edge of every card. The deck was published circa 2000. A booklet by Colette Silvestre-Haeberle accompanies the deck, but the artist is unidentified. The double-ended back design is architectural motifs in blue on blue.

Collection of the author

Astrologie Tarot
From *Die Geheimnisvolle Welt der Astrologie,* 1998

Véritable Tarot de Marseille (True Tarot of Marseilles)   Kris Hadar, Les Editions de Mortagne, 1996

Tarot of Marseilles   Alexandre Jodorowsky and Philippe Camoin, Camoin, 1997

Le Mat

Le Bateleur

La Papesse

L'Impératrice

L'Empereur

Le Pape

L'Amoureux

L'Hermite

La Roue de Fortune

La Force

Le Pendu

Tempérance

Le Diable

L'Etoile

La Lune

Le Soleil

Le Monde

Roi de Deniers

Nouveau Tarot de Marseille   FJP France Jeux Production, 2000

THE ANCIENT EGYPTIAN TEMPLE

Collection of Laurie Amato

 Laurie Amato writes of her Ancient Egyptian Tarot Temple, "The model…is a faithful replica of an edifice described by French occultist Paul Christian in his book *Histoire de la Magie* in 1870. Christian recounted a secret initiation ceremony of the ancient Egyptians in which an initiate was led through a hidden entranceway between the paws of the giant sphinx. After many gruelling tests of courage, the initiate was finally led into a chamber lined with twenty-two sacred images, which are known today as tarot cards."

The claim that the tarot was the work of ancient Egyptians was initiated by French occultist Antoine Court de Gebelin in his 1781 book *Le Monde Primitif*. The keen interest that the French took in things Egyptian was no doubt fueled by exploration and colonization of the Middle East by European powers. During that time, many Egyptian antiquities found their way back to Europe—though none was known to be a tarot deck.

The concept of ancient Egyptian roots for the tarot is intriguing, but as Amato affirms, no tarot temple has ever been unearthed and, in fact, ancient Egypt has never yielded tarot images.

The Egyptian theory may not stand up to scholarship, but it has stood the test of time. Famous occultists Eliphas Levi (Alphonse Louis Constant), Falconnier, Etteille (Alliette), Papus (Gerard Encausse), and Aleister Crowley all adapted Egyptian symbolism, or at least their interpretation of it, to the tarot.

Decks with ancient Egyptian themes continue to proliferate today. Thanks to them, the entry to the tarot temple is no longer hidden, and even the most timid

Egyptian Tarot Temple   Laurie Amato and Josef Machynka   Amato created her temple in 1997, and it was displayed at the 1997 World Tarot Congress in Chicago. The initiate enters the temple by going up the stairs between the huge sphinxes. The images inside are from the Ibis Tarot, by Josef Machynka.

"armchair initiate" need not tremble on entering "The Ancient Egyptian Temple."

Ibis Tarot   The Ibis Tarot was modeled on the deck illustrated in *Practical Astrology*, by Comte de Saint-Germain, published in 1901. Machynka began work on his deck in conjunction with New Akropolis, an organization dedicated to philosophy, symbology, anthropology, and so on. According to the booklet accompanying the deck, the figures are based on measurements of ancient Egyptian paintings. The deck is named after the bird that accompanies the god Thoth, who is shown with Ibis head on the backs of the cards. The cards are numbered I through LXXVIII, with suits of swords, sceptres, cups, and pentacles, and courts of master, mistress, warrior, and slave. The deck was published by AGMüller of Switzerland in 1991.

The "Ancient Egyptian Temple" section includes both published and unpublished tarot designs, arranged in chronological order of completion or first publication (except for the Ibis Tarot). Spellings of the Egyptian words and names vary according to the text accompanying each deck.

Ibis Tarot Josef Machynka, AGMüller, 1991 Descriptions are based on those in the booklet by Machynka.

TOP ROW: **I The Magician** is like a pillar connecting heaven and earth. His left hand points to earth, symbolizing his mastery over matter. The white ibis on the altar is the god Thoth. It devours the eggs of the crocodile, the offspring of lower, unconscious matter. A comet heralds the dawning of a New Age. **II The Gate of the Sanctuary** shows an aspect of the veiled Isis, representing intuition. She guards the entry to a temple and is flanked by the pillars of duality. The partially hidden scroll shows her as the keeper of secret knowledge. Below her breast is the symbol of continuous creation. **IV The Cubic Stone.** The Emperor sits cross-legged on a cubic throne. His clothes form a triangle pointed heavenward. His body forms the symbol for Jupiter. He symbolizes complete authority of spirit over matter. **VII The Chariot of Osiris** shows Osiris riding his cubic vehicle to war, surrounded by four pillars, symbols of the four elements of his personality. **VIII The Balance and the Sword.** A female figure sits on a throne at the top of three steps, which represent the three worlds. Behind her is a pair of winged twins, adorned with the feathers of Ma'at, goddess of cosmic order, harmony, and justice.

BOTTOM ROW: **IX The Veiled Lamp.** A bearded man carries an oil lamp, whose three flames light his path. His square coat represents his personality, created of the four elements. The old man is a candidate for initiation into the Mysteries, and therefore sworn to silence. **X The Sphinx.** On one hand, Bastet, the Light, is rising, while on the other side, Typhon, the darkness, descends. Atop the wheel is the Sphinx, an embodiment of the mysterious force that perpetually spins the wheel of karmic cycles of death and rebirth. At the foot of the column supporting the wheel, two vipers of power and wisdom raise their heads. **XI The Tamed Lion.** A female figure, secretly uniting within herself male and female attributes, opens and closes the mouth of a lion without using force. She is crowned with the vulture goddess Nechbeth, her guardian and protector, and the Uraus serpent, her awareness and wakefulness. **XII The Victim** hangs between two palms. His legs are crossed above his head, signifying that he has surrendered to the lure of materialism. The four coins are "the spoils of his exploits," the four elements of his personality which he must now sacrifice. **XIV The Two Urns.** The angel is a symbol for Thoth or Mercury as the Divine Alchemist. He conducts a unifying process that produces the Elixir of Life. He wears the wings of the goddess Noot, the eternity of cosmic space.

Ibis Tarot (continued)

TOP ROW: **XV Typhon.** Seth Typhon is a strange conjunction of human and animal parts. His bat wings show him as a kind of dark angel. The flame of awareness burns above his head. His crocodile's head, goat's hooves, bloated hippopotamus body, and the black serpent of sensuality coming from his belly demonstrate his relationships to material life. He has shattered the temple walls around him with his scepter. The goat heads of the people below symbolize the power of the sun, which means that the power to free themselves is within. **XVI The Thunderstruck Tower.** Kings and slaves fall from the shattered pyramid, indicating that all layers of society are affected by the blow and must return to their spiritual source. **XVII The Star of the Magicians.** A female figure pours out hot and cold liquid. The unity of male and female is reflected in the black and white pyramids above. The butterfly, symbol of the changeability of the psyche, drinks the nectar from the source of life. **XVIII The**

Twilight. The black jackal is an embodiment of the god Anubis. The black pyramid is sealed. A scorpion emerges from the water, ready to kill the lower passions. The time between day and night is considered a magical time. **XXI The Crown of the Magicians.** A female figure plays a three-stringed harp, representing the threefold harmony in human life of body, mind, and spirit. Above, in a circle of threefold lotus blossoms, floats a winged creature, half fish, half bird. It is the human spirit rising above the material plane.

BOTTOM ROW: **XXII The Crocodile.** The man, shouldering two bags of karma and experience, is blindly walking toward the mouth of a crocodile. The "monster" represents man's passions and the mercilessness of fate, which will devour the blind and ignorant. **XXVI Slave of Sceptres. XXXVIII Mistress of Cups. LXVII Warrior of Pentacles. LIX Five of Swords.**

Exoteric Timeline of the Egyptian Tarot

This list is not comprehensive, but, rather, notes the books and illustrations that have been most influential in the development of Egyptian-style decks.

1781 Publication of *Le Monde Primitif*, by Antoine Court de Gebelin, describing the Egyptian "Book of Thoth" as taking the form of a tarot deck. The deck illustrated in the book is the Tarot of Marseilles, with some cards altered. (See *The Encyclopedia of Tarot*, volume I, page 139).

1783 Publication of Etteilla's book *Les Tarots ou Manière de se Récréer avec le Jeu de Cartes Nommées Tarot*, which furthered Court de Gebelin's outlook. The first Etteilla Tarot was published by Grimaud, France, based on the works of Etteilla, circa 1800.

1854 Publication of Eliphas Lévi's *Le Dogme et Rituel de la Haute Magique*. Lévi called the tarot "The Book of Hermes." His only known illustration of a tarot card is VII The Chariot, which was the first to substitute sphinxes for horses.

1870 Publication of *Histoire de la Magie*, by Paul Christian (pen-name for Jean-Baptiste Pitois), which describes the Egyptian Temple initiation. His 1863 novel *L'Homme Rouge des Tuileries* gave much the same description. No illustrations were shown of tarot cards or the temple.

1888 Oswald Wirth published his tarot designs under the title *Le Livre de Thot* (The Book of Thoth). The images reflect the Tarot of Marseilles, with only a few Egyptianate details.

Eliphas Lévi's illustration of VII The Chariot

1896 René Falconnier published *Les XXII Lames Hermétique du Tarot Divinatoire* (The 22 Hermetic Pages of the Divinatory Tarot). The subtitle translates: "Exactly reconstituted after the sacred texts, and after the tradition of the Magi of Ancient Egypt." The book was illustrated with Major Arcana by Otto Wegener. (See *The Encyclopedia of Tarot*, volume II, pp. 394–395.)

1901 Publication of *Practical Astrology*, by Comte de Saint-Germain. The book was illustrated with a deck copied from the Falconnier/Wegener deck, with card II The Gate of the Sanctuary altered in some details. (See *The Encyclopedia of Tarot*, volume I, pp. 189–191.)

1909 Publication of *Le Tarot Divinatoire*, by Papus (Gerard Encausse). The book included illustrations of a full deck by Gabriel Goulinat. (See *The Encyclopedia of Tarot*, volume I, pp. 211.)

1936 Publication of *Sacred Tarot*, by C.C. Zain, with tarot illustratrations by Gloria Beresford. The illustrations were based on Falconnier's. The deck was originally published as Egyptian Tarot Cards, then Brotherhood of Light Tarot, then Church of Light Tarot. (See *The Encyclopedia of Tarot*, volume I, pp. 240–241.)

1975 Egipcios Kier Tarot deck, artist unknown, published by Egipcios Kier of Argentina. Based on Falconnier/Wegener deck, with original elements as well. The Minor Arcana do not have suits, but rather are numbered 23 through 78, with interpretive words as titles. (See *The Encyclopedia of Tarot*, volume I, page 585.)

Etteilla-type Tarot A tarot hand-drawn by an unknown artist was modeled on the Etteilla tarots of the nineteenth century, with traces of influence by Eliphas Levi. The titles are in English, at times misspelled, and the numbering departs from traditional or Etteilla schemes. The deck seems to have been created for personal use by someone well-versed in occult symbolism, although not a scholar. The script at the top of the Minor Arcana possibly makes alchemical references. The deck comprises twenty-two Major Arcana, sixteen court cards—master, mistress, knight, and slave—and four aces in suits swords, scepters, cups, and shekels. It was probably created at the end of the nineteenth century.

Ancient Esoteric Tarot (Tarocchi di Etteilla) Etteilla first gained prominence as a cartomancer in late-nineteenth-century France. The deck reproduced here is a facsimile of a deck that was printed as an Etteilla tarot around 1870 by an unknown printer in France. Although the images and the numbering of the cards as 1 through 78 are suggestive of Etteilla's tarot, the sequence of the cards varies from typical Etteilla decks. The facsimile includes divinatory meanings in five languages, and comes with a title card, advertising card and instructional leaflet. The back design is a pattern of Egyptian motifs in brown on white.

Lo Scarabeo also published a miniature version of cards 1 through 22 and 78. The miniature version is an exact (though reduced in size) facsimile of the original deck, including the French divinatory meanings and titles. The miniature deck is titled I Tarocchi di Etteilla "Libro di Thot," and its back design is star-like figures in gold on bright green. The decks were published by Lo Scarabeo, of Turin, Italy, in 2000.

702

Etteilla-type Tarot   Late nineteenth century

Ancient Esoteric Tarot (Tarocchi di Etteilla)   Circa 1870, reproduction by Lo Scarabeo, 2000   All cards are shown at sixty percent of their original size.   TOP ROW, SECOND ROW: From the miniature deck.   THIRD ROW, BOTTOM ROW: From seventy-eight-card deck.

Tarocchi Egizi Original designs by Comte de Saint-Germain, 1901; reproduction by Lo Scarabeo, 1989 TOP ROW: 0 Il Coccodrillo (The Crocodile). 1 Il Mago (The Magician). 2 La Porta del Santuario Occulto (The Gate of the Occult Sanctuary). 3 Iside Urania (Isis Urania). 4 La Pietra Cubica (The Cubic Stone). 5 Il Maestro degli Arcana (The Master of the Arcana). BOTTOM ROW: 6 Le Due Strade (The Two Ways). 9 La Lampada Velata (The Veiled Lamp). 10 La Sfinge (The Sphinx). 11 Il Leone Domato (The Conquered Lion). 17 La Stelle dei Magi (The Star of the Magi). 21 La Corona dei Magi (The Crown of the Magi).

Tarocchi Egizi (Egyptian Tarot) The designs of the Tarocchi Egizi are reproduced from *Practical Astrology,* by Comte de Saint-Germain, published in 1901. The twenty-two-card deck was issued in a numbered, limited edition of 1,123 copies. The images are printed in black on stock with a metallic gold background, and the titles, in Italian, are based on de Saint-Germain's titles. The box and the presentation card are black textured paper print-ed in gold. The back design is a photo of an ancient Egyptian bas-relief of a pharaoh in reddish brown on white. The deck was published by Lo Scarabeo, Turin, Italy, in 1989.

Junya Suzue Papus Tarot Japanese artist Junya Suzue created tarot designs based on the Papus Tarot in 1987.

Junya Suzue Papus Tarot Original Papus Tarot by Gabriel Goulinat, 1909; unpublished reproduction, 1987

Tarocchi di Papus (Papus Tarot)   Cosimo Musio, Lo Scarabeo, 1990

Tarocchi di Papus (Papus Tarot)   Italian artist Cosimo Musio's version of the Papus Tarot was published in 1990 by Lo Scarabeo of Turin in a numbered, limited edition of fifty decks of Major Arcana only, printed on soft, tex-

tured paper. The cards have titles in Italian, and the backs are blank. The deck includes a presentation card with the artist's signature.

Taro dos Bohemios   Gabriel Goulinat, 1909; redrawn by Martius Americano do Brasil, Thot Livaria e Editora Esoterica, circa 1991

Taro dos Bohemios (Papus Tarot) The Taro dos Bohemios, based on the images by Gabriel Goulinat, was illustrated by Brazilian artist Martius Americano do Brasil, and published circa 1991 by Thot Livaria e Editora Esoterica. The Major Arcana feature a Hebrew letter and titles in Portuguese, English, and French. The Minor Arcana repeat the designs for each pip card within the suit, with the only variation being the number of the card. The back design is blue with four fleurs-de-lis. The backs of the cards are unvarnished, although the fronts are varnished. 0 The Fool is also counted as card XXI; The World is card XXII.

Hofman-Barth Egyptian Tarot Barth Hofman, published by the artist, 1990

Hofman-Barth Egyptian Tarot Barth Hofman of Bonn, Germany, created twenty-two designs as Major Arcana postcards. The cards were published by the artist in 1990.

Way of the Jackal Tarot   Billie John, artist, and David Goddard, unpublished, 1992

Way of the Jackal Tarot "The depicted god-forms, the colors, the landscapes and each precise detail [on the cards] are an exact formula. Each card is, in fact, a potent visual suggestion to the unconscious mind of the user, unlocking their paranormal powers." David Goddard thus designed his Egyptian tarot deck. Billie John executed the designs in 1992.

Egyptian Tarot   Esther Casla illustrated the Egyptian Tarot with simple images mostly of human figures in ancient Egyptian clothes, with only a few if any objects in the background. The Egyptian Tarot is patterned after the Egipcios Kier Tarot; the Major Arcana are numbered and titled according to tarot tradition, but the Minor Arcana continue the numbering sequence with 23 through 78 and are not divided into suits.

The cards are titled in English and Spanish, and the deck includes a presentation card and an advertising card, plus an instructional brochure in four languages. The double-ended back design is of a scarab. The Egyptian Tarot deck was published in 1993 by Naipes Heraclio Fournier, Vitoria, Spain.

Tarot Egyptien d'Esméralda   The Tarot Egyptien d'Esméralda has designs by Thierry Biancamaria, made under the direction of Esméralda. The deck was published in Nice, France, in 1993. The deck includes a title card and a card giving credits. The back design is of a green scarab.

Ancient Egyptian Tarot   Clive Barrett spent over five years to research and paint the Ancient Egyptian Tarot. The structure of the Major Arcana is based on the cycle of myth about Osiris, the god of the underworld and consort of Isis. In the book accompanying the deck, Barrett says, "There is no reason to believe that the tarot originated in Ancient Egypt. However, there is strong reason to believe that the tarot as a collection of mystical images draws upon Ancient Egyptian sources." Barrett bases this belief on the archetypal nature of the tarot, and the fact that it came forth during the Renaissance, a time when Europeans were rediscovering ancient Rome, Greece, and the Celts. The deck was published in 1994 by Thorsons of England.

Tarots Egyptiens   The structure of the tarot deck designed by A. Taccori is based on the Etteilla Tarot, with new art in keeping with the Egyptian themes favored by Etteilla. The heavy, large cards are made of textured cardboard. The faces are printed to give the appearance of papyrus, and the back design is of Egyptian hieroglyphs in brown on cream. The cards include upright and reversed divinatory meanings in French. The deck was published in 1995 by Editions de Vecchi of Paris, and it was accompanied by a book by Laura Tuan.

Tarocchi Egiziani (Egyptian Tarots)   Artist Silvana Alasia based her tarot deck on the designs by Falconnier and Wegener. She painted them in tempera on paper, to resemble ancient papyrus.

The deck, published by Lo Scarabeo, was issued in 1996 as a seventy-eight-card deck, and in 1998 as a twenty-two-card supplement to *Astra* magazine. The titles in the seventy-eight-card deck are traditional, whereas the titles of the twenty-two-card deck are Italian translations of the Falconnier titles. Both decks have a back design of a scarab surrounded by Egyptian motifs.

The twenty-two-card deck has titles in Italian and the back design is in teal on white. It is accompanied by a title card and three instructional cards in Italian. The seventy-eight-card deck has titles in four languages, and backs in brown on white. It comes with a title card and nine instructional cards in four languages.

Divination Egyptian Tarot   The Divination Egyptian Tarot was designed by Margarita Arnal Moscardo and illustrated by Jordi Bernaus. About the deck, the artist says in correspondence with Stuart Kaplan, "My long sojourn in Egypt and the studies of old documents (papyrus), which are in the most important museums in the world, have been the basis for the creation of this tarot." The deck, published in 1998 by Negsa/Naipes Comas, was patterned after the Egipcios Kier Tarot. The Divination Egyptian deck is accompanied by a title card, a presentation card, and an instructional leaflet.

Egyptian Tarot Esther Casla, Naipes Heraclio Fournier, 1993

Tarot Egyptien d'Esméralda   Thierry Biancamaria, artist, and Esméralda, published by the artist, 1993

Ancient Egyptian Tarot   Clive Barrett, Thorsons, 1994
The descriptions are based on the book accompanying the
deck.

TOP ROW: **0 The Fool** shows Amun, the creator god. He
holds the feather of Ma'at, goddess of truth. The cosmic egg
containing the god Horus is in the background. Mut, Amun's
consort and mother goddess, is in the form of a vulture
overhead. The dog represents the dog star, Sirius. **II The
High Priestess** is Isis, the lunar goddess, and sister and consort of Osiris. The ankh she holds represents the unity of
male and female, heaven and earth. The veil between the pillars conceals the horizon, representing the darkness before
dawn, or the imminence of enlightenment. The white dove is
a symbol of purity. **IV The Emperor** is the sun god Amun-
Ra. He is associated with the head of the zodiac, Aries, and
hence wears a ram mask. The dry cliffs denote the arid
sterility of his masculine realm. **VIII Strength** shows the
lion goddess Sekhmet, daughter of the sun god Ra. The snake
in front of the lion represents here the divine power of the
gods. The Uraeus, with its rearing cobra, on the head of
Sekhmet represents the destructive and protective power of
fire. **XII The Hanged Man** is suspended between heaven

and earth by a noose that suggests an inverted ankh. The lin-
tel is decorated with a solar barque, supported on the shoulders of the god Nun. The pillars show the Nile god of abundance, Hapi.

SECOND ROW: **XVI The Tower** symbolizes the end of a
dynasty. The fallen Djed in the foreground symbolizes Osiris's
death. **XVII The Star** shows Isis, crowned by the hieroglyph
of her name, kneeling on the banks of the Nile. The bird is an
ibis, sacred to Isis and symbol of the human soul. The star
that represents the card is Sirius. The time of year that Sirius
rose at dawn coincided with the life-giving flood of the Nile.
XVIII The Moon rises over two pillars at the gate of life
and death. The jackals on either side are creatures of Anubis.
The coffin of Osiris floats, as yet undiscovered, in the waters.
XIX The Sun shines on two children. The girl wears a
crown of daisies, literally, "day's eyes," and the boy wears the
sidelock of youth. They are pure and symbolize humankind
freed of hatred and guilt. **XX Judgement** depicts Osiris
resurrected. His robe is made of feathers in white for purity,
red for vitality, green for resurrection and joy, and black for
the underworld. The three people represent the eternal triad
of mother, father, and child. The left sarcophagus bears the

Tarot Egyptiens   A. Taccori, Editions De Vecchi, 1995

image of Ba, the wandering spirit of the dead. The middle one depicts outstretched hands for Ka, the vital spirit or "double" of the deceased. The right depicts the crested ibis called Aakh or Khu, the imperishable spirit-soul.

BOTTOM ROW: **XXI The World** depicts Nuit, Lady of the Stars. She holds the lotus and papyrus wands of upper and lower Egypt. The red disks on her body represent the Kabbalistic Sephiroth Malkuth, Tiphareth, and Kether. She treads on the head of the serpent, enemy of Ra, indicating that it is under her control. **Six of Swords. Eight of Wands. Two of Cups. Prince of Disks.**

Tarocchi Egiziani (Egyptian Tarots) Silvana Alasia, Lo Scarabeo, 1996 (From twenty-two-card deck) TOP ROW: 0 Il Coccodrillo (The Crocodile). 1 Il Mago (The Magician). 3 Iside Urania (Isis Urania). 4 La Pietra Cubica (The Cubic Stone). 6 Le Due Strade (The Two Ways). SECOND ROW: 8 La Bilancia e la Spada (The Scale and the Sword). 9 La Lampada Velata (The Veiled Lamp). 11 Il Leone Domato (The Conquered Lion). 13 Anubi (Anubis). 15 Tifone (Typhon). (From the seventy-eight-card deck) THIRD ROW: XVI The Tower. XVII The Stars. XVIII The Moon. XIX The Sun. XX Judgement. BOTTOM ROW: XXI The World. Knave of Swords. 1 of Wands. 1 of Cups. 2 of Pentacles.

714

Divination Egyptian Tarot   Margarita Arnal Moscardo and Jordi Bernaus, artist, Negsa and Naipes Comas, 1998

Tarot de los Dioses Egipcios (Tarot of the Egyptian Deities) Sebastián Vázquez conceptualized a tarot deck that was illustrated by Cristina Garcia G. The deck was published by Editorial EDAF of Madrid, in 2000. The Major Arcana are titled with the names of ancient Egyptian deities. 20 El juicio de los muertos (Judgment of the dead) is in a horizontal format. The suits are ankh (swords), djed (batons), nun (cups), and udjet (coins). The ankh is a symbol of life; the djed is a column; the nun is a boat, and udjet is the eye of god. Courts are el faraón (the pharaoh, the king), la reina (the queen), el sacerdote (the priest, the knight), and el escriba (the scribe, the page). The deck includes a title card. The back design shows the goddess Nut in a starry sky.

Ramses: Tarot of Eternity Giordano Berti of Lo Scarabeo, Turin, created a "storyboard" of ancient Egypt, illustrated by Severino Baldi. The deck focuses on a specific period of Egyptian history, from approximately 1304 BCE to 1224 BCE, the life span of Ramses II. Only two cards show people from outside the period, 0 The Fool, which shows Akenaton, and XX Judgement, which shows Moses. The Major Arcana show scenes from the life of Pharaoh Ramses II, and the Minor Arcana show scenes from the lives of ordinary people. The deck was published in 2003. The back design shows the pharaoh with flail and crook.

Tarocchi della Sfinge (Tarots of the Sphynx) The Tarot of the Sphinxes was painted by Silvana Alasia and published by Lo Scarabeo, of Turin, in 1998. It includes a title card and an advertising card. The background is black, and the artwork is done in a way to resemble papyrus.

The same artwork was published as **Nefertari's Tarot** in 1999 by Lo Scarabeo. The images are reversed, and the backgrounds are white with a blue border. The seventy-eight cards of Nefertari's Tarot each have a gold foil background and titles in Italian, English, French, German, and Spanish.

The deck is named after Nefertari, wife of Ramses II, the Egyptian pharaoh of the nineteenth dynasty. From the leaflet accompanying the deck: "Ramses worshiped her, calling her the Charming Queen and the Sweetest Lover. When she died he built for her a beautiful sepulcher that survived almost intact to our time. Inside the sepulcher the fascination and even the mystery of Egyptian culture [was] conserved through the objects that belonged to the queen. This deck tries to recreate the atmosphere and the symbology so loved by Nefertari, Light of Egypt and symbol of the most beautiful aspects of this civilization."

Ramses: Tarot of Eternity Giordano Berti and Severino Baldi, artist, Lo Scarabeo, 2003

0 — Khons   1 — Thot   2 — Isis   3 — Mut   5 — Haroeris

6 — Khnum   7 — Horus   9 — Ptah   10 — Khephri   11 — Maat

13 — Anubis   14 — Nephtis   16 — Imhotep   17 — Hathor   18 — Selket

19 — Ra

20 — El juicio de los muertos

Tarot de los Dioses Egipcios (Tarot of the Egyptian Deities)   Sebastián Vázquez and Cristina Garcia G., artist, Editorial EDAF, 2000

Faraón

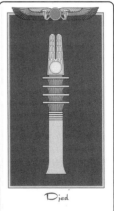

Djed

Nefertari's Tarot Silvana Alasia, Lo Scarabeo, 1999
TOP ROW: 0 The Fool. I The Magician. II The High Priestess. III The Empress. IV The Emperor. SECOND ROW: V The Hierophant. VI The Lover. VII The Chariot. VIII Justice. IX The Hermit. THIRD ROW: XIV Temperance. XVIII The Moon. XXI The World. 9 of Wands. 5 of Chalices.

**Tarocchi della Sfinge
(Tarots of the Sphynx)**
Silvana Alasia, Lo Scarabeo,
1998

Miss Cleo Tarot Power Deck "Miss Cleo's Mind and Spirit Psychic Network" was launched on television in 1999. In two years, it became the most popular telephone psychic service in the country. Miss Cleo claimed to be a shaman from Jamaica and spoke in a dialect to her audience. One of the two advertising cards accompanying Miss Cleo's deck says, "Experience the power of a real tarot reading from a true Shaman. There is no substitute." However, it was not Miss Cleo (Youree Cleomili Harris) who answered the phone, but rather "psychic associates." This and other issues attracted federal and state charges of fraud against the network.

Miss Cleo's Tarot Power Deck was designed by J.F.

Lambert and Seth Stephens and published by Radar Communications in 2001. The double-ended back design is a geometrical ornament with grasses and winged solar disks in purple on white. The scenes on the Minor Arcana pips are obviously inspired by the Rider-Waite Tarot, but the illustrations of both Minor and Major Arcana cards have originality and character.

Miss Cleo says in the booklet accompanying the deck, "The Tarot is not something that can be taken lightly. You've heard me say a thousand times, 'Dah cards dem neva lie!' It never ceases to amaze, my Dears. Open up your heart and your mind and receive the power of the Tarot."

Miss Cleo's Tarot Power Deck   J.F. Lambert and Seth Stephens, Radar Communications, 2001

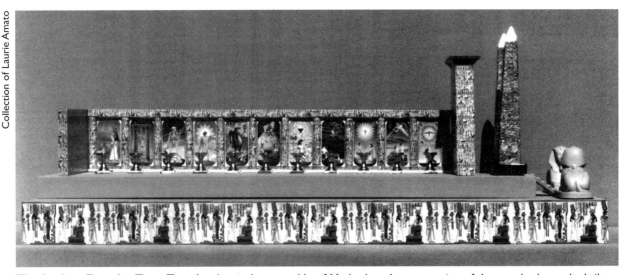

Collection of Laurie Amato

The Ancient Egyptian Tarot Temple   Laurie Amato and Josef Machynka   A cross-section of the temple shows the brilliant images of the Ibis Tarot, by Josef Machynka. Oil lamps are in front of each card.

Other Egyptianate tarot decks featured in *The Encyclopedia of Tarot* are:

IV

TAROCK PACKS

The term tarock is used to describe tarot decks used only for gaming. The Majors, or Trumps, do not feature allegorical pictures. Tarock decks have twenty-two Trumps and fifty-six or thirty-two Minors. Rather than 0 The Fool, tarock packs have an unnumbered, untitled Joker card. Suits are usually spades, clubs, hearts, and diamonds. The shortened packs have cards seven through ten plus courts in the black suits, and ace through four in the red suits.

The decks in this chapter are arranged as a section of pre-World War II decks, in chronological order, then later decks in alphabetical order (by title).

PRE-WWII TAROCK DECKS

Habsburger Tarock   Piatnik of Vienna issued a facsimile of an Austrian deck originally published in 1850. The knight of clubs bears the engraver's and maker's names and addresses (respectively): "Fabrik Schottenfeld, Herrngasse, no. 407 / Ferd. Piatnik verm'als A. Moser in Wien." The Ace of Hearts shows a tax stamp issued by Ferdinand I of Austria. The "W" indicates the tax stamp office, and 20 K indicates a value of 20 kreuzer. The date 1850 is in the center of the stamp. The Ace of Hearts also bears a stamp: "F. Piatnik / Wien 1850." Each of the Trumps shows historical or legendary scenes from the Habsburg (Hapsburg) empire. The court cards show folk heroes and other historical figures. The deck comprises twenty-two Trumps, and fifty-four Minors. The back design is brown on cream. The facsimile is undated.

Hungarian tax stamp   This tax stamp on the Ace of Hearts of the Ungarisches Ansichten Tarock was in use in Hungary from 1883 to 1896.

Ungarisches Ansichten Tarock (Hungarian Scenic Tarock)   The artwork for the Hungarian Scenic Tarock was first made in 1857 by István Giergl. In 1875, the deck was reprinted by Elsó Magyar Kártyagyári Részvénytársulat (First Hungarian Card Manufacturer). The tax stamp on the Ace of Hearts was in use from 1883 to 1896. A facsimile of the deck was issued by Ferdinand Piatnik & Söhne, Vienna, in 1993, as indicated on an extra card in the deck. The deck comprises twenty-two Trumps and sixteen courts, but only the tens of spades and clubs, and the aces of hearts and diamonds.

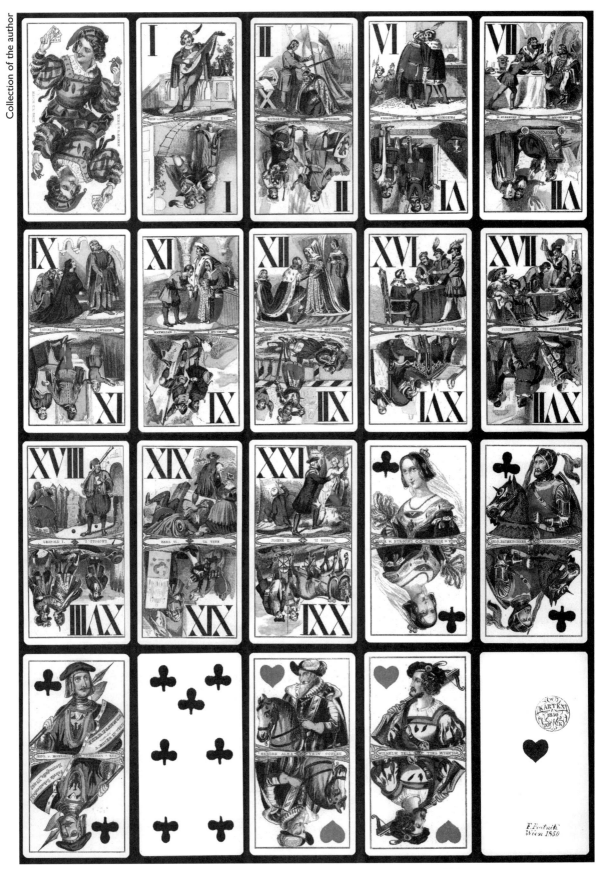

Habsburger Tarock   Engravings by Fabrik Schottenfeld, Piatnik, 1850; reproduction, circa 1990

Ungarisches Ansichten Tarock (Hungarian Scenic Tarock)   István Giergl, 1857; reprint Elsó Magyar Kártyagyári Részvénytársulat (First Hungarian Card Manufacturer), 1875; facsimile Ferdinand Piatnik & Söhne, 1993   The artwork on the Trump cards shows scenes in Hungary.

Grazer Tarock   V. Ferd. Pittner, circa 1865; facsimile Piatnik, 1989

Grazer Tarock   The Grazer Tarock is a facsimile of deck issued circa 1865 by Ferdinand Pittner, cardmaker of Graz, Austria. The Trumps feature scenes of Graz and its locale. Tarock decks featuring landscapes were popular in the mid-nineteenth century, inspired by advances in engraving as well as the rise of tourism. The original maker's name and location are on the knave of spades and knave of hearts, respectively. The maker of the facsimile, Ferd. Piatnik and Söhne of Vienna, and the date, 1989, are given on the Ace of Hearts. The original of this deck was featured in *The Encyclopedia of Tarot,* volume II, page 460.

Wiener Verduten Tarock   A scenic tarot from the late nineteenth century was produced in facsimile by Ferd. Piatnik & Söhne, Vienna, in 1993. The Austrian deck was originally published by Ferdinand Piatnik, whose name appears on the page of clubs and on the ace of hearts. The date and maker of the facsimile are also shown on the Ace of Hearts. The tax stamp was valid from 1882 to 1889, and was used in Vienna only.

Sehr Feine Tarock Nr. 84   ASS Vereinigte Altenburger und Stralsunder Spielkarten-Fabriken published an Industrie und Glück tarock, "Nr. 84." The deck has fifty-four cards (trumps, courts, and red pips ace through four and black pips five through ten). Although the deck is based on nineteenth-century decks, it was probably published in the early twentieth century. The maker's name is found on the pages of clubs and diamonds, and the ASS logo is on the ace of diamonds. The back design is a red and black pattern. The deck does not bear a tax stamp.

Eagle Vienna Taroc Playing Cards (Wiener Taroc Spielkarten) Eagle Taroc Co. of St. Louis, Missouri, published a fifty-four-card tarock pack, based on a deck that Piatnik published circa 1920 (see Keller, AUS 233). Several cards, including the Joker, are missing from the deck in the author's collection, but it seems that all of the Trumps, except probably the Joker, repeat the same four designs from the Piatnik original. The back design is brown and blue tarotée. The German and English packaging indicates that the deck was marketed to the German immigrant community in the United States.

Austrian tax stamp, actual size   The tax stamp is two-colored, with the eagle in red and the text in blue. The duty is 30 kreuzer. This stamp was valid from 1882 to 1889, and was used in Vienna only. (From the Wiener Verduten deck)

Wiener Verduten   Original Piatnik, late nineteenth century; facsimile Piatnik, 1993

Sehr Feine Tarock Nr. 84   ASS Vereinigte Altenburger und Stralsunder Spielkarten-Fabriken, early twentieth century

Eagle Vienna Taroc Playing Cards (Wiener Taroc Spielkarten)   Eagle Taroc Co., based on a Piatnik deck of circa 1920

Yugoslavian Tarock no. 9   Yugoslavian Tarock no. 9 has fifty-four cards and was made circa 1920. The package and the ace of hearts has the tax stamp showing the old Carniolan (Slovenian) coat of arms and is inscribed "Giavna carinarnica - Ljubljana" (Customs Ljubljana). The text on the wrapper says (translated): "The finest club tarot *(tarok)* cards / number 9 / 54 cards / First Yugoslav Playing Cards Manufactory Ltd in Ljubljana." The back design is green and red tarotée. The Hungarian publisher's name appears on the pages of clubs and diamonds. The deck is nearly identical to the Coffee House Tarock no. 9A issued by Piatnik in the late nineteenth century (see *The Encylopedia of Tarot,* volume I, page 324). The eagle and shield on card II differ, and the borders of 9a have rounded corners, whereas those of 9 are squared.

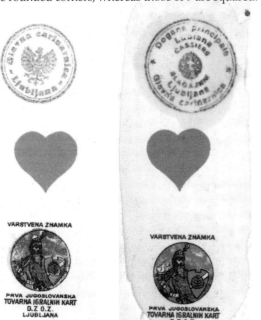

Yugoslavian Tarock no. 103   Yugoslavian Tarock no. 103 has fifty-four cards and was made circa 1930. The text on the wrapper says (translated): "The finest tarot *(tarok)* cards / number 103 / 54 cards / First Yugoslav Playing Cards Manufactory Ltd in Ljubljana." The back design is green and red tarotée. The deck has the same designs as the Yugoslavian Tarock no. 9, but the border is a single line with rounded corners, the margins are narrower, and the cards are smaller overall. The publisher's name is on the pages of clubs and diamonds.

The deck was sold during the Italian occupation of Yugoslavia, during World War II, as indicated by the tax stamps on one of the decks in the author's collection. The tax stamp on the wrapper shows the fascist coat of arms and the inscription: "Provincia di Lubiana / Dogana Principale / Lubiana / Ljubijana / Giavana Carinarnica / Ljubljanska pokrajina." The tax stamp on the ace of hearts differs slightly, with the inscription: "Dogana Principale / Lubiana / Cassiero / Blagajunk (?) / Ljubijana / Giavana Carinarnica." An identical deck has the same tax stamps as Yugoslavian Tarock no. 9, indicating that the deck was first published before the Italian occupation.

Yugoslavian Tarock no. 103
Tax stamp and maker's seal on wrapper. The stamp was used during the Italian occupation of Yugoslavia.

Yugoslavian tax stamps on ace of hearts
LEFT TO RIGHT: **Yugoslavian Tarock no. 9**   Deck is circa 1920. The tax stamp is at the top; the maker's seal is below the heart.
Yugoslavian Tarock no. 103   Tax stamp and maker's seal on ace of hearts. The stamps and seals were visible through an opening in the wrapper of the deck. The tax stamp was in use during World War II.

Yugoslavian Tarock no. 9   First Yugoslav Playing Cards Manufactory, circa 1920

Yugoslavian Tarock no. 103   First Yugoslav Playing Cards Manufactory Ltd, circa 1930

POST WWII TAROCK DECKS

Tarot Asterix   The popular French comic character has a tarot deck all his own. Asterix is a Gaulish warrior whose zany adventures take place around 50 BCE. Each Major Arcana card features a double-ended cartoon, by Albert René, with a different Asterix cartoon on each end. The deck also includes a title card and a card giving tarot game values. The back design features sound effects and phrases familiar to Asterix lovers. The deck was published in 1997 by France Cartes-Grimaud-Ducale-Heron.

Droopy Tarots   The Droopy Tarots are based on the cartoon character "Droopy Dog." Droopy, a phlegmatic detective dog, was created by American cartoonist Tex Avery and appeared on film and TV from 1943 on. The deck was issued for tarock players in France, where Droopy's fame lives on beyond his TV series in the United States. The deck was published in 1997 by A.P.M. under license from Turner Entertainment Company. It includes a title card and a card giving point values in French.

Tarot Epoque Napoleon III   Heron of France published a tarock deck illustrated with scenes from everyday life during the time of Napoleon III, who ruled France from 1848 to 1870. The deck was published circa 1999 and includes a presentation card and a card giving values for the game of tarock. The double-ended back design is the letter N with a crown and ribbons, in blue on tan. The deck was created by J.-P. Broche.

Gendarmerie Tarock II (Military Police Tarock II)   In honor of the French military police, Grimaud of France issued a seventy-eight-card tarock deck that shows the various branches and duties of the Gendarmerie. The photographs, from Laboratoire Photographique Central Gendarmerie, were assembled by gendarme Erick Bernard. The cards are double-ended, and include the logo of the cardmaker on each end between the numbers. Most of the photographs show the police in action, with no gore spared, as shown by the bloody murder scene on card 3. The back design is double-ended in blue, gray, and black.

The Gendarmerie II deck was issued circa 1995. A card accompanying the deck identifies the branches represented by the different cards, and another card gives tarock point values. The courts and pips are the old-fashioned design used by Grimaud for tarock decks. The first Gendarmerie deck was issued by Grimaud in 1980; see *The Encyclopedia of Tarot*, volume II.

Tarot de la Havane   The Havana tarock deck was created by Jean-Marc Poiriez for the magazine *L'Amateur de Cigare*, Paris. The double-ended Trumps feature pictures of Cuba, with many of the pictures showing the tobacco harvest and the manufacturing of Havana's famous cigars. The joker portrays the Cuban revolutionary, Che Guevera. The logo of Carta Mundi, Belgium, appears on the ace of spades. The deck includes a card promoting the magazine and a card giving card values. It was published circa 2000.

Tarot L'Incal   Artist Jean Giraud (Moebius) and writer Alexandro Jodorowsky created the science fiction *bandes dessinées* series "L'Incal," whose hero is named John Difool. The series first appeared in 1989. The deck was published circa 2000 by Editions le Diouris in a limited edition of 2,500. The backs of the cards show the Incal motif of joined pyramids in black and white. A title card and a values card are included.

Tarot Asterix   France-Cartes-Grimaud-Ducale-Heron, 1997   Title card is at bottom right.

Droopy Tarots   Tex Avery, A.P.M., 1997   The cavaliers (knights) and the suit of spades feature Screwball Squirrel. Miss Vavoom is for the dames (queens) and the suit of hearts. McWolf is the valets (pages) and star of the suit of spades. Roi (king), of course, is Droopy Dog, and he is also the mascot for the suit of diamonds.

731

Tarot Epoque Napoleon III   J.-P. Broche, Heron, circa 1999

Collection of the author

Gendarmerie Tarock II (Military Police Tarock)   Erick Bernard, Grimaud, circa 1995   TOP ROW: Joker (Excuse) shows a male and a female gendarme. 1: a young gendarme swearing in / stained glass window of Sainte-Geneviève, patron of the Gendarmerie. 2, 3, 4: Gendarmerie départmentale (one of the main branches of the Gendarmerie; provides support and citizen liaison, and includes forensics and investigation).   SECOND ROW: 6: Gendarmerie mobile (the other main branch of the Gendarmerie, maintains order). 7, 8: La garde républicaine (government security and ceremonial functions). 9: Gendarmerie de l'air (security on air force bases). 10: Gendarmerie maritime (security in naval installations and ocean rescues).   THIRD ROW: 11: Gendarmerie d'outre-mer (gendarmes overseas). 14: Mountain rescue. 15: Water rescue. 16 E.P.I.G.N. (the pararchutist formation of the Gendarmerie). 17: Spelunking.   BOTTOM ROW: 18: Canine corps. 19: Medical evacuation by helicopter. 20: Boats. 21: Uniforms throughout history, and today. 1 of clubs shows the maker.

Tarot de la Havane   Jean-Marc Poiriez, L'Amateur de Cigare and Carta Mundi, circa 2000

Tarot L'Incal   Moebius and Alexandro Jodorowsky, Éditions le Diouris, circa 2000

Joe Bar Team   Christian Debarre and Stéphane Deteindre (BAR2), Carta Mundi, 2000.

Joe Bar Team   "Joe Bar Team" is a *bandes dessinées* series created by BAR2, France. The tarock deck was published by Carta Mundi, Belgium, under license of Vents d'Ouest in 2000. The design and scenarios of Joe Bar are by Christian Debarre and Stéphane Deteindre, collectively called BAR2. The deck includes two extra cards. The back shows design the Joe Bar Team on a blue checkered background.

Lanfeust Tarot   "Lanfeust de Troy" is a *bandes dessinées* series that takes place in a magical world called Troy. The illustrator is Didier Tarquin, and the writer is Scotch Arleston (Christophe Pelinq). The series was published by Soleil. The tarot deck was published by Editions le Diouris in 2002. The back design is a pattern of blue spirals on green. A title card and values card are included.

Largo Winch Tarot   "Without family or attachments, rebel, womanizer, vagabond, iconoclast, and brawler, he finds himself, at twenty-six, at the head of an empire worth ten billion dollars. Discover Largo Winch, the billionaire in blue jeans—and fasten your seat belts!" Thus the title card of the tarock deck describes the action hero Largo Winch. Winch began life as the protagonist of a *bandes dessinées* series, published by Dupuis/Editions le Diouris, and continued to star in a French television series. The creators of Winch are Phillippe Francq and Jean Van Hamme, and their art illustrates the tarock deck. B.P. Grimaud published the deck in 1998. The back design shows a one-hundred-dollar bill. The maker's name is on the ace of clubs. The deck includes a title card and a card giving values for the game of tarot.

Marseille Tarot   Artist Anne Le Dantec brings the color and culture of the great port city of France to the tarot in the Marseille Tarot. Marseilles' place as a crossroads of Mediterranean cultures is reflected in the court cards, which show various types of Marseilles people, with a caption in dialect. The Trumps have on one end words in the dialect of Marseilles and on the other vignettes. The back design is of sardines and lemon slices. The deck was published in 1995 by Vigno of Marseilles and includes two extra cards giving rules, in French, for the game of tarock.

Lanfeust Tarot Didier Tarquin and Scotch Arleston, Editions le Diouris, 2002

Largo Winch Tarot　　Phillippe Francq and Jean Van Hamme, Grimaud, 1998

Marseille Tarot   Anne Le Dantec, Vigno, 1995

1900-2000: Les Hommes et les femmes qui ont illustré le siécle The court cards of a fifty-four-card tarock deck published by Heron of Méringnac, France, portray men and women who made an impact on history during the twentieth century. The court illustrations are by Marie-France Gary. Each has a caption in French naming and describing the figure portrayed. The Trumps are genre scenes with no connection to the courts. The deck was published circa 2000. A title card and a card giving card values for tarock are included.

L'Oevre Cinematographique de Marcel Pagnol A tarock deck published circa 2000 by Vigno of Marseille celebrates the film work of French director Marcel Pagnol. The films were produced between 1930 and 1960. The double-ended back design shows a strip of film and a tree. The four suits focus on characters from four films: diamonds represent *Triologie;* clubs represent *Topaze;* hearts represent *La Femme du Boulanger;* and clubs represent *Manon des Sources.* The deck includes two cards giving rules for the game of tarot.

Tarocchi del Palio di Siena The famous horse race of Siena is commemorated in a deck designed by Maruska Pradelli Rossi under direction of Arrigo Pecchioli. The deck's Major Arcana cards illustrate the animals associated with different neighborhoods of Siena. Four extra cards show the heraldic shields of Siena and its three main sections. The deck also includes a title card and a presentation card. The back design is an abstract black pattern. The deck was published in 1988 by Edizioni d'Italia, Rome. The suit cards are numbered 1 through 14, with cards 11 through 14 as courts.

Tarot Philatelique (Stamp Collector Tarot) The Tarot Philatelique features French stamps on the Major Arcana, court cards and aces. The back design is of postmarks. The tarot was created by Jacques Hiver, with the authorization of La Poste, the post office of France. Editions Yvert & Tellier worked with Grimaud to publish the deck in 1990. The Trumps and aces show stamps that feature sites and monuments. Court cards present art, with a different century represented by each suit: diamonds show medieval art; spades fifteenth century; hearts seventeenth century; clubs nineteenth century; and the Joker shows art from the twentieth century. The seventy-eight-card deck includes an explanatory card and a card giving the card values for the game of tarot.

Tarot de la Révolution Artist Hélène Bouboulis created a tarock deck illustrated with images of the people and events of the French Revolution, in which the monarchy was overthrown. The deck includes a card giving the values of the cards in the game of tarot, and the equivalents of the four suits: Sacré-Coeur des Chouans (Sacred Heart of Chouans) is hearts; drapeau tricolore (tricolor flag) is spades; bonnet phrygian (Phrygian cap) is diamonds; lys royal (royal lily) is clubs. The deck was published by Heron of France circa 2000. The back design is red, blue and white stripes.

Tarot XIII Artist William Vance and writer Jean Van Hamme created the *bandes dessinées* series "XIII," a cliché-ridden action story with lots of guns, busty women, hairy bad guys, and combinations thereof. The hero is a macho American tormented by amnesia; the creators of the series are Belgian. The deck was published by Editions le Diouris in 1997. The back design shows the hero of the series in white on black. A title card and a values card are included.

Tarot Thorgal Artist Grzegorz Rosinski and writer Jean Van Hamme created the adventure *bandes dessinées* series "Thorgal." The series, which began in 1980, is about a mysterious man in medieval Scandinavia. The Vikings name him Thorgal Aegirsson, son of Storms and the Sea. The deck portraying the characters of Thorgal was published in 1998 by EDL - B&M, under license of Hyphen. The deck includes a title card and a card giving values for the tarot game. The ace of clubs has the name of the manufacturer, B.P. Grimaud of Paris. The back design is red with dog's heads in two corners.

1900-2000: Les Hommes et les femmes qui ont illustré le siécle Marie-France Gary, Heron, circa 2000 The descriptions are translated from the captions on the cards.

TOP ROW: **Joker:** Wilbur Wright. 1930. Two brothers experimented with a flying machine. 12 seconds in flight! Aviation is born. **King of Spades:** General De Gaulle. Politician and illustrious Resistance figure.

SECOND ROW: **Queen of Spades:** Amy Johnson. English woman who was the first to fly solo between England and Australia. **Knight of Spades:** Marcel Proust. Writer who dominated the French novel of the twentieth century with *Remembrance of Things Past.* **Page of Spades:** Charlie Chaplin. He created the funny and sad character of Charlie. His films are known throughout the world. **King of Clubs:** Sigmund Freud. Father of psychoanalysis. He made the unconscious conscious. **Queen of Clubs:** Marie Curie. Received the Nobel Prize for Physics for her research on radioactivity.

THIRD ROW: **Knight of Clubs:** Youri Gargarine. Began the conquest of space. He was the first astronaut. **Page of Clubs:** Robert Falcon Scott. Explorer of the Antarctic. His second expedition failed and ended in the death of himself and his companions. **King of Hearts:** Captain Dreyfus. Accused of espionage and later pardoned. The "Dreyfus Affair" mobilized public opinion. **Queen of Hearts:** Marilyn Monroe. Sex symbol of the 1960s. She was a mythic figure in the world of film. **Knight of Hearts:** Orville Wright (same caption as Joker).

BOTTOM ROW: **Page of Hearts:** Professor Barnard. He achieved success with the first heart transplant in 1967. **King of Diamonds:** Albert Einstein. Physics scholar, he created the Theory of Relativity. **Queen of Diamonds:** Simone de Beauvoir. Woman of letters, disciple of Jean-Paul Sartre, essayist, and writer of novels and plays. **Knight of Diamonds:** André Breton. Pope of the Dadaist movement. A founder of Surrealism. **Page of Diamonds:** Neil Armstrong. First man to walk on the moon. A planetary exploit.

Wilbur WRIGHT
1930. Deux frères expérimentent leur engin volant. 12 secondes de vol! l'Aviation est née.

Général DE GAULLE
Homme politique, figure illustre de la Résistance.

Amy JOHNSON
De nationalité Anglaise elle est la première femme a avoir entrepris seule, le premier vol Angleterre /Australie.

Marcel PROUST
Ecrivain, Il domine le roman français du 20ème siècle, avec: "A la recherche du temps perdu".

Charly CHAPLIN
Il crée le célèbre personnage, drôle et douloureux à la fois de CHARLOT. Ses films sont connus dans le monde entier.

Sigmund FREUD
Père de la psychanalyse. Il prend conscience de l'inconscient.

Marie CURIE
Prix Nobel de Physique pour ses recherches sur la radioactivité.

Youri GARGARINE
Début de la conquête de l'espace. Il est le premier homme a effectuer un vol spatial.

Robert falcon SCOTT
Explorateur de l'Antartique, sa deuxième expédition échoue et se solde par sa mort et celle de ses compagnons.

Capitaine DREYFUS
Accusé d'espionnage, gracié puis réhabilité. "L'Affaire" mobilise avec force l'opinion publique.

Marylin MONROE
Sex symbol des années 60. Elle est une figure mythique de l'univers cinématographique.

Orville WRIGHT
1930. Deux frères expérimentent leur engin volant. 12 secondes de vol! l'Aviation est née.

Professeur BARNARD
Il tenta avec succès la première transplantation cardiaque en 1967

Albert EINSTEIN
Physicien, il crée la Théorie de la Relativité.

Simone DE BEAUVOIR
Femme de lettres, disciple de Sartre, auteur d'essais, de romans, de pièces de théâtre.

André BRETON
Pape du mouvement "DADA". Un des fondateurs de l'Ecole surréaliste.

Neil AMSTRONG
Premier homme a marcher sur la lune. Un exploit planétaire.

L'Oevre Cinematographique de Marcel Pagnol   Vigno, circa 2000

Tarocchi del Palio di Siena   Maruska Pradelli Rossi and Arrigo Pecchioli, Edizioni d'Italia, 1988   The Montone, bottom row, is the Joker. Terzo Citta is an extra card illustrating the heraldic device of a section of Siena.

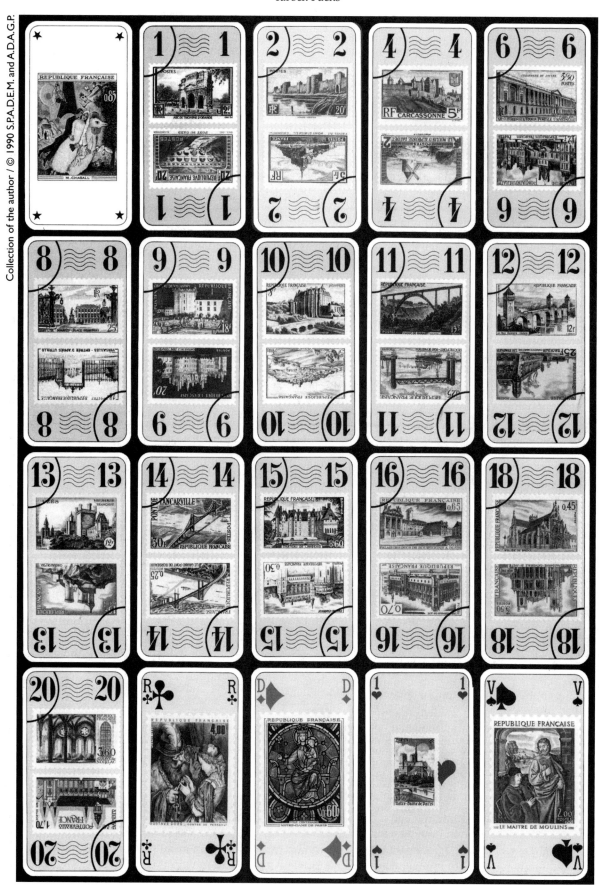

Tarot Philatelique (Stamp Collector Tarot)   Jacques Hiver and La Poste, Editions Yvert & Tellier and Grimaud, 1990

Tarot de la Révolution   Hélène Bouboulis, Heron, circa 2000

Tarot XIII   William Vance and Jean Van Hamme, Editions le Diouris, 1997

Tarot Thorgal   Grzegorz Rosinski and Jean Van Hamme, EDL - B&M and Grimaud, 1998

Does the Tarot Work?

The following essay by Allen Stairs, of the Department of Philosophy, University of Maryland, tackles one of the big questions of tarotists: Does the tarot "work"?

One of the questions that seems to come up most frequently in connection with tarot is, "Does it work?" What people generally mean is, "Can tarot really predict the future?"

For the moment, suppose it can; but think about another, much more ordinary context in which we ask questions about the future: the weather. Under some conditions, we can make extremely accurate predictions of the weather. Under other conditions, our predictions are not very good at all. There are three main reasons for this.

First, weather systems are chaotic: small differences in conditions can make large differences in the outcome. Our knowledge of the conditions is not nearly precise enough to allow stable long-term predictions, and is often too imprecise to be reliable even over the short run. Second, unexpected perturbing factors, celestial or human-generated, affect the weather and render predictions obsolete. Third, errors of measurement occur. For example, a thermometer does not read temperature with one hundred percent accuracy.

The conditions of a tarot reading are similarly chaotic and changing, and the instrument itself, the tarot deck, is not one hundred percent precise. Life and the world are simply too complicated for that.

Two additional factors bear on the accuracy of tarot predictions. First, the tarot cards don't interpret themselves. They must be read, and different readers faced with the same spread may very well disagree about some aspects of its interpretation.

Another factor is so obvious that it may escape notice. Most of us have had the experience of hesitating over a card in a draw. We may draw it nonetheless, or we may draw another. If we end up drawing the "wrong" card, the reading could obviously be affected. Someone might reply that the card we actually settled on was right for that very reason. But surely this is controversial at best! After all, even an experienced musician will occasionally put her finger on the wrong key. Why should a draw from the tarot deck not be subject to similar fumblings of the fingers?

Correct cards or not, the number of possible spreads is huge. Take a full deck of seventy-eight tarot cards. The popular Celtic Cross spread involves ten cards, arranged in a specific order. The number of different Celtic Cross spreads possible using the seventy-eight cards is 4,566,176,969,818,464,000.

Another popular use of the cards is to draw three cards to represent one's day. If the order of the cards is important (e.g., past, present, future, or body, mind, spirit), then there are 456,456 such three-card spreads. If the order doesn't matter, there are 76,076 possible clusterings of three cards. If you considered one of these three-card clusters a day, it would take over 200 years to get through all of them!

Is there a moral in this unpredictability? A small one, perhaps. One should be careful not to over-interpret the cards, whether they be "bad" or "good." Meteorology and many other "non-occult" branches of science—economics, psychology, sociology, and the like—approach predictions with a certain measure of caution.

Another issue comes up in tarot card reading. There is a tension between the belief that our futures can be predicted and the belief that we are free, responsible individuals. The interplay between human freedom and the forces that swirl around us is complex, but the belief that we are to some extent free, and that our choices and actions can really make a difference is not one we should surrender lightly.

Sallie Nichols, the author of *Jung and Tarot,* writes that even after twenty years of professional tarot reading, "I never use the cards to predict specific future events for myself or others. I feel that to do so is generally not helpful and may, in fact, prove harmful. Instead, I view the cards as symbolic of archetypal forces operating in all aspects of life at various times—forces that demand our attention now in the present moment." In Nichols' view, the real significance of the tarot lies in the richness and depth of its symbols. She writes further that "reading the tarot symbolically rather than literally doesn't predict a given future; rather, it offers us opportunities to participate in the creation of a new and unpredictable future."

The question of whether tarot can tell us what is going to happen need not be seen as a simple "Yes/No" question. Tarot is valuable quite apart from whether it has any power to predict the future. Indeed, whether the tarot can predict the future is not the most important question to ask. What makes tarot valuable lies elsewhere. Tarot is a rich set of symbols that allows us ample room for thinking about our lives in creative ways. And that, it seems to me, is saying quite a bit.

The Math: Allen Stairs' big number shows all possible ten-card spreads using a seventy-eight-card deck. Spreads that comprise the same ten cards, but with those cards laid in different configurations, are each counted.

The equation has ten numbers, one number for each card in a ten-card spread.

For card 1, in the first position, you have 78 possibilites. This leaves you with 77 cards for the second position, then 76 cards for the third position, and so on. So, the equation is:

$$78 \times 77 \times 76 \times 75 \times 74 \times 73 \times 72 \times 71 \times 70 \times 69$$
$$= 4,566,176,969,818,464,000.$$

ANNOTATED BIBLIOGRAPHY

THIS COMPREHENSIVE LISTING comprises books, manuscripts, films, sound recordings, and magazine articles not included in the bibliographies of volumes I, II, and III of *The Encyclopedia of Tarot*. Most of the books deal with tarot: its history, symbolism, collecting, and uses. Books of historical interest on playing cards and gambling are also included. Works that do not directly concern tarot or playing cards, by authors such as A.E. Waite and Aleister Crowley, are included since those authors had a significant impact on tarot. Films and sound recordings are listed by title. Works designated with a single asterisk (*) are from the private collection of Stuart R. Kaplan; works with a double asterisk (**) denotes a photocopy in Stuart R. Kaplan's collection. The Web is a treasure trove of tarot information, and many of the artists featured in the Encyclopedia have their own websites. However, no internet sites are included in this bibliography, because they often are unfortunately ephemeral. The reader is strongly encouraged to search the Web in order to learn more about the tarot and the artists who have created such a beautiful variety of tarot images.

A

AABO, Birgit. "Hvis De vil vide Mere!" *Politiken Magasinet* (1995): 8–9. Ill. Article in Copenhagen newspaper on Danish tarotist Ulrik Goldnoff.

* **AALTONEN**, Kalervo. *Kalevala Tarot.* Stamford, CT: U.S. Games Systems, 1995. Ill. 222 pp. 18 cm. (paper) Book accompanying the Kalervo Tarot, illustrated by Taina Pailos.

* **ABADIE**, M. J. *The Everything Tarot Book: Discover Your Past, Present, and Future: It's in the Cards!* Holbrook, MA: Adams Media Corp., 1999. Ill. xv, 285 pp. 23 cm. Divination with the tarot.

ABADIE, M. J., *Tarot for Teens.* Rochester, VT: Bindu Books, 2002. Ill. 256 pp. (paper) 22 cm. Basic tarot.

* **ABBAMONTE**, Mary Francis. *The 13th Sign: The Zodiac Has Changed: So Have You—Find Out How and Why.* 1st Books Library, 2002. Ill. 168 pp. Includes section on XIII Death of the tarot.

* **ABBEY**, Christopher, and Morgana Abbey. *The Wonderland Tarot.* Stamford, CT: U.S. Games Systems, 1989. (paper) Book accompanying the deck illustrated by Morgana Abbey.

** **ABBOTT**, Stephen. "Strength Key 8: The White Lady of Fiery Light." *Gnostica,* 49 (January/February 1979): 46–47. Meditation on Strength, based on Rider-Waite image.

* **ABRAHAM**, Sylvia. *Cómo Leer del Tarot.* Madrid: Editorial Edaf, 2003. 208 pp. (paper) 17 cm. Spanish-language edition of *How to Read the Tarot.*

* **ABRAHAM**, Sylvia. *How to Read the Tarot: The Key Word System.* St. Paul, MN: Llewellyn Publications, 1994. Ill. 260 pp. (paper) 18 cm. Very basic meanings. Illustrated with the Rider-Waite Tarot.

* **ABRAHAM**, Sylvia. *How to Use Tarot Spreads.* St. Paul, MN: Llewellyn Publications, 1997. Ill. ix, 274 pp. (paper) 17 cm. Reading the cards for various situations in life; includes sample readings.

* **ABRAHAM**, Sylvia. *Lecturas con el Tarot.* Madrid: Editorial Edaf, 2003. 264 pp. (paper) 22 cm. Spanish-language edition of *How to Use Tarot Spreads.*

* **ABRAMS**, Carol Herzer. *Astral Mandala.* Privately published, New York, 1987. No pagination. Handmade book.

* **ACEVES**, Octavio. *La Otra Vertiente del Tarot.* Barcelona: Ediciones Obelisco, 1990. 150 pp. (paper) 22 cm. In Spanish. Reflections on the tarot and our times. Illustrated in color with the Oswald Wirth Tarot.

ACQUELIN, José, and Robert Cadot. *Tarokado.* Québec: Editions de Mortagne, circa 1990. Book on Tarokado deck, illustrated by Robert Cadot.

* **ADER PICARD TAJAN.** *Collection Alan Borvo: Cartes à Jouer Tarots Aluettes.* June 1994. Ill. Auction catalog.

* **ADER PICARD TAJAN.** *Collection Unique de 340 Jeux de Cartes.* March 1986. Ill. (paper) Catalogue for auction, including antique tarot decks.

AFLALO, Michel. "Is the Self-Expression Workshop a Place for and an Aspect of Rehabilitation?" *International Journal of Mental Health* 25, 1 (Spring 1996): 80–86. Group work on creating a film results in "Tarot Makeup Squiggle" session video.

AGRELL, Sigurd. *Die pergamenische zauberscheibe und das tarockspiel.* Lund, 1936. Ill. 24 cm. In German.

* **AKRON** and H.R. Giger. *Baphomet: Tarot der Unterwelt.* Switzerland: Urania Verlag, 1992. Ill. 507 pp. Book accompanying Baphomet Tarot, with artwork by H.A. Giger. (Akron is penname of C.F. Frey.)

* **AKRON.** *Baphomet: The Tarot of the Underworld.* Neuhausen, Switzerland: AGMüller, 1993. Ill. 137 pp. Booklet accompanying the English-language edition of the Baphomet Tarot. Abridged from original. Packaged with the Major Arcana Baphomet Tarot, illustrated by H.R. Giger, and with a music CD by the rock group Epilepsy.

* **AKRON** and Hajo Banzhaf. *Der Crowley Tarot.* Germany: Hugendubel, 1992. Ill. 219 pp.

* **AKRON** and Hajo Banzhaf. *The Crowley Tarot: The Handbook to the Cards.* Stamford, CT: U.S. Games Systems, 1995. Ill. 221 pp. (paper) 26 cm. Translation of *Der Crowley Tarot.*

* **ALARNAH**, Tobin-Gray, and Llyle Wentworth. *Time Tarot.* Australia: Simon and Schuster, 2002. Ill. 164 pp. (paper) 22 cm. Predicting with cards, including time lines. Illustrated with the Rider-Waite Tarot.

* **ALBA**, Alberto Suarez. *A Vitoria, Barajas.* Vitoria, Spain: Museo Fournier de Naipes, 1991. History of the museum. In Spanish, with English translation included.

* **ALBIÑANA**, José María Doria. *Tarot of the Universe.* Canary Islands, Spain: Antakaran, 1988. Ill. 160 pp. (paper) Book accompanying Tarot of the Universe. Illustrated by Rafael Trelles.

ALL AROUND THE TAROT. Virginia Le Delp, editor. Los Angeles: APA, 1992. Ill. Newsletter.

ALL ARTIST'S TAROT. 1995. Ill. 12 pp. Tarot images by different artists.

ALLI, Antero *Angel Tech: A Modern Shamans Guide to Reality Selection.* AZ: Falcon Press, 1986. Ill. Described by K. Frank Jensen: "This discordian work is illustrated with tarot cards in the discordian taste."

ALLI, Antero. "The Neuro-Tarot." *Whole Earth Review,* Fall 1991: 28–33. Includes illustrations by the author.

ALMOND, Jocelyn, and Keith Seddon. *Tarot for Lovers: A Practical Guide to Understanding Love and Sex from Tarot Reading.* London: Thorsons, 1990. Ill. 175 pp. (paper) Illustrated with the Norse Tarot by Clive Barrett.

ALMOND, Jocelyn and Keith Seddon. *Understanding Tarot.* England: Aquarian Press, 1991; St. Paul, MN: Llewellyn Publications, 1991. Ill. 160 pp.

ALPERT, Richard. (See Ram Das.)

AMANO, Yoshitako. *The Illustrations for the Tarot Cards of Yoshitaka Amano.* Japan, 1997. Ill. 111 pp. (paper) In Japanese.

* **AMARAL**, Geraldine, and Nancy Brady Cunningham. *Tarot Celebrations: Honoring the Inner Voice.* York Beach, ME: Samuel Weiser, 1997. Ill. xxi, 312 pp. (paper) 21 cm. Exercises and meditations for each of the Major Arcana. Illustrated with the Rider-Waite Tarot.

* **AMATO**, Laurie. *Tarot Insights.* Unpublished manuscript, 2003. Interpretation of the tarot for self-realization.

* **AMBESI**, A.C. "I Tarocchi del Mantegna." *Esopo* 12 (1981): 49–63.

* **AMERICAN ANTIQUE DECK COLLECTORS CLUB.** Ongoing. Membership Roster.

AMERY, Colin. *New Atlantis: The Secret of the Sphinx.* London: Regency, 1976. 139 pp.

ANANDO (Irmgard Gleichauf), ed. *Tarot: Ein Blick in Verschlusselte Weisheiten.* Germany: Connection Verlag, 1991. Ill. 96 pp. Special tarot issue from the German magazine *Connection.* Includes articles by Herman Haindl, Mario Montano, Hajo Banzhaf.

ANDEL, Gabriele. *I Tarocchi dei Visconti.* Bergamo, Italy: Monumenta Longobardica, 1974. Ill. 32 pp. 22 cm. Pamphlet accompanying reproduction of Visconti Tarot deck.

ANDERSON, FW Chris. *The Metaphysical Tarot Workbook.* Privately published, 1999. Ill. 93 pp. (paper, comb-bound) Observations on the Major Arcana, with illustrations by the author. Signed and numbered edition of 100 copies.

* **ANDERSON**, Hilary. "Destiny Spread: A Process for Self-Transformation." In *Wheel of Tarot.* James Wanless and Angeles Arrien, eds. Tarot spread that uses two decks at once.

* **ANDERSON**, Jim. "Archetypes and Tarot Cards." *Printmaking Today* 8, 4 (Winter 1999): 6–7.

ANDERSON, Vikki. *Totally Tarot: How to Be a Tarot Detective.* Wayne, NJ: Libraland Publishing, 1998. Ill. 158 pp. (paper, comb-bound). Reprint. Rose International Publishing House, 2000. Ill. 148 pp. (paper)

Reading the cards. Illustrated with the Rider-Waite Tarot.

* **ANDO**, Arnell. *Transformational Tarot.* USA: Ink Well Publications, 1995. Ill. 96 pp. (paper) Book accompanying Transformational Tarot by Ando.

ANDRES, Marquinez Casas. "Un Tarot para Macondo." In *XX Congreso Nacional de Literatura, Linguistica y Semiotica.* 1998.

* **ANDREWS**, Ted. *The Animal-Wise Tarot.* Jackson, TN: Dragonhawk Publications, 1999. 246 pp. (paper) 21 cm. Book accompanying the Animal-Wise Tarot, by Andrews.

* **ANNETT**, Sally, and Rowena Shepherd. *The Atavist Tarot.* London: Quantum, 2003. Ill. 256 pp. (paper) Guide to the Atavist Tarot.

ANONYMOUS. *L'Actuel* 51 (1983). Ill. Magazine including an untitled article featuring a set of satirical photographic tarot cards.

* **ANONYMOUS.** "Als je wereld instort." *Troubadour* 24 (1999): 10–11. Review of *When Things Fall Apart,* by Tibetan Buddhist nun Pema Chödrön, is illustrated with The Tower from an unknown Dutch tarot.

ANONYMOUS. *The A.M.O.S. Path of Light.* USA, circa 1930. 50 pp. Volume VII. Volume on tarot, from a series by the Ancient Mystical Order of Seekers.

* **ANONYMOUS.** *Antiche Carte Italiane da Tarocchi.* Rome: Edindustria Editoriale, 1961. Unpaginated. (hardcover) 28 cm. In Italian: *Antique Italian Tarot Cards.* Features color plates of historical decks.

* **ANONYMOUS.** "Antique Playing Cards and Card Games." *Antiques & Auction News* 27, 22 (May 31, 1996): 1, 2. Article on exhibition at the Bruce Museum, Connecticut.

* **ANONYMOUS.** "Bei Neuesten Licht Besehen." *Frauen und Film* 41 (December 1986): 84–89. In German: "Seeing in a New Light." German film critics speak about the representation of men in German cinema, especially the films *Tarot* and *Männer.*

* **ANONYMOUS.** "Businessman Finds His Fortune." *Playthings Magazine* (November 1970). On the launch of U.S. Games Systems' tarot products.

* **ANONYMOUS.** "Cards on the Table: The Sola-Busca Tarot Cards." *FMR* 90 (February/March 1998): 107–128.

* **ANONYMOUS.** *The Complete Book of the Tarot for Mastering Practical Use: The Theory of Macrocosmos and Microcosmos.* Japan: Kokusho, 2000. Ill. 385 pp. (cloth) 23 cm. In Japanese. Illustrated with the Rider-Waite Tarot.

* **ANONYMOUS.** "Dancing Figures with Tarot Cards." *Art News* 5, 100 (May 2001): 16.

ANONYMOUS. *Der Daumenlange Hansel mit dem Ellenlangen Barte: Erzahl oder Vorlesebuch.* Austria: Bibliothek der Provinz, 1989. 112 pp. A children's story with tipped-in reproductions of an animal tarot by Gobi, made in Linz, in 1716. Packaged with the deck as well.

* **ANONYMOUS.** "Domenico Balbi." *Le Arti* 6, 22 (June 1972): 192–193.

* **ANONYMOUS.** *The Economist* (May 14, 1994): cover. Cover features four tarot cards.

ANONYMOUS. *Ezekiel's Vision: Tarot of the Magi.* Carrollton, TX: School of Light Publications, 1991. Ill. Instruction book for Tarot of the Magi.

* **ANONYMOUS.** "Gentilini's Tarot Cards." *Graphis* 33.

* **ANONYMOUS.** *El Gran Libro Practico del Tarot.* Barcelona: Editorial De Vecchi, 1998. 202 pp. 25 cm.

* **ANONYMOUS.** *History of Playing Cards in Belgium.* Brussels, circa 1960.

* **ANONYMOUS.** "House of Cards: Niki de Saint-Phalle's Tuscan Fantasy. *Architectural Digest* (1987): 124–131.

* **ANONYMOUS.** "Issy-les-Moulineaux: Musee Francais de la Carte Jouer." *Revue du Louvre et des Musees de France* 47 (October 1997): 31. Article on the reopening of the French museum of playing cards in Issy-les-Moulineaux.

* **ANONYMOUS.** *Juegos de naipes españoles: Guía fácil y rápida.* Vitoria, Spain: Naipes Fournier, 1997. 24th edition. 128 pp. (paper) In Spanish.

ANONYMOUS. *Mongol-Kinai Jóskönyv.* Hungary, circa 1990. Ill. Book on I Ching, with reference to connection with tarot. In Hungarian.

* **ANONYMOUS.** "Naked Tarot." *Entertainment Design* 35, 3 (March 2001): 14–16.

* **ANONYMOUS.** *Niki de Saint Phalle.* Bonn: Kunst und Ausstellungshalle der Bundesrepublik Deutschland, 1992. Ill. 209 pp. (paper) Catalog of an exhibition of photographs of Niki de Saint Phalle's tarot garden.

ANONYMOUS. *The 1988 Encyclopedia of Grand Prediction and Fortune Telling.* Japan, 1988. Ill. 175 pp. In Japanese.

* **ANONYMOUS.** "Play Your Cards!" *Antiques and the Arts Weekly* (January 12, 1996). Article on exhibition at the Bruce Museum, Connecticut.

* **ANONYMOUS.** *Playthings as Art Objects: Playing Cards.* Birmingham, England: Ethnographic Resources for Art Education Project, 1991. One of five booklets on historical, ethnographic, and play traditions of various world cultures. The fourth booklet focuses on history of playing cards, including tarot cards.

* **ANONYMOUS.** *Psychic Powers.* Alexandria, VA: Time-Life Books, 1987. Ill. 160 pp. (hardcover) 28 cm. Includes picture of psychic using

cards from the Tarot of the Cat People.

* **ANONYMOUS.** *Quick & Easy Tarot.* Privately published, circa 1995. Ill. 42 pp. (paper, comb-bound) 22 cm. Basic meanings and spreads.

** **ANONYMOUS.** "A Sampling of Tarot Decks." Survey of decks, dividing them into categories such as Historic, Esoteric, and Classic Readers' Decks. (Pages 187–195, photocopied from an unknown book.)

* **ANONYMOUS.** "Seelenlandschaften des H. Haindl." *Esotera* 11 (November 1989): 61–64. Ill. In German: "H. Haindl's Landscape of the Soul." On the Haindl Tarot, by Hermann Haindl.

* **ANONYMOUS.** *Six Ways of Forecasting.* Donghak Publishing, circa 1999. In Japanese. Includes illustrations of the Rider-Waite Tarot.

* **ANONYMOUS.** *Spielkarten aus aller Welt vom Mittelalter bis zur Gegenwart aus dem Museum der Vereinigten Altenburger und Stralsunder Spielkartenfabriken Leinfelden bei Stuttgart und aus deutschen Sammlungen.* Stuttgart: Staatsgalerie Stuttgart, 1968. Catalog for exhibition that took place September to November 1968, featuring playing cards from Museum der Vereinigten Altenburger und Stralsunder Spielkartenfabriken.

* **ANONYMOUS.** *Tarot.* Barcelona: Oceano Grupo Editorial, 1997. Ill. 96 pp. (hardcover) 26 cm. In Spanish. Part of a four-volume set "Ciencia y Predicción." Illustrated primarily with Fournier's Tarot of Marseilles.

* **ANONYMOUS.** *Tarot.* Munich: arsEdition, 1996. German version of *The Tarot,* published by Thames and Hudson.

* **ANONYMOUS.** *The Tarot.* New York: Thames and Hudson, 1995. Ill. (unpaged) 14 cm. Richly illustrated with a variety of tarot cards, including some interesting antique decks.

* **ANONYMOUS.** *Tarot.* Scotland: Geddes & Grosset, 2000. Ill. 286 pp. (paper) Symbolism of the tarot.

* **ANONYMOUS.** *Tarot Agenda.* Amsterdam: Uitgeverij Schors, 1993 on. Yearly pocket calender illustrated with various tarot decks, for example: 1993: Book of Thoth Tarot, by Aleister Crowley and Frieda Harris. 1995: Hanson-Roberts Tarot, by Mary Hanson-Roberts. 1997: Tarot of the Ages, by Rufus Camphausen. 1999: Tarot of the Cat People, by Karen Kuykendall. 2000: Tarot of the Witches.

* **ANONYMOUS.** *Tarot Cards in Sculpture by Niki de Saint Phalle.* Milan: Giuseppe Ponsio, 1985. Ill. 40 pp.

* **ANONYMOUS.** *Tarot Cue Cards.* Melbourne: Dynamo House, circa 2004. Ill. 6 pp. Small cards, attached with a rivet, giving short meanings for each tarot card. Illustrated with the Rider-Waite Tarot.

* **ANONYMOUS.** *Tarot de Marseille dans votre poche.* Paris: Creation Créatom, circa 2000. (paper) Foldout guide to tarot, with three wheels that give meanings of Major Arcana cards in context of health, money, and love.

ANONYMOUS. *El Tarot: el futuro en las cartas.* Madrid: Ediciones UVE, circa 1980. Ill. 137 pp. 17 cm. In Spanish: *The Tarot: The Future in the Cards.*

ANONYMOUS. *Tarot Lays: Reflective Patterns of the Tarot.* 1980. Reprint. San Francisco: Pomegranate Artbooks, 1993. 31 pp. (paper) Tarot spreads, using the Rider-Waite Tarot.

ANONYMOUS. *Tarot Quinze: Paris-Varsovia.* Esplugas de Llobregat: Ariel, 1975. Ill. 22 pp. 21 cm.

ANONYMOUS. "Tarot Series: Le Magicien." *Beaux Arts Magazine* 197 (October 2000): 163.

* **ANONYMOUS.** *Visions and Prophecies.* Alexandria, VA: Time-Life Books, 1988. Ill. 160 pp. (hardcover) Includes section on tarot.

** **ANONYMOUS.** "Wins by Witchery in London Drawing Rooms." *Brooklyn Daily Eagle* (November 1, 1904). Article on Pamela Colman Smith, "closely related to many prominent families, and her strange career." Includes photos of Smith and reproductions of some of her work.

* **ANONYMOUS.** "Your Romantic Destiny Revealed." *YM* (Young and Modern) (February 1998): 50–51. Article on reading cards includes cards intended to be cut out.

ANPU, Ebony, Lotte Lieb, and Bill Heidrik. "Talking Tarot: A History of The Book of Thoth Tarot Deck." *Magical Blend.* pp. 32–35. Ill.

* **ANTAL**, Jánoska. *Tarokk Album: Kártyakészítes és tarokk-játék a XIX–XX. Századi Magyarországon.* Hungary: Pallas Stúdió, 1998. Ill. 231 pp. (cloth) 32 cm. In Hungarian. Cards illustrated are historical, but seem to be recolored for the book.

ANTHONY, Piers. *Tarot.* New York: Ace Books, 1987. xxiii, 616 pp. (paper) 21 cm. Fantasy novel.

ANTONORSI BLANCO, Marcel. *Los 10 primeros casos de Franklin Quiñones W.: investigador privado y social. Asesor, taxista, tarot (es lo que dice su tarjeta de visita).* Venezuela: Editorial Planeta Venezolana, 1996. Ill. 116 pp. 19 cm.

* **ANTONOWICZ-WLAZINSKA**, Barbara. *Tarot Intuicyjny: Wielkie Arkana Wielkie tajemnice zycia.* Bialystok, Poland: Studio Astropsychologii, 2000. Ill. 311 pp. (hardcover) In Polish. Illustrated with the Rider-Waite Tarot.

* **ANTONS-VOLMERG**, Klaus. "Wandlungen eines Rationalisten." *Gruppendynamik* 20, 4 (November 1989): 381–388. In German: "Conversion of a Rationalist." Personal transformation from working with the esoteric tarot.

ANUPAM, Swami Anand. *Spiel Tarot—Spiel Leben.* Germany: Sannyas Verlag, 1983. Ill. 134 pp.

AOUMIEL (Ann Moura). *Tarot for the Green Witch.* St. Paul, MN: Llewellyn Publications, 2003. Wiccan-style tarot work. Illustrated with Sacred Circle Tarot, Buckland Romani Tarot, Robin Wood Tarot, Nigel Jackson Tarot and Witches Tarot, all decks from Llewellyn.

APA TAROT. Privately published, USA, 1985 ongoing. Ill. Magazine on tarot.

* **APPELBAUM,** Stanley. *The Triumph of Maximilian I.* New York: Dover Publications, 1964. Ill. 140 pp. (paper) 29 cm. Not about tarot, but outstanding examples of "triumphs," these from circa 1512, commissioned by the German Holy Roman Emperor. Many reflect the iconography of the tarot.

* **AQUARIAN PRESS.** *The Fool's Journey.* England: Aquarian Press, 1993. Ill. Fool cards from various tarot decks, most published by Aquarian Press, in the format of bound postcards.

* *AQUARIAN VOICES: A Journal of Arcana Advice for Everyday Living.* 1990 ongoing. Ill. New Age journal, which features articles on tarot.

* *ARCANUM: A Magickal Journal.* New York: Tarot School. A bi-monthly journal, including articles on tarot.

* **ARCARTI,** Kristyna. *Tarot for Beginners.* London: Hodder & Stoughton Educational, 1993. Ill. 84 pp. (paper) 20 cm. Illustrated with the Swiss 1JJ Tarot.

ARIENTI, Vito. *1981 Auguri.* Milan: Editions del Solleone, 1980. Ill. Calendar featuring Gumpenberg Neoclassical Tarot. Issued as limited edition of 500.

* **ARIGOS,** Alba. *El Tarot Profetico de Babilonia.* Argentina: Editorial Kier, 1991. Ill. 160 pp.

* **ARLENEA,** Willow, and Jasmin Lee Cori. *The Tarot of Transformation.* Boston: Weiser Books, 2002. Ill. 139 pp. (paper) 21 cm. Companion book to Tarot of Transformation, illustrated by Arlenea.

ARNOTT, Nancy. *Tarot: It's in the cards!* Kansas City: Andrews and McMeel, 1997. 78 pp. 10 mm. Miniature book on basic tarot.

ARONSON, David. *Il Tarot di Purgatorio.* Privately published, 2001. Ill. 22 pp. (paper) Collages of the Major Arcana.

* **ARRIEN,** Angeles. *Handbuch zum Crowley Tarot.* Germany: Urania Verlag, 1991. Ill. 439 pp. (paper) 20 cm. Translation of *The Tarot Handbook.*

ARRIEN, Angeles. "Tarot: An Esoteric Psychology." *New Realities* 5, 2: 56–58. Self expression in the East and the West, compared and connected with the principles of the tarot.

* **ARRIEN,** Angeles. *The Tarot Handbook: Practical Applications of Ancient Visual Symbols.* Sonoma, CA, 1987. Reprint. New York: Jeremy P. Tarcher/Putnam, 1997. Ill. 320 pp. 28 cm. Illustrated with the Crowley Book of Thoth Tarot. 1997 edition has a new introduction by the author.

* **ARYA,** Rohit. *The Money Tarot Book: Make the Right Decisions to Attract Financial Abundance.* India: Yogi Impressions, 2001. 302 pp. (paper) 22 cm.

* **ASCARI,** A., et al. *Tarocchi: Arte e Magia.* Faenza: Edizioni Le Tarot, 1995. 152 pp. 30 cm. In Italian: *Tarot: Art and Magic.* Revised edition of *Tarrocchi, le carte del destino.* History and symbolism of the tarot, featuring illustrations of historical decks and also paintings that have images similar to tarot.

ASCARI, A., et al. *Tarrocchi, le carte del destino.* Faenza: Edizioni Le Tarot, 1994. 152 pp. 30 cm.

ASECOIN (Association of Spanish Playing Card Collectors). *Naipes Españoles Modernos de la Guerra Civil a Nuestros Dias.* Privately published, Madrid, 1989. Ill. 340 pp. Spanish playing cards from the Spanish Civil War until 1989. Includes tarot decks.

* **ASHCROFT-NOWICKI,** Dolores. *Inner Landscapes: A Journey into Awareness by Pathworking.* England: Aquarian Press, 1990. Ill. 160 pp. Illustrated with Josephine Gill's Servants of the Light Tarot.

* **ASHCROFT-NOWICKI,** Dolores. *The Servants of the Light.* England: Aquarian Press, 1991. Ill. 126 pp. Explanatory book accompanying the Servants of the Light Tarot, by Josephine Gill.

* **ASHCROFT-NOWICKI,** Dolores. *The Shakespearian Tarot.* England: Aquarian Press, 1993. Ill. 156 pp. Book describing the Shakespearian Tarot illustrated by Paul Hardy.

ASHPLANT, Trudy J. *Tarot: Intermediate Handbook.* Privately printed, 2001. 43 pp. (paper) Astrological, elemental, and numerological meanings.

ASSAD, Richard M. *The Archetypal Symbology of the Tarot, Meditation, and Psychological Change.* Dissertation, Boston University, 1984.

* *ATA NEWSLETTER, The.* Newsletter of the American Tarot Association. Formerly called *The Spread.*

ATKINSON, Belinda. *Tarot of the Soul.* Newberg, OR: Swan-Raven & Co., 1995. Ill. 80 pp. 21 cm.

AUDOIN, P. "Ambassadors of the Hermetic Tradition: The Genealogy of New Images." *XXe Siecle* 46 (June 1977): 54–65.

* **AUGER,** Emily E. *Tarot and Other Meditation Decks: History, Theory, Aesthetics, Typology.* Jefferson, NC & London: McFarland & Company, 2004. Ill. 214 pp. (paper) 25 cm. Scholarly look at tarot, concentrating on aesthetics and cultural references. Auger classifies tarot decks as Annotative (drawn largely from the Rider-Waite Tarot) and Discursive (departing from the Rider-Waite Tarot). Book also includes Meditative type decks (non tarot).

* **AUTRIVE,** Valérie. *Votre Avenir en 78 Lames.* Paris: Librarie de l'Inconnu, 2002. Ill. 240 pp. (paper) 24 cm.

AVENI, Anthony. *Behind the Crystal Ball: Magic, Science, and the Occult from Antiquity through the New Age.* New York: Random House, 1996. 406 pp. (paper) Brief mention of tarot.

AVIRAZ, Zeev. *Ha-Orakl ha-meshulash.* Tel-Aviv: Zéev Aviraz, 1995. Ill. 187 pp. 22 cm. In Hebrew: *Oracle of the Triad.*

* **AVIRAZ,** Zéez. *Hermetic Tarot.* 1994. 347 pp. (hardcover) 22 cm. In Hebrew.

* **AVIZA,** Edward A. *Thinking Tarot: Be Your Own Reader and Adviser.* New York: Fireside, 1997. Ill. 217 pp. (paper) 24 cm. Includes a CD-ROM for tarot spreads. (Copy in author's collection is advance proof.)

B

BACCHIAZ, Diana. *I Tarocchi di Pier Canosa.* Italy: Guido Tamoni Editore, 1990. Ill. 134 pp. Book accompanying deck illustrated by Pier Canosa. Limited edition of 1078.

* **BACHMANN,** Yvonne, and Christa Dettwiler. *Tarot-Karten als Lebenspfad.* Düsseldorf: Patmos Verlag, 2004. Ill. 239 pp. 21 cm. Reprint of *Tarot: Stufen der Selbsterfahrung in Bildern.*

BACHMANN, Yvonne, and Christa Dettwiler. *Tarot: Stufen der Selbsterfahrung in Bildern.* Zürich: Walter, 1997. Ill. 239 pp. 21 cm. In German: *Tarot: Steps of the Self-journey in Pictures.*

BALDERRAMA, David. *Tarot poemático.* Culiacán: Dirección de Investigación y Fomento de Cultura Regional, 2000. 82 pp. 21 cm. In Spanish.

BALDWIN, Margaret. *Fortune Telling.* New York: J. Messner, 1984. Ill. 96 pp. 23 cm. Discusses fortune-telling through the use of tarot cards, crystal balls, palm reading, and tea leaves.

* **BANZHAF,** Hajo. *Aprenda a Consultar el Tarot: Método práctico con la baraja Rider.* Madrid: Editorial Edaf, 1992. 190 pp. (paper) 26 cm. Spanish-language edition of *Das Arbeitsbuch zum Tarot.*

BANZHAF, Hajo. *Das Arbeitsbuch zum Tarot.* Munich: Diederichs, 1988. Ill. 187 pp. Reprint. Germany: Heinrich Hugendubel Verlag, 2003.

* **BANZHAF,** Hajo. *The Crowley Tarot Handbook.* Stamford, CT: U.S. Games Systems, 1995. Ill. (paper)

BANZHAF, Hajo. *Das Geheimnis der Hohenpriesterin.* Germany: Heinrich Hugendubel, 1989. Ill. 62 pp. In German: *The Secret of the High Priestess.* Includes posters with spreads and a Rider-Waite Tarot deck.

* **BANZHAF,** Hajo. *Las Llaves del Tarot.* Madrid: Editorial Edaf, 1998. 294 pp. (paper) 22 cm. Spanish-language edition of *Schlüsselworte zum Tarot.*

* **BANZHAF,** Hajo. *Schlusselworte zum Tarot.* Munich: Goldmann Verlag, 1990. Ill. 214 pp. Reprint. Germany: Orbis Verlag, 1992. In German: *Keywords to the Tarot.* Illustrated with the Rider-Waite Tarot.

* **BANZHOF,** Bajo, and Elisa Hemmerlein. *Tarot als Wegbegleiter: Der Zuverlässige Ratbeger für den Nächsten Schritt.* Munich: Heinrich Hugendubel Verlag, 1993. Ill. 213 pp. (hardcover) 22 cm. In German. Illustrated with the Rider-Waite Tarot and the Book of Thoth Tarot.

* **BANZHAF,** Hajo. *Tarot and the Journey of the Hero.* York Beach, ME: Samuel Weiser, 2000. Ill. xi, 236 pp. (paper) 26 cm. Translation of *Tarot und die Reise des Helden.*

* **BANZHAF,** Hajo. *The Tarot Handbook.* Stamford, CT: U.S. Games Systems, 1993. 184 pp. Ill. 26 cm. Translation of *Tarot Handbuch.*

* **BANZHAF,** Hajo. *Tarot und die Reise des Helden.* Munich: Heinrich Hugendubel Verlag, 1997. Ill. 174 pp. (paper) 26 cm. The Major Arcana as illustrations of the phases, characters, and events in the archetypal journey of the hero. Illustrated with the Rider-Waite Tarot.

* **BANZHAF,** Hajo. *El Tarot y el Viaje del Héroe.* Madrid: Editorial Edaf,

2001. 252 pp. (paper) 26 cm. Spanish-language edition of *Tarot und die Reise des Helden.*

* **BANZHAF,** Hajo. *Das Tarotbuch.* Munich: Wilhelm Goldmann Verlag, 2001. Ill. 208 pp. (hardcover) 27 cm. Meanings of the cards in various positions in a spread. Illustrated with the Rider-Waite Tarot.

BANZHAF, Hajo, and Irene Dalikow. "Tarot und Kabbalah." *Esotera* (circa 1990). Ill. Articles, including an interview with Mario Montana.

* **BANZHAF,** Hajo, and Elisa Hemmerlein. *Guía de los Tarots: Rider, Crowley y Marsella.* Madrid: Editorial Edaf, 1990. 200 pp. (paper) 21 cm. Spanish-language edition of *Tarot as Your Companion.*

* **BANZHAF,** Hajo, and Elisa Hemmerlein. *Tarot as Your Companion: A Practical Guide to the Rider-Waite and Crowley Tarot Decks: The Reliable Adviser for the Next Step.* Stamford, CT: U.S. Games Systems, 1999. (paper) Translation of *Tarot als Wegbegleiter.*

BANZHAF, Hajo, and Brigitte Theler. *Key Words for the Crowley Tarot.* York Beach, ME: Weiser Books, 2001. Ill. vi, 244 pp. 21 cm. (paper) Translation of *Schlüsselworte zum Crowley-Tarot.*

* **BARGELLINI,** Ovidio. *Il Giuoco Pratico o sieno Capitoli Diversi.* Bologna, 1760.

BARNWELL, John. *The Arcana of Light on the Path.* Bloomfield Hills, MI: Verticordia Press, 2000. Ill. 200 pp. (paper) Spiritual lessons from the tarot. Includes forty-two Grail diagrams.

* **BARRETT,** Clive. *The Ancient Egyptian Tarot.* England: Aquarian Press, 1994. Ill. 152 pp. Book accompanying the Ancient Egyptian Tarot by Barrett.

* **BARRETT,** Clive. *El Antiguo Tarot Egipcio: Una Obra que Devuelve el Tarot a sus Orígenes.* Madrid: Editorial Edaf, 2003. 190 pp. (paper) 26 cm. Spanish-language edition of *Ancient Egyptian Tarot.*

* **BARRETT,** Clive. *The Norse Tarot: Gods, Sagas and Runes from the Lives of the Vikings.* London: Aquarian Press, 1991. Ill. 160 pp. (paper) 18 cm. Book for the Norse Tarot, by Barrett.

* **BARRETT,** David V. *Tarot.* London, New York: Dorling Kindersley, 1995. Ill. 61 pp. (hardcover) 17 cm. Basic tarot. Illustrated in color with cards from a variety of decks.

BARRETT, David. V. *Tarot: Kennis and Magie.* Holland: Uitgiveriji Bosch & Kenning, 1996. Ill. Translation of *Tarot* into Dutch.

BARROETA, Maria B. "'El Ermitano del reloj': Simbologia y misterio." *Cifra Nueva* 3–4 (Oct 1996): 149–169.

BARRY'S GIFT. Francis Xavier, director. 1999. Film of a psychic and tarot reader turned resurrection man, literally. The action starts when his efforts to exploit his talent and his clients backfire.

* **BARTLETT,** Sarah. *The Love Tarot: Use the Power of the Mystic Deck to Guide You in Love, Romance, and Sex.* Boston: Bulfinch Press, 1995. 96 pp. (hardcover) 14 cm. Book accompanying Love Tarot illustrated by Nancy Tolford.

BASILIDE, T. *Le Symbolisme du Tarot.* Paris: Chacornac Freres, 1942. Ill. 53 pp.

BASTA, Sp. M. *Anviisning til at spille l'hombre, whist, boston og tarock.* Copenhagen: H. C. Klein, 1846. Description of games of ombre, whist and tarot.

* **BATHON,** Ute. *Das Neue Tarot-Buch.* Dorfen, Germany: Kompetenz Verlag, 1995. Ill. 240 pp. (hc) 21 cm. Illustrated with the Motherpeace Tarot.

BATTEY, Rev. Don. *Adventure into Other Dimensions: A Practical Guide to Developing Psychic Ability and Becoming a Reader.* Virginia: Educational Programs, 1990. Ill. 180 pp.

BAUER, Erich. *Psycho Tarot: Das Erlebnis-Programm zur Arbeit mit den psychologischen Bedeutungen der Tarot-karten.* Germany: Heyne Verlag, 1991. Ill. 252 pp. Working with the psychological meanings of the tarot. Illustrated with tarot designs by Linde Famira (see *The Encyclopedia of Tarot,* volume III.)

* **BAUM,** Marlene. "Meine Arbeit ist Autobiographisch: Zur Symbolik in Werk und Vita von Niki de Saint Phalle." *Bruckmanns Pantheon* 50 (1992): 161–167.

BAXTER, Aza. *Sense Dominance Tarot Workbook.* Longview, WA: Intuitive Psychology Press, 1995. 79 pp. (paper, comb-bound) The Major Arcana as steps in a spiritual journey.

BAYARD, Jean Pierre. *La Pratique du Tarot: Symbolisme, Tirages,*

Interprétations. St-Jean-de-Braye, France: Editions Dangles, 1987. Ill. 392 pp. 21 cm.

BAYER, William. *Tarot.* Manuscript, 1996. 209 pp. Novel based on tarot.

BAYER, William. *Tarot Literature in New York Public Library and in Harvard Libraries.* Privately published, 1993. Data base search.

* **BEATTIE,** Patricia. *Quester: The Journey of the Brave.* Dorset, UK: Element Books, 1999. Ill. 215 pp. (cloth) 20 cm. Book accompanying the Quester deck, illustrated by Mike Giddens.

BEEBE, John. "A Tarot Reading on the Possibility of Nuclear War." *Psychological Perspectives* 16, 1 (Spring 1986): 97–106.

BEHAEGHEL, Julien. *Le Tarot du Fou.* Brussels: Editions Labor, 1991. Ill. 333 pp. (cloth) Includes illustrations of a tarot by the author.

BEIERHOLM, Helle Agathe. "Tarot: en udviklingsvej." *Nyt aspekt* 5 (September 1989): 12–15. Ill. Article on tarot with references to Rachel Pollack's books.

* **BELAND,** Nicole. "Play Cosmo's Love Tarot and Learn Your Romantic Destiny." *Cosmopolitan* (August 1999): 204.

BELLENGHI, Alessandro. *Cartomancy.* London: Ebury Press, 1988. Ill. 158 pp. (cloth) Translation from Italian.

BEN `AMI, Tseviyah. *Tarot ve-Kabalah.* Hod ha-Sharon, Israel: Astrolog, 1996. Ill. 208 pp. 22 cm. In Hebrew.

BENARES, Camden. *Common Sense Tarot: The Complete Guide to Tarot Reading.* Van Nuys, CA: Newcastle Publishing, 1992. 171 pp. 21 cm.

BENAVIDES, Rodolfo. *Tarot 0 Baraja Egipcia.* Mexico: Editorial Diana, 1990. Ill. 141 pp. Book accompanying tarot deck by Benavides.

BENDER, Eleanor. "Marge Piercy's Laying Down the Tower: A Feminist Tarot Reading." In *Ways of Knowing: Essays on Marge Piercy,* edited by Sue Walker and Eugenie Hamner. 1991.

BENEDI, J. A. Lopez. *El Tarot al Benedi.* Spain: Case de Horus, 1992. 123 pp. Book accompanying Tarot al Benedi.

* **BENI,** Luisa. *Il Libro dei Tarocchi: La magia dei Tarocchi.* Milan: De Vecchi Editore, 1987. Ill. 188 pp. Emphasis on divinatory meanings. Illustrated with Tarot of Marseilles.

* **BENNETT,** Stella. *The Star that Never Walks Around.* Boston: Red Wheel/Weiser, 2002. Ill. 200 pp. (paper) 15 cm. Book accompanying Star that Never Walks Around deck illustrated by Stella Bennett.

* **BENÖ,** Zsoldos. "Kártyafestök Pesten." *Budapest* (September 1976): 39–41. Illustrated with Hungarian decks, including tarock.

* **BERGEN,** David. "Magic Mirror Tarot." Unpublished manuscript, 1998. Text written to accompany Bergen's Magic Mirror Tarot.

* **BERGES,** John. *Sacred Vessel of the Mysteries: The Great Invocation, Words of Power; Gift of Love.* Northfield, NJ: Planetwork Press, 1997. Ill. 492 pp. (paper) 23 cm. Analysis of Christ-centered prayer, including commentary on tarot cards.

BERND AND MERTZ. *Der Agyptische Tarot: Ein Einweihungsweg.* Germany: Bauer Verlag, 1987. Ill. 217 pp.

* **BERRES,** Janet. *Textbook of the Tarot.* Morton Grove, IL: International Tarot Society, 1990. Ill. 105 pp. (paper) 23 cm. Basic tarot divination. Illustrated with the Rider-Waite Tarot.

BERTI, Giordano, and Andrea Vitali. *Le Carte di Corte. I Tarocchi Gioco e Magia alia Corte degli Estensi.* Ferrara, Italy: Nuova Alfa Editoriale, 1987. 234 pp. ill. In Italian: *Courtly Cards: Tarot Game and Magic at the Estensi Court.*

* **BERTI,** Giordano, and Antonio Lupatelli. *I Tarocchi degli Gnomi: Favole, giochi e magie del Mondo di Esir.* Turin, Italy: Edizioni Lo Scarabeo, 1990. Ill. 106 pp. (paper) 24 cm. Book describing the Tarot of the Gnomes illustrated by Lupatelli.

* **BERTI,** Geordano, and Tiberio Gonard. *I Tarocchi dei Visconti.* Turin, Italy: Edizioni d'Arte Lo Scarabeo, 1997. Ill. 96 pp. (paper) Book accompanying edition of the Renaissance Visconti Tarot.

BERTI, Giordano. *Il Tarocco Esoterico in Francia.* 1987. Reprint. Faenza, Italy: Associazione Culturale le Tarot, 1989. 32 pp. (paper) Information on Court de Gebelin, Etteilla, Eliphas Levi, Paul Christian, and Papus. In Italian.

* **BERTI,** Giordano, and Antonio Lupatelli. *El Tarot de los Gnomos.* Barcelona: Ediciones Obelisco, 1992. 112 pp. (paper) 28 cm. Fantasy based on the Tarot of the Gnomes, illustrated by Lupatelli.

BETA, Caliph Hymenmus. *A Brief History of the Thoth Tarot.* Los Angeles: O.T.O International, 1988. Ill. Extracts from *The Magical Link* 2–3, 1988. Article on Frieda Harris' work with Aleister Crowley. Letters between them are included. Illustrated with early versions of Book of Thoth Tarot cards.

* **BETTS,** T. A. *Tarot and the Millennium: The Story of Who's on the Cards and Why.* Rancho Palos Verdes, CA: New Perspective Media, 1998. Ill. 383 pp. 22 cm. Historical roots of the iconography of the tarot.

BETZ, Charlie. "The Lord of the Rings Tarot Deck: Not Necessarily Middle-Earth." *Journal of the Tolkien Society* 36 (November 1998): 13–15.

* **BEVILACQUA,** Marguerite. *Cartes et Tarots a la Portée de Tous.* Paris: Editions Trajectoire, 2004. Ill. 184 pp. (paper) 24 cm. Reading tarot and tarock cards.

* **BIAS,** Clifford, ed. *Qabalah, Tarot and the Western Mystery Tradition: The 22 Connecting Paths on the Tree of Life.* York Beach, ME: Samuel Weiser Books, 1997. Ill. xxiv, 156 pp. 21 cm. Includes rituals based on the Major

Arcana as they relate to the Kabbalah.

BIBLIOTHÈQUE VOLANTE, LA. *Le Tarot.* April 1971. Ill. 55 pp. (paper) Catalogue on an exhibition that took place in Paris.

BIEDERMANN, Klaus D. *Tarot: Ihr innerer Spiegel—Lebenshilfe aus dem Unbewussten.* Wiesbaden, Germany: Dr. Werner Jopp Verlag, 1989. Ill. 172 pp.

BIEHL, Kathy. "Re-envisioning the Tarot." *Rubberstampmadness* 21, 109: 54–50. Review of the Artists's Inner Vision Tarot, a mail-art tarot coordinated by Stephanie King.

BIRD, Isobel. *What the Cards Said.* New York: Avon Books, 2001. 234 pp. 18 cm. Novel for young adults, featuring witchcraft and the tarot.

BIRVEN, Henri Clemens. *Der tarot.* Gelnhausen-Gettenbach, Germany: H. Schwab, 1960. Ill. 79 pp. 21 cm.

BLACKMORE, Susan. *The Adventures of a Parapsychologist.* Buffalo, NY: Prometheus Books, 1986. 249 pp. (cloth) Includes chapter on ESP experiments using tarot cards.

** **BLACKMORE,** Susan J. "Divination with Tarot Cards: An Empirical Study." *Journal of the Society for Psychical Research,* 52: 97–101. Study of ten university students, concluding that no paranormal activity by tarot cards or tarot reader was necessary for students to accept validity of readings. (The ten students surveyed accepted general readings uncritically.)

* **BLACKMORE,** Susan. *In Search of the Light: Adventures of a Parapsychologist.* Amherst, NY: Prometheus Books, 1996. (paper) Updated edition of *The Adventures of a Parapsychologist.*

* **BLAKSTAR,** Alexander. *Beyond Witchcraft: The Tigers-Eye and the Way of the Yin.* Danbury, CT: Blakstar Press, 1993. 66 pp. Ill. (comb-bound) Neo-pagan magic. Includes an illustration of the Magician from Crowley's Book of Thoth Tarot.

BLANK, William. *Torah, Tarot and Tantra: A Guide to Jewish Spiritual Growth.* Boston, London: Coventure, 1991. 235 pp.

BLASER, Robin, and John Granger. "A Plan for a Book on Tarot." *Boundary* 6 (1977): 25–29.

BLEAKLEY, Alan. *Earth's Embrace: Facing the Shadow of the New Age.* Bath, England: Gateway Books, 1989. Critique of New Age therapies and call for recognizing the "shadow side" of our psyches.

* **BLOXSOM,** Daniel. *Book of Formation Cards (Sepher Yetzirah).* Privately published, California, 1953/1971. Ill. 75 pp. Includes a set of color photocopied triangular cards, mixing tarot and kabbalistic traditions.

BOAK, Gerald. *Weissagebuch der Taromantie: Die Neue Methode der Zukunftsdeutung.* Germany: Econ Taschen Buch, 1987. Ill. 166 pp.

BOCCONI, Andrea. *Il Matto e il Mondo: Il Simbolismo dei Tarocchi nel Processo di Transformazione della Personalità in Chiave Psicosintetica: Con Specifici Esercizi Psicologici per Ogni Arcano Maggiore.* Rome: Nomina, 2001. Ill. 219 pp. 21 cm. In Italian: *The Fool and the World: The Symbolism of Tarot in the Transformative Process of the Personality...*

* **BOHNENKAMP,** Axel. *Tarot for Partners.* Freiburg, Germany: Bauer Verlag, 1989. Ill. 175 pp. Tarot for partners, with special spreads.

BOHNING, Gabriele. "Seelenlandschaften des H. Haindl: Das Werk des Maiers und Visionars Hermann Haindl: 'Symbole der Wandlung.'" *Esotera* (November 1989): 60–64. Ill. In German. Article on Hermann Haindl and his tarot deck.

BONIFACY, Pierre. *Les vingt-deux portes du château d'Emeraude: 22 méditations sur les arcanes majeures du tarot; suivi de Dédale et Icare.* Troyes, France: Librairie Bleue, 1991. 59 pp. 21 cm.

* **BONNER,** John, and Susan Jameson. *Via Tarot: The Path of Life.* Neuhausen, Switzerland: Urania Verlag AG Müller, 2002. Ill. 166 pp. (paper) 18 cm. Book accompanying the Via Tarot illustrated by Susan Jameson.

* **BORECKY,** Vladimir. *Imaginace a Kultura.* Prague: Univerzita Karlova, 1996. 144 pp. (paper) 20 pp. Has a picture of the Magician on the cover, and includes reference to tarot.

BOUCHET, Gervais. *Le tarot égyptien, ses symboles, ses nombres, son alphabet.* Vichy: Bouchet-Dreyfus, 1922. Ill. 26 cm. On the Etteilla Tarot.

BOUGEAREL, Alain-Jacques. *Origines et histoire du Tarot: Le Tarot médiéval; Eléments de tarologie.* Toulouse, France: Editions Envol, 1997. Ill. 150 pp. (paper) In French: *Origins and History of the Tarot: The Medieval Tarot; Elements of Tarology.*

* **BOULTER,** Carment. *Angels and Archetypes.* Rapid City, SD: Swan Raven Co., 1997. Ill. 282 pp. 22 cm. (paper) Feminine archetypes, with correlations to tarot cards.

* **BOWES,** Susan. *Life Magic: The Power of Positive Witchcraft.* New York: Simon and Schuster, 1999. Ill. 176 pp. (cloth) 21 cm. Richly illustrated and eclectic survey of sacred and occult symbolism, including a brief, basic description of tarot, illustrated with the 1JJ Swiss Tarot deck.

BRADEN, Nina Lee. *Tarot for Self Discovery.* St. Paul, MN: Llewellyn Publications, 2002. xii, 152 pp. 23 cm. Introduction by Mary K. Greer.

* **BRAFF,** Phyllis. "Nanas, Guns and Gardens." *Art in America* 80, 12 (December 1992): 102–107. Article on sculptor Niki de Saint Phalle.

* **BRAUN,** Franz. *Schriftenreihe "Spielkarten."* Privately published, 1988 ongoing. Ill. (paper) 30 cm. Playing cards in Germany. Multiple volumes.

* **BREGOLI-RUSSO,** Mauda. "I Tarocchi nel Rinascimento Italiano."

Letteratura Italiana e Arti Figurative: Atti del XII Convegno dell'Associazione Internazionale per gli Studi di Lingua e Letteratura Italiana. Firenze: L.S. Olschki, 1988. In Italian: "The Tarot in Renaissance Italy."

BRÊTHE, Alain. *L'Interpretations dynamique du tarot: Tous les assemblages des Arcane Majeurs.* Paris: Alain Brêthe, 1995. 413 pp. (paper) In French. Interpretations of over 450 pairs of Major Arcana.

BRÊTHE, Alain. *L'Interpretation humaniste du tarot: Les Arcane Majeurs.* Paris: Alain Brêthe, 1996. 306 pp. (paper) In French. Spiritual, professional, and alchemical meanings for the Major Arcana cards.

* **BRIDGES,** Carol. *The Medicine Woman Inner Guidebook: A Woman's Guide to Her Unique Powers, Using the Medicine Woman Tarot Deck Created by Carol Bridges.* Revised edition. Stamford, CT: U.S. Games Systems, 1991. Ill. xiv, 239 pp. (paper) 18 cm.

* **BRIER,** Bob. "Parapsychological Principles from Anthropological Studies." *Parapsychology Review* 5, 1 (January 1974): 3–8. The survival of tarot (and I Ching and astrology) due to the possibility of their validity.

* **BROCHKA,** Kamina, and Charly Samson. *Les Tarots à la Portée de Tous.* Paris: Librairie de l'Inconnu Editions, 2004. Ill. 272 pp. (paper) 22 cm.

BROCKHAUS, Heinrich. "Ein Edles Geduldspiel: Die Leitung der Welt oder die Himmelsleiter 'die sogenannten Tarok Mantegnas vom Jahre 1459–60.'" In *Miscellana di Storia Dell'Arten.* Firenze, Italy: Olschki, 1933. III. pp. 397–416.

** **BROMAGE,** Bernard. "The Tarot." *The Occult Observer,* no. 4 (circa 1950): 269–274. Survey of tarot. Includes some interesting observations. "In London, at the present day, the set designed by Pamela Colman Smith and published by Messrs. Rider, can be seen for a modest figure and gives the beginner a good idea of the meaning and history of the cards. Lady Harris has quite recently exhibited her own very expressive drawings at Oxford...." Bromage describes the Etteilla deck as "executed in a typical eighteenth century manner—'red-cao' figures, astrological hints and chaste Directoire costumes."

* **BROMER BOOKSELLERS.** *Gleanings for the Devoted Collector: Catalog 98.* Includes German 1850s fortune-telling cards.

* **BROWN,** Eric. *The Pocket Guide to Tarot.* Australia: Si-Kik, 1998. Ill. 128 pp. (paper) 13 cm. Basic tarot interpretations; illustrated with the Rider-Waite Tarot.

* **BROWN,** Steven. *The Everlasting: Book of the Unliving.* LaGrange, GA: Visionary Entertainment Studio, 1997. Ill. 316 pp. (paper) 28 cm. Guide to a role-playing game. Includes short section on tarot "for added atmosphere and built-in props."

* **BROZZI,** Abel Raúl. *El Arte del Leer el Tarot.* Buenos Aires: Editorial Siete Llaves, 2000. 95 pp. (paper) 20 cm. In Spanish: *The Art of Reading the Tarot.*

* **BRZESC-COLONGES,** Régine. *Le Clefs du Tarot de Wirth.* Paris: Yves Peynet Editions, 2003. Ill. 186 pp. (paper) 25 cm. In French: *Keys to the Wirth Tarot.*

* **BRZESC-COLONGES,** Régine. *Le Tarot: Science de L'Etre.* Corcelles-le-Jorat, Switzerland: Yva Peyret Editeur, 1991. 207 pp. Symbolism of the tarot, based on the Oswald Wirth Tarot. In French. (Copy in author's collection is an unpaginated editorial proof.)

BUCHELT, Lisabeth C. "Alchemical and Tarot Imagery in Yeat's Later Plays: The Resurrection and a Full Moon in March." *Studies in Hermeticism* 16, no. 1 (Spring 1997): 1–9.

* **BUCKLAND,** Raymond. *The Buckland Romani Tarot: The Gypsy Book of Wisdom.* St. Paul, MN: Llewellyn Publications, 2001. Ill. 239 pp. 21 cm. (paper) Book accompanying the Buckland Romani Tarot illustrated by Lissanne Lake.

* **BUCKLAND,** Raymond. *Complete Book of Witchcraft.* Revised and expanded edition. St. Paul, MN: Llewellyn Publications, 1986. Ill. 348 pp. (paper) 28 cm. Witchcraft as a series of lesson, including a lesson on divination, illustrated with the Rider-Waite Tarot.

BUCKLAND, Raymond. *Gypsy Fortune Telling and Tarot Reading.* 2nd ed. St. Paul, MN: Llewellyn Publications, 1998. Ill. xiv, 222 pp. (paper) 21 cm.

BUCKLAND, Raymond. *Secrets of Gypsy Fortunetelling.* St. Paul, MN: Llewellyn Publications, 1996. Ill. xiii, 219 pp. (paper) 18 cm.

BUESS, Lynn M. *The Tarot and Transformation.* Lakemont, GA: Tarnhelm Press, 1973. Ill. 256 pp.

* **BÜHLER,** Weiss. *Clave del Tarot Verdadero.* Buenos Aires: Editorial CAYMI, 1991. 96 pp. (paper) 19 cm. In Spanish. Basic Tarot.

* **BUNKER,** Dusty. *The Two-Timing Corpse: The Number Mysteries.* San Jose: Mystery and Suspense Press, 2002. Ill. 235 pp. 22 cm. Murder mystery in which a tarot card layout gives the clues. Includes an illustration of a Rider-Waite spread.

* **BUNNING,** Joan. *Curso Prático de Tarot.* Barcelona: Ediciones Urano, 2000. Ill. 367 pp. (paper) 23 cm. Spanish edition of *Learning the Tarot.*

* **BUNNING,** Joan. *Learning Tarot Reversals: A Tarot Book for Beginners.* York Beach, ME: Weiser Books, 2003. Ill. x, 173 pp. (paper) 23 cm. Reading reversed tarot cards. Illustrated with the Universal Waite Tarot.

BURCH, Kathleen. *Indicia: A Romance.* Santa Fe, NM: Burning Books,

1990. 60 pp. Introduction to games, tarot, and divination.

* **BURGER**, Evelin, and Johannes Fiebig. *Complete Book of Tarot Spreads.* New York: Sterling, 1997. Ill. 176 pp. 23 cm. Translation of *Tarot Praxis.*

* **BURGER**, Evelin, and Johannes Fiebig. *De Crowley Tarot: De Weg der Verandering.* Amsterdam: Uitgeverij Schors, 1997. Ill. 238 pp. (paper) 22 cm. Translation into Flemish of *Tarot, Wege der Wandlung.*

* **BÜRGER**, Evelin, and Johannes Fiebig. *Tarot Básico para Principiantes.* Madrid: Eidciones Karma, 2003. 160 pp. (paper) 22 cm. Spanish-language edition of *Tarot für Einsteiger/innen.* Accompanied by a deck of pocket-sized Rider-Waite cards.

* **BURGER**, Evelin, and Johannes Fiebig. *Tarot Basics.* New York: Sterling, 1997. Ill. 128 p. 23 cm. Translation of *Tarot für Einsteiger.*

  BURGER, Evelin, and Johannes Fiebig. *Tarot: Spiegel deiner Möglichkeiten.* Bonn, Germany: Verlag Kleine Schritte, 1984. Ill. In German: *Tarot: Mirror of Your Possibilities.*

* **BURGER**, Evelin, and Johannes Fiebig. *Tarot voor Beginners.* Amsterdam: Uitgeverij Schors, 1995. Ill. 137 pp. (paper) 22 cm. Translation into Flemish of *Tarot für Einsteigerinnen.*

* **BURGER**, Evelin, and Johannes Fiebig. *Tarot: Wege des Glücks.* Germany: Königsfort, 1996. Ill. 236 pp. (paper) 20 cm. Interpretation of the Rider-Waite Tarot.

* **BURGER**, Evelin, and Johannes Fiebig. *Tarot: Wege der Wandlung.* Germany: Königsfort, 1996. Ill. 236 pp. (paper) 20 cm. Interpretation of Crowley's Book of Thoth Tarot.

  BURGHARDT, Marlies. "Landkarten für den Lebensraum." *Esotera* 3 (1995): 86–91. Illustrated article on tarot connected to the Kabbalistic Tree of Life.

  BURGOYNE, T .H. *The Tarot.* 1983. Reprint. Ontario: John Ballantrae, circa 1989. Reprint of a series of articles that appeared in *The Platonist.*

* **BURNHAM**, J. "Huebler's Pinwheel and the Letter Tau." *Arts Magazine* 49, 2 (October 1974): 32–35.

  BURNS, Jane, and Dale Gottlieb. *Wise Gal Tarot: Amazing Ways to Read Your Fortune!* New York: Crown Publishers, 2000. Ill. 61 pp. 23 cm. (paper)

  BURNS, Jerry. *The Way: A Trip in Tao-Tarot Time.* San Francisco, CA: Goliards Press, 1968. 25 pp. 23 cm.

* **BURYN**, Ed. "Notes for the William Blake Tarot." USA: Tools and Rites of Transformation, 1995. 25 pp. Detailed list of Blake's works used for the creation of Buryn's Blake Tarot deck.

* **BURYN**, Ed. *The William Blake Tarot of the Creative Imagination.* San Francisco: HarperSanFrancisco, 1995. Ill. vii, 160 pp. 18 cm. Book accompanying the Blake Tarot, created by Ed Buryn, based on the works of William Blake.

  BYARS, Betsy Cromer. *Tarot Says Beware.* New York: Viking, 1995. vi, 151 pp. 22 cm. Mystery novel in which Herculeah Jones and her bumbling pal, Meat, investigate the murder of a palm reader.

C

* **CALVINO**, Italo. *Tarots: The Visconti Pack in Bergamo and New York.* New York: Rizzoli International, 1976. Ill.

  CAMP, John. *The Empress File.* New York: Henry Holt and Company, 1991. 231 pp. (cloth) Mystery that includes tarot readings.

  CAMP, John. *The Fool's Run.* New York: Henry Holt and Company, 1989. 254 pp. (cloth) Mystery that includes tarot readings.

* **CAMPHAUSEN**, Rufus C. *Spiegel des Lebens: Tarot und Kabbala.* Basel: Sphinx Pocket, 1983. 125 pp. ill. (paper) In German: *Mirror of Life: Tarot and Kabbalah.*

  CANDUCCI, Monica. *Gli Arcani Della Soglia* Genova, Italy: Edizioni Culturali Internazionali Genova, 1988. Ill. 183 pp. According to K. Frank Jensen: "An unusual Major Arcana set accompanies this book."

  CANO, José Luis. *Tarot Cano: Zaragoza, Museo Camón Aznar Ibercaja, del 17 de octubre al 16 de diciembre de 2001.* Zaragoza: Obra Social y Cultural de Ibercaja, 2001. Ill. 58 pp. 28 cm.

  CANOVA, Patricia. *Tarot Sutra: An Intimate Guide to Exploring Sex through the Tarot.* New York: Dorling Kindersley, 2000. Ill. 128 pp. 17 cm.

Includes a seventy-eight-card tarot deck in a kit.

  CANSELIET, Eugene. *Le Realisme Symbolique de MICHEL DESIMON. La Femme et L'Oeuf philosophical en Alchimie.* Paris: Editions du Cygne, 1979. Ill. 120 pp. According to K. Frank Jensen: "Desimon is a French philosopher and painter whose esoteric imagery is stunning. Eroticism plays an important role in his artistic universe. The art includes tarot imagery."

* **CANTIN**, Candis, and Michael Tierra. *The Spirit of Herbs: A Guide to the Herbal Tarot.* Stamford, CT: U.S. Games Systems, 1993. Ill. 222 pp. 18 cm. Book accompanying the Herbal Tarot illustrated by Candis Cantin.

* **CAPITANI**, Mauro. *Tarocchi: I 22 Trionfi di Mauro Capitano.* Sienna, Italy: Monte dei Paschi di Siena, 1998. Ill. 63 pp. (paper) In Italian. Booklet accompanying the author's deck.

  CAROLL, Amy Elaine. *The Angelic Tarot: Invocational Prayer of The Starward Path.* Carmel, CA: Starfire Publications, 1982. Ill. 95 pp. Book accompanying Caroll's Angelic Tarot.

  CAROLL, Amy Elaine. *The Starward Path.* Carmel, CA: Starfire Publications, 1982. Ill. 95 pp. Book accompanying Caroll's Angelic Tarot.

* **CARTOPHILIA HELVETICA.** Ongoing series of bulletins for card collectors. The March 2000 edition includes an article on U.S. Games Systems.

* **CARTORAMA.** Catalog of antiquarian cards, including tarot and tarock. Ill. (paper)

  CARUSO, Luciano. *Gli Arcana Maggiori: 22 Tarocchi.* Livorno, Italy: Belforte Editore Libraio, 1993. Ill. 27 pp. (paper) Color illustrations of Caruso's abstract Major Arcana. In Italian.

  CASE, Paul Foster. *The Book of Tokens. Tarot Meditation.* Los Angeles: Builders of the Adytum, 1989. Ill. 200 pp. Fourteenth edition is the first that has colored illustrations of the BOTA tarot deck.

  CASE, Paul Foster. *The Oracle of Tarot in Qabalah: Authorized Religious Practices and Teachings of B.O.T.A., Based upon the Holy Qabalah and Tarot.* Los Angeles, Builders of the Adytum, 1969. Ill. 29 cm. Completely revised and enlarged edition.

  CASE, Paul Foster. *Schlössel zur Ewigen Weisheit des Tarot.* Switzerland: Urania Verlag, 1992. Ill. 196 pp. First German edition of Case's *Key to the Wisdom of the Ages.*

  CASE, Paul Foster. *The Tarot: A Key to the Wisdom of the Ages.* Los Angeles: Builders of the Adytum, Temple of Tarot and Holy Qabalah, 1990. Ill. 223 pp. 22 cm. First revised edition.

  CASE, Paul Foster. *Tarot Fundamentals.* 1936.

  CASTANIÉ, Gérard. *Et in Arcadia ego: Le tarot du hautboïste: 22 pièces pour hautbois solo.* Paris: Leduc, 1990. Twenty-two pieces of music composed for oboe.

  CAUWET, Thierry. *Les fonctions du repentir.* France: Editions Al Dante, 1997. Ill. 59 pp. (paper) Process used by the author to create tarot cards.

  CAVENDISH, Richard. *The Tarot.* London: M. Joseph, 1975. Reprint. New York: Crescent Books, 1986. Ill. 191 pp. 29 cm.

* **CELEBRATING THE TAROT: A NEWSLETTER FOR TAROT ENTHUSIASTS.** Quarterly dedicated to tarot. From Arlington, Virginia.

* **CHAPNICK**, Debbie. *Tarot Tip Sheet.* New York: Datura Press, 2000. Ill. 4 pp. (paper) Fold-out giving basic meanings of the tarot cards, and a few spreads. Illustrated with the Rider-Waite Tarot.

  CHEVALIER, Pierre. *Tarot: Poetic Revelations and Other Verses.* New York: Writers Club Press, 2000. 200 pp. (paper)

  CHICOREL, Marietta, ed. *Chicorel Index to Parapsychology and Occult Books.* Chicorel Index Series, vol. 24. New York: Chicorel Library Publishing Group. Includes section on tarot.

  CHIH-HSU OU-I. *The Buddhist Tarot.* Boston: Shambhala Publications, 1987. 236 pp. (paper) About the I-Ching, which translator Thomas Cleary calls a "Buddhist tarot."

  CHILDREN OF THE ARCANA. Pearry Reginald Teo, director. 2003. 21 minute video. The protagonist, Gordion, sews into his body six tarot cards made out of human skin. He dies during the ensuing ritual and goes to Purgatory where he meets "The Keeper," who will decide his ultimate fate: heaven or hell—or being The Keeper's "best friend."

* **CHRISTOPHER.** "In My Own Words." *Heart Beat* XIV (Fall 2000): 4–8. Channeled meditations on relationships, including reference to VI The Lovers and an illustration from the Rider-Waite Tarot.

  CICERO, Chic, and Sandra Tabatha Cicero. *The Golden Dawn Journal: Book 1: Divination.* St. Paul, MN: Llewellyn Publications, 1994. Ill. 286 pp. A collection of articles on various divination methods related to the Golden Dawn.

  CICERO, Chic, and Sandra Tabatha Cicero, eds. *The Golden Dawn Journal: Book 2: Quabalah: Theory and Magic* St. Paul, MN: Llewellyn, 1994. Ill. 425 pp. Compilations of articles on Golden Dawn themes.

* **CICERO**, Chic, and Sandra Tabatha Cicero. *The Golden Dawn Magical Tarot: Keys to the Rituals, Symbolism, Magic, and Divination.* St. Paul, MN: Llewellyn Publications, 2000. Ill. 192 pp. Book accompanying the Golden Dawn Magical Tarot.

* **CICERO**, Chic, and Sandra Tabatha Cicero. *The New Golden Dawn Ritual Tarot: Keys to the Rituals, Symbolism, Magic, and Divination.* St. Paul, MN: Llewellyn Publications, 1991. Book accompanying the

Golden Dawn Ritual Tarot (republished in 2000 as Golden Dawn Magical Tarot).

* **CLARSON**, Laura E. *The Cosmic Tarot: Signposts along the Path.* Portland, OR: Visionary Enterprises, 1995. Ill. 144 pp. (paper) 21 cm. Book for Cosmic Tarot, illustrated by Norbert Lösche.

* *CLEAR THE DECKS.* Ongoing. Official newsletter of 52 Plus Joker: The American Antique Deck Collectors Club. Ill. (paper)

CLIFTON, Chas S. "The Unexamined Tarot." *Gnosis* 18, (Winter 1991): 44–51. Ill. Origin of the tarot.

CLOUDS. *The Color of Dark.* Novus, 1989. Sound recording of jazz music, including a piece called Tarot. Clyde Criner, piano and synthesizers, with Clouds ensemble; and vocals by the Darryl Douglas Workshop Company.

COHEN, Richard. *By the Sword.* New York: Random House, 2002. Ill. 519 pp. (cloth) 24 cm. History of fencing. A footnote on pages 28–29 describes connection of the Spanish word *espada,* "sword," to playing cards and tarot. Cohen places the origin of playing cards in China and credits Germans as being the first to mass-produce playing cards, citing Anthony Holden's *Big Deal: One Year as a Professional Poker Player* (New York, 1995).

* **COLBY**, Laura. "In Full Bloom." *ARTnews* 93, 10 (December 1994): 130–133. About Niki de Saint Phalle's Tarot Garden.

COLLINS, Patricia. *Psychic New York: A Guide to Astrologers, Tarot Readers, Psychics, Palmists & Numerologists.* New York: City & Company, 1996. Ill. 143 pp. 18 cm. (paper)

COLQUHOUN, Ithell. "The Taro as Colour." *Sangreal* (1977). The author, who prefers to spell tarot "taro," describes her tarot paintings, which are based on Golden Dawn color values.

COMPTON, Madonna. *Archetypes on the Tree of Life: The Tarot as Pathwork.* St. Paul, MN: Llewellyn, 1991. Ill. xix, 309 pp. 23 cm. The Major Arcana and Kabbalah.

CONFORD, David. "The Tarot Fool in English and American Novels." In *Fools and Jesters in Literature, Art, and History.* Vicki K Janik, ed. 1998. 552 pp.

* **CONNOLLY**, Eileen. *Tarot: The First Handbook for the Master.* Van Nuys, CA: Newcastle Publishing, 1994. Ill. 300 pp. (paper) 25 cm. Advanced tarot studies, building on Connolly's "Handbooks." Illustrated with the Connolly Tarot.

* **CONWAY**, D. J. *A Guide to the Celtic Dragon Tarot.* St. Paul, MN: Llewellyn Publications, 1999. Ill. xv, 218 pp. (paper) 23 cm. Book accompanying the Celtic Dragon Tarot illustrated by Lisa Hunt.

* **CONWAY**, D.J., and Sirona Knight. *Shapeshifter Tarot.* 1998. Reprint. St. Paul, MN: Llewellyn Publications, 2001. Ill. 238 pp. 23 cm. (paper). Book accompanying the Shapeshifter Tarot deck illustrated by Lisa Hunt.

* **COOK**, Catherine, and Dwariko von Sommaruga. *Songs for the Journey Home.* Devonport, Aukland, NZ: Alchemists and Artists, 1993. Ill. Descriptions of the tarot Songs for the Journey Home.

COOKE, John Star. *Community: A Game: Tarot Insights from Three Ages.* Privately published. 34 pp. K. Frank Jensen describes: "Alice Cooke Kent published her brother's game, which includes three different Major Arcana decks. The introduction includes a short biography of John Star Cooke. Includes a deck of tarot cards."

COOKE, John S. *Prophesy of the Royal Maze.* USA: Circa 1975/1994. Video starring John S. Cooke, author of New Tarot for the Aquarian Age.

COOKE, John Star. *The Word of One Tarot Workbook.* Los Angeles: Catalyst Enterprises, 1993. 70 pp. (hardcover) Book accompanying the 1993 edition of Cooke's T: The New Tarot the Aquarian Age. Also includes the Atlantean Tarot and the Medieval Tarot.

* **COOPER**, D. Jason. *The Astral Grail: A Novel Approach to Astral Projection, Tarot, and Qabbalah.* Niceville, FL: Spilled Candy Books, 2002. 198 pp. (paper) Fantasy novel.

* **COOPER**, James. "Tarot Cards." *Eye* (October 1968): 44. Includes tarot centerfold, with Major Arcana arranged as a poster.

COOPER, John Charles. *Throwing the Sticks: Occult Self-Therapy.* Bristol, IN: Wyndham Hall Press, 1985. 121 pp. (paper) Includes section on reading the tarot.

CORTELLESI, Linda. *The User-Friendly Tarot Guidebook.* Worthington: Chalice Moon Publications, 1996.

* **CORTEZ**, Ana, and C.J. Freeman. *The Playing Card Oracles: A Source Book for Divination.* Denver, CO: Two Sisters Press, 2002. Ill. (paper) 21 cm. A father-daughter team created a method of divination based on regular playing cards. Not tarot, but interesting in that Freeman's illustrations of a fifty-two-card deck are like those of a tarot deck.

COWIE, Norma. *Exploring the Patterns of the Tarot.* Canada: N.C. Publishing, 1987. Ill. 246 pp.

CRASE, Sharon N. *Dream Interpretation through the Tarot.* Privately printed, 1979. 14 pp. (paper) Book of Thoth Tarot is used.

CREEKMORE, Betsey. "The Tarot Fortune in 'The Waste Land.'" *ELH* 49, no. 4 (Winter 1982): 908–928.

* **CREMERS**, Filip, ed. *Yvonne Jensen: Heel de Mens: Tarok in Textiel.* Turnhout: National Museum van de Speelkart, 1991. Ill. 37 pp. Catalog

for exhibition of tarot art by Yvonne Jensen.

* **CRESTIN-BILLET**, Frédérique. *La Folie des Cartes à Jouer.* Paris: Flammarion, 2002. Ill. 380 pp. History of playing and divinatory cards, with color illustrations on nearly every page.

* **CRONSTEDT**, Marie Louise. *Levande Symboler.* Denmark: Algiz Förlag, 2002. Ill. 174 pp. (paper) 22 cm. Connects tarot with folk and fairy tales. Illustrated with Rider-Waite Tarot and other examples.

CROWLEY, Aleister (as Master Therion). *The Book of Thoth.* New York: Lancer Books, circa 1975. Ill. 287 pp.

CROWLEY, Aleister. *The Book of Thoth: A Short Essay on the Tarot of the Egyptians, Being the Equinox, Volume III, No. V / by the Master Therion.* London: OTO (Ordo Templi Orientis, 1944. Ill. xii, 287 pp. 26 cm. Limited edition of 200 copies. Originally published in the *Equinox,* Vol. III, no. V. Features tipped in prints of Frieda Harris's artwork. Reprint. New York: Samual Weiser, 1969.

* **CROWLEY**, Aleister. *Das Buch Thoth.* Switzerland: Urania Verlag, 1994. Ill. 278 pp. Ill. Book included a "50 Jahre Crowley Thoth Tarot," a limited edition of Crowley's *Book of Thoth* book and tarot deck, issued fifty years after the first publication. Includes a compact disc with invocations by Crowley and a poster.

* **CROWLEY**, Aleister. *Le Livre du Thoth.* Ill. 263 pp. (paper) 23 cm. Neuhausen, Switzerland: Urania Verlag, 1994. French language edition of *The Book of Thoth.*

CRYSTAL. *The Inner Truth and Wisdom of the Tarot.* Mermaid Press, 1988. Ill. 225 pp. (paper) Includes Major Arcana illustrations by the author, and Minor Arcana from the Rider-Waite Tarot.

CULBERSON, Mary John Cobb. *The Relationship between Transpersonal Symbols.* PhD Thesis, California Institute of Transpersonal Psychology, 1982. Microfilm. Ann Arbor, MI.: University Microfilms International, 1984. Ill. viii, 294 pp.

* **CUNNINGHAM**, Tosca. *Tarot Tutor.* Unpublished manuscript, 1998. 170 pp. (looseleaf bound) Basic card reading, illustrated with the Royal Fez Moroccan Tarot.

CURRIE, Robert. "Eliot and the Tarot." *ELH* 46 (1979): 722–733.

CURTISS, Harriette Augusta, and F. Homer Curtiss. *The Key of Destiny: Sequel to "The Key to the Universe."* New York: E.P. Dutton, 1919. Reprint. 4th ed. San Bernardino, CA: Borgo Press, 1983. Ill. x, 340 pp. 21 cm. Symbolism of numbers.

CURTISS, Harriette Augusta, and F. Homer Curtiss. *The Key to the Universe, or: A Spiritual Interpretation of Numbers and Symbols.* 6th and rev. ed. San Bernardino, CA: Borgo Press, 1983. Ill. 404 pp. 22 cm.

D

* **DACHS**, Monika. "Antonio Cicognara als 'Restaurator': Die Uberarbeitung der Colleoni-Tarocchi aus dem Atelier der Cremoneser Familie Bembo." *Bruckmanns Pantheon* 50 (1992): 175–178.

DAFFI, Marco (Spirit). *Il tarocco secondo la Mensa isiaca e l'I king* Genova: Alkaest, 1980. Ill. 98 pp. 17 cm. In Italian, about tarot and the I Ching.

* **D'AGOSTINO**, Joseph D. *Tarot: The Path to Wisdom.* York Beach, ME: Samuel Weiser, 1994. Ill. x, 117 pp. (paper) 22 cm.

DALI, Salvador. *The Tarot.* Salem, NH: Salem House, 1985.

DALICHOW, Irene. "Am Anfang war die Energie." *Esotera* 8 (1993): 16–21. Ill. Article and interview with Hans-Dieter Leuenberger, who asserts the importance of looking at the underlying energies of tarot cards.

DALICHOW, Irene. "Ein Fest fur meine Ahninnen." *Esotera* (May 1990): 50–53. Ill. Article about Louisa Francia, author of *Hexentarot.*

DALICHOW, Irene. "Eintritts-Karten in die Anderswelt." *Esotera* 5 (1990): 60–64 Ill. Article on Margarete Petersen and her Major Arcana artwork (see *The Encyclopedia of Tarot,* volume III).

DALICHOW, Irene. "Der Schatten Tarot." *Esotera* 12 (December 1992): 22–27. Ill. In German: "The Shadows Tarot." Article on Giger's Baphomet Tarot and Akron's accompanying book. Includes an interview with Akron.

DALICHOW, Irene. "Siegeszug des Tarot: 78 'Geheimnisse' erobem die Herzen." *Esotera* 8 (August 1992): 14–19. Ill. Article on tarot in Germany.

DALICHOW, Irene. "Tarot oder I-Ching: Weisheit Zweier Welten." *Esotera* 5 (May 1994): 40–44. Ill. Interview with Ruth Zehnhausern and Jilrgen vom Scheidt on using tarot and I Ching in therapeutic work.

DALICHOW, Irene. "Wie Frauen Tarot Spielt." *Esotera* 10 (October 1989): 46–50. Ill. In German: "How Women Play Tarot."

* **D'ALLEMAGNE**, Henry René. *Antique Playing Cards: A Pictorial Treasury.* Carol Belanger Grafton, ed. Mineola, NY: Dover Publications, 1996. Ill. 91 pp. (paper) 31 cm. Illustrations from D'Allemagne's *Les Cartes à Jouer.*

D'AMATO-NEFF, Adam Lee. *The Pleidian Tarot: Fundamentals of Divination.* New York, NY: Writers Club Press. 96 pp. (paper) Astrological analysis of the tarot.

* **DAN**, Calin. "Misterele cartii." *Arta* 36, 4 (1989): 16–17. In Romanian: "Mysteries of the Cards."

* **DANIELS**, Kooch N., and Victor Daniels. *Tarot d'Amour: Find Love, Sex, and Romance in the Cards.* York Beach, ME: Red Wheel/Weiser, 2003. Ill.

248 pp. (paper) 23 cm. Illustrated with the Universal Waite Tarot, with an original illustration, by Molly Dickerson, of VI The Lovers on the cover.

* **DANTE.** *Share.* Hollywood, CA: Peyto Books, 1993. Ill. 20 pp. (paper) Includes color illustrations by Dante of fourteen tarot cards.

DAPHINOFF, Dimiter. "Der Narr im Tarot." In *Der Narr: Beiträge zu einem interdisziplinären Gespräch.* Freiburg, Switzerland: Universitätsverlag, 1991. 177 pp. Ill. 23 cm. Papers presented at a seminar held at the Universität Freiburg in 1989, on fools and jesters in art.

* **DARCHE,** Claude. *Pratique du Tarot de Marseille: Spiritualite et Divination.* France: Editions du Rocher, 1994. Ill. 239 pp. (paper) 22 cm. In French: *Using the Tarot of Marseilles for Spirituality and Divination.* Illustrated with Grimaud Tarot of Marseilles.

* **DARRIGOL,** Jean. "Agnés Varda: Les Cartes Buissonières." *Mensuel du Cinéma* 17 (May 1994): 48–52. Director Varda discusses her films and her interest in tarot cards.

DAS, Ram. *Questa,* NM: Seed, circa 1975. Ill. 210 pp. Includes a deck of cards, part of which is a major arcana tarot, plus a huge game board.

DASHIELL, David Cannon. *Invert, Oracle.* San Francisco: Ethan J. Wagner, 1989. Ill. 113 pp. (paper) Exhibition catalog of artist Dashiell's work. Author relates personal experiences of the tarot.

* **DAUBIER,** Jean. *Le Grand Livre des Tirage du Tarot de Marseille.* Paris: Editions Trajectoire, 2003. 256 pp. (paper) 24 cm. In French: *The Big Book of Reading the Tarot of Marseilles.*

DAVIDSON, Leah. "Foresight and Insight: The Art of the Ancient Tarot." *Journal of the American Academy of Psychoanalysis* 29, no. 3 (Fall 2001): 491–501.

DAVIES, Ann. *Meditational Ascent on the Tree of Livingness: Authorized Religious Practices and Teachings of B.O.T.A., Based upon the Holy Qabalah and Tarot.* Los Angeles: Builders of the Adytum, 1975. Ill. 573 pp. 29 cm.

DAVIES, Ann. *Tarot Series.* Los Angeles: Builder of the Adytum, 1980. Eleven sound cassettes (analog, stereo). Presents instruction in reading tarot cards.

* **DAVIS,** David H. *Seven Rays Book Store.* Unpublished manuscript, 1991. An account of the author's founding of his bookstore, Seven Rays (in Syracuse, NY) with the Major Arcana providing "our map for New Age Bookstoreism." For example, Davis interprets the snake biting its tail as "a customer dance, a dance of people that come back at very periodic rates."

DAVIS, Erik. "The Gods of the Funny Books." *Gnosis* 32 (Summer 1994): 12–17. An interview with writers Rachel Pollack and Neil Gaiman, in an issue dealing with pop culture and the esoteric.

* **DAY,** Paula. *Tarot.* Shaftesbury, Dorset, UK; Rockport, MA: Element Books, 1997. Ill. 56 pp. 19 cm. Basic tarot. Illustrated with Swiss 1JJ Tarot and Tarot of Marseilles (versions of decks published by U.S. Games Systems).

THE DAY THE EARTH CAUGHT FIRE. City Boy. New York: Atlantic Records, 1979. Rock and roll recording that includes song "Me and My Tarot."

* **DE AMBROSINI,** Silvia. "Kirin: Arte y arcanos mayores." *Artinf* 23, 103–104 (Autumn 1999): 32. In Spanish: "Kirin: Art and Major Arcana."

* **DE BURGH,** Julian. *The Celtic Tarot: Instruction Book.* New York: St. Martin's Press, 2000. Ill. 175 pp. 22 cm. Book accompanying deck illustrated by Mary Guinan.

* **DE GÜLER,** Maritxu Erlanz. *Tarot: Ciencia o Revlacion?* Spain: Museum of Fine Arts, 1989. Ill. 15 pp. (paper) 28 cm. In Spanish. Catalogue of exhibition of Fournier collection. Illustrated in color with various antique tarot and tarock decks.

DE SURANY, Marguerite. *Medical Graphology.* York Beach, ME: Samuel Weiser, 1991. Ill. 178 pp. (paper) English translation of *Essai de Graphologie Médicale.* Tarot and handwriting analysis. Illustrated with the Oswald Wirth Tarot.

DE VEER, Olenka. *Les Secrets du Tarot Divinatoire.* Paris: Solar/Votre Beaute, 1986. 80 pp. In French.

DE VLEESCHAUWER, Rudy. *Gesprekken met El Sabio: De symboliek van*

de Tarot. Belgium, 1988. Ill. 74 pp. Esoteric tarot. A color plate with sixteen cards is included.

* **DEAN,** Liz. *The Art of Tarot.* London: Cico Books; New York: Barnes & Noble, 2001. (paper and hardcover) Book accompanying deck illustrated by Emma Garner.

* **DEBELLE,** Katherine. *S'Initier Facilement au Tarot de Marseille.* Paris: Editions Trajectoire, 2003. Ill. 250 pp. (paper) 22 cm.

DECKER, Ron. "The Steele Manuscript." *The Journal of the International Playing Card Society* XVII, 3 (February 1989)

* **DECKER,** Ronald, Thierry Depaulis, and Michael Dummett. *A Wicked Pack of Cards: The Origins of the Occult Tarot.* Reprint. New York: St. Martin's Press, 1996. Ill. xii, 308 pp. 24 cm.

* **DEE,** Jonathan. *Tarot: An Easy-to-Follow Illustrated Guide to the Mysteries of the Tarot.* 1996. Reprint. New York: Barnes & Noble Books, 1998. Ill. 64 pp. (cloth) Packaged with a deck illustrated by Shirley Barker.

DEGUY, Michel. "Reponse a l'envoi de Tarot." *Oevres & Critiques* 15, 1 (1990): 45–37.

DEISSING, Gotthold. *Tarot Mysterien Spiel.* Privately published, Germany, 1989. Ill. Board game based on tarot, including a gameboard poster.

* **DELCLOS,** Marie. *Le Grand Livre du Tarot Chinois.* Paris: Editions Trajectoire, 2003. Ill. 208 pp. (paper) 24 cm. In French. Book accompanying Tarot Chinois, by Jean-Louis Victor.

* **DELGADO,** Santiago. *Tarot Murciano.* Spain: Ars Gratia Artis, 1989. Book accompanying Tarot Murciano, illustrated by Ignacio Garcia. Issued in a limited edition of 3000.

* **DELISI,** Elizabeth. *Fatal Fortune.* Jackson, TN: Petals of Life, 1998. Ill. 155 pp. (paper) 22 cm. Mystery novel. Illustrated with cards from the Rider-Waite Tarot.

* **DENICOLA,** Anthony T. A. *Fool's Journey.* 24 pp. (paper) 22 cm. Poems on each of the Major Arcana. Cover illustration is 0 The Fool from the Rider-Waite Tarot.

* **DÉNIZ,** Octavio. *Fundamentos del tarot: adivinación y crecimiento personal.* St. Paul, MN: Llewellyn Español, 2001. xvi, 320 pp. Ill. 24 cm. In Spanish. Illustrated with the Universal Waite Tarot.

* **DENNING,** Melita, and Osborne Phillips. *The Llewellyn Practical Guide to the Magick of the Tarot.* St. Paul, MN: Llewellyn Publications, 1983. xxii, 252 pp. Ill. (paper) 21 cm.

* **DENNING,** Trevor. *The Playing Cards of Spain: A Guide for Historians and Collectors.* Cranbury, NJ: Fairleigh Dickinson Press, 1996. Ill. 183 pp. (cloth) 27 cm.

* **DENNIS,** Regen. *Tarot for Cats.* New York: MacMillan, 1996. Ill. 68 pp. (hardcover) 13 cm. Book accompanying deck illustrated by Kipling West.

* **DEPAULIS,** Thierry. *Tarot, Jeu et Magie.* Paris: Bibliothèque Nationale, 1984. Ill. 152 pp. 24 cm. Catalog of exhibition held at the Galerie Mazarine, October 17, 1984, to January 6, 1985.

* **DEPAULIS,** Thierry. "Tarot: Nouvelles Découvertes à la Bibliothèque Nationale." *Nouvelles de l'Estampe* 80 (May 1985): 4–5. In French: "Tarot: New Discoveries at the Bibliothèque Nationale."

* **DEPLAZES,** C. "Troccas: Das Tarockspiel in Graubuenden." *Schweizerisches Archiv für Volkskunde* 83 (1987): 41–59.

DESAI, Narendra. [*Fortune Telling by 52 Playing Cards*] India, 1980. Ill. In Gurajati. The Jean Chaboseau Tarot and other European decks are used for illustrations.

DESSUART (Le Mage). *La Cartomancie: Devins et Destins.* Paris: Nathan, 1987. Ill. 142 pp. K. Frank Jensen describes the book: "This lavishly illustrated volume is such a rare thing as a book on the history of cartomancy and its practitioners. Several famous and less famous card readers are mentioned, and many card decks are shown, some of them rare ones."

DEVINE, Mary Virginia. *Brujería: A Study of Mexican-American Folk Magic.* St. Paul, MN: Llewellyn Publications, 1982. 239 pp. (paper) 20 cm. Includes a chapter "The Bruja's Tarot."

* **DG DIFFUSION.** *Le Tarot Divinatoires.* Toulouse: DG Diffusion, 1994. Ill. Catalogue of tarot, cartomancy, and playing cards for sale. All decks are illustrated in color.

DH. *The Friendly Tarot.* Privately published, circa 1990. Ill. 68 pp. (paper, comb-bound) Includes black and white cards to punch out and color.

DHÉNIN, Nathalie. *Le Tarot contemporain.* Montreal: Editions Rebis, 1996. 117 pp. (paper) Meanings of two-card combinations. Includes a color set of Major Arcana cards. In French.

DHINGRA, Guneeta. *All You Wanted to Know about Tarot.* New Delhi: New Dawn, 2000. Ill. 176 pp. (paper) Divinatory meanings of tarot cards.

* **DI VINCENZO,** Sofia. *Sola Busca Tarot.* Stamford, CT: U.S. Games Systems, 1998. Ill. 208 pp. (paper) 18 cm. With a preface by Giordano Berti and afterword by Marisa Chiesa.

* **DIASIO,** Daniel. *Treasure of the Tarot: A Modern Day Treasure Hunt.* New York: Vantage Press, 1994. A book with clues as to the location of a diamond, emerald, and gold pendant showing the Fool from the Rider-Waite Tarot. Illustrated with the Rider-Waite Tarot.

DICKERMAN, Alexandra Collins. *Following Your Path: A Self-discovery*

Adventure Journal using Myths, Symbols, and Images. Fair Oaks, CA: New Dimensions, 1989. Ill. xvi, 324 pp. 28 cm. Self-development, using tarot and the Kabbalah.

DICTA and Françoise. *Mythes et Tarots: Le Voyage du Bateleur.* France: Mercure de France, 1991. Ill. 206 pp. (cloth) 22 cm. In French: *Myths and Tarot: The Voyage of the Magician.* Relates each of the Major Arcana to a myth.

DICTA and Françoise. *Tarot de Marseille.* Paris: Mercure de France, 1980. Ill. 188 pp. 22 cm.

* **DIDIER,** Colin. *El Gran Libro Practico del Tarot: 5000 Respuestas Inmediatas a sus preguntas.* Barcelona: Ediciones Martínez Roca, 1991. Ill. 507 pp. (paper) 25 cm. Spanish-language edition of *Le Tarot et votre avenir.*

DIDIER, Yaguel. *Le Jeu Divinatoire.* France: Editions Robert Laffon, 1991. 185 pp. Ill. The book includes a tarot-based cartomancy deck by Marina Karella, which was also published in the magazine *Madame Figaro.*

** **DILLON,** Judith. *A Faerie Tale: Black Sea Goddesses, Magic Alphabets & The Origin of Ogham.* Unpublished manuscript, 1997. 413, xx pp. Includes a few references to tarot cards.

DINKELMANN, Anna. *Tarot: In den Bildern von der anderen Seite Lesen.* Privately published, Bielefeld, Germany, 1982. 115 pp. Ill. In German. Feministic outlook on tarot.

DOANE, Doris Chase. *Blending Astrology, Numerology, and the Tarot.* Tempe, AZ: American Federation of Astrologers, 1997. Ill. xii, 184 pp. 22 cm.

* **DOANE,** Doris Chase. *Secret Symbolism of the Tarot.* Tempe, AZ: American Federation of Astrologers, 1993. 104 pp. (paper) Explanation of Brotherhood of Light Tarot.

DOBBS, John. *The Ninth Hour.* New York: Greenwich Book Publishers, 1960. 270 pp. (cloth) The author puts forth the idea that the Christian bible was derived from the "holy tarot" created in ancient Egypt. A new religious system is proposed, with the tarot as the means of propogation.

* **DOBRATZ,** Gudrun. *The Basic Tarot.* Neuhausen, Switzerland: AGM AGMüller, 1997. (paper) 15 cm. Book accompanying the Basic Tarot, illustrated by Dobratz.

DOCTERS VAN LEUWEN, Onno, and Rob Docters van Leuwen. *De Tarot in de Herstelde Orde.* Holland: Servire Uitgevers, 1995. Ill. 416 pp. Theorizes that the Major Arcana originally had twenty-four cards, including Juno and Jupiter as the missing two.

DOG EARED MAGAZINE: A Journal of Book Arts. Issue Nine: Decks of Cards. Seattle, WA: Turtle Press, 2003. Ill. 46 pp. Includes articles on tarot cards, with illustrations.

* **DOMINGO,** Margarida, and María Krishna Lapuente. *Tarot y numerología tántrica comparados.* Barcelona: Editorial Alas, 2001. 236 pp. 22 cm.

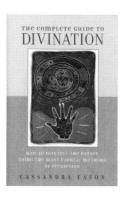

* **DONALDSON,** Terry. *The Dragon Tarot.* Stamford, CT: U.S. Games Systems, 1996. Ill. xi, 178 pp. (paper) 18 cm. Book accompanying the Dragon Tarot illustrated by Peter Pracownik.

* **DONALDSON,** Terry. *The Lord of the Rings Tarot.* Stamford, CT: U.S. Games Systems, 1997. Ill. 268 pp. 18 cm. Book to go with the Lord of the Rings Tarot, illustrated by Peter Pracownik under direction of Terry Donaldson.

* **DONALDSON,** Terry. *Principles of Tarot.* London: Thorsons, 1996. Ill. 170 pp. (paper) 19 cm. Emphasis is on reading the cards.

* **DONALDSON,** Terry. *El Señor de los Anillos Tarot.* Spain: Edaf/La Tabla de Esmerelda, 1999. Ill. 267 pp. 18 cm. (paper) In Spanish: *The Lord of the Rings Tarot.* Goes with the deck illustrated by Peter Pracownik under direction of Donaldson.

* **DONALDSON,** Terry. *Step-by-Step Tarot.* London, San Francisco: Thorsons, 1995. Ill. 215 pp. (paper) 22 cm. Illustrated with the Morgan-Greer Tarot.

* **DONALDSON,** Terry. *The Tarot Spellcaster: Over 40 Spells to Enhance Your Life with the Power of Tarot Magic.* Hauppauge, NY: Barron's, 2001. Ill. 128 pp.

* **DONALDSON,** Terry. *El Tarot y Sus Poderes Magicos.* Madrid: Editorial Edaf, 2001. Ill. 128 pp. (paper) 23 cm. Spanish-language edition of *The Tarot Spellcaster.* Illustrated with the Morgan-Greer Tarot and Grimaud's Tarot of Marseilles.

* **DONELLI,** I. *Les Tarots des Gitans.* Paris: Editions de Vecchi, 2000. Ill. 156 pp. (paper) 16 cm. Book accompanying Tarots des Gitans illustrated by M. Ameli.

DONOVAN, Lawrence. "Donovan's Tarot." *Spirit: A Magazine of Poetry* LI. Poetry and drawings of each of the Major Arcana.

* **DRANE,** John, Ross Clifford, and Philip Johnson. *Beyond Prediction: The Tarot and Your Spirituality.* Oxford: Lion Publishing, 2001. Ill. 135 pp. (paper) Spiritual lessons in the tarot. Illustrated with the Rider-Waite Tarot.

* **DROESBEKE,** Erna. *De Tarot van Isis.* Antwerp: Uitgeverej Parsifal, 1993. Ill. 310 pp. (paper) 23 cm. The illustrations by Droesbeke are not of an actual tarot deck.

DRURY, Nevill. *Inner Visions: Explorations in Magical Consciousness.* 1979. Reprint. London: Arkana/Penguin Books, 1994. Ill. 142 pp. (paper) Contains chapter on tarot and transformation.

* **DRURY,** Nevill. *The Tarot Workbook: A Step-by-Step Guide to Discovering the Wisdom of the Cards.* Sydney: Lansdowne Publishing, 2004. Ill. 192 pp. (paper) An overview of tarot divination and meditation. Illustrated with cards from various tarot decks.

* **DUKE,** Charles R., ed. *Writing Exercises from "Excercises Exchange."* Volume 2. Urbana, IL: National Council of Teachers of English, 1984. Includes exercise using tarot in composition class.

* **DUMMETT,** Michael A. E. *Il mondo e l'angelo: i tarocchi e la loro storia.* Naples: Bibliopolis, 1993. Ill. 489 pp. 25 cm. In Italian: *The World and the Angel: The Tarot and Its Lore.*

DUMMETT, Michael A. E. *I tarocchi siciliani.* Palermo: Edizioni La Zisa, 1995. Ill. 176 pp. 22 cm. In Italian: *The Sicilian Tarot.* Preface by Gianluigi Oliveri.

* **DUMMETT,** Michael A. E. *Twelve Tarot Games.* London: Duckworth, 1980. Ill. 242 pp. 22 cm. (paper)

* **DUQUETTE,** Lon Milo. *The Chicken Qabalah of Rabbi Lamed Ben Clifford: A Dilettante's Guide to What You Do and Do Not Need to Know to Become a Qabalist.* York Beach, ME: Weiser Books, 2001. Ill. xxii, 233 pp. 21 cm.

* **DUQUETTE,** Lon Milo. *Tarot of Ceremonial Magick: A Pictorial Synthesis of Three Great Pillars of Magick: Enochian, Goetia, Astrology.* York Beach, ME: Samuel Weiser, 1995. Ill. xxv, 275 pp. 21 cm. Companion book to the Tarot of Ceremonial Magick.

* **DUQUETTE,** Lon Milo, and Christopher S. Hyatt. *Aleister Crowley's Illustrated Goetia.* Scottsdale, AZ: New Falcon Publications, 1992. Illustrated by David Wilson.

* **DUQUETTE,** Lon Milo, and Christopher S. Hyatt. *Enochian World of Aleister Crowley.* Phoenix, AZ: New Falcon Publications, 1991. The illustrations, by David Wilson, were later made into the Tarot of Ceremonial Magick.

* **DUQUETTE,** Lon Milo, and Christopher S. Hyatt. *Sex Magic, Tantra, and Tarot: The Way of the Secret Lover.* Phoenix, AZ: New Falcon Publications, 1991.

* **DUSAULX,** M. *De la Passion du Jeu.* Paris, 1779.

E

* **EAKINS,** Pamela. *Priestess: Woman as Sacred Celebrant.* York Beach, ME: Samuel Weiser, 1996. viii, 296 pp. (paper) 23 cm. Cover has an illustration, by Joyce Eakins, of II The High Priestess from the Tarot of the Spirit.

* **EAKINS,** Pamela. *Tarot of the Spirit.* York Beach, ME: Samuel Weiser, 1992. Ill. xviii, 424 pp. (paper) 23 cm. Book on Tarot of the Spirit, illustrated by Joyce Eakins.

EASON, Cassandra. *The Complete Book of Tarot.* Freedom, CA: Crossing Press, 1999. Ill. 256 pp. (paper) 23 cm. Basic tarot.

* **EASON,** Cassandra. *The Complete Guide to Divination: How to Foretell the Future Using the Most Popular Methods of Prediction.* Freedom, CA: Crossing Press, 2003. Ill. 314 pp. (paper) 23 cm. Includes a chapter on tarot illustrated with the Rider-Waite deck.

EASON, Cassandra. *Tarot Divination for Today's Woman.* Berkshire, England: Foulsham, 1992. Ill. 155 pp. Feminist tarot interpretations.

* **EASON,** Cassandra. *Tarot Talks to the Woman Within: Teach Yourself to Rely on Her Support. Self-empowerment for women, using the tarot.* UK: Quantum, 2000. Ill. Illustrated with the Universal Waite Tarot.

* **EASTERN ILLINOIS UNIVERSITY.** Warbler, 1996. 352 pp. (hardcover) College yearbook includes photograph of a Rider-Waite Tarot tarot spread.

ECHOLS, Signe E., Robert Mueller, and Sandra A. Thomson. *Spiritual Tarot: Seventy-eight Paths to Personal Development.* New York: Avon Books, 1996. Ill. xv, 335 pp. (paper) 21 cm.

* **EDGHILL,** Rosemary. *Book of Moons: A Bast Mystery.* New York: Tom Dougherty Associates, 1995. 220 pp. (cloth) Murder mystery whose milieu is New York occult scene. Cover is illustrated with XVIII The Moon by Deirdre Snowdon-Romer.

EDMONDSON, C. Melody. *The Complete Reference Book for Tarot Divination: Trebreh.* Aptos, CA: MJP Pub., 2001. Ill. xvi, 240 pp. 22 cm.

EERENBEEMT, Noud van den. *Sleutel tot de Tarot.* Leiden: Tango, 1973. Ill. 156 pp. 21 cm.

* **EGOROV,** Alexander. *Pictorial Art of Space.* Privately published, circa 1995. Ill. 24 pp. (paper) 23 cm. Illustrations of Egorov's works, in color. Some of the designs were applied by the artist to tarot cards.

* **ELEUZEL.** *Apologia del Libro de Thoth.* South America: Editorial Barath, 1980. (unbound portfolio) 34 cm. Major Arcana, in Egyptian style, and verse.

* **EMETERIO,** E. San. *Le Grand Livre de l'Etteilla – Tarots Egyptiens.* Paris: Editions Trajectoire, 2003. 168 pp. (paper) 24 cm. In French.

* **ENCHANTÉ:** *The Journal for the Urbane Pagan.* John Yohalem, editor. 1989 ongoing. Number 8 was a special issue on tarot.

ENDREI, Walter. *Spiele und Unterhaltung im alten Europa.* Hanau, Germany: Verlag Werner Dausien, 1988. Ill. 196 pp. In German: *Games and Pastimes in Old Europe.* Translation from Hungarian book.

ENEL. *Triologie de Rota: Manuel de Cabbale Pratique.* Toulon, France: 1931. Ill. Includes illustrations of tarot cards.

* **THE ENGLISH PLAYING CARD SOCIETY.** Ongoing. Newsletter.

ENGLISH, Jane. *Tarot and Physics.* Dissertation, 1981. Ill. 22 pp.

ENGLISH, Maurice, and Frederick Morgan. *The Tarot of Cornelius Agrippa.* Gertrude Clarke Whittall Poetry and Literature Fund, 1978; Archive of Recorded Poetry and Literature, U.S. Library of Congress. Sound recording. Maurice English and Frederick Morgan reading their poems. Includes four poems by Morgan from his collection *The Tarot of Cornelius Agrippa.* Recorded Nov. 14, 1978, at the Library of Congress in Washington, D.C.

ENGSTROM, Alfred. "Gerard de Nerval's Lobster and the Tarot Cards." *Romance Notes* 6 (1964): 33–36.

ENNERS, Marilyn Jean. *Keys to Self-Realization: A Self-Counseling Manual.* West Chester, PA: Whitford Press, circa 2000. 413 pp. (paper) Spiritual lessons from the Tarot.

* **EPHEMERA NEWS.** Ongoing newsleter of Ephemera Society of America, Schoharie, NY. Occasionally includes articles on tarot and playing cards.

* **EPHEMERA SOCIETY OF AMERICA.** Membership Roster. Ongoing. Includes collectors of playing and tarot cards.

* **ERANZ DE GÜLER,** Maritxu. *Basque Country Tarot (Tarot de Euskaherria).* Vitoria, Spain: Heraclio Fournier, 1991. Book accompanying the Basque Country Tarot, illustrated by Alfredo Fermin Cemillán Mintxo.

ERTE, Asta. See K. Frank Jensen.

ESKENAZI, Enrique. *Tarot: El arte de adivinar.* Barcelona: Dopesa, 1978. 251 pp. Ill. 20 cm.

ETIENVRE, Jean-Pierre. "Le Symbolisme de la carte a jouer dans l'Espagne des XVIe et XVIIe siecles." In *Les Jeux a la Renaissance,* edited by Philippe Arles and Jean-Claude Margolin. 1982. 736 pp. In French: "The Symbolism of Spanish Playing Cards of the XVIth and XVIIth Centuries."

ETTEILLA. *Das Eteilla Tarot: Das ursprüngliche Buch Tarot.* Germany: Fourier Verlag, 1900. Ill. 62+78 pp. In German. Reprint of an Etteilla book, illustrated by a black and white rendition of an Etteilla deck.

ETTEILLA. *Tharoth.* 2 vols. Ill. 17 cm. A collection of separately published works by Etteilla [Alliette]. Title was taken by U.S. Library of Congress from the binder's title on spine.

* **ETUDE TAJAN.** *Cartes a Jouer Estampes.* Paris, May 1996. Catalog for prints and playing cards.

* **EVANS,** David W. "Eliot and the Sense of the Occult." *Accent* (Spring 1954): 148–155. Tarot and Eliot's poem "The Waste Land."

* **EYAL,** Arik. *Tarot: Masà le-tokh hayekha.* Tel-Aviv: Yedi`ot aharonot: Sifre hemed, 2000. Ill. 175 pp. (paper) 24 cm. In Hebrew: *Tarot: A Journey into Your Life.* Illustrated with the Rider-Waite Tarot.

F

FAIRCHILD, Dennis. *The Fortune Telling Handbook: The Interactive Guide to Tarot, Palm Reading, and More.* Philadelphia, PA: Running Press, 2003.

* **FAIRCHILD,** Dennis. *Reading the Tarot.* Philadelphia: Running Press, 1996. Ill. 12 pp. (paper) Book accompanying fortune-telling kit, including the Tarot Nova, illustrated by Julie Paschkis.

* **FAIRCHILD,** Dennis. *Tarot.* Philadelphia, PA: Running Press Book Pub., 1999. Miniature book.

FAIRFIELD, Gail. *Choice-Centered Relating and the Tarot.* Foreword by James Wanless. York Beach, ME: Samuel Weiser, 2000. xiv, 335 pp. 23 cm.

* **FAIRFIELD,** Gail. *Cómo Tomar Decisiones con el Tarot.* Barcelona: Ediciones Urano, 1998. 208 pp. (paper) 22 cm. Spanish-language edition of *Choice-Centered Relating.*

* **FAIRFIELD,** Gail, and Patti Provo. *Inspiration Tarot: A Workbook for Understanding and Creating Your Own Tarot Deck.* York Beach, ME: Samuel Weiser, 1991. 212 pp. (paper) 26 cm.

FALLON, Jim, and Laura James. *Kriya Yoga and the Tarot.* USA: Mystic Insights Publishers, 1992. Ill. 130 pp. Tarot used as a tool for yoga exercises.

FALORIO, Linda. *The Shadow Tarot.* Privately published, Pittsburgh, PA, 1988. Ill. 51 pp. Reprint. Pittsburg, PA: Black Moon Publishing, 1994. Ill. 82 pp. (paper) Book accompanying Linda Falorio's Shadow Tarot.

FAMILIARI, Rocco. *Don Giovanni e il suo servo: dramma: illustrazioni tratte dai Tarot d'Epinal.* Firenze: La casa Usher, 1982. Ill. 99 pp. 24 cm.

* **FARBER,** Monte. *The Enchanted Tarot.* New York: St. Martin's Press, 1990. Ill. 184 pp. Book accompanying Enchanted Tarot, illustrated by Amy Zerner.

* **FARBER,** Monte. *The Instant Tarot Reader.* New York: St. Martin's Press, 1997. Ill. 342 pp. 22 cm. Book accompanying deck illustrated by Amy Zerner.

FARBER, Monte. *Paradise Found: The Visionary Art of Amy Zerner.* Boston: Journey Editions, 1995. Ill. 204 pp. (cloth) Includes chapter on the Enchanted Tarot.

FARBER, Monte, and Zerner, Amy. *The Enchanted Tarot Calendar, 1991.* Berkeley, CA: Zephyr Press, 1990. Ill. Wall calendar with illustrations by Amy Zerner and text by Monte Farber.

* **FENTON,** Sasha. *Super Tarot: New Techniques for Improving Your Tarot Reading.* London: Aquarian Press, 1991. 176 pp. (paper) 22 cm. Techniques for reading the cards.

FENTON, Sasha. *Tarot Oraklet: Lad tarotkortene tyde din fremtid.* Copenhagen: Strubes Forlag, 1985 Ill. 162 pp. *The Tarot Revealed,* translated into Danish by K. Frank Jensen.

* **FENTON,** Sasha. *Tarot: Your Color Guide to the Fascinating World of Tarot.* New York: Smithmark Publishing, 1998. Ill. 64 pp. (hardcover) 17 cm. Book in set with deck illustrated by Samantha Bale. Basic tarot.

* **FENTON-SMITH,** Paul. *The Tarot Revealed: A Simple Guide for Unlocking the Secrets of the Tarot.* Australia: Simon and Schuster, 1995. Ill. 240 pp. (paper) 22 cm. Illustrated with the Rider-Waite Tarot.

* **FERGUSON,** Anna-Marie. *Legend: El Tarot del Rey Arturo.* Madrid: Arkano Books, 1999. 280 pp. (paper) In Spanish. Book accompanying the tarot by Ferguson.

* **FERGUSON,** Anna-Marie, and Ray Rue. *A Keeper of Words.* St. Paul, MN: Llewellyn Publications, 1995. Second edition, 1999. Ill. xvi, 282 pp. (paper) 23 cm. Book accompanying Legend: The Arthurian Tarot, illustrated by Anna-Marie Ferguson, with poetry by Ray Rue.

* **FERNÁNDEZ,** Celia T. *Qué es el Tarot?* Buenos Aires: Editorial Kier, 2002. 142 pp. (paper) 22 cm. In Spanish: *What is the Tarot?*

* **FETTERMAN,** William. *John Cage's Theatre Pieces: Notations and Performances.* Amsterdam: Harwood Academic Publishers, 1996. Ill. 282 pp. (paper) 24 cm. Section on Cage's use of tarot cards to compose 4'33" in 1952. Cage recalled that he probably used the "Horseshoe Spread" (see *The Encyclopedia of Tarot,* volume I). Fetterman surmises that the recollection was correct, in that it is a complicated spread, and has three sections, which would correspond to the three movements of the piece. Cage used a home-made deck of cards. "It was done just like a piece of music, except there were no sounds—but there were durations," said Cage in a later interview. "It was dealing these cards—shuffling them, on which there were durations, and then dealing them—and using the tarot to know how to use them."

FIEBIG, Johannes. "Die Vielen Geschichter des Tarot." *Esotera* 4 (1994): 24–28. Ill. In German: "The Four Stories of the Tarot."

* **FILIPPI,** Pina. *Il Grande Libro dei Tarocchi.* Italy: Marziano Genovese Edizioni, 1995. Ill. 182 pp. Esoteric tarot. Illustrations based on the Wirth tarot.

* **FIMLAID,** Louise. *The Spiritual Study of the Tarot Including the Kabalah, Numerology & Astrology.* Privately published, circa 1998. Audio cassettes.

* **FIMLAID,** Louise. *The Spiritual Study of the Tarot Including the Kabalah, Numerology & Astrology.* St. Petersburg, FL: Galaxy Publishing House, 1998. Ill. 289 pp. (paper) 22 cm. Book illustrated with the Rider-Waite Tarot.

* **FIMLAID,** Louise. *The Tarot: The Major Arcana.* Unpublished, 1997. VHS Video of Fimlaid teaching basics of the tarot, using the Rider-Waite Tarot.

* **FINER, STEVE, RARE BOOKS.** *Circus, Gambling, Games, Magic, Popular Impositions, Puzzles, Sports & Theater.* Catalogues.

FINN, Edouard. *L'Escalier de la Grande Déesse.* Quebec: Les Editions de Mortagne, 1994. 251 pp. (paper) In French: *Staircase of the Grand [female] Deity.* Discussion of feminine archetypes in the tarot.

FINN, J. Edward. *And the One Became Two.* New York: Vantage Press, 1992. 132 pp. 20 cm. Discussion of Egypt and the Bible.

* **FINOCCHI,** Daniela. "Giacinto Gaudenzi." *Zoom* 8 (May–June 1995): 63–65. In Italian, on artist Gaudenzi.

* **FIORINI,** Jeanne. *Invitation to Wonder: Real Life Insights through the Tarot.* Privately published, 2002. Ill. 136 pp. (paper) 28 cm. Tarot readings, with many examples drawn from the author's practice. Illustrated with the Rider-Waite Tarot.

FLENDROVSKY, Friedrich. *Tarock: Ein Wegweiser durch das königliche*

Spiel. Vienna: F. Flendrovsky, circa 1991. Ill. 269 pp. 21 cm. In German: *Tarot: A Path through the Kingly Game.*

* **FLEURY,** Rene. *El Tarot.* Barcelona: Ediciones Dalmau Socías, 1990. 150 pp. (paper) 22 cm. In Spanish. Basic tarot, with a chapter aligning history of tarot with different Spanish rulers.

* **FLORA,** Charlene M. *Reflection to Self-Proficiency: A Guide to Achieving Wisdom and Understanding through Individual Translation Using Tarot Cards.* 5 pp. (paper) 22 cm. Meditative card spread.

FLUCH, Hans Norbert. *Osterreichisches Tarock im 19. Jahrhundert.* Vienna: Piatnik & Sohne, 1981. Ill. In German: *Austrian Tarock in the 19th Century.* A catalogue from the first exhibition of Piatnik's collection.

FOA, Simona. "I Tarocchi di Matteo Maria Boiardo dalla corte estense alla tipografia veneziana." In *Passare il tempo: La letteratura del giuoco e dell'intrattenimento dal XII al XVI secolo.* 1993.

* **FONTANA,** David. *The Secret Language of Symbols: A Visual Key to Symbols and Their Meaning.* San Francisco: Chronicle Books, 1994. Ill. 192 pp. (paper) 23 cm. Includes a section on tarot, illustrated with fascinating antique decks from the British Museum.

FORTE, Andrea, et al. *I Tarocchi Perduti.* Italy: Alia uno, 1988. Ill. 186 pages. Book on the Tarocchi Perduti set of decks, which has both male and female cards of each major.

* **FOSTER,** Margaret L. *Virtual Tarot.* Sunnyvale, CA: Virtual Media Works, 1995. Software for tarot card spreads.

* **FOURNIER.** Calendar. 1973, 1974, 1975, 1977. Calendars with large illustrations of historical decks.

* **FRADELLA,** Frank. *Fradella Adventure Tarot.* Stamford, CT: U.S. Games Systems, 2002. Ill. 146 pp. (paper) Book accompanying the Fradella Adventure Tarot, illustrated by JP Dupras.

* **FRANCE CARTES.** Ongoing. Catalog of playing and tarot cards, from Saint-Max, France. Includes Grimaud, Ducale, and Heron cards.

FRANCIA, Louisa. *Hexentarot.* Zürich: Stechapeel, circa 1982. Ill. 59 pp. In German: *Witches Tarot.*

* **FRANKLIN,** Anna. *The Sacred Circle Tarot: A Celtic Pagan Journey.* St. Paul, MN: Llewellyn Publications, 1998. Book accompanying the Sacred Circle Tarot, illustrated by Paul Mason.

* **FRANOV,** Enrique. *El Tarot: Testigo de la Realidad.* Barcelona: Ediciones Indigo y Enrique Franov, 1987. 402 pp. (paper) 23 cm. In Spanish.

* **FREDERICKS,** Emmi. *The Smart Girl's Guide to Tarot.* New York: St. Martin's Press, 2004. Ill. 192 pp. (paper) 21 cm. Basic tarot, "with a young, hip attitude," as the publisher describes it.

FREY, C.F. See Akron.

FRIIS, Ronald J. "The Devil, the Tower, and the Hanged Man: The Hermetic Tarot of the Numancia. In *A Star-Crossed Golden Age.* Frederick A De Armas, ed. 1998. 247 pp.

FRITZ, Jürgen. *Spiele als Spiegel ihrer Zeit: Glücksspiele, Tarot, Puppen, Videospiele.* Mainz, Germany: Matthias-Grünewald-Verlag, 1992. Ill. 152 pp. 21 cm. In German: *Games as Mirror into their Time: Gambling, Tarot, Puppets and Videogames.* How games reflects their milieu.

* **FRONTERAS,** Adam. *The Tarot: The Traditional Tarot Reinterpreted for the Modern World.* New York: Steward, Tabori and Chang, 1996. Ill. 128 pp. (paper) Book accompanying a recolored version of the Rider-Waite Tarot.

* **FUENTES,** Salvador Tena. *Testimoni Històric de Naipes Comas.* Spain: Naipes y Especialidades Gráficas, 1994. Ill. 142 + unpaginated. (paper) 21 cm. History of Naipes Comas card manufacturer. Includes many color illustrations of cards and original woodblocks.

FULLWOOD, Nancy. *The Flaming Sword.* New York: Macoy Publishing Co., 1935. 59 pp. 21 cm.

FULLWOOD, Nancy. *On the Road to Damascus.* New York, Macoy Publishing Co., 1935. 94 pp. 21 cm.

FULLWOOD, Nancy. *The Tower of Light.* New York: Macoy Publishing Co., 1931. 120 pp.

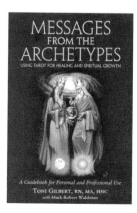

G

* **GAD,** Irene. *Tarot and Individuation: Correspondences with Cabala and Alchemy.* York Beach, ME: Nicolas-Hays, 1994. Ill. xxxvii, 472 pp. 23 cm. Jungian outlook on tarot, individuation, kabbalah and alchemy. Fascinating illustrations paralleling alchemical engravings and tarot images.

* **GAIMAN,** Neil. *The Books of Magic.* New York: DC Comics, 1993. Ill. 26 cm. Graphic novel on a boy's initiation as a magician. Tarot readings and characters interweave in the plot.

** **GALBREATH,** Robert. "Arthur Edward Waite Occult Scholar and Christian Mystic: A Chronological Bibliography." *Bulletin of Bibliography* 30 (1973): 55–61.

* **GALENORN,** Yasmine. *Tarot Journeys: Adventures in Self-Transformation.* St. Paul, MN: Llewellyn Publishers, 1999. Ill. 288 pp. (paper) Guided meditation, or lyrical story, for each of the Major Arcana. Includes an audio CD with selected meditations from the book.

GALLEGO RIPOLL, Federico. *Tarot.* Madrid: Libertarias, 1991. Ill. 58 pp. 25 cm. Illustrated by the author.

* **GAME RESEARCHERS' NOTES.** Lewiston, ME. Ongoing newsletter of American Game Collectors Association. Occasionally includes articles on tarot and playing cards.

* **GANTHER,** Eric. *The Cosmic Tribe Tarot.* Rochester, VT: Destiny Books, 1998. Ill. 199 pp. 24 cm. Book accompanying the Cosmic Tribe Tarot, illustrated by Stevee Postman.

GARCIA, Carole. *Tarot Poetry.* London: Avon Books, 1997. Ill. 45 pp. Illustrated with original designs.

* **GAREN,** Nancy. *Creating Your Own Tarot Cards.* New York: Simon & Schuster, 1991. Ill. 271 pp. 24 cm.

* **GAREN,** Nancy. *The Tarot According to You: A Workbook.* New York: Simon & Schuster, 2001. 431 pp. 24 cm. Encourages reflection on the tarot cards through questions.

* **GAREN,** Nancy. *Tarot Made Easy.* New York: Fireside, Simon & Schuster, 1989. Ill. 383 pp. 24 cm. Illustrated with the Rider-Waite Tarot. Meanings for each card for different situations.

* **GARGIULO-SHERMAN,** Johanna. *Guide to the Sacred Rose Tarot.* Stamford, CT: U.S. Games Systems, 1999. 240 pp. Ill. 18 cm. Illustrated by the author.

* **GEMMING,** Mary. *Mystical Secrets of the Stars.* Tempe, AZ: American Federation of Astrologers. Ill. 75 pp. (paper) 29 cm. Astrology, with Major Arcana linked to the different signs. Illustrated with the Rider-Waite Tarot.

* **GENETTI,** Alexandra. *The Wheel of Change Tarot.* Rochester, VT: Destiny Books, 1997. Ill. 383 pp. (paper) 23 cm. Book accompanying the Wheel of Change Tarot deck.

GERINGER, Mary Steiner. *Tarot als Selbsterfahrung.* Cologne, Germany: Eugen Diedrich, 1985. Ill. 236 pp. In German: *Tarot as a Journey of the Self.*

GERINGER, Mary Steiner, and Sergius Golowin. *Die XXII Arcana des Tarot: Die Welt als Spiel.* Switzerland: Rene Simmen, 1968. Ill. 122 pp. In German: *The XXII Arcana of the Tarot: The World as a Game.* Book accompanying Henri Steiner's limited edition tarot deck. Book and deck packaged in metal box.

* **GERM,** Tine. "Simbolizem Tarocka: Renasancni Neoplatonizem I Ikonografija Zgodnjih Italijanskih Tarokov." *Zbornik za Umetnostno Zgodovino* 30 (1994): 27–42.

* **GERM,** Tine. "Slovanski tarok Hinka Smrekarja." *Zbornik za Umetnostno Zgodovino* 31–32 (1995–1996): 119–125.

GIBBONS, Tom. "The Waste Land Tarot Identified." *Journal of Modern Literature* 2 (1972): 560–565.

* **GILBERT,** Toni. *Messages from the Archetypes: Using Tarot for Healing and Spiritual Growth.* Ashland, OR: White Cloud Press, 2004. Ill. 179 pp.

(paper) 23 cm. Illustrated with Osho Zen Tarot, Voyager Tarot, and Rider-Waite Tarot. Includes case histories of card readings helping people facing crises in their lives.

GILCHRIST, Cherry. *Divination: The Search for Meaning.* London: Dryad Press Limited, 1987. 159 pp. (paper) Includes a chapter on tarot.

* **GILES**, Cynthia Elizabeth. *Russian Tarot of St. Petersburg.* Stamford, CT: U.S. Games Systems, 1996. Ill. ix, 326 pp. 18 cm. Book accompanying tarot illustrated by Yury Shakov.

* **GILES**, Cynthia Elizabeth. *The Tarot: History, Mystery, and Lore.* New York: Paragon House, 1992. Reprint. New York: Fireside/Simon & Schuster, 1994. Ill. xvi, 238 pp. 24 cm. Esoteric tarot through the ages.

* **GILES**, Cynthia Elizabeth. *The Tarot: Methods, Mastery, and More.* New York: Simon & Schuster, 1996. Ill. 238 pp. 24 cm. Tarot in context of the culture of the late 1990s, including leading tarotists.

* **GILL**, Elizabeth Josephine. *The Gill Tarot.* Stamford, CT: U.S. Games Systems, 1996. Ill. 213 pp. 18 cm. Book accompanying the Gill Tarot.

GILLABEL, Dirk. (Medicator) *Egyptian Gods Tarot.* Privately published, Belgium, 1991. 13 pp. Description of Medicator's Egyptian Gods Tarot.

GILLABEL, Dirk. (Medicator) *Greek Gods Tarot.* Privately published, Belgium, 1991. 9 pp. A description of the Gillabel's Greek Gods Tarot.

* **GILLABEL**, Dirk. (Medicator) *The Medicator Tarot.* Privately published, Belgium 1987. Ill. Approx. 200 pp. Limited and numbered edition of 5.

GILLABEL, Dirk. (Medicator) *9.9 Tarot.* Privately published, Belgium, circa 1987. 22 pp. Booklet accompanying deck by author.

* **GILLABEL**, Guido. *The Cosmic Egg. Tarot and the philosophy of the Holy Trinity.* Privately published, Mechelen, Belgium/Woodstock, NY, 1989. Ill. 32 pp. Guidebook to Carol Herzer's Cosmic Egg Tarot.

* **GILLABEL**, Guido. *De Hierofants Alchemisten Tarot.* De Hierofant, Belgium, 1987. 46 pp. ill. Booklet describing the Alchemisten-Tarot.

GILLABEL, Guido, ed. *Tarot-illustrationer.* Belgium, 1980. Enlargements, wrapping paper, and so on, depicting tarot imagery produced by Guido Gillabel, Belgium.

GILLABEL, Guido, ed. (Untitled). Privately published, 1994. 13 pp. Ill. Guido Gillabel's collection of tarot decks and items.

GIOVANNONI, Giannino. *Mantova e i tarocchi del Mantegna.* Mantova: Provincia di Mantova, Casa del Mantegna & Faenza: Associazione culturale le tarot, 1987. Ill. 78 pp. 24 cm. Catalog for exhibition of Mantegna tarot cards.

GIRIÉ, Jacques, and Amédée de Miribel. *Le Tarot sacré: manuel initiatique.* Marseilles: Editions J. Laffitte, 1984. Ill. 99 pp. 22 cm.

* **GLAS**, Johan. "De Verborgen Betekenis van het Tarotspiel." *Paravisie* 5 (May 1991): 62–66. Esoteric tarot, illustrated with cards from Book of Thoth, Tarot of Marseilles, and Wirth Tarot.

* **GODING**, Jessica, and Lauren O'Leary. *The World Spirit Tarot.* St. Paul, MN: Llewellyn Publishers, 2001. Ill. 164 pp. (paper) 13 cm. Book accompanying the World Spirit Tarot deck, illustrated by Lauren O'Leary.

GODO, Carlos. *O tarô de Marselha.* São Paulo: Editora Pensamento, 1985. Ill. 124 pp. 20 cm. In Portuguese: *The Tarot of Marseilles.* Preface by Luis Pellegrini.

* **GODWIN**, David. *How to Choose Your Own Tarot.* St. Paul, MN: Llewellyn Publications, 1995. Ill. 178 pp. (paper) 18 cm. How to choose among tarot decks.

* **GOEPFERD**, Michael, and Brian Williams. *The Light and Shadow Tarot.* Rochester, VT: Destiny Books, 1997. Ill. xii, 194 pp. 14 cm. Book accompanying Light and Shadow Tarot, illustrated with block prints by Michael Goepferd.

* **GOFFREDO**, Christopher A.M. *Order in the Court: A Journey through the Elements of the Royal Tarot.* Privately published, 1998. 49 pp. (paper, comb-bound) Elemental and astrological significance of the court cards.

GOLODNOFF, Ulrik. *Tarot ABC.* Copenhagen: Sphinx, 1997. Ill. 228 pp. Reprint. 2001. 160 pp. (paper) Correspondence course in basic tarot. 2001 edition accompanied by Universal Waite Tarot.

GOLODNOFF, Ulrik. *Tarot: Den Individuelle Indvielsesvej,* vol. 1. Ill. 54 pp. Home study course in three volumes. First volume deals with the 40 numbered Minor Arcana.

* **GOMBOLD**, Dori. "The Psychodynamic Effect of Tarot Symbolism." In *Wheel of Tarot.* James Wanless and Angeles Arrien, ed. pp. 187–202. Description of B.O.T.A courses in tarot symbology.

* **GONZALEZ**, Federico. *La Rueda: Una Imagen Simbólica del Cosmos.* Barcelona: Symbolos, 1986. 262 pp.

* **GONZALEZ**, Federico. *El Tarot de los Cabalistas, Vehículo Mágic.* Buenos Aires: Eitorial Kier, 1993. 192 pp.

* **GONZÁLEZ**, Federico, with Fernando Trejos. *El tarot de los cabalista: vehículo mágico.* Buenos Aires: Editorial Kier, 1993. Ill. 189 pp. (paper) Illustrated with Grimaud Tarot of Marseilles.

* **GOODALL**, Michael H. *British Playing Card Manufacture in the 19th Century.* Privately published, Surrey, 1993. Ill. Unpaginated. Gathers photocopies from various sources on playing card manufacture.

Does not include tarot, but is interesting for its information and illustrations concerning manufacture of cards.

GOODRICH, Peter H. "Arthurian Legend in Tarot." In *King Arthur in Popular Culture.* Sklar, Elizabeth S., and Donald Hoffman, eds. Jefferson, N.C.: McFarland, 2002.

* **GORDEN**, S.A. *The Deuce of Pentacles.* Crossroads Pub, 1997. Reprint. Deer River, MN: Taconite Runes, 2002. Ill. 159 pp. (paper) Murder mystery featuring tarot. Each chapter is titled with a tarot card, including an illustration from the Rider-Waite Tarot. (Also in collection of SRK: unpublished manuscript.)

* **GORDON**, Richard, with Dixie Taylor. *The Intuitive Tarot: A Metaphysical Approach to Reading the Tarot Cards.* Nevada City, CA: Blue Dolphin Pub., 1994. Ill. xii, 143 pp. 22 cm. Rituals and meditations using the tarot. Illustrated with the Universal Waite Tarot deck.

GORKOM, J. van. *Tarot.* Wassenaar, Servire, 1973. Ill. 142 pp. 22 cm.

GOSSMAN, Ann. "The Greater Trumps." *Descant: The Texas Christian University Literary Journal* 20, no. 3 (1976): 41–48.

* **GOTTHOLD**, Shirley. *The Transformational Tarot: An Appropriate Tool for a Time of Transition.* Berkeley, CA: Foolscap Press, 1995. Ill. 178 pp. 26 cm. Book accompanying the Transformational Tarot illustrated by Peggy Gotthold.

* **GOVER**, Jane. "Women of the Photo-Secession and Alfred Stieglitz." *AB: Bookman's Weekly* (November 2, 1987): 1690–1698. Includes a brief reference to Pamela Colman Smith: "The first non-photographic exhibit at the Little Galleries was the work of a young, relatively unknown painter, Pamela Colman Smith."

GRAF, Eckhard. *Lexicon des Tarot.* Stuttgart: Verlag Stephanie Nagelschmied, 1991. Ill. 222 pp. In German. Describes 254 tarot decks available in 1990.

GRAF, Eckhard. *Mythos Tarot: Historische Fakten.* Germany: Param Verlag Günter Koch, 1989. Ill. 192 pp. History of the tarot. In German.

* **GRAF**, Eckhard. "Sibylle der Salons." *Biella Intern* (August 1995): 19–21. History of tarot, illustrated with the Pierpont Morgan-Bergamo deck.

* **GRANEN PORRUA**, Isabel. "El tarto mexicano del siglo XVI." *Gutenberg-Jahrbuch* 69 (1994): 158–169.

* **GRANT**, Julia L. *LItarotURE: Tarot as a Metafictional Device in Twentieth-century Literature.* MA Thesis, University of Western Ontario, 2000. 104 pp.

GRAUF, Heike Pauline. *Der dreimalgrösste Eulenspiegel: Eine philosophische Hermetik des Narren am Spiegel des Tarot.* Freiburg im Breisgau: Rombach, 1996. Ill. 299 pp. 23 cm. In German: *The Triple Eulenspiegel: A Hermetic Philosophy of the Fool in the Mirror of the Tarot.*

GRAY, Eden. *Het Geheim van de Tarot: De Magische Kaarten die Verleden en Toekomst Onthullen.* Ultrecht: Kosmos-Z&K Uitgevers, 1986. Ill. 135 pp. (paper) 18 cm. Flemish translation of *The Tarot Revealed.*

GRAY, Eden. *The Tarot Revealed: A Modern Guide to Reading the Tarot Cards.* New York: Inspiration House 1960. Ill. 121 pp. 24 cm. Revised and updated edition. New York: New American Library, 1988. Ill. 242 pp. 18 cm.

GRAY, William G. *Growing the Tree Within: Patterns of the Unconscious Revealed by the Qabbalah.* St. Paul, MN: Llewellyn Publications, 1991. Ill. xxvi, 434 pp. (paper) 23 cm. Originally published as *The Talking Tree* (New York: Samuel Weiser, 1977).

GREBE, Coralee. "Tarot Card Symbolism in the Star Wars Films." *Mythlore: A Journal of J.R.R. Tolkien, C.S. Lewis, Charles Williams, and the Genres of Myth and Fantasy* 76 (Spring 1994): 27–31.

GREER, Mary K. *An Audio Exploration of the Tarot: A Visualized Journey through the Major and Minor Arcana.* Los Angeles: Audio Renaissance Tapes, 1988. Includes a black and white version of the Rider-Waite Tarot.

* **GREER**, Mary K. *The Complete Book of Tarot Reversals.* St. Paul, MN: Llewellyn Publications, 2002. Ill. xii, 274 pp. (paper) 23 cm.

* **GREER**, Mary K. *The Essence of Magic: Tarot, Ritual, and Aromatherapy.* North Hollywood, CA: Newcastle Publishing, 1993. Ill. ix, 192 pp. 22 cm.

* **GREER**, Mary K. "Permutations: On the Celtic Cross Spread." In *Wheel of Tarot.* James Wanless and Angeles Arrien, eds. pp. 49–67. Analysis and modem use of the spread first published by A.E. Waite.

* **GREER**, Mary K., and Rachel Pollack. *New Thoughts on Tarot.* North Hollywood: Newcastle Publishing Co., 1989.

GREGORY, James. *How to Perform a Psychic Reading: A Beginner's Guide to Reading Tarot Cards.* Colorado Springs, CO: Zymore Press, Inc., 1999. Ill. 91 pp. (paper) Includes questions most commonly asked in readings.

* **GRIMASSI**, Raven. *Wiccan Magick: Inner Teachings of the Craft.* Ill. 244 pp. (paper) 23 cm. Includes a chapter on I The Magician card, illustrated by the Visconti-Sforza version, and including a section on the Rider-Waite Magician.

* **GROTH**, Morten. "Tarot: Sjelens speil." *Alternativt Nettverk* (September 1995): 20, 21, 36, 37. Illustrated with the Morgan-Greer Tarot.

GRUE SORENSEN, Bodil, ed. *Udviklinger: Narren, Kejseren og*

Yppersteprrestinden: 78 kort med symbolsk betydning. Copenhagen, April 1994. A taped national broadcast on tarot. K. Frank Jensen is interviewed about the historical background of tarot and its development and spread.

* **GUFFY,** Margaret. *El Tarot Secreto: Cómo Adivinar el Futuro.* Spain: Ediciones Didáctica, 2001. 128 pp. (paper) 20 cm. In Spanish: *The Secret Tarot: How to Tell the Future.*

* **GUILEY,** Rosemary Ellen. *The Angels Tarot.* San Francisco: HarperSanFrancisco, 1995. Ill. xii, 115 pp. (paper) 16 cm. Book accompanying the Angels Tarot, illustrated Robert Michael Place.

GUILEY, Rosemary Ellen. *The Encyclopedia of Witches and Witchcraft.* New York: Facts On File, 1989. Ill. 421 pp. (cloth) 29 cm. Includes information on tarot cards.

* **GUILEY,** Rosemary Ellen. *The Mystical Tarot.* New York: Signet Books, 1991. Ill. 371 pp. (paper) 17 cm. Basic tarot, with focus on reading the cards.

GÜIRALDES, Florencia. *Los Arcanos en seda.* Buenos Aires: Amandaro, 1998. Ill. 117 pp. 32 cm. In Spanish: *The Arcana in Silk.* Poems by Güiraldes, illustrated with reproductions of tapestries by Latin American textile artist Silke.

* **GULDAGER,** Anne Grethe. *Religion 6.* Denmark: Alinea, 1997. Ill. 64 pp. (hardcover) 24 cm. In Danish. Includes section on paranormal with illustrations from the Hermetic Tarot.

* **GULFOSS,** Henrik. *Svaerdsvingere Lynslyngere: Tarotlortenes Univers.* Faabog, Denmark: Zosma, 2001. Ill. 151 pp. (paper) 23 cm. In Danish. Illustrated with the Aquarian Tarot.

* **GULFOSS,** Henrik. *Tarot: En innføring I tarotkortenes magiske verden.* Oslo: Orion Forlag, 1995. Ill. 157 pp. (hardcover) 20 cm. In Swedish. Illustrated with the Rider-Waite Tarot.

* **GUNASINGHE,** Zora. "Giardino dei Tarocchi." *Tableau* 12, 1 (September 1989): 110–112. Ill. In Italian: "Garden of Tarot."

GUTHRIE, Al. *Murder by Tarot.* New York: Zebra Group/Kensington Publishing Corp., 1992. 288 pp. (paper) Mystery in which a tarot reading provides clues.

GUTIÉRREZ VEGA, Hugo. *Poetry reading.* Sound recording, 1986. Archive of Hispanic Literature on Tape (Library of Congress) Includes selections from the poet's work, *Tarot.* Recorded April 25, 1986, at the Library of Congress.

GUTIÉRREZ VEGA, Hugo. *Tarot de Valverde de la vera.* Madrid: Taller Prometeo de Poesía Nueva, 1981. Ill. 43 pp. 22 cm. Poems with theme of tarot.

* **GWAIN,** Rose. *Discovering Your Self through the Tarot: A Jungian Guide to Archetypes & Personality.* Rochester, VT: Destiny Books; New York: Inner Traditions, 1993. Ill. ix, 198 pp. 23 cm. Jungian archetypes in the tarot.

H

HADAR, Kris. *Le Grande livre du tarot: Méthode pratique d'art divinatoire.* Boucherville, Quebec: Les Editions de Mortagne, 1988. 558 pp. (paper) Tarot card combinations in readings.

HADFIELD, Duncan. "Under the Tarot: A Reading of a Volcanic Sub-Level." *The Malcolm Lowry Review* 23–24 (Fall 1988–Spring 1989): 40–77.

HAGA, Enoch. *TAROsolution: A Complete Guide to Interpreting the Tarot.* Ill. Livermore, CA: E. Haga, 1994. Ill. v, 40 pp. 29 cm. (cloth and paper)

* **HAGER,** Günter. *Numerologie und Tarot.* Neuhausen, Switzerland: Urania Verlag, 1992. Ill. 117 pp. (paper) Handbook for the Prager Tarot, illustrated by Jan Bouzek.

* **HAGER,** Günter. *Le Tarot Pratique.* Neuhausen, Switzerland: AGMüller, 1985. Ill. 135 pp. (paper) 14 cm. Illustrated with Rider-Waite Tarot and Swiss 1JJ Tarot. In French.

* **HAICH,** Elisabeth. *The Wisdom of the Tarot.* London: Unwin Paperbacks, 1985. Ill. 174 pp.

* **HAINDL,** Hermann, Ricarda Scherzer, and Erika Haindl. *Hermann Haindl und Seine Welt des Tarot.* Privately published, circa 1993. Ill. 48 pp. (paper) 21 cm. Beautiful book on the making of the Haindl Tarot.

HAJDU, Istvan. "The Graphic Artist Tamas Kovacs." *Hungarian Book Revue* 1 (1989): 41–43. Ill. On Tamas Kovacs' tarot decorations for the Flamenco Occidental Hotel in Budapest. The nine images were later issued as copper engravings on three sheets.

* **HALL,** Manley P. *The Secret Teachings of the Ages: An Encyclopedic Outline of Masonic, Hermetic, Quabalistic and Rosicrucian Symbolical Philosophy.* CA: Philosophical Research Society, 1978. Ill. 245 pp. Includes information on tarot.

* **HALOEYES.** *Tarot: The Halo Method.* Privately published, 2002. Ill. 154 pp. (paper) Introduction to tarot.

HAMAKER-ZONDAG, Karen. *Tarot as a Way of Life: A Jungian Approach to the Tarot.* York Beach, ME: Samuel Weiser, 1997. Ill. xiv, 271 pp. 21 cm. Translation of *Tarot als Levensweg.*

* **HAMAKER-ZONDAG,** Karen. *El Tarot como Vía de Conocimiento.* Barcelona: Ediciones Urano, 1999. 317 pp. 21 cm. In Spanish. Translation of *De Tarot als Levensweg.* Illustrated with Rider-Waite Tarot.

* **HAMAKER-ZONDAG,** Karen. *The Way of the Tarot: A Jungian Approach*

for Working More Deeply with the Tarot. London: Judy Piatkus Publishers, 1998. Ill. 271 pp. (paper) 24 cm. Reprint of *Tarot as a Way of Life.*

* **HAMILTON,** Jean. *Playing Cards in the Victoria & Albert Museum.* London: Her Majesty's Stationary Office, 1988. Ill. 79 pp. (paper) 24 cm. Catalog of regular playing cards and tarot.

HANLEY, Timothy. *Miracles, Money and Mastery through the Tarot.* Alexander, NC: WorldComm, 1995. (paper)

* **HANSSON,** Susan. *The Hanson-Roberts Tarot Companion.* Stamford, CT: U.S. Games Systems, 1998. Ill. 191 pp. (paper) 18 cm. Book accompanying deck illustrated by Mary Hanson-Roberts.

* **HANSSON,** Susan. *Reading Tarot Cards: A Guide to the New Palladini Tarot.* Stamford, CT: U.S. Games Systems, 1996. Ill. x, 218 pp. (paper) 18 cm. Illustrated by David Palladini.

HARDING, M.E. *Tarot: Book One. Key to the Inner Sanctum—Path of the Initiate.* Privately published, circa 1990. 59 pp. (paper, comb-bound)

* **HARPER,** George Mills, and Walter K. Hood. *A Critical Edition of Yeat's "A Vision."* England: McMillan Press, 1978.

HARRIS, Rosemary. *A Wicked Pack of Cards.* New York: Walker and Company, 1969. 216 pp. (cloth) Romantic mystery involving tarot cards.

HARROW, Judy. *Low Bridge: Divination, A Technique for Pagan Religious Counselling.* Los Angeles: APA-Tarot, 1992. 12 pp.

* **HARTER,** Maurice. "Wisdom at Your Fingertips: A Consumer's Guide to Tarot." *The Monthly Aspectarian* 14, 1 (September 1992): 52–63. Brief history of tarot, and review of different decks, with illustrations.

* **HARTUNG & HARTUNG.** *Spielkarten.* Munich, 1994. Ill. Auction catalog.

HASBROUCK, Muriel Bruce. *Tarot and Astrology: The Pursuit of Destiny.* New York: Destiny Books, 1986. Ill. 224 pp. (paper) 20 cm. Reprint of *The Pursuit of Destiny.*

* **HAWES,** Bob and Rhonda. *Playing Card Auction.* November 1996 (and ongoing). Hamden, CT.

* **HAZEL,** Elizabeth. *Tarot Decoded: Understanding and Using Dignities and Correspondences.* Boston/York Beach, ME: Weiser Books, 2004. 187 pp. (paper) 23 cm. Hazel says, "Dignity is the relationship between cards in a spread." The book looks at these relationships in different lights, including elemental and astrological.

* **HEENAN,** Jan Ferris. "Divination = Divine Sales." *Publishers Weekly* 248, 21 (May 21, 2002): 46.

* **HEFTER-GOROL,** Renate. *Tarot für Teens: Das Orakelbuch für junge Leute.* Munich: Heinrich Hugendubel Verlag, 1995. Ill. 196 pp. (hardcover) 23 cm. In German: *Tarot for Teens: The Oracle for Young People.* Illustrated with the Rider-Waite Tarot.

* **HENDERSON,** Mary. *Star Wars: The Magic of Myth.* New York: Bantam Books, 1997. Ill. 214 pp. (paper) 27 cm. Companion to Star Wars exhibition at the National Air and Space Museum of the Smithsonian Institution. Page 22 has an illustration of 0 The Fool, from the Rider-Waite Tarot. "As the trilogy opens, Luke [Skywalker] is like the Fool... This card shows an inexperienced youth setting out on a journey; the way ahead is unknown, and the youth is completely unaware of the dangers that await him. In some decks, the youth may even be shown unwittingly on the verge of stepping off a high cliff. Like this archetype, Luke's character as the story begins is unformed and untested, innocent of a wider experience of the world and unaware of what lies ahead.

* **HERMAND,** Marie-Odile. *Le Tarot Divinitoire: Guide et Initiation.* Paris: Editions du Rocher, 1995. Ill. 167 pp. (paper) 22 cm. Illustrated with the Papus Tarot.

* **HEROLD,** Thea, et. al. *Tarot der Europa.* Berlin: Parthas, 1999. Ill. 143 pp. 30 cm. Catalog of an exhibition sponsored by the Kunstverein Bad Salzdetfurth and the Neuer Sächsischer Kunstverein. Includes text by Veit Stiller and Thea Herold, and an interview with Antoinette von Wolfgang Nützenadel. In German.

* **HET SPEL.** Ill. Dutch quarterly magazine about playing cards, board games, and puzzles.

HETMANN, Frederik. *Madru, oder, Der grosse Wald: ein Märchen.* Köln: E. Diederichs, 1984. Ill. 317 pp. (paper) 22 cm. A novel in which tarot figures in the plot. The cover is the Baum Tarot, illustrated by Tilman Michalski, printed so that the cards can be removed and used as a deck.

DE HIEROFANT. Guido Gillabel, editor. A periodical published by Guido Gillabel of Belgium in late 1980s.

HIGHWATER, Jamake. *The Language of Vision: Meditations on Myth and Metaphor.* New York: Grove Press, 1994. 342 pp. (cloth) Myth, art, and contemporary culture related to tarot.

* **HILL,** Douglas. "Fortune and the Tarot." *Fate and Fortune* 2: 42–48. Ill. How to read the tarot. Illustrated with Book of Thoth and Tarot of Marseilles.

* **HILL,** Sally. *Tarot Affirmations.* Stamford, CT: U.S. Games Systems, circa 1998. Ill. (unbound) The Rider-Waite Tarot, with affirmations alongside each card illustration.

* **HINTON,** W. Ladson. "Buffoni, Buffoneria e Senso del Ridiculo." *Rivista di Psicologia Analitica* 12, 23 (March 1981): 129–141. In Italian: "Fools, Buffoonery, and the Sense of the Ridiculous." Analyzes archetypal, magical, ritual, and dynamic functions of laughter and the laughable, linking them with creative psychotherapy. Includes the symbolism of 0 The Fool.

HINZ, Manfred. "Tarock und Literatur: Calvino's Castello dei destini incrociati." *Romanistische Zeitschrift für Literaturgeschichte/Cahiers d'Histoire des Litteratures Romanes* 19, nos. 3–4 (1995): 395–409.

* **HOELLER,** Stephan A. *The Fool's Pilgrimage: Kabbalistic Meditations on the Tarot.* Wheaton, IL: Theosophical Publishing House, 1975. Ill. 132 pp. (paper) 23 cm. Second edition 2004. The revised edition includes author's connection of tarot with Gnosticism and an audio compact disc with guided meditations read by the author. Illustrated with the Universal Waite Tarot.

* **HOFFMAN,** Detlef. *Kultur- und Kunstgeschichte der Spielkarte.* Marburg, Germany: Jonas Verlag, 1995. Ill. 270 pp. (paper) 24 cm. Culture and art history of playing cards. Illustrated with cards in the collection of the Deutsches Spielkarten-Museum.

* **HOFFMANN,** Detlef. *Schweitzer Spielkarten 1: Die Anfänge im 15. und 16. Jahrhundert.* Schaffhausen, Switzerland: Museum zu Allerheiligen Schaffhausen & Cartophilia Helvetica, 1998. Ill. 147 pp. (paper) 28 cm. In German: "Swiss Playing Cards 1: The Beginning in 15th and 16th centuries."

* **HOFFMAN,** Detlef. "Spielen, Wahrsagen, Lehren." *Weltkunst* 56, 10 (1986): 1427–1429.

* **HOFFMAN,** Detleff. "Tarot, Jeu et Magie à la Bibliothèque Nationale." *Nouvelles de l'Estampe* 79 (1985): 38–41.

* **HOFFMAN,** Detlef. *Wahrsagespiele, Los- und Orakelbücher aus Fünf Jahrhunderten.* Ill. 129 pp. (paper) 24 cm. Catalog for exhibition at Schloss Klessheim, August 27 through October 1997.

* **HOFFMANN,** Detlef. "Wenn der freche Karnöffel den König sticht." *Die Waage: Zeitschrift der Grünenthal GmbH* 4, 21 (1982): 147–153. History of playing cards. In German.

* **HOFFMANN,** Detlef, and Margot Dietrich. *Tarot Art.* Leinfelden, Germany: Deutsches Spielkarten Museum, 1989. III. 68 pp. + enclosures. Catalogue from an exhibition of Modern Art Tarot, November 1989.

* **HOLLANDER,** Hans, and Christiane Zangs. *Mit Glück und Verstand: Zur Kunst- und Kultur- geschichte der Brett- und Kartenspiele. 15. bis 17 Jahrhundert.* Germany: Thouet Verlag, 1994. Ill. 289 pp. Profusely illustrated large format catalog from an exhibition in Museum Schloss Rheydt, Monchengladbach, Germany, held July through September 1994. Includes articles on board games and playing cards.

* **HOLLANDER,** P. Scott. *Tarot for Beginners: An Easy Guide to Understanding & Interpreting the Tarot.* St. Paul, MN: Llewellyn Publications, 1995. Ill. xvi, 359 pp. 21 cm. Basic tarot, with illustrations from various decks.

* **HOLLANDER,** P. Scott. *Tarot para principiantes: Una Guía fácil para entender e interpretar el tarot.* St. Paul, MN: Llewellyn Español, 2000. Translation into Spanish of *Tarot for Beginners.*

* **HOLT,** Nancy D. "Stuart R. Kaplan, U.S. Games Systems." *The Wall Street Journal* (August 27, 2003). Part of a column "Workspaces: A Look at Where People Work." Brief history of U.S. Games Systems and description of the Stamford, Connecticut offices, and Stuart Kaplan's collection. Photograph accompanying the article features a rare look at Kaplan's office with no stray papers in sight.

HONEY TONGUE. Ayers, Jen, and Graham McNeill. Sound recording. Includes song, "Tarot."

* **HOOVER,** Tracey. *The Ancestral Path Tarot.* Stamford, CT: U.S. Games Systems, 1996. (paper) Book accompanying Ancestral Path Tarot, illustrated by Julia Cuccia-Watts.

* **HOOVER,** Tracey A. *To the Cosmic Joker.* Unpublished, 1977. Mainly tarot, but runes and ogham are also discussed.

* **HOTEMA,** Hilton. *Ancient Tarot Symbolism Revealed.* Reprint. Canada: John Ballantrae, undated. Ill. 213 pp.

HOUNSOME, Steve. *Tarot Therapy.* Berkshire, UK: Capall Bann Publishing, 1999. 322 pp. (paper) Guide to reading the tarot professionally.

* *HOUSE OF CARDS.* (Ongoing) New Jersey auction catalogs for collectible cards.

* **HUBER,** Holly, and Tracy LeCocq. *Santa Fe Tarot.* Stamford, CT: U.S. Games Systems, 1995. (paper) Book for the Sante Fe Taot, illustrated by Huber and LeCocq.

* **HUETS,** Jean. *The Cosmic Tarot.* Stamford, CT: U.S. Games Systems, 1996. Ill. xi, 162 pp. 18 cm. Book accompanying the Cosmic Tarot, illustrated by Norbert Lösche. Huets was senior editor with U.S. Games Systems during the 1980s.

** **HUETS,** Jean. *Garuda at the Source.* Manuscript. Novel, with several episodes that include tarot readings, descriptions of cards, and card games.

HULSE, David Allen. *The Key of It All.* St. Paul, MN: Llewellyn, 1994. Ill. 577 pages. The Western tradition, including tarot, runes and Enochian alphabets. Says K. Frank Jenssen: "The study on tarot is comprehensive and points to many new details."

HULSE, David Allen. *New Dimensions for the Cube of Space: The Path of Initiation Revealed by the Tarot upon the Qabalistic Cube.* York Beach, ME: Samuel Weiser, 2000. Ill. xvi, 145 pp. 26 cm.

* **HURLBUTT GALLERY.** *Five Centuries of Tarot: Fortune-telling Cards and Antique Playing Cards.* Catalog from exhibition at the Greenwich Library, Greenwich, CT, April 2–29, 1976.

* **HUSON,** Paul. *Djaevelens billedbog: Tarokbogen.* Copenhagen: Stig Vendelkrer, 1981. Ill. 254 pp. Danish translation of *The Devil's Picturebook.*

HUTTAR, Charles. "Charles Williams's Christmas Novel: The Greater Trumps." *Seven: An Anglo-American Literary Review* 4 (1983): 68-83.

* **HYATT,** Christopher S., and Lon Milo Duquette. *Sex Magic, Tantra & Tarot: The Way of the Secret Lover.* Tempe, AZ: New Falcon Publications, 1996. Ill. 191 pp. 22 cm. Expanded and revised edition of *The Way of the Secret Lover.*

* **HYATT,** Christopher S., and Lon Milo Duquette. *The Way of the Secret Lover.* Tempe, AZ: New Falcon Publications, 1991. Ill. 158 pp. The black and white line drawings by David Wilson follow Aleister Crowley's *Ritual of the Secret Lover.*

* **HYDE,** Richard. "T .S. Elliot and Tarot: The Quest for Wholeness." In *Wheel of Tarot.* James Wanless and Angeles Arrien, eds. 1992. pp. 231–241. Analysis of Elliot's "The Waste Land," with references to the tarot card imagery that inspired the poet.

I

* **ICHAZO,** Oscar. *The Arica Tarot: Colouring Cards for the Game of the Scarab.* New York: Arica Institute Press, undated. Ill. Photocopy of workshop material, on tarot.

* **IMWINKELRIED,** Rita. "Ein Magischer Garten der Mutter–Göttin." *Das Kunstmagazine* 6 (June 1993): 36–44, 46–47. Ill. In German: "A Magical Garden of the Mother Goddess." On Nikki de Saint-Phalle's tarot garden.

IN THE BEGINNING. Malice (ensemble). New York: Atlantic, 1985. Sound recording. Rock and roll album, including a piece titled "Tarot Dealer."

* **INDIRA,** Madame, and Colette Silvestre-Haéberlé. *Le tarot persan de Madame Indira: méthode d'interprétation.* Paris: J. Grancher, 1993. Ill. 177 pp. 22 cm.

* **INTERNATIONAL TAROT SOCIETY.** *Second World Tarot Congress.* July 1999. Audio cassettes of speakers at the Congress.

* **IRIS MUNDI.** *Naipeteca del Museo Fournier de Naipes.* Registry of makers of Spanish playing cards.

* **IRWIN,** Lee. *Gnostic Tarot: Mandalas for Spiritual Transformation.* York Beach, ME: Samuel Weiser, 1998. Ill. vi, 358 pp. 23 cm. Hermetic and gnostic interpretation of the tarot, including a survey on esoteric tarot through the 1990s.

J

JÁSNIAK, Aleksandra. *Wrózba z kart TAROT: podstawowe wiadomósci dla zainteresowanych tajemnica przyszlósci.* Chicago: Chemigraph, 1990 Ill. 303 pp. 22 cm. In Polish.

* **JACKSON**, Eric. *Book of the Tarot: An Introduction to the Tarot Cards.* USA: Tome Press, circa 1992. Ill. A short introductory text with line drawings of the Major Arcana, by various comic book artists.

* **JACKSON**, Nigel. *The Nigel Jackson Tarot.* St. Paul, MN: Llewellyn Publications, 2000. Ill. 143 pp. 14 cm. Book accompanying the tarot, illustrated by the author.

JACOB, Max, and Claude Valence. *Miroir d'astrologie. Éd. définitive, contenant des extraits du Livre d'Arcandam, les analogies se rapportant à chaque constellation, les correspondances astrologiques, des lames du tarot ainsi que des emblêmes proposés pour chaque signe et les dames des décans.* Paris: Gallimard, 1949. 252 pp. 19 cm. Astrology and its correspondence with the Major Arcana.

JACOBS, Michael. *Ten and Twenty-two: A Journey through the Paths of Wisdom.* Jason Aronson, Inc., 1997. Ill. 128 pp. (cloth) Tarot as paths on the Tree of Life.

JAPIKSE, Carl. *Exploring the Tarot.* Ohio: Ariel Press, 1989. Ill. 298 pp. Illustrated with the Aquarian Tarot, by David Palladini.

* **JAYANTI**, Amber. *Living the Tarot: Applying an Ancient Oracle to the Challenges of Modern Life.* New Castle Pub., 1988. Reprint. San Bernardino, Calif.: Borgo Press, 1989. xvi, 309 pp. Ill. 28 cm. Reprint. St. Paul, MN, U.S.A.: Llewellyn, 1993. xx, 345 pp. Ill. 26 cm.

JAYANTI, Amber. *Stepping through Addictive & Codependent Behavior: A Practical Guide and Workbook Using the Seven Steps of Spiritual Unfoldment Depicted by the Ancient Qabalistic Tarot.* Privately published, 1993. 37 pp. (paper, comb-bound)

* **JAYANTI**, Amber. *Tarot for Dummies.* New York: Hungry Minds, 2001. Ill. xxii, 334 pp. 24 cm. Introduction to tarot, illustrated with the Rider-Waite Tarot.

* **JEAN-DIDIER**. *Méthode de Tirage Express du Tarot.* Paris: Editions Bussiére, 1990. Ill. 159 pp. (paper) 24 cm. In French: *Express Method of Reading the Tarot.* Illustrated with Grimaud's Tarot of Marseilles. Jean-Didier's method rests on using only the Major Arcana. Also includes an illustration of Jean-Didier's own designs "Le Tarot Express de Jean-Didier," which were published as Taromino.

JEDRZIEWSKI, Anna. *Tarot as a Tool for Personal Growth: The Sacred Geometry Spreads.* New York: Inanna Works, 1997. 117 pp. (paper, comb-bound) Spreads using geometric patterns.

* **JENSEN**, K. Frank. *Bibliography of Books in Spilkammeret.* Privately published, 1993. Ill. 258 pp. (paper) Bibliography with Jensen's commentary. Includes section on tarot.

* **JENSEN**, K. Frank. *Books in Spilkammeret: Accessions 1993-1997.* Privately published, 1973. (paper) Continues where Jensen's 1993 bibliography leaves off.

* **JENSEN**, K. Frank. *A Collectors Guide to Playing Cards in Denmark.* Roskilde, Denmark: Ourobouros, 1993. Ill. (unpaginated) Includes tarot and tarock.

* **JENSEN**, K. Frank (as Asta Erte). *The Fake Mail Interview with K. Frank Jensen* Roskilde, Denmark: Ourobouros, 1997. Ill. 24 pp. (paper) Called a "fake" interview because Jensen actually "interviews" himself about mail art.

* **JENSEN**, K. Frank, ed. *The Fish Tail Tarot.* Copenhagen, 1976. Ill. Compilation of material identifying a German animal tarot deck by Zimmermann in Lubeck, circa 1820.

* **JENSEN**, K. Frank, ed. *Flowers on Gebelin's Tombstone: A silent visual zine.* Privately published, Roskilde, Denmark, from 1992 ongoing.

JENSEN, K. Frank. *Individuel Tarot: En arbejdsbog.* Roskilde, Denmark: Ouroboros, 1983. Various editions. Originally material used in workshops, later developed into a workbook to be used with Jensen's *Den personlige Tarot.*

* **JENSEN**, K. Frank, ed. *Mail Artist's Tarot.* Roskilde, Denmark: Spilkammeret, 1993. Ill. 20 pp. Documentation of the Mail Art project: Mail Artist's Tarot, initiated by Spilkammeret. Entries from all over the world are illustrated.

* **JENSEN**, K. Frank, ed. *Mail Artist's Tarot 1994.* Roskilde, Denmark: Ourbouros, 1994. 20 pp., loose color pages. Contributions to Spilkammeret's 1994 edition of Mail Artist's Tarot project. Profusely illustrated with almost all contributor's works.

* **JENSEN**, K. Frank, ed. *Mail Artist's Tarot 1995.* Roskilde, Denmark: Ouroboros, 1995. Ill. No pagination (20 pages). Documentation for the 1995 Mail Artist's Tarot project. Works by forty contributors are reproduced.

JENSEN, K. Frank, ed. *Mail Artist's Tarot 1996.* Roskilde, Denmark: Ouroboros, 1997. Ill. No pagination. Two ringbinders with original contributions to the mail art project plus the final color-illustrated documentation.

JENSEN, K. Frank, ed. *Mail Artist's Tarot 1995: The Contributions Received.* Roskilde, 1995. Ill. A ringbinder with all the original contri-

butione received for the Mail Artist's Tarot 1995 project. Includes a twenty-page magazine.

* **JENSEN**, K. Frank, ed. *The Manteia Catalog of Mantic Tools.* Privately published, 1998. (Limited edition of 14 copies) Ill. 250 pp. List of tarot and cartomancy decks not included in volumes 1-3 of *The Encyclopedia of Tarot* (by Stuart Kaplan), volumes 1-3 of *The Prophetic Cards*, or volumes 1-4 of *Manteia* magazine.

* **JENSEN**, K. Frank. *Mayers Danske Dyretarot.* Odense, Denmark: Hagen & Sorensen, 1978. Introductory booklet to the reproduction of Mayers Danske Dyretarot (animal tarot) at the National Museum in Copenhagen.

* **JENSEN**, K. Frank. *Mulleposten.* 1985 ongoing. Jensen's contribution to APA-Tarot. APA stands for Amateur Press Association. Anyone could join and contribute.

* **JENSEN**, K. Frank. *The Organization of a Collection of Playing Cards.* Privately published, Roskilde, Denmark, circa 1991. Jensen's method of cataloguing his immense collection.

* **JENSEN**, K. Frank. *The Prophetic Cards: Vol III.* Roskilde, Denmark: Ouroboros, 1996. Ill. Not paginated. (paper) 29 cm. 184 cartomancy decks from the collection of Spilkammert.

* **JENSEN**, K. Frank. *Tarot.* Copenhagen: Strubes Forlag, 1975. 201 pp. Reprint. 1981. 231 pp. Second edition was revised, especially chapter on tarot history.

JENSEN, K. Frank. *Tarot: Oprindelse, historie, symbolik (foredrag).* Unpublished manuscript, 1982. 19 pp. In Danish. Manuscript for a series of talks accompanied by slides.

* **JENSEN**, K. Frank, ed. *The Tarot Vocabulary 1992.* Roskilde, Denmark: Ouroboros, 1992. 8 pp. A tarot glossary, with an appendix on groups of tarot and cartomancy decks. Made in cooperation with Bob Jervis and APA-Tarot.

* **JENSEN**, K. Frank (as Asta Erte). *Tarotlen: Den evige billedbog.* Asta Erte is a pseudonym for K. Frank Jensen.

* **JENSEN**, K. Frank (as Asta Erte). *25 Years with Tarot.* Roskilde, Denmark: Ourobouros, 1999. Ill. 12 pp. (paper) Jensen's reflections on tarot, extracted from his journal *Manteia 1998–1999.*

* **JENSEN**, K. Frank. *The World of L.P. Holmblad.* Privately published, 1993. Ill. 24 pp. (paper) Paper on Danish cardmaker, presented by Jensen to the International Playing Card Society.

JENSEN, K. Frank. See also Erte, Asta.

JENSEN, Poul. *Tarok.* Privately published, Humlebrek, Denmark, circa 1983. Rules for the game of tarock as played in Denmark.

* **JETTE**, Christine. *Tarot for All Seasons: Celebrating the Days and Nights of Power.* St. Paul, MN: Llewellyn, 2001. Ill. xii, 154 pp. (paper) 23 cm.

JETTE, Christine. *Tarot for the Healing Heart: Using Inner Wisdom to Heal Body and Mind.* St. Paul, MN: Llewellyn Publications, 2001. Ill. xiv, 217 pp. 23 cm.

JETTE, Christine. *Tarot Shadow Work: Using the Dark Symbols to Heal.* St. Paul, MN: Llewellyn Publications, 2000. Ill. xii, 222 pp. 23 cm.

* **JIMÉNEZ**, Sebastián Vázquez. *El Tarot de los Dioses Egypcios.* Madrid: La Tabla de Esmeralda, 2000. Ill. 340 pp. (paper) 18 cm. Connects ancient Egyptian deities with the tarot. Illustrated with an Egyptian style tarot, by Cristina García Ganga.

* **JOHNSON**, Cait. *Tarot for Every Day: Ideas and Activities for Bringing Tarot Wisdom into Your Daily Life.* Wappingers Falls, N.Y.: Shawangunk Press, 1994. Ill. 170 pp. 22 cm. (paper). Self-actualization through tarot. Foreword by Z. Budapest.

JOHNSON, Cait, and Maura D. Shaw. *Tarot Games: 45 Playful Ways to Explore Tarot Cards Together; A New Vision for the Circle of Community.* San Francisco: HarperSanFrancisco, 1994. Ill. xvi, 112 pp. (paper) 24 cm. Games with tarot that build community and intimacy.

* **JOHNSON**, Don. "Card Sharks Look for a Winning Hand." *Antique Week* (January 29, 1996). On collecting playing cards, with focus on the collection of Stuart R. Kaplan.

JOHNSTON, Wayne. "The Tarot Reader." In *Atlantica: Stories from the Maritimes and Newfoundland.* Lesley Choyce, ed. Fredericton, N.B.: Goose Lane, 2001. Fiction story.

* **JONES**, Granny (Rebecca Jones). *Granny Jones Australian Tarot Book.* Australia: Kangaroo Press, 1994. Ill. 168 pp. Book accompanying the Granny Jones Tarot.

* **JONSSON**, Thomas. *Tarot: Den indre varldsomseglingen.* Sverige, Denmark: Solrosens Forlag, 1991. Ill. 216 pp. Jungian approach to tarot.

* **JORGENSEN**, Danny Lynn. "Divinatory Discourse." *Symbolic Interaction* 7, 2 (Fall 1984): 135–153. Observation of tarot readings to study occult claims to knowledge.

* **JORGENSEN**, Danny Lynn. *The Esoteric Scene, Cultic Milieu, and Occult Tarot.* New York: Garland Publishing, 1992. 269 pp. (cloth) Sociological study of tarot card readers.

* **JORGENSEN**, Danny Lynn. "Social Meanings of the Occult." *Sociological Quarterly* 23, 3 (Summer 1982): 373–389. Data from fifty professional tarot readers is used to explore the social meanings of modern occultism.

JOURNEY CONTINUES. Tantra (ensemble). New York: Importe/12,

1982. Rock and roll sound recording including pieces titled: "The Tarot Suite," "A Place Called Tarot," "The Tarot Reprise," "The Guitars of Tarot."

* **JUDHWANNA.** *Tarot Has Been Made Easy with a Little Help from Our Friends.* Weatherford, TX: Triad Publishing, 1995. Ill. 142 pp. (paper) Meanings of the cards in spreads. Illustrated with the Rider-Waite Tarot.

* **JUNJULAS,** Craig. *El Tarot Psíquico.* Mexico: Editorial Diana, 1998. Ill. 192 pp. (paper) 22 cm. *The Psychic Tarot* in Spanish, illustrated with the Aquarian Tarot by David Palladini.

K

* **K,** Amber, and Azrael Arynn K. *Heart of Tarot: An Intuitive Approach.* St. Paul, MN: Llewellyn Publications, 2002. Ill. 272 pp.

KABALEB. *Le Grand livre du tarot cabalistique.* Paris: Editions Bussière, 1991. 317 pp. (paper) Book explaining Le Tarot Cabalistique. In French.

* **KAHANER,** Laurel. "Queen of Wands." *Meditation* (1987).

* **KALLEN,** Stuart A. *Fortune-Telling.* Farmington Hills, MI: Lucent Books, 2004. Ill. 112 pp. (hardcover) 23 cm. Includes a chapter on tarot cards, and a sample reading for film actress Jennifer Aniston (not at Aniston's request). Several of the illustrations are photographs of fortune-tellers from around the world.

* **KALTENBRUNNER,** Regina. "Pagat und Sküs: Zu einer Austellung des Salzburger Museums Carolino Augusteum." *Weltkunst* 66, 6 (1996): 634–635.

* **KAPLAN,** Stuart R. *The Encyclopedia of Tarot.* Vol. III. Stamford, CT: U.S. Games Systems, 1990. Ill. 694 pp. (cloth) Mostly twentieth century decks. Includes a chapter devoted to Pamela Colman Smith.

* **KAPLAN,** Stuart R. *Klassicsches Tarot.* Neuhausen, Switzerland: Urania Verlag, 1999. Ill. 256 pp. (paper) 22 cm. German translation of *Tarot Classic.* Illustrated with various tarot decks, including Tarot Classic.

* **KAPLAN,** Stuart R. *Libro Para el Tarot James Bond 007.* Vitoria, Spain; Heraclio Fournier; Stamford, CT: U.S. Games Systems Inc. Ill. 104 pp. Spanish translation of the James Bond Tarot *Tarot of the Witches.*

* **KAPLAN,** Stuart R. *Play Your Cards: The Stuart and Marilyn R. Kaplan Playing Card Collection.* Greenwich, CT: Bruce Museum, 1995. Ill. vi, 96 pp. (paper) A catalog of the exhibition held at the Bruce Museum, Connecticut, December 1995 through February 1996.

* **KAPLAN,** Stuart R. *Tarot Classic.* Japan: Triangle Company, 1985. Ill. 66 pp. (paper) 18 cm. Japanese translation of Tarot Classic.

* **KAPLAN,** Stuart R., and Jean Huets. *The Encyclopedia of Tarot.* Vol. IV. Stamford, CT: U.S. Games Systems, 2005. Ill. 816 pp. (cloth) Mostly tarot decks from 1980 through 2004, but also includes tarock and antique decks.

KARAFCHOW, David. *Listening to the Soul: A Cabalistic Guide to the Tarot.* Woodstock, NY: Shadiam Press, 2002. 151 pp. (paper)

* **KARELYN.** *Karelyn's Instructional Tarot Workbook.* Iyi Publications: Palm Coast, FL, 2000. Ill. 170 pp. (comb-bound) Reading tarot cards. Illustrated with the Rider-Waite Tarot.

* **KÄRTNER,** Rosmarie. *TarAstro: Ihr Leben auf einem Blick.* Freiburg im Breisgau, Germany: Verlag Hermann Bauer, 2002. Ill. 136 pp. (paper) 18 cm. In German: *TarAstro: Your Life in the Blink of an Eye.* Tarot connected with astrology. Accompanied by a mini Rider-Waite Tarot deck.

* **KASER,** R. T. *Tarot in Ten Minutes.* New York: Avon Books, 1992. Ill. xiv, 346 pp. 21 cm. (paper) Illustrated with the Rider-Waite Tarot. Emphasis on reading the cards. Gives meanings according to position and relation with other cards.

* **KASHER,** Robert J. *Tarot of Baseball.* Stamford, CT: U.S. Games Systems, 1996. Ill. 115 pp. (paper) 18 cm. Book accompanying the Tarot of Baseball, illustrated by Beverley Ransom.

* **KAZANLÁR,** Amin Emil. *Tarot: Nagy Arkánumok.* Budapest: Kassák Kiadó, 1992. Ill. 87 pp. (cloth) 25 cm. A beautiful book, illustrated with the Kazanlár Major Arcana. The dust jacket of the book can be split into Major Arcana cards. The pages showing XVIII The Moon and XIX The Sun are silver and gold, respectively.

* **KAZANLAR,** Emil. *Kazanlar Tarot.* Switzerland: Urania Verlag, 1996. Ill. 223 pp. Book accompanying the Kazanlar Tarot.

KEDAR, Dorit. *Kalfe tarot: shelavim le-hàatsamat ha-mudàut ba-yomyom.* Tel Aviv: Yaron Golan, 1999. Ill. 127 pp. 21 cm. In Hebrew: *Tarot Cards: Phases towards Enhancing Daily Conciousness.*

* **KELLY,** Dorothy. *Combinaciones con el Tarot.* Madrid: Editorial Edaf, 1997. 376 pp. (paper) 21 cm. Spanish-language edition of *Tarot Card Combinations.*

* **KELLY,** Dorothy. *Tarot Card Combinations.* York Beach, ME: Samuel Weiser, 1995. Ill. x, 354 pp. 23 cm. Illustrated with the Rider-Waite Tarot. Hundreds of different meanings for combined tarot cards.

KENT-WEBSTER, Roger St. John. *The "Teach Yourself" Tarot Course and How to Do the Cabbalistic Wheel.* Devon, England: Arthur H. Stockwell, Ltd., 2002. 96 pp. (paper)

KETCH, Tina. *Get a Life: Resolving Past Life Karma. Archetypal Personalities as Seen through Tarot.* Privately published, 1991. Ill. 74 pp. (paper) Releasing fears with the tarot. Illustrated with the Rider-Waite Tarot.

KETTLEWELL, Sarah. *Guide to Tarot.* London: Caxton Editions, 2000. Ill. 237 pp. (paper) Divinatory meanings of Rider-Waite Tarot.

* **KIELCE,** Anton. *Tarot: Geheimnissvolle Krafte.* Munich: Wilhelm Heine, 1984. Ill. 156 pp. In German.

KIES, Cosette N. *The Occult in the Western World: An Annotated Bibliography.* Hamden, CT: Library Professional Publications, 1986. 233 pp. (cloth) Includes a section on tarot.

* **KI'ILEHUA,** Morgan. *Learning to Read the Symbolism of the Tarot.* Irvine, CA: Body and Mind Productions, 2000. VHS video on tarot, using the Rider-Waite Tarot.

* **KI'ILEHUA,** Morgan. *Rider-Waite: Learning to Read the Tarot Intuitively.* Irvine, CA: Body and Mind Productions, 2000. VHS video on tarot, using the Rider-Waite Tarot.

* **KING,** Francis X. *Nostradamus: Prophecies Fulfilled and Predictions for the Millenium & Beyond.* New York: St. Martin's Press, 1994. Ill. 176 pp. (paper) 28 cm. Includes a section "The Coming of the Antichrist," illustrated with XI Lust from the Book of Thoth Tarot, and reference to Aleister Crowley, who called himself the "Antichrist."

KIRCHNER, William. *Arcana for the New Dark Age.* San Francisco: Pomegranate Artbooks, 1994. Ill. 50 pp. (paper) Postcards of Major Arcana bound as a book.

KIRKPATRICK, Catriona. *Guide to the Tarot.* London: Brockhampton Press, 1996. 188 pp. (cloth) Divinatory meanings of the Rider-Waite Tarot.

* **KITHARA.** *Das Geheime Wissen einer Modernen Hexe.* Munich: W. Ludwig Buchverlag, 1996. Ill. 160 pp. (hardcover) 22 cm. Witch's handbook. Includes section on tarot, illustrated with the Rider-Waite Tarot.

* **KLIEGMAN,** Isabel Radow. *Tarot and the Tree of Life: Finding Everyday Wisdom in the Minor Arcana.* Wheaton, IL: Theosophical Publishing House, 1997. Ill. xxv, 220 pp. (paper) 23 cm.

* **KLUGMANN,** Susanna, and Alberto Milano. *Far le Carte Creazioni e proposte di carte da gioco e tarocchi.* Italy: Grafad, 1997. Ill. 58 pp. Catalog of an exhibition in Trieste, September through October 1997. Illustrated with tarot and playing cards.

* **KLUGMANN,** Susanna, et al. *Due Secoli di Carte da Gioco a Trieste.* Trieste, Italy: Grafad, 1989. Ill. 117 pp. (cloth) 20 cm. In Italian: *Two Centuries of Playing Cards in Trieste.* Book on occasion of an exhibition in Trieste, at the Palazzo della Sopritendenz, October through November 1989.

* **KLUMPER,** Ds. W. Tj. *Gestalie: Symboliek in Mystiek Friesland.* Netherlands: Geesteswetenschappelijk Centrum, undated. Ill. 16 pp. Tarot imagery in the Friesland part of the Netherlands.

* **KNIGHT,** Gareth. *The Magical World of the Tarot: Fourfold Mirror of the Universe.* London: Aquarian Press, 1991. Reprint. York Beach, ME: Samuel Weiser, 1996. Ill. 210 pp. 21 cm. (paper) An exploration of the Tarot of Marseilles, presented so as to engage the reader's imagination to "enter" the cards.

* **KNIGHT,** Gareth. *Tarot and Magic: Images for Ritual and Pathworking.* Rochester, VT: Destiny Books, 1991. Ill. 192 pp. (paper) 22 cm. Illustrated with the Tarot of Marseilles. Tarot as a meditative key to expanding consciousness.

* **KNIGHT,** Gareth. *The Tarot: Four-fold Mirror of the Universe.* Privately published, 1987. 16 pp. (paper) Introduction to history of tarot.

* **KNIGHT,** Gareth. *El Tarot Mágico: Curso Completo.* Madrid: Arkano Books, 1999. 282 pp. (paper) 22 cm. Spanish-language edition of *The Magical World of the Tarot.*

KOLLMAN, Judith. "Grendel and the Tarot." In *Spectrum of the Fantastic.* Donald Palumbo, ed. 1988.

KONRAAD, Sandor. *Classic Tarot Spreads.* Gloucester, MA: Para Research, 1985. 160 pp. Ill. (paper) 24 cm.

* **KONRAAD,** Sandor. *Numerology: Key to the Tarot.* Gloucester, MA: Para Research, 1983. Ill. 234 pp. Tarot and kabbalistic numerology.

* **KOPP,** Jonathan B. *The Use of Tarot Cards as an Archetypal Projective Instrument.* Dissertation, California School of Professional Psychology, 1984. Use of Major Arcana as thematic archetypal projective instrument.

KOPP, Karl. *Tarot Poems.* Three Rivers, MI: Three Herons Press, 1974. 55 pp. (paper)

* **KOPP,** Sheldon B. *Kopfunter hängend sehe ich alles anders: Psychotherapie und die Krafte des Dunkels.* Germany: Diederichs, 1986. Ill. 220 pp. In German: *Head-down, I See All Others: Psychotherapy and the Strength of Darkness.*

* **KÖRBEL,** Thomas. *Hermeneutik der Esoterik: Ein Phänomenologie des Kartenspiels Tarot als Beitrag zum Verständnis von Parareligiostät.* Münster: Lit Verlag, 2001. Ill. 452 pp. (paper) 23 cm.

* **KOSARIN,** Jenni. *The Everything Divining the Future Book.* Avon, MA: Adams Media Corporation, 2003. Ill. 304 pp. (paper) 21 cm. Includes information on tarot.

KOSSATS, Gummar. *The World of Tarot: The Ultimate Virtual Tarot Game.* Germany: The Magic Vision, 1995. Software for tarot readings, with nine tarot decks to choose among.

KRAGORA, Harold. *Tarot: Fotokunst.* Vienna: Aram Verlag, 1987. In German: *Tarot and photo-art.*

KRAIG, Donald Michael. *Tarot & Magic*. St. Paul, MN: Llewellyn Publications, 2002.

* **KREFTING**, Miki. *Adrian Tarot*. Switzerland: Urania Verlag, 1996. Ill. 235 pp. (paper) Book accompanying Adrian Tarot, by Adrian Koehli.

* **KREFTING**, Miki. *Einführung in den Crowley-Tarot*. Urania, 1991. Ill. 142 pp. Book accompanying Crowley Book of Thoth Tarot.

* **KREFTIG**, Miki. *Der Golden Rider Tarot: Die Bedeutung der Karten und Wie Man Sie Liegt*. Neuhausen, Switzerland: Urania Verlag, 1992. Ill. 204 pp. (paper) 18 cm. In German: *The Golden Rider Tarot: Meanings of the Cards and How to Lay Them Out.*

KRUGER, Kathryn Sullivan. "The Tarot in Yeats's Stories of Red Hanrahan." *Eire-Ireland: A Journal of Irish Studies* 26, no. 2 (Summer 1991): 62–77.

KÜNTZ, Darcy, ed. *The Sacred Book of Henoch Tarot: Synthetic and Kabbalistic Studies on the Sacred Book of Henoch Attributed to Hermes Trismegistus*. Edmonds, WA: Holmes Publishing Group, 1997. 28 pp. (paper) Golden Dawn Studies Series 17.

KURTZMAN, Mary. "Plath's 'Ariel' and Tarot." *The Centennial Review* 32, 3 (Summer 1988): 286–295.

* **KUYKENDALL**, Karen. *Cat People Tarot Handbuch*. Neuhausen, Switzerland: Urania Verlag, 1995. Ill. 187 pp. (paper) 18 cm. German translation of *Tarot of the Cat People.*

* **KUYKENDALL**, Karen. *Tarot of the Cat People: A Traveler's Report*. Stamford, CT: U.S. Games Systems, 1991. Ill. ix, 179 pp. 18 cm. Description of the Cat People Tarot, describing the different realms, costumes, and customs of the Cat People.

KYOKO, Inoue. *The Complete Book of the Tarot for Mastering Practical Use*. Japan, 2000. Ill. (cloth in slipcase) In Japanese.

* **KYSTER**, Ole. "Tarottens mange ansigter." *Solkysten* (1989). Article on tarot in magazine for Scandinavians living in Spain.

L

LA PORTA, Gabriele. *I tarocchi di Giordano Bruno: Le carte della memoria*. Milan: Jaca Book, 1984. Ill. 92 pp. 24 cm. Connecting Giordano Bruno (1548–1600) to tarot. Packaged with a tarot deck.

LABORDE, Genie Z. "Tarot: As a Hook for Fishing." *New Realities* 5, 2: 50–54. Psychological processes as taught and illustrated with the tarot, for fun and therapy.

LAMMEY, William C. *Karmic Tarot: A Profound System for Finding and Following Your Life's Path*. North Hollywood, CA: Newcastle Publishing, 1988. Reprint. San Bernardino, CA: Borgo Press, 1989, 1988. xix, 147 pp. Ill. 26 cm. Reprint. Franklin Lakes, NJ: New Page Books, 2002. Ill. 384 pp. The tarot as it corresponds to phases in life.

LANDAU, Elaine. *Fortune Telling*. Brookfield, CN: Millbrook Press, 1996. Ill. 48 pp. 23 cm. Explores palmistry, tarot card reading, crystal gazing, and other techniques that purport to foretell the future.

* **LANDERT**, Erika. "Tarot: Wenn die Seele zum Menschen spricht." *MenschSein* (February/March 1999): 21–25. In German: "Tarot: When the Souls of People Speak." Illustrated with the Rider-Waite Tarot.

LANTIERE, Joe. *Professional Tarot Reading Secrets*. Oakville, CA: Joe Lantiere Books, 1992. 41 pp. (paper) Advice on how to conduct professional tarot readings.

* **LASENIC**, Pierre. *Tarot: Klíč Iniciaci*. Prague: Trigon, 1994. Ill. 240 pp. (paper)

* **LATTANZI**, Bernardino. "La Mostra dei Tarocchi a Foligno." *Bollettino Storico della Città di Foligno* 14 (1990): 565–572.

* **LAU**, Kwan. *The I Ching Tarot: A Game of Divination and Discovery*. New York: Tengu Books, 1996. Ill. 231 pp. (paper) 18 cm. Not actually tarot. Includes 64 trigram cards illustrated by Patricia Pardini.

LAURITSEN, John. "Uranian Love in the Tarot." *Gay Books Bulletin* 5 (Spring 1981): 18–23.

LAVIOLETTE, Paul A. *Beyond the Big Bang*. Rochester, VT: Park Street Press, 1995. Ill. 374 pp. (cloth) Physics and the Egyptian tarot temple.

LAWRENCE, D. Baloti. *Tarot: Twenty-two Steps to a Higher Path*. Stamford, CT: Longmeadow Press, 1992. Ill. 160 pp. 21 cm. Self-actualization.

LEARY, Timothy. *The Game of Life: The 24 Stages of Your Neurological Tarot*. Arizona: New Falcon Publications, 1993. Ill. 288 pp. New edition.

LEARY, Timothy. *Das Spiel des Lebens: Neurologisches Tarot*. Basel, Switzerland: Sphinx Verlag, 1984. Ill. 218 pp. German translation of *The Game of Life.*

LEE, Karin. *The Amazing Fortune-telling Book*. New York: Hyperion Paperbacks for Children, 1997. Ill. 60 pp. 21 cm. Explains how to read fortunes using a variety of popular Eastern and Western methods. Includes a set of tarot cards illustrated by Kipling West.

* **LEE**, Karin. *The Halloween Tarot*. Stamford, CT: U.S. Games Systems, 1996. Ill. viii, 137 pp. (paper) 18 cm. Book accompanying the Halloween Tarot, illustrated by Kipling West.

* **LEE**, Rebecca Carol. *The Three Resurrections: Kaballistically Decoding the Book of Revelations: Correlating the three Resurrections Given in Code in the 22 Chapters of the Book of Revelation: The 22 Major Arcana of the Tarot and the 22 Hebrew Letters*. Williamstown, NC: KnightVision Press, 1999. Ill. 168 pp. Includes illustrations from the Rider-Waite Tarot.

* **LEEB**, Christian, and Michael Kassner, eds. *Tarot und Wahrsagekarten*. Munich: Münzgalerie München, 1990 ongoing. Ill. Dealer's catalog.

LEES, Jacqui. *A Complete Course in the Tarot and Psychic Development*. London: Pen Press, 1998. Ill. 115 pp. (paper) Material, emotional, physical, and spiritual interpretations of the cards. Illustrated with Zolar's Astrological Tarot Fortune-Telling cards.

LEM, Carol. *The Hermit's Journey*. Temple City, CA: Peddler Press, 1993. Ill. 51 pp. (paper) Poems for each of the Major Arcana. Illustrated with the Rider-Waite Tarot.

LEMARCHAND, Mlle. *Les récréations de la cartomancie*, Paris, Chez tous les marchands de nouveautés. 1856. Ill. 90 pp. 14 cm. Includes information on tarot cards.

* **LEONE**, Paul. *Tarot para Todos*. Buenos Aires: Ediciones Porteñas, 1996. 238 pp. (paper) 22 cm. In Spanish.

* **LERNER**, Isha. *Inner Child Cards: A Fairy Tale Tarot*. Rochester, VT: Bear & Co., 2002. Reprint of *Inner Child Cards: A Journey into Fairy Tales, Myth, and Nature.*

LERNER, Isha. *The Inner Child Cards Workbook: Further Exercises and Mystical Teachings from the Fairy-tale Tarot*. Rochester, VT: Bear & Co., 2002. Illustrated by Christopher Guilfoil.

* **LERNER**, Isha. *The Triple Goddess Tarot*. Rochester, VT: Bear and Company, 2002. Ill. 231 pp. (paper) 22 cm. Book accompanying the Triple Goddess Tarot illustrated by Mara Friedman.

* **LERNER**, Isha, and Mark Lerner. *Inner Child Cards: A Journey into Fairy Tales, Myth, and Nature*. Santa Fe, NM: Bear & Co. Pub., 1992. Ill. xxvi, 293 pp. 23 cm. Book accompanying deck of cards adapted from traditional tarot, illustrated by Christopher Guilfoil.

* **LERNER**, Mark, and Laura Philips. *Baseball Tarot: The Cards Explained*. New York: Workman Pub., 1999. Book for the tarot deck illustrated by Dan Gardiner.

* **LESUEUR**, Christine. *Le Tarot d'amour*. France: Editions Ipomée, 1985. Ill. 60 pp. (cloth) 32 cm. Accompanies deck illustrated by the author.

LEUENBERGER, Hans-Dieter. *Schule des Tarot I: Das Rad des Lebens; Ein praktischer Weg durch die großen Arkana*. Freiburg: Herman Bauer Verlag, 1993. (paper)

LEUENBERGER, Hans-Dieter. *Schule des Tarot II: Der Baum des Lebens; Tarot und Kabbala*. Freiburg: Herman Bauer Verlag, 1993. (paper)

LEUENBERGER, Hans-Dieter. *Schule des Tarot III: Das Spiel des Lebens; Tarot als Weg praktischer Esoterik*. Freiburg: Herman Bauer Verlag, 1993. (paper)

LEUENBERGER, Hans-Dieter. *Tarot: Kurz und Bündig*. Germany: Bauer Verlag, 1993. Ill. 183 pp. Divination with the tarot. In German.

* **LEUENBAERGER**, Hans-Dieter. *Tarot: Kurz und Praktisch*. Freiburg: Herman Bauer Verlag, 1995. (paper)

* **LEUENBERGER**, Hans-Dieter. "Weisheit auf losen Blättern." *Esotera* 7 (1986): 44–47 Ill. In German: "Wisdom of loose leaves."

* **LEVINE**, Leah, and Bertram Wallrath. *Tantra Tarot*. Neuhausen, Switzerland: Urania Verlag, 2002. Ill. 191 pp. (paper) 18 cm. Book accompanying the Tantric Tarot illustrated by the authors.

* **LEVITT**, Susan. *Introduction to Tarot*. Stamford, CT: U.S. Games Systems, 2002. Ill. 246 pp. (paper; spiral bound) 22 cm. As the title says, the book introduces the tarot, but differs from most treatments by covering a variety of topics and ways to interpret and work with the tarot. Illustrated mainly with the Rider-Waite Tarot and Book of Thoth Tarot.

* **LEVITT**, Susan. *Tarot Journal*. Stamford, CT: U.S. Games Systems, 2002. Ill. 166 pp. (paper; spiral bound) 22 cm. Workbook that guides one through different spreads. Accompanies Levitt's *Introduction to Tarot.*

LHOTE, Jean-Marie. *Court de Gebelin: Le Tarot, présenté et commenté*. Paris: Berg International Editeurs, 1983. 195 pp. (paper) Analysis of *Le Monde Primitif*, by Court de Gebelin. In French.

LICHTENBERG, Jacqueline. *Never Cross a Palm with Silver. The Biblical Tarot*. Laceyville, PA: Belfry Books, 1997. Ill. 184 pp. (paper) Christian interpretation of the tarot.

* **LIEBENSON**, Bess. "300 Years of Human Experience, All on the Cards." *New York Times* (January 7, 1996). Article on collection of Stuart

Kaplan, on occasion of the exhibition at the Bruce Museum, Connecticut.

LINDEN, Michlen. *Typhonian Taratomas: The Shadows of the Abyss.* Cincinnati: Black Moon Publishing, 1991. About Shadow Tarot, illustrated by Linda Falorio.

* **LINDGREN,** Viveka. "Se in I de Magiska Kortens Värld!" *Hemmets Journal* (April 24, 1995): 80–85. Illustrated with the Rider-Waite Tarot.

* **LIONNET,** Annie. *Los Secretos del Tarot.* Hohenzollernring, Germany: Taschen, 2003. 224 pp. (hardcover) 13 cm. Spanish-language editin of *Secrets of the Tarot.*

LIONNET, Annie. *Secrets of Tarot.* New York: Dorling Kindersley Pub., 2000. Ill. 224 pp. 14 cm.

* **LIONNET,** Annie. *The Tarot Directory.* Edison, NJ: Chartwell Books, 2002. Ill. 207 pp. (hardcover) 22 cm. Basic tarot. Includes two pages listing "useful websites and books."

* *LIVE AND LET DIE.* Brochure from premier of the film. Cover is illustrated with tarot cards featuring the characters from the film.

* **LLAUGÉ,** Félix. *Tarot Básico.* Barcelona: Ediciones Martínez Roca, 1995. 298 pp. (paper) 24 cm. In Spanish.

* *LO SCARABEO.* Catalog of Italian card publisher. From Turin.

LOGUE, Carol Jean. *PC Gypsy.* Spirit Lake, ID: Rosehips Ink, circa 1989. Divination software.

* **LOGUE,** Carol Jean. *The Tarot Gypsy Tales.* Spirit Lake, ID: Rosehips Ink, 1989. Ill. 287 pp. (cloth) Poetry and paintings of the tarot.

* **LOGUE,** Carol Jean. *Tarot Gypsy Tapes.* Northern Electron Works, 1989. 2 computer floppy disks with a user's manual (107 pp.) + 1 brochure. Program lets users explore the symbols and history of tarot cards. Users can ask questions of the "Gypsy", choose cards and store their readings. Accompanied by sound cassette *The Tarot Gypsy Tapes* (90 min.: analog) and book *The Tarot Gypsy Tales* (Ill. 287 pp. 15 cm.). In velvet pouch.

LOPARCO, Marie Berg. *The Tarot: A Study of the Historical and Contemporary Illustration of Seven Feminine Archetypes of the Major Arcana.* Master of Fine Arts Thesis, Syracuse University, 1990. 224 pp.

* **LÖSCHE,** Norbert. *Tarot Cosmic.* Madrid: Arkano Books, 1999. 192 pp. (paper) In Spanish. Book accompanying the Cosmic Tarot.

* **LOTTERHAND,** Jason C. *The Thursday Night Tarot.* Arisa Victor, ed. North Hollywood, CA: New Castle Publishing, 1989. Ill. 355 pp. (paper) Tarot based on Paul Foster Case's ideas.

* **LOUIS,** Anthony. *Tarot Plain and Simple.* St. Paul, MN: Llewellyn Publications, 1996. Ill. ix, 322 pp. (paper) 23 cm. Illustrated with Robin Wood Tarot.

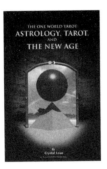

* **LOVE,** Crystal. *The One World Tarot: Astrology, Tarot, and the New Age.* Stamford, CT: U.S. Games Systems, 2002. Ill. 290 pp. (paper) 17 cm. Companion book to the One World Tarot, illustrated by the author's son, Michael Hobbs.

* **LOZAR-PODLOGAR,** Helena. "Slovanske sege na tarok kartah Hinka Smrekarja." *Traditions* 21 (1992): 213-226.

* **LUBLINER,** Larry. *Playing Card Auction of the Fred G. Taylor Collection.* February 1998. Ill. Includes tarock.

LUCIA, Lina. *Releasing through the Tarot.* Stone Mountain, GA: Lucia Publishing Company, 1988. Ill. 122 pp. Techniques to release psychological problems, using the tarot.

* **LÜDELING,** Ingeborg M. *Steine, Bäume, Menschenträume: Ein Spirituelles Erlebnisbuch mit 24 übungen.* Freiburg im Breisgau, Germany: Verlag Hermann Bauer, 1997. Ill. 220 pp. (paper) 21 cm. In German: *Stones, Trees and Dreams: A Spiritual Lesson Book of 24 Lessons.* Includes some references to tarot cards XII The Hanged Man and IX The Hermit, illustrated with the Rider-Waite Tarot.

* **LUETGEBRUNE,** Barbara. *Heilung Durch Erkenntnis: Das Kosmische Tarot.* Germany: Windpferd Verlag, 1988. Ill. 189 pp. In German: *Healing through Knowledge: The Cosmic Tarot.* Tarot as therapy; not connected with the Cosmic Tarot deck by Norbert Lösche.

* **LUZ,** Angela. *Curso Practico Tarot Profesional.* Buenos Aires: Blotta & Blotta, 2004. 256 pp. (paper) 21 cm. In Spanish: *Practical Course in Professional Tarot.*

* **LYLE,** Jane. *The Key to the Tarot.* San Francisco: HarperCollins, 1995. Ill.

Unpaginated. (cloth) 17 cm. Illustrated with Fournier's Tarot of Marseilles.

* **LYLE,** Jane. *The Lovers' Tarot: For Affairs of the Heart.* New York: St. Martin's Press, 1992. Ill. 160 pp. 22 cm. (cloth) Includes Major Arcana deck illustrated by Oliver Burston.

* **LYLE,** Jane. *The Renaissance Tarot.* New York: Fireside, 1998. Ill. 192 pp. (paper) 21 cm. Book accompanying the Renaissance Tarot illustrated by Helen Jones.

* **LYLE,** Jane. *Tarot.* London: Hamlyn; USA: Mallard Press, 1990. Ill. 160 pp. 31 cm. Introduction to tarot.

* **LYLE,** Jane. *El Tarot del Renacimiento.* Madrid: Editorial Sirio, 2001. Spanish-language edition of *The Renaissance Tarot.*

LYONS, Albert S. *Predicting the Future.* New York: Harry N. Abrams, 1990. Ill. 431 pp. (cloth) Survey of divination, with a chapter dedicated to tarot.

M

MACGREGOR, T.J. *The Hanged Man.* New York: Kensington Publishing Corp., 1998. 314 pp. (cloth) Mystery novel featuring the tarot.

* **MACGREGOR,** Trish, and Phyllis Vega. *Power Tarot: More than 100 Spreads that Give Specific Answers to Your Most Important Questions.* New York: Simon & Schuster, 1998. Ill. 288 pp. 22 cm.

* **MACNAB,** Geoffrey. "Tarot and Toads in Coats." *Sight & Sound* 9, 6 (June 1999): 58-59. Interview with Alexandro Jodorowsky, director of the film *The Holy Mountain.*

MACOU, Jacqueline. *Le Tarot Psychologique.* Paris: Editions Dervy, 1993. 208 pp. (paper) Numerological and astrological correspondances. In French.

* *MAGICAL LINK.* New York, NY. Newsletter of the Ordo Templi Orientis. Vol 2, No. 3 (September/October 1988) includes correspondence between Aleister Crowley and Frieda Harris concerning the Book of Thoth Tarot, a work in progress at the time.

* **MAIZELS,** John. "Fantasy Worlds." *Raw Vision* 28 (Fall 1999): 34-35.

* **MALA,** Matthias. *Orakelspiele: Verspielte Anworten auf Schicksalhafte Fragen.* Munich: Hugendubel Verlag, 1996. Ill. 212 pp. (hardcover) 23 cm. In German. Fortune-telling with playing cards. Cover is illustrated with the Seven of Cups from the Royal Fez Moroccan Tarot.

* **MALA,** Matthias. *Das Tarot Losbuch: Ein Spiel für Alle Lebenslagen.* Munich: Hugendubel Verlag, 1994. Ill. 184 pp. (hardcover) 23 cm. In German. Illustrated with the Royal Fez Moroccan Tarot. Reading the tarot cards, with affirmations for different outcomes.

* **MANDEL,** Gabriele. *I Tarocchi.* Legnano, Italy: Gruppo editorale EdiCart, 1994. Ill. 60 pp. History of tarot, with information on card-makers. In Italian.

* **MANDEL,** Gabriele. *I Tarocchini.* Italy: Grafica Gutenberg, 1978. 20 pp. 22 cm. (paper) Booklet accompanying the Tarot of Giuseppe Maria Mitelli. In Italian.

* **MANN,** A. E. *Techikos: Songs of Berenice and Tarot.* Privately published, 1990. Ill. 22 cm. Verses on tarot, illustrated with the Swiss 1JJ Tarot.

* **MANN,** A. T. *The Elements of Tarot.* England: Element Books, 1993. Ill. 152 pages. Basic tarot, with affirmations. Illustrated with the Rider-Waite Tarot.

MANN, A. T. *Tarot: Den nye guide til tarotkortene.* Copenhagen, Denmark: Lindhardt & Ringhof, 1995. Ill. 151 pages. Danish edition of *The Elements of Tarot.*

* **MANN,** A.T. *The Secrets of the Tarot: A Guide to Inner Wisdom.* London: Thorsons, 2002. Ill. 167 pp. (paper) trade. Originally published as *The Elements of Tarot.*

* **MANN,** A. T. *The Tarot: An Introductory Guide to Unlocking the Secrets of the Tarot.* Shaftesbury, Dorset; Rockport, MA: Element, 1999. Ill. 128 pp. 20 cm. Originally published as *The Elements of Tarot.*

MANN, William F. *The Labyrinth of the Grail.* Grand Bay, AL: Laughing Owl Pub., 1999. Ill. xviii, 325 pp.

* **MARGRE,** Maurice. *La clef des choses cachées.* Paris, Fasquelle, 1935. 106 pp. 19 cm. In French: *The Key to Hidden Things.* Covers Druids and druidism, Grail legends, and tarot.

* **MARIOTTO,** Florent. *Cours sur le Tarot.* Paris: Editions Trajectoire, 2004. Ill. 288 pp. (paper) 24 cm.

* **MARIOTTI,** Giovanni. "Tarocchi: Il destino si svela nel giardino dei giganti colorati." *Arte* 287 (July 1997): 22–23. In Italian: "Tarot cards: Destiny reveals itself in the garden of colored giants." About Niki de Saint Phalle's Tarot Garden.

* **MARIUS,** Docteur. *Divining Cards: Suits of Love.* New York: Modiano Graphic Arts, 1950. Ill. 71 pp. (paper) Divination with playing cards.

MARKEY, Constance. "The Tarot Cards as Subversive Tool in Italo Calvino." In *Aspects of Fantasy: Selected Essays from the Second International Conference on the Fantastic in Literature and Film.* William Coyle, ed. 1986.

* **MARKS,** Londa. *Crow's Magick.* Stamford, CT: U.S. Games Systems, 2001. Ill. 191 pp. (paper) 18 cm. Book accompanying the Crow's Magick Tarot by Marks.

MARKS, Londa. *Londa Marks.* USA: Wicca Gallery Video, 1994. A promotional video with Londa Marks.

* **MARQUES-RIVIÈRE,** Jean. *Histoire des Doctrines Esoteriques.* Paris: Payot, 1940. Ill. In French: *History of Esoteric Doctrines.* Includes information on tarot.

* **MARSALA,** Jackie. *Le Tirage Sacrée.* Paris: Editions Trajectoire, 2003. 192 pp. (paper) 24 cm. Accompanies a large Major Arcana Tarot of Marseilles.

* **MARTELLO,** Leo Louis. *Reading the Tarot.* Garden City Park, NY: Avery Publishing Group, 1990. Ill. 202 pp. (paper) 21 cm. Includes combinations of cards and memnomic rhymes on the meanings.

MARTÍ I POL, Miquel. *Cinc esgrafiats a la mateixa paret.* Barcelona: Lumen, 1975. Ill. 16 pp. 25 cm.

* **MARTIN,** Elizabeth. *El Tarot de Sirio.* Madrid: Editorial Sirio, 2001. 260 pp. (paper) 21 cm. In Spanish. Book about the Sirio Tarot, by Marcela Garcia.

* **MARTIN,** Joseph Ernest. *The Compass: Guide to the Quest Tarot.* St. Paul, MN: Llewellyn Publications, 2003. Ill. 296 pp. (paper) 22 cm. Companion book to Martin's Quest Tarot.

* **MARTIN,** Pat. "Proactive Tarot." *New Pentacle* 2, 4 (Summer 1998): 45–48. Using tarot as a tool to create circumstances, versus predictions.

* **MARTIN,** Pat. "Spoilt for Choice: Tarot Decks and How to Select One." *New Pentacle* 2, 2 (Winter 1998): 19–22. Survey of popular decks and books.

* **MARTIN,** Pat. "Tarot: Old Magic, New Age." *New Pentacle* 2, 1 (Autumn 1998): 43–45. On the popularization of tarot.

* **MARTIN,** Pat. "Technotarot." *New Pentacle* 2, 3 (Spring 1998): 37–39. Ethical considerations of on-line tarot reading.

* **MARTINIÉ,** Louis. *The New Orleans Voodoo Tarot.* Rochester, VT: Destiny Book, 1992. Ill. 276 pp. 23 cm. (paper). Book accompanying New Orleans Voodoo Tarot illustrated by Sallie Ann Glassman. .

* **MASINO,** Marcia. *Easy Tarot Guide.* San Diego, CA: ACS Publications, 1987. Ill. 270 pp. (paper) 21 cm. Lessons on the tarot, illustrated with the Rider-Waite Tarot. Includes exercises.

MASSACRIER, Jacques. *Le jeu de tarot par l'image: avec les symboles traditionnels des arcanes majeurs pour les atouts.* Paris: A. Michel, 1983. Ill. 32 pp. 31 cm. In French. Symbolism of the Major Arcana.

* **MATTEI,** Luigi E. *Luigi E. Mattei: Sculptura a grafica.* Bologna, 1991. Ill. In Italian: *Luigi E. Mattei: Sculptor and Artist.*

* **MATTHEWS,** Caitlin, and John Matthews. *The Arthurian Tarot: A Hallowquest Handbook.* London: Thorsons, 1990. Ill. 190 pp. 23 cm. (paper) Book accompanying the Arthurian Tarot illustrated by Miranda Gray.

* **MATTHEWS,** Caitlin. *The Arthurian Tarot Course: A Quest for All Seasons.* Wellingborough, Northamptonshire: Thorsons/HarperCollins, 1993. Ill. 267 pp. The author describes the book as "a year's journey into the Celtic Otherworld." Based on the Arthurian Tarot. The material differs from the book that accompanies the deck and from the author's *Hallowquest.* Includes activities such as meditations, rituals, and card spreads.

THE CELTIC WISDOM TAROT
Caitlin Matthews

* **MATTHEWS,** Caitlin. *The Celtic Wisdom Tarot.* Rochester, VT: Destiny Books, 1999. Ill. 143 pp. 21 cm. Book accompanying tarot deck illustrated by Olivia Rayner.

* **MATTHEWS,** Caitlin, and John Matthews. *Hallowquest: Tarot Magic and the Arthurian Mysteries.* London: Aquarian Press, 1990. Ill. 303 pp. (paper) 21 cm. On the Arthurian Tarot, with an exploration of Arthurian lore.

* **MATTHEWS,** Caitlin, and John Matthews. *El Tarot Artúrucio.* Madrid: Editorial Edaf, 2004. 174 pp. (paper) 23 cm. Spanish-language edition of *The Arthurian Tarot.*

MATZAK, Kurt Hildebrand. *Tarok, Rota, Tarot: Das Geheimnis der Tarokkarte* Graz; Wien: Leykam Verlag, 1976. Ill. 87 pp. 24 cm.

MATZAK, Kurt Hildebrand. *Das Geheimnis des Kartenschlagens von Johannes Trismegistus.* Graz; Wien: Leykam Verlag, 1978. Ill. 106 pp. A re-edition of a book on fortune-telling by cards, originally published in Ulm, Germany, in 1846. Includes commentary on Major Arcana.

* **MAYER-RECHNITZ,** Cecilia. *Tarot.* Privately published, Chile, circa

1991. 22 pp. Handwritten book accompanying tarot deck by author.

MCCARROLL, Amber. *The Kaleidoscope of Day Dreams.* Atlanta, GA: JJ Publishing, 1998. Ill. 112 pp. (paper) Poetry for the Major Arcana, with artwork by Veronique Pignatta.

MCCARROLL, Tolbert. *Exploring the Inner World: A Guidebook for Personal Growth and Renewal.* New York: Julian Press, 1971. 222 pp.

MCCLOSKEY, Michael. *Tarocco.* Privately published, 1973. 24 pp. (paper) A short poem for each of the Major Arcana.

* **MCCLUSKEY,** John William. *Amazing Mystic Tarot.* East Hampton, NY: Arden Book Company, 2002. Ill. 239 pp. (paper) Divinatory meanings for the Rider-Waite Tarot.

MCCORMACK, Kathleen. *Beginner's Tarot.* Hauppauge, NY: Barron's, 2001. Ill. 80 pp. 20 cm. Book accompanying the Beginner's Tarot, illustrated by John Woodcock.

* **MCCORMACK,** Kathleen. *Tarot Decoder.* Hauppauge, NY: Barron's Educational Series, 1998. Ill. 148 pp. (paper) 28 cm. Basics of tarot, illustrated with various decks.

MCCORMACK, Kathleen. *The Tarot Workbook: An IQ Book for the Tarot Practitioner.* Hauppauge, NY: Barron's, 2002. Ill. 128 pp. (paper) 25 cm.

* **MCCUSKER,** Brian, and Cherie Sutherland. "Probability and the Psyche: A Reproducible Experiment Using Tarot, and the Theory of Probability." *Journal of the Society for Psychical Research* 57, 822 (January 1991): 344–353.

MCDANIEL, Ellen. "The Magus: Fowles's Tarot Quest." *Journal of Modern Literature* 8, no. 2 (1980–1981): 247–260.

MCKIE, Jyoti, and David McKie. *The Healing Earth Tarot: A Journey in Self-discovery, Empowerment and Planetary Healing.* St. Paul, MN: Llewellyn Publications, 1994. Ill. xvii, 262 pp. (paper) 20 cm. Book accompanying Healing Earth Tarot.

MCLAINE, Patricia. *The Wheel of Destiny: The Tarot Reveals Your Master Plan: The Master Spread of the Tarot Major Arcana.* St. Paul, MN: Llewellyn Publications, 1991. Ill. 461 pp. (paper) 26 cm. Tarot interpreted through astrology.

* **MCVITIE,** Anne. *Teach Yourself Tarot the Easy Way.* Glasgow: Flashback Communications, 1996. Video to learn Celtic Cross spread. Packaged with the Connolly Tarot.

MEDICATOR. See Dirk Gillabel.

* **MEDICI,** Marina. *Good Magic.* New York: Simon and Schuster, 1988. Ill. 252 pp. (paper) 23 cm. Incantations, herbs, stones, and so on, with a short section on tarot for divination.

* **MELDI,** Diego. *Tarot: La Historia, el Simbolismo, y el Juego.* Buenos Aires: Editorial el Ateneo, 2001. 352 pp. (paper) 25 cm. Spanish-language edition of *I Tarocchi.*

MELODY. *Love Is in the Earth: Crystal Tarot: The Tarot for the Millennium* Wheat Ridge, CO: Earth-Love Pub. House, 2001. 171 pp. 23 cm. Book accompanying Crystal Tarot, illustrated by Steve Goins.

MELTON, J. Gordon. *Magic, Witchcraft, and Paganism in America: A Bibliography.* New York: Garland Publishing, 1982. 231 pp. (cloth) Includes references to tarot.

MELTON, J. Gordon. *New Age Encyclopedia.* Detroit: Gale Research, 1990. Ill. 586 pp. (cloth) Includes section on history of tarot, attributing the Major Arcana to Hellenistic Egypt, and the Minor Arcana to the ancient Celts.

MEMO, Nino. *Arcana: Alchimia del Simbolo.* Venice: Edizioni Galleria d'Arte Ravagnan, 1990. Ill. 37 pp. Catalogue from exhibition of alchemical and symbolic lithographs by Memo.

* **MENDOZA,** Staci, and David Bourne. *Tarot: Your Destiny Revealed in the Cards.* Australia: Southwater, 2000. Ill. 64 pp. (paper) Basic tarot, with illustrations from various decks. Also includes illustrations of Major Arcana themes from other sources.

* **MENDOZA,** Staci, and David Bourne. *The Element Tarot.* London: Element Books, 2002. Ill. 151 pp. (paper) 18 cm. Book accompanying the Element Tarot (formerly Dreamers Tarot), by Mendoza and Bourne.

* **MERTZ,** B.A., and Paul Struck. *Astrologie und Tarot.* Switzerland: Ansata Verlag, 1981. Ill. 202 pp. In German: *Astrology and Tarot.* Accompanies deck of cards.

* **MERTZ,** Bernd. *Tarot für Alle Decks.* Germany: Falken-Verlag, 1996. Ill. 144 pp. (paper) 18 cm. Basic tarot, illustrated with various decks.

* **MGM JOKER KG.** *Spielkartenangebot.* Ongoing. Catalog of antiquarian playing cards, including tarot.

* **MICHELSEN,** Teresa. *Designing Your Own Tarot Spreads.* St. Paul, MN: Llewellyn, 2003. Ill. 156 pp. (paper) 23 cm. Tarot spreads for all occasions.

MILCOVITCH, Mircea. *Des symboles universels a la spiritualité chrétienne.* Paris: Editions Retz, 1991. Ill. 190 pp. 23 cm. Includes commentary on tarot.

MILLER, Carol. *El profeta alado.* Mexico: Editorial Diana, 1990. 281 pp. 21 cm. Spanish edition of *The Winged Prophet.*

MILLER, Carol, and Guadalupe Rivera. *The Winged Prophet from Hermes to Quetzalcoatl: An Introduction to the Mesoamerican Deities through the Tarot.* York Beach, ME: Samuel Weiser, 1994. Ill. xvi, 323 pp. (paper) 23 cm.

* **MILLER,** Christopher. "The Changing Fortunes of Georges de la

Tour." *Art and Antiquities* (December 1996): 48–55. Nothing on tarot, but a beautiful (though cropped) two-page spread of de la Tour's "The Cheat with the Ace of Clubs."

MILLER, Lynn C. *The Fool's Journey: A Romance.* Houston: Winedale Publishing, 2002. 290 pp. (paper) Romance novel featuring tarot.

* MILLER, Maxwell. *The Universal Tarot.* Scotland: Findhorn Press; York Beach, ME: Samuel Weiser, 1996. (paper) Book accompanying Universal Tarot by Miller.

MÍNGUEZ NEGRE, Núria. *Tarot per un mort: Novella.* Barcelona: Edicions Paraula Magna, 1996. 257 pp. 22 cm.

MIRANDE, Bernard. *Le Tarot Initiatique et les Reves.* Paris: Editions Francois de Villac, 1991. Ill. 396 pp. Illustrated with a tarot deck based on the Oswald Wirth designs.

* MITELLI, G.M. *Das Tarockspiel aus Bologna.* Wurzburg: Popp, 1979. Ill. 20 pp.

* MOAKLEY, Gertrude. "Ancient Chinese Book Started this Collection." *Hobbies* (March 1958): 122. A personal account of Moakley's passion for collecting cards.

* MOAKLEY, Gertrude. *Memorabilia.* A treasury of tarotist Moakley's collection of tarot memorabilia, including two volumes of scrapbooks, manuscripts, correspondence, "wish list" of decks for her collection, and more.

MOENCH & MORROW. *The Spectre.* DC Comics (June 15, 1988). Comic book in which the characters enter into tarot cards.

MOISE, Edwin. "The 'Hanged Man' in 'The Waste Land.'" *Notes and Queries* 39, no. 2 (June 1992): 193.

MÖLLER, Ingrid. *Das La Fontaine-Tarock des Leipziger Kaufmanns Peter Friedrich Ulrich.* Würzburg: Edition Popp, 1980. Ill. 168 pp. 11 cm. Text in English and German. La Fontaine Tarock by cardmaker Peter Friedrich Ulrich, made Leipzig circa 1778.

* MONREAL, Violeta. *El Rey Negro.* Madrid: Revista Punto de Encuentro, 1995. Ill. 24 pp. (paper) 14 cm.

* MONTALBAN, Madeline. *The Prediction Book of the Tarot.* Poole, Dorset: Blandford Press; New York, NY: Sterling Pub. Co., 1983. Ill. 127 pp. (paper) 22 cm. Relates pre-Columbian symbolism with symbolism of the tarot.

* MONTANGERO, Nina. *Le Tarot Médiéval.* Montreaux, Switzerland: Editions Indigo–Montangero, 2002. Ill. 245 pp. (paper) 21 cm. In French. Book accompanying Tarot Médiéval, illustrated by Pal Degome.

* MONTANGERO, Nina. *Le Tarot: Outil de développement personnel.* Lausanne: Editions Indigo–Montangero, 2001. Ill. 213 pp. (paper) 21 cm. In French: *The Tarot: Tool for Personal Development.* Includes section that matches tarot cards with the chakras.

* MONTANO, Mario. *Meister Tarot.* Switzerland: AGMüller/Urania, 1996. Ill. 253 pages. Book accompanying the Meister Tarot (Tarot of the Master) illustrated by Amerigo Folchi.

* MONTANO, Mario. *Poker mit dem Unbewussten.* Germany: Hermann Bauer, 1990. Ill. 316 pp. In German: *Poker with the Unknown.* Although the book is about using tarot, the deck accompanying the book is not a traditional tarot.

MONTANO, Mario. *Tarot. Livets Spil.* Copenhagen, Denmark: Sphinx, 1993. 144 pp. Translation of *Tarot: Spiegel des Lebens.* Accompanies Danish edition of the Rider-Waite Tarot deck (deck with Danish titles).

* MONTANO, Mario. *Tarot Rider: El Espejo de la Vida.* Madrid: Arkano Books, 1999. In Spanish. Book accompanying the Rider-Waite Tarot.

MONTANO, Mario, and Mauro De Matteis. *Tarot: Spiegel deiner Liebe.* Neuhausen, Switzerland: Urania Verlag, 1994. Ill. 157 pp. In German: *Tarot: Mirror of Your Love.* Book accompanying Tarot der Liebe.

MOORE, Alan, J.H. Williams, Mich Gray, Jeromy Cox, Todd Klein, and Jose Willarrubia. *Promethea* 12. La Jolia, CA: America's Best Comics, 2000. Comic book on tarot.

MOORE, Francis, Edwin J. Nigg, and Karl Spiesberger. *Secrets of the New Age.* New York: Bell Pub. Co., 1989. Ill. 24 cm. Three books reproduced and bound together, including Nigg's "Reveal the Secrets of the Tarot."

* MORAG, Hali. *The Complete Guide to Tarot Reading.* Israel: Astrolog Publishing, 1998. Ill. 160 pp. (paper) 21 cm. Basic tarot, illustrated with the Rider-Waite Tarot.

* MORGAN, Chris. *The Fortune Telling Kit: A Fun Guide to the Future!* New York: Barron's, 1996. 64 pp. (pape) 31 cm. Book is packaged with tarot cards, rune stones with a drawstring pouch, and Chinese coins.

* MORGAN, David, and Sally M. Promey. *The Visual Culture of American Religions.* Berkeley, CA: University of California Press, 2001. Ill. xiv, 437 pp. (paper) 25 cm. Includes commentary on interpreting tarot cards.

* MORGAN, Diane. *Magical Tarot, Mystical Tao: Unlocking the Hidden Power of the Tarot Using the Ancient Secrets of the Tao Te Ching.* New York: St. Martin's Griffin, 2003. 261 pp. (paper) 23 cm. Tarot aligned with Tao Te Ching. Illustrated with the Rider-Waite Tarot.

* MORGAN, Ffiona. *Daughters of the Moon Tarot.* Willits, CA: Daughters of the Moon, 1984. Reprint. Novato, CA: Daughters of the Moon, 1991. 2000. 88 pp. Ill. 21 cm. On the Daughters of the Moon Tarot.

* MORGAN, Ffiona. *Mysteries of the Goddess: Astrology, Tarot and the*

Magical Arts. Graton, CA: Daughters of the Moon Publishing, 1991. Ill. 179 pp. (paper) Guidebook to Daughters of the Moon Tarot. Originally published as *Wild Witches Don't Get the Blues.*

* MORGAN, Ffiona. *Wild Witches Don't Get the Blues.* Novata, CA: Daughters of the Moon Publishing, 1991. Ill. 284 pp. Book on the Daughters of the Moon Tarot.

MORGAN, Keith. *Read the Tarot in 7 Days.* London: Pentacle Enterprises, 1991. Ill. 34 pp. (paper) A complete course for learning to use the tarot for divination in seven days.

MORGAN, Michele. *A Magical Course in Tarot: Reading the Cards in a Whole New Way.* Berkeley, CA: Conari Press, 2002. Ill. 245 pp. 18 cm.

* MORLEY, Lord. (Henry Parker). *Tryumphes of Fraunces Petrarcke: The First English Translation of the Trionfi.* D.D. Carnicelli, ed. London: Oxford University Press, 1971.

* MORRIS, Christopher. *The Hanging Figure: On Suspense and the Films of Alfred Hitchcock.* Westport, CT: Praeger Publishers, 2002. Ill. 315 pp. (cloth) 24 cm. Page 80–82 are about XII The Hanged Man, including an illustration from the Universal Waite Tarot.

MORRISON, Dorothy. *Everyday Tarot Magic: Meditation & Spells.* St. Paul, MN: Llewellyn Publications, 2002.

* MORRISON, Dorothy. *The Whimsical Tarot: A Deck for Children and the Young at Heart.* Stamford, CT: U.S. Games Systems, 2001. Ill. 204 pp. (paper) 18 cm. Book accompanying the Whimsical Tarot, illustrated by Mary Hanson-Roberts.

* MOSCARDÓ, Margarita Arnal. *El Tarot Egipcio.* Barcelona: Plaza & Janes Editores, 1992. Book accompanying Tarot Egipcio, by the author.

* MUELLER, Robert E., and Signe E. Echols, with Sandra A. Thomson. *The Lovers' Tarot.* New York: Avon Books, 1993. Ill. xiv, 305 pp. 21 cm. Relationships and the tarot. Illustrated with the Rider-Waite Tarot.

* MULLEN, Dikki-Jo. "Tarot Magic." *Horoscope Guide* 88, 8 (August 1990): 16–19. Connection of zodiac with tarot Major Arcana. Illustrated with the Rider-Waite Tarot.

MULLER, Marcia. *Ask the Cards a Question.* New York: Mysterious Press, 1990. 209 pp. (paper) Mystery involving a tarot reader.

* MUSEO FOURNIER DE NAIPES DE ALAVA. *Catalogo.* Multiple volumes. Spain: Museo Fournier de Naipes, circa 2000. Catalog of Museo Fournier's holdings, with color illustrations.

* MUSIC OF THE TAROT. David and Steve Gordan. Topanga, CA: Sequoia Records, 1993. Sound recording. Music composed for groups of tarot cards.

* MYSTIC MEG. *Mystic Tarot.* UK: Carlton Books, 1997. Ill. 128 pp. (paper) 18 cm. Book accompanying deck illustrated by Caroline Smith.

* MYSTIC MEG. "Play My Tarot Game of Fortune, I dare you!" *Luxury Lifestyles of the Rich and Famous* (May 1996): 30, 31. Meanings of various tarot cards, randomly selected. Illustrated with the Universal Waite Tarot. The game is played by flipping a coin onto the pages of the magazine, then reading the fortune where the coin falls.

* MYSTIC MIMI. "Tarot Revealed: The Lovers." *The Twelfth House* 1, 2: 29, 38. Article on VI The Lovers.

N

NAIFF, Nei. *Curso Completo de Tarô.* Brazil: Record/Nova Era, 2002. Illustrated with designs later issued as Tarô Clássico, by Thais de Linhares.

* NAIFF, Nei. *Tarô, Ocultismo & Modernidade.* Brazil: Elevação, 2000. Ill. 392 pp. (paper) 20 cm.

NAMRON. *The Secrets of the Marseilles Tarot.* London: Namron Books, 1990. Ill. 144 pp.

NAMRON. *Shade of the Marseilles Tarot.* London: Namron Books, 1996. 340 pp. (paper) Numerological and mythological meanings for the cards.

NANNY, Max. "'Cards Are Queer': A New Reading of the Tarot in The Waste Land." *English Studies: A Journal of English Language and Literature* 62, no. 4 (August 1981): 335–347.

NEIMARK, Jill. "Do the Spirits Move You?" *Psychology Today* 29, 5:

48–54. Investigation into the paranormal, illustrated with photographic tarot cards.

* **NETTLES**, Bea. *Knights of Assisi: A Journey through the Tarot.* Ill. 24 pp. (paper) 22 cm. Photographs based on the male characters of the tarot. Shot on location in Assisi, Italy. Nettles created the first photographic tarot, Mountain Dream Tarot.

NEUTZSKY-WULFF, Erwin. *AME Tarok.* Copenhagen: Sphinx, 1994. 31 pp. Booklet accompanying second edition of Neutzsky-Wulff's "Tarot Majora Extensa."

* **NEUTZSKY-WULFF**, Erwin. *Magi.* Copenhagen: Borgens Forlag, 1986. Ill. 247 pp. In Danish: *Magic.* Includes illustrations of a tarot deck by Ole Mikkelsen.

* **NEUTZSKY-WULFF**, Erwin. *Okkultism.* Copenhagen: Borgens Forlag, 1985. Ill. 239 pp. In Danish: *Occultism.* Includes section on tarot.

* **NEVILLE**, E.W. *Tarot for Lovers.* West Chester, PA: Whitford Press, 1997. 188 pp. (paper) 23 cm. Reading the tarot in the context of relating to others.

* *NEW PENTACLE MAGAZINE: A Quarterly Magazine of the Esoteric.* From Australia, a zine that began publishing in 1997.

NICHOLS, Sallie. "The Devil in the Tarot." From *Meeting the Shadow: The Hidden Power of the Dark Side of Human Nature.* Jeremiah Abrams and Connie Zweig, eds. Los Angeles: J.P. Tarcher, 1991. xxv, 335 pp. 24 cm. Using the tarot for "shadow-work," to release negative projections and emotions.

* **NICHOLS**, Sallie. *Jung y el Tarot.* Barcelona: Edición Kairós, 1988. 538 pp. (paper) 21 cm. Spanish-language edition of *Jung and Tarot.*

* **NOBLE**, Vicki. "Letting Nature Take Its Course." *Women and Therapy* 24, 3–4 (2001): 193–208. Use of ancient arts, such as oracles and astrology, can enhance work with women clients, whose natural condition may predispose them to "letting nature take its course."

NOBLE, Vicki. *Making Ritual with Motherpeace Cards: Multicultural, Women-Centered Practices for Spiritual Growth.* New York: Three Rivers Press, 1998. Ill. 195 pp. 20 cm.

* **NOBLE**, Vicki. *Rituals and Practices with the Motherpeace Tarot.* Rochester, VT: Bear & Co., 2003. Ill. 208 pp. (paper) 15 cm. Re-edition of Noble's *Making Ritual with Motherpeace Cards.*

* **NoMONET.** *Artists Inner Vision Tarot.* NoMonet Full Court Press, 1999. Handmade book accompanying Artist's Inner Vision Tarot, by various artists (mail art project). The print run was 4,750 sets, with a special limited, numbered edition of 250.

NORDIC, Rolla. *Let's Talk about the Tarot: A Tarot Story for Children and the Young at Heart.* New York: Vantage Press, 1992. Ill. xiii, 92 pp. 22 cm. Explanation of tarot for children.

NORTON, Andre. *The Mark of the Cat.* New York: Ace Books, 1992. Ill. 248 pp. 22 cm. Based on the 'Outer Regions' as created by Karen Kuykendall in the Tarot of the Cat People.

NUNSEXMONKROCK. Nina Hagen. New York: Columbia, 1982. Sound recording. Rock and roll album includes piece titled "Taitschi tarot."

O

OBERMAIR, Gilbert. *Der Schlüssel zum Tarot.* Munich: Heyne Verlag, 1985. Ill. 128 pp. In German: *The Key to the Tarot.* Includes Major Arcana deck by Obermair.

O'BRIEN, Keith (ed.) *Kardz.* Privately published, 1992. Ill. Magazine that features comic type tarot images with animal characters by various artists. Artwork is intended to be used for making rubber stamps.

* *THE OCCULT DIGEST: A Periodical of Reprint and Research.* Includes articles on tarot. From Chicago.

* **ODYSEUZ.** *Ksiazka O Taroku.* Warsaw: Wydawnictwo Glodnych Duchow, 1991. Ill. 75 pp. In Polish.

* **OKEN**, Alan. *Pocket Guide to the Tarot.* Freedom, CA: Crossing Press, 1996. 151 pp. Ill. 16 cm. Gives "Primary principle," key words for each card, along with the meaning. Illustrated with the Rider-Waite Tarot.

* **OLDHAM**, Brian H. *Tarot Assistant for Windows.* Oakland, CA: Sea Point Software, 1997. Software that helps in reading the Rider-Waite Tarot.

OLMSTEAD, Kathleen. *The Girls' Guide to Tarot.* New York: Sterling Pub., 2002. Ill. 128 pp. 24 cm. Full instructions on how to use tarot cards. Includes ideas for birthdays, parties, storytelling, keeping a journal, and designing one's own tarot cards.

* **OLSEN**, Christina. *The Art of Tarot.* New York: Abbeville Press, 1995. Ill. 319 pp. 12 cm. Tarot art, most of well-known, but also includes rare art.

OLSEN, Christina. *Carte da Trionfi: The Development of Tarot in Fifteenth-Century Italy.* PhD dissertation, University of Pennsylvania, 1994.

* **OLSZEWSKA**, Manuela Klara. *Tarot: Lekarz Dusz.* Poland: Studio Astropsychologh, 1999. Ill. 146 pp. (paper) In Polish: *Tarot: Physician of the Soul.* Illustrated in color with original deck by Jadwiga Kalmus, as an insert intended to be cut out.

* **OLSZEWSKA**, Manuela Klara. *Tarot Terapia Slowem.* Poland: Studio Astropsychologh, 1999.

* **ÓMICRON**, Equipo. *El Tarot para Predicir el Futuro.* Barcelona: Editorial De Vecchi, 1995. 128 pp. (paper) 21 cm. In Spanish: *The Tarot to Predict the Future.*

* **OMWAKE**, John. *Autobiographical Notes.* Cincinatti: Stewart Kidd, 1922. Ill. 40 pp. (hardcover) 23 cm. Autobiography of former president of U.S. Playing Cards Company, addressed to his daughter.

OORTGIJSEN, David. *Rota: De Tarot met je Lijf.* The Netherlands: Mirananda, 1983. Ill. 125 pp. Book on tarot yoga, inspired by Bhagwan Shree Rajneesh (later called Osho).

* **OPSOPAUS**, John. *Guide to the Pythagorean Tarot: An Interpretation Based on Pythagorean & Alchemical Principles.* St. Paul, MN: Llewellyn Publications, 2001. Ill. ix, 470 pp. (paper) 23 cm. Book accompanying the Pythagorean Tarot.

OSHO. *The Osho Transformation Tarot: Insights and Parables for Renewal in Everyday Life.* New York: St. Martin's Press, 1999. Ill. 144 pp. (paper) 17 cm. Book accompanying sixty-card Osho Transformation Tarot. Deck is not actually tarot, but illustrations of parables from different traditions.

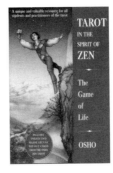

* **OSHO.** *Osho Zen Tarot: The Transcendental Game of Zen.* Cologne, Germany: Rebel House Pub., 1994. 176 pp. (paper) 22 cm. Book accompanying Osho Zen Tarot deck.

* **OSHO.** *Tarot in the Spirit of Zen: The Game of Life.* New York: St. Martin's Press/Griffin, 2003. Ill. 206 pp. (paper) 21 cm. Book on the Osho Zen Tarot. Includes glossy pages with "pop-out" Major Arcana from the Osho Zen Tarot.

OUSPENSKY, P.D. See Uspenskii, P.D.

* **OVENALL**, Sarah, and Georg Patterson. *Victoria Regina Tarot Companion.* St. Paul, MN: Llewellyn Publications, 2002. Ill. 270 pp. (paper) 23 cm. Book that accompanies the Victoria Regina Tarot deck, by Sarah Ovenall.

* **OZANIEC**, Naomi. *The Element Tarot Handbook: An Initiation into the Key Elements of the Tarot.* Shaftesbury, Dorset; Rockport, MA: Element, 1994. Ill. 180 pp. (paper) 24 cm. Symbolism of the tarot.

* **OZANIEC**, Naomi. *The Illustrated Guide to Tarot.* New York: Sterling Pub., 1999. Ill. 128 pp. (cloth) 27 cm. Survey of tarot, including symbolism, history, Kabbalah, and different ways of using the tarot, for self-realization, healing, and divination.

* **OZANIEC**, Naomi. *Teach Yourself Tarot.* Lincolnwood, IL: National Textbook Company, 1998. (paper) Tarot for divination and self-realization, illustrated with the Zolar Astrological Tarot.

P

* *PAGAN VOICE: A Non-Christian Networking Newsletter.* Rose Clark, ed. Zine that began publishing in 1991. Includes articles on tarot.

* **PAGE**, James Lynn. *Everyday Tarot Essentials.* Berkshire, England: W. Foulsham & Co., 2003. Ill. 192 pp. (paper) 15 cm. Basic tarot. Illustrated with the Universal Waite Tarot.

* **PALIN**, Poppy. *Stories of the Wild Spirit.* St. Paul, MN: Llewellyn Publications, 2002. Ill. xviii, 283 pp. (paper) Book accompanying the Waking the Wild Spirit Tarot.

* **PALM**, Guy. *All Things Are Numbers.* Unpublished manuscript, 1999. Cross-reference of ideas and numerological symbolism of the tarot.

* **PALUMBO**, Donald. "Tarot Reading as a Recombinant Narrative: Literature as Game/Game as Literature." *CEA Forum* 12, 2 (December 12, 1981): 9–12. Using the tarot to generate stories. Demonstrates that the basic elements of narrative are inherent in and arise from the structure of a tarot reading.

PANERO, Leopoldo María. *El tarot del inconsciente anónimo.* Madrid: Valdemar, 1997. Ill. 135 pp. 23 cm. Includes Major Arcana illustrated by Jabier Herrero.

* **PARENT**, Sylvie. *Arcani: Nanda Lanfranco.* Toronto: Istituto Italiano di Cultura, 1997. Ill. 21 pp.

* **PARISIOUS**, Roger. "Figures in a Dance: W.B. Yeats and the Waite/Rider Tarot." *The Hermetic Journal* (1987). Transcription of a talk given by Parisious at a Golden Dawn conference.

PARKER, Derek, and Julia Parker. *The Future Now: How to Use All Methods of Prediction from Astrology to Tarot to Discover Your Future.* New York: Prentice Hall Press, 1988. Ill. 224 pp. 28 cm.

PARKER, Derek, and Julia Parker. *Parkers' Prediction Pack: A Compelling Guide to Divination: Look into the Future and Plan Your Life Using Three Systems of Prediction: I Ching, Tarot, Runes.* New York: DK Pub., 1999.

* **PARRA**, Danièle, and Daniel Sauvaget. "Rüdiger Vogler: 'Un caractère assez proche de ma vie.'" *Revue du Cinéma* 419 (September 1986): 14–15, 61–64. German actor Vogler recalls work on film *Tarot*, directed by Rudolf Thome. Thome explains origin of project, which was adapted from a Goethe novel.

* **PARSONS**, Melinda Boyd. "Beyond the Veil: Magic, Mythology, and Music in the Visionary Painting of Pamela Colman Smith, Artist of the Rider-Waite Tarot Cards." Unpublished manuscript, 1992. Introduction and chapters 1 through 3.

PARSONS, Melinda Boyd. "Mysticism in London: The 'Golden Dawn,' Synaesthesia, and 'Psychic Automism' in the Art of Pamela Colman Smith." In *The Spiritual Image in Modern Art*, edited by Kathleen J. Regier. Wheaton, IL: The Theosophical Publishing House, 1987. Ill. 201 pp. (paper)

* **PARSONS**, Melinda Boyd. "Pamela Colman Smith and Alfred Stieglitz: Modernism at 291." *History of Photography* 20, 4 (Winter 1996): 285–292.

PARSONS, Melinda Boyd. *The Rediscovery of Pamela Colman Smith.* MA Thesis, University of Delaware, 1975. Ill. 122 pages.

* **PATERSON**, Helena. *The Celtic Tarot.* London: Aquarian Press, 1990. Ill. 160 pp. (paper) 18 cm. Reprint. London: Element, 2002. 152 pp. (paper) 15 cm. Book accompanying the Celtic Tarot illustrated by Courtney Davis.

* **PAUVERT**, Jean-Jacques, ed. *Le Tarot.* Paris: La Bibliotheque Volante, 1971. Ill. Special tarot issue of French magazine.

PAVAN, Monique. *Les Secrets du Tarot à Jouer: Chemin Initiatique des Bohémiens.* Sainte-Michel-de-Boulogne, France: Editions St.-Michel, 1993. 191 pp. (paper) Numerological and symbolic analysis of the tarot. In French.

* **PAVIC**, Milorad. *Last Love in Constantinople: A Tarot Novel for Divination.* Chester Springs, PA: Dufour Editions, Inc., 1998. Ill. 183 pp. (cloth) Translation from Yugoslavian *Poslednja ljubav u Carigradu.* The novel takes place in Serbia at the turn of the nineteenth century and is about the military and romantic adventures of two Serbian families. Illustrated by the author. The novel comes with a pack of tarot cards and the way they turn up determines the sequence in which the chapters should be read. First published in Beograd, Yugoslavia in 1993.

* **PAYNE**, Robin. *Tarot 2000: The Pagan Tarot.* Cornwall, England: Alexander Associates, 1999. 128 pp. (paper) Book accompanying the Pagan Tarot, illustrated by Rosemarie Lewsey under direction of Robin Payne. Sonnets for each Major Arcana card.

* **PAYNE-TOWLER**, Christine. *The Underground Stream: Esoteric Tarot Revealed.* Eugene, OR: Noreah Press, 1999. Ill. 160 pp. (paper) 27 cm. Includes an interesting section on choosing a personal tarot "lineage," or system.

* **PEACH**, Emily. *Discover Tarot: Understanding and Using Tarot Symbolism.* London: Aquarian Press, 1990. Ill. 256 pp. (paper) 21 cm. Originally published as *The Tarot Workbook.*

* **PEACH**, Emily. *Tarot for Tomorrow: An Advanced Handbook of Tarot Prediction.* Wellingborough, Northamptonshire, England: Aquarian Press, 1988. Ill. 288 pp. 22 cm. Basic and esoteric tarot. Illustrated with the Prediction Tarot.

* **PECCHIOLI**, Arrigo. *I Tarocchi del Palio di Siena.* Rome: Editalia-Edizioni d'Italia, 1988. Ill. 136 pp. Descriptions of the heraldry and symbols shown on the cards of the accompanying tarot deck, including history of the city of Siena, Italy. In Italian.

PEIRCE, Carol. "'Intimations of Powers Within': Durrell's Heavenly Game of the Tarot." In *Critical Essays on Lawrence Durrell.* Alan Warren Friedman, ed. 251 pp.

* **PELEGRY**, Laurence. *Divination par le Tarot.* Paris: Editions Trajectoire, 2004. Ill. 192 pp. (paper) 24 cm.

* **PELOSINI**, Giovanni. *I Tarocchi Aurei.* Italy: Il Mosaico Gruppo Editoriale De Agostini, 1997. Ill. 128 pp. Book accompanying the Major Arcana deck painted by Roberto Granchi.

* **PENNICK**, Nigel. *The Complete Illustrated Guide to Runes.* Shaftesbury, Dorset, UK: Element Books, 1999. Ill. 192 pp. (paper) 28 cm. Includes information on tarot cards, with parallels to divination with runes.

* **PERADEJORDI**, Julio. *Los Templarios y el Tarot: Las Cartas del Santo Grial.* Barcelona: Ediciones Obelisco, 2004. 110 pp. (paper) 22 cm. In Spanish: *The Templars and the Tarot: Cards of the Holy Grail.*

PEREZ-VIGO, J. Fernando. *El Necronomicon (Libro de los numbres muertos).* Spain: Casa de Horus, 1992 Ill. 161 pp. Book accompanying the tarot deck. In Spanish.

PERRIN, Oliver. "Reflections on the Tarocchi of Mantegna." *Alexandria: The Journal of Western Cosmological Traditions* 3 (1995): 283–305.

PERRY, Susan. "The Tarot as Alternate Structure in Yeats's 'The Circus Animals' Desertion.'" *Yeats Eliot Review* 14, no. 4 (Spring 1997): 11–17.

PETERSEN, Margarete. *Tarot-Postkartenbuch.* Krummwisch, Germany: Königsfurt Verlag, 1988. Ill. 50 pp. (paper) Postcard book of Margarete Petersen's tarot.

PETIBON, Andrée. *L'alchimie mystique au seuil de l'ère du Verseau, examinée à la lumière du Tarot.* Paris: Éditions de la Maisnie, 1979. Ill. 238 pp. 22 cm. In French. Alchemy examined in the light of tarot.

* **PIANTANIDA**, Donato. *La Magia de los Tarots: Esoterismo y Adivinación.* Buenos Aires: Robin Book, 1995. 184 pp. (paper) 23 cm. In Spanish: *The Magic of the Tarot: Esoteric and Divinatory.*

* **PICINI**, Andrea. *I Tarocchi Carte Segrete.* Bergamo, Italy: Galleria Antenna, circa 1979. Ill. In Italian: *Secret Cards of the Tarot.* On Picini's tarot artwork.

* **PICINI**, Andrea. *I Tarocchi.* Italy: Galeria Eros, 1976. Ill. Exhibition catalog for Major Arcana by Picini. Tipped in color illustrations.

* **PIEDILATO**, Janet Riche. *Iconography of the Transcendent: An Experiential Hermeneutic Method Applied to Personal Development (Altered States of Consciousness).* Dissertation, Saybrook Institute, 2000. A method of self-realization based on production of altered states of consciousness and the subsequent analysis of mental imagery produced in those states. The author was her own subject, and produced a tarot deck.

* **PIELMEIER**, Heidemarie, and Markus Schirner. *Illustrated Tarot Spreads.* New York: Sterling Pub., 1999. Ill. 96 pp. (paper) 21 cm. Translation of *Tarot-Welten.*

* **PIELMEIER**, Heidemarie, and Markus Schirner. *Tarot-Welten.* Darmstadt, Germany: Schirner Verlag, 1995. Ill. 95 pp. (cloth) 21 cm. In German: *Tarot World.* Seventy-eight different tarot spreads. Illustrated with cards from various decks.

* **PIERRE**. *New Age 2.* Japan: Onon, 1997. Ill. 250 pp. (paper) 22 cm. Illustrated and accompanied by the Visconti-Sforza Pierpont Morgan deck, as printed by U.S. Games Systems.

* **PILZ**, Ananda Kurz. *Ananda Tarot.* Neuhausen, Switzerland: Urania Verlag, 2001. Ill. 292 pp. (paper) 18 cm. Book accompanying the Ananda Tarot, illustrated by Pilz.

PITA RODRÍGUEZ, Félix. *Tarot de la poesía.* Havana: Unión de Escritores y Artistas de Cuba, 1976. Ill. 92 pp. 22 cm.

PITOIS, Jean-Baptiste (Paul Christian). *Tarocchi Egizi e Misteri dell'Oroscopo.* Turin, Italy: Edizioni Lo Scarabeo, 1988. 87 pp. Italian translation of *Histoire de la Magie.*

* **PLACE,** Robert Michael. *A Gnostic Book of Saints.* St. Paul, MN: Llewellyn Publications, 2001. Ill. 248 pp. (paper) 23 cm. Book accompanying the Tarot of the Saints, illustrated by Place.

* **PLACE,** Robert Michael, and Rosemary Ellen Guiley. *The Alchemical Tarot.* England: Thorsons, 1995; New York: Harper Collins, 1995. Ill. 176 pp. (paper) Book accompanying the Alchemical Tarot.

* **PLATT,** Charles. *Card Fortune Telling: A Lucid Treatise Dealing with All the Popular and More Abstruse Methods.* London: W. Foulsham & Co., circa 1925. Ill. 155 pp. (cloth) 18 cm. Mainly concerns divination with regular playing cards (called "Western" by the author), but includes historical information on tarot, especially as it evolved into standard playing cards.

* *PLAYING CARD COLLECTORS' ASSOCIATION.* Ongoing newsletters, from Cleveland, OH.

POINSOT, M.C. *Encyclopedia of the Occult Sciences.* 1939. Reprint. 1968. Ill. 496 pp. Includes information on tarot.

POLLACK, Rachel. *The Complete Illustrated Guide to Tarot.* Boston: Element, 1999. (paper)

POLLACK, Rachel. *The Forest of Souls: A Walk through the Tarot.* St. Paul, MN: Llewellyn Publications, 2002. Ill. xxiv, 278 pp. (paper) 23 cm.

POLLACK, Rachel. *The Haindl Tarot: The Major Arcana.* Franklin Lakes, NJ: New Page Books, 2002. Ill. 272 pp. 21 cm. Revised edition.

* **POLLACK,** Rachel. *The Haindl Tarot: A Reader's Handbook.* Stamford, CT: U.S. Games Systems, 1999. Ill. 203 pp. (paper) 23 cm. Book to accompany the Haindl Tarot.

POLLACK, Rachel. *The New Tarot.* London: Aquarian Press, 1989. Reprint. Woodstock, N.Y.: Overlook Press, 1990. Ill. 169 pp. 25 cm. Describes a variety of decks published between 1975 and 1990.

* **POLLACK,** Rachel. *Lo Setenta y Ocho Grados de Sabiduría del Tarot: Arcanos Mayores.* Barcelona: Ediciones Urano, 1987. 192 pp. (paper) 23 cm. Spanish-language edition of *Seventy-Eight Degrees of Wisdom: The Major Arcana.*

* **POLLACK,** Rachel. *Lo Setenta y Ocho Grados de Sabiduría del Tarot: Arcanos Menores y Lecturas.* Barcelona: Ediciones Urano, 1987. 255 pp. (paper) 23 cm. Spanish-language edition of *Seventy-Eight Degrees of Wisdom: The Minor Arcana and Readings.*

* **POLLACK,** Rachel. *The Shining Tribe Tarot.* St. Paul, MN: Llewellyn Publications, 2001. Ill. 332 pp. 23 cm. Detailed descriptions and interpretations of the cards of the Shining Tribe Tarot.

* **POLLACK,** Rachel. *Shining Woman Tarot Guide.* London: Aquarian Press, 1992. Ill. 158 pp. Detailed descriptions and interpretations of the cards of the Shining Woman Tarot. Expanded and republished in 2001 as *The Shining Tribe Tarot.*

* **POLLACK,** Rachel. *Le Tarot de Salvador Dali.* Paris: Seghers, 1985. 175 pp. Translation into French of *Salvador Dali's Tarot.*

* **POLLACK,** Rachel. *Tarot: El Labertinto Abierto.* Barcelona: Ediciones Urano, 1988. 192 pp. (paper) 23 cm. Spanish-language edition of *Tarot: The Open Labyrinth.*

* **POLLACK,** Rachel. *Das Tarot Ubungsbuch.* Munich: Knaur Esoterik, 1987. Ill 231 pp. German translation of *Tarot: The Open Labyrinth.*

POLLACK, Rachel. *Teach Yourself Fortune Telling: Palmistry, the Crystal Ball, Runes, Tea Leaves, the Tarot.* New York: H. Holt, 1986. Ill. 144 pp. 24 cm. (paper): Originally published as *A Practical Guide to Fortunetelling.*

* **POLLACK,** Rachel. *The Vertigo Tarot.* New York: DC Comics, 1995. Ill. 128 pp. (paper) Book accompanying the Vertigo Tarot. Illustrated by Dave McKean.

POLLACK, Rachel, and Mary K. Greer, eds. *New Thoughts on Tarot: Transcripts from the First International Newcastle Tarot Symposium.* North

Hollywood, CA: Newcastle Pub. Co., 1989. Ill. vi, 174 pp. 26 cm. Symposium was held September 1988 in Los Angeles.

PORRUA, Isabel Granen. "El tarot mexicano del siglo XVI." *Gutenberg-Jahrbuch* 69 (1994): 158–169.

* **PORTELA,** J. A. *Manual Práctico del Tarot.* Barcelona: Ediciones Indigo, 1994. 326 pp. (paper) 22 cm. In Spanish: *Practical Manual for the Tarot.*

PORTELA, J.A. *El Poder de los Tattwas.* Spain: Ediciones Indigo, circa 1995. 228 pp. (paper) 22 cm. In Spanish: *The Power of the Tattwas.* Includes description of Portela's Tarot de Tattwas.

* **PORTELA,** José Antonio. *El Tarot Superfácil.* Madrid: Arcano Books, 2004. 192 pp. (paper) 20 cm. In Spanish: *Supereasy Tarot.*

* **PORTER,** Tracy. *Tarot Companion: An Essential Reference Guide.* St. Paul, MN: Llewellyn Publications, 2000. Ill. xiv, 242 pp. (paper) 21 cm. General tarot, with emphasis on reading cards. Illustrated with the Rider-Waite Tarot.

POTENZAT, Gianmaria. *I Tarocchi: Le Arcane radici dell' Alberto della vita Milano.* Italy: Electa, 1990. Ill. xv, 70 pages. In Italian, with English translation provided as a separate booket. Catalog from an exhibition of tarot paintings, with the Major Arcana set illustrated in color.

* **POTTENGER,** Milton Alberto. *Symbolism, Astro Cards.* Sacramento, CA: Symbol Publishing, 1905. Reprint. 1994. 275 pp. (Photocopy, comb bound.) Includes analysis of the Major Arcana, illustrated with the Oswald Wirth Tarot, and of the regular playing card deck.

* **POTTS,** Billie. *Ein Neues Tarot der Frauen.* Munich: Frauenoffensive, 1984. Ill. 84 pp. German translation of *A New Women's Tarot.*

POWERS, Tim. *Last Call.* New York: Morrow, 1992. 479 pp. 25 cm. Novel on cardplaying; includes reference to tarot.

* **PRAMAD,** Veet. *Curso de Tarot: El Uso Terapéutico del Tarot.* Mexico: Editora y Distribuidora Yug, 2001. Ill. 362 pp. (paper) 27 cm. In Spanish: *A Course on Tarot: Its Therapeutic Applications.* Includes in-depth study of Crowley's Book of Thoth Tarot.

* **PRATESI,** Franco, and Marzia Faietti. "Storica di un Gioco: Cultura Ludicia." *Ilooein* 3 (1992): 61–81. In Italian, with English summary. On the Sola-Busca Tarot.

* **PREDIERI,** Gianni. *I Tarocchi Veneziani.* Venice: Centro Internazionale della Grafica di Venezia, 1981. Ill. 54 pp. Book with Predieri's Major Arcana tarot. (Limited edition of 800.)

* **PRINKE,** Rafal T. *Tarot: Dzieje Niezwyklej talii kart.* Warsaw: Wydawnictwo Glodnych Duchów, 1991. Ill. 200 pp. (paper) Survey of tarot. In Polish.

PRITCHARD, Paul D. *Ca$h from Tarot.* Kent, UK: Finbarr International, 1992. 53 pp. (paper) How to set up a tarot reading business.

PROMETTI, Enrico. *I Tarocchi.* Bergamo, Italy: El Bagan, 1994. Ill. (No pagination) Catalog for Prometti's tarot exhibition. Limited edition of 300.

* **PROSAPIO,** Richard, with Elizabeth Prosapio. *Intuitive Tarot: Discovering and Reinforcing the Power of Your Intuition: Using the Tarot as a Tool.* Dobbs Ferry, NY: Morgan & Morgan, 1990. 96 pp. Ill. 25 cm. 2nd ed. Stamford, CT: U.S. Games Systems, 1996. Ill. xvi, 92 pp. 25 cm. Illustrated with the Morgan-Greer Tarot.

* **PROSE,** Francine. "Hers." *New York Times* (April 11, 1985): C2. Column for women, this one about fortune-telling, and the author's experiences, during college, of reading cards for money. Includes the following: "The Waite deck, with its quaint imagery suggestive of some slightly hallucinogenic 19th-century children's classic, dealt in abstract, archetypal situations."

* **PROVOOST,** Eric. "Minotarot: En Suivant le Fil des Cartes se Déroule le dédale des Couloirs du Labyrinthe et des Destins de Thésée." *Coloquio: Artes* 65 (June 1985): 23–29.

* **PUENTE,** Oscar. *Tarot Egipcio: Teoria y Practica.* Privately published, 1997. 256 pp. (paper) In Spanish: *Egyptian Tarot: Theory and Practice.*

* **PUGA,** Alejandro. "El tarot de Kirin." *Artinf* 23, 103–104 (Autumn 1999): 33. In Spanish: "The tarot of Kirin."

Q

* **QUIGLEY,** David. "From Sex and Romance to Love and Oneness." In *Wheel of Tarot.* James Wanless and Angeles Arrien, eds. pp. 150–160. References to the chakras in the New Tarot for the Aquarian Age.

* **QUNTANNA,** Beatrex, with Cody Cammbell. *Tarot, a Universal Language: A Glossary of the Tarot and Its Symbols.* Carlsbad, CA: Art Ala Carte Pub., 1989. Ill. iii, 89 pp. (paper; comb bound) 29 cm.

R

RABBEN, Mascha. *Tarot 2000: Einstieg in die Neue Zeit.* Neuhausen, Switzerland: Urania Verlag, 1990. 125 pp. Book accompanying the Tarot 2000. In German.

RADÓ, María. *Paradiso Perdido.* Buenos Aires: Editorial Nueva Generacíon, 2002. Ill. 165 pp. (paper) Novel for teenagers, in Spanish. Illustrated with the Rider-Waite Tarot.

RAINBOW RISING. Ritchie Blackmore and Ronnie Dio, composers; Rainbow ensemble. New York: Polydor, 1976. Sound recording. Includes composition "Tarot Woman." Rock and roll music, performed by Rainbow and Munich Philharmonic Orchestra; Rainer Pietsch, arranger and conductor.

RÂKÓCZI, Basil Ivan. *La Roulotte Initiatique.* Paris: Editions Adyar, 1967. Ill. 248 pp. French edition of the *The Painted Waggon* (Holland, 1954). The French edition illustrates all seventy-eight cards of the deck, which was illustrated only in part in the Dutch edition.

* **RANDEL,** Carla. *Farbe, Tarot und Kabbala: Die mythologische Entschlüsselung der Beiden Paradiesbäume durch das Marseiller Tarot.* Munich: Heinrich Hugendubel Verlag, 1994. Ill. 253 pp. (hardcover) 27 cm. In German: *Color, Tarot and Kabbalah: The Mythological Development of the Two Trees of Paradise in the Marseilles Tarot.*

RANDEL, Carla. *Der Mensch als Abbild und Gleichnis Gottes. Die Deutung der Genesis durch das Marseiller Tarot.* Frankfurt: Cornelia Goethe Akademieverlag, 2002. Ill. 794 pp. 22 cm. In German: *People as Illustrations and Parables of God: The Interpretation of Genesis through the Tarot of Marseilles.*

RAZZINI, Carla. *I Tarocchi: Una Strada verso il Sè: La Via Umida e il Principio Femminile.* Milano: Kemi, 1980. 207 pp. 23 cm.

* **REA,** Nicky Rea and Jackie Cassada. *Mage: The Ascension.* Clarkston, CA: White Wolf, 1995. 296 pp. (cloth) 26 cm. Book accompanying tarot deck, illustrated by various artists.

REATL, Fernando. "Los Signos del tarot y el fin de la rason occidental en America: Daimon, de Abel Posse." *American Journal of Cultural Histories and Theories* 20, no. 47 (1997): 93–108.

THE RED VIOLIN. François Girard, director. 1998. Film that follows a seventeenth-century Italian violin with a red varnish through the hands of various musicians to a twentieth-century auction. The narrative is supported by a five-card tarot reading by an Italian soothsayer. The cards used are based on seventeenth-century French decks, but seem to have been created for the film. Unfortunately, the artist is not credited. Besides the five cards shown in the film, more cards appear in the credits.

REDGROVE, Peter. *Dressed as for a Tarot Pack.* Devon, England: Taxus, 1990. 56 pp. (paper) A poem on the tarot.

REED, Ellen Cannon. *The Witches' Qabala.* St. Paul, MN: Llewellyn Publications. Ill. 21 cm. (paper) Includes chapter on tarot.

* **REED,** Ellen Cannon. *The Witches Tarot.* St. Paul, MN: Llewellyn Publications, 1989. Ill. 320 pp. (paper) Book accompanying the Witches Tarot deck, illustrated by Martin Cannon.

* **REGARDIE,** Israel. *The Golden Dawn.* Sixth corrected edition. St. Paul, MN: Llewellyn Publications, 1989. Ill. 807 pp. (paper) 23 cm. Originally published as four volumes.

REIFF, Stephanie. *Visions of the Future: Magic Numbers and Cards.* New York: Contemporary Perspectives, 1977. Ill. 48 pp. 24 cm. Numerology and tarot.

* **REIHER,** Jim. *The Message in the Tarot.* Privately published, 1998. 117 pp. (paper) 20 cm. Philosophical musings on the Major Arcana, with extracts from the Old and New Testaments.

* **REINERTSEN,** Maud. "Tarot: If You Don't Make the Effort, You Won't Know the Secrets." *Magical Blend* 19 (May-June-July 1998): 98–103. Interview with Jason Lotterhand.

* **REISINGER,** Klaus. *Von Lyon nach Wien.* Privately printed, Vienna, 2000. Ill. 280 pp. (cloth) 30 cm. Limited edition. Color illustrations and explications of court cards on antique playing cards. In German: *From Lyon to Vienna.*

* **RENAUD,** J. "Kittie Bruneau, Inheritor of Surrealism." *Vie des Arts* 22, 90 (Spring 1978): 61–63.

* **RENÉE,** Janina. *Tarot for a New Generation.* St. Paul, MN: Llewellyn Publications, 2001. Ill. xvi, 368 pp. (paper) 23 cm. Reading tarot cards; aimed at young adults. Illustrated with Arthurian Tarot, World Spirit Tarot and Universal Tarot (Rider-Waite, redrawn by R. De Angelis).

* **RENÉE,** Janina. *Tarot Spells.* St. Paul, MN: Llewellyn Publications, 1990. xvii, 258 pp. (paper) 23 cm. Reprint. St. Paul, MN: Llewellyn Publications, 2000. (Rev. ed.) Ill. xvi, 294 pp. 24 cm. Use of the tarot in various life situations. Illustrated with the Robin Wood Tarot.

* **RENÉE,** Janina. *Tarot: Your Everyday Guide: Practical Problem Solving and Everyday Advice.* St. Paul, MN: Llewellyn Publications, 2000. Ill. xiii, 270 pp. 24 cm. Meanings of the cards in readings. Illustrated with various decks.

RESNICK, Rosalind. "Check Your Fate Here." *Computer Life* (April 1995): 32. Review of tarot software.

* **REVELL,** Lindel Barker. *The Tarot & You: A Simple Guide to Using the Cards for Self-discovery and Prophecy.* New York: Smithmark Publishers, 1999. Book for tarot deck illustrated by Penny Lovelock.

RICE, Valeta. *Possibilities: Know Your Name through Tarot & Numerology.* Gilroy, CA: Privately published, circa 2000. 119 pp. (paper) Numerological analysis of the tarot.

RICHARDSON, Alan. *Magical Gateways.* St. Paul, MN: Llewellyn Publications, 1992. Ill. 184 pp. (paper) Popular introduction to various forms of esoterism, including Kabbalah and tarot.

RICHARDSON, John. *A Life of Picasso.* New York: Random House, 1991. 548 pp. (cloth) Volume I, pages 270–275, discusses the influence of the Tarot of Marseilles on Picasso's work.

* **RICHER,** J. "Le Recours à la Symbolique du Tarot dans l'Oevre d'A.

Dürer." *Hamsa Paris* 8 (1977): 2–13.

* **RICHER,** J. "La Symbolique du Tarot dans *Le Roi Lear* de Shakespeare et *L'Aurelia* de Nerval." *Diotima* 10 (1982): 107–111. In French: "The Symbolism of the Tarot in Shakespeare's *King Lear* and Nerval's *L'Aurelia.*" Author parallels main characters in *King Lear* to tarot cards; for example, Cordelia is Fortitude and King Lear is The Emperor. Demonstrates that Nerval's *L'Aurelia* describes the succession of the Major Arcana.

RICKETTS, Mark, et al. *Book of the Tarot.* Plymouth, MI: Caliber Comics, 1997. Ill. 64 pp. (paper) Comic book format, with each card illustrated by a different artist.

* **RICKLEF,** James. *Tarot Tells the Tale: Explore Three-Card Readings through Familiar Stories.* St. Paul, MN: Llewellyn Publications, 2003. Ill. 269 pp. (paper) 23 cm. Characters ranging from Hamlet to the Ugly Duckling ask advice of tarot reader "KnightHawk." The answers are given as tarot readings. Entertaining and effective way of demonstrating how the cards can be interpreted in different situations. Feedback on each reading is also given.

* **RIERA,** Anna. "Niki de Saint Phalle y el Jardin de los Tarots." *Goya* 270 (May-June 1998): 173–178. In Spanish: "Niki de Saint-Phalle and the Giardino dei Tarocchi."

* **RIJNBERK,** Gérard van. *Le Tarot: Histoire, Iconographie, Esoterisme.* Paris: Editions de la Maisnie, 1981. 363 pp. In French: *Tarot: History, Iconography, Esotericism.*

RILEY, Jana. *The Tarot Book: Basic Instruction for Reading Cards.* York Beach, ME: Samuel Weiser, 1992. Ill. 203 pp. (paper) 22 cm.

* **RILEY,** Jana. *Tarot Dictionary and Compendium.* York Beach, ME: Samuel Weiser, 1995. xxx, 286 pp. 21 cm. (paper) English translation of *Tarot: Handbuch der Kartendeutungen.* Meanings of the cards excerpted from different authors, including Greer, Crowley, Waite, Wirth, Noble, Pollack. Illustrated with cards from various decks.

* **RILEY,** Jana. *Tarot: Handbuch der Kartendeutungen.* Germany: Urania Verlag, 1991. Ill. 328 pp. (paper).

* **RIVIÈRE,** Emile. *Jeux de Cartes Etrangers et Jeux Français de Cartes Historiques Impériales.* Paris, 1917. Ill. In French: *Foreign and French Historic Imperial Playing Cards.*

* **RIZZOLI,** Bianca Maria. *Tarocchi: Storia e significato simbolico.* Italy: Antonio Vallardi Editore, 1997. Ill. 336 pp. In Italian. History and symbolism of the tarot, illustrated with Tarot of Marseilles and other examples.

* **ROBERTS,** Richard. *The Original Tarot & You.* San Anselmo, CA: Vernal Equinox Press, 1987. 296 pp. (paper) 22 cm. Reprint of *Tarot and You.*

* **ROBERTS,** Robert E. *Ethnicity and Health: Mexican Americans: A Guide for Health Care Providers.* Bethesda, MD: National Institutes of Mental Health, 1984. Perspectives of traditional Mexican Americans, including five major types of indigenous health care providers: healers, herbalists, folk chiropractors, tarot card readers, and midwives.

* **ROBERTSON,** Sandy. *The Aleister Crowley Scrapbook.* York Beach, ME: Samuel Weiser, 1988. Ill. 127 pp. (paper) 24 cm. Fascinating look at Crowley, much of it illustrated with clippings and photos from Robertson's personal collection.

* **ROCCO,** Gustavo Andres. *Metodo Karmico-Cabalistico para la consulta del Tarot.* Argentina: Albatros, 1991. Ill. 195 pp. Book accompanying tarot deck.

RODGERS-WEBB, Angelic. "Diving for Pearls: Using the Tarot as Subtext in 'The Waste Land.'" *Yeats Eliot Review* 16, no. 2 (Winter 1999): 18–27.

RODIK, Belinda. *Das Tarot Lexikon.* Germany: Delphi bei Droemer, 1998. Ill. 336 pp. (cloth) In German: *The Tarot Dictionary.*

* **RODWAY,** Howard. *Tarot of the Old Path.* Neuhausen, Switzerland: Urania Verlag, 1990. Ill. 160 pp. (paper) Book accompanying deck illustrated by Sylvia Gainsford.

* **ROELEN,** Jerry. *Rock Art Tarot.* Stamford, CT: U.S. Games Systems,

1996. Ill. vii, 207 pp. (paper) 18 cm. Book accompanying the Roelen's Rock Art Tarot.

ROGERS, Brett. "Yeats's 'Blood and the Moon'." *Explicator* 49 (Summer 1991): 224–225.

* **ROHR,** Wulfing von, and Gayan S. Winter. *The Tarot of Love: A Tarot for Creative Living and Positive Solutions in Personal Relations.* Stamford, CT: U.S. Games Systems, 1990. Ill. xv, 159 pp. (paper) 18 cm. Book accompanying Tarot of Love illustrated by Marcia Perry

* **ROHRIG,** Carl-W. *Carl-W. Rohrig Tarot: Das Spiel der Inspiration und Fantasie.* Germany: Aquamarin Verlag, 1993. Ill. 132 pp. Röhrig Tarot illustrated in large size, with commentary.

RÖHRIG, Carl-W., and Francesca Marzano-Fritz. *The Röhrig-Tarot Book.* Woodside, CA: Bluestar Communications, 1997. Ill. 160 pp. (paper) 20 cm. Companion to the Röhrig Tarot deck.

* **ROLAND,** Francis. *Cómo Consultar el Tarot: El Metodo Roland.* Buenos Aires: E. Edris Ediciones, 1993. 96 pp. (paper) 21 cm. In Spanish: *How to Consult the Tarot: The Roland Method.*

* **ROMANOWSKI,** Hubert. "Media Art: Festwal-WRO'95." *Sztuka* 19, 1–6 (1995): 21. In Polish.

* **ROMÉE,** Per. *Tarotkorten I spadom och spel.* Privately published, Trelleborg, Sweden, 1985. Ill. 55 pp. Illustrated with the Tarot of Marseilles.

RONEY-DOUGAL, Serena. "An Exploration of Blackmore's Tarot Experiment in a Classroom Situation." *The Parapsychological Association 34th Annual Convention: Proceedings of Presented Papers.* 1991. A replication of Susan Blackmore's experiments, run over two years in Adult Education Parapsychology classes, confirms Blackmore's results, but with some reservations on methodology.

ROSBO, Patrick de. *Le tarot des comédiens.* Paris: Editions Clancier-Guénaud, 1987. 21 cm.

* **ROSCHER,** Michael. *Die Stier Persönlichkeit.* Munich: Wilhelm Goldmann Verlag, 1999. Ill. 192 pp. (paper) 18 cm. In German. Book on the astrological sign Taurus. An illustration of the Rider-Waite Tarot Four of Coins is on page 33.

** **ROSE,** Barbara. "A Garden of Earthly Delights." *Vogue* (December 1987): 268–272. An article about Niki de Saint Phalle's tarot garden in Italy.

ROSE, Carol Jean. *Tarot Comparisons: 78 Packs of 78 Cards.* Spirit Lake, ID: Rosehips Productions, 1999. Ill. 342 pp. (cloth) Reviews of seventy-eight decks.

ROSE, Carol Jean. *The Tarot Gypsy Trips.* Spirit Lake, ID: Rosehips Productions, 1996. 532 pp. (cloth)

ROSE, Donna. *The Tarot.* Hialeah, FL: MI-World Publishing Company, 1994. (paper) Pamphlet on reading the tarot.

ROSENFELD, Hellmutt. "Zur Vor- und Frühgeschichte und Morphogenese von Kartenspiel und Tarock." *Archiv für Kulturgeschichte.* Cologne, Germany, 1970. In German. History and evolution of playing cards and tarot.

* **ROSENGARTEN,** Arthur E., Jr. *Accessing the Unconscious: A Comparitive Study of Dreams, the TAT, and Tarot.* Dissertation. California Institute of Integral Studies, San Francisco, 1985. 180 pp. (cloth) Psychological evaluations through dreams, TAT and tarot compared.

* **ROSENGARTEN,** Arthur. *Tarot and Psychology: Spectrums of Possibility.* St. Paul, MN: Paragon House, 2000. Ill. xx + 293 pp. 24 cm. Illustrated with Rider-Waite Tarot.

ROSENGARTEN, Art. *Tarot Research Project.* Presentation at Anaheim Tarot Symposium, 1996. Privately printed. 17 pp. Study on using tarot readings as part of court-ordered counseling for men and women involved in domestic violence, as perpetrators and victims.

* **ROSS,** Gary. "The Court Cards: Nature's Archetypes." In *Wheel of Tarot.* James Wanless and Angeles Arrien, eds. pp. 105–124. An analysis of the tarot's court cards as elemental archetypes.

* **ROUSSEAU,** Claudia. "Cézanne, Dr. Gachet, and the Hanged Man." *Notes in the History of Art* 6, 1 (Fall 1986): 29–35.

ROVELLI, Paul Joseph. *The Whole Tarot Workbook.* Birdland

Communications, 1993. Basic tarot. Published in a limited edition of 200.

ROZHON, Judith. *Dictionary of the Minor Arcana: Thoth Deck.* Privately printed, 1985. 16 pp. (paper) Divinatory meanings of the cards.

* **RUISINGER,** Karl. "Tarot, Tarock, Tarocchi: Karten zwischen Spiel und Metaphysik." *Gruss Aus* (1989): 20–24. Ill. In German: "Tarot: Cards between Game and Metaphysics."

* **RUIZ,** Juan De Dios Agudo. *Los Naipes en España.* Vitoria, Spain: Museo Fournier de Naipes, 2000. Includes history of the printing of playing cards.

* **RUIZ,** Juan De Dios Agudo. *Playing Cards in Spain.* Vitoria, Spain: Museo Fournier de Naipes, 2000. English translation of *Los Naipes en España.*

* **RUSHKOFF,** Douglas. *Cyber Tarot: Electronic oracle.* New York, NY: HarperCollins Interactive, 1994. Software that enables user to perform complete tarot reading. Contains full-color Cyber Tarot and Rider-Waite decks; maintains statistical and graphical records of all saved readings; and offers computer "shuffling" or simulation of manual shuffling.

* **RYAN,** Mark, and Chesca Potter. *The Greenwood Tarot: Pre-Celtic Shamanism of the Mythic Forest.* London: Thorsons, 1996; New York: Harper/Collins, 1996. Ill. 118 pages. Book accompanying deck illustrated by Chesca Potter.

S

* **SACKETT,** Martha. "Tarot: A Deck Stacked in Your Favor." *Fate* (January 1997): 34, 35. Article on reading tarot, illustrated with Rider-Waite Tarot cards, recolored and accompanying a book by Adama Fronteras (Stewart, Tabori & Chang, England, 1996). The article incorrectly identifies the cards as from the Papus Tarot published by U.S. Games Systems.

* **SADHU,** Mouni. *Tarot: Curso Contemporaneo de la Quinta Esencia del Ocultismo Hermetico.* Buenos Aires: Editorial Kier, 2003. 514 pp. (paper) 23 cm. Spanish-language edition of *A Contemporary Course of the Quintessence of Hermetic Occultism.*

SAINT-GEORGE, Edith. "Le Tarots: La vie cartes sur table." *Télestar* (January 2000). Magazine with bonus of tarot illustrations, by Kantaro, intended to be cut out.

SAINT PHALLE, Niki de. *Le Jardin des Tarots.* Berne: Benteli, 1997. Ill. 75 pp.

SAINT PHALLE, Niki de. *Niki de Saint Phalle: The Tarot Garden.* Anna Mazzanti, editor. Milan: Charta, 1998. Ill. 114 pp. 24 cm. The first Italian edition of this book was created on the occasion of the exhibition Il Giardino dei Tarocchi di Niki de Saint Phalle at Polveriera Guzman, Orbetello, in 1997.

* **SAINT PHALLE,** Niki. "Niki tire les cartes du jardin des tarots pour Beaux Arts Magazine." *Beaux Arts Magazine* 159 (August 1997): 48–57. In French: "Niki draws the cards of the tarot garden for Beaux Arts Magazine."

SAINT PHALLE, Niki de. *Tarot Cards in Sculpture.* Milan: Giuseppe Ponsio, 1985. USA and England: Gimpel, 1985. Ill. 40 pp. (paper) Photographs of the construction of the Niki de Sainte Phalle's Tarot Garden.

* **SAMSON,** Donald C. "Using the Tarot in Composition Class." *Exercise Exchange* 22, 1 (Fall 1977): 40–44. Describes the use of tarot cards to help students achieve clairty in descriptive writing and learn how to interpret symbols.

* **SAMUL,** A. L. *Wisdom in the Cards.* Stamford, CT: U.S. Games Systems, 2002. Ill. 300 pp. (paper) 18 cm. Book accompanying the Hudes Tarot deck, illustrated by Susan Hudes. Includes affirmations and prayers for each card.

* **SANFO,** Valerio. *El Gran Libro del Tarot.* Barcelona: Editorial De Vecchi, 1999. 256 pp. (paper) 22 cm. In Spanish: *The Big Book of the Tarot.* Illustrated with redrawn Oswald Wirth Tarot.

SARGENT, Carl. *Personality, Divination, and the Tarot.* Rochester, VT: Destiny Books, 1988. Ill. viii, 222 pp. 20 cm.

* **SARIOL,** Elsa M. *Tarot of an Old Gypsy.* New York: Writers Club Press, 2000. 186 pp. (paper) Brief meanings of the cards, for readings. Illustrated with the Universal Waite Tarot.

* **SATTERWAIT,** Walter. *The Death Card.* New York: St. Martins Press, 1994. Ill. 258 pp. (cloth) Originally published as *The Hanged Man.*

* **SATTERWAIT,** Walter. *The Hanged Man.* New York: St. Martin's Press, 1993. Ill. 258 pp. (cloth) Mystery novel in which each chapter is titled with a tarot card. Illustrated with the Rider-Waite Tarot.

* **SAVAGE,** Audrey, and Paula Scott Frantz. *Dance of Life Cards: An Intimate Tarot.* Indianapolis: Book Weaver Publishing Company, 2000. Ill. 308 pp. (paper) 21 cm. Companion book to Dance of Life Tarot, illustrated by Paula Scott Frantz.

* **SCAPINI,** Luigi. *Shakespeare Tarot (Tarocchi di Giulietta e Romeo).* Treviso, Italy: Dal Negro Spa, circa 1990. Book accompanying deck by Luigi Scapini, in English and Italian.

* **SCHEAR,** Dayle. *Tarot for the Beginner: A Simple and Easy Step-by-Step Guide in Reading the Tarot Cards in One Hour or Less!* CA: Blue Dolphin

Publishing, 1994. 56 pp. (paper) 19 cm. Illustrated with the Rider-Waite Tarot.

* **SCHMITZ,** Stefan. *Psychologie: Eine Umfassende Darstellung aus Ganzheitlicher Sicht.* Petersberg, Germany: Verlag Via Nova, 2000. Ill. 340 pp. (paper) 23 cm. In German. Jungian psychology. Includes section on archetypes, illustrated with the Rider-Waite Tarot.

SCHOLDER, Fritz. *Tarot.* Tempe, Ariz.: Nomadic Press, 1987. 12 x 7 cm. Portfolio of six cards by Fritz Scholder: L'amoureux (The lovers), La mort (Death), Le pendu (The hanged man), Le diable (The devil), and Le fol (The fool). Edition limited to fifty sets signed by the artist.

* **SCHOLIN,** Nora. *Transitional Tarot: A New Approach to Card Reading.* Ill. Unpaged. (paper; spiral bound) 17 cm. Book on the author's triangular Transitional Tarot.

SCHÖLLMANN, Peter C. *Tarot: Für Gitarre.* Cologne, Germany: C. Schöllmann, 1992. 23 pp. Sheet music of tarot songs for the guitar: Die Welt (The World), Der Mond (The Moon), Die Herrscherin (The Empress), La tempérance – Die Mässigkeit (Temperance), Ceda, Die Gelassenheit (Equanimity), Der Herrscher (The Emperor), Der Wagen (The Chariot), Der Magier (The Magician).

SCHROBER-PAWESKA, Peter. *Das Rider-Waite Tarot Handbuch.* Germany: Windpferd Verlag, 1993. Ill. 279 pp. In German: *The Rider-Waite Tarot Handbook.*

* **SCHUBERT,** Ursula, and Wolfgang Neutzler. *Heilkraft des Tarot.* Munich: Verlag Peter Erd, 1991. Ill. 234 pp. In German. Introduction to tarot.

* **SCHUELER,** Gerald J. *The Enochian Tarot.* St. Paul, MN: Llewellyn Publications, 1989. Ill. 334 pp. (paper) 21 cm. 2nd ed. 2000. Ill. 128 pp. 15 cm. Book accompanying deck created by Gerald and Betty Schueler, painted by Sallie Ann Glassman.

SCHUELER, Gerald J., and Betty Schueler. *The Enochian Workbook: An Introduction to the Enochian Magical System.* St. Paul, MN: Llewellyn Publications, 1993. Ill. 309 pp. Enochian magic described in detail. Includes Enochian chess and Enochian tarot.

* **SCHWARTZ,** Jack. *Human Energy Systems: A Way of Good Health Using Our Electromagnetic Fields.* Mendocino, CA: Schwartz Publishing, 1980. Ill. 252 pp. (cloth) Includes a chapter on using tarot for healing.

SCORPIUS, Faustus, and Juha Vuorma. *Satanic Tarot: Dark Pathways.* New Zealand: Realist Publications, 1991. Ill. 17 pp. Booklet accompanying Major Arcana tarot.

SEABURY, William Marston. *The Tarot Cards and Dante's Divine Comedy.* Privately printed, New York, 1951. Ill. 29 cm.

SEDDON, Keith, and Jocelyn Almond. *The Faceless Tarot.* London: Dunscaith Publishing Ltd., 1989. Ill. 155 pp. (paper) Novel using tarot cards in the struggle between good and evil. With illustrations by Jocelyn Almond.

SÉDILLOT, Carole, Claude Trapet, and Elisabeth Zana. *Le tarot du Chat: Le Livre et le Jeu de 22 Arcanes.* Paris: Editions Jean Bouly, 1989. Ill. 190 pp. In French: *The Tarot of the Cat.* Packaged with a deck of Major Arcana featuring cat pictures

SÉDILLOT, Carole, and Claude Trapet. *Le Tarot du Chien.* France: Editions NoSme, 1992. Ill. 256 pp. In French: *The Tarot of the Dog.* Book describing the symbolism of the tarot illustrations by Claude Trapet.

* **SEGETH,** Uwe-Volker. *Spielkarten: Jugendstil und Art Déco.* Vienna: Edition Christian Brandstätter, 1994. Ill. 159 pp. (cloth) 31 cm. Includes tarot and tarock decks, illustrated in color.

* **SEGETH,** Uwe-Volker. *Unspielbar, aber schön: Spielkarten der Wiener Secession.* Weltkunst 64, 20 (October 15, 1994): 2673–76. Ill. In German: *Unplayable but Beautiful: Playing cards of the Viennese Secession.*

* **SEIDMAN,** Richard. *The Oracle of Kabbalah: Mystical Teachings of the Hebrew Letters.* New York: St. Martin's Press, 2001. Ill. xviii, 190 pp. (paper) 18 cm. Book accompanying deck printed with Hebrew letters. Although not tarot, it provides an accessible, contemporary study of the Kabbalah.

* **SEMETSKY,** Inna R. *Semiotica 2000,* 130, 3–4: 283–300. Tarot as symbols to be decoded.

* **SETTANNI,** Pino. *Tarot Settani.* Neuhausen, Switzerland: Urania Art, 1999. Ill. 91 pp. (cloth) 30 cm. Book illustrated with the Tarot Settanni, by Pino Settani.

7 TRUMPS FROM THE TAROT CARDS. Ruth S. White. Pinions. Sound recording. Electronic music described as "a choreography about symbolic flight, intended for ballet.

* **SEXTON,** David. *The Tarot of Oz.* St. Paul, MN: Llewellyn Publications, 2002. Ill. 180 pp. (paper) 18 cm. Book accompanying the Tarot of Oz.

* **SGOUROS,** Marios Ra. *Ra Smaragdenpfad Tarokspiel.* Michelstadt, Germany: Marlies Klamp, 1983. Ill. 146 pp. Book about a tarot deck which was printed on the cover.

* **SHAFFER,** William J., and Donald L. Johnson. *Bartholomew.* Norway: GP Books, 1990. Ill. 203 pp. (paper) 19 cm. Fictional biography of a Druid magician and teacher in the court of King Arthur. Each chapter begins with an illustration from the Rider-Waite Tarot.

* **SHARMAN-BURKE,** Juliet. *Beginner's Guide to Tarot.* New York: St. Martin's Griffin, 2001. Ill. 159 pp. (paper) 18 cm. Book accompanying deck illustrated by Giovanni Caselli.

* **SHARMAN-BURKE,** Juliet. *Mastering the Tarot: An Advanced Personal Teaching Guide.* New York: St. Martin's Griffin, 2000. Ill. 144 pp. (paper) Symbolism of the tarot. Illustrated in color with cards from various decks.

* **SHARMAN-BURKE,** Juliet. *The Mythic Tarot Workbook.* New York: Simon & Schuster, 1988. Ill. 160 pp. (paper) 24 cm. Illustrated in color with a variety of decks.

* **SHARMAN-BURKE,** Juliet. *Understanding the Tarot: A Personal Teaching Guide.* New York: St. Martin's Griffin, 1998. Ill. 128 pp. (paper) 26 cm. Descriptions of tarot cards, using examples from various decks. Includes sample readings.

* **SHARMAN-BURKE,** Juliet, and Liz Greene. *The Mythic Tarot.* 1986. Reprint. New York: Simon & Schuster, 2001. Book accompanying deck illustrated by Tricia Newell.

* **SHAVICK,** Nancy. *Nancy Shavick's Tarot Universe.* Santa Monica, CA: Santa Monica Press, 2000. Ill. 336 pp. (paper) 22 cm. Tarot reading, with topices for each card: Romance, Work & Business, Spiritual Growth.

* **SHAVIK,** Nancy. *The Tarot.* New York: Berkley Books, 1988. 140 pp. (paper) Card reading and self-actualization.

SHAVICK, Nancy. *The Tarot Guide to Love and Relationships.* New York: Berkley Books, 1993. Ill. 160 pp. 19 cm.

SHAVICK, Nancy. *The Tarot Reader.* New York: Berkley Books, 1991. Ill. 159 pp. 18 cm.

* **SHAW,** Dona. *Native American Tarot Interpreted.* Bakersfield, CA: Snow Walker Originals, 1993. Ill. 258 pp. (paper) 22 cm. Additional insights on the Native American Tarot by Magda and J.A. Gonzalez.

SHERMAN, Johanna. See Gargiulo-Sherman, Johanna.

SHIMIZU, Reiko. *Waltz.* Japan, 1995. Ill. 83 pp. (paper) Illustrations of the Miracle Tarot.

* **SHINE,** Raven. *The Journey Home: A Beginner's Guide to Reading Tarot Cards.* Privately published, 2003. Ill. 201 pp. (paper) 28 cm. Illustrated with the Rider-Waite Tarot.

SHOOK, Gary. *Introduction to the Tarot: The First Book You Need to Learn the Tarot.* California: Usul Press, 1991. Ill. 143 pp.

* **SIEGEL,** Suzie. "Tarot through the Ages." *Tampa Tribune* (August 20, 1993). Article on the tarot and its popularity. Includes a profile of Gertrude Moakley.

SILVA, Esmeralda da. *Tarot.* London: New Holland, 1997. Ill. 63 pp. 17 cm.

* **SILVA,** Rita H. *God's Numbers: Their Hidden Meaning.* Hayward, CA: The Silva House, 2001. Ill. 64 pp. (paper) 28 cm. Numerology, with some illustrations from the Classic Tarot deck.

SILVERS, Terry, and Theresa Cheung. *Teen Tarot.* Avon, MA: Adams Media Corp., 2003. A guide for using tarot cards to help deal with problems in many areas of life, including school, home, work, dating, physical health and appearance, and dreams.

* **SILVESTRE,** Colette. *Le Grand Livre des Jeux de Cartes et de Tarots.* Paris: Editions Trajectoire, 2004. Ill. 360 pp. (paper) 24 cm.

* **SILVESTRE,** Colette. *Réponses Immédiates à Toutes Vos Questions par le Tarot de Marseilles.* Paris: Editions Trajectoire, 2003. 228 pp. (paper) 24 cm. In French: *Immediate Responses to All Your Questions by the Tarot of Marseilles.* Accompanies Tarot of Marseilles deck.

* **SILVESTRE,** Colette. *Le Tarot de la Réussite.* Paris: Librairie de l'Inconnu Editions, 2003. Ill. 128 pp. (paper) 21 cm.

* **SILVESTRE,** Collette. *24 Leçons pour Apprendre Seul le Tarot de Marseille.* Paris: Editions Trajectoire, 2003. Ill. 156 pp. (paper) 24 cm.

SILVESTRE-HAEBERLE, Colette. *ABC de la symbolique du tarot.* France: Jacques Grancher, Editeur, 1992. Ill. 168 pp. (paper) Symbolism of the Major Arcana. In French.

* **SINGH,** Sunny Saninder. *Kismet.* Richmond, VA: 13 Enterprises, 1998. Spiritual journal. Includes a transcript of a tarot card reading, illustrated with the Universal Waite Tarot.

* **SISSON,** Pat. *The Royal Path: A Layman's Look at the Tarot.* Knoxville, TN: Earthtide Publications, 1989. Ill. 72 pp. (paper) 22 cm. Divinatory meanings of the tarot. Illustrated by Daniel McPheeters.

SLADE, Michael. *Ripper.* New York: Signet, 1994. 416 pages. Horror story whose plot includes tarot symbolism.

* **SMITH,** Caroline, and John Astrop. *Elemental Tarot.* New York: Doubleday, 1988. Ill. 128 pp. (paper) 16 cm. Book accompanying the Elemental Tarot illustrated by Smith.

* **SMITH,** Guy D. *The Digital Crystal Ball: Your Personal Electronic Astrology, Tarot, Numerology, and I Ching Advisor.* Glen Ellen, CA: LightSpeed Pub, 1996. Ill. vii, 211 pp. 23 cm. Book accompanying CD-ROM that includes the software "Virtual Tarot" for tarot readings by computer. Illustrated with the Rider-Waite Tarot.

SMITH, Malcolm K. *Poems of the Tarot.* Independence, MO: International University Press, 1985.

SOCIÉTÉ DES BIBLIOPHILES FRANÇOIS, PARIS. *Jeux de cartes tarots et de cartes numérales du quatorzième au dix-huitième siècle, représentés en cent planches d'après les originaux, avec un précis historique et explicatif; publiés par la Société des bibliophiles français.* Paris: Crapelet, 1844. Ill. 22 pp. 36 cm. In French. History of tarot cards from the fourteenth through the sixteenth centuries.

SOL E LUNA. Valet, Alain, ed. Mail art tarot magazine, based on mail art project "Alchemy Tarot." Begun in 1994.

* **SOLARI**, Ernesto. *Gli Arcani Occultati di Leonardo.* Italy: Editrice Saval, 1989. Ill. 123 pp. Solari describes how Leonardo da Vinci's artwork is grounded in astrology, alchemy, and the kabbalah. A companion to Solari's circa 1990 deck I 22 Arcani di Leonardo.

* **SOLDAT**, Hans-Georg. "Päpstin, Tod und Teufel." *Spielbox* (October 1989): 38–41. In German: "Poppess, Death and Devil." Commentary on tarot from toy-seller's point of view. Illustrated with various decks.

* **SØRENSEN**, Anne. *Alle har evnerne: Om brugen af Tarotkort.* Denmark: CáLuna, 1996. Ill. 224 pp. (paper) 21 cm. In Danish. Meanings of the tarot cards. Illustrated with the Rider-Waite Tarot.

* **SORRENTINO**, Gilbert. *Crystal Vision.* Normal, IL: Dalkey Archive Press, 1999. 289 pp. 23 cm. Fiction with tarot in the plot.

* **SPECTOR**, Richard. "Case Study 3: Strategic Tarot." *Family Therapy Networker* 10, 5 (September/October 1986): 36, 37, 68, 69. Describes a case study in which the therapist communicated with a fifteen-year-old boy by using tarot cards.

* **SPIESBERGER**, Karl, and Edwin J. Nigg. *Secrets of the New Age.* New York: Bell Publishing Company, 1989. Ill. 387 pp. (cloth) Four volumes in one: *Old Moore's Dream Book* (1985); *Reveal the Powers of the Pendulum* (1987); *Old Moore's Book of Fate* (1986); *Reveal the Secrets of the Tarot* (1986).

SPOTO, Salvatore. *Le Carte da Gioco: Storia e mistero.* Rome: Logart Press, 1993. Ill. 183 pp. The history of playing cards. Many illustrations, partly from the collection of Vito Arienti. Color illustrations of the Gringonneur Tarot.

* **STAR**, Suzanne. *In Search of Unicorns: A Guide to the Unicorn Tarot.* Stamford, CT: U.S. Games Systems, 1997. Ill. 165 pp. 18 cm. Book accompanying the Unicorn Tarot, illustrated by Liz Hilton.

* **STARBIRD**, Margaret. *The Tarot Trumps and the Holy Grail: Great Secrets of the Middle Ages.* Boulder, CO: WovenWord Press, 2000. Ill. 74 pp. (paper) Includes illustrations of the Gringonnier trumps. Medieval history and the tarot. Author connects tarot, specifically the Gringonneur Tarot, with the Albigensian heresy.

* **STARBIRD**, Margaret. *The Woman with the Alabaster Jar: Mary Magdalen and the Holy Grail.* Ill. 198 pp. (paper) 23 cm. Exploration of the Albigensian Heresy. Includes illustrations of the Gringonneur trumps.

STATE OF MIND. Icarus. London: Russian Roulette Records, circa 1980. Reggae music, sound recording. Includes piece titled "Land of Tarot."

* **STEIN**, Diane. *The Women's Spirituality Book.* St. Paul, MN: Llewellyn Publications, 1988. Ill. 262 pp. (paper) Includes section on tarot.

STEINER-GERINGER, Marie, and Heiri Steiner. *Die XXII [Zweiundzwanzig] Grossen Arkane: Das Tarot; Die Welt als Spiel.* Zürich, R. Simmen, 1968. Ill. 122 pp. 17 cm. In German: *The XXII Major Arcana: The Tarot: The World as a Game.* Book accompanying twenty-two-card deck illustrated by Sergius Golowin.

* **STEPANEK**, Marcia. "Tarot Cards Go Digital." *Business Week* (March 20, 2000): 10.

STEPANICH, Kisma K. *Faery Wicca Tarot.* St. Paul, MN: Llewellyn Publications, 1998. Ill. xi, 416 pp. (paper) 23 cm. Book accompanying the Faery Wicca Tarot, illustrated by Renee Christine Yates. Based on the folk traditions and myths of Ireland.

* **STERLING**, Stephen Walter. *Tarot Awareness: Exploring the Spiritual Path.* St. Paul, MN: Llewellyn Publications 2000. Ill. xiii, 392 pp. (paper) 24 cm. Meditations and meanings of the tarot, including poems by the author. Illustrated with the BOTA Tarot and the Universal Waite Tarot.

* **STEVENTON**, Kay. *Spiral Tarot: A Story of the Cycles of Life.* Stamford, CT: U.S. Games Systems, 1998. Ill. 157 pp. (paper) 18 cm. Book to go with the Spiral Tarot, illustrated by Kay Steventon.

* **STEWART**, James. "Fairytale Tarot." Unpublished manuscript, circa 1990.

* **STEWART**, Louis. *Life Forces: A Contemporary Guide to the Cult and Occult.* Kansas City, MO: Andrews and McMeel, 1980. Ill. 567 pp.

(cloth) Includes chapter on tarot (pp. 94–107).

* **STEWART**, R.J. *The Complete Merlin Tarot.* London: Aquarian Press, 1992. Ill. 353 pp. (paper) 23 cm. Detailed descriptions of the symbolism and myths of the cards of the Merlin Tarot, illustrated by Miranda Gray.

* **STEWART**, R.J. *The Dreampower Tarot.* London: Aquarian/Thorsons, 1993. Ill. 186 pp. (paper) Book accompanying Dreampower Tarot, illustrated by Stuart Littlejohn. Deck is not traditional tarot, but has cards that correspond to the Major Arcana.

* **STEWART**, R.J. *The Merlin Tarot.* London: Element Books, 2002. Ill. 155 pp. (paper) 18 cm. Reprint of *The Merlin Tarot Handbook.*

* **STEWART**, R.J. *The Merlin Tarot Handbook.* London: Aquarian Press, 1992. Ill. 155 pp. (paper) 18 cm. Book accompanying the Merlin Tarot, illustrated by Miranda Gray.

* **STONE**, MJ. "Zero in the Tarot: Whirling through the Major Arcana." *Parabola* (Fall 2001): 87–90. Meditation in first person, on the Fool through history.

* **STRACHAM**, Francoise, ed. *The Fortune Tellers.* New York: Black Watch, 1974. Ill. 128 pp. Includes information on tarot.

* **STRAUGHN**, R.A. *The Oracle of Thoth: The Kabalistical Tarot.* Bronx, NY: Oracle of Thoth Publishing Company, 1977. Ill. 167 pp. (paper, comb-bound) Spiritual laws of the tarot. Illustrated with line drawings by Paul Stephen.

* **STREIFF MORETTI**, Monique. "L'Isis des Tarot ou la Naissance d'un Mythe. In *Isis, Narcisse, Psyché: Entre Lumières et Romantisme: Mythe et Ecritures, Ecritures du Myth.* Clermont-Ferrand: Presses Universitaires Blaise-Pascal, 2000. In French: "Isis of the Tarot, or the Birth of a Myth."

* *STRICTLY SUPERNATURAL: TAROT.* Video. Directed by Justin Hardy and Ludo Graham; produced by Andre Singer. 50 minutes. Episode of the A&E network television series, *Strictly Supernatural,* that featured tarot. Included are interviews with Stuart Kaplan and Michael Dummett. In the video, a tarot reader explains how she told a client that a potential husband had had a vasectomy.

STRIEGLER, Per Genvej til. *Kabbalah: Livets Trae.* Privately published, Denmark, 1995. Multimedia software that gives correspondences to the Kabbalistic Tree of Life. Text about tarot is from K. Frank Jensen's *Tarot.*

STROHM, Eckhard F.E. *Mesterviden fra Atlantis.* Kibaek, Denmark: Povl Clement Sørensen. Ill. 263 pp. Book accompanying Atlantean Tarot.

* **STRUTHERS**, Jane. *Read Your Future: The Ultimate Guide to Tarot, Astrology, the I Ching, and Other Divination Techniques from Around the World.* New York: St. Martin's Griffin, 2002. Reprint of *Tell Your Own Fortune.*

* **STRUTHERS**, Jane. *Tell Your Own Fortune.* London: Kyle Cathie, 2001. Ill. 256 pp. 25 cm. Tarot section illustrated with the Universal Waite Tarot.

STUART, Anne. *Prince of Swords.* Unity, ME: Five Star, 1997. 304 pp. (hardcover) 22 cm. Historical romance featuring tarot.

* **STUART**, Rowenna. *Tarot.* Glasgow: HarperCollins Publishers, 1998. Ill. 254 pp. (paper) 11 cm. Guide to symbolism and reading of tarot. Illustrated with Tarot of Marseilles (from U.S. Games Systems, Inc.).

STURZAKER, James. *Tarot Symbolism Revealed.* UK: Mark Saunders Books, 1987. Analysis of symbolic elements on the cards.

* **SULIGA**, Jan Witold. *Biblia Satana.* Lodz, Poland: Krajowa Agencja Wydawnicza, 1991. Ill 159 pp. In Polish.

* **SULIGA**, Jan Witold. *Tarot: Karty, Które Wróżą.* Lodz, Poland: Wydawnictwo Lódzkie. Ill. 112 pp. In Polish. Includes deck of cards.

SUMMERS, Catherine, and Julian Vayne. *The Inner Space Workbook.* Berks, England: Capall Bann Publishing, 1994. 188 pp. (paper) Magic and the tarot.

* **SUMMERS**, Catherine, and Julian Vayne. *Personal Development with the Tarot.* London: Quantum, 2002. Ill. 160 pp. (paper) Illustrated with Crowley's Book of Thoth Tarot. Tarot used to access inner psyche.

* **SUSTER**, Gerald. *The Truth about the Tarot.* London: Skoob Books, 1990. 107 pp. Self-actualization through tarot.

* **SUSTER**, Gerald. *La Verda Sobre el Tarot.* Madrid: Equipo Difusor del Libro, 2001. 160 pp. (paper) 22 cm. Spanish-language edition of *The Truth about the Tarot.*

SUZANNE. *Secrets of the Tarot Revealed.* Grand Forks, ND: Psychic Training Institute, 2002. Ill. 17 pp. (paper) Introduction to tarot card reading.

* **SWANSON**, Scott. *The Mysteries of Tarot: A Computerized Guide to the Tarot.* Unpublished, 1990. Includes booklet by Swanson.

* **SWEIKHARDT**, Karen Marie. *Tarot of a Moon Garden.* Stamford, CT: U.S. Games Systems, 1998. Ill. 153 pp. (paper) 18 cm. Book to go with Tarot of a Moon Garden, illustrated by Sweikhardt.

* *SWIAT ASTROLOGII: ODKRYJ SZTUKI TAJEMNE.* Polish magazine that includes articles on tarot.

* **SYBILA**, Charles de. *Tarot: Una Lectura para Acuario.* Colombia: Elektra Editores, 1993. 200 pp. (cloth) 22 cm.

SZEPES, Maria. *A Tarot Bölcsessége.* Budapest, Hungary: Edesvíz Kiadó, 1993. Ill. 256 pp. In Hungarian.

T

T BYRON G. *Gilgamesh!* (Reannotated Revision of *I Gilgamesh: The Synthesismyth*). Privately published, 1995. 224 pp. (paper) Guide to the Gilgamesh Tarot.

T BYRON G. *Synthesis: The Hermetic Tarot.* Privately printed, circa 1990. Illustrated with a Major Arcana by the author.

* *TALON: Osterreichisch-Ungarischer Spielkartenverein.* Magazine periodical for collectors of Austrian and Hungarian playing and tarot cards. Illustrated with historical decks.

TAPESTRY: A Magazine for the Tarot Community. Quarterly magazine From Lansdale, PA.

TAROT. West Germany: WEA, 1988. Sound recording. Performed by Juliane Werding. Includes composition, "Tarot."

TAROT. Rudolf Thome, director. German film based on Goethe's novel, *Die Wahlverwandtschaften* (Elective Affinities). Includes card reading scene.

* *TAROT INTERPRETER: Newsletter of TI Publications.* Sugar Creek, Missouri.

* *TAROT NEWS: A Journal for Tarot Enthusiasts.* Published by American Mensa, in Quincy, IL.

TAROT SUITE. Batt, Mike. Epic, 1979. Rock and roll sound recording. Contents include "Introduction (The Journey of a Fool)," "The Valley of Swords," "Tarota."

TAROT TALK. Norma Cowie, editor. Canada: N.C. Publishing, 1982 ongoing. Ill. Newsletter on tarot.

* *TAROZINE.* Canada: W.W.P., 1994. Ill. 12 pp. (paper; accordion folded leaflet) Monthly publication, in which the reader scratches a surface to reveal a tarot card, for a four-card spread. Illustrated with the Sacred Rose Tarot, by Johanna Gargiulo-Sherman.

TATHAM, Campbell. "Tarot and Gravity's Rainbow." *Modern Fiction Studies* 32, no 4 (Winter 1986): 581–590.

* **TAYLOR,** Brian. "Tarot-Scope." *Faze.* Ongoing column on reading tarot cards, illustrated by the Rider-Waite Tarot.

TAYLOR, Ken. *Tarot for Today.* London: London House, 2000. 155 pp. (paper) Introduction to tarot.

* **TCHALAI.** *Le Véritable Tarot Tzigane.* Paris, 2003. Ill. 112 pp. (paper) 22 cm. In French. Book accompanying deck by Tchalai.

TEGTMEIER, Ralph. *Tarot: Geschichte eines Schicksalspiel.* Cologne: Dumont Taschenbücher, 1986. Ill. 181 pp. In German: *Tarot: History of a Fortune-Telling Game.*

* **TEIKEMEIER,** Lothar. "New Thoughts about the Old Tarocchi." Unpublished manuscript, 1993. Teikemeier advances the theory that the Renaissance Italian decks never had twenty-two Major Arcana (versus the idea that cards were lost from twenty-two trumps).

* **TENZIN-DOLMA,** Lisa. *The Glastonbury Tarot: Timeless Wisdom from The Isle of Avalon.* Glastonbury: Gothic Image Publications; York Beach, ME: Samuel Weiser, Inc., 1999. Ill. 167 pp. (paper) 19 cm. Book for the Glastonbury Tarot deck.

TERESCHENKO, Nicolas. "A New Look at an Old Anachronism." *Hermetic Journal* (1989): 126–134. Called by K. Frank Jensen "epoch-making theories on the structure of tarot."

* **TERESCHENKO,** Nicolas. *Le Trésors du Tarot.* Paris: Editions Atlas/Guy Tredaniel, 1986. Ill. 445 pp. Accompanies Cosmos Tarot, illustrated by Maria Sky.

* **TESSIER,** Andrée. *The Wheel of Destiny: Instruction and Interpretation Guide.* Québec: A.S.T. Distributions, 1996. Booklet accompanying Wheel of Destiny deck.

* *THIRD EYE: Magazine for Popularization of Alternative Healing and Spirituality.* Includes series of articles on tarot, illustrated by the Rider-Waite Tarot.

* **THOMAS,** Edith Ann. *It's in the Cards: An Easy Guide to Reading and Understanding the Mysteries of the Tarot Cards.* Palm Springs, CA: International Guild of Advanced Sciences, 1995. Ill. 125 pp. 29 cm. Basic meanings and symbolism of tarot cards. Illustrated with the Rider-Waite Tarot.

* **THOMAS,** J. Philip. *Tarot de Paris.* New York: St. Martin's Press, 2002. Ill. 160 pp. (hardcover) 22 cm. Book accompanying the Tarot de Paris deck, illustrated by Thomas.

* **THOMPSON,** Andrew. *Arcane Mysteries: Tarot Magic.* Mystic Eye Games, 2003. Ill. 87 pp. (paper) Companion book to "Dungeons and Dragons" role-playing game.

THOMPSON, Claude G. *Le Tarot sur l'Enneagramme de Gurdjieff.* France: Louise Courteau, Editrice, 1989. Ill. 128 pp. (paper) Placement of the Major Arcana on the Enneagram by the teacher G.I. Gurdjieff. In French.

* **THOMPSON,** David. "Timon of Athens." *Illuminations: Stories of the Plays for the 1997 Season:* 23-25. Oregon Shakespeare Festival. Booklet includes an illustration of the Six of Pentacles, from the Rider-Waite Tarot, as an illustration of Timon, who "freely dispenses his wealth to anybody who asks and will not accept payment in return, thereby assuring that those who benefit from his generosity can never become his equals and are always in his debt."

* **THOMSON,** Karen M. "Joseph Campbell, Jung, Anne Tyler, and 'The Cards': The Spiritual Journey in *Searching for Caleb.*" Paper presented at the Annual Meeting of the College English Association, 1991. The ancient and metaphysical routine of reading cards for guidance, counseling, and predictions is shown in mainstream literature as a positive part of one's spiritual journey.

* **THOMSON,** Sandra A. *Pictures from the Heart: A Tarot Dictionary.* New York: St. Martin's Press, 2003. Ill. 467 pp. (paper) Tarot dictionary. (Also in author's collection, bound uncorrected advance proof.)

* **THOMSON,** Sandra A., Robert E. Mueller, and Signe E. Echols. *The Heart of the Tarot: The Two-Card Layout: Easy, Fast, and Insightful.* San Francisco: HarperSanFrancisco, 2000. Ill. xii, 303 pp. (paper) 20 cm. Basic tarot, illustrated with the Rider-Waite Tarot and the Morgan Greer Tarot.

THORIN, J. *De la Prohibition et de la Tolérance des Jeux.* Paris: Chez Delaunay, 1818. In French: *On the Prohibition and Tolerance of Games.*

THORMANN, Janet. *The Tarot Suite.* White Rabbit Press, 1964. 21 pp. (paper) A poem for each Major Arcana card.

TICOULAT, Anna-Maria. *Tarot d'instants: Poemes.* Ciutadela de Menorca: Consell Insular de Menorca: Ajuntament, 1994. Ill. 86 pp. 22 cm. Poems on tarot.

* **TIFFANY,** Eugene. "Tiffany Tarot." Unpublished manuscript, 1995. Ill. 128 pp. About the author's Tiffany Tarot, and how to read the tarot.

* **TIME-LIFE BOOKS.** *Visions and Prophecies.* New York: Time-Life Books, 1998. Ill. 160 pp. (hardcover) 28 cm. Includes extensive section on tarot, and descriptions of several decks.

* **TISCHER,** Stefan. "Der Tarotgarten von Niki de Saint Phalle." *Gardtenkunst* 2, 5 (1993): 213–263.

TOGNETTI, Arlene, and Lisa Lenard. *The Complete Idiot's Guide to Tarot and Fortune Telling.* New York, NY: Alpha Books, 1998. New York: Macmillan Publishing, 1999.

* **TOLAND,** Diane. *Inner Pathways to the Divine.* Hygiene, CO: SunShine Press Publications, 2001. Ill. 128 pp. (paper) Descriptions and affirmations for the Major Arcana. Illustrated with the Rider-Waite Tarot.

* *TOOLS AND RITES OF TRANSFORMATION.* Ongoing quarterly newsletter. Includes information on William Black Tarot and reviews of others. Published by Ed Buryn.

* **TOROK,** Judit. "A Tarokk-kert es tarsai." *Uj Muveszet* 11, 7 (July 2000): 12–15. In Hungarian: "The Tarot Garden and Its Associates."

* **TOSONOTTI,** Pina Andronico. *Fantastico Viaggio di un Manichino da Pittore.* Milan: Edizioni Il Meneghello, 1993. In Italian: *The Fantastic Voyage of an Artist's Mannequin.* Book accompanying deck illustrated by Osvaldo Menegazzi. The set was issued in a signed, numbered edition of 800.

* **TOWNLEY,** Kevin. *The Cube of Space: Container of Creation.* Boulder, CO: Archive Press; Montreal, Quebec: Editions Le Chaos, 1993. Ill. 271 pp. (paper) 24 cm. Tarot cards placed on the "cube of space" diagram. Illustrated with the BOTA Tarot.

TOWNLEY, Kevin. *Meditations on the Cube of Space.* Los Angeles: Archer Books, 2003. (paper and cloth) Tarot and the kabbalah.

TRAVERS, Christopher. "The Tarot." *Prediction Magazine* 1997–1998. Series of articles on tarot.

TROCCHI, Cecilia Gatto. *I Tarocchi.* Italy: Tascabili Economici Newton, 1995. 95 pp. Introduction to tarot. In Italian.

* **TSAINIS,** Kathrin. "Tarot: Wie funktioniert es, und was steckt dahinter?" *Young Miss* (June 1998): 54–57. In German: "Tarot: How does it work and what does it mean?" Illustrated with the Rider-Waite Tarot.

* **TUAN,** Laura. *Interpretar el Tarot.* Barcelona: Editorial De Vecchi, 2001. 94 pp. (paper) 25 cm. New edition of *Tarot: Interpretación - Adivinación.*

* **TUAN,** Laura. *El Lenguaje Secreto del Tarot.* Barcelona: Editorial De Vecchi, 2000. 270 pp. (paper) 25 cm. In Spanish: *The Secret Language of the Tarot.*

* **TUAN,** Laura. *Tarocchi: Interpretazione—Divinazione.* Milan: De Vecchi Editore, 1998. Divination with the tarot, illustrated with a

Gumppenberg-type deck.

* **TUAN**, Laura. *Tarot: Interpretación - Adivinación.* Barcelona: Editorial De Vecchi, 1998. 94 pp. (paper) 23 cm.
* **TUAN**, Laura. *Le Tarots.* Paris: Editions de Vecchi, 1994. Ill. 159 pp. (paper) 16 cm. Book accompanying reproduction of deck by Teodoro Dotti.
* **TUAN**, L. *Les Tarots Celtiques.* Paris: Editions De Vecchi, 1998. 174 pp. (paper) 16 cm. In French. Book packaged with Tarots Celtiques, illustrated by M. Ameli.
* **TUAN**, Laura. *Les Tarot Egyptiens.* Paris: Editions de Vecchi, 1995. Ill. 212 pp. (paper) 16 cm. Book accompanying Etteilla-style tarot deck illustrated by A. Taccori.
* **TURK**, Julia A. *Navigators Tarot of the Mystic SEA.* Stamford, CT: U.S. Games Systems, 1997. Ill. 235 pp. 23 cm. Book accompanying Navigators Tarot of the Mystic SEA.

U

UCLA, Bernard. "Les Arcanes majeurs du tarot initiatique dans Le Capitaine Fracasse." *Bulletin de la Societe Theophile Gautier* 20 (1998): 98–124. In French: "The Major Arcana of the Initiatory Tarot in Captain Fracasse."
* **UECKER**, E. Z. *Tarot Looking Glass: Alternative New Age Guide to the Psychology of Tarot.* Salt Lake City: Mass Media Publications, 1994. Ill. 193 pp. (paper) Use of projection techniques for insight.
* **UMMAN**, Jost. *Kartenspielbuch.* Munich, 1880. Ill. In German: *Playing Card Book.*

USPENSKII, P. D. *The Major Arcana of the Tarot as Described by P. D. Ouspensky.* Taylor McCall, ed. St. Petersburg, Russia: Trood Print. and Pub. Co., 1913. Reprint. Santa Fe: Bocaccio, 1975. Ill. 58 cm. Limited edition of 150 copies. Ouspensky's *The Symbolism of the Tarot,* in a portfolio with Major Arcana illustrated by Taylor McCall.

USPENSKII, P. D. *A New Model of the Universe: Principles of the Psychological Method in Its Application to Problems of Science, Religion, and Art.* New York: A. Knopf, 1931. Includes section: "The Symbolism of the Tarot."
* **UXKULL**, Woldemar von. *Die Einweihung im Alten Agypten.* Germany: Avalon Verlag, 1957. Ill. 174 pp. In German. Describes initation in ancient Egypt, in tarot-illustrated room.

V

VALLYON, Imre. *The Lightning-Struck Tower of Wisdom.* New Zealand: Sounding-Light, circa 1980. Teachings by the Hungarian-born guru Vallyon.
* **VAUGHAN**, Hal. "Cycle: A Poetic View of Tarot." Unpublished manuscript, circa 1990.

VEGA, Phyllis. *Romancing the Tarot: How to Use Tarot to Find True Love, Spice Up Your Sex Life, or Let Go of a Bad Relationship.* New York: Fireside, 2001. Ill. 255 pp. 22 cm.
* **VERAME**, Jean. *La Toma del Cielo y de la Tierra: Coleccion de Juegos del Mundo y su Obra.* Spain: Sala Amarica, 2003. Ill. 79 pp. (paper) 30 cm. In Spanish, Basque, and French. Catalogue for an exhibition of the cards and games collection of Jean Verame, as well as original artwork by Verame.
* **VERCELLESI**, Pia, and Giampaolo Gasparri. *Tarocchi e Chakra.* Milan: Xenia Edizioni, 1999. In Italian: *Tarot and Chakra.* Book accompanying the Energy Tarot, by the authors.

VIA, Claudia Cieri. *I tarocchi detti del Mantegna.* Pavia: Torchio dé Ricci, 1992. Ill. 132 pp. 24 cm. In Italian, with text also in English.

VICTOR, Cameo. *A Self-Guided Tour to the State of Happiness: Cameo Tarot Collages.* Privately published, 1999. 95 pp. (paper; spiral bound). Original tarot collages with commentary.
* **VICTOR**, Jean-Louis. *Tarot Settanni.* Neuhausen, Switzerland: Urania Art, 1995. Book accompanying deck by Pino Settanni.

VILELA, Beatrix. *Tarot Hipocampo.* Brazil: Editora Hipocampo, 1990. Ill. 62 pp. Book accompanying Tarot Hipocampo, designed by F.D. di Venus.

* **VITALI**, Andrea. *I Tarocchi Visconti-Sforza.* Milan: Edizioni "Il Meneghello", 1996. Unpaged. (paper) In Italian. Booklet accompanying Il Meneghello's edition of the Visconti-Sforza Tarot.
* **VIVIEN**, Jean-Denis. *A Vous de Jouer.* Ill. Catalog for an exhibition at Galerie Gerard Guerre, Avignon, France, June through September 1998.
* **VOGEL**, Karen. *Motherpeace Tarot Guidebook.* Stamford, CT: U.S. Games Systems, 1995. Ill. xi, 127 pp. 18 cm. Book accompanying the deck illustrated by Vicki Nobel and Karen Vogel.
* **VOGT**, Kenneth D. "Demonstrating Biological Classification." *The American Biology Teacher* 57 (May 1995): 282–283. Shows how phenetic and phylogenetic classification can be explored more dispassionately using a deck of tarot cards.
* **VON ROHR**, Wulfing, and Gayan S. Winter. *Tarot der Liebe.* Munich: Ariston Verlag, 1989. In German: *Tarot of Love.* Includes Major Arcana deck illustrated by Marcia Perry.
* **VON ROHR**, Wulfing, and Gayan S. Winter. *Tarot of Love.* Stamford, CT: U.S. Games Systems, 1990. Ill. 159 pp. (paper) Book accompanying Tarot of Love, illustrated by Marcia Perry.
* **VURM**, Bohumil. *Tajemství karet: Encyklopedie Tarotu.* Prague: Tarot Mania, 1995. Ill. 136 pp. History and symbolism of the tarot. In Czech.

WXYZ

* **WAHODI**, Paul. *Fins and Bindings.* Privately published, 1992. 24 pp. (paper; combbound) 28 cm. Meditations on tarot. Inspired by the Universal Waite Tarot.

WAITE, A.E. *Alchemists through the Ages.* New York: Rudolf Steiner Publications, 1970. Reprint of *Lives of the Alchemical Philosophers,* with introduction by Paul M. Allen added.

WAITE, A.E. *Azoth: Or, The Star in the East.* London: Theosophical Publishing Society, 1893. A study on alchemy.

WAITE, A.E. *Belle and the Dragon: An Elfin Comedy.* London: James Elliott, 1894. A fairytale.

WAITE, A.E. *The Book of Black Magic and of Pacts, Including the Rites and Mysteries of Goetic Theurgy, Sorcery, and Infernal Necromancy.* London: George Redway, 1898.

WAITE, A.E. *The Book of Ceremonial Magic: The Secret Tradition in Goetia, Including the Rites and Mysteries of Goetic Theurgy, Sorcery, and Infernal Necromancy.* London: William Rider & Son, 1911. Revised edition of *The Book of Black Magic and Pacts.*

WAITE, A.E. (as Grand Orient). *The Book of Destiny, and the Art of Reading Therein.* London: William Rider & Son, 1912.

WAITE, A.E. *A Book of Mystery and Vision.* London: Philip Welby; New York: Brentano's, 1902. Poetry.

WAITE, A.E. *The Book of the Holy Graal.* London: John M. Watkins, 1921. Poetry.

WAITE, A.E. *The Collected Poems of Arthur Edward Waite.* London: William Rider & Son, 1914.

WAITE, A.E. *Devil Worship in France: Or, The Question of Lucifer: A Record of Things Seen and Heard in the Secret Societies According to the Evidence of Initiates.* London: George Redway, 1896. About a hoax concerning a supposedly Satanic order of Freemasons.

WAITE, A.E. *The Doctrine and Literature of the Kabalah.* London: Theosophical Publishing Society, 1902.

WAITE, A.E. *The Golden Stairs: Tales from the Wonder-World.* London: Theosophical Publishing Society, 1893. New York: Path, 1893. Fairytales.

WAITE, A.E., and Machen, Arthur. *The House of the Hidden Light: Manifested and Set Forth in Certain Letters Communicated from a Lodge of the Adepts by The High Fratres FILIUS AQUARUM and ELIA ARTISTA.*

Privately printed, 1904. Possibly issued for members of the Golden Dawn.

WAITE, A.E. *Israfel: Letters, Visions and Poems.* London: E. W. Allen, 1886. London: James Elliott & Co., 1894.

WAITE, A.E. *Lamps of Western Mysticism: Essays on the Life of the Soul in God.* London: Kegan Paul, Trench, Trubner & Co.; New York: Alfred A. Knopf, 1923.

WAITE, A. E. *Lives of the Alchemical Philosophers.* London: George Redway, 1888. Based on a work attributed to Francis Barrett (1814, 1815). Includes a bibliography of alchemy and hermetic philosophy.

WAITE, A.E. *Lucasta: Parables and Poems.* London: James Elliott, 1894.

WAITE, A. E. *A Lyric of the Fairyland and Other Poems.* London: Catty, 1879.

WAITE, A.E. *Manual of Occult Divination.* New Hyde Park, NY: University Books, 1972. Reprint of *The Book of Destiny.*

WAITE, A.E. *A New Encyclopedia of Freemasonry.* London: William Rider & Son; Philadelphia: David McKay Co., 1921. Reprint. New Hyde Park, NY: University Books, 1970.

WAITE, A.E. *The Occult Sciences: A Compendium of Transcendental Doctrine and Experiment, Embracing an Account of Magical Practices; of Secret Sciences in Connection with Magic; of the Professors of Magical Arts; and of Modern Spiritualism, Mesmerism, and Theosophy.* London: Kegan, Paul, Trench, Trubner & Co., 1891.

WAITE, A. E. *An Ode to Astronomy and Other Poems.* Privately printed, circa 1874–1879. Quarto. Poetry by Waite, self-published in a limited edition of 100 copies.

WAITE, A.E. *The Open Vision: A Selection from the Poems of Arthur Edward Waite.* Eton, Berkshire: Shakespeare Head Press, 1959.

WAITE, A.E. *The Quest of the Golden Stairs: A Mystery of Kinghood in Faerie.* London: Theosophical Publishing House, 1927. Reprints of Waite's *Prince Starbeam* and *The Golden Stairs.*

WAITE, Arthur Edward. *The Pictorial Key to the Tarot: Being Fragments of a Secret Tradition under the Veil of Divination.* Blauvelt, N.Y.: Steiner Publications, 1971. Ill. xii, 340 pp. 18 cm. With introduction by Paul M. Allen. Reprint. San Francisco: Harper & Row, 1980. Ill. ix, 340 pp. (paper) 20 cm. The book, illustrated by Pamela Colman Smith.

WAITE, A.E. *Prince Starbeam: A Tale of Fairyland.* London: J. Burns, 1889. London: James Elliott, 1894. A fairytale.

WAITE, A.E. *Raymund Lully, Illuminated Doctor, Alchemist and Christian Mystic.* London: William Rider & Son, 1922.

WAITE, A. E. *The Real History of the Rosicrucians Founded on Their Own Manifestoes and on Facts and Documents Collected from the Writings of Initiated Brethren.* London: George Redway, 1887. New York: J.W. Bouton, 1888. First edition of book later revised and titled *The Brotherhood of the Rosy Cross.*

WAITE, A.E. *Saint-Martin the French Mystic and the Story of Modern Martinism.* London: William Rider & Son, 1922.

WAITE, A.E. *The Secret Doctrine of Israel: A Study of the Zohar and Its Connections.* London: William Rider & Son, 1913. New York: Samuel Weiser, 1970.

WAITE, A.E. *The Secret Tradition of Freemasonry.* London: Rebman Limited; New York: Rebman Company, 1911. London: Rider & Co., 1937. Revised and expanded edition.

WAITE, A.E. *A Soul's Comedy: The Spiritual History of Jasper Cartwright.* London: George Redway, 1887. Poetry.

WAITE, A.E. *Steps to the Crown.* London: Philip Wellby, 1907. Aphorisms.

WAITE, A.E. *Strange Houses of Sleep.* London: Philip Sinclair Wellby, 1906. Poetry.

WAITE, A.E. *Studies in Mysticism and Certain Aspects of the Secret Tradition.* London: Hodder and Stoughton, 1906.

WAITE, A.E. *The Way of Divine Union: Being a Doctrine of Experience in the Life of Sanctity, Considered on the Faith of Its Testimonies and Interpreted after a New Manner.* London: William Rider & Son, 1915.

* **WAITE,** Edith. *El Tarot Universal de Waite.* Buenos Aires: Editorial Sirio, 2002. 264 pp. (paper) 21 cm. In Spanish: *The Universal Tarot of Waite.* Illustrations, by Guillermo Dominguez Elizarrarás, are based on the Rider-Waite Tarot. Author is not related to A. E. Waite.

* **WAKELING,** Edward. *Alice in Wonderland Puzzle and Game Book.* Stamford, CT: U.S. Games Systems, 1996. Ill. 88 pp. (paper) Games and puzzles by Lewis Carroll and by Edward Wakeling. Accompanies the Alice in Wonderland deck of playing cards.

* **WALDHERR,** Kris. *The Goddess Tarot.* Stamford, CT: U.S. Games Systems, 1999. Ill. 207 pp. (paper) 18 cm. Book to accompany the Goddess Tarot, illustrated by Waldherr.

* **WALDHERR,** Kris. *The Goddess Tarot Workbook.* Stamford, CT: U.S. Games Systems, 2000. Ill. 258 pp. (paper) 26 cm. Workbook to go with Waldherr's Goddess Tarot.

* **WALKER,** Ann. *The Living Tarot.* UK: Broomtail Publications, 1988. Reprint, 1993. Ill. 83 pp. (paper) 20 cm. Reprint. UK: Capall Bann Publishing, 1994. 109 pp. Introduction to tarot, illustrated with the Hanson-Roberts Tarot.

WALL, Rosalind, and John S. Cooke, eds. *The World of One: The*

Aquarian Tarot Revelation. GA: Naylor Pub., 1975. 414 pp. (paper)

WALLIS, Shirley. *Discover the Tarot.* London: Blandford, 1991. Ill. 126 pp. 22 cm.

* **WALSH,** Allyson. *The Sacred Tarot Unveiled.* Brooklandville, MD: Allyson Universal Ministry, 1994. Ill. ii, 249 pp. 23 cm. Religious interpretation of the tarot. Illustrated with Rider-Waite Tarot.

* **WALSH,** Chad. *God at Large.* New York: The Seabury Press, 1971. Ill. 137 pp. (cloth) Christian meditations. Includes pages illustrated with the BOTA Tarot, and other images and text, with suggestions of cutting them out and using them as a "meditation kit."

WALZ, Karin. "Visionen fur die Firma." *Esotera* 2 (1994): 82–85. Ill. Tarot as a tool for business management. A special card deck is illustrated.

* **WANG,** Robert. *Handbuch für das Jungianische Tarot.* Neuhausen, Switzerland: Urania Verlag, 1988. German translation of *Tarot Psychology*, book for the Jungian Tarot, by Wang.

* **WANG,** Robert. *The Jungian Tarot: An Iconological Study in Cross-Cultural Archetypal Imagery.* Neuhausen, Switzerland: Urania Verlag, 1988. Companion to Wang's deck, with more detail than *Tarot Psychology.*

* **WANG,** Robert. *Jungian Tarot and Its Archetypal Imagery.* Columbia, MD: Marcus Aurelius Press, 2001. Reprint of *The Jungian Tarot: An Iconological Study in Cross-Cultural Archetypal Imagery.*

* **WANG,** Robert. *Tarot Psychology: A Practical Guide to the Jungian Tarot.* Stamford, CT: U.S. Games Systems, 1992. Ill. 140 pp. (paper) 18 cm. Reprint of *Tarot Psychology: Handbook for the Jungian Tarot* (Urania Verlag: Neuhausen, 1988).

* **WANLESS,** James. *Prophecy 1987: Where Are We Going?* Carmel, CA: Merrill-West Publishing, 1987. 53 pp. (paper) 21 cm. "150 tarot readings for the planet Earth," primarily using the Voyager Tarot.

* **WANLESS,** James. *Strategic Intuition for the 21st Century: Tarot for Business.* New York: Three Rivers Press, 1996. Ill. xi, 193 pp. (paper) 23 cm. Business forecasting with Tarot. Illustrated with the Voyager Tarot.

* **WANLESS,** James, and Angeles Arrien, eds. *Wheel of Tarot: A New Revolution.* Carmel, CA: Merrill-West Publishing, 1992. Ill. 303 pp. Symposium on tarot, covering a variety of topics.

WARD, Brian. *Het zesde zintuig.* The Netherlands: Het Spectrum, 1978. Ill. 95 pages. In Dutch: *The Sixth Sense.* Includes a color illustration of one of the versions of Aleister Crowley's and Frieda Harris's Magician card.

WARWICK-SMITH, Kate. *The Tarot Court Cards: Archetypal Patterns of Relationship in the Minor Arcana.* New York: Destiny Books, 2003. Ill. 224 pp. (paper) 15 cm.

* **WASSERMAN,** James. *Art and Symbols of the Occult: Images of Power and Wisdom.* Vermont: Destiny Books, 1993. Ill. 128 pp. Large format. Heavily illustrated, with chapters on astrology, initiation, magic, sexuality, alchemy and tarot.

* **WATTERS,** Joanna. *Tarot for Today.* Ill. 160 pp. (paper) 25 cm. Illustrated with the Universal Waite Tarot. Basic tarot, with astrological information.

WEATHERLY, Joan. "Yeats, the Tarot, and the Fool. *College Literature* 13, no 1 (Winter 1986): 112–121.

WEINSTEIN, Marion. *Marion Weinstein's Handy Guide to Tarot Cards.* New York: Earth Magic Productions, 2000. 90 pp. (paper) How to do readings, for beginners.

WEOR, Samael Aun. *The Initiatic Path in the Arcana of Tarot and Kabalah.* Melbourne: Gnostic Editions, 1996. Ill. 358 pp. (paper) English translation of *El Sendero Initiatico en los Arcanos del Tarot y Cabala* (Mexico, 1979).

WESTFEHLING, Uwe, ed. *"Tarocchi": Menschenwelt und Kosmos: Ladenspelder, Dürer und die "Tarock-Karten des Mantegnä: Wallraf-Richartz-Museum Köln, 9. Nov. 1988 bis 22. Jan. 1989.* In German: "'Tarots': The world of men and the cosmos: Ladenspelder, Dürer and the 'Tarot cards of Mantegna.'" Catalog for exhibition at Richartz-Museum, Cologne, Germany, which featured playing card designs attributed to Johann Ladenspelder, circa 1511–circa 1580 and Albrecht Dürer, 1471–1528.

WHELDRAKE, Elizabeth. *Tarot.* Australia: Axiom Publishing, 1999. Ill. 56 pp. (paper) Introduction to tarot.

* **WHITAKER,** Hazel. *Tarot Talk: The Language of Intuition.* England: Gary Allen Pty, 2001. Ill. vi, 136 pp. (paper) 23 cm. Divination with the tarot. Illustrated with the Rider-Waite Tarot.

* **WHITE,** Jeffrey. *Intro to Tarot.* West Palm Beach, FL: Rebel Vision, 1994. Video.

* *WHITE SUN: JOURNAL OF D.O.M.E., THE INNER GUIDE MEDITATION CENTER.* From Los Angeles. Includes tarot articles.

* **WILLIAMS,** Allan D. *Simply Tarot.* Privately published, 2000. Ill. 48 pp. (comb-bound) Basic reading. Includes laminated one-page "Quick Reference Guide" with card meanings.

* **WILLIAMS,** Brian. *Book of Fools.* St. Paul, MN: Llewellyn Publications, 2002. Ill. xviii, 207 pp. (paper) 23 cm. Book accompanying the Ship of Fools Tarot, by Williams.

WILLIAMS, Brian. *The Minchiate Tarot: The 97-Card Tarot of the*

Renaissance, Complete with the 12 Astrological Signs and the 4 Elements. Rochester, VT: Destiny Books, 1999.

* **WILLIAMS,** Brian. *The Pomo Tarot: A Postmodern Deck for Navigating the Next Millennium.* San Francisco: HarperSanFrancisco, 1994. 120 pp. (paper) 16 cm. Book accompanying Williams' Pomo [Postmodern] Tarot deck.

* **WILLIAMS,** Brian. *A Renaissance Tarot: A Guide to the Renaissance Tarot.* Stamford, CT: U.S. Games Systems, 1994. Ill. ix, 197 pp. (paper) 26 cm. Book describing in detail Williams' Renaissance Tarot, illustrated with additional line drawings by the author.

* **WILLIAMS,** Cecilia Maiocco. *Understanding the Tarot: A Workbook and Journal to Help You Learn the Key to Unlocking the Mysteries of the Tarot.* Privately published, 1998. Ill. 123 pp. (paper; combbound) Basics of reading tarot cards.

WILLIAMS, J.M. *Tarot: Learning the Basics.* Privately published, 2002. 22 pp. (paper) Charts of definitions for the cards.

* **WILLIS,** Tony. *Magic and the Tarot: Using Tarot to Manipulate the Unseen Powers of the Universe.* Wellingborough, Northamptonshire: Aquarian Press. Ill. 272 pp. 22 cm. Spells and charms for each tarot card. Illustrated with the Magickal Tarot by Anthony Clark.

WILLIS, Tony. *The Magickal Tarot.* London: Aquarian Press, 1992. Ill. 192 pp. (paper) 18 cm. Based on tarot symbolism in Crowley's Book of Thoth, illustrated with Anthony Clark's Magickal Tarot.

** **WILSON,** Erika. "Paper II: Display Techniques, TLC for Boxed Games, Fire & Water Damage." Photocopied from an unknown source, page 160–161. Wilson is a member of the American Game Collectors Association.

WIND, Barry. "A Note on Card Symbolism in Caravaggio and His Followers." *Paragone* 40, 475 (September 1989): 15–18.

WINKELMANN, Joachim. *Tarot for Indviede.* Copenhagen: Sphinx, 1992. Ill. 128 pp. Danish translation of German work: *Tarot der Eingeweihten.*

WINTERSON, Jeanette. *Gut Symmetries.* New York: Alfred A. Knopf, 1997. 223 pp. (cloth) Novel. Each chapter is titled with a tarot card.

* **WOLFF,** Emil. *Tarot.* Copenhagen: Hagerups forlag, 1899. 102 pp. K. Frank Jensen calls this "the oldest Danish book dealing with the rules for the game of tarot."

WOOD, Juliette. "The Celtic Tarot and the Secret Tradition: A Study in Modern Legend Making." *Folklore* 109 (1998): 15–24.

* **WOOD,** Monica. *My Only Story.* San Francisco: Chronicle Books, 2000. 293 pp. (cloth) Novel in which the character refers to tarot cards.

WOODRUFF, Frederick. *Secrets of a Telephone Psychic.* Hillsboro, OR: Beyond Words Publishing, 1998. 149 pp. (paper) Personal account of a telephone psychic.

* **WORLD TAROT CONGRESS 1997.** *ITS,* 1997. Ill. (paper, comb bound) Program for the World Tarot Congress of 1997, coordinated by the International Tarot Society. Includes biographical sketches of the speakers at the congress.

WORLEY, Lloyd. "Joyce, Yeats, Tarot, and the Structure of Dubliners." *The Shape of the Fantastic,* edited by H. Olena. 1990.

* **WORRELL,** Trish. *A Collection of Designs from the Rider-Waite Tarot Deck in Cross Stitch.* Privately published, 1995. Unpaginated. (paper) 28 cm. Instructions for creating cross-stitched images of the Rider-Waite Tarot Major Arcana.

* **WOUDHUYSEN,** Jan. *Das Tarotbuch: Das Weg der narren.* Munich: Kösel Verlag, 1984. Ill. 252 pp. *Tarotmania* in German.

WOUDHUYSEN, Jan. *Tarotmania, or, Why only an Idiot Would Want to Become a Fool.* London: Wildwood House; Sydney: Bookwise Australia, 1979. Ill. 203 pp. 22 cm.

* **WYATT,** Martin J. *Tarot: Its Meaning, Mythology, and Methods of Divination.* Hove, England: Valdarro Books, 1976. Ill. 148 pp.

* **WYNNE,** Patrice, ed. *The Womanspirit Sourcebook.* San Francisco: Harper & Row, 1988. Ill. xxv, 277 pp. 28 cm. Catalog of books, periodicals, music, calendars, and tarot cards, organizations, video and audio tapes, bookstores, interviews, meditations, art.

YAOUANC, Hadès A. *Manuel complet d'interprétation du tarot [par] Hadès.* Paris, N. Bussiere, 1968.

YOHALEM, John, ed. See Enchanté.

YOUNG, Alexa. *Verses, Symbols & Techniques of Tarot Magic.* Privately printed, 1994. 281 pp. (paper, comb-bound) Tarot poetry and affirmations.

ZANGS, Christiane, and Hans Holländer. *Mit Glück und Verstand.* Aachen: Thouet, 1994. Ill. 289 pp. 30 cm. Catalog for exhibition at Städtisches Museum Schloss Rheydt, Germany, July 29 to September 25, 1994, on games, including tarot cards.

* **ZANNOS,** Susan. *Human Types: Essence and the Enneagram.* York Beach, ME: Samuel Weiser, 1997. Ill. 322 pp. (paper) 22 cm. Human typology based on the Gurdjieff "Fourth Way." Includes some comments on playing cards, and a foldout page on court cards of regular playing cards related to types.

* **ZELAZNY,** Roger, and Neil Randall. *Roger Zelazny's Visual Guide to Castle Amber.* New York: Avon Books, 1988. Ill. 220 pp. Shows the Amber Tarot, illustrated by Florence Magnin.

* **ZERNER,** Amy, and Monte Farber. *Le Tarot Enchanté.* Paris: Editions Solar, 1991. Ill. 183 pp. (hardcover) 22 cm. French translation of *The Enchanted Tarot.*

* **ZIEGLER,** Gerd. *Tarot: Mirror of Your Relationships.* Neuhausen: Urania Verlag, 1989. Ill. 175 pp. (paper) 18 cm. The Crowley Tarot used to interpret personal relations.

ZIEGLER, Gert. *Tarot: Sjaalens Spejl.* Copenhagen: Sphinx, 1991. 144 pp. Danish translation of *Tarot: Mirror of the Soul.*

* **ZOLRAK.** *The Tarot of the Orishas: The Bi-lingual English/Spanish Guide to All 77 Cards of the Orisha Tarot* St. Paul, MN: Llewellyn Publications, 1994. Ill. xlvii, 341 pp. 24 cm. Illustrated by Dürkön.

ZORLI, Girolamo. *Il Tarocchino Bolognese.* Bologna: A. Forni, 1992. Ill. 119 pp. 24 cm. In Italian: *The Bolognese Tarot.*

* **ZUCKER,** Mark. "The Master of the Sola-Busca Tarocchi and the Rediscovery of Some Ferrarese Engravings of the Fifteenth Century." *Artibus et Historiae* 18, 35 (1997): 181–194.

INDEX

The titles of cards vary greatly. To facilitate comparison of equivalent cards, titles that commonly used in modern decks are given in the index. Some examples of the equivalents are: High Priestess includes Popess; Hierophant includes Pope; Death includes Transformation; wands includes batons; coins includes pentacles.

A

A.P.M.   729, 731
ASS (see Altenburger und Stralsunder Spielkarten)
Aaltonen, Kalervo   389, 392
Abbey, Christopher   198, 200, 597, 599
Abbey, Morgana   198, 200, 597, 599
Abizdris, Esther   64, 66
Abrams, Carol (see Herzer, Carol)
Academia de Cultura Arcana   435, 436
Accademia Carrara   669
Acquelin, José   544, 546
Acquiescent Tarot   1, 3
Adflatus Tarot   1, 2
Adler, Margot   444, 446
Adobe Photoshop   55, 58, 60–61, 110, 111, 177, 178, 179, 494, 495
Adrian Tarot   207, **208–209**
Affirmations, Tarot   **490**
African symbolism   131, 132, 183, 184–185, 207, 209–210, 427
African Tarot   207, **209–210**
Afrodite, Tarocco di   **4**
Age of Mythology Tarot   **610**
Aghem, Mara   335, 338
AGMüller   207, 208, 231, 235, 235, 237, 240, 304, 308, 329, 343, 351, 374, 377, 393, 394, 408, 419, 421, 442, 443, 444, 446, 486, 488, 494, 500, 541, 543, 580, 581, 585, 586, 699, 700
Ah! My Goddess Tarot   **610**
Ai no Tarot Uranai   **628**
Ai to Shinpi no Tarot Uranai   **651**
AIC Studio   610, 661
Akemi, Takada   645
Akimoto, Nami   666
Akron   235, 237
Akuma-Kun   630
Akutsu, Kazumi   642
Alasia, Silvana   285, 324, 328, 709, 714, 716, 718
Alba Dorato, Tarocchi dell'   320, 321
Albano-Waite Tarot   **486**
Alchemical Tarot   207, **210–211**
Alchemisten Tarot   207, **212**

Alchemy   207, 210–211, 212, 563, 564
Aldez Belgium   259, 262
Aleph-Beth Tarot   4, **5**
Alexander Associates   450, 455
Alexander, Kathya   77
Alien Tarot   4, **6**
Alien, The (movie)   235
Alligo, Piero   342, 344, 567
Almeida e Sousa   467
Amano Tarot   **611**
Amano, Yoshitaka   611
Amato, Laurie   25, 27, 100, 101, 102, 176, 200, 201, 537, 540, 668, 699, 700, 720
Amazing Tarot   **612**
Ameli, M.   267, 272, 354, 356
Americano do Brasil, Martius   242, 244, 707
Anan Tarot   **613**
Ananda Tarot   213, **214**
Ancestral Path Tarot   213, **215**
Ancient East, Tarot of   7
Ancient Egyptian Tarot   709, **712–713**
Ancient Esoteric Tarot   **704**
Ancient Etruria Minchiate (see Etruria Minchiate)
Ancient Italian Tarot (see Avondo Brothers–Cartiera Italiana Tarot)
Ancient Millennium Tarot   8, **9**
Ancient Minchiate Etruria (see Etruria Minchiate)
Ancient Tarot of Liguria–Piedmont (see Guala, Giovanbattista, Tarot)
Ancient Tarots of Bologna (see Zoni, Giacomo, Tarot)
Anderson, Lora   173
Ando, Arnell   141, 560
Andrews, Ted   217, 218
Angel CLAMP Tarot   **613**
Angel Mithra Divination, Tarot   **614**
Angel of Divination Tarot   **614**
Angel Playing Card   647
Angel Sanctuary Tarot   **615, 616**
Angelique Innocence Tarot   **617**
Angelique Tarot   **616, 617**
Angels   8, 213, 216, 320, 323, 596, 597

Angels Tarot   213, **216**
Angels, Tarot of   **8**
Angry Moon, Tarot of the   9, **10**
Animal Tarot (Gibby)   **213**
Animal Tarot (anonymous Japanese)   **618**
Animal–Wise Tarot   217, **218**
Animé   609, 610, 613–619, 621–625, 627, 630, 632–637, 640, 641, 645–647, 654–664, 666–668
Annett, Sally   222, 227
Anonymous 1797 Tarot of Marseilles   689, **670**
Anonymous Italian Tarot of Marseilles   689, **691**
Anonymous Dutch Tarot   217, **219**
Anonymous French Tarot   217, **220**
Antakarana   572
Antichi Tarocchi Divinatori (see Guala, Giovanbattista, Tarot)
Antonazzo, Ivan A.   141
Antoni Tarot   **9**
Antonio Delfino Editore   456, 457
Apocalisse, Tarocchi dell'   217, **221**
Aquamarin Verlag   320, 323
Aquarian Press   222, 310, 312, 422, 425, 442, 518, 519
Aquarian Voices magazine   21
Arai, Kiyoko   630
Araki, Noma   641
Arcana Tarot   **619**
Arcanum magazine   560, 561
Arcus Arcanum Tarot   304, **308**
Argentina   435, 437
Arlenea, Willow   560, 561
Arleston, Scotch   736, 737
Arnsten-Russell, Susan   110
Arrien, Angeles   490
Arriola, Cindy C.   150, 151
Ars Gratias Artas   433
Art Nouveau, Tarocchi   222, **223**
Art of Tarot   222, **224**
Arthurian legend   94, 95, 136, 183, 184–185, 213, 215, 222, 224, 225, 232, 234–235, 354, 357–358, 393, 397, 422, 425
Arthurian Tarot   222, **224–225**
Artiste, Tarot des   11, **12**
artists & alchemists   528, 530

G

H

K

L

X

Y

Z